ADVENTURES FOR READERS

BOOK TWO

The Adventures
in Literature Program

═══

ADVENTURES FOR READERS: BOOK ONE
Teacher's Manual
Test Booklet
Reading/Writing Workshop, Grade 7

ADVENTURES FOR READERS: BOOK TWO
Teacher's Manual
Test Booklet
Reading/Writing Workshop, Grade 8

ADVENTURES IN READING
Teacher's Manual
Test Booklet
Reading/Writing Workshop, Grade 9

ADVENTURES IN APPRECIATION
Teacher's Manual
Test Booklet
Reading/Writing Workshop, Grade 10

ADVENTURES IN AMERICAN LITERATURE
Teacher's Manual
Test Booklet
Lessons in Critical Reading and Writing:
Henry James's *Washington Square* and *Daisy Miller*

ADVENTURES IN ENGLISH LITERATURE
Teacher's Manual
Test Booklet
Lessons in Critical Reading and Writing: Shakespeare's *Hamlet*

EGBERT W. NIEMAN

Byron Junior High School, Shaker Heights, Ohio

ELIZABETH C. O'DALY

New York City Schools, New York, New York

FINE ARTS PROGRAM

THOMAS M. FOLDS

Dean of Education, The Metropolitan Museum of Art
New York, New York

ADVENTURES
for Readers

BOOK TWO

CLASSIC   EDITION

Harcourt, Brace & World, Inc.

NEW YORK   CHICAGO   SAN FRANCISCO   ATLANTA   DALLAS

EGBERT W. NIEMAN is principal of Byron Junior High School in Shaker Heights, Ohio. He has served as president of the Greater Cleveland Council of Teachers of English and is a member of the National Education Association, National Council of Teachers of English, National Secondary School Principals Association, and the Association for Supervision and Curriculum Development. He has served as president of the Council for Junior High School Administration. His teaching experience has been in junior and senior high schools in Wood County, Ohio, and in Shaker Heights. A teacher of English for many years, Mr. Nieman was chairman of the English department at Shaker Heights Junior High School. At various times, he has been a student adviser, the assistant principal of a junior high school, and the director of guidance and special services for the Shaker Heights schools.

ELIZABETH C. O'DALY is an assistant superintendent of schools in New York City, in charge of the More Effective Schools program. She was formerly in charge of language arts in the junior high schools and later head of a Brooklyn school district. She has served as president of the Brooklyn Teachers Association and vice-president of the Junior High School Principals Association. Mrs. O'Daly is a member of the Academy of Public Education and the American Association of School Administrators. She has been program chairman of the New York State Council of English and a panel speaker for the National Council of Teachers of English and the International Reading Association. A former elementary and junior high school principal, she has taught English at Sarah J. Hale Vocational High School in Brooklyn, has given courses in the language arts, and has lectured at various colleges.

THOMAS M. FOLDS is Dean of Education at the Metropolitan Museum of Art in New York City. A graduate of Yale College and the Yale School of Fine Arts, Mr. Folds has been an instructor of English and art director at the Phillips Exeter Academy, New Hampshire, and a professor of art and chairman of the department of art at Northwestern University.

Special Acknowledgment: G. B. HARRISON, Emeritus Professor of English at the University of Michigan, has served as special consultant for the section on Shakespeare in this book.

Front cover photo by Susan McCartney.

Coin used as colophon courtesy of The American Numismatic Society.

Printed in the United States of America

Contents

PART ONE | THEMES IN LITERATURE

	Unit 1	*The Concept of Courage*
Jerome Ross and Larry Marcus	The Stone	3
Homer	Odysseus and the Cyclops FROM *The Odyssey*	15
Dorothy Heiderstadt	Sir Gawain	26
Howard Pyle	Will Stutely's Rescue FROM *The Merry Adventures of Robin Hood*	32
James Ramsey Ullman	Top Man	42
Alfred, Lord Tennyson	The Charge of the Light Brigade	58
Robert Nathan	Dunkirk	60
Mary O'Hara	My Friend Flicka	64
Paul Gallico	Lou Gehrig's Epic of Courage	87
Emily Dickinson	We Never Know How High	98

PRACTICE IN READING AND WRITING: DESCRIPTION   99

Unit 2 *The Search for Values*

Edith Hamilton	Baucis and Philemon	103
Olivia E. Coolidge	Midas 107	
John Godfrey Saxe	The Blind Men and the Elephant	113
Russell G. Davis and Brent K. Ashabranner	The Gift and the Giver 114	
James Street	Weep No More, My Lady 118	
Emily Dickinson	A Word 132	
Phyllis McGinley	A Choice of Weapons 132	
Stephen Crane	Think As I Think 132	
Phyllis McGinley	A Garland of Precepts 133	
Kathryn Forbes	Mama and the Graduation Present 134	
Richard Y. Thurman	The Countess and the Impossible	139
Abioseh Nicol	As the Night the Day 144	

PRACTICE IN READING AND WRITING: NARRATION   155

Unit 3 *Our American Heritage*

Esther Forbes	Salt-Water Tea FROM *Johnny Tremain* 159	
Henry Wadsworth Longfellow	Paul Revere's Ride 171	
Ralph Waldo Emerson	The Concord Hymn 176	
Oliver Wendell Holmes	Old Ironsides 177	
Edward Everett Hale	The Man Without a Country	187
Ray Bradbury	The Drummer Boy of Shiloh 202	
Abraham Lincoln	The Gettysburg Address 208	
Walt Whitman	O Captain! My Captain! 210	
Conrad Richter	Smoke over the Prairie 212	
C. B. Wall	Incandescent Genius 235	
Eleanor R. Van Zandt	Sing an Old Song 249	

PRACTICE IN READING AND WRITING: EXPOSITION   254

PART TWO | FORMS OF LITERATURE

Unit 4 Stories

Washington Irving   The Legend of Sleepy Hollow   259

O. Henry   The Ransom of Red Chief   283

Sir Arthur Conan Doyle   The Red-headed League   301

Dorothy Canfield   The Apprentice   320

PRACTICE IN READING AND WRITING: STORIES   329

Unit 5 Plays

Robert Louis Stevenson   The Sire de Maletroit's Door   333

Thornton Wilder   The Happy Journey to Trenton and Camden   351

A. A. Milne   The Ugly Duckling   363

PRACTICE IN READING AND WRITING: DIALOGUE   379

Unit 6 Nonfiction

Robert Benchley   Your Change   383

William Allen White   Mary White   385

Florence Crannell Means   George Washington Carver FROM Carver's George   390

Robert Creamer   First Pitch   409

Paul Engle   An Old-fashioned Iowa Christmas   410

Edwin Way Teale   From Spring to Summer   417

Arthur C. Clarke   Where's Everybody?   423

PRACTICE IN READING AND WRITING: NONFICTION   431

Unit 7 Poems

HUMOROUS VERSE

Lewis Carroll — Jabberwocky   435

Ernest Lawrence Thayer — Casey at the Bat   436

Ogden Nash — The Panther   438

The Porcupine   438

The Eel   438

The Termite   438

T. S. Eliot — The Naming of Cats   439

NARRATIVE POEMS

Sir Walter Scott — Lochinvar   441

Edgar Allan Poe — The Raven   444

LYRIC POEMS

Five Japanese Poems   449

PICTURES IN POETRY

Carl Sandburg — Fog   451

John Ciardi — The River Is a Piece of Sky   451

William Carlos Williams — The Lonely Street   452

T. S. Eliot — Prelude I: The Winter Evening   452

Percy Bysshe Shelley — A Widow Bird   453

EXPERIENCES IN POETRY

William Wordsworth — The Daffodils   454

John Greenleaf Whittier — The Hearth Fire   455

Robert Burns — Jean   456

Herbert Clark Johnson — Crossing a Creek   456

Robert Hillyer — The Wise Old Apple Tree in Spring   457

Pilot-Officer John Gillespie Magee, Jr., RCAF — High Flight   458

Edna St. Vincent Millay — Exiled   458

DEEPER MEANINGS IN POETRY

Edwin Arlington Robinson The Dark Hills 461

Thomas Hardy Last Week in October 461

E. E. Cummings what if a much of a which
of a wind 462

Langston Hughes Kid in the Park 463

DIFFERENT VIEWS IN POETRY

Theodore Roethke Night Journey 464

Emily Dickinson I Like to See It Lap the Miles 465

PRACTICE IN READING AND WRITING: POETRY 466

PART THREE | A CLOSE LOOK AT FOUR AUTHORS

Mark Twain INTRODUCTION 471

Boyhood Reminiscences
FROM *The Autobiography
of Mark Twain* 472

Cub Pilot on the Mississippi
FROM *Life On the Mississippi* 481

The Celebrated Jumping Frog of
Calaveras County 497

Lost in a Snowstorm
FROM *Roughing It* 503

Punch, Brothers, Punch 511

Robert Frost   INTRODUCTION   516

The Pasture   517

A Time to Talk   517

The Birthplace   518

The Road Not Taken   519

Stopping by Woods on a Snowy
Evening   520

The Last Word of a Bluebird   521

Mending Wall   522

Dust of Snow   524

The Armful   524

Fire and Ice   525

What Fifty Said   525

James Thurber   INTRODUCTION   527

The Night the Bed Fell   528

The Dog That Bit People   532

Memorial   537

The Spreading "*You* Know"   539

The Little Girl and the Wolf   541

The Princess and the Tin Box   542

The Tiger Who Would Be King   544

The Kingfisher and the Phoebe   545

Thurber's Cartoons   546

William Shakespeare   INTRODUCTION   549

A Father's Advice to His Son
FROM *Hamlet*   550

Good Name   FROM *Othello*   552

Sonnet 71   553

Advice to Actors   FROM *Hamlet*   554

Pyramus and Thisby   FROM *A
Midsummer Night's Dream*   555

PRACTICE IN WRITING: HOW TO WRITE ABOUT LITERATURE   572

PART FOUR OUR HERITAGE FROM ROME

Bella Koral   The Wooden Horse   577

Virgil   The Adventures of Aeneas   582

Henry W. Lanier   How Horatius Held the Bridge   597

Robert Silverberg   The Battle of Zama   602

Plutarch   Julius Caesar   610

William Shakespeare   Lines from *Julius Caesar*

Cassius Speaks of Ceasar to
Brutus   621

Caesar to Antony   621

Caesar to Calpurnia   622

Antony's Oration at Caesar's
Funeral   622

Antony Speaks of Brutus   624

Pliny   The Eruption of Vesuvius   625

Gilbert Highet   The Heart of the City   631

PRACTICE IN READING AND WRITING: EXPOSITION   639

Fine Arts Program

MASTERPIECES OF ART   Paintings by Old Masters   79

The American Heritage in
Painting   179

How Painters Express Action   293

Movement and Rhythm
in Painting   401

Winslow Homer   489

Roman Art   589

Authors' Biographies   641

The Reading Program   652

The Composition Program   654

Index of Contents by Types   656

Index of Fine Art   658

Glossary   659

Index of Authors and Titles   671

PART ONE

Stephen Crane

Old North Bridge on the Concord River, Massachusetts

Themes in Literature

Unit 1
The Concept of Courage

1

UNIT 1 The Concept of Courage

The word *courage* was handed down to us by the ancient Romans. It comes from a Latin word meaning "heart." One of Rome's great writers, Plautus, once said that a man with courage has every blessing.

Courageous men and women have lived in all times, and the concept of courage has been a recurring theme in the literature of all countries. The first four stories in this unit come from ancient and medieval times. They tell some world-famous stories about the courageous spirit of man.

The Stone by Jerome Ross and Larry Marcus:
  A dramatization of the Biblical story of David and his challenge to the giant Goliath.
Odysseus and the Cyclops by Homer:
  A famous adventure in which the daredevil hero of ancient Greece meets a one-eyed giant.
Sir Gawain retold by Dorothy Heiderstadt:
  A strange medieval legend about a knight whose courage and honor lead him to submit to an impossible test.
Will Stutely's Rescue by Howard Pyle:
  One of the legends about the cowardly Sheriff of Nottingham and Robin Hood, the outlaw hero of medieval England.

The other stories and poems in this unit come from modern times. They show that courage is a quality that may lie deep within any one of us.

Top Man by James Ramsey Ullman:
  A modern writer's suspenseful story of two mountain climbers.
The Charge of the Light Brigade by Alfred, Lord Tennyson:
  A poem about a doomed yet obedient company of soldiers.
Dunkirk by Robert Nathan:
  A poem about a young boy and girl and a dramatic rescue.
My Friend Flicka by Mary O'Hara:
  A story about a misunderstood boy whose love for a horse brings him to a moment of courage.
Lou Gehrig's Epic of Courage by Paul Gallico:
  A true story about a great baseball player and a brave man.
We Never Know How High by Emily Dickinson:
  A poem suggesting that we may not use our store of courage.

The Stone

JEROME ROSS *and* LARRY MARCUS

The Biblical tale of David and Goliath is one of the earliest stories of courage. Here, two modern authors have put this traditional story into dramatic form for television.

Characters

GOLIATH'S VOICE, *voice of the champion of the Philistines, a powerful people who were enemies of the Israelites*

DAVID, *a young Israelite shepherd*

KING SAUL, *King of the Israelites*

PRINCESS MICHAL (mī′kal), *Saul's daughter*

SHAMMAH (sham′ma) ⎱
ELIAB (ē·lī′ab)   ⎰ *David's* BROTHERS
ABINADAB (a·bin′a·dàb)

CAPTAIN

ABNER, *commander of Saul's army*   *the* OFFICERS

JOAB (jō′ab), *deputy commander of Saul's army*

SOLDIERS

GUARDS

The Stone by Jerome Ross and Larry Marcus, a photoplay produced by Revue Studios, a segment of the General Electric Theater Series. Reprinted by permission of Larry Marcus.

SCENE 1

SETTING. *The Israelite camp*

[*Out of the mist comes a huge voice.*]

GOLIATH'S VOICE. Soldiers of Israel! And you — Saul — King of the Israelites! Hear me! Hear Goliath of Gath, you cowards and weaklings. Today is the thirty-ninth day! And where is he? Where is the man among you who'll dare to fight with me? Where is your hero to meet my challenge? Hear me! For the thirty-ninth morning, *I*, Goliath of Gath, repeat my offer! Let one of you defeat me and the war will be over! The Philistines will become your slaves! (*Mockingly*) Is there *no one* of you to take up my challenge? Are you an army of women and children? (DAVID *now appears. He glances incredulously at various* SOLDIERS *as the booming voice continues.*) Where is this God of yours called Jehovah? Surely he'll give your champion the strength to kill Goliath of Gath. (*He laughs mockingly.*)

DAVID (*to* FIRST SOLDIER). It is always like this? Every morning like this?

[FIRST SOLDIER *turns away.*]

GOLIATH'S VOICE. Or have you found that your Jehovah is false? Is that why you hold back? Hear me, Israelites! I say that your Lord Jehovah is false!

DAVID. Why has no one answered him? Why? What's happened to our army? We heard rumors of this back in Bethlehem. But it's worse, much worse, than they said.

FIRST SOLDIER (*angrily*). Then go home if you can't stand the sound of it.

DAVID (*incredulous*). But he mocks the Lord, our God!

FIRST SOLDIER. We don't talk of it. Do you understand? No one here talks of it!

[*David's three* BROTHERS *approach.*]

SHAMMAH. David! What brings you here?

[*The two others add their surprise.*]

DAVID. Shammah — Eliab — Abinadab —

SHAMMAH (*to other* SOLDIERS). He's our brother, the youngest.

DAVID. Father sent me with provisions for you. Corn and bread, a gift of cheese for your captain.

[*The* BROTHERS *laugh affectionately.*]

ELIAB. Are things well at home, David?

DAVID. Better than here, Eliab. Much better. (*The mood of merriment dies.*) I stood waiting — waiting for one man, one among our thousands, to shout out: "I'll meet you, Goliath! I'll teach you to taunt the Lord!"

SHAMMAH. Huh! The poet speaks.

ELIAB. That's right. Our brother who sits home on the hillside tending sheep and making songs.

SHAMMAH. Listen, David! We don't like this any more than you do. But who has a chance against this giant?

ELIAB. It would be suicide.

DAVID. But somebody *must* fight him. What about our generals? Warriors like Abner, like Joab?

ELIAB (*shrugging*). We don't know. We're only soldiers.

DAVID. What about King Saul? Why does *he* keep silent?

[*The* BROTHERS *glance around uneasily.*]

ELIAB. David, hold your tongue ——

SHAMMAH. If one of the captains hears you ——

DAVID. Saul is the strongest and the bravest among us. He conquered Edom and Ammon; he destroyed the Amalekites.[1] Remember when the King passed through our village, and I played my harp for him? Years ago — but I've never forgotten the sight of him. Such majesty and dignity! Certainly King Saul is *not* afraid of this Philistine!

[*A* CAPTAIN *comes over suspiciously.*]

CAPTAIN. Who's this boy with the loose tongue?

ELIAB (*hastily*). Don't mind him, Captain; he's our brother.

SHAMMAH. He's a shepherd boy, Captain — roams the mountains — always full of strange ideas —

ELIAB. Alone with his flock of sheep, he even talks to himself ——

CAPTAIN (*to* DAVID). What's your business in camp?

DAVID. I — I came to see my brothers ——

---

[1] **Amalekites** (am'ə·lek·īts).

CAPTAIN. Well, you've seen them. Now send him away. Busybodies from home won't help our situation. (*Exits.*)

ELIAB. Go home before you make more trouble for us.

DAVID. How? By praising the King? By saying that he's always been my hero? (DAVID *looks at the King's tent with deep respect and hope.*) He'd remember me, I think.

[DAVID *makes an impulsive move toward the tent. His* BROTHERS *restrain him.*]

SCENE 2

SETTING. *King's tent, richly furnished*

[*Several* OFFICERS *are standing around. The* KING *is slumped in a chair, tormented by a headache. Beside him is his daughter, the beautiful* PRINCESS MICHAL.]

JOAB. The Philistines now await us with ten thousand troops and two hundred war chariots.

ABNER. Sire, did you hear? Ten thousand of them. Twice our number and we have no chariots.

KING (*wearily*). I know, Abner.

ABNER. Each day, for each new man we recruit, five men desert in terror. This Goliath will shrink our army to a handful, and then they'll fall on us.

KING (*flaring up*). I know!

ABNER (*impatiently*). Sire — give me a plan. Give me your orders. We must make up our minds to something!

MICHAL (*jumps up, furiously*). My father is ill; he's in pain. Why must you torment him?

ABNER (*with a trace of sarcasm*). Because he's our king, Princess Michal. He's our leader.

[*The* KING *rises slowly, in pain.*]

KING (*brokenly*). I can read your hearts. You're all asking yourselves: Is this Saul, our warrior King, anointed by Samuel? [1] Is *this* the same Saul who led us to old victories? Why doesn't he lead us from this wilderness we're in? (*Shouting in desperation*) I cannot give the answer! Some poison has taken hold of me. I'm without strength! without hope! without faith!

[1] **Samuel:** a great judge and prophet of ancient Israel.

MICHAL (*sharply*). Father, stop it! Don't listen to him. It will pass. His illness makes him talk this way.

KING. I have no answer. You'll have to make your own decisions.

[*There is a general hubbub outside, and the camera moves from the interior of the tent to focus on the entrance.* DAVID *is being barred by the* CAPTAIN *and two* GUARDS.]

CAPTAIN. You cannot enter!

DAVID. I must talk to the King.

CAPTAIN (*drawing sword*). Stand aside, or we'll run you through!

BROTHERS. David — have you gone mad? Men have been whipped for less! Go home, boy — leave us in peace.

DAVID. He knows me. He'll remember me. . . . I must talk to him! Let me in!

[*Inside the King's tent again*]

MICHAL. Help! An assassin — to kill my father!

[ABNER *and* MICHAL *go to the entrance and see* DAVID *struggling in the grip of a burly* GUARD *and the* CAPTAIN.]

MICHAL. What does this mean? Who are you?

CAPTAIN. He's a shepherd boy, Princess. He says he knows the King and wants an audience.

KING. Let him in.

DAVID. Sire, I wouldn't have dared to come to you, except that you know me.

KING (*puzzled*). I know you . . .?

DAVID. In our village of Bethlehem, a few years ago, I brought my harp and sang you some of my verses, the ones I make up when I'm alone at night with my flocks.

KING. Your harp . . .? Your verses . . .?

DAVID (*eagerly*). It was during your campaign against Moab. You said you *liked* them — you said they were beautiful. You said they ended your melancholy. Don't you remember?

KING (*shakes his head*). I've passed through a thousand villages.

DAVID (*pained*). But there was one special song. You said——

[*The* KING *rises wearily. He cuts* DAVID *off with a gesture of dismissal.*]

KING. I'm sorry.

MICHAL. Do you think my father has nothing better to do than talk to every stray shepherd boy who ever crossed his path?

KING (*to* DAVID). Be a good lad and leave me. You have my blessing.

DAVID. You don't recognize me — and, by the same token, I hardly recognize you, sire. You're not so tall as you were. You wore your armor then; you're not wearing it now. In the midst of a war, you stand without armor.

[*Others in tent are staring at* DAVID.]

KING (*irritably*). Who sent this boy to goad me?

DAVID. Sire, I'll go soon enough, and peacefully, but first I'd like to hear it from your own lips.

MICHAL (*indignantly*). Hear what?

DAVID. That my King Saul of the Tribe of Benjamin accepts the challenge of Goliath of Gath——

KING. What?

DAVID. —— and puts an end to this mocking of the Lord.

MICHAL. How dare you? How dare you tell the King what to do?

ABNER. Shall I order fifty lashes for him?

DAVID. If not you, sire, then who else? Who else can ——

KING (*interrupting*). STOP!

DAVID (*despairingly*). You were the last hope of our soldiers, of our people. (*He turns away from the* KING.)

ABNER (*angrily to the* KING). I'll have him flogged.

[*The* KING *shakes his head.*]

KING. What's your name, boy?

DAVID. David.

KING. Well, hear me out, David. Don't you suppose that for thirty-nine mornings I've wanted to strap on my armor and go down the mountainside?

DAVID. What stopped you, sire?

KING. I'm the King. I haven't the right.

DAVID (*shocked*). Haven't the right . . .?

KING. A king's life isn't his own; it holds our people together, our towns, our fields, our faith. If I am killed, Israel is lost.

DAVID (*simply*). What is happening to Israel *now*?

[*His honest manner, his refusal to be persuaded by debate, suddenly infuriate the* KING.]

KING (*explosively*). THESE ARE NOT EXCUSES! Look at me! In my time, the strongest of all — and now, forcing myself into cowardice! How easy for a boy, off tending sheep somewhere, to decide, "Let the King do it!" You little fool!

MICHAL. You're driving my father to fury.

ABNER. My advice is to leave, boy.

[*The* KING *seizes a sword lying on the officers' table, moves toward* DAVID.]

KING. Yes! Before I strike him down!

[*His arm is upraised; he towers over* DAVID. *For a moment he really intends to kill this youthful intruder.* DAVID *stands waiting for the blow, not flinching. Suddenly, the* KING *lets the sword fall to the ground. There is a radiance about* DAVID, *a kind of joyous determination. For a moment he seems not to be a shy, uncertain country youth, but a leader divinely inspired.*]

DAVID. I WILL BE THE ONE! I will meet Goliath!

MICHAL (*with a burst of laughter*). Behold our champion!

[*The* SOLDIERS *and* OFFICERS *join her merriment.*]

ABNER. Good idea. Goliath will die of laughter!

JOAB. They'll fight with wool shears.

[*The* KING *remains quiet and motionless, his eyes fixed on* DAVID.]

DAVID. Sire, I ask your permission to meet tomorrow with Goliath in the Valley of Elah.

[*The laughter dies. There is a brief silence. They are all impressed.*]

KING (*suddenly angry*). No — this is madness! (*To* ABNER) Tell him what you saw the giant do at Leasa!

ABNER. He tore *men* apart as you would tear the wings and legs from a chicken. (*Contemptuously at* DAVID) *Men.*

KING. His height is more than nine

feet. His coat of mail weighs over two hundred pounds. What weapon would you use against him?

DAVID. I — I hadn't thought, sire.

MICHAL. Put your mind on it, shepherd boy.

DAVID. Sometimes, Princess, the Lord's hand is weapon enough. (*To the* KING) Once, a lion and a bear came on my flock and seized a lamb. I slew them both. The Lord that delivered me out of the paw of the lion and the paw of the bear will deliver me out of the hand of this Philistine.

KING. I can't let you do it.

DAVID. Think it over, sire. Someone must do it. Let *me*. I'll be waiting outside your tent for your decision. (*Exits.*)

MICHAL (*mockingly*). I know. He's heard that absurd rumor — that the King will marry me to the slayer of Goliath! The idiot *believes* it!

[*Laughter from the* OFFICERS]

KING. BE SILENT!

MICHAL. Father, surely you don't take the boy seriously?

KING. Of course not. It would be madness. All the same, it's very strange.

MICHAL. Strange?

KING. What is there about him? The pain of my headache is suddenly gone.

SCENE 3

SETTING. *A stream on the hillside*

[DAVID *is stooped beside the stream, examining stones. Some* SOLDIERS *approach.*]

SECOND SOLDIER. Look — pebbles! He's going to fight with pebbles!

[*David's three* BROTHERS *appear. They are very angry.*]

ELIAB. Go home and tend your sheep! The whole camp's laughing at us!

ABINADAB. You're making us look ridiculous!

SHAMMAH. You've made fools of us!

DAVID. As the giant is making fools out of all Israel?

SECOND SOLDIER. Pretend I'm the giant. I stand before you. I DEFY you, shepherd boy!

[*Again there is laughter.* DAVID *flushes angrily, and almost faster than the eye can follow, he fits a stone into his sling, whirls the sling once, and sends the stone flashing through the air. The stone smashes into the soldier's iron helmet which lies at his feet. The helmet topples and rolls five feet. Everyone is startled. The* SOLDIERS *stare at* DAVID, *highly impressed.*]

SCENE 4

SETTING. *Outside the King's tent*

[DAVID *is seated on a large rock, waiting.* PRINCESS MICHAL *comes out and approaches* DAVID, *followed by the* CAPTAIN *and two* GUARDS *carrying the King's armor.*]

DAVID. Do you bring me word from your father?

MICHAL. If I had my way, it would be to run you out of camp! What's this nonsense I hear, that you expect to kill the giant with a small stone?

DAVID. You told me to think of what weapon to use.

MICHAL. STOP MAKING FOOLS OF US! (*She slaps his face.* DAVID *takes it calmly, without flinching.*) Imagine! A warrior with a harp! When will you sing me love songs, my hero? And we can't let you go into battle wearing your shepherd's vest. I've had the Captain bring the King's own armor. (*To* CAPTAIN) Put it on him!

[*The* CAPTAIN *and a* SOLDIER *fasten the heavy iron breastplate on* DAVID, *which comes to his knees, and set the too-large helmet on his head. The sight draws laughter from bystanders.*]

MICHAL. A turtle! We're sending a *turtle* to fight Goliath! He will throw a stone, then pull in his head!

[*The* KING *enters.*]

KING. What game is this — baiting the shepherd boy?

MICHAL. He's a troublemaker!

[DAVID *now stands uncovered, without the armor. The taunting seems not to have touched him at all.*]

DAVID. I'm still waiting for your decision, sire.

[*The camera follows the* KING, JOAB, *and* ABNER *as they enter the tent. The flaps close, shutting off the view of* DAVID *and all the others outside.*]

KING (*wonderingly*). I can hardly blame my daughter and the soldiers for making sport. And yet, what *is* there about that boy?

ABNER. Sire, if the shepherd wants to be a martyr, then let him be a martyr.

[*The* KING *looks surprised.*]

ABNER. You saw our men just now, howling with laughter at the ridiculous sight. Think, sire! Think of how the Philistines will watch him as he comes down the hillside tomorrow morning.

JOAB (*laughing*). Waddling down, weaving his way down ——

ABNER. Every soul in the Philistine camp will hasten into the valley to see the fun. Down there, the morning mist will hide us from them. THIS would be the moment to strike camp!

KING. And retreat? Use the boy as — as a decoy?

ABNER. While they're watching the hilarious duel, we'll be sending the men back by a dozen different trails. (*Quickly*) Of course, the shepherd boy needn't know.

KING. Abner! Oh, Abner! How low have we fallen?

ABNER (*losing patience*). Sire, you agree that the stalemate must be ended, and yet you offer no suggestions of your own.

JOAB. Isn't this the perfect chance to withdraw without heavy casualties? With *no* casualties. (*To* ABNER) Later, the shepherd — what's left of him — can be buried with full honors.

KING. Do as you please.

[ABNER *goes to the tent entrance.*]

ABNER. Send in David, the shepherd boy!

SCENE 5

SETTING. *A hillside just overlooking the army camp. It is night.*

[DAVID *begins to play his harp.*]

DAVID (*very softly*).
Blessed is the man that walketh not in the counsel of the ungodly,
Nor standeth in the way of sinners,
Nor sitteth in the seat of the scornful.
But his delight is in the law of the Lord;
And in his law doth he meditate day and night.
And he shall be like a tree planted by the rivers of water,

That bringeth forth his fruit in his season;
His leaf also shall not wither;
And whatsoever he doeth shall prosper.
The ungodly are not so:
But are like the chaff which the wind driveth away.
Therefore the ungodly shall not stand in the judgment,
Nor sinners in the congregation of the righteous.
For the Lord knoweth the way of the righteous:
But the way of the ungodly shall perish.

[MICHAL, *awakened by David's playing, goes to the hillside.*]

MICHAL (*surprised*). So it's you, the shepherd boy, who's making this music! I heard it first in my sleep. Then I woke and listened. Then it seemed to draw me half-awake outside.

DAVID. I felt the need to sing tonight.

MICHAL (*smiling a bit patronizingly*). Well, sing then. I'm listening.

DAVID.
Hear my cry, O God;
Attend unto my prayer.

From the end of the earth will I cry
    unto thee,
When my heart is overwhelmed:
Lead me to the rock that is higher
    than I.

MICHAL. Why — why — that's lovely!

DAVID. Thank you.

MICHAL. Where did you learn such
verses?

DAVID. I make them up.

MICHAL. *You* make them up?

DAVID (*smiling*). The words sort of
come to me. They come to me — well,
when I look down at a lamb nestled in
the grass, or else up at a star, and . . .
(*He breaks off.*) You don't believe me.

MICHAL. I — I'm not sure.

DAVID. They also come to me when
I'm alone with my flock in the night —
when I need my faith to fight my fears.
And tonight, Princess Michal, I have
fears. That's why I'm playing my harp,
saying my verses of praise to the Lord
— because I'm frightened. I'll meet
Goliath because it must be done. But
I'm trembling inside.

[ABNER *is standing not far away, listening.*]

MICHAL (*softly, after a pause*). Give
it up, David. Run away.

DAVID (*shaking his head*). I can't.

[MICHAL *suddenly kisses* DAVID. *He
stares at her.*]

MICHAL (*wonderingly*). What made
me do that?

[*For a moment, they look at each
other.*]

DAVID. I'm glad you did.

MICHAL. May the Lord be with you,
David.

[MICHAL *hurries away.* DAVID *picks up a
stone and weighs it in his hand.
There is a look of grim determination
on his face; her tenderness has given
him a new courage.* ABNER *enters.*]

ABNER. I couldn't help hearing what
you told the Princess. (DAVID *looks up,
startled.*) So you're not just being
blindly, stupidly courageous, h'm?
You're frightened, shepherd boy?

DAVID. I was, yes.

ABNER. A man must know fear before he can have real courage.

DAVID. A man must also know faith.

SCENE 6

SETTING. *At camp, inside the King's
tent, are* DAVID *and the* KING. *It is almost
morning.*

KING. They tell me it was you who
played during the night.

DAVID. I hope I didn't disturb you,
sire.

KING. David, I forbid you to meet
Goliath.

DAVID. But, sire ——

KING. I can't have your death on my
conscience. I can't have my people saying, "The boy refused armor and a
sword, and Saul let him go down with
only a sling for his weapon. . . ."

DAVID (*breaking in*). But, sire — *you*
were once a shepherd. (*He holds up his
slingshot for the* KING *to see.*) You know
how in the fields this can kill wild animals. (*Eagerly*) Please! Share my faith
in what the Lord will have it do to our
enemy.

KING. All the faith, all the courage, is gone, David.

DAVID (*angrily*). I won't believe it of you!

KING (*angrily*). Be quiet! Let me tell you something! We were going to use you! While the Philistines watched Goliath tear you apart, we planned to strike camp and retreat. (DAVID *stares at him.*) Now you know! Go home, boy; go home to your flock.

DAVID. I want you to make use of me, sire! But not to retreat. Why not attack the Philistines? Why not come down the mountainside and take them by surprise?

KING. We're outnumbered.

DAVID. We were outnumbered in the days of Moab, in the days of the Amalekites. We are *always* outnumbered!

KING (*half to himself*). Attack, eh? It might work — it might just work.

DAVID. It *must* work! Put on your armor, sire, and attack!

[*There is a moment of silence. They are facing each other. The* KING *stands motionless, trying to make up his mind.*]

GOLIATH'S VOICE. Soldiers of Israel! Hear me, you cowards and weaklings. Today it is the *fortieth* day — and where is he? Where is your champion?

DAVID. Sire, give me your answer. Why do you look at me that way?

KING. It was in the village of Bethlehem. I remember now. They brought you to me, and you sang songs of praise to the Lord, our God ——

GOLIATH'S VOICE. For the fortieth morning, Goliath of Gath repeats his challenge!

KING. You spoke one verse — it was the most beautiful of all. I forget it now. But it drove my melancholy away. It restored my lost faith.

DAVID (*joyously*). Yes, sire, yes!

[GOLIATH'S VOICE *booms louder.*]

GOLIATH'S VOICE. Where is this God of yours called Jehovah? If he is true, why does he not smite me?

[*The* KING *smiles at* DAVID. *Suddenly, there is real majesty about the* KING.]

KING. Go, David, and the Lord be with you.

[*At once* DAVID *begins stripping off his goatskin vest and faces the* KING.]

DAVID. The verse I sang to you that night, long ago, I remember it . . . (*A pause, then he sings.*)
The Lord is my shepherd; I shall not want.

KING. Yes, yes! That was it!

DAVID.
He maketh me to lie down in green pastures:
He leadeth me beside the still waters.

KING. Captain! My armor! Abner! Joab! Prepare to attack!

SCENE 7

SETTING. *The valley*

[DAVID *is walking into the valley. His voice continues the psalm.*]

DAVID.
He restoreth my soul:
He leadeth me in the paths of righteousness for His Name's sake.
Yea, though I walk through the valley of the shadow of death,

I will fear no evil: for Thou art with
me;
Thy rod and Thy staff they comfort me.

[*Out of the mist, we begin to see the
enormous shadow of Goliath.*]

Thou preparest a table before me in
the presence of mine enemies:
Thou anointest my head with oil; my
cup runneth over.

[DAVID *pauses and fits a stone to his
sling. Then he advances again.*]

Surely goodness and mercy shall fol-
low me all the days of my life:
And I will dwell in the house of the
Lord forever.

[DAVID, *a tiny figure, still advances
toward the enormous shadow.* DAVID
*stops, swinging his sling. The huge
shadow advances.* DAVID *releases the
stone. The shadow falls with a loud
crash.*]

[*The End*]

COURAGE AND FAITH — A BIBLE TALE

1. What were David's reactions to Goliath's tauntings at the opening of the
play? How did the first soldier, the brothers, and the captain react to David's questions?

2. What questions did David ask Saul?
What is unusual about the kind of questions David asked? How did Saul react to
David's questions? How did Saul then explain his lack of leadership?

3. What happened when Saul raised his
sword to strike David? After this, David
offered to meet Goliath. How did the various people in the tent react to David's offer? What did the soldiers and his brothers say to David? How did Michal try to
humiliate him?

4. How did Abner and Joab suggest using David? How did David's singing in the
night affect Michal? Describe the morning
talk between David and Saul, and its results.

5. Even from early times, people have
been concerned about what makes one
man courageous and another fearful. Was
David's courage dependent on the attitudes of the people around him? Upon

what conviction was his courage based? Why did David seem foolish to others? Was this because of something lacking in them? Explain.

6. At one point Abner says to David: "A man must know fear before he can have real courage." What did he mean? What is the difference between courage and foolhardiness? Do you think that courageous people are ever afraid?

7. What things make children afraid? How do they learn to overcome such fears? What can help an individual to conquer his fears?

8. Can you think of examples from modern times in which an individual put himself or herself into danger in order to help other people? Do you personally know any such person?

WORDS: SOUND AND SPELLING

In English, we often have difficulty pronouncing words. One reason is that one letter may be used to indicate several different sounds. For example, the letter *a* indicates different sounds in the words *add, ace, account,* and *father.* Pronounce each of these words to see how the sound of the letter *a* varies. Also, combinations of letters are often pronounced in different ways. For example, the letters *ough* are sounded differently in the words *though* and *bough.*

Since writing, then, does not always represent the sounds of speech exactly, we often need to refer to a dictionary or a glossary in order to find the pronunciations of new words. In the back of this book you will find a glossary. Study and be ready to discuss the preface to this glossary. Be sure that you know how to use the pronunciation key. See if you can make use of this key and correctly pronounce the names of the characters listed at the opening of the play.

SENTENCES: PUNCTUATION AND MEANING

When we speak, we use our voices to help indicate what we mean. In writing, punctuation marks aid us in signaling meaning. However, since we have only a few punctuation devices, they stand for only some of the things we can do with our voices.

In speaking, we often use pauses to signal meaning. In writing, a comma signals a pause. Notice how a pause before the word *Abner* can change the meaning of the following sentences. Read the sentences aloud: *I know Abner. I know, Abner.*

A speaker often indicates meaning by putting heavy emphasis or stress on a certain word or syllable in the sentence. Sometimes, though not too often, a writer will use italics to indicate that a word should be stressed. Notice how these same words now change slightly in meaning when you stress the word *I: I know Abner.* How can you change the meaning of this sentence by stressing different words?

The next three sentences are from *The Stone.* Read each one aloud. How can you change the meaning of each sentence by changing the pitch of your voice, by pausing in different places, or by stressing different words? Can you use different punctuation devices to signal all these changes in meaning?

"We're sending a turtle to fight Goliath."
"You make them up?"
"It *must* work."

ORAL READING

Read aloud the first speech from *The Stone.* Check with your teacher to see if you are reading with the right pitch and with the right pauses to signal the meaning the playwright intended. Notice that the playwright has put three words in italics. How should these words be read?

Odysseus and the Cyclops

HOMER

Translated by Samuel Butler

Courage was highly valued by the ancient Greeks. In the Greek epic *The Odyssey*, the poet Homer tells of the adventures of Odysseus, one of the Greek leaders in the Trojan War. After helping to destroy the city of Troy, Odysseus set sail for home. The journey was so filled with trials that it took ten years to complete. This selection tells of one of the most famous tests of Odysseus' courage and daring. Odysseus himself narrates the story.

WE SAILED AWAY always in much distress, till we came to the land of the lawless and inhuman Cyclopes.[1] Now the Cyclopes neither plant nor plow, but trust in providence, and live on such wheat, barley, and grapes as grow wild without any kind of tillage, and their wild grapes yield them wine as the sun and the rain may grow them. They have no laws or assemblies of the people, but live in caves on the tops of high mountains; each is lord and master in his family, and they take no account of their neighbors.

Now off their harbor there lies a wooded and fertile island not quite close to the land of the Cyclopes, but still not far. It is overrun with wild goats that breed there in great numbers and are never disturbed by foot of man. For sportsmen — who as a rule will suffer so much hardship in forest or among mountain precipices — do not go there, nor yet again is it ever plowed or fed down, but it lies a wilderness untilled and unsown from year to year, and has no living thing upon it but only goats. For the Cyclopes have no ships, nor shipwrights who could make ships for them. They cannot, therefore, go from city to city or sail over the sea to one another's country, as people who have ships can do. If they had had these they would have

---

[1] **Cyclopes** (sī·klō′pēz): plural form of *Cyclops.* The word means "round-eyed." A Cyclops had only one eye, set in the middle of his forehead.

"Odysseus and the Cyclops" from *The Odyssey of Homer* by Samuel Butler. Reprinted by permission of Walter J. Black, Inc.

colonized the island, for it is a very good one, and would yield everything in due season. There are meadows that in some places come right down to the seashore, well watered and full of luscious grass; grapes would do there excellently; there is level land for plowing, and it would always yield heavily at harvest time, for the soil is deep. There is a good harbor where no cables are wanted, nor anchors, nor need a ship be moored, but all one has to do is to beach one's vessel and stay there till the wind becomes fair for putting out to sea again. At the head of the harbor there is a spring of clear water coming out of a cave, and there are poplars growing all round it.

Here we entered, but so dark was the night that some god must have brought us in, for there was nothing whatever to be seen. A thick mist hung all round our ships; the moon was hidden behind a mass of clouds so that no one could have seen the island if he had looked for it, nor were there any breakers to tell us we were close in shore before we found ourselves upon the land itself. When, however, we had beached the ships, we took down the sails, went ashore, and camped upon the beach till daybreak.

When the child of morning, rosy-fingered Dawn, appeared, we admired the island and wandered all over it, while the nymphs, Zeus'[1] daughters, roused the wild goats that we might get some meat for our dinner. On this we fetched our spears and bows and arrows from the ships and, dividing ourselves into three bands, began to

shoot the goats. Heaven sent us excellent sport; I had twelve ships with me, and each ship got nine goats, while my own ship got ten; thus, through the livelong day to the going down of the sun, we ate and drank our fill, and we had plenty of wine left, for each one of us had taken many jars full when we sacked the city of the Cicones [2] and this had not yet run out. While we were feasting we kept turning our eyes toward the land of the Cyclops, which was hard by, and saw the smoke of their stubble fires. We could almost fancy we heard their voices and the bleating of their sheep and goats, but when the sun went down and it came on dark, we camped down upon the beach, and next morning I called a council.

"Stay here, my brave fellows," said I, "all the rest of you, while I go with my ship and explore these people myself. I want to see if they are uncivilized savages, or a hospitable and humane race."

I went on board, bidding my men to do so also and loose the hawsers; [3] so they took their places and smote the gray sea with their oars. When we got to the land, which was not far, there, on the face of a cliff near the sea, we saw a great cave overhung with laurels. It was a station for a great many sheep and goats, and outside there was a large yard, with a high wall round it made of stones built into the ground and of trees both pine and oak. This was the abode of a huge monster who was then away from home shepherding

---

[1] Zeus (zo͞os) was the supreme Greek god.

[2] **Cicones** (sĭk'ō·nēz).

[3] **hawsers** (hô'zərz): ropes used for mooring ships.

his flocks. He would have nothing to do with other people, but led the life of an outlaw. He was a horrid creature, not like a human being at all, but resembling rather some crag that stands out boldly against the sky on the top of a high mountain.

I told my men to draw the ship ashore and stay where they were, all but the twelve best among them, who were to go along with myself. I also took a goatskin of sweet black wine which had been given me by Maron, a priest of Apollo, who lived within the wooded precincts of the temple. When we were sacking the city we respected him, and spared his life, as also his wife and child; so he made me some presents of great value — seven talents of fine gold, and a bowl of silver, with twelve jars of sweet wine, unblended,

and of the most exquisite flavor. Not a man or maid in the house knew about it, but only himself, his wife, and one housekeeper. When he drank it he mixed twenty parts of water to one of wine, and yet the fragrance from the mixing bowl was so exquisite that it was impossible to refrain from drinking. I filled a large skin with this wine and took a wallet full of provisions with me, for my mind misgave me that I might have to deal with some savage who would be of great strength and would respect neither right nor law.

We soon reached the Cyclops' cave, but he was out shepherding, so we went inside and took stock of all that we could see. His cheese racks were loaded with cheeses, and he had more lambs and kids than his pens could hold. They were kept in separate flocks;

first there were the hoggets,[1] then the oldest of the younger lambs, and lastly the very young ones, all kept apart from one another. As for his dairy, all the vessels, bowls, and milk pails into which he milked were swimming with whey. When they saw all this, my men begged me to let them first steal some cheeses and make off with them to the ship; they would then return, drive down the lambs and kids, put them on board, and sail away with them. It would have been indeed better if we had done so, but I would not listen to them, for I wanted to see the owner himself, in the hope that he might give me a present.[2] When, however, we saw him, my poor men found him ill to deal with.

We lit a fire, offered some of the cheeses in sacrifice, ate others of them, and then sat waiting till the Cyclops should come in with his sheep. When he came, he brought in with him a huge load of dry firewood to light the fire for his supper, and this he flung with such a noise onto the floor of his cave that we hid ourselves for fear at the far end of the cavern. Meanwhile he drove all the ewes inside, as well as the she-goats that he was going to milk, leaving the males, both rams and he-goats, outside in the yards. Then he rolled a huge stone to the mouth of the cave — so huge that two-and-twenty strong, four-wheeled wagons would not be enough to draw it from its place against the doorway. When he had so done, he sat down and milked his ewes and goats, all in due

course, and then let each of them have her own young. He curdled half the milk and set it aside in wicker strainers, but the other half he poured into bowls that he might drink it for his supper. When he had got through with all his work, he lit the fire, and then caught sight of us, whereon he said, "Strangers, who are you? Where do you sail from? Are you traders, or do you sail the sea as rovers, with your hands against every man, and every man's hand against you?"

We were frightened out of our senses by his loud voice and monstrous form, but I managed to say, "We are Achaeans[3] on our way home from Troy, but by the will of Zeus and stress of weather we have been driven far out of our course. We are the people of Agamemnon, son of Atreus,[4] who has won infinite renown throughout the whole world by sacking so great a city and killing so many people. We therefore humbly pray you to show us some hospitality, and otherwise make us such presents as visitors may reasonably expect. May your excellency fear the wrath of heaven, for we are your suppliants, and Zeus takes all respectable travelers under his protection, for he is the avenger of all suppliants and foreigners in distress."

To this he gave me but a pitiless answer. "Stranger," said he, "you are a fool, or else you know nothing of this country. Talk to me, indeed, about fearing the gods or shunning their anger? We Cyclopes do not care about

---

[1] hoggets: young sheep.
[2] These Greeks looked upon hospitality to visitors as a religious duty.

[3] Achaeans (ə·kē′ənz): Greeks.
[4] Agamemnon . . . Atreus (ā′trōōs): Agamemnon was chief of the Greek army in the war against Troy.

Zeus or any of your blessed gods, for we are ever so much stronger than they. I shall not spare either yourself or your companions out of any regard for Zeus, unless I am in the humor for doing so. And now tell me where you made your ship fast when you came on shore. Was it round the point, or is she lying straight off the land?"

He said this to draw me out, but I was too cunning to be caught in that way, so I answered with a lie. "Poseidon,"[1] said I, "sent my ship on the rocks at the far end of your country, and wrecked it. We were driven onto them from the open sea, but I and those who are with me escaped the jaws of death."

The cruel wretch vouchsafed me not one word of answer, but with a sudden clutch he gripped up two of my men at once and dashed them down upon the ground as though they had been puppies. Their brains were shed upon the ground, and the earth was wet with their blood. Then he tore them limb from limb and supped upon them. He gobbled them up like a lion in the wilderness, flesh, bones, marrow, and entrails, without leaving anything un-eaten. As for us, we wept and lifted up our hands to heaven on seeing such a horrid sight, for we did not know what else to do; but when the Cyclops had filled his huge paunch and had washed down his meal of human flesh with a drink of neat milk,[2] he stretched himself full length upon the ground among his sheep and went to sleep. I was at first inclined to seize my sword, draw it, and drive it into his vitals, but

[1] **Poseidon** (pō·sī′dən): god of the sea.
[2] **neat milk**: cow's milk.

I reflected that if I did we should all certainly be lost, for we should never be able to shift the stone which the monster had put in front of the door. So we stayed sobbing and sighing where we were till morning came.

When dawn appeared, he again lit his fire, milked his goats and ewes, all quite rightly, and then let each have her own young one; as soon as he had got through with all his work, he clutched up two more of my men and began eating them for his morning's meal. Presently, with the utmost ease, he rolled the stone away from the door and drove out his sheep, but he at once put it back again — as easily as though he were merely clapping the lid on to a quiver full of arrows. As soon as he had done so he shouted and cried, "Shoo, shoo," after his sheep to drive them on to the mountain; so I was left to scheme some way of taking my revenge and covering myself with glory.

In the end I deemed it would be the best plan to do as follows. The Cyclops had a great club which was lying near one of the sheep pens; it was of green olive wood, and he had cut it intending to use it for a staff as soon as it should be dry. It was so huge that we could only compare it to the mast of a twenty-oared merchant vessel of large burden, able to venture out into open sea. I went up to this club and cut off about six feet of it; I then gave this piece to the men and told them to fine it evenly off at one end, which they proceeded to do, and lastly I brought it to a point myself, charring the end in the fire to make it harder. When I had done this I hid it under the dung, which was lying about all over the cave, and told the men to cast lots which of them should venture along with myself to lift it and bore it into the monster's eye while he was asleep. The lot fell upon the very four whom I should have chosen, and I myself made five. In the evening the wretch came back from shepherding and drove his flocks into the cave — this time driving them all inside and not leaving any in the yards; I suppose some fancy must have taken him, or a god must have prompted him to do so. As soon as he had put the stone back to its place against the door, he sat down, milked his ewes and his goats all quite rightly, and then let each have her own young one; when he had got through with all this work, he gripped up two more of my men and made his supper off them. So I went up to him with an ivy-wood bowl of black wine in my hands.

"Look here, Cyclops," said I, "you have been eating a great deal of man's flesh, so take this and drink some wine, that you may see what kind of liquor we had on board my ship. I was bringing it to you as a drink offering, in the hope that you would take compassion upon me and further me on my way home, whereas all you do is to go on ranting and raving most intolerably. You ought to be ashamed of yourself. How can you expect people to come and see you any more if you treat them in this way?"

He then took the cup and drank. He was so delighted with the taste of the wine that he begged me for another bowl full. "Be so kind," he said, "as to give me some more, and tell me your name at once. I want to make you a present that you will be glad to have. We have wine even in this country, for our soil grows grapes and the sun ripens them, but this drink is like nectar and ambrosia [1] all in one."

I then gave him some more; three times did I fill the bowl for him and three times did he drain it without thought or heed. Then, when I saw that the wine had got into his head, I said to him as plausibly as I could: "Cyclops, you ask my name and I will tell it to you; give me, therefore, the present you promised me. My name is No Man; this is what my father and mother and my friends have always called me."

But the cruel wretch said, "Then I will eat all No Man's comrades before No Man himself, and will keep No Man for the last. This is the present that I will make him."

As he spoke, he reeled and fell sprawling face upwards on the ground. His great neck hung heavily backwards and a deep sleep took hold upon him. Presently he turned sick, and threw up both wine and the gobbets of human flesh on which he had been gorging, for he was very drunk. Then I thrust the beam of wood far into the embers to heat it, and encouraged my men lest any of them should turn fainthearted. When the wood, green though it was, was about to blaze, I drew it out of the fire glowing with heat, and my men gathered round me, for heaven had filled their hearts with courage. We drove the sharp end of the beam into the monster's eye, and

[1] **nectar and ambrosia:** the drink and food of the gods.

bearing upon it with all my weight I kept turning it round and round as though I were boring a hole in a ship's plank with an auger, which two men with a wheel and strap can keep on turning as long as they choose. Even thus did we bore the red-hot beam into his eye, till the boiling blood bubbled all over it as we worked it round and round, so that the steam from the burning eyeball scalded his eyelids and eyebrows, and the roots of the eye sputtered in the fire. As a blacksmith plunges an ax or hatchet into cold water to temper it — for it is this that gives strength to the iron — and it makes a great hiss as he does so, even thus did the Cyclops' eye hiss round the beam of olive wood, and his hideous yells made the cave ring again. We ran away in a fright, but he plucked the beam all besmirched with gore from his eye, and hurled it from him in a frenzy of rage and pain, shouting as he did so to the other Cyclopes who lived on the bleak headlands near him. So they gathered from all quarters round his cave when they heard him crying, and asked what was the matter with him.

"What ails you, Polyphemus," [1] said they, "that you make such a noise, breaking the stillness of the night and preventing us from being able to sleep? Surely no man is carrying off your sheep? Surely no man is trying to kill you either by fraud or by force?"

But Polyphemus shouted to them from inside the cave, "No Man is killing me by fraud! No Man is killing me by force!"

"Then," said they, "if no man is attacking you, you must be ill; when Zeus makes people ill, there is no help for it, and you had better pray to your father Poseidon."

Then they went away, and I laughed inwardly at the success of my clever stratagem, but the Cyclops, groaning and in an agony of pain, felt about with his hands till he found the stone and took it from the door; then he sat in the doorway and stretched his hands in front of it to catch anyone going out with the sheep, for he thought I might be foolish enough to attempt this.

As for myself, I kept on puzzling to think how I could best save my own life and those of my companions. I schemed and schemed, as one who knows that his life depends upon it, for the danger was very great. In the end I deemed that this plan would be the best. The male sheep were well grown, and carried a heavy black fleece, so I bound them noiselessly together in threes, with some of the withies [2] on which the wicked monster used to sleep. There was to be a man under the middle sheep, and the two on either side were to cover him, so that there were three sheep to each man. As for myself, there was a ram finer than any of the others, so I caught hold of him by the back, ensconced [3] myself in the thick wool under his belly, and hung on patiently to his fleece, face upward, keeping a firm hold on it all the time.

Thus, then, did we wait in great fear of mind till morning came, but when

---

[1] **Polyphemus** (pol'i·fē'məs).

[2] **withies:** flexible, slender twigs.
[3] **ensconced:** hid.

dawn appeared, the male sheep hurried out to feed, while the ewes remained bleating about the pens waiting to be milked, for their udders were full to bursting; but their master, in spite of all his pain, felt the backs of all the sheep as they stood upright, without being sharp enough to find out that the men were underneath their bellies. As the ram was going out, last of all, heavy with its fleece and with the weight of my crafty self, Polyphemus laid hold of it and said:

"My good ram, what is it that makes you the last to leave my cave this morning? You are not wont to let the ewes go before you, but lead the mob with a run, whether to flowery meadow or bubbling fountain, and are the first to come home again at night; but now you lag last of all. Is it because you know your master has lost his eye, and you are sorry because that wicked No Man and his horrid crew have got him down in his drink and blinded him? But I will have his life yet. If you could understand and talk, you would tell me where the wretch is hiding, and I would dash his brains upon the ground till they flew all over

the cave. I should thus have some satisfaction for the harm this no-good No Man has done me."

As he spoke he drove the ram outside. When we were a little way out from the cave and yards, I first got from under the ram's belly and then freed my comrades. As for the sheep, which were very fat, by constantly heading them in the right direction we managed to drive them down to the ship. The crew rejoiced greatly at seeing those of us who had escaped death, but they wept for the others, whom the Cyclops had killed. However, I made signs to them by nodding and frowning that they were to hush their crying, and told them to get all the sheep on board at once and put out to sea. So they went aboard, took their places, and smote the gray sea with their oars. Then, when I had got as far out as my voice would reach, I began to jeer at the Cyclops.

"Cyclops," said I, "you should have taken better measure of your man before eating up his comrades in your cave. You wretch, eat up your visitors in your own house? You might have known that your sin would find you out, and now Zeus and the other gods have punished you."

He got more and more furious as he heard me, and he tore the top off from a high mountain and flung it just in front of my ship, so that it was within a little of hitting the end of the rudder. The sea quaked as the rock fell into it, and the wash of the wave it raised carried us back toward the mainland, and forced us toward the shore. But I snatched up a long pole and kept the ship off — making signs to my men, by nodding my head, that they must row for their lives, whereon they laid out with a will. When we had got twice as far as we were before, I was for jeering at the Cyclops again, but the men begged and prayed of me to hold my tongue.

"Do not," they exclaimed, "be mad enough to provoke this savage creature further. He has thrown one rock at us already which drove us back again to the mainland, and we were sure it would be the death of us. If he hears any further sound of voices, he will pound our heads and our ship's timbers into a jelly with rugged rocks, for he can throw them a long way."

But I would not listen to them, and shouted out to him in my rage, "Cyclops, if anyone asks you who it was that put your eye out and spoiled your beauty, say it was the valiant warrior Odysseus, son of Laertes,[1] who lives in Ithaca."

On this he groaned, and cried out, "Alas, alas, then the old prophecy about me is coming true. There was a prophet here, at one time, a man both brave and of great stature, Telemus, son of Eurymus,[2] who was an excellent seer and did all the prophesying for the Cyclopes till he grew old. He told me that all this would happen to me some day, and said I should lose my sight by the hand of Odysseus. I have been all along expecting someone of imposing presence and superhuman strength, whereas he turns out to be a little insignificant weakling who has managed to blind my eye by taking advantage of me in my drink. Come here, then, Odysseus, that I may make you presents to show my hospitality and urge Poseidon to help you forward on your journey — for Poseidon and I are father and son. He, if he so wills, shall heal me, which no one else, neither god nor man, can do."

Then I said, "I wish I could be as sure of killing you outright and sending you down to the house of Hades, as I am that it will take more than Poseidon to cure that eye of yours."

On this he lifted up his hands to the firmament of heaven and prayed, saying: "Hear me, great Poseidon! If I am indeed your own true-begotten son, grant that Odysseus may never reach his home alive; or, if he must get back to his friends at last, let him do so late and in sore plight after losing all his men. Let him reach his home in another man's ship and find trouble in his house."

Thus did he pray, and Poseidon heard his prayer. Then he picked up a rock much larger than the first, swung it aloft and hurled it with prodigious force. It fell just short of the ship but

---

[1] Laertes (lā·ûr′tēz).

[2] Eurymus (yōō′ri·məs).

was within a little of hitting the end of the rudder. The sea quaked as the rock fell into it, and the wash of the wave it raised drove us onward on our way toward the shore of the island.

When at last we got to the island where we had left the rest of our ships, we found our comrades lamenting us and anxiously awaiting our return. We ran our vessel upon the sands and got out of her onto the seashore. We also landed the Cyclops' sheep, and divided them equitably among us, so that none might have reason to complain. As for the ram, my companions agreed that I should have it as an extra share; so I sacrificed it on the seashore and burned its thighbones to Zeus, who is the lord of all. But he heeded not my sacrifice and only thought how he might destroy both my ships and my comrades.

Thus through the livelong day to the going down of the sun we feasted our fill on meat and drink, but when the sun went down and it became dark, we camped upon the beach. When dawn appeared, I bade my men go on board and loose the hawsers. Then they took their places and smote the gray sea with their oars. So we sailed on, with sorrow in our hearts because we had lost our comrades, but glad to have escaped death ourselves.

COURAGE AND DARING — AN OLD GREEK LEGEND

1. What reason did Odysseus give for wanting to visit the land of the Cyclopes? What misgivings did he have? What did his men want to do when they saw the Cyclops' cave? Why was this not done?

2. Describe the reception the Greeks got from the giant. Why did Odysseus have to remain in the cave?

3. What plan did Odysseus devise for their escape? Tell in detail how the plan worked out.

4. After their escape, what actions of Odysseus did his men disapprove of? What prayer did the Cyclops make to his father, the god Poseidon?

5. In what ways does Odysseus seem less noble than David, in *The Stone?* How would you describe the courage of Odysseus? Were the risks he took necessary?

6. Odysseus expected his men to share his dangers and to face them with equal courage. What is your reaction to this fact? Did Odysseus seem to care for his men and to shown concern for them? Explain.

7. Would you consider Odysseus foolhardy rather than courageous? Discuss.

8. Can you think of men today who, like Odysseus, go out of their way to face danger? Why do they do this? Would you consider them courageous?

9. Have you ever gone out of your way to take a chance? If so, why did you do it? Were you more like David or Odysseus at the time? In what ways?

WORDS: ACCENT, PRONUNCIATION, AND MEANING

The word *exquisite* is used in this narrative to describe the flavor of wine. Say *exquisite* aloud. Which syllable did you stress: *EXquisite?* or *exQUISite?* Look in your glossary or dictionary to find out which pronunciation is more commonly used. When you speak or read aloud, you are expected to stress a word in the way that most other educated speakers of English do.

Sometimes a shift in accent or a change in pronunciation indicates a change in a word's function. For example, when we pronounce the word *separate* as sep′ə·rāt, the word is a verb. When we say sep′ər·it the word is an adjective.

The following words can be pronounced in more than one way. Look in your dictionary to find out which pronunciation is more commonly used. Do different pronunciations signal different functions, or even different meanings, in any of these words?

either	present
apparatus	elaborate
permit	minute

SENTENCES: WORD ORDER

Here is a group of words that could tell about something that happened in this story: *Cyclops of took cave the twelve his Odysseus of to the men best.*

Why don't these words make sense? Let's see if the problem is that they aren't arranged in the right order. Here are the same words arranged in different ways:

The Cyclops took twelve of his best men to the cave of Odysseus.

Twelve of his best men took Odysseus to the cave of the Cyclops.

Odysseus took twelve of his best men to the cave of the Cyclops.

Now each group should say something to you, for each is arranged in an order that makes sense in English. But the statements do not mean the same thing. Which statement corresponds with what really happened in the story?

You see that word order is one of the most important ways to signal meaning in English. By changing the order of words, we can change the meaning.

Arrange the following group of words in various ways that make sense. Then underline the group that tells what happened in the story: *the gave him Odysseus enough make to sweet drunk Cyclops wine.*

COMPOSITION: DETAILS IN DESCRIPTION

When an author tells a story, he usually includes descriptions of people and places. In the second paragraph of this story, Homer describes the island where the events of the story take place. Reread this paragraph, and then list the details that help you to picture the setting.

"Now off their harbor there lies a wooded and fertile island not quite close to the land of the Cyclops, but still not far. It is overrun with wild goats that breed there in great numbers and are never disturbed by foot of man. For sportsmen . . . do not go there, nor yet again is it ever plowed or fed down, but it lies a wilderness untilled and unsown from year to year, and has no living thing upon it but only goats. . . . There are meadows that in some places come right down to the seashore, well-watered and full of luscious grass; grapes would do there excellently; there is level land for plowing, and it would always yield heavily at harvest time, for the soil is deep. There is a good harbor where no cables are wanted, nor anchors, nor need a ship be moored, but all one has to do is to beach one's vessel and stay there till the wind becomes fair for putting out to sea again. At the head of the harbor there is a spring of clear water coming out of a cave and there are poplars growing all around it."

Look also at the brief third paragraph of "Odysseus and the Cyclops." What specific details help you to picture the darkness and gloom as Odysseus' ship enters the harbor at night? Can you find any other descriptions in this story that help you picture settings or characters?

In one paragraph, describe some setting with which you are familiar. Include details that will give the reader a clear picture of this place.

Sir Gawain

DOROTHY HEIDERSTADT

In England in the Middle Ages, courage was linked with chivalry and honor. Among the knights of King Arthur's Round Table, Sir Gawain was known for both of these virtues. In this retelling of the famous medieval legend, Sir Gawain accepts an unusual challenge that puts his courage to a test.

THE COLD WINTER SUNLIGHT streamed through the narrow windows onto the rushes strewn on the stone floor for warmth. The knights' shields hung on the walls; each had its own decoration, which served to identify its owner when he was dressed in his battle armor. Banners stirred in the wintry drafts, even though a great fire blazed on the hearth. Shivering pages ran about, lighting tapers in the silver sconces against the early winter darkness.

Suddenly King Arthur lifted his head sharply, for he heard a horn in the distance. Sir Gawain, his favorite nephew, heard it too, and stopped his

"Sir Gawain" from *Knights and Champions* by Dorothy Heiderstadt, © 1960 by Dorothy Heiderstadt. Reprinted by permission of Thomas Nelson & Sons.

idle, gallant chatter with a lady to listen. Then all the company could hear horns blowing, high-pitched and shrill, and all knew that these were no ordinary horns. The casements shook, and the flames of the candles trembled. As the knights sprang up to seize their swords and shields, the great doors of the hall burst open as if pushed by violent hands, and, on a gust of icy wind, a strange figure entered.

He was a giant knight on horseback, and he was dressed in green armor from head to toe. Even the plumes and trappings on his horse were green. In his right hand the knight carried a green battle-ax, in his left hand a bough of holly. His eyes gleamed like two emeralds through the visor of his helmet. He leaped from his saddle and stood laughing at the astonished knights and ladies.

"Knights of the Round Table," he cried, "stand forth! Take up your battle-ax, one of you, and strike at me!"

Arthur's knights looked at one another uneasily. All sorts of visitors came to Camelot, but there had never been one so strange as this man.

"Why should one of us strike at

you?" asked the King. "That would be poor hospitality on this festive day. Have you wronged us?"

"I have wronged no one," said the Green Knight. "I was told that here I would find the bravest knights in the world. I come only for adventure's sake."

Everyone could understand that statement, for there was not a man present who did not love adventure for adventure's sake. Sir Gawain, the King's nephew, leaned forward, gazing at the stranger with interest.

"Well," said the Green Knight impatiently, "will no one trade blows with me? Let the bravest among you strike me. Then let him agree to take the same blow from me a year and a day from now. Come, come, is there no one among you venturesome enough?"

At these words, King Arthur himself drew his sword and started up. But Gawain cried quickly, "Dear Uncle, let me claim this adventure!" The King hesitated, then smiled and waved his hand in consent.

"I will trade blows with you!" cried Gawain, leaping to his feet and going to stand before the Green Knight.

"Good!" cried the knight. He planted his feet firmly on the floor and removed his helmet to reveal a great, flowing green beard and a green face. Gawain lifted his sword.

"That paltry thing!" jeered the knight. "Strike me a real blow with your battle-ax! Or are you afraid of the mighty blow you may expect from me in return?"

Gawain reddened with anger, and, thrusting his sword into its scabbard with a clang, he seized his battle-ax.

"You will not live to return this blow!" he cried; gripping the battle-ax in both hands, he swung it above his head.

The Green Knight laughed and dropped to his knees before Gawain, shaking the long green hair from his neck. "Strike!" he said. "Then I will tell you my name and where you can find me, a year and a day from now!"

Gawain made no answer, but swinging his ax with all his strength he cut off the Green Knight's head. Whereupon, the stranger picked up his head and set it back on his shoulders.

"I am the Knight of the Green Chapel," he announced, "and that is where you must meet me, the day after next New Year's Day, Sir Gawain! There I will return your blow. You will

be a coward and shamed before all men if you fail to come."

So saying, the strange knight mounted his charger and rode out of the hall, leaving Arthur's knights to stare into one another's faces. Once more they heard the wild horns blowing, and then all was still.

"That was no man, but a monster," someone breathed. And the others agreed, "Yes, it was a monster. No human being could prevail against it. Do not keep the tryst, Gawain."

But Gawain was resolved to go. All that year, as he fought in tournaments and rode forth to right wrongs and rescue maidens in distress, he thought about the Green Knight.

When the year had nearly gone and it was Christmastide, Gawain knew that it was time for him to go. He must seek out the Green Chapel and receive the deadly blow which was his due. He knew that he could not survive such a blow, for he had not the magic powers of the Green Knight. Yet he had no thought of failing to keep the agreement.

On the morning of his departure, he called to his page to fetch his arms. Servants spread a carpet on the floor, and Gawain stood on it. And first, his men put upon him a doublet of silk and a well-made hood. They set steel shoes on his feet and encased his legs and arms in steel armor. Gloves of metal were placed upon his hands. Then the men enclosed his body in coat armor, his spurs were fixed to the heels of his shoes, and his sword was fastened to his side by a silken girdle.

Thus arrayed, Gawain went to hear Mass and then took leave of King Arthur. His mighty horse, Gringolet, awaited him, encased in armor, too, which glittered like sunlight. Gringolet stood patiently while his master, in his heavy armor, was assisted into the saddle. Sir Gawain then set his helmet upon his head, and took up his shield and lance. Bidding all "Farewell," he spurred his horse and rode out of the castle courtyard. Not one of those left behind expected to see him alive again.

Gringolet's hoofs, clattering across the wooden drawbridge, were echoed by the hoofbeats of the charger belonging to Gawain's young squire, his only companion. The squire was taken along to look after Gawain's horse and his armor, and to arrange for the burial of his body after his death. It was the custom for knights to be accompanied by their squires, and according to the chivalric code no squire could be harmed, for he rode unarmed. It was probable that even so outlandish a being as the Green Knight would observe the code.

Gawain and his squire heard the drawbridge being pulled up behind them after they had crossed over. Sleet was falling, and later there was hail and snow, for it was an uncommonly bitter winter. Into Wales they traveled, over hills and through deep valleys, and across the River Dee. At last, on Christmas night, they came to a fine castle in the midst of a forest of oak trees. Here they were made welcome by a handsome lord and royally entertained.

Knights and squires led them into the hall and took Gawain's helmet and sword. They helped him remove his armor and brought rich robes for him to wear. A chair was placed for him beside the fireplace, and a table drawn up before it. Gawain sat down to a hearty meal of baked fish and meat well seasoned and spiced.

"Why do you wander abroad at Christmastide in such bitter weather, when most folk are at home?" his host asked curiously. Gawain willingly told his story.

"The Knight of the Green Chapel! I know him well," said the lord of the castle when Gawain had finished. "The Green Chapel is two miles from here, and the name of the knight is Bernlak de Hautdesert.[1] Some say he is a madman, and some say he is not human, but a monster. Whatever he is, it would be better, young sir, to give up your quest and return to King Arthur's court where more worthy adventures must surely await you."

"No, I have given my word," said Gawain. "I will not turn aside from this adventure."

"Stay here then, until the appointed day," said his host. "On the day after New Year's Day I will send a servant to guide you to the Green Chapel. I would not go there myself for all the gold in the world."

Gawain willingly remained for a week at the fine castle, where he was well entertained. On the appointed day he set out with the guide and the squire to seek the Green Chapel. Through a wild valley they rode, among great, sweeping hills covered with leafless oak trees white with frost. They saw hazel and hawthorn trees, on whose boughs huddled unhappy birds crying

piteously with the cold. Presently the riders came to a roaring stream; beside it there was a mound overgrown with green moss, with a thorn tree growing before it. They could hear a whining sound, as though an ax were being sharpened. The green mound looked like a cave, for it had great openings at one end and on either side.

"They call this the Green Chapel," said the old servant, reining his horse before the mound. "It is guarded by the Green Knight, who is so cruel and merciless that he kills everyone who passes. Good Sir Gawain, return with me to my lord's castle, and let the Green Knight alone. Or, if you will, ride home. I will never tell anyone that you had wisdom enough to run away!"

Gawain glanced at his squire, and observed that the boy was looking at him with confidence. Squire and knight smiled at one another and exchanged a wordless sentence: This poor, fearful old man has never known adventure for adventure's sake!

"No, I thank you," Gawain said courteously to the old servant. "I must fulfill my part of the bargain."

The servant, seeing that it was useless to reason further, bowed his head and rode homeward, leaving Gawain to his fate. Now the two, knight and squire, dismounted and stood listening to the noise of the ax being sharpened on the whetstone.

Then Gawain saw a great horn hanging on one limb of the thorn tree before him. He set the horn to his lips and blew a mighty blast upon it.

"I am Gawain of King Arthur's court!" he cried, "and I have come to keep tryst with the Knight of the Green

---

[1] **Bernlak de Hautdesert** (hŏ′dez·ərt).

Chapel! Sir Knight, come forward if you are not afraid!"

"Wait!" roared a voice, and there came forth from the mound the Green Knight in his strange armor, ax in hand. "You have been true to your promise," he said. "Are you ready to receive the blow?"

"It is for that I have come," replied Gawain, approaching the knight and taking off his helmet to bare his head.

"This will be a fatal blow," the Green Knight said, and he whirled the blade around his head, making it sing in the frosty air.

"I am ready," answered Gawain.

Then the Green Knight bent forward and looked at Gawain with narrowed eyes. "You are young to die," he said. "Beg for mercy, and perhaps I will let you go free."

"I have never yet begged for mercy," said Gawain carelessly, and he stood smiling at the Green Knight.

"Then kneel!" thundered his adversary.

Gawain knelt before him and bowed his head. All was still. The birds which had cried so piteously were silent, and even the wind had stopped blowing. Gawain waited, but the expected blow did not fall.

"Arise, Sir Gawain," said the Green Knight gruffly. "I can see that the tales I have heard of King Arthur's knights are indeed true: they are the bravest knights in the world. The blow, had I given it, would have finished you; though I tempted you to beg for mercy, you would not. Know you now, had you weakened you would have died for it. Go now; return to your King, and peace go with you."

The Green Knight threw down his battle-ax and saluted Gawain with his lifted sword. Then Gawain and his young squire rode back to King Arthur's court.

When they rode into the courtyard at Camelot, trumpets sounded on the battlements of the castle, and banners were unfurled in celebration of Sir Gawain's return. Bells were rung in the highest tower in honor of Gawain, and King Arthur himself came out to greet him. Then the knight was led into the castle to tell the tale of his adventure at the Green Chapel. Sir Gawain continued to be one of the bravest and best loved of Arthur's knights, until his death from a wound in the war waged by Arthur against his evil nephew, Modred.

COURAGE AND HONOR — A MEDIEVAL LEGEND

1. What was unusual about the appearance and actions of the Green Knight? What challenge did he present to the Knights of the Round Table?

2. How did the Green Knight anger Gawain? What magical occurrence surprised the knights? What did they advise Gawain to do?

3. Why did Gawain resolve to meet the Green Knight? Describe his preparations for meeting the Green Knight. Why did he take his squire?

4. Tell about the events that concluded Gawain's tryst with the Green Knight.

5. In what ways did supernatural or magical elements play a part in this story? Do you think these elements made Gawain even more courageous and knightly? Explain. In what other stories have you seen the supernatural at work?

6. In what ways are Gawain and Odys-

seus similar? In what ways are they different? How does David differ from both?

7. How did Gawain's sense of honor contribute to making him courageous?

8. Whom would you rather have as a leader on a search for adventure — David, Odysseus, or Gawain? Why?

9. If each of these three heroes were living today, in what kind of activity might each be engaged?

WORDS:
CONTEXT CLUES TO MEANING

Notice the use of the word *rushes* in the first sentence of this story:

"The cold winter sunlight streamed through the narrow window onto the *rushes* strewn on the stone floor for warmth."

Usually you would think of *rushes* as an action verb meaning to hurry, to plunge, or to move with violence. What told you that *rushes* was used here as a noun? The rest of the sentence, or the word's context, told you that the sunlight was shining on the rushes and also that the rushes were lying on the floor. It told you that the rushes were there to aid in giving warmth. You perhaps concluded that the rushes were a kind of covering for the floor. Such intelligent guessing of the meaning of words through the use of context clues is an important reading skill.

Try to guess from the context of this fourth sentence the meaning of the words *pages, tapers,* and *sconces.*

"Shivering *pages* ran about, lighting *tapers* in the silver *sconces* against the early winter darkness."

BASIC SENTENCES

A few words provide the key to the meaning of almost every English sentence. These words are the subject and the verb. Often the subject and verb are followed by an object or a complement. These key words are in italics in the following sentences.

"*Banners stirred* in the wintry drafts . . ." (subject-verb)

"Suddenly *King Arthur lifted* his *head* sharply . . ." (subject-verb-object)

"*He was* a giant *knight* on horseback . . ." (subject - linking verb - complement)

These basic patterns show you the foundations on which many English sentences are formed.

Make up three sentences of your own and underline the key words. Try to make up one sentence for each of the basic patterns mentioned above.

COMPOSITION:
UNITY IN DESCRIPTION

The purpose of the third paragraph of this story is to describe the Green Knight. We say that this paragraph has unity because every detail in it helps to give a picture of this strange person.

"He was a giant knight on horseback, and he was dressed in green armor from head to toe. Even the plumes and trappings on his horse were green. In his right hand the knight carried a green battle-ax, in his left hand a bough of holly. His eyes gleamed like two emeralds through the visor of his helmet. He leaped from his saddle and stood laughing at the astonished knights and ladies."

Can you find any sentence in this paragraph that does not describe some aspect of the Knight?

Write a short paragraph describing a painting or photograph. Try to include details that will help your reader to visualize what the painting or photograph depicts. Be sure to make your paragraph unified. Do not include any details that are not relevant to your description.

Will Stutely's Rescue

HOWARD PYLE

From medieval England comes the legend of the generous "outlaw" hero, Robin Hood, who took from the rich to help the poor. This clash between Robin and the corrupt Sheriff is from Pyle's book The Merry Adventures of Robin Hood.

NOW WHEN THE SHERIFF found that neither law nor guile could overcome Robin Hood, he was much perplexed, and said to himself, "Fool that I am! Had I not told our King about Robin Hood, I would not have gotten myself into such a coil; but now I must either take him captive or have wrath visited upon my head from his most gracious Majesty. I have tried law, and I have tried guile, and I have failed in both; so I will try what may be done with might."

Thus communing within himself, he called his constables together and told them what was in his mind. "Now take ye each four men, all armed in proof," [1] said he, "and get ye gone to the forest, at different points, and lay in wait for this same Robin Hood. But if any con-stable finds too many men against him, let him sound a horn, and then let each band within hearing come with all speed and join the party that calls them. Thus, I think, shall we take this green-clad knave. Furthermore, to him that first meeteth with Robin Hood shall one hundred pounds of silver money be given if he be brought to me dead or alive; and to him that meeteth with any of his band shall twoscore [2] pounds be given, if such be brought to me dead or alive. So, be ye bold and be ye crafty."

So thus they went in threescore companies of five to Sherwood Forest, to take Robin Hood, each constable wishing that he might be the one to find the bold outlaw, or at least one of his band. For seven days and nights they hunted through the forest glades, but never saw so much as a single man in Lincoln green; for tidings of all this had been brought to Robin Hood by trusty Eadom [3] of the Blue Boar.

When he first heard the news, Robin said, "If the Sheriff dare send force to

[1] **proof:** armor.

[2] **twoscore:** forty. One score is twenty.
[3] **Eadom** (eʹdəm).

meet force, woe will it be for him and many a better man beside, for blood will flow, and there will be great trouble for all. But fain would I shun blood and battle, and fain would I not deal sorrow to womenfolk and wives because good stout yeomen lose their lives. Once I slew a man, and never do I wish to slay a man again, for it is bitter for the soul to think thereon. So now we will abide silently in Sherwood Forest, so that it may be well for all; but should we be forced to defend ourselves, or any of our band, then let each man draw bow and brand with might and main."

At this speech many of the band shook their heads, and said to themselves, "Now the Sheriff will think that we are cowards, and folk will scoff throughout the countryside, saying that we fear to meet these men." But they said nothing aloud, swallowing their words, and doing as Robin bade them.

Thus they hid in the depths of Sherwood Forest for seven days and seven nights, and never showed their faces abroad in all that time; but early in the morning of the eighth day Robin Hood called the band together and said, "Now who will go and find what the Sheriff's men are at by this time? For I know right well they will not bide forever within Sherwood shades."

At this a great shout arose, and each man waved his bow aloft and cried that he might be the one to go. Then Robin Hood's heart was proud when he looked around on his stout, brave fellows, and he said, "Brave and true are ye all, my merry men, and a right stout band of good fellows are ye; but ye cannot all go, so I will choose one from

amongst you, and it shall be good Will Stutely, for he is as sly as e'er an old dog fox in Sherwood Forest."

Then Will Stutely leaped high aloft and laughed loudly, clapping his hands, for pure joy that he should have been chosen from among them all. "Now thanks, good master," quoth he, "and if I bring not news of those knaves to thee, call me no more thy sly Will Stutely."

Then he clad himself in a friar's gown, and underneath the robe he hung a good broadsword in such a place that he could easily lay hands upon it. Thus clad, he set forth upon his quest, until he came to the verge of the forest, and so to the highway. He saw two bands of the Sheriff's men, yet he turned neither to the right nor the left, but only drew his cowl the closer over his face, folding his hands as if in meditation. So at last he came to the Sign of the Blue Boar. "For," quoth he to himself, "our good friend Eadom will tell me all the news."

At the Sign of the Blue Boar he found a band of the Sheriff's men drinking right lustily; so, without speaking to any one, he sat down upon a distant bench, his staff in his hand, and his head bowed forward as though he were meditating. Thus he sat waiting until he might see the landlord apart, and Eadom did not know him, but thought him to be some poor tired friar, so he let him sit without saying a word to him or molesting him, though he liked not the cloth. "For," said he to himself, "it is a hard heart that kicks the lame dog from off the sill."

As Stutely sat thus, there came a great house cat and rubbed against his knee, raising his robe a palm's breadth high. Stutely pushed his robe quickly down again, but the constable who commanded the Sheriff's men saw what had passed, and saw also fair Lincoln green beneath the friar's robe. He said nothing at the time, but communed within himself in this wise: "Yon is no friar of orders gray, and also, I wot, no honest yeoman goeth about in priest's garb, nor doth a thief go so for naught. Now I think in good sooth that is one of Robin Hood's own men." So, presently, he said aloud: "O holy Father, wilt thou not take a good pot of March beer to slake thy thirsty soul withal?" But Stutely shook his head silently, for he said to himself, "Maybe there be those here who know my voice."

Then the constable said again, "Whither goest thou, holy friar, upon this hot summer's day?"

"I go a pilgrim to Canterbury Town," answered Will Stutely, speaking gruffly, so that none might know his voice.

Then the constable said, for the third time, "Now tell me, holy Father, do pilgrims to Canterbury wear good Lincoln green beneath their robes? Ha! By my faith, I take thee to be some lusty thief, and perhaps one of Robin Hood's own band! Now, by Our Lady's grace, if thou movest hand or foot, I will run thee through the body with my sword!"

Then he flashed forth his bright sword and leaped upon Will Stutely, thinking he would take him unaware; but Stutely had his own sword tightly held in his hand, beneath his robe, so he drew it forth before the constable came upon him. Then the stout constable struck a mighty blow; but he

THE CONCEPT OF COURAGE

struck no more in all that fight, for Stutely, parrying the blow right deftly, smote the constable back again with all his might. Then he would have escaped, but could not, for the other, all dizzy with the wound and with the flowing blood, seized him by the knees with his arms even as he reeled and fell. Then the others rushed upon him, and Stutely struck again at another of the Sheriff's men, but the steel cap glanced the blow, and though the blade bit deep, it did not kill. Meanwhile, the constable, fainting as he was, drew Stutely downward, and the others, seeing the yeoman hampered so, rushed upon him again, and one smote him a blow upon the crown so that the blood ran down his face and blinded him. Then, staggering, he fell, and all sprang upon him, though he struggled so manfully that they could hardly hold him fast. Then they bound him with stout hempen cords so that he could not move either hand or foot, and thus they overcame him. But it was a doleful day's doings for two of that band; for the constable was sorely wounded, and the other, whom Stutely smote upon the crown, lay sick for many a day ere he was the stout man that he had been before this famous fight.

Robin Hood stood under the greenwood tree, thinking of Will Stutely and how he might be faring, when suddenly he saw two of his stout yeomen come running down the forest path, and betwixt them ran buxom Maken of the Blue Boar. Then Robin's heart fell, for he knew they were the bearers of ill tidings.

"Will Stutely hath been taken," cried they, when they had come to where he stood.

"And is it thou that hast brought such doleful news?" said Robin to the lass.

"Ay, marry, for I saw it all," cried she, panting as the hare pants when it has escaped the hounds; "and I fear he is wounded sore, for one smote him main shrewdly in the crown. They have bound him and taken him to Nottingham Town, and ere I left the Blue Boar I heard that he should be hanged tomorrow day."

"He shall not be hanged tomorrow day," cried Robin; "or, if he be, full many a one shall gnaw the sod, and many shall have cause to cry alack-a-day!"

Then he clapped his horn to his lips and blew three blasts right loudly, and presently his good yeomen came running through the greenwood until sevenscore bold blades were gathered around him.

"Now hark you all!" cried Robin. "Our dear companion, Will Stutely, hath been taken by that vile Sheriff's men; therefore doth it behoove us to take bow and brand in hand to bring him off again; for I wot that we ought to risk life and limb for him, as he hath risked life and limb for us. Is it not so, my merry men all?" Then all cried, "Ay!" with a great voice.

"Now," quoth Robin again, "if there be any here that care not to risk life and limb, let them bide within Sherwood shades, for I constrain no man to my will; but tomorrow I will bring Will Stutely back or I will die with him."

Then up spake stout Little John.

"Thinkest thou, good master," he said, "that there be one among us all that would not risk life and limb for a fellow in trouble? If such there be, then do not I know every man in this company of stout yeomen. And, moreover, if there be such, I wot he should be stripped and beaten from out our merry woodlands. Is it not so, good friends?"

Then all cried, "Ay!" again, for there was not one man among them all that would not venture everything for a friend in need.

So the next day they all wended their way from Sherwood Forest, but by different paths, for it behooved them to be very crafty; so the band separated into parties of twos and threes, which were all to meet again in a tangled dell that lay near to Nottingham Town. Then, when they had all gathered together at the place of meeting, Robin spoke to them thus: "Now we will lie here in ambush until we can get news, for it doth behoove us to be cunning and wary if we would bring our friend, Will Stutely, off from the Sheriff's clutches."

So they lay hidden a long time, until the sun stood high in the sky. The day was warm and the dusty road was bare of travelers, except an aged palmer [1] who walked slowly along the highroad that led close beside the gray castle wall of Nottingham Town. When Robin saw that no other wayfarer was within sight, he called young David of Doncaster, who was a shrewd man for his years, and said to him, "Now get thee forth, young David, and speak to yonder palmer that walks beside the town wall, for he hath come but now from Nottingham Town, and may tell thee news of good Stutely, perchance."

[1] **palmer:** one who has visited Palestine and brought back a palm branch as a token of the pilgrimage.

So David strode forth, and when he came up to the pilgrim, he saluted him and said: "Good morrow, holy Father, and canst thou tell me when Will Stutely will be hanged upon the gallows tree? I fain would not miss the sight, for I have come from afar to see so sturdy a rogue hanged."

"Now, out upon thee, young man," cried the palmer, "that thou shouldst speak so when a good stout man is to be hanged for nothing but guarding his own life!" And he struck his staff upon the ground in anger. "Alas, say I, that this thing should be! For even this day, toward evening, when the sun falleth low, he shall be hanged, fourscore rods from the great town gate of Nottingham, where three roads meet; for there the Sheriff sweareth he shall die as a warning to all outlaws in Nottinghamshire. But yet, I say again, alas! For, though Robin Hood and his band may be outlaws, yet he taketh only from the rich and the strong and the dishonest man, while there is not a poor widow nor a peasant with many children, nigh to Sherwood, but has barley flour enough all the year long through him. It grieves my heart to see one as gallant as this Stutely die, for I have been a good Saxon [1] yeoman in my day, ere I turned palmer, and well I know a stout hand and one that smiteth shrewdly at a cruel Norman or a proud abbot with fat money bags. Had good Stutely's master but known how his man was compassed about with perils, perchance he might send succor to bring

[1] **Saxon:** The Saxons of England had been defeated by the Norman French invaders in 1066. There was still at this time bad feeling between the Normans, who were mostly of the ruling class, and the Saxons.

him out of the hand of his enemies."

"Ay, marry, that is true," cried the young man. "If Robin and his men be nigh this place, I wot right well they will strive to bring him forth from his peril. But fare thee well, thou good old man, and believe me, that, if Will Stutely die, he shall be right well avenged."

Then he turned and strode rapidly away; but the palmer looked after him, muttering, "I wot that youth is no country hind [2] that hath come to see a good man die. Well, well, perchance Robin Hood is not so far away but that there will be stout doings this day." So he went upon his way, muttering to himself.

When David of Doncaster told Robin Hood what the palmer had said to him, Robin called the band around him and spoke to them thus:

"Now let us get straightway into Nottingham Town, and mix ourselves with the people there; but keep ye one another in sight, pressing as near the prisoner and his guards as ye can, when they come outside the walls. Strike no man without need, for I would fain avoid bloodshed, but if ye do strike, strike hard, and see that there be no need to strike again. Then keep all together until we come again to Sherwood, and let no man leave his fellows."

The sun was low in the western sky when a bugle note sounded from the castle wall. Then all was bustle in Nottingham Town and crowds filled the streets, for all knew that the famous Will Stutely was to be hanged that

[2] **hind** (archaic): peasant.

day. Presently the castle gates opened wide and a great array of men-at-arms came forth with noise and clatter, the Sheriff, all clad in shining mail of linked chain, riding at their head. In the midst of all the guard, in a cart, with a halter about his neck, rode Will Stutely. His face was pale with his wound and with loss of blood, like the moon in broad daylight, and his fair hair was clotted in points upon his forehead, where the blood had hardened. When he came forth from the castle he looked up and he looked down, but though he saw some faces that showed pity and some that showed friendliness, he saw none that he knew. Then his heart sank within him like a plummet of lead, but nevertheless he spoke up boldly.

"Give a sword into my hand, Sir Sheriff," said he, "and wounded man though I be, I will fight thee and all thy men till life and strength be gone."

"Nay, thou naughty varlet," quoth the Sheriff, turning his head and looking right grimly upon Will Stutely, "thou shalt have no sword but shall die a mean death, as beseemeth a vile thief like thee."

"Then do but untie my hands and I will fight thee and thy men with no weapon but only my naked fists. I crave no weapon, but let me not be meanly hanged this day."

Then the Sheriff laughed aloud. "Why, how now," quoth he, "is thy proud stomach qualing? Shrive thyself,[1] thou vile knave, for I mean that thou shalt hang this day, and that

where three roads meet, so that all men shall see thee hang, for carrion crows and daws to peck at."

"O thou dastard heart!" cried Will Stutely, gnashing his teeth at the Sheriff. "Thou coward hind! If ever my good master meet thee, thou shalt pay dearly for this day's work! He doth scorn thee, and so do all brave hearts. Knowest thou not that thou and thy name are jests upon the lips of every brave yeoman? Such a one as thou art, thou wretched craven,[2] will never be able to subdue bold Robin Hood."

"Ha!" cried the Sheriff, in a rage, "Is it even so? Am I a jest with thy master, as thou callest him? Now I will make a jest of thee and a sorry jest withal, for I will quarter thee limb from limb, after thou art hanged." Then he spurred his horse forward and said no more to Stutely.

At last they came to the great town gate, through which Stutely saw the fair country beyond, with hills and dales all clothed in verdure,[3] and far away the dusky line of Sherwood's skirts. Then when he saw the slanting sunlight lying on field and fallow, shining redly here and there on cottage and farmhouse, and when he heard the sweet birds singing their vespers and the sheep bleating upon the hillside and beheld the swallows flying in the bright air, there came a great fullness to his heart so that all things blurred to his sight through salt tears, and he bowed his head lest the folk should think him unmanly when they saw the tears in his eyes. Thus he kept his head

---

[1] **shrive** (shrīv) **thyself:** make your confession.

[2] **craven** (krā′vən): coward.

[3] **verdure** (vûr′jər): green.

bowed till they had passed through the gate and were outside the walls of the town. But when he looked up again he felt his heart leap within him and then stand still for pure joy, for he saw the face of one of his own dear companions of merry Sherwood; then glancing quickly around he saw well-known faces upon all sides of him, crowding closely upon the men-at-arms who were guarding him. Then of a sudden the blood sprang to his cheeks, for he saw for a moment his own good master in the press, and, seeing him, knew that Robin Hood and all his band were there. Yet betwixt him and them was a line of men-at-arms.

"Now, stand back!" cried the Sheriff in a mighty voice, for the crowd pressed around on all sides. "What mean ye, varlets, that ye push upon us so? Stand back, I say!"

Then came a bustle and a noise, and one strove to push between the men-at-arms so as to reach the cart, and Stutely saw that it was Little John that made all that stir.

"Now stand thou back!" cried one of the men-at-arms whom Little John pushed with his elbows.

"Now stand thou back thine own self," quoth Little John, and straightway smote the man a buffet beside his head that felled him as a butcher fells an ox; and then he leaped to the cart where Stutely sat.

"I pray thee take leave of thy friends ere thou diest, Will," quoth he, "or maybe I will die with thee if thou must die, for I could never have better company." Then with one stroke he cut the bonds that bound the other's arms and

legs, and Stutely leaped straightway from the cart.

"Now as I live," cried the Sheriff, "yon valet I know right well is a sturdy rebel! Take him, I bid you all, and let him not go!"

So saying he spurred his horse upon Little John, and rising in his stirrups smote with might and main, but Little John ducked quickly underneath the horse's belly, and the blow whistled harmlessly over his head.

"Nay, good Sir Sheriff," cried he, leaping up again when the blow had passed, "I must e'en borrow thy most worshipful sword." Thereupon he twitched the weapon deftly from out the Sheriff's hand. "Here, Stutely," he cried, "the Sheriff hath lent thee his sword! Back to back with me, man, and defend thyself, for help is nigh!"

"Down with them!" bellowed the Sheriff in a voice like an angry bull, and he spurred his horse upon the two who now stood back to back, forgetting in his rage that he had no weapon with which to defend himself.

"Stand back, Sheriff!" cried Little John; and even as he spoke, a bugle horn sounded shrilly, and a clothyard shaft [1] whistled within an inch of the Sheriff's head. Then there came a swaying hither and thither and oaths and cries and groans and clashing of steel, and swords flashed in the setting sun, and a score of arrows whistled through the air; and some cried "Help, help!" and some, "A rescue, a rescue!"

"Treason!" cried the Sheriff in a loud voice. "Bear back! Bear back! Else we be all dead men!" Thereupon he reined his horse backward through the thickest of the crowd.

Now Robin Hood and his band might have slain half of the Sheriff's men had they desired to do so, but they let them push out of the press and get them gone, only sending a bunch of arrows after them to hurry them in their flight.

"Oh stay!" shouted Will Stutely after the Sheriff. "Thou wilt never catch bold Robin Hood if thou dost not stand to meet him face to face." But the Sheriff, bowing along his horse's back, made no answer but only spurred the faster.

Then Will Stutely turned to Little John and looked him in the face till the tears ran down from his eyes, and he wept aloud, and kissed his friend's cheek. "O Little John!" quoth he, "mine

own true friend, and he that I love better than man or woman in all the world beside! Little did I reckon to see thy face this day, or to meet thee this side of Paradise." And Little John could make no answer, but wept also.

Then Robin Hood gathered his band together in a close rank, with Will Stutely in the midst, and thus they moved slowly away toward Sherwood and were gone, as a storm cloud moves away from the spot where a tempest has swept the land. But they left ten of the Sheriff's men lying along the ground wounded — some more, some less — yet no one knew who smote them down.

Thus the Sheriff of Nottingham tried thrice to take Robin Hood and failed each time; and the last time he was frightened, for he felt how near he had come to losing his life; so he said: "These men fear neither God nor man, nor King nor King's officers. I would sooner lose my office than my life, so I will trouble them no more." So he kept close within his castle for many a day and dared not show his face outside of his own household, and all the time he was gloomy and would speak to no one, for he was ashamed of what had happened that day.

COURAGE AND LOYALTY —
   A MEDIEVAL LEGEND

1. Why did the Sheriff send out a search party for Robin Hood? Why did Robin not fight the Sheriff's men immediately? What did Robin's men think of this?

2. Why did Will Stutely go to the Sign of the Blue Boar? How did a cat ruin Will's scheme? What plans did Robin Hood make as a result? What did the

---

[1] **clothyard shaft:** an arrow, about twenty-seven inches long.

palmer reveal about the way the common people felt toward Robin Hood?

3. Describe how Will Stutely was rescued.

4. Loyalty is often a motivation for courage. Describe how loyalty prompted acts of courage by Will Stutely, by Robin Hood, by Little John, and by Robin Hood's other men. What did Will's and Little John's tears show us about their characters?

5. Think back to the acts of courage of David, Odysseus, and Gawain. Which was most like the courage of Robin Hood? How did Robin Hood differ from the other heroes?

6. Do you know of any incident in which someone courageously came to the aid of a friend, or in which family loyalty played a part?

ARCHAIC WORDS

By his choice of words, Howard Pyle gives his story the flavor and atmosphere of early England. Many words in this story are not used at all today. A few others no longer have the meaning they had in Robin Hood's time. For example, the Sheriff said, ". . . I would not have gotten myself into such a *coil*." We no longer use *coil* to mean trouble. Most dictionaries list this meaning of *coil* as "archaic," or, in other words, "old-fashioned" or "belonging to an earlier period."

Here are some other archaic words from the story: *ye, fain, yon, wot, sooth, withal, betwixt,* and *varlets*. Look for these words and try to figure out their meanings from context. A large dictionary will help you to locate their exact meanings.

SENTENCES: COMPOUND PARTS

Notice in the following sentences that some key parts are compound, that is, at least two subjects, verbs, objects, or complements are used. How many short and simple sentences can you make from each of these longer structures?

"Then Will Stutely *leaped* high aloft and *laughed* loudly . . ." (two verbs)

"Then he *clapped* his *horn* to his lips and *blew* three *blasts* . . ." (two verbs, two objects)

"'*Brave* and *true* are ye all . . .'" (two complements)

"Now *Robin Hood* and his *band* might have slain half of the Sheriff's men . . ." (two subjects)

Make up four sentences having compound parts.

COMPOSITION:
SENSORY APPEAL IN DESCRIPTION

As the author tells about Will Stutely being taken to his execution, he describes the English countryside. Notice the details the author uses in these two sentences of description:

"At last they came to the great town gate, through which Stutely saw the fair country beyond, with hills and dales all clothed in verdure, and far away the dusky line of Sherwood's skirts. Then . . . he saw the slanting sunlight lying on field and fallow, shining redly here and there on cottage and farmhouse, and . . . he heard the sweet birds singing their vespers and the sheep bleating upon the hillside and beheld the swallows flying in the bright air . . ."

A writer of description wants to put our senses to work. List the details in this passage that help you to see and to hear what Will Stutely saw and heard on his way to execution.

Write a brief paragraph describing your route to school each morning. Be sure to use several specific details that will tell your reader exactly what you see and hear — and perhaps even what you can smell — along your way.

Top Man

JAMES RAMSEY ULLMAN

THE GORGE BENT. The walls fell suddenly away, and we came out on the edge of a bleak, boulder-strewn valley. . . . *And there it was.*

Osborn saw it first. He had been leading the column, threading his way slowly among the huge rock masses of the gorge's mouth. Then he came to the first flat bare place and stopped. He neither pointed nor cried out, but every man behind him knew instantly what it was. The long file sprang taut, like a jerked rope. As swiftly as we could, but in complete silence, we came out one by one into the open space where Osborn stood, and we raised our eyes with his.

In the records of the Indian Topographical Survey it says: "Kalpurtha: altitude 27,930 feet. The highest peak in the Garhwal Himalayas and probably fourth highest in the world. Also known as K3. A Tertiary formation of sedimentary limestone. . . ."

There were men among us who had spent months of their lives — in some cases years — reading, thinking, planning about what now lay before us; but at that moment statistics and geology,

knowledge, thought, and plans, were as remote and forgotten as the faraway western cities from which we had come. We were men bereft of everything but eyes, everything but the single electric perception: *there it was!*

Before us the valley stretched into miles of rocky desolation. To right and left it was bounded by low ridges, which, as the eye followed them, slowly mounted and drew closer together, until the valley was no longer a valley at all, but a narrowing, rising corridor between the cliffs. What happened then I can describe only as a stupendous crash of music. At the end of the corridor and above it — so far above it that it shut out half the sky — hung the blinding white mass of K3.

It was like the many pictures I had seen, and at the same time utterly unlike them. The shape was there, and the familiar distinguishing features: the sweeping skirt of glaciers; the monstrous vertical precipices of the face and the jagged ice-line of the east ridge; finally, the symmetrical summit pyramid that transfixed the sky. But whereas in the pictures the mountain had always seemed unreal — a dream-image of cloud, snow, and crystal — it was now no longer an image at all. It was a mass:

solid, immanent, appalling. We were still too far away to see the windy whipping of its snow plumes or to hear the cannonading of its avalanches, but in that sudden silent moment every man of us was for the first time aware of it not as a picture in his mind, but as a thing, an antagonist. For all its twenty-eight thousand feet of lofty grandeur it seemed, somehow, less to tower than to crouch — a white-hooded giant, secret and remote, but living. Living and on guard.

I turned my eyes from the dazzling glare and looked at my companions. Osborn still stood a little in front of the others. He was absolutely motionless, his young face tense and shining, his eyes devouring the mountain as a lover's might devour the form of his beloved. One could feel in the very set of his body the overwhelming desire that swelled in him to act, to come to grips, to conquer. A little behind him were ranged the other white men of the expedition: Randolph, our leader, Wittmer and Johns, Dr. Schlapp and Bixler. All were still, their eyes cast upward. Off to one side a little stood Nace, the Englishman, the only one among us who was not staring at K3 for the first time. He had been the last to come up out of the gorge and stood now with arms folded on his chest, squinting at the great peak he had known so long and fought so tirelessly and fiercely. His lean British face, under its mask of stubble and windburn, was expressionless. His lips were a thin line, and his eyes seemed almost shut. Behind the sahibs [1] ranged the porters, bent for-

---

[1] **sahibs** (sä′ibs): a word used in India to refer to people of high rank.

ward over their staffs, their brown seamed faces straining upward from beneath their loads.

For a long while no one spoke or moved. The only sounds between earth and sky were the soft hiss of our breathing and the pounding of our hearts.

Through the long afternoon we wound slowly between the great boulders of the valley and at sundown pitched camp in the bed of a dried-up stream. The porters ate their rations in silence, wrapped themselves in their blankets, and fell asleep under the stars. The rest of us, as was our custom, sat close about the fire that blazed in the circle of tents, discussing the events of the day and the plans for the next. It was a flawlessly clear Himalayan night, and K3 tiered [2] up into the blackness like a monstrous beacon lighted from within. There was no wind, but a great tide of cold air crept down the valley from the ice fields above, penetrating our clothing, pressing gently against the canvas of the tents.

"Another night or two and we'll be needing the sleeping bags," commented Randolph.

Osborn nodded. "We could use them tonight would be my guess."

Randolph turned to Nace. "What do you say, Martin?"

The Englishman puffed at his pipe a moment. "Rather think it might be better to wait," he said at last.

"Wait? Why?" Osborn jerked his head up.

"Well, it gets pretty nippy high up, you know. I've seen it thirty below at twenty-five thousand on the east ridge.

---

[2] **tiered** (tērd) **up:** rose upward in rows or *tiers*.

Longer we wait for the bags, better acclimated we'll get."

Osborn snorted. "A lot of good being acclimated will do, if we have frozen feet."

"Easy, Paul, easy," cautioned Randolph. "It seems to me Martin's right."

Osborn bit his lip, but said nothing. The other men entered the conversation, and soon it had veered to other matters: the weather, the porters and pack animals, routes, camps, and strategy, the inevitable, inexhaustible topics of the climber's world.

There were all kinds of men among the eight of us, men with a great diversity of background and interest. Sayre Randolph, whom the Alpine Club had named leader of our expedition, had for years been a well-known explorer and lecturer. Now in his middle fifties, he was no longer equal to the grueling physical demands of high climbing, but served as planner and organizer of the enterprise. Wittmer was a Seattle lawyer, who had recently made a name for himself by a series of difficult ascents in the Coast Range of British Columbia. Johns was an Alaskan, a fantastically strong, able sourdough,[1] who had been a ranger in the U.S. Forestry Service and had accompanied many famous Alaskan expeditions. Schlapp was a practicing physician from Milwaukee, Bixler a government meteorologist with a talent for photography. I, at the time, was an assistant professor of geology at an eastern university.

Finally, and preeminently, there were Osborn and Nace. I say "preeminently" because, even at this time,

when we had been together as a party for little more than a month, I believe all of us realized that these were the two key men of our venture. None, to my knowledge, ever expressed it in words, but the conviction was none the less there that if any of us were eventually to stand on the summit of K3, it would be one of them, or both. They were utterly dissimilar men. Osborn was twenty-three and a year out of college, a compact, buoyant mass of energy and high spirits. He seemed to be wholly unaffected by either the physical or mental hazards of mountaineering and had already, by virtue of many spectacular ascents in the Alps and Rockies, won a reputation as the most skilled and audacious of younger American climbers. Nace was in his forties — lean, taciturn,[2] introspective. An official in the Indian Civil Service, he had explored and climbed in the Himalayas for twenty years. He had been a member of all five of the unsuccessful British expeditions to K3, and in his last attempt had attained to within five hundred feet of the summit, the highest point which any man had reached on the unconquered giant. This had been the famous, tragic attempt in which his fellow climber and lifelong friend, Captain Furness, had slipped and fallen ten thousand feet to his death. Nace rarely mentioned his name, but on the steel head of his ice ax were engraved the words: TO MARTIN FROM JOHN. If fate were to grant that the ax of any one of us should be planted upon the summit of K3, I hoped it would be this one.

Such were the men who huddled

[1] **sourdough:** a slang word meaning "pioneer" or "prospector."

[2] **taciturn** (tas′ə·tûrn): reserved, quiet.

about the fire in the deep, still cold of a Himalayan night. There were many differences among us, in temperament as well as in background. In one or two cases, notably that of Osborn and Nace, there had already been a certain amount of friction, and as the venture continued and the struggles and hardships of the actual ascent began, it would, I knew, increase. But differences were unimportant. What mattered — all that mattered — was that our purpose was one: to conquer the monster of rock and ice that now loomed above us in the night; to stand for a moment where no man, no living thing, had ever stood before. To that end we had come from half a world away, across oceans and continents to the fastnesses [1] of inner Asia. To that end we were prepared to endure cold, exhaustion, and danger, even to the very last extremity of human endurance. . . . Why? There is no answer, and at the same time every man among us knew the answer; every man who has ever looked upon a great

[1] **fastnesses:** fortresses or strongholds. Here, the author is comparing the mountains to fortresses.

mountain and felt the fever in his blood to climb and conquer knows the answer. George Leigh Mallory, greatest of mountaineers, expressed it once and for all when he was asked why he wanted to climb unconquered Everest.

"I want to climb it," said Mallory, "because it is there."

Day after day we crept on and upward. Sometimes the mountain was brilliant above us, as it had been when we first saw it; sometimes it was partially or wholly obscured by tiers of clouds. The naked desolation of the valley was unrelieved by any motion, color, or sound; and as we progressed, the great rock walls that enclosed it grew so high and steep that its floor received the sun for less than two hours each day. The rest of the time it lay in ashen half-light, its gloom intensified by the dazzling brilliance of the ice slopes above. As long as we remained there we had the sensation of imprisonment; it was like being trapped at the bottom of a deep well or in a sealed court between great skyscrapers. Soon we were thinking of the ascent of the shining mountain not only as an end in itself, but as an escape.

In our nightly discussions around the fire our conversation narrowed more and more to the immediate problems confronting us, and during them I began to realize that the tension between Osborn and Nace went deeper than I had at first surmised. There was rarely any outright argument between them — they were both far too able mountain men to disagree on fundamentals — but I saw that at almost every turn they were rubbing each other the wrong way. It was a matter of person-alities, chiefly. Osborn was talkative, enthusiastic, optimistic, always chafing to be up and at it, always wanting to take the short straight line to the given point. Nace, on the other hand, was matter-of-fact, cautious, slow. He was the apostle of trial-and-error and watchful waiting. Because of his far greater experience and intimate knowl-edge of K3, Randolph almost invaria-bly followed his advice, rather than Os-born's, when a difference of opinion arose. The younger man usually capit-ulated with good grace, but I could tell that he was irked.

During the days in the valley I had few occasions to talk privately with ei-ther of them, and only once did either mention the other in any but the most casual manner. Even then, the remarks they made seemed unimportant and I remember them only in view of what happened later.

My conversation with Osborn oc-curred first. It was while we were on the march, and Osborn, who was di-rectly behind me, came up suddenly to my side. "You're a geologist, Frank," he began without preamble. "What do you think of Nace's theory about the ridge?"

"What theory?" I asked.

"He believes we should traverse [1] un-der it from the glacier up. Says the ridge itself is too exposed."

"It looks pretty mean through the tel-escope."

"But it's been done before. He's done it himself. All right, it's tough — I'll ad-mit that. But a decent climber could

---

[1] **traverse** (trav'ərs): To traverse a mountain is to crisscross it instead of climbing straight up.

make it in half the time the traverse will take."

"Nace knows the traverse is longer," I said. "But he seems certain it will be much easier for us."

"Easier for *him* is what he means." Osborn paused, looking moodily at the ground. "He was a great climber in his day. It's a shame a man can't be honest enough with himself to know when he's through." He fell silent and a moment later dropped back into his place in line.

It was that same night, I think, that I awoke to find Nace sitting up in his blanket and staring at the mountain.

"How clear it is!" I whispered.

The Englishman pointed. "See the ridge?"

I nodded, my eyes fixed on the great, twisting spine of ice that climbed into the sky. I could see now, more clearly than in the blinding sunlight, its huge indentations and jagged, wind-swept pitches. "It looks impossible," I said.

"No, it can be done. Trouble is, when you've made it you're too done in for the summit."

"Osborn seems to think its shortness would make up for its difficulty."

Nace was silent a long moment be-fore answering. Then for the first and only time I heard him speak the name of his dead companion. "That's what Furness thought," he said quietly. Then he lay down and wrapped himself in his blanket.

For the next two weeks the upper-most point of the valley was our home and workshop. We established our base camp as close to the mountain as we could, less than half a mile from the tongue of its lowest glacier, and plunged into the arduous tasks of preparation for the ascent. Our food and equipment were unpacked, inspected and sorted, and finally repacked in lighter loads for transportation to more advanced camps. Hours were spent poring over maps and charts and studying the monstrous heights above us through telescope and binoculars. Under Nace's supervision, a thorough reconnaissance of the glacier was made and the route across it laid out; then began the backbreaking labor of moving up supplies and establishing the chain of camps.

Camps I and II were set up on the glacier itself, in the most sheltered sites we could find. Camp III we built at its upper end, as near as possible to the point where the great rock spine of K3 thrust itself free of ice and began its precipitous ascent. According to our plans, this would be the advance base of operations during the climb. The camps to be established higher up, on the mountain proper, would be too small and too exposed to serve as anything more than one or two nights' shelter. The total distance between the base camp and Camp III was only fifteen miles, but the utmost daily progress of our porters was five miles, and it was essential that we should never be more than twelve hours' march from food and shelter. Hour after hour, day after day, the long file of men wound up and down among the hummocks [1] and crevasses of the glacier, and finally the time arrived when we were ready to advance.

Leaving Dr. Schlapp in charge of

[1] **hummocks:** here, mounds of ice.

eight porters at the base camp, we proceeded easily and on schedule, reaching Camp I the first night, Camp II the second, and the advance base the third. No men were left at Camps I and II, inasmuch as they were designed simply as caches for food and equipment; and furthermore we knew we would need all the manpower available for the establishment of the higher camps on the mountain proper.

For more than three weeks now the weather had held perfectly, but on our first night at the advance base, as if by malignant prearrangement of nature, we had our first taste of the fury of a high Himalayan storm. It began with great streamers of lightning that flashed about the mountain like a halo; then heavily through the weird glare, snow began to fall. The wind rose. At first it was only sound — a remote, desolate moaning in the night high above us — but soon it descended, sucked down the deep valley as if into a gigantic funnel. Hour after hour it howled about the tents with hurricane frenzy, and the wild flapping of the canvas dinned in our ears like machine-gun fire.

There was no sleep for us that night or the next. For thirty-six hours the storm raged without lull, while we huddled in the icy gloom of the tents, exerting our last ounce of strength to keep from being buried alive or blown into eternity. At last, on the third morning, it was over, and we came out into a world transformed by a twelve-foot cloak of snow. No single landmark remained as it had been before, and our supplies and equipment were in the wildest confusion. Fortunately there had not been a single serious injury, but it was another three days before we had regained our strength and put the camp in order.

Then we waited. The storm did not return, and the sky beyond the ridges gleamed flawlessly clear; but night and day we could hear the roaring thunder of avalanches on the mountain above us. To have ventured so much as one step into that savage vertical wilderness before the new-fallen snow froze tight would have been suicidal. We chafed or waited patiently, according to our individual temperaments, while the days dragged by.

It was late one afternoon that Osborn returned from a short reconnaissance up the ridge. His eyes were shining and his voice jubilant.

"It's tight!" he cried. "Tight as a drum. We can go!" All of us stopped whatever we were doing. His excitement leaped like an electric spark from one to another. "I went about a thousand feet, and it's sound all the way. What do you say, Sayre? Tomorrow?"

Randolph hesitated, then looked at Nace.

"Better give it another day or two," said the Englishman.

Osborn glared at him. "Why?" he challenged.

"It's usually safer to wait till ——"

"Wait! Wait!" Osborn exploded. "Don't you ever think of anything but waiting? My God, man, the snow's firm, I tell you!"

"It's firm down here," Nace replied quietly, "because the sun hits it only two hours a day. Up above it gets the sun twelve hours. It may not have frozen yet."

"The avalanches have stopped."

"That doesn't necessarily mean it will hold a man's weight."

"It seems to me Martin's point ——" Randolph began.

Osborn wheeled on him. "Sure," he snapped. "I know. Martin's right. The cautious bloody English are always right. Let him have his way, and we'll be sitting here chewing our nails until the mountain falls down on us." His eyes flashed to Nace. "Maybe with a little less of that bloody cautiousness you English wouldn't have made such a mess of Everest. Maybe your pals Mallory and Furness wouldn't be dead."

"Osborn!" commanded Randolph sharply.

The youngster stared at Nace for another moment, breathing heavily. Then abruptly he turned away.

The next two days were clear and windless, but we still waited, following Nace's advice. There were no further brushes between him and Osborn, but an unpleasant air of restlessness and tension hung over the camp. I found myself chafing almost as impatiently as Osborn himself for the moment when we would break out of that maddening inactivity and begin the assault.

At last the day came. With the first paling of the sky a roped file of men, bent almost double beneath heavy loads, began slowly to climb the ice slope, just beneath the jagged line of the great east ridge. In accordance with prearranged plan, we proceeded in relays, this first group consisting of Nace, Johns, myself, and eight porters. It was our job to ascend approximately two thousand feet in a day's climbing and establish Camp IV at the most level and sheltered site we could find. We would spend the night there and return to the advance base next day, while the second relay, consisting of Osborn, Wittmer, and eight more porters, went up with their loads. This process was to continue until all necessary supplies were at Camp IV, and then the whole thing would be repeated between Camps IV and V and V and VI. From VI, at an altitude of about twenty-six thousand feet, the ablest and fittest men — presumably Nace and Osborn — would make the direct assault on the summit. Randolph and Bixler were to remain at the advance base throughout the operations, acting as directors and co-ordinators. We were under the strictest orders that any man — sahib or porter — who suffered illness or injury should be brought down immediately.

How shall I describe those next two weeks beneath the great ice ridge of K3? In a sense there was no occurrence of importance, and at the same time everything happened that could possibly happen, short of actual disaster. We established Camp IV, came down again, went up again, came down again. Then we crept laboriously higher. With our axes we hacked uncountable thousands of steps in the gleaming walls of ice. Among the rocky outcroppings of the cliffs we clung to holds and strained at ropes until we thought our arms would spring from their sockets. Storms swooped down on us, battered us, and passed. The wind increased, and the air grew steadily colder and more difficult to breathe. One morning two of the porters awoke with their feet frozen black; they had to be sent down. A short while later Johns developed an uncontrollable nosebleed and was forced to descend to a lower camp. Wittmer was suffering from racking headaches and I from a continually dry throat. But providentially, the one enemy we feared the most in that icy gale-lashed hell did not again attack us. No snow fell. And day by day, foot by foot, we ascended.

It is during ordeals like this that the surface trappings of a man are shed and his secret mettle [1] laid bare. There were no shirkers or quitters among us — I had known that from the beginning — but now, with each passing day, it became more manifest which were the strongest and ablest among us. Beyond all argument, these were Osborn and Nace.

Osborn was magnificent. All the boyish impatience and moodiness which he had exhibited earlier were gone, and, now that he was at last at work in his natural element, he emerged as the

---

[1] **mettle** (met'l): courage, spirit.

peerless mountaineer he was. His energy was inexhaustible, his speed, both on rock and ice, almost twice that of any other man in the party. He was always discovering new routes and short cuts. Often he ascended by the ridge itself, instead of using the traverse beneath it, as had been officially prescribed; but his craftsmanship was so sure and his performance so brilliant that no one ever thought of taking him to task. Indeed, there was such vigor, buoyancy, and youth in everything he did that it gave heart to all the rest of us.

In contrast, Nace was slow, methodical, unspectacular. Since he and I worked in the same relay, I was with him almost constantly, and to this day I carry in my mind the clear image of the man: his tall body bent almost double against endless shimmering slopes of ice; his lean brown face bent in utter concentration on the problem in hand, then raised searchingly to the next; the bright prong of his ax rising, falling, rising, falling, with tireless rhythm, until the steps in the glassy incline were so wide and deep that the most clumsy of the porters could not have slipped from them had he tried. Osborn attacked the mountain head-on. Nace studied it, sparred with it, wore it down. His spirit did not flap from his sleeve like a pennon;[1] it was deep inside him — patient, indomitable.

The day soon came when I learned from him what it is to be a great mountaineer. We were making the ascent from Camp IV to V, and an almost perpendicular ice wall had made it neces-

sary for us to come out for a few yards on the exposed crest of the ridge. There were six of us in the party, roped together, with Nace leading, myself second, and four porters bringing up the rear. The ridge at this particular point was free of snow, but razor-thin, and the rocks were covered with a smooth glaze of ice. On either side the mountain dropped away in sheer precipices of five thousand feet.

Suddenly the last porter slipped. I heard the ominous scraping of boot nails behind me and, turning, saw a gesticulating figure plunge sideways into the abyss. There was a scream as the next porter was jerked off too. I remember trying frantically to dig into the ridge with my ax, realizing at the same time it would no more hold against the weight of the falling men than a pin stuck in a wall. Then I heard Nace shout, "Jump!" As he said it, the rope went tight about my waist, and I went hurtling after him into space on the opposite side of the ridge. After me came the nearest porter. . . .

What happened then must have happened in five yards and a fifth of a second. I heard myself cry out, and the glacier, a mile below, rushed up at me, spinning. Then both were blotted out in a violent spasm, as the rope jerked taut. I hung for a moment, an inert mass, feeling that my body had been cut in two; then I swung in slowly to the side of the mountain. Above me the rope lay tight and motionless across the crest of the ridge, our weight exactly counterbalancing that of the men who had fallen on the far slope.

Nace's voice came up from below. "You chaps on the other side!" he

---

[1] **pennon** (pen′ən): flag.

shouted. "Start climbing slowly. We're climbing too."

In five minutes we had all regained the ridge. The porters and I crouched panting on the jagged rocks, our eyes closed, the sweat beading our faces in frozen drops. Nace carefully examined the rope that again hung loosely between us.

"All right, men," he said presently. "Let's get on to camp for a cup of tea."

Above Camp V the whole aspect of the ascent changed. The angle of the ridge eased off, and the ice, which lower down had covered the mountain like a sheath, lay only in scattered patches between the rocks. Fresh enemies, however, instantly appeared to take the place of the old. We were now laboring at an altitude of more than twenty-five thousand feet — well above the summits of the highest surrounding peaks — and

day and night, without protection or respite, we were buffeted by the fury of the wind. Worse than this was that the atmosphere had become so rarefied it could scarcely support life. Breathing itself was a major physical effort, and our progress upward consisted of two or three painful steps followed by a long period of rest in which our hearts pounded wildly and our burning lungs gasped for air. Each of us carried a small cylinder of oxygen in his pack, but we used it only in emergencies and found that, while its immediate effect was salutary, it left us later even worse off than before. My throat dried and contracted until it felt as if it were lined with brass. The faces of all of us, under our beards and windburn, grew haggard and strained.

But the great struggle was now mental as much as physical. The lack of air induced a lethargy of mind and spirit; confidence and the powers of thought and decision waned, and dark foreboding crept out from the secret recesses of the subconscious. The wind seemed to carry strange sounds, and we kept imagining we saw things which we knew were not there. The mountain, to all of us, was no longer a mere giant of rock and ice; it had become a living thing, an enemy, watching us, waiting for us, hostile, relentless, and aware. Inch by inch we crept upward through that empty forgotten world above the world, and only one last thing remained to us of human consciousness and human will: to go on. To go on.

On the fifteenth day after we had first left the advance base we pitched Camp VI at an altitude of almost twenty-six thousand feet. It was located near the uppermost extremity of the great east ridge, directly beneath the so-called shoulder of the mountain. On the far side of the shoulder the monstrous north face of K3 fell sheer to the glaciers, two miles below. And above it and to the left rose the symmetrical bulk of the summit pyramid. The topmost rocks of its highest pinnacle were clearly visible from the shoulder, and the intervening two thousand feet seemed to offer no insuperable obstacles.

Camp VI, which was in reality no camp at all, but a single tent, was large enough to accommodate only three men. Osborn established it with the aid of Wittmer and one porter; then, the following morning, Wittmer and the porter descended to Camp V, and Nace and I went up. It was our plan that Osborn and Nace should launch the final assault — the next day, if the weather held — with myself in support, following their progress through binoculars and going to their aid or summoning help from below if anything went wrong. As the three of us lay in the tent that night, the summit seemed already within arm's reach, victory securely in our grasp.

And then the blow fell. With malignant timing, which no power on earth could have made us believe was a simple accident of nature, the mountain hurled at us its last line of defense. It snowed.

For a day and a night the great flakes drove down on us, swirling and swooping in the wind, blotting out the summit, the shoulder, everything beyond the tiny white-walled radius of our tents. Hour after hour we lay in our sleeping bags, stirring only to eat or to secure the straining rope and canvas. Our feet froze under their thick layers of wool and rawhide. Our heads and bodies throbbed with a dull nameless aching, and time crept over our numbed minds like a glacier. At last, during the morning of the following day, it cleared. The sun came out in a thin blue sky, and the summit pyramid again appeared above us, now whitely robed in fresh snow. But still we waited. Until the snow either froze or was blown away by the wind it would have been the rashest courting of destruction for us to have ascended a foot beyond the camp. Another day passed. And another.

By the third nightfall our nerves were at the breaking point. For hours on end we had scarcely moved or spoken, and the only sounds in all the world were the endless moaning of the wind outside and the harsh sucking noise of our breathing. I knew that, one way or another, the end had come. Our meager food supply was running out; even with careful rationing there was enough left for only two more days.

Presently Nace stirred in his sleeping bag and sat up. "We'll have to go down tomorrow," he said quietly.

For a moment there was silence in the tent. Then Osborn struggled to a sitting position and faced him.

"No," he said.

"There's still too much loose snow above. We can't make it."

"But it's clear. As long as we can see —— "

Nace shook his head. "Too dangerous. We'll go down tomorrow and lay in a fresh supply. Then we'll try again."

"Once we go down we're licked. You know it."

Nace shrugged. "Better to be licked than . . ." The strain of speech was suddenly too much for him and he fell into a violent paroxysm of coughing. When it had passed there was a long silence.

Then suddenly Osborn spoke again. "Look, Nace," he said, "I'm going up tomorrow."

The Englishman shook his head.

"I'm going — understand?"

For the first time since I had known him I saw Nace's eyes flash in anger. "I'm the senior member of this group," he said. "I forbid you to go!"

Osborn jerked himself to his knees, almost upsetting the tiny tent. "You forbid me? This may be your sixth time on this mountain, and all that, but you don't *own* it! I know what you're up to. You haven't got it in you to make the top yourself, so you don't want anyone else to make it. That's it, isn't it? Isn't it?" He sat down again suddenly, gasping for breath.

Nace looked at him with level eyes. "This mountain has beaten me five times," he said softly. "It killed my best friend. It means more to me to climb it than anything else in the world. Maybe I'll make it and maybe I won't. But if I do, it will be as a rational intelligent human being — not as a fool throwing my life away. . . ."

He collapsed into another fit of coughing and fell back in his sleeping bag. Osborn, too, was still. They lay there inert, panting, too exhausted for speech.

It was hours later that I awoke from dull, uneasy sleep. In the faint light I saw Nace fumbling with the flap of the tent.

"What is it?" I asked.

"Osborn. He's gone."

The words cut like a blade through my lethargy. I struggled to my feet and followed Nace from the tent.

Outside, the dawn was seeping up the eastern sky. It was very cold, but the wind had fallen and the mountain seemed to hang suspended in a vast stillness. Above us the summit pyramid climbed bleakly into space, like the last outpost of a spent and lifeless planet. Raising my binoculars, I swept them over the gray waste. At first I saw nothing but rock and ice; then, suddenly, something moved.

"I've got him," I whispered.

As I spoke, the figure of Osborn sprang into clear focus against a patch of ice. He took three or four slow upward steps, stopped, went on again. I handed the glasses to Nace.

The Englishman squinted through them, returned them to me, and reentered the tent. When I followed, he had already laced his boots and was pulling on his outer gloves.

"He's not far," he said. "Can't have been gone more than half an hour." He seized his ice ax and started out again.

"Wait," I said. "I'm going with you."

Nace shook his head. "Better stay here."

"I'm going with you," I said.

He said nothing further, but waited while I made ready. In a few moments we left the tent, roped up, and started off.

Almost immediately we were on the shoulder and confronted with the paralyzing two-mile drop of the north face;

but we negotiated the short exposed stretch without mishap, and in ten minutes were working up the base of the summit pyramid. The going here was easier, in a purely climbing sense: the angle of ascent was not steep, and there was firm rock for hand- and foot-holds between the patches of snow and ice. Our progress, however, was creepingly slow. There seemed to be literally no air at all to breathe, and after almost every step we were forced to rest, panting and gasping as we leaned forward against our axes. My heart swelled and throbbed with every movement until I thought it would explode.

The minutes crawled into hours and still we climbed. Presently the sun came up. Its level rays streamed across the clouds, far below, and glinted from the summits of distant peaks. But, although the pinnacle of K3 soared a full three thousand feet above anything in the surrounding world, we had scarcely any sense of height. The wilderness of mountain valley and glacier that spread beneath us to the horizon was flattened and remote, an unreal, insubstantial landscape seen in a dream. We had no connection with it, or it with us. All living, all awareness, purpose, and will, was concentrated in the last step and the next: to put one foot before the other; to breathe; to ascend. We struggled on in silence.

I do not know how long it was since we had left the camp — it might have been two hours, it might have been six — when we suddenly sighted Osborn. We had not been able to find him again since our first glimpse through the binoculars; but now, unexpectedly and abruptly, as we came up over a jagged outcropping of rock, there he was. He was at a point, only a few yards above us, where the mountain steepened into an almost vertical wall. The smooth surface directly in front of him was obviously unclimbable, but two alternate routes were presented. To the left, a chimney [1] cut obliquely across the wall, forbiddingly steep, but seeming to offer adequate holds. To the right was a gentle slope of snow that curved upward and out of sight behind the rocks. As we watched, Osborn ascended to the edge of the snow, stopped, and probed it with his ax. Then, apparently satisfied that it would bear his weight he stepped out on the slope.

I felt Nace's body tense. "Paul!" he cried out.

His voice was too weak and hoarse to carry. Osborn continued his ascent.

Nace cupped his hands and called his name again, and this time Osborn turned. "Wait!" cried the Englishman.

Osborn stood still, watching us, as we struggled up the few yards to the edge of the snow slope. Nace's breath came in shuddering gasps, but he climbed faster than I had ever seen him climb before.

"Come back!" he called. "Come off the snow!"

"It's all right. The crust is firm," Osborn called back.

"But it's melting. There's . . ." Nace paused, fighting for air. "There's nothing underneath!"

In a sudden sickening flash I saw what he meant. Looked at from directly below, at the point where Osborn had come to it, the slope on which

[1] **chimney:** formation of rock resembling a chimney.

he stood appeared as a harmless covering of snow over the rocks. From where we were now, however, a little to one side, it could be seen that it was in reality no covering at all, but merely a cornice or unsupported platform clinging to the side of the mountain. Below it was not rock, but ten thousand feet of blue air.

"Come back!" I cried. "Come back!"

Osborn hesitated, then took a downward step. But he never took the next. For in that same instant the snow directly in front of him disappeared. It did not seem to fall or to break away. It was just soundlessly and magically no longer there. In the spot where Osborn had been about to set his foot there was now revealed the abysmal drop of the north face of K3.

I shut my eyes, but only for a second, and when I reopened them Osborn was still, miraculously, there. Nace was shouting, "Don't move! Don't move an inch!"

"The rope —" I heard myself saying.

The Englishman shook his head. "We'd have to throw it, and the impact would be too much. Brace yourself and play it out." As he spoke, his eyes were traveling over the rocks that bordered the snow bridge. Then he moved forward.

I wedged myself into a cleft in the wall and let out the rope which extended between us. A few yards away Osborn stood in the snow, transfixed, one foot a little in front of the other. But my eyes now were on Nace. Cautiously, but with astonishing rapidity, he edged along the rocks beside the cornice. There was a moment when his only support was an inch-wide ledge beneath his feet, another where there was nothing under his feet at all, and he supported himself wholly by his elbows and hands. But he advanced steadily and at last reached a shelf wide enough for him to turn around on. At this point he was perhaps six feet away from Osborn.

"It's wide enough here to hold both of us," he said in a quiet voice. "I'm going to reach out my ax. Don't move until you're sure you have a grip on it. When I pull, jump."

He searched the wall behind him and found a hold for his left hand. Then he slowly extended his ice ax, head foremost, until it was within two feet of Osborn's shoulder. "Grip it!" he cried suddenly. Osborn's hands shot out and seized the ax. "Jump!"

There was a flash of steel in the sunlight and a hunched figure hurtled inward from the snow to the ledge. Simultaneously another figure hurtled out. The haft [1] of the ax jerked suddenly from Nace's hand, and he lurched forward and downward. A violent spasm convulsed his body as the rope went taut. Then it was gone. Nace did not seem to hit the snow; he simply disappeared through it, soundlessly. In the same instant the snow itself was gone. The frayed, yellow end of broken rope spun lazily in space. . . .

Somehow my eyes went to Osborn. He was crouched on the ledge where Nace had been a moment before, staring dully at the ax he held in his hands. Beyond his head, not two hundred feet above, the white untrodden pinnacle of K3 stabbed the sky.

---

[1] **haft:** handle.

Perhaps ten minutes passed, perhaps a half hour. I closed my eyes and leaned forward motionless against the rock, my face against my arm. I neither thought nor felt; my body and mind alike were enveloped in a suffocating numbness. Through it at last came the sound of Osborn moving. Looking up, I saw he was standing beside me.

"I'm going to try for the top," he said tonelessly.

I merely stared at him.

"Will you come?"

"No," I said.

Osborn hesitated; then turned and began slowly climbing the steep chimney above us. Halfway up he paused, struggling for breath. Then he resumed his laborious upward progress and presently disappeared beyond the crest.

I stayed where I was, and the hours passed. The sun reached its zenith above the peak and sloped away behind it. And at last I heard above me the sound of Osborn returning. As I looked up, his figure appeared at the top of the chimney and began the descent. His clothing was in tatters, and I could tell from his movements that only the thin flame of his will stood between him and collapse. In another few minutes he was standing beside me.

"Did you get there?" I asked dully.

He shook his head. "I couldn't make it," he answered. "I didn't have what it takes."

We roped together silently and began the descent to the camp.

There is nothing more to be told of the sixth assault on K3 — at least not from the experiences of the men who made it. Osborn and I reached Camp V in safety, and three days later the entire expedition gathered at the advance base. It was decided, in view of the tragedy that had occurred, to make no further attempt on the summit, and by the end of the week we had begun the evacuation of the mountain.

It remained for another year and other men to reveal the epilogue.

The summer following our attempt a combined English-Swiss expedition stormed the peak successfully. After weeks of hardship and struggle they attained the topmost pinnacle of the giant, only to find that what should have been their great moment of triumph was, instead, a moment of the bitterest disappointment. For when they came out at last upon the summit they saw that they were *not* the first. An ax stood there. Its haft was embedded in rock and ice and on its steel head were the engraved words: TO MARTIN FROM JOHN.

They were sporting men. On their return to civilization they told their story, and the name of the conqueror of K3 was made known to the world.

TOP COURAGE

1. Describe the two conflicts in this story: the conflict between Nace and Osborn and the conflict between the exploring party and the natural obstacles they faced. In which conflict were you more interested? Why?

2. In what ways were Nace and Osborn different? Refer to paragraphs in the story that bring out these differences.

3. The two conflicts are resolved at the end of the story. How did they turn out?

4. What do you think the ax symbolized

or meant in the story? Why did Osborn place it on the top of the mountain?

5. Both Nace and Osborn showed courage in different ways. Do you think that Nace knew that saving Osborn would result in his own death? Why do you think Nace made this final, generous act of courage? What, in your opinion, was Osborn's greatest act of courage — his reaching the top of K3 or his generous denial of his achievement? Who do you think is the "top man" of the title?

6. Sometimes men of courage in modern fictional stories are very much like those in old legends and myths. In what ways are Nace and Osborn like David, Odysseus, Gawain, and Robin Hood? The narrator says that these men wanted to climb K3 "because it is there." Did any other men in this unit show courage for reasons similar to this? Give examples to support your answer.

7. What weaknesses were found in the characters of Nace and Osborn? How did these weaknesses almost destroy Osborn? Are the heroes of myth and legend portrayed as realistically as Nace and Osborn?

8. What is your reaction to the ideas in the sentence on page 49 which begins "It is during ordeals like this that the surface trappings of a man are shed . . ."? What other forces of nature have challenged men? Do you know of any men who have shown unusual courage in fighting such forces? What were their motives?

WORDS: INFLECTIONS IN ENGLISH

In most languages, certain words can be inflected; that is, they can be changed in form to signify tense, person, number, possession, or comparison. Over the centuries, the English language has kept only a few of its original inflections.

In English we still add *–ed* or *–ing* to some verbs to show tense: *I talk; I talked; I was talking.* We also add *–s* to some verbs to show a change in person: *I talk, but she talks.*

Many nouns in English can be inflected by adding *–s* or *–s* with an apostrophe to show plural or possession: *books, book's, books'.*

Some adjectives and adverbs can be inflected by adding *–er* or *–est* to show comparison: *sadder, saddest.*

Which of the following words can be inflected, either to show tense, person, number, possession, or comparison? Can any of these words not be inflected at all?

fox	four	yet
he	sand	milk
bad	pet	put

COMPOSITION:
SENSORY APPEAL IN DESCRIPTION

Notice that the italicized words in the following sentence from "Top Man" help you to see the fury of the Himalayan storm:

"It began with *great streamers of lightning* that *flashed* about the mountain like a *halo;* then *heavily* through the *weird glare, snow* began to fall."

This passage describing the storm continues with the following sentences. Point out the words in these sentences which appeal to your sense of hearing:

"The wind rose. At first it was only sound — a remote, desolate moaning in the night high above us — but soon it descended, sucked down the deep valley as if into a gigantic funnel. Hour after hour it howled about the tents with hurricane frenzy, and the wild flapping of the canvas dinned in our ears like machine-gun fire."

Write several sentences of your own about a game, a fight, a race, or other contest, in which you try to describe an action vividly by choosing words with sensory appeal.

The Charge of the Light Brigade

ALFRED, LORD TENNYSON

In 1854, during the Crimean War, the English Light Brigade, armed only with swords, was ordered by mistake to attack well-fortified Russian gun positions. The results were disastrous. This poem was written soon after the news of the slaughter reached England. It has kept the memory of that gallant brigade alive ever since.

Half a league,° half a league,
Half a league onward,
All in the valley of death
 Rode the six hundred.

"Forward, the Light Brigade! 5
Charge for the guns!" he said:
Into the valley of death
 Rode the six hundred.

1. **league** (lēg): a measure of distance, about three miles.

"Forward, the Light Brigade!"
Was there a man dismayed?   10
Not though the soldier knew
    Someone had blundered;
Theirs not to make reply,
Theirs not to reason why,
Theirs but to do and die;   15
Into the valley of death
    Rode the six hundred.

Cannon to right of them,
Cannon to left of them,
Cannon in front of them   20
    Volleyed and thundered;
Stormed at with shot and shell,
Boldly they rode and well,
Into the jaws of death,
Into the mouth of hell   25
    Rode the six hundred.

Flashed all their sabers bare,
Flashed as they turned in air
Sab'ring the gunners there,
Charging an army, while   30
    All the world wondered.

Plunged in the battery smoke,
Right through the line they broke;
Cossack and Russian
Reeled from the saber-stroke,   35
    Shattered and sundered.
Then they rode back, but not,
    Not the six hundred.

Cannon to right of them,
Cannon to left of them,   40
Cannon behind them
    Volleyed and thundered;
Stormed at with shot and shell,
While horse and hero fell,
They that had fought so well   45
Came through the jaws of death,
Back from the mouth of hell,
All that was left of them,
    Left of six hundred.

When can their glory fade?   50
Oh, the wild charge they made!
    All the world wondered.
Honor the charge they made,
Honor the Light Brigade,
    Noble six hundred!   55

COURAGE AND OBEDIENCE

1. What order was given to the brigade? What lines in the poem tell that a mistake had been made? What was the result of this blunder?

2. Which lines tell about a soldier's duty in the face of a command? Do you think a soldier can choose to obey or disobey orders?

3. Twice Tennyson says "All the world wondered." Do you think he means that the world marvelled at the soldiers' bravery, or that it wondered about the mistake that sent the men to their deaths? Explain your answer.

4. Compare the position of these soldiers with that of Odysseus' and Robin Hood's men.

SOUND EFFECTS IN POETRY

Did you notice how Tennyson created the feeling of battle? The short, staccato lines suggest gunshots, quick movements, heedless action, and confusion. The repetitions of rhymes suggest the mechanical actions of the soldiers as they respond to the commands, almost like wound-up toy soldiers. Read the poem aloud, emphasizing these sound effects.

Dunkirk

ROBERT NATHAN

It happened at the end of May in 1940. World War II was less than a year old, yet already Hitler's Nazi armies were within sight of victory. Poland, Norway, and Denmark had fallen; Luxembourg, Holland, and Belgium had been overrun; France was tottering. England's army of 338,000 men was trapped around Dunkirk on the French coast, and if the army surrendered, the war might well end there.

But then a call went out to all the sailors of England, and they answered heroically. Luxurious yachts and little fishing boats crossed the English Channel, into the heart of the battle, to rescue England's soldiers. Among them were young people like the boy and girl in this story.

> Will came back from school that day,
> And he had little to say.
> But he stood a long time looking down
> To where the gray-green Channel water
> Slapped at the foot of the little town,   5
> And to where his boat, the *Sarah P,*
> Bobbed at the tide on an even keel,
> With her one old sail, patched at the leech,°
> Furled like a slattern down at heel.
>
> He stood for a while above the beach;   10
> He saw how the wind and current caught her.
> He looked a long time out to sea.
> There was steady wind and the sky was pale
> And a haze in the east that looked like smoke.
>
> Will went back to the house to dress.   15
> He was halfway through when his sister Bess,
> Who was near fourteen and younger than he
> By just two years, came home from play.
> She asked him, "Where are you going, Will?"
> He said, "For a good long sail."   20
> "Can I come along?"

8. **leech:** edge of the sail.

"No, Bess," he spoke.
"I may be gone for a night and a day."
Bess looked at him. She kept very still.
She had heard the news of the Flanders rout,
How the English were trapped above Dunkirk,   25
And the fleet had gone to get them out —
But everyone thought that it wouldn't work.
There was too much fear; there was too much doubt.
She looked at him, and he looked at her.
They were English children, born and bred.   30
He frowned her down, but she wouldn't stir.
She shook her proud young head.
"You'll need a crew," she said.

They raised the sail on the *Sarah P*,
Like a pennoncel° on a young knight's lance,   35
And headed the *Sarah* out to sea,
To bring their soldiers home from France.

There was no command, there was no set plan,
But six hundred boats went out with them
On the gray-green waters, sailing fast,   40
River excursion and fisherman,
Tug and schooner and racing M,°
And the little boats came following last.

From every harbor and town they went
Who had sailed their craft in the sun and rain,   45
From the South Downs, from the cliffs of Kent,
From the village street, from the country lane.
There are twenty miles of rolling sea
From coast to coast, by the sea gull's flight,
But the tides were fair and the wind was free,   50
And they raised° Dunkirk by the fall of night.

They raised Dunkirk with its harbor torn
By the blasted stern and the sunken prow;
They had raced for fun on an English tide,
They were English children bred and born,   55
And whether they lived or whether they died,
They raced for England now.

35. **pennoncel** (pen'ən·sel): small flag.   42. **racing M**: a class of boats built to certain specifications.   51. **raised**: saw on the horizon.

Bess was as white as the *Sarah*'s sail,
She set her teeth and smiled at Will.
He held his course for the smoky veil   60
Where the harbor narrowed thin and long.
The British ships were firing strong.

He took the *Sarah* into his hands,
He drove her in through fire and death
To the wet men waiting on the sands.   65
He got his load and he got his breath,
And she came about, and the wind fought her.
He shut his eyes and he tried to pray.
He saw his England where she lay.
The wind's green home, the sea's proud daughter,   70
Still in the moonlight, dreaming deep,
The English cliffs and the English loam —
He had fourteen men to get away.
And the moon was clear and the night like day
For planes to see where the white sails creep   75
Over the black water.

He closed his eyes and he prayed for her;
He prayed to the men who had made her great,
Who had built her land of forest and park,
Who had made the seas an English lake;   80
He prayed for a fog to bring the dark;
He prayed to get home for England's sake.
And the fog came down on the rolling sea,
And covered the ships with English mist.
The diving planes were baffled and blind.   85

For Nelson was there in the *Victory*,°
With his one good eye, and his sullen twist,
And the guns were out on *The Golden Hind*,°
Their shot flashed over the *Sarah P.*
He could hear them cheer as he came about.   90

By burning wharves, by battered slips,
Galleon, frigate, and brigantine,
The old dead captains fought their ships,
And the great dead admirals led the line.
It was England's night, it was England's sea.   95

The fog rolled over the harbor key.
Bess held to the stays° and conned° him out.
And all through the dark, while the *Sarah's* wake
Hissed behind him, and vanished in foam,
There at his side sat Francis Drake,   100
And held him true and steered him home.

86. *Victory:* the flagship of Lord Nelson who defeated the French at the Battle of
Trafalgar in 1805.   88. *The Golden Hind:* the ship in which Sir Francis Drake sailed
around the world, 1577–1580.   97. **stays:** cables.   **conned:** directed.

COURAGE IN DEFEAT

1. Describe how Will and Bess came to be on their way to Dunkirk. How do lines 38–51 make this more than a poem about Will and Bess?

2. Reread the lines that tell of the dangers in the harbor at Dunkirk and of Will's tremendous task. For what did Will hope and pray?

3. Why, do you suppose, the poet chose two young people like Will and Bess as the central characters of his poem?

4. The retreat at Dunkirk was a terrible defeat for the English. How does this poet make it end in a British triumph?

5. Discuss the reasons for the courage shown by these two school children and by the other Englishmen who rescued the soldiers from Dunkirk. In what ways did Drake and Nelson and the other dead heroes of England help them through?

6. Compare the courage of these "civilian soldiers" with that of the soldiers of the Light Brigade in Tennyson's poem. Do you think the motives of both groups of soldiers were different, or the same? Does one deserve more honor than the other?

CONVERSATIONAL STYLE

You know that rhyming, or the repetition of end sounds of words, is a device often used by poets. Usually the poet plans a definite and regular rhyme scheme or pattern. However, in "Dunkirk" the rhyming is irregular, with no repetition of rhyme schemes from stanza to stanza. This lack of a repeated pattern helps to give the poem a conversational style.

As you read the poem aloud, try to give it a normal conversational tone, accenting the rhymes but not overemphasizing them.

My Friend Flicka

MARY O'HARA

REPORT CARDS for the second semester were sent out soon after school closed in mid-June.

Kennie's was a shock to the whole family.

"If I could have a colt all for my own," said Kennie, "I might do better."

Rob McLaughlin glared at his son. "Just as a matter of curiosity," he said, "how do you go about it to get a *zero* in an examination? Forty in arithmetic; seventeen in history! But a *zero?* Just as one man to another, what goes on in your head?"

"Yes, tell us how you do it, Ken," chirped Howard.

"Eat your breakfast, Howard," snapped his mother.

Kennie's blond head bent over his plate until his face was almost hidden. His cheeks burned.

McLaughlin finished his coffee and pushed his chair back. "You'll do an hour a day on your lessons all through the summer."

Nell McLaughlin saw Kennie wince

as if something had actually hurt him.

Lessons and study in the summertime, when the long winter was just over and there weren't hours enough in the day for all the things he wanted to do!

Kennie took things hard. His eyes turned to the wide-open window with a look almost of despair.

The hill opposite the house, covered with arrow-straight jack pines, was sharply etched in the thin air of the eight-thousand-foot altitude. Where it fell away, vivid green grass ran up to meet it; and over range and upland poured the strong Wyoming sunlight that stung everything into burning color. A big jack rabbit sat under one of the pines, waving his long ears back and forth.

Ken had to look at his plate and blink back tears before he could turn to his father and say carelessly, "Can I help you in the corral with the horses this morning, Dad?"

"You'll do your study every morning before you do anything else." And McLaughlin's scarred boots and heavy spurs clattered across the kitchen floor.

"I'm disgusted with you. Come, Howard."

Howard strode after his father, nobly refraining from looking at Kennie.

"Help me with the dishes, Kennie," said Nell McLaughlin as she rose, tied on a big apron, and began to clear the table.

Kennie looked at her in despair. She poured steaming water into the dishpan and sent him for the soap powder.

"If I could have a colt," he muttered again.

"Now get busy with that dish towel, Ken. It's eight o'clock. You can study till nine and then go up to the corral. They'll still be there."

At supper that night, Kennie said, "But Dad, Howard had a colt all of his own when he was only eight. And he trained it and schooled it all himself; and now he's eleven and Highboy is three, and he's riding him. I'm nine now, and even if you did give me a colt now, I couldn't catch up to Howard because I couldn't ride it till it was a three-year-old and then I'd be twelve."

Nell laughed. "Nothing wrong with that arithmetic."

But Rob said, "Howard never gets less than seventy-five average at school, and hasn't disgraced himself and his family by getting more demerits than any other boy in his class."

Kennie didn't answer. He couldn't figure it out. He tried hard; he spent hours poring over his books. That was supposed to get you good marks, but it never did. Everyone said he was bright; why was it that when he studied he didn't learn? He had a vague feeling that perhaps he looked out the window too much, or looked through the walls to see clouds and sky and hills and wonder what was happening out there. Sometimes it wasn't even a wonder but just a pleasant drifting feeling of nothing at all, as if nothing mattered, as if there was always plenty of time, as if the lessons would get done of themselves. And then the bell would ring and study period was over.

If he had a colt . . .

When the boys had gone to bed that night, Nell McLaughlin sat down with her overflowing mending basket and glanced at her husband.

He was at his desk as usual, working on account books and inventories.

Nell threaded a darning needle and thought, "It's either that whacking big bill from the vet for the mare that died or the last half of the tax bill."

It didn't seem just the auspicious moment to plead Kennie's cause. But then, these days, there was always a line between Rob's eyes and a harsh note in his voice.

"Rob," she began.

He flung down his pencil and turned around.

"That law!" he exclaimed.

"What law?"

"The state law that puts high taxes on pedigreed stock. I'll have to do as the rest of 'em do — drop the papers."

"Drop the papers! But you'll never get decent prices if you don't have registered horses."

"I don't get decent prices now."

"But you will some day, if you don't drop the papers."

"Maybe." He bent again over the desk.

Rob, thought Nell, was a lot like Kennie himself. He set his heart. Oh, how stubbornly he set his heart on just some one thing he wanted above everything else. He had set his heart on horses and ranching way back when he had been a crack rider at West Point; and he had resigned and thrown away his army career just for the horses. Well, he'd got what he wanted . . .

She drew a deep breath, snipped her thread, laid down the sock, and again looked across at her husband as she unrolled another length of darning cotton.

To get what you want is one thing, she was thinking. The three-thousand-acre ranch and the hundred head of horses. But to make it pay — for a dozen or more years they had been trying to make it pay. People said ranching hadn't paid since the beef barons ran their herds on public land; people said the only prosperous ranchers in Wyoming were the dude ranchers; people said . . .

But suddenly she gave her head a little rebellious, gallant shake. Rob would always be fighting and struggling against something, like Kennie, perhaps like herself too. Even those first years when there was no water piped into the house, when every day brought a new difficulty or danger, how she had loved it! How she still loved it!

She ran the darning ball into the toe of a sock, Kennie's sock. The length of it gave her a shock. Yes, the boys were growing up fast, and now Kennie — Kennie and the colt . . .

After a while she said, "Give Kennie a colt, Rob."

"He doesn't deserve it." The answer was short. Rob pushed away his papers and took out his pipe.

"Howard's too far ahead of him; older and bigger and quicker and his wits about him, and . . ."

"Ken doesn't half try, doesn't stick at anything."

She put down her sewing. "He's crazy for a colt of his own. He hasn't had another idea in his head since you gave Highboy to Howard."

"I don't believe in bribing children to do their duty."

"Not a bribe." She hesitated.

"No? What would you call it?"

She tried to think it out. "I just have a feeling Ken isn't going to pull anything off, and" — her eyes sought Rob's — "it's time he did. It isn't the school marks alone, but I just don't want things to go on any longer with Ken never coming out at the right end of anything."

"I'm beginning to think he's just dumb."

"He's not dumb. Maybe a little thing like this — if he had a colt of his own, trained him, rode him . . ."

Rob interrupted. "But it isn't a little thing, nor an easy thing, to break and school a colt the way Howard has schooled Highboy. I'm not going to have a good horse spoiled by Ken's careless ways. He goes woolgathering. He never knows what he's doing."

"But he'd *love* a colt of his own, Rob. If he could do it, it might make a big difference in him."

"*If* he could do it! But that's a big if."

At breakfast next morning, Kennie's father said to him, "When you've done your study, come out to the barn. I'm going in the car up to section twenty-one this morning to look over the brood mares. You can go with me."

"Can I go too, Dad?" cried Howard.

McLaughlin frowned at Howard. "You turned Highboy out last evening with dirty legs."

Howard wriggled. "I groomed him . . ."

"Yes, down to his knees."

"He kicks."

"And whose fault is that? You don't get on his back again until I see his legs clean."

The two boys eyed each other, Kennie secretly triumphant and Howard chagrined. McLaughlin turned at the door, "And, Ken, a week from today I'll give you a colt. Between now and then you can decide what one you want."

Kennie shot out of his chair and stared at his father. "A — a — spring colt, Dad, or a yearling?"

McLaughlin was somewhat taken aback, but his wife concealed a smile. If Kennie got a yearling colt, he would be even up with Howard.

"A yearling colt, your father means, Ken," she said smoothly. "Now hurry with your lessons. Howard will wipe."

Kennie found himself the most important personage on the ranch. Prestige lifted his head, gave him an inch more of height and a bold stare, and made him feel different all the way through. Even Gus and Tim Murphy, the ranch hands, were more interested in Kennie's choice of a colt than anything else.

Howard was fidgety with suspense. "Who'll you pick, Ken? Say — pick Doughboy, why don't you? Then when he grows up, he'll be sort of twins with mine, in his name anyway. Doughboy, Highboy, see?"

The boys were sitting on the worn wooden step of the door which led from the tack room into the corral, busy with rags and polish, shining their bridles.

Ken looked at his brother with scorn. Doughboy would never have half of Highboy's speed.

"Lassie, then," suggested Howard. "She's black as ink, like mine. And she'll be fast . . ."

"Dad says Lassie'll never go over fifteen hands."

Nell McLaughlin saw the change in Kennie and her hopes rose. He went to his books in the morning with determination and really studied. A new alertness took the place of the daydreaming. Examples in arithmetic were neatly written out, and, as she passed his door before breakfast, she often heard the monotonous drone of his voice as he read his American history aloud.

Each night, when he kissed her, he flung his arms around her and held her fiercely for a moment, then, with a winsome and blissful smile into her eyes, turned away to bed.

He spent days inspecting the different bands of horses and colts. He sat for hours on the corral fence, very important, chewing straws. He rode off on one of the ponies for half the day, wandering through the mile-square pastures that ran down toward the Colorado border.

And when the week was up, he announced his decision. "I'll take that yearling filly of Rocket's. The sorrel [1] with the cream tail and mane."

His father looked at him in surprise. "The one that got tangled in the barbed wire? that's never been named?"

In a second all Kennie's new pride was gone. He hung his head defensively. "Yes."

"You've made a bad choice, Son. You couldn't have picked a worse."

"She's fast, Dad. And Rocket's fast . . ."

"It's the worst line of horses I've got. There's never one among them with real sense. The mares are hellions and the stallions outlaws; they're untamable."

"I'll tame her."

Rob guffawed. "Not I, nor anyone, has ever really been able to tame any one of them."

Kennie's chest heaved.

"Better change your mind, Ken. You want a horse that'll be a real friend to you, don't you?"

"Yes" — Kennie's voice was unsteady.

"Well, you'll never make a friend of that filly. She's all cut and scarred up already with tearing through barbed wire after that no-good mother of hers. No fence'll hold 'em . . ."

[1] **sorrel** (sôr'əl): here, a horse of reddish- or yellowish-brown color.

"I know," said Kennie, still more faintly.

"Change your mind?" asked Howard briskly.

"No."

Rob was grim and put out. He couldn't go back on his word. The boy had to have a reasonable amount of help in breaking and taming the filly, and he could envision precious hours, whole days, wasted in the struggle.

Nell McLaughlin despaired. Once again Ken seemed to have taken the wrong turn and was back where he had begun, stoical, silent, defensive.

But there was a difference that only Ken could know. The way he felt about his colt. The way his heart sang. The pride and joy that filled him so full that sometimes he hung his head so they wouldn't see it shining out of his eyes.

He had known from the very first that he would choose that particular yearling because he was in love with her.

The year before, he had been out working with Gus, the big Swedish ranch hand, on the irrigation ditch, when they had noticed Rocket standing in a gully on the hillside, quiet for once and eying them cautiously.

"Ay bet she got a colt," said Gus, and they walked carefully up the draw.[2] Rocket gave a wild snort, thrust her feet out, shook her head wickedly, then fled away. And as they reached the spot, they saw standing there the wavering, pinkish colt, barely able to keep its feet. It gave a little squeak and started after its mother on crooked, wobbling legs.

[2] **draw**: gully.

"Yee whiz! Luk at de little *flicka!*" said Gus.

"What does *flicka* mean, Gus?"

"Swedish for little gurl, Ken . . ."

Ken announced at supper, "You said she'd never been named. I've named her. Her name is Flicka."

The first thing to do was to get her in. She was running with a band of yearlings on the saddleback,[1] cut with ravines and gullies, on section twenty.

They all went out after her, Ken, as owner, on old Rob Roy, the wisest horse on the ranch.

Ken was entranced to watch Flicka when the wild band of youngsters discovered that they were being pursued and took off across the mountain. Footing made no difference to her. She

[1] **saddleback:** hill or ridge shaped like a saddle on top.

floated across the ravines, always two lengths ahead of the others. Her pink mane and tail whipped in the wind. Her long, delicate legs had only to aim, it seemed, at a particular spot for her to reach it and sail on. She seemed to Ken a fairy horse.

He sat motionless, just watching and holding Rob Roy in, when his father thundered past on Sultan and shouted, "Well, what's the matter? Why didn't you turn 'em?"

Kennie woke up and galloped after.

Rob Roy brought in the whole band. The corral gates were closed, and an hour was spent shunting the ponies in and out and through the chutes, until Flicka was left alone in the small round corral in which the baby colts were branded. Gus drove the others away, out of the gate, and up the saddleback.

But Flicka did not intend to be left. She hurled herself against the poles which walled the corral. She tried to jump them. They were seven feet high. She caught her front feet over the top rung, clung, scrambled, while Kennie held his breath for fear the slender legs would be caught between the bars and snapped. Her hold broke; she fell over backward, rolled, screamed, tore around the corral. Kennie had a sick feeling in the pit of his stomach, and his father looked disgusted.

One of the bars broke. She hurled herself again. Another went. She saw the opening and, as neatly as a dog crawls through a fence, inserted her head and forefeet, scrambled through, and fled away, bleeding in a dozen places.

As Gus was coming back, just about to close the gate to the upper range, the sorrel whipped through it, sailed across the road and ditch with her inimitable floating leap, and went up the side of the saddleback like a jack rabbit.

From way up the mountain, Gus heard excited whinnies, as she joined the band he had just driven up, and the last he saw of them they were strung out along the crest running like deer.

"Yee whiz!" said Gus, and stood motionless and staring until the ponies had disappeared over the ridge. Then he closed the gate, remounted Rob Roy, and rode back to the corral.

Rob McLaughlin gave Kennie one more chance to change his mind. "Last chance, Son. Better pick a horse that you have some hope of riding one day. I'd have got rid of this whole line of stock if they weren't so fast that I've had the fool idea that some day there might turn out one gentle one in the lot — and I'd have a racehorse. But there's never been one so far, and it's not going to be Flicka."

"It's not going to be Flicka," chanted Howard.

"Perhaps she *might* be gentled," said Kennie; and Nell, watching, saw that although his lips quivered, there was fanatical determination in his eye.

"Ken," said Rob, "it's up to you. If you say you want her, we'll get her. But she wouldn't be the first of that line to die rather than give in. They're beautiful and they're fast, but let me tell you this, young man, they're *loco!*" [1]

Kennie flinched under his father's direct glance.

"If I go after her again, I'll not give up whatever comes, understand what I mean by that?"

"Yes."

"What do you say?"

"I want her."

They brought her in again. They had better luck this time. She jumped over the Dutch half-door of the stable and crashed inside. The men slammed the upper half of the door shut and she was caught.

The rest of the band were driven away, and Kennie stood outside the stable, listening to the wild hoofs beating, the screams, the crashes. His Flicka inside there! He was drenched with perspiration.

"We'll leave her to think it over," said Rob when dinnertime came. "Afterward, we'll go up and feed and water her."

[1] *loco* (lō′kō): a Spanish word meaning "crazy."

But when they went up afterward, there was no Flicka in the barn. One of the windows, higher than the mangers, was broken.

The window opened into a pasture an eighth of a mile square, fenced in barbed wire six feet high. Near the stable stood a wagonload of hay. When they went around the back of the stable to see where Flicka had hidden herself, they found her between the stable and the hay wagon, eating.

At their approach she leaped away, then headed east across the pasture.

"If she's like her mother," said Rob, "she'll go right through the wire."

"Ay bet she'll go over," said Gus. "She yumps like a deer."

"No horse can jump that," said McLaughlin.

Kennie said nothing because he could not speak. It was, perhaps, the most terrible moment of his life. He watched Flicka racing toward the eastern wire.

A few yards from it, she swerved, turned, and raced diagonally south.

"It turned her! It turned her!" cried Kennie, almost sobbing. It was the first sign of hope for Flicka. "Oh, Dad! She has got sense. She has! She has!"

Flicka turned again as she met the southern boundary of the pasture; again at the northern; she avoided the barn. Without abating anything of her whirlwind speed, following a precise, accurate calculation and turning each time on a dime, she investigated every possibility. Then, seeing that there was no hope, she raced south toward the range where she had spent her life, gathered herself, and shot into the air.

Each of the three men watching had the impulse to cover his eyes, and Kennie gave a sort of howl of despair.

Twenty yards of fence came down with her as she hurled herself through. Caught on the upper strands, she turned a complete somersault, landing on her back, her four legs dragging the wires down on top of her, and tangling herself in them beyond hope of escape.

"Blasted wire!" said McLaughlin. "If I could afford decent fences . . ."

Kennie followed the men miserably as they walked to the filly. They stood in a circle, watching while she kicked and fought and thrashed until the wire was tightly wound and knotted about her, cutting, piercing, and tearing great three-cornered pieces of flesh and hide. At last she was unconscious, streams of blood running on her golden coat, and pools of crimson widening and spreading on the grass beneath her.

With the wire cutter which Gus always carried in the hip pocket of his overalls, he cut all the wire away, and they drew her into the pasture, repaired the fence, placed hay, a box of oats, and a tub of water near her, and called it a day.

"I don't think she'll pull out of it," said McLaughlin.

Next morning Kennie was up at five, doing his lessons. At six he went out to Flicka.

She had not moved. Food and water were untouched. She was no longer bleeding, but the wounds were swollen and caked over.

Kennie got a bucket of fresh water and poured it over her mouth. Then he leaped away, for Flicka came to life, scrambled up, got her balance, and stood swaying.

Kennie went a few feet away and sat down to watch her. When he went in to breakfast, she had drunk deeply of the water and was mouthing the oats.

There began, then, a sort of recovery. She ate, drank, limped about the pasture; stood for hours with hanging head and weakly splayed-out legs, under the clump of cottonwood trees. The swollen wounds scabbed and began to heal.

Kennie lived in the pasture, too. He followed her around; he talked to her. He too lay snoozing or sat under the cottonwoods; and often, coaxing her with hand outstretched, he walked very quietly toward her. But she would not let him come near her.

Often she stood with her head at the south fence, looking off to the mountain. It made the tears come to Kennie's eyes to see the way she longed to get away.

Still Rob said she wouldn't pull out of it. There was no use putting a halter on her. She had no strength.

One morning, as Ken came out of the house, Gus met him and said, "De filly's down."

Kennie ran to the pasture, Howard close behind him. The right hind leg, which had been badly swollen at the knee joint, had opened in a festering wound, and Flicka lay flat and motionless, with staring eyes.

"Don't you wish now you'd chosen Doughboy?" asked Howard.

"Go away!" shouted Ken.

Howard stood watching while Kennie sat down on the ground and took Flicka's head on his lap. Though she was conscious and moved a little, she did not struggle or seem frightened.

Tears rolled down Kennie's cheeks as he talked to her and petted her. After a few moments, Howard walked away.

"Mother, what do you do for an infection when it's a horse?" asked Kennie.

"Just what you'd do if it was a person. Wet dressings. I'll help you, Ken. We mustn't let those wounds close or scab over until they're clean. I'll make a poultice for that hind leg and help you put it on. Now that she'll let us get close to her, we can help her a lot."

"The thing to do is see that she eats," said Rob. "Keep up her strength."

But he himself would not go near her. "She won't pull out of it," he said. "I don't want to see her or think about her."

Kennie and his mother nursed the filly. The big poultice was bandaged on the hind leg. It drew out much poisoned matter, and Flicka felt better and was able to stand again.

She watched for Kennie now and followed him like a dog, hopping on three legs, holding up the right hind leg with its huge knob of a bandage in comical fashion.

"Dad, Flicka's my friend now; she likes me," said Ken.

His father looked at him. "I'm glad of that, Son. It's a fine thing to have a horse for a friend."

Kennie found a nicer place for her. In the lower pasture the brook ran over cool stones. There was a grassy bank, the size of a corral, almost on a level with the water. Here she could lie softly, eat grass, drink fresh running water. From the grass, a twenty-foot hill sloped up, crested with overhanging trees. She was enclosed, as it were, in a green, open-air nursery.

Kennie carried her oats, morning and evening. She would watch for him to come, eyes and ears pointed to the hill. And one evening, Ken, still some distance off, came to a stop and a wide grin spread over his face. He had heard her nicker. She had caught sight of him coming and was calling to him!

He placed the box of oats under her nose, and she ate while he stood beside her, his hand smoothing the satin-soft skin under her mane. It had a nap as deep as plush. He played with her long, cream-colored tresses, arranged her forelock neatly between her eyes. She was a bit dish-faced, like an Arab, with eyes set far apart. He lightly groomed and brushed her while she stood turning her head to him whichever way he went.

He spoiled her. Soon she would not

step to the stream to drink but he must hold a bucket for her. And she would drink, then lift her dripping muzzle, rest it on the shoulder of his blue chambray shirt, her golden eyes dreaming off into the distance; then daintily dip her mouth to drink again.

When she turned her head to the south and pricked her ears and stood tense and listening, Ken knew she heard the other colts galloping on the upland.

"You'll go back there some day, Flicka," he whispered. "You'll be three and I'll be eleven. You'll be so strong you won't know I'm on your back, and we'll fly like the wind. We'll stand on the very top where we can look over the whole world and smell the snow from the Never-Summer Range. Maybe we'll see antelope . . ."

This was the happiest month of Kennie's life.

With the morning, Flicka always had new strength and would hop three-legged up the hill to stand broadside to the early sun, as horses love to do.

The moment Ken woke, he'd go to the window and see her there; and when he was dressed and at his table studying, he sat so that he could raise his head and see Flicka.

After breakfast, she would be waiting for him and the box of oats at the gate, and for Nell McLaughlin with fresh bandages and buckets of disinfectant; and all three would go together to the brook, Flicka hopping along ahead of them, as if she were leading the way.

But Rob McLaughlin would not look at her.

One day all the wounds were swollen again. Presently they opened, one by one; and Kennie and his mother made more poultices.

Still the little filly climbed the hill in the early morning and ran about on three legs. Then she began to go down in flesh and almost overnight wasted away to nothing. Every rib showed; the glossy hide was dull and brittle, and was pulled over the skeleton as if she were a dead horse.

Gus said, "It's de fever. It burns up her flesh. If you could stop de fever she might get vell."

McLaughlin was standing in his window one morning and saw the little skeleton hopping about three-legged in the sunshine, and he said, "That's the end. I won't have a thing like that on my place."

Kennie had to understand that Flicka had not been getting well all this time; she had been slowly dying.

"She still eats her oats," he said mechanically.

They were all sorry for Ken. Nell McLaughlin stopped disinfecting and dressing the wounds. "It's no use, Ken," she said gently. "You know Flicka's going to die, don't you?"

"Yes, Mother."

Ken stopped eating. Howard said, "Ken doesn't eat anything any more. Don't he have to eat his dinner, Mother?"

But Nell answered, "Leave him alone."

Because the shooting of wounded animals is all in the day's work on the western plains, and sickening to everyone, Rob's voice, when he gave the order to have Flicka shot, was as flat as if he had been telling Gus to kill a chicken for dinner.

"Here's the Marlin, Gus. Pick out a time when Ken's not around and put the filly out of her misery."

Gus took the rifle. "Ja, Boss . . ."

Ever since Ken had known that Flicka was to be shot, he had kept his eye on the rack which held the firearms. His father allowed no firearms in the bunkhouse. The gun rack was in the dining room of the ranch house; and, going through it to the kitchen three times a day for meals, Ken's eye scanned the weapons to make sure that they were all there.

That night they were not all there. The Marlin rifle was missing.

When Kennie saw that, he stopped walking. He felt dizzy. He kept staring at the gun rack, telling himself that it surely was there — he counted again and again — he couldn't see clearly . . .

Then he felt an arm across his shoulders and heard his father's voice.

"I know, Son. Some things are awful hard to take. We just have to take 'em. I have to, too."

Kennie got hold of his father's hand and held on. It helped steady him.

Finally he looked up. Rob looked down and smiled at him and gave him a little shake and squeeze. Ken managed a smile too.

"All right now?"

"All right, Dad."

They walked in to supper together.

Ken even ate a little. But Nell looked thoughtfully at the ashen color of his face, and at the little pulse that was beating in the side of his neck.

After supper he carried Flicka her oats, but he had to coax her and she would only eat a little. She stood with her head hanging, but when he stroked it and talked to her, she pressed her face into his chest and was content. He could feel the burning heat of her body. It didn't seem possible that anything so thin could be alive.

Presently Kennie saw Gus come into the pasture, carrying the Marlin. When he saw Ken, he changed his direction and sauntered along as if he were out to shoot some cottontails.

Ken ran to him. "When are you going to do it, Gus?"

"Ay was goin' down soon now, before it got dark . . ."

"Gus, don't do it tonight. Wait till morning. Just one more night, Gus."

"Vell, in de morning, den, but it got to be done, Ken. Yer fader gives de order."

"I know. I won't say anything more."

An hour after the family had gone to bed, Ken got up and put on his clothes. It was a warm moonlit night. He ran down to the brook, calling softly, "Flicka! Flicka!"

But Flicka did not answer with a little nicker, and she was not in the nursery nor hopping about the pasture. Ken hunted for an hour.

At last he found her down the creek, lying in the water. Her head had been on the bank, but as she lay there, the current of the stream had sucked and pulled at her, and she had had no strength to resist; and little by little her head had slipped down until when Ken got there only the muzzle was resting on the bank, and the body and legs were swinging in the stream.

Kennie slid into the water, sitting on the bank, and he hauled at her head. But she was heavy, and the current dragged like a weight; and he began to sob because he had no strength to draw her out.

Then he found a leverage for his heels against some rocks in the bed of the stream, and he braced himself against these and pulled with all his might; and her head came up onto his knees, and he held it cradled in his arms.

He was glad that she had died of her own accord, in the cool water, under the moon, instead of being shot by Gus. Then, putting his face close to hers and looking searchingly into her eyes, he saw that she was alive and looking back at him.

And then he burst out crying and hugged her and said, "Oh, my little Flicka, my little Flicka."

The long night passed.

The moon slid slowly across the heavens.

The water rippled over Kennie's legs and over Flicka's body. And gradually the heat and fever went out of her. And the cool running water washed and washed her wounds.

When Gus went down in the morning with the rifle, they hadn't moved. There they were, Kennie sitting in water over his thighs and hips, with Flicka's head in his arms.

Gus seized Flicka by the head and hauled her out on the grassy bank, and then, seeing that Kennie couldn't move, cold and stiff and half paralyzed as he was, lifted him in his arms and carried him to the house.

"Gus," said Ken through chattering teeth, "don't shoot her, Gus."

"It ain't fur me to say, Ken. You know dat."

"But the fever's left her, Gus."

"Ay wait a little, Ken . . ."

Rob McLaughlin drove to Laramie to get the doctor, for Ken was in violent chills that would not stop. His mother had him in bed, wrapped in hot blankets, when they got back.

He looked at his father imploringly as the doctor shook down the thermometer.

"She might get well now, Dad. The fever's left her. It went out of her when the moon went down."

"All right, Son. Don't worry. Gus'll feed her, morning and night, as long as she's . . ."

"As long as I can't do it," finished Ken happily.

The doctor put the thermometer in his mouth and told him to keep it shut.

All day Gus went about his work, thinking of Flicka. He had not been back to look at her. He had been given no more orders. If she was alive, the order to shoot her was still in effect. But Kennie was ill; McLaughlin, making his second trip to town, taking the doctor home, would not be back till long after dark.

After their supper in the bunkhouse, Gus and Tim walked down to the brook. They did not speak as they approached the filly, lying stretched out flat on the grassy bank, but their eyes were straining at her to see if she was dead or alive.

She raised her head as they reached her.

"By the powers!" exclaimed Tim, "there she is!"

She dropped her head, raised it again, and moved her legs and became tense as if struggling to rise. But to do so she must use her right hind leg to brace herself against the earth. That was the damaged leg, and at the first bit of pressure with it, she gave up and fell back.

"We'll swing her on to the other side," said Tim. "Then she can help herself."

"Ja . . ."

Standing behind her, they leaned over, grabbed hold of her left legs, front and back, and gently hauled her over. Flicka was as lax and willing as a puppy. But the moment she found herself lying on her right side, she began to scramble, braced herself with her good left leg, and tried to rise.

"Yee whiz!" said Gus. "She got plenty strength yet."

"Hi!" cheered Tim. "She's up!"

But Flicka wavered, slid down again, and lay flat. This time she gave notice that she would not try again by heaving a deep sigh and closing her eyes.

Gus took his pipe out of his mouth and thought it over. Orders or no orders, he would try to save the filly. Ken had gone too far to be let down.

"Ay'm goin' to rig a blanket sling fur her, Tim, and get her on her feet and keep her up."

There was bright moonlight to work by. They brought down the posthole digger and set two aspen poles deep into the ground on either side of the filly, then, with ropes attached to the blanket, hoisted her by a pulley.

Not at all disconcerted, she rested comfortably in the blanket under her belly, touched her feet on the ground, and reached for the bucket of water Gus held for her.

Kennie was sick a long time. He nearly died. But Flicka picked up. Every day Gus passed the word to Nell, who carried it to Ken. "She's cleaning up her oats.". . . "She's out of the sling.". . . "She bears a little weight on the bad leg."

Tim declared it was a real miracle. They argued about it, eating their supper.

"Na," said Gus. "It was de cold water, washin' de fever outa her. And more dan dot — it was Ken — you tink it don't count? All night dot boy sits dere and says, 'Hold on, Flicka, Ay'm here wid you. Ay'm standin' by, two of us togedder' . . ."

Tim stared at Gus without answering, while he thought it over. In the silence, a coyote yapped far off on the plains, and the wind made a rushing sound high up in the jack pines on the hill.

Gus filled his pipe.

"Sure," said Tim finally. "Sure, that's it."

Then came the day when Rob McLaughlin stood smiling at the foot of Kennie's bed and said, "Listen! Hear your friend?"

Ken listened and heard Flicka's high, eager whinny.

"She don't spend much time by the brook any more. She's up at the gate of the corral half the time, nickering for you."

"For me!"

Rob wrapped a blanket around the boy and carried him out to the corral gate.

Kennie gazed at Flicka. There was a look of marveling in his eyes. He felt as if he had been living in a world where everything was dreadful and hurting but awfully real; and *this* couldn't be real; this was all soft and happy, nothing to struggle over or worry about or fight for any more. Even his father was proud of him! He could feel it in the way Rob's big arms held him. It was all like a dream and far away. He couldn't, yet, get close to anything.

But Flicka — Flicka — alive, well, pressing up to him, recognizing him, nickering . . .

Kennie put out a hand — weak and white — and laid it on her face. His thin little fingers straightened her forelock the way he used to do, while Rob looked at the two with a strange expression about his mouth and a glow in his eyes that was not often there.

"She's still poor, Dad, but she's on four legs now."

"She's picking up."

Ken turned his face up, suddenly remembering. "Dad! She did get gentled, didn't she?"

"Gentle — as — a kitten. . . ."

They put a cot down by the brook for Ken, and boy and filly got well together.

COURAGE IN EVERYDAY LIFE

1. How does the author lead us to sympathize with Kennie at the opening of the story? How did Kennie's mother convince his father that Kennie should have a horse of his own?

2. Why did Kennie choose Flicka? What made this a hard decision for Kennie? Why was it difficult for Kennie's father to let Kennie hold to this decision? Do you think Kennie's father was fair to him?

3. Describe the rounding up of the horses and Flicka's attempts at escape. What were Kennie's reactions to these events?

4. Tell about Kennie's nursing and taming of Flicka. What saved Flicka?

5. This story tells about courage in everyday life. A boy makes a decision and has the courage to stand by it. How did the attitudes of his father and brother make it hard for Kennie to hold to his decision? What outside circumstances and events tested his courage even more?

6. We should not confuse courage with stubbornness. Do you think there were elements of each in Kennie's actions? Is there any difference between stubbornness and singleness of purpose? Discuss your answers.

7. Have you, or someone you know well, ever had to make a difficult decision? Did it call for courage as great as Kennie's to make the decision and to carry it out?

8. At what times must men in public life be courageous? Give examples to illustrate your answer.

WORDS: FORMING ADJECTIVES

Observe the italicized words in these sentences:

The *wind* is blowing today.
It is a *windy* day.
The road has *bumps*.
It is a *bumpy* road.

You can see that by adding the letter *y* to two nouns, we have made them into adjectives.

Make up some pairs of sentences like those above to illustrate how the following nouns can be changed to adjectives: *fish, sun, jingle, rose, tub*.

Can you think of some nouns that cannot be changed into adjectives by the addition of –*y*?

SENTENCES: MODIFYING THE NOUN

We have seen how modifiers make more detailed sentences. In the sentences below, you will see some of the different kinds of modifiers that can be added to nouns.

"There was *bright* moonlight . . ."
"Examples *in arithmetic* were neatly written out . . ."
"She hurled herself against the poles *which walled the corral*."

In the first sentence, an adjective, *bright*, modifies the noun *moonlight*. In the second sentence, a prepositional phrase, *in arithmetic*, modifies the noun *examples*. In the third sentence, a clause, *which walled the corral*, modifies the noun *poles*.

Write three sentences and modify one of the nouns in each sentence. Use each kind of modifier illustrated above.

COMPOSITION: TOTAL IMPRESSION

Read this paragraph from page 69, and notice how all the details work together to give us a strong impression of Flicka's lightness and swiftness:

"Ken was entranced to watch Flicka when the wild band of youngsters discovered that they were being pursued and took off across the mountain. Footing made no difference to her. She floated across the ravines, always two lengths ahead of the others. Her pink mane and tail whipped in the wind. Her long, delicate legs had only to aim, it seemed, at a particular spot for her to reach it and sail on. She seemed to Ken a fairy horse."

Do you agree that this writer has created a strong impression of lightness and swiftness by using words like *floated, delicate, sail,* and *fairy*?

Write a short paragraph describing an animal, in which you emphasize a particularly outstanding quality — perhaps heaviness or playfulness or sneakiness.

MASTERPIECES OF ART

Paintings by Old Masters

You have probably heard certain painters spoken of as "old masters." These are painters who lived before our time, but whose pictures are still admired today. Everyone has heard of Rembrandt, for instance — the great Dutch painter of the seventeenth century. Rembrandt painted so many fine pictures that it would be difficult to single out any one as his masterpiece. Let us just take an example, a painting called *The Polish Rider* (PLATE 1). We don't know who the Polish rider was — whether he actually existed or whether Rembrandt invented him. But whoever he may have been, this young man on horseback is certainly made to look impressive. He turns boldly toward us with one hand on his hip. We seem to be looking up at him, as if our eye level were somewhere between his knee and his foot, which makes his figure tower above us like a statue and thus appear even more impressive. Notice the background provided by the distant hill which rises up from both sides of the picture, reaching its summit to the left of the rider's head.

Around 1635, the great Spanish artist Diego Velásquez painted a huge picture to commemorate the surrender of the Dutch town of Breda ten years earlier, after a long siege by the Spanish army. In this painting (PLATE 2) we see Justinus of Nassau offering the victorious Spanish general the key to the town while soldiers of both armies look on. Many of the faces are so well defined that they seem like individual portraits, yet Velásquez had seen most of these people only in other pictures. He had never been to Breda in his life!

Although Velásquez has compressed many figures within a shallow space in the foreground, he has left ample room in the center in order to focus our attention on the two main figures and on the large key, which you can see more closely in PLATE 3. Then he leads us suddenly back into space, for as we look beyond the key we can make out another group of soldiers in the middle distance and beyond them a landscape stretching away for miles. Undoubtedly, in real life the surrender was an anxious moment, yet Velásquez has expressed here an over-all feeling of calm. He has counterbalanced all the shapes in the foreground with a row of vertical lances and has filled the distant sky with a gentle haze of smoke and clouds. All this provides a setting for the Spanish general's compassionate gesture as he accepts the Dutch surrender.

In the next painting, *Courtyard of a House in Delft* (PLATE 4), nothing much seems to be happening at all. A woman simply leads a little girl down the steps of a house, and in the archway to the left another woman stands with her back to us, looking into the next courtyard. Pieter de Hooch, who painted this picture, had no real story to tell, no important event to record. But how skillfully he leads our eye from one detail to another! Even the bricks of the houses and the stones of the court hold our attention for a few moments as we examine their many subtle changes in texture and color. But what attracts us most is the quality of the light in the archway and the court beyond.

If a wealthy Dutchman of the early seventeenth century wanted his portrait painted, he could choose between two great masters living in his own country. One was Rembrandt. The other was Frans Hals, a Flemish-born painter who had settled in the Dutch town of Haarlem. PLATE 5 shows one of Hals's most stunning portraits, *The Laughing Cavalier*. This is a curious title (not the artist's own, by the way), for this jaunty military officer does not appear to be laughing. He merely seems amused. At any rate, you can see that Hals has captured a momentary facial expression, almost like the effect of a camera snapshot. But note how different it really is from a photograph. Notice particularly the brisk way Hals has painted the cavalier's face and the crackling brushwork defining the gold embroidery on his sleeve.

Of the five old masters we have chosen to discuss here, the earliest was Pieter Bruegel, a Flemish painter of the sixteenth century. He is known to us mainly for pictures of festive village and country scenes, such as *The Peasant Wedding* (PLATE 6). With so many things going on at once, you might expect nothing but confusion from such a painting. But Bruegel has composed his picture so skillfully that we can examine its many interesting details without ever losing sight of its over-all unity. Notice how each corner in the foreground is filled like the corners of a stage. Our eye is led inward diagonally from the tray of pies, past the man who serves the food, and along the banquet table to the crowd bursting in through the doorway at the rear.

PLATE 1. REMBRANDT VAN RIJN (Dutch, 1606–1669): *The Polish Rider*. About 1655. Oil on canvas, 46 x 55 inches. (Copyright The Frick Collection, New York)

PLATE 2. DIEGO VELÁSQUEZ (Spanish, 1599–1660): *The Surrender of Breda.* 1635. Oil on canvas, 121⅛ x 144¾ inches. (The Prado, Madrid)

PLATE 3. Detail from PLATE 2.

PLATE 4. PIETER DE HOOCH (Dutch, 1632–1683): *Courtyard of a House in Delft.*
1658. Oil on canvas, 30¾ x 25⅝ inches. (Reproduced by courtesy of the Trustees, The
National Gallery, London)

84

PLATE 5. FRANS HALS (Dutch, 1580/81–1666): *The Laughing Cavalier*. 1624. Oil on canvas, 33¾ x 27 inches. (Reproduced by permission of the Trustees of the Wallace Collection, London)

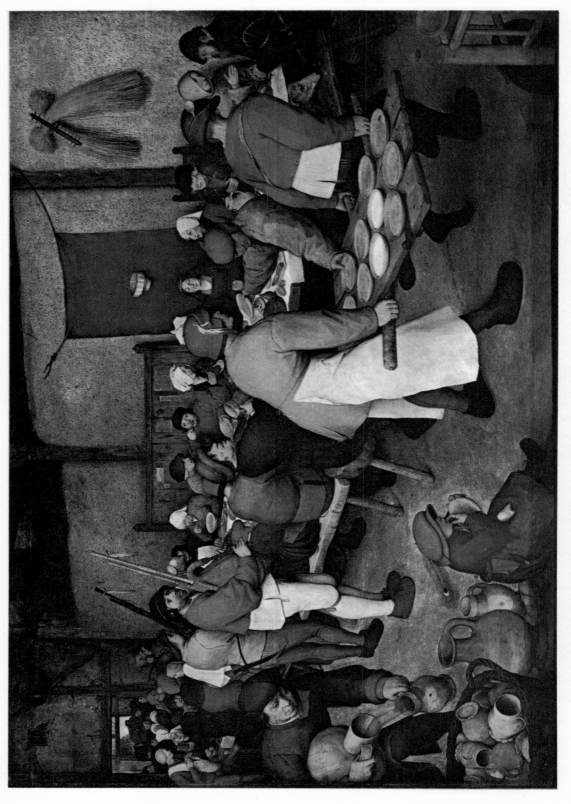

PLATE 6. PIETER BRUEGEL, THE ELDER (Flemish, about 1525–1569) : *The Peasant Wedding*. About 1565. Oil on wood, 44⅞ x 64 inches. (Kunsthistorisches Museum, Vienna)

Lou Gehrig's Epic of Courage

PAUL GALLICO

Success in full measure came to Henry Louis Gehrig, the American-born son of immigrant German parents. He had fame, money, popularity, love, and companionship, and, thanks to his wife Eleanor, even a little self-assurance.

The awkward boy who could neither bat nor field as a youngster had, by his unswerving persistence, his gnawing ambition, his tenacity and iron will power, made himself into the greatest first baseman in the history of organized baseball. The ballplayer whose cultural tastes seldom rose above a B movie found his interest awakened in music, books, and the theater.

I remember writing years ago about Gehrig: "To my mind there is no greater inspiration to any American boy than Lou Gehrig and his career. For if the awkward, inept, and downright clumsy Gehrig that I knew and saw in the beginning could turn himself into the finest first-base-covering machine in

all baseball, through sheer drive and determination, then nothing is impossible to any man or boy in this country."

Men like Connie Mack and Hughie Fullerton, baseball encyclopedias who spanned generations of players, unhesitantly placed Lou Gehrig at first base on any "All" team.

When the "All-Star" games were played each summer, there was bitter controversy about who should play many of the positions. But it was almost automatically conceded that Lou Gehrig should play first base for the American Leaguers.

In 1934 Lou won the triple batting championship of the American League, and gave it to his Eleanor as a first-anniversary present. He led his league in hitting that year, batting .363, hitting 49 home runs, and driving in 165 runs.

It is interesting to note Ruth's [1] waning record for the same year. He hit .288, knocked 22 out of the park, and batted in 84 runs.

[1] **Ruth's:** Babe Ruth's.

In 1935, Lou Gehrig was out from beneath the shadow of Babe Ruth. The Babe was no longer with the Yankee team. Wear and tear and time had tapped Ruth. But actually, Gehrig had begun to emerge even before Ruth's retirement. For toward the end, as the figures indicate, not even the Babe could cast a shadow large enough to blanket the Iron Horse.

Gehrig's modesty and self-deprecation continued to keep him in the background, but his deeds, his amazing vitality, durability, and the quality of his play refused to be submerged any longer.

Sincere tributes to the man appeared in the sports columns. From the Olympian slopes of the press box, the sports writers began to look down with honest affection at the piano legs, the broad rear porch which had earned him the name of Biscuit Pants, the powerful, smooth-swinging shoulders and the young and pleasant face of "that big dumb Dutchman."

Success! The Golden Decade was buried in the limbo of beautiful dreams. There was a new era and a new team. With Lou as captain, the Bronx Bombers won the American League pennant in 1936–7–8. They won three World Series in a row, two from the Giants, 4–2 and 4–1, and one from the helpless Cubs in straight games.

In 1936, Lou was again named the most valuable player in the American League, exactly nine years after he had first achieved this honor. His salary had been mounting steadily, and in 1938 he signed for the largest sum he ever received for playing ball, $39,000.

Toward the end of the last decade, the name, the figure, and above all, the simple engaging personality of Lou Gehrig became welded into the national scene. Came the baseball season, came Gehrig. Came Gehrig, came home runs, triples, doubles, excitement, and faultless play around first base. And his consecutive-games record went on and on. Sick or well, he never missed a game.

Sick or well. I wonder whether you know what that means to a ballplayer, and particularly one who plays at first base, where the bumps are many and there is daily danger both from ball and man.

Lou played with colds. He played with fevers. He played so doubled over with lumbago [1] that it was impossible for him to straighten up, and bent over at the plate, he still got himself a single.

In 1934, the year he won the triple crown, he fractured a toe. He played on. He was knocked unconscious by a wild pitch, suffered a concussion that would hospitalize the average man for two weeks. He was at his position the next day and collected four hits. When, late in his career, his hands were X-rayed, they found seventeen assorted fractures that had healed by themselves. He had broken every finger on both hands and some twice, and *hadn't even mentioned it* to anyone.

The fantastic thing about all this is not that he was able to endure the pain of breaks, strains, sprains, pulled and torn tendons, muscles, and ligaments,

---

[1] **lumbago** (lum·bā′gō): aching in the small of the back.

but that it failed to impair his efficiency. On the contrary, if he had something the matter with him it was the signal for him to try all the harder, so that no one, least of all his own severe conscience, could accuse him of being a handicap to his team while playing in a crippled condition.

When, in 1939, Lou Gehrig found himself slow in spring training, he began to punish his body for a failure that was unaccountable and to drive it harder than ever before.

It had begun before that, the slow tragedy of disintegration. Signs and symptoms had been mistaken. During most of 1938, Gehrig had been on a strict diet. That year had not been a good one for him. In the early winter of 1939 he had taken a $5,000 salary slash. Baseball players are paid by the records they compile. That winter, as usual, Lou and Eleanor went ice skating together. Lou was a fine skater. But, strangely, he kept falling all the time.

The teams went south for the 1939 training season and the sports writers went along with them. And the boys with one accord began sending back stories that must have saddened them to write. I know sports writers. When you grow to love an athlete the way they loved Lou Gehrig, it isn't fun to oil your typewriter with his blood and be the first to write the story of the passing from the sports scene of a once-great figure.

What they saw was not unfamiliar to them. The useful playing lifetime of a top-flight professional athlete is on the average shockingly short. A sports writer is quick to notice the first symp-

toms of slowing up. They were obvious with Gehrig at St. Petersburg. He was slow afoot, afield, and at bat. And while he fought like a rookie to hold his position, no improvement was evident. Sadly the sports writers wrote that the old Iron Horse was running down.

But the players on the Yankee ball club were saying something else. They were close to Gehrig — close enough to touch. They noticed things that worried and depressed them. And they had knowledge of their craft and of themselves. One of the things they knew was that a ballplayer slows up only gradually. His legs go, imperceptibly at first, then noticeably as he no longer covers the ground in the field that he used to cover. But he doesn't come apart all at one time, and in chunks.

I talked to Tony Lazzeri at his neat little home in San Francisco. Tony watched Lou in practice in Florida in 1939. Once Lou was up at the plate and ducked back from a close one. And he couldn't stop himself. He just kept on staggering backward, unable to regain his balance, until he crashed into one of the other players, who righted him again.

The ballplayers knew that wasn't right.

Bill Dickey, Lou's closest friend, was worried sick. He began to watch over Lou the way a father watches over a child. And nobody would say anything to Gehrig, because, rough and tough though the ballplayer may be, he is a sensitive fellow and a respecter of private feelings.

There are grim tales of things that happened in the locker room, and one

Lou Gehrig, at the peak of his career, is seen above and right. Below, in an emotional moment on the day Lou Gehrig said good-bye to baseball, Babe Ruth embraces his former teammate.

is macabre with overtones of manly nobility. It tells of Gehrig dressing, leaning over to lace his spikes and falling forward to the floor, to lie momentarily helpless. And it tells further of tough men with the fine instincts to look away and not to hurt his already tortured soul the more by offering to help. Quickly they left the locker room, leaving him to struggle to his feet alone with no eyes to see his weakness.

Few men can have gone through what Gehrig did during those days.

Among the elements that go to make up a hero is the capacity for quiet, uncomplaining suffering; the ability to take it and never let the world suspect that you are taking it. This was Lou Gehrig. Not even his wife knew wholly, though she must have suspected, how terribly Gehrig suffered during those days when his speed and skill were deserting him.

Picture the fear, the worry, the helpless bewilderment that must have filled Lou's soul as he found that he could not bat, could not run, could not field. Life for him took on nightmarish aspects. All the fearful dreams to which humans are prone, dreams of shameful failure, dreams of not being able to run when pursued, dreams of performing some well-remembered daily office with grotesque results, now haunted his waking hours.

The strain and terror of it lined his face in a few short months and brought gray to his hair. But it could not force a complaint from his lips.

Gehrig's most powerful reaction when it became apparent that there was something wrong with him was to drive himself still harder, to punish his flagging muscles and sick body relentlessly. He was certain it was work he needed. It never occurred to him to blame for his apparent lack of condition something quite outside his own power to control.

His performance during the early part of 1939 was pitiful. And yet, so great was the spell cast by his integrity, his honest attempts to please, and his service over the long years, that that worst-mannered, worst-tempered, and most boorish individual in the world, the baseball fan, forebore to heckle him.

On Sunday, April 30, 1939, the Yankees played the Senators in Washington. Lou Gehrig came to bat four times with runners on base. He failed even to meet the ball, and the Yankees lost.

Something else happened on that day. There was a toss ball at first. The pitcher fielded a one-hop grounder, ran over toward first, and tossed the ball underhand to Lou, as pitchers frequently do when there is time.

Lou muffed the throw.

Monday was an "off" day. Lou went to Larchmont, New York. He did a lot of thinking, but he did it to himself. He had the toughest decision of his life to make. But he had to make it alone.

Tuesday, May 2, the team met in Detroit to open a series against the Tigers. Joe McCarthy flew in from Buffalo. Lou met him in the dugout and said the fateful words:

"Joe, I always said that when I felt I couldn't help the team any more I would take myself out of the line-up.

I guess that time has come."

"When do you want to quit, Lou?" asked McCarthy.

Gehrig looked at him steadily and said, "Now. Put Babe Dahlgren in."

Later, alone in the dugout, he wept. The record ended at 2,130 games.

The newspapers and the sports world buzzed with the sensation of Lou Gehrig's departure from the Yankee line-up.

At the urging of Eleanor, Lou went to the Mayo Clinic in Rochester, Minnesota, for a checkup.

There was a lull in the news. Then out of a clear sky the storm burst again. Black headlines tore across the page tops like clouds and lightninged their messages: GEHRIG HAS INFANTILE PARALYSIS. GEHRIG FIGHTS PARALYZING ILLNESS.

The New York Yankees released the report of the doctors at the clinic. It was a disease diagnosed as amyotrophic lateral sclerosis, interpreted for the layman as a form of infantile paralysis, and the mystery of the too-sudden decline and passing of Henry Louis Gehrig, perennial Yankee first baseman, was solved.

Before Gehrig came home from the Mayo Clinic, Eleanor went to their family physician, gave him the name of the disease, and asked to be told the truth about it. The doctor knew her well. He said quietly, "I think you can take it. And I think you should know."

Then he told her that her husband could not live more than two years.

Eleanor went home. She closed her door upon herself, shutting out the world. But before she could give in to grief and shock for the first and last time, she telephoned the Mayo Clinic. She had but one question to ask of the doctors there: "Have you told my husband?"

Gehrig had so captivated the staff that they had not yet had the heart to tell him the truth, and they so advised Eleanor.

She begged, "Please promise me that you never will. Don't ever let him know. I don't want him to find out."

They promised. Only then did Eleanor permit herself to weep.

The time of weeping was short. Lou came home. He came home full of smiles and jokes, and the girl who met him was smiling and laughing too, though neither noticed that in the laughter of the other there was something feverish. They were too busy to notice — too busy with their magnificent deception of each other.

Lou's cheer was based outwardly on the fact that he hadn't been just an aging ballplayer, that his sudden disintegration had been caused by disease — a disease of which he promised Eleanor he would be cured before he learned to pronounce its name.

Eleanor fought a constant fight to keep the truth from Lou. She had to be on the spot always to answer the telephone; to watch over him so that people did not get to him; to look at the mail before he saw it. Ever present was the menace of the one crackpot who might slip through the shields of love she placed about her husband and tell him that his case was hopeless.

As to what Lou knew — he never told anybody.

To all intents and purposes, Gehrig

Gehrig bows his head as 60,000 fans and his teammates say good-bye on July 4, 1939.

went into the battle with his chin up and his determination blazing. If the knowledge was clear within him that the cards were stacked against him and he could not win, he fought, nevertheless. He would have fought if only to keep up Eleanor's courage, to prevent her from realizing the hopelessness of his situation.

On July 4, 1939, there took place the most tragic and touching scene ever enacted on a baseball diamond — the funeral services for Henry Louis Gehrig.

Lou Gehrig attended them in person.

Lou Gehrig Appreciation Day, as it was called, was a gesture of love and appreciation on the part of everyone concerned, a spontaneous reaching out to a man who had been good and kind and decent, to thank him for having been so.

The suggestion that there be a Geh-rig Day began in the sports column of Bill Corum of the *Journal-American*. Other columnists concurred, and the event was set between the games of a Fourth of July double-header.

The most touching demonstration of what the day meant was the coming from the ends of the country of Gehrig's former teammates, the famous Murderers' Row, the powerful Yankees of 1927.

Bob Meusel; balding Benny Bengough, Gehrig's first pal; gray-eyed Mark Koenig; dead-panned Poosh-'em-up Tony Lazzeri, the clown of the team; tall, skinny Joe Dugan, and even taller and skinnier Pipp the Pickler, the Yankee first baseman whose place Gehrig had taken so many years ago, all came.

Little Everett Scott turned up, the man whose endurance record Gehrig had conquered so decisively, and the great pitching staff of other days: Herb

Pennock, from his Pennsylvania fox farm; Waite Hoyt from the broadcasting booths. George Pipgras was there too, but wearing the blue uniform of an umpire. Early Combs and Art Fletcher still were in Yankee uniforms as coaches.

And finally there was George Herman Ruth. The Babe and Lou hadn't got along very well the last years they played together, and after Babe retired, he had criticized Lou's long playing record in a newspaper interview. The original feud was a childish affair which gains nothing in dignity or sense in the retelling. Suffice it to say that the Babe was there on that Requiem Day, with an arm around Lou and a whispered pleasantry that came at a time when Gehrig was very near to collapse from the emotions that turmoiled within him. It needed Babe's Rabelaisian [1] nonsense to make him smile.

Present, too, were Lou's more recent teammates, the Bronx Bombers under Joe McCarthy, and the Washington Senators, who were the opponents of the Yankees for the doubleheader.

Sid Mercer, president of the Baseball Writers' Association, was the master of ceremonies. The principal speakers were Jim Farley, Postmaster General, and Mayor Fiorello La Guardia. Sixty-one thousand, eight hundred and eight were in the stands. It was what was known as a Great Day.

To Lou Gehrig, it was good-bye to everything that he had known and loved.

It was good-bye to baseball: to the big steel and concrete stadium where he had served so long; to the neat green diamond with the smooth dirt paths cut by the sharp steel baseball cleats; to the towering stands with the waving pennons;[2] to the crowds, their roar and color.

Good-bye, too, to the men with whom he had played for fourteen years, the happy, friendly men who had been his shipmates through life.

In the stands were all that he held dear: his mother and father seated in a box, unaware of his doom; his wife seated in another. Lifelong friends were in the boxes, cheering and applauding. And as Lou observed them gathered there in his honor, he knew he was seeing them thus for the last time.

For he was the living dead, and this was his funeral.

Gifts piled up for him: a silver service, smoking sets, writing sets, fishing tackle. They were from the Yankees; from their great rivals the Giants; from the baseball writers; and even from the ushers in the stadium and the peanut boys. The objects were a mockery, because Lou could no longer possess them. But the warmth of the feeling that prompted their presentation melted the iron reserve in him and broke him down.

It was so human and so heroic that Gehrig should have wept there in public before the sixty-one thousand, not for pity of himself, nor yet for the beauty and sweetness of the world he

[1] **Rabelaisian** (rab'ə·lā'zē·ən): like Rabelais (1494?–1553), a French writer whose stories were robust and earthy.

[2] **pennons** (pen'ənz): flags.

would soon leave, but because the boy who all his life had convinced himself that he had no worth, that he did not matter and never would, understood on this day, for the first time, perhaps, how much people loved him.

Not only were his parents, his adored wife, and his personal friends broadcasting their warmth to him, but huge masses of plain, simple people with whom he felt a deep kinship. He was the lone receiving station. To tune in suddenly upon so much love was nearly too much for him.

The speeches were ended at last, the gifts given, and the stadium rocked as wave after wave of cheers rolled down from the stands and broke over him. For a little while, as he stood at the microphones, it seemed as if the huge combers[1] of sound might engulf him. He stood with his head bowed to the tumult and pressed a handkerchief to his eyes.

But when at last, encouraged by his friend Ed Barrow, a burly bear of a man with the kindest of hearts, he faced the instruments and the people behind them, the noise stopped abruptly. Everyone waited for what he would say. With a curled finger he dashed away the tears that would not stay back, lifted his head, and brought his obsequies[2] to their heartbreaking, never-to-be-forgotten finish when he spoke his epitaph:

"For the past two weeks you have been reading about a bad break I got. Yet today I consider myself the luckiest man on the face of the earth . . ."

The clangy, iron echo of the Yankee Stadium picked up the sentence that poured from the loud-speakers and hurled it forth into the world. "The luckiest man on the face of the earth . . . the luckiest man on the face of the earth . . . luckiest man . . ."

EPILOGUE

There is an epilogue, because although the tale of "Lou Gehrig — An American Hero" really ends above, he lived for quite a while longer, and perhaps in the simple story of how he lived what time was left to him is to be found his greatest gallantry.

For life is not the work of a master dramatist. The hero does not vanish in a cloud of fire at the supreme moment. No, life must be lived on until the curtain falls of its own accord, and that calls for the greatest heroism of all — the heroism of little things: the breaking smile, the cheery word, the laugh that covers pain, the light phrase that denies hopelessness and a sinking heart.

Almost two more years had to pass before the end came to Henry Louis Gehrig, and Eleanor says that during that time he was always laughing, cheerful, interested in everything, impatient only of unasked-for sympathy. In short, he lived his daily life.

But he did more. And here we come to the final bit of heroism. With his doom sealed and his parting inevitable from the woman who had given him the only real happiness he had ever known, he chose to spend his last days, not in one final feverish attempt to suck from life in two years all that he

---

[1] **combers:** waves.
[2] **obsequies** (ob′sə·kwēz): funeral services.

might have had in forty, but in work and service.

Mayor La Guardia appointed him a city parole commissioner. And so, for the next months, as long as he was able to walk even with the assistance of others, Gehrig went daily to his office and did his work. He listened to cases, studied them; he brought to the job his thoroughness and his innate kindness and understanding.

He sat at his desk even when no longer able to move his arms. When he wanted a cigarette, his wife or his secretary lit it for him and put it between his lips, removed it to shake the ash, replaced it.

He listened to thief, vagabond, and narcotic addict. When there was help to be given, he gave it unstintingly from what strength there was left to him. He would not give in. He would not give up. He did not give up.

On June 2, 1941, Lou Gehrig died in the arms of his wife in their home in Riverdale, New York.

But the final beauty of his story is that, in a way, the tenacious man who had overcome every obstacle that ever faced him overcame that last one too.

Gehrig achieved the life everlasting in that he left behind a vital part of himself in the hearts and minds of men. They have tried to express it in the perpetuating of his playing number "4" and his locker in the Yankee Stadium; in the naming of the intersection at Grand Concourse and East 161st Street Gehrig Plaza; in the dedication of a World Series to him; in the screening by Samuel Goldwyn of a picture patterned after his life.

But the light that really shines like a friendly, beckoning beacon in the darkness of a disillusioned world is that of the spirit of a clean, honest, decent, kindly fellow. It is not so much the man whom our weary souls have canonized, as the things by which he lived and died. And for the seeing of those we must all of us be very grateful.

THE HEROISM OF A GALLANT MAN

1. Describe Lou Gehrig's success as a ballplayer. How was he affected by minor illnesses and injuries during his career?

2. What were some of the early signs of Lou's last illness? In its later stages, how did this sickness affect him? Describe some of his struggles with it.

3. Relate the events of Lou Gehrig Appreciation Day. Why does the author call it Lou Gehrig's "funeral"?

4. At one point the author says this:

"Among the elements that go to make up a hero is the capacity for quiet, uncomplaining suffering; the ability to take it and never let the world suspect that you are taking it."

Show how Lou lived up to this quality of a hero.

5. How does Lou Gehrig's courage compare with that of the other heroes in this unit?

6. Do you think that Lou and his wife Eleanor could have helped each other more if they had admitted to each other the seriousness of Lou's illness? What do you think of Lou's decision to work during his last years?

WORDS: FINDING WORD CLASSES

Lou Gehrig batted in many runs. Someone just learning English might be confused at hearing the word *runs* used as a noun in this way. He would know about the verb *runs* that means to move fast with one's feet. But if he looked in the dictionary, he would find many meanings for *run* as a verb, noun, and adjective. The dictionary also shows that *run* can be used in combination with other words: *run down, run out, run off, run through.*

The dictionary, then, tells you the various classes in which a word is used and also the various meanings it may have under each of those classes. Use the dictionary to make a study of the word *go*. Write sentences for some of the different uses of *go*.

SENTENCES: MODIFYING THE VERB

In the following sentence, a single-word adverb modifies the verb:

> "*Sadly* the sports writers wrote that the old Iron Horse was running down."

A prepositional phrase might have been used instead. Do you think this phrase is as effective?

> *With sadness,* the sports writers wrote that the old Iron Horse was running down.

Verbs may be modified by one word, like *sadly*, or they may be modified by groups of words. In the sentences below, the modifiers are in italics. What words do they modify? What question does each modifier answer?

> "His salary had been mounting *steadily* . . ."
> "It tells of Gehrig . . . falling forward *to the floor* . . ."
> ". . . it isn't fun to oil your typewriter *with his blood* . . ."

COMPOSITION:
DESCRIBING CHARACTER

In this biographical essay you probably got a good feeling for the kind of man Lou Gehrig was. The author gives you an impression of his character by showing how Lou Gehrig worked and how he treated others. The incidents narrated in this article emphasized that Lou Gehrig had heroic courage.

Write a character sketch describing a person that you know well. Choose details to emphasize one quality of this person's character, perhaps his kindness, courage, humor, or perseverance.

READING WORD GROUPS

You can improve your reading speed and comprehension by applying your knowledge about English sentences. You know that the key words in a sentence are the subject and the verb. You know also that the subject may be expanded by having one or more word, phrase, or clause modifiers clustered around it. The verb, too, may take modifiers. Instead of reading single words you should now be reading groups of words that belong together in the sentence; subject clusters and verb clusters can be read as units. Thus, in a sentence of twenty to fifty words, instead of reading twenty to fifty separate words and then trying to put them together, you should read only two, three, or four large clusters of words, and put these few parts together. Let's see how you might do this in a sentence from this account of Lou Gehrig's life:

> "The awkward boy who could neither bat nor field as a youngster / had, by his unswerving persistence, his gnawing ambition, his tenacity and iron will power, / made himself into the greatest first baseman in the history of organized baseball."

You see that there are several large clusters of words in this sentence. The verb cluster is divided into two parts, because of its length.

Show how three other sentences from this selection may be divided into word clusters to make reading them easier.

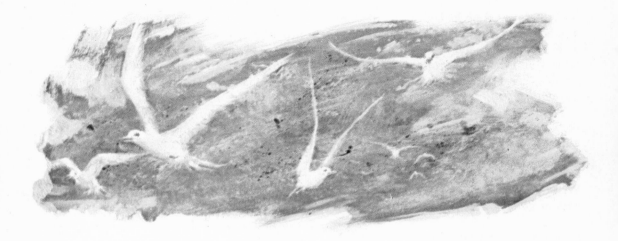

We Never Know How High

EMILY DICKINSON

We never know how high we are
  Till we are called to rise;
And then, if we are true to plan,
  Our statures touch the skies.

The heroism we recite
  Would be a daily thing,
Did not ourselves the cubits warp
  For fear to be a king.

TOUCHING THE SKIES

1. Think of situations in life that might lead an ordinary person to do extraordinary things.

2. Do you agree with the poet that we hold ourselves back? Why do you think some people are afraid to do as well as they might?

3. In what ways does this poem apply to the heroes that you have read about in this unit? Which of these heroes were ordinary people who faced incidents that brought out their courage?

PARAPHRASING

Putting into other words the thought or meaning of what someone has said or written is called paraphrasing. Here is how lines 1–2 of this poem might be paraphrased:

Most people do not really know the possibilities that lie within themselves until something happens that calls upon these inner resources.

Paraphrase the remainder of this poem, but first discuss the meaning of the line "Did not ourselves the cubits warp."

Description

Read carefully this passage from "Sir Gawain" by Dorothy Heiderstadt, describing the journey taken by Sir Gawain, his squire, and a guide, as they rode forth to meet the Green Knight.

Through a wild valley they rode, among great, sweeping hills covered with leafless oak trees white with frost. They saw hazel and hawthorn trees, on whose boughs huddled unhappy birds crying piteously with the cold. Presently the riders came to a roaring stream; beside it there was a mound overgrown with green moss, with a thorn tree growing before it. They could hear a whining sound, as though an ax were being sharpened.   (page 29)

READING DESCRIPTION

1. *Learn to recognize and remember important descriptive details.* Go back and reread the model paragraph in the way that you should read all descriptive paragraphs — noting the specific details used to describe the setting, the characters, and the action. After you have reread the paragraph, make a list of these specific details. Which details do you think are more important than others?

2. *Be aware of the general impression created by a descriptive passage.* You should be able to distinguish this impression from the single details that work together to form it. Which of the three statements that follow best summarizes the general impression of the setting described in this passage about Gawain's journey?

a. The scenery was bleak.

b. The trees were white with frost.

c. The birds were crying piteously.

Look back at "Top Man." State in your own words the general impression you receive of the mountain K3 after reading the two paragraphs on pages 42–43 beginning "Before us the valley . . ." and ending "Living and on guard."

3. *Be sure you understand the meanings of the specific, descriptive words the writer uses.* In the model passage about Sir Gawain's journey, for example, the writer has deliberately mentioned several kinds of trees. What are they? Do you know exactly what a thorn tree looks like? Do you know what moss looks and feels like? How does this knowledge help to create a more vivid impression for you?

Look back again at pages 42–43 of "Top Man," at the two paragraphs just cited. Do you know what is meant by a "symmetrical summit pyramid"? What are glaciers, and what do they look like? What does a ridge look like? In what ways is your understanding of these details essential to your understanding of the action of the story?

4. *When you read description, you must be prepared to understand comparisons.* Do you understand these comparisons used in "Top Man"? Can you explain what each italicized word means here? (First, go back and read these words in their contexts, on pages 42–43.)

"the sweeping *skirt* of glaciers"

"its snow *plumes*"

"the *cannonading* of its avalanches"

"it [the mountain] seemed . . . less to tower than to *crouch*"

WRITING DESCRIPTION

1. *To write effective description, choose details that are as specific as possible.*

2. *Tell, if you can, not only how things look, but also how they smell, sound, taste, or feel.* Refer back to the model passage from "Sir Gawain." Note the words that remind you of sounds: "crying piteously," "roaring stream," "whining sound." What details give you the sensation of cold? If Sir Gawain were to enter the cave, what might he smell in there? Write a sentence answering this question.

3. *Use precise nouns, verbs, and modifiers in description.* For example, in the second sentence of the model passage from "Sir Gawain," the writer says that the birds "huddled" on boughs. How much more descriptive is the verb *huddled* than the more general verb *sat! Huddled* helps us picture the birds crowded closely and miserably together. Here are two sentences from "My Friend Flicka." Replace the italicized verbs with more descriptive verbs. Then check to see which verbs the author used to fit the contexts.

Flicka came to life, *got* up, got her balance, and stood swaying. (See page 71.)

The water *went* over Kennie's legs and over Flicka's body. (See page 75.)

4. *Before you write, decide precisely what impression you have formed of the object or person or place you are about to describe.* As you write, use words that will help your reader form this impression.

Write a description of two of the following things. Try to tell precisely how the things look, smell, taste, sound, and feel. Tell your general impression of each thing.

a piece of pie   your lunch
grass   someone's shoes

Or, write a description of an imaginary person, perhaps of the man who will be President in the year 2900, or of the prehistoric man who huddled in caves. Describe the way this imaginary person dresses, what his face is like, what his voice sounds like. What is your general impression of this person?

Sentence Study. A modifying word group is italicized in the first sentence below. It has been reduced to a one-word modifier in the second sentence. Which sentence reads more smoothly?

The hills were covered with oak trees *that were leafless.*

The hills were covered with *leafless* oak trees.

Reread the model passage from "Sir Gawain." How did the author describe the oak trees? Did he use the long modifying word group or the one-word modifier?

Read the following sentences aloud. Then reduce each italicized word group to a single-word modifier. Where will you place each modifier? Does your rewording make each sentence read more smoothly? How did the authors phrase them?

I turned my face from the glare, *which was dazzling,* and looked at my companions. (See page 43.)

But suddenly she gave her head a little shake *which was rebellious and gallant.* (See page 66.)

ART AND LITERATURE

Look at the paintings on pages 81–86. Imagine that you are a writer, standing alongside the artists as they paint these scenes from life. Write a paragraph describing the scene that appeals to you most or least. Besides describing the visual details that the artist has portrayed, add details of your own, describing what you might hear and smell as you look on the scene. Try to communicate to the reader your general impression of the scene.

Themes in Literature

Unit 2
The Search for Values

UNIT 2 The Search for Values

At the heart of all great literature are questions of values. Problems of right and wrong and struggles between good and evil have always concerned writers.

In this unit, man's search for values is viewed first in several myths and folk tales.

Baucis and Philemon retold by Edith Hamilton:
A myth told in ancient Greece and Rome, about people whose kindness is put to a severe test.

Midas retold by Olivia E. Coolidge:
An ancient Greek story about a vain king and the lessons in humility he learns from the gods.

The Blind Men and the Elephant by John Godfrey Saxe:
A fable from India, revealing that there is more than one kind of blindness.

The Gift and the Giver retold by Russell Davis and B. Ashabranner:
An African folk tale about the true value of a gift.

The other stories and poems in this unit come from modern times. They, too, look at different aspects of man's search for values. Many tell about an experience that helped to shape someone's life. Perhaps you will respond as deeply to these stories as you would to an experience of your own.

Weep No More, My Lady by James Street:
A story of a dog and of a boy's agonizing decision.

A Word by Emily Dickinson:
A brief poem about the long life of the spoken word.

A Choice of Weapons by Phyllis McGinley:
Four lines on the destructive power of words.

Think As I Think by Stephen Crane:
A terse poem about name-calling.

A Garland of Precepts by Phyllis McGinley:
A humorous but thoughtful poem about giving advice.

Mama and the Graduation Present by Kathryn Forbes:
A story about a girl who learns what true generosity is.

The Countess and the Impossible by Richard Y. Thurman:
A true article about a Countess who gives a boy a challenge he remembers all his life.

As the Night the Day by Abioseh Nicol:
A modern African story about prejudice and honesty.

Baucis and Philemon

EDITH HAMILTON

Many of the ancient myths tell about mortals whose values were put to a test by the gods. In this famous story, the king of the gods, Jupiter, goes down to earth to test the hospitality of the men and women living there.

IN THE PHRYGIAN [1] HILL COUNTRY there were once two trees which all the peasants near and far pointed out as a great marvel, and no wonder, for one was an oak and the other a linden, yet they grew from a single trunk. The story of how this came about is a proof of the immeasurable power of the gods and also of the way they reward the humble and the pious.

Sometimes when Jupiter was tired of eating ambrosia and drinking nectar up in Olympus and even a little weary of listening to Apollo's lyre and watching the Graces [2] dance, he would come down to the earth, disguise himself as a mortal, and go looking for adventures. His favorite companion on these tours was Mercury, the most entertaining of all the gods, the shrewdest, and the most resourceful. On this particular trip Jupiter had determined to find out how hospitable the people of Phrygia were. Hospitality was, of course, very important to him, since all guests, all who seek shelter in a strange land, were under his especial protection.

The two gods, accordingly, took on the appearance of poor wayfarers and wandered through the land, knocking at each lowly hut or great house they came to and asking for food and a place to rest in. Not one would admit them; every time they were dismissed insolently and the door barred against them. They made trial of hundreds; all treated them in the same way. At last they came upon a little hovel of the humblest sort, poorer than any they had yet found, with a roof made only of reeds. But here, when they knocked, the door was opened wide and a cheerful voice bade them enter. They had to stoop to pass through the low entrance, but once inside they found themselves in a snug and very clean room, where a kindly-faced old man and woman welcomed them in the friendliest fashion and bustled about to make them comfortable.

The old man set a bench near the fire and told them to stretch out on it and rest their tired limbs, and the old woman threw a soft covering over it. Her name was Baucis, she told the strangers, and her husband was called Philemon. They had lived in that cottage all their married life and had always been happy. "We are poor folk," she said, "but poverty isn't so bad when you're willing to own up to it, and a contented spirit is a great help, too." All the while she was talking, she was busy doing things for them. The coals under the ashes on the dark hearth she fanned to life until a cheerful fire was burning. Over this she hung a little kettle full of water, and just as it began to boil, her husband came in with a fine cabbage he had got from the garden. Into the kettle it went, with a piece of the pork which was hanging from one of the beams. While this cooked, Baucis set the table with her trembling old hands. One table leg was too short, but she propped it up with a bit of broken dish. On the board she placed olives and radishes and several eggs that she had roasted in the ashes. By this time the cabbage and bacon were done, and the old man pushed two rickety couches up to the table and bade his guests recline and eat.

Presently he brought them cups of beechwood and an earthenware mixing bowl which held some wine very like vinegar, plentifully diluted with

water. Philemon, however, was clearly proud and happy at being able to add such cheer to the supper, and he kept on the watch to refill each cup as soon as it was emptied. The two old folks were so pleased and excited by the success of their hospitality that only very slowly a strange thing dawned upon them. The mixing bowl kept full. No matter how many cups were poured out from it, the level of the wine stayed the same, up to the brim. As they saw this wonder, each looked in terror at the other, and dropping their eyes they prayed silently. Then in quavering voices and trembling all over they begged their guests to pardon the poor refreshments they had offered. "We have a goose," the old man said, "which we ought to have given your lordships. But if you will only wait, it shall be done at once." To catch the goose, however, proved beyond their powers. They tried in vain until they were worn out, while Jupiter and Mercury watched them greatly entertained.

But when both Philemon and Baucis had to give up the chase, panting and exhausted, the gods felt that the time had come for them to take action. They were really very kind. "You have been hosts to gods," they said, "and you shall have your reward. This wicked country which despises the poor stranger will be bitterly punished, but not you." They then escorted the two out of the hut and told them to look around them. To their amazement all they saw was water. The whole countryside had disappeared. A great lake surrounded them. Their neighbors had not been good to the old couple; nevertheless, standing there they wept for them. But of a sudden their tears were dried by an overwhelming wonder. Before their eyes, the tiny, lowly hut which had been their home for so long was turned into a stately pillared temple of whitest marble with a golden roof.

"Good people," Jupiter said, "ask whatever you want and you shall have your wish." The old people exchanged a hurried whisper, then Philemon spoke. "Let us be your priests, guarding this temple for you — and oh, since we have lived so long together, let neither of us ever have to live alone. Grant that we may die together."

The gods assented, well pleased with the two. A long time they served in that grand building, and the story does not say whether they ever missed their little cozy room with its cheerful hearth. But one day, standing before the marble and golden magnificence,

they fell to talking about that former life, which had been so hard and yet so happy. By now both were in extreme old age. Suddenly, as they exchanged memories, each saw the other putting forth leaves. Then bark was growing around them. They had time only to cry, "Farewell, dear companion." As the words passed their lips, they became trees, but still they were together. The linden and the oak grew from one trunk.

From far and wide people came to admire the wonder, and always wreaths of flowers hung on the branches in honor of the pious and faithful pair.

KINDNESS TO OTHERS — A MYTH

1. How did Jupiter and Mercury happen to be knocking on Baucis and Philemon's door? How had they been treated up to then?

2. Describe the couple and their cottage. What did they do to make the strangers welcome? What miraculous thing happened to their mixing bowl?

3. What happened to the neighbors of the old couple? What wish did the couple make? Tell how their wish was fulfilled.

4. Myths were often used in ancient times to teach people how to live in the world. Several values are pointed out in this myth. What does it say about the way people should treat others?

5. Another value is illustrated in the old couple's wish. Baucis and Philemon could have had anything they wanted. What does their wish tell you about the thing they valued most in the world?

6. Are the values contained in this ancient story still esteemed by people today? Explain. How do you think poor people asking from house to house for food and lodgings would be received today?

7. Can you think of any other stories in which floods or other disasters were used to punish people for their wickedness? Do you know of other stories in which people were rewarded for their goodness?

WORDS: LATIN ROOTS

In this myth the god Jupiter disguises himself as a mortal. The word *mortal* comes from the Latin word *mors*, meaning "death." A mortal is a creature subject to death. In the myths, mortals are human beings.

Several other English words are built on the Latin root *mors*. Check in the dictionary to see how "death" is part of the meaning of each of these words: *mortality, immortal, mortally*. Many English words are built on other Latin roots. Name some other words that are built on each of the following Latin roots.

Root	Meaning	Word
audire	to hear	audience
credere	to believe	credible
manus	hand	manual

SENTENCES: ADVERB CLAUSES

Adverb clauses can often be moved around in a sentence for variety or emphasis, as you can see from these examples:

Each looked in terror at the other *as they saw this wonder.*

As they saw this wonder, each looked in terror at the other.

Though the general meaning of the sentence is unchanged when this clause is switched around, there is a change in emphasis. Read these sentences aloud. Which arrangement sounds best to you? Which arrangement places more emphasis on the fact that each looked at the other? Look back at the story, on page 104, to see which arrangement the author used.

The adverb clause in the following sentence is placed in a poor position. Put it in two other positions that are better than this one. In which position is the adverb clause least emphatic? In which position does it sound best?

A door was opened wide and then a cheerful voice bade them enter *when they knocked.*

COMPOSITION:
A NARRATIVE PARAGRAPH

A narrative tells about a series of related events. The following narrative tells about some of the events that occurred when Baucis and Philemon were visited by the gods.

"All the while she was talking, she was busy doing things for them. The coals under the ashes on the dark hearth she fanned to life until a cheerful fire was burning. Over this she hung a little kettle full of water, and just as it began to boil, her husband came in with a fine cabbage he had got from the garden. Into the kettle it went, with a piece of the pork which was hanging from one of the beams. While this cooked, Baucis set the table with her trembling, old hands. One table leg was too short, but she propped it up with a bit of broken dish. On the board she placed olives and radishes and several eggs that she had roasted in the ashes. By this time the cabbage and bacon were done, and the old man pushed two rickety couches up to the table and bade his guests recline and eat."

List the events in this narrative. Are they all clearly related to one another?

Write a narrative about certain events. You might use one of these topics:

The game seesawed, with the outcome always in doubt.

The astronaut made a search of the strange moon-house.

Midas

OLIVIA E. COOLIDGE

Not all the ancient myths are about virtuous people. One of the most widely read of all the myths is this story about a foolish king whose mistaken sense of values gets him into trouble.

Midas was King in Phrygia,[1] which is a land in Asia Minor, and he was both powerful and rich. Nevertheless, he was foolish, obstinate, and hasty, without the sense to appreciate good advice.

It happened one time that Dionysus[2] with his dancing nymphs and satyrs passed through Phrygia. As they went, the old, fat Silenus,[3] nodding on an ass, strayed from the others, who danced on without missing him. The ass took his half-conscious master wherever he wanted, until some hours later, as they came to a great rose garden, the old man tumbled off. The King's gardeners found him there and roused him, still sleepy and staggering, not quite sure who or where he was. Since, however, the revels of Dionysus had

[1] **Phrygia** (frij'ē·ə).
[2] **Dionysus** (dī'ə·nī'səs): god of wine.
[3] **Silenus** (sī·lē'nəs).

spread throughout the land, they recognized him as the god's companion and made much of him. They wreathed his neck with roses and, one on each side and one behind, they supported him to the palace and up the steps, while another went to fetch Midas.

The King came out to meet Silenus, overjoyed at the honor done him. He clapped his hands for his servants and demanded such a feast as never was. There was much running to and fro, setting up of tables, fetching of wine, and bringing up of sweet-scented oil. While slaves festooned the hall with roses and made garlands for the feasters, Midas conducted his guest to the bath with all honor, that he might refresh himself and put on clean garments for the feast.

A magnificent celebration followed. For ten days, by daylight and by torchlight, the palace of the King stood open, and all the notables of Phrygia came up and down its steps. There were sounds of lyre and pipe and singing. There was dancing. Everywhere the scent of roses and of wine mingled with the costly perfumes of King Midas in the hot summer air. In ten days' time, as the revels were dying down from sheer exhaustion, Dionysus came in person to seek his friend. When he found how Silenus had been entertained and honored, he was greatly pleased and promised Midas any gift he cared to name, no matter what it was.

The King thought a little, glancing back through his doors at the chaos in his hall of scattered rose petals, overturned tables, bowls for the wine mixing, and drinking cups. It had been a good feast, the sort of feast a king should give, only he was very weary now and could not think. A king should entertain thus and give kingly presents to his guests, cups of beaten gold, such as he had seen once, with lifelike pictures of a hunt running round them, or the golden honeycomb which Daedalus [1] made exactly as though it were the work of bees. Gods, like these guests, should have golden statues. Even a king never had enough.

"Give me," he said to Dionysus sud-

[1] **Daedalus** (ded′ə·ləs): in Greek mythology, a mortal who was a famous architect and inventor.

denly, "the power to turn all I touch to gold."

"That is a rash thing to ask," said Dionysus solemnly. "Think again." But Eastern kings are never contradicted, and Midas only felt annoyed.

"It is my wish," he answered coldly.

Dionysus nodded. "You shall have it, he said. "As you part from me here in the garden, it shall be yours."

Midas was so excited when he came back through the garden that he could not make up his mind what to touch first. Presently he decided on the branch of an oak tree which overhung his path. He took a look at it first, counting the leaves, noticing the little veins in them, the jagged edges, the fact that one of them had been eaten half away. He put out his hand to break it off. He never saw it change. One moment it was brown and green; the next it wasn't. There it was, stiff and shining, nibbled leaf and all. It was hard and satisfyingly heavy and more natural far than anything Daedalus ever made.

Now he was the greatest king in the world. Midas looked down at the grass he was walking over. It was still green; the touch was evidently in his hands. He picked up a stone to see; it became a lump of gold. He tried a clod of earth and found himself with another lump. Midas was beside himself with joy; he went into his palace to see what he could do. In the doorway he stopped at a sudden thought. He went outside again and walked down all the long row of pillars, laying his hands on each one. No king in the world had pillars of solid gold. He considered having a gold house but rejected the idea; the gold pillars looked better against the stone. Midas picked a gold apple and went inside again to eat.

His servants set his table for him, and he amused himself by turning the cups and dishes into gold. He touched the table too by mistake — not that it really mattered, but he would have to be careful. Absently he picked up a piece of bread and bit it and nearly broke his teeth. Midas sat with the golden bread in his hand and looked at it a long time. He was horribly frightened. "I shall have to eat it without touching it with my hands," he said to himself after a while, and he put his head down on the table and tried that way. It was no good. The moment his lips touched the bread, he felt it turn hard and cold. In his shock he groped wildly for his winecup and took a big gulp. The stuff flowed into his mouth all right, but it wasn't wine any more. He spat it out hastily before he choked himself. This time he was more than frightened; he was desperate. "Great Dionysus," he prayed earnestly with

uplifted hands, "forgive my foolishness, and take away your gift."

"Go to the mountain of Tmolus,"[1] said the voice of the god into his ear, "and bathe in the stream that springs there so that the golden touch may be washed away. The next time think more carefully before you set your judgment against that of the gods."

Midas thanked the god with his whole heart, but he paid more attention to his promise than to his advice. He lost no time in journeying to the mountain and dipping himself in the stream. There the golden touch was washed away from Midas, but the sand of the river bottom shone bright gold as the power passed into the water, so that the stream flowed over golden sand from that time on.

Midas had learned his lesson in a way but was still conceited. He had realized at least that gold was not the

[1] **Tmolus** (tmō′ləs): Tmolus was a god who had been turned into a mountain as a consequence of a punishment.

most important thing. Indeed, having had too much gold at one time, he took a violent dislike to it and to luxury in general. He spent his time in the open country now, listening to the music of the streams and the woodlands, while his kingdom ran itself as best it might. He wanted neither his elaborate palace, his embroidered robes, his splendid feasts, nor his trained dancers and musicians. Instead he wished to be at home in the woodlands with simple things that were natural and unspoiled.

It happened at the time that in the woods of Tmolus, the goat-god Pan had made himself a pipe. It was a simple hollow reed with holes for stops cut in it, and the god played simple tunes on it like birdcalls and the various noises of the animals he had heard. Only he was very skillful and could play them fast and slow, mixed together or repeated, until the listener felt that the woods themselves were alive with little creatures. The birds and beasts made answer to the pipe so that it seemed the whole wood was an orchestra of music. Midas himself was charmed to ecstasy with the beauty of it and begged the shaggy god to play hour by hour till the very birds were weary of the calls. This Pan was quite ready to do, since he was proud of his invention. He even wanted to challenge Apollo [1] himself, sure that any judge would put his instrument above Apollo's golden lyre.

Apollo accepted the challenge, and Tmolus, the mountain, was himself to be the judge. Tmolus was naturally a woodland god and friendly to Pan, so

[1] **Apollo:** god of music, poetry, prophecy, and medicine.

he listened with solemn pleasure as the pipe trilled airs more varied and more natural than it had ever played before. The woods echoed, and the happy Midas, who had followed Pan to the contest, was almost beside himself with delight at the gaiety and abandon of it all. When, however, Tmolus heard Apollo play the music of gods and heroes, of love, longing, heroism, and the mighty dead, he forgot his own woods around him and the animals listening in their tiny nests and holes. He seemed to see into the hearts of men and understand the pity of their lives and the beauty that they longed for.

Even after the song had died away, Tmolus sat there in forgetful silence with his thoughts on the loves and struggles of the ages and the half-dried tears on his cheeks. There was a great quiet around him too, he realized, as he came to his senses. Even Pan had put down his pipe thoughtfully on the grass.

Tmolus gave the prize to Apollo, and in the whole woodland there was no one to protest but Midas. Midas had shut his ears to Apollo; he would neither listen nor care. Now he forgot where he was and in whose presence. All he remembered was that he was a great king who always gave his opinion and who, his courtiers told him, was always right. Leaping up, he protested loudly to Tmolus and was not even quiet when the mountain silently frowned on him. Getting no answer, he turned to Apollo, still objecting furiously to the unfairness of the judgment.

Apollo looked the insistent mortal up and down. "The fault is in your ears, O King. We must give them their true

shape," he said. With that he turned away and was gone to Olympus, while the unfortunate Midas put his hands to his ears and found them long and furry. He could even wriggle them about. Apollo had given him asses' ears in punishment for his folly.

From that time on King Midas wore a scarlet turban and tried to make it seem as though wearing this were a privilege that only the king could enjoy. He wore it day and night — he was so fond of it. Presently, however, his hair began to grow so long and straggly that something had to be done. The royal barber had to be called.

The barber of King Midas was a royal slave, so it was easy enough to threaten him with the most horrible punishment if, whether waking or sleeping, he ever let fall the slightest hint of what was wrong with the King. The barber was thoroughly frightened. Unfortunately he was too frightened, and the King's threats preyed on his

mind. He began to dream he had told his secret to somebody, and what was worse, his fellow servants began to complain that he was making noises in his sleep, so that he was desperately afraid he would talk. At last it seemed that if he could only tell somebody once and get it over, his mind would be at rest. Yet tell somebody was just what he dared not do. Finally, he went down to a meadow which was seldom crossed because it was waterlogged, and there, where he could see there was no one around to hear him, he dug a hole in the ground, put his face close down, and whispered into the wet mud, "King Midas has asses' ears." Then he threw some earth on top and went away, feeling somehow much relieved.

Nothing happened for a while except that the hole filled up with water. Presently, though, some reeds began to grow in it. They grew taller and rustled as the wind went through them.

After a while someone happened to go down that way and came racing back, half-amused and half-terrified. Everyone crowded around to listen to him. It was certainly queer, but it was a bit amusing too.

Everybody streamed down the path to investigate. Sure enough, as they came close to it, they could hear the whole thing distinctly. The reeds were not rustling in the wind; they were whispering to one another, "King Midas has asses' ears . . . asses' ears . . . asses' ears."

THE FOLLY OF A KING — A MYTH

1. Why did Dionysus grant Midas any gift he wanted? How did Midas behave immediately after he received the golden touch?

2. What discovery led Midas to pray to be relieved of the gift? What advice did the god then give him? How did Midas change after his experience with the golden touch?

3. Tell about the contest between Pan and Apollo. How did Midas show poor judgment again? How did Apollo punish Midas for this second example of folly? What part did Midas' barber play in the story? How did everyone come to know Midas' secret?

4. There are several points made in this story of Midas. What personal qualities led Midas to go against the wisdom of the gods? What undesirable human traits are we warned against in this myth?

5. In what ways were Midas' values different from those of Baucis and Philemon?

6. If you were told you could have anything you wished, what would you wish for?

7. What do we mean nowadays when we say that someone has "the Midas touch"? Do you think that a "Midas touch" necessarily brings unhappiness to its possessor? Explain.

WORDS: CONTEXT AND MEANING

If you see or hear the word *rose* used by itself, you cannot really tell what it means. But when, in the story of Midas, you read "they came to a great rose garden," you knew at once from its context that *rose* meant a type of flower. What is the meaning of *rose* in these two contexts? *The sun rose. The people rose against the tyrant.*

It is context that helps us determine a word's meaning. What is the meaning of the word *land* as it is used in the first sentence of "Midas"? Use *land* in sentences that will give it two other meanings.

COMPOSITION: CHRONOLOGICAL ORDER

The events in most narratives are told in the order in which they happened. This is called time order or chronological order. Notice how the events included in this narrative paragraph are arranged. Are they in chronological order?

"The King came out to meet Silenus, overjoyed at the honor done him. He clapped his hands for his servants and demanded such a feast as never was. There was much running to and fro, setting up of tables, fetching of wine, and bringing up of sweet-scented oil. While slaves festooned the hall with roses and made garlands for the feasters, Midas conducted his guest to the bath with all honor, that he might refresh himself and put on clean garments for the feast."

Write a narrative paragraph of your own, telling about something unusual or interesting that happened to you recently or about something that happened to someone else. Arrange the events of your narrative in chronological order.

The Blind Men and the Elephant

JOHN GODFREY SAXE

It was six men of Indostan°
  To learning much inclined,
Who went to see the Elephant
  (Though all of them were blind),
That each by observation   5
  Might satisfy his mind.

The *First* approached the Elephant,
  And happening to fall
Against his broad and sturdy side,
  At once began to bawl: 10
"God bless me! But the Elephant
  Is very like a wall!"

The *Second*, feeling of the tusk,
  Cried, "Ho! What have we here
So very round and smooth and sharp?
  To me 'tis mighty clear   16
This wonder of an Elephant
  Is very like a spear!"

The *Third* approached the animal,
  And happening to take   20
The squirming trunk within his hands,
  Thus boldly up and spake:
"I see," quoth he, "the Elephant
  Is very like a snake!"

1. **Indostan** (in'dō·stan'): Hindustan, a region of India.

The *Fourth* reached out an eager hand,
  And felt about the knee.   26
"What most this wondrous beast is like
  Is mighty plain," quoth he;
" 'Tis clear enough the Elephant
  Is very like a tree!"   30

The *Fifth*, who chanced to touch the ear,
  Said: "E'en the blindest man
Can tell what this resembles most;
  Deny the fact who can,
This marvel of an Elephant   35
  Is very like a fan!"

The *Sixth* no sooner had begun
  About the beast to grope,
Than, seizing on the swinging tail
  That fell within his scope,   40
"I see," quoth he, "the Elephant
  Is very like a rope!"

And so these men of Indostan
  Disputed loud and long,
Each in his own opinion   45
  Exceeding stiff and strong,
Though each was partly in the right,
  And all were in the wrong!

MANY VIEWS — AN INDIAN FABLE

1. Tell in your own words the story of this fable. What conception did each blind man have of the elephant? How was each "partly in the right"?

2. Each man in this fable based his conclusions about the elephant on his own limited experience. What might have happened if they had listened to one another? What value does this folk tale illustrate?

3. Have you ever heard, or taken part in, a discussion in which people have acted like these blind men? Why do you think people behave this way?

"The Blind Men and the Elephant" by John Godfrey Saxe. Reprinted by permission of Houghton Mifflin Company.

The Gift and the Giver

RUSSELL G. DAVIS *and*
BRENT K. ASHABRANNER

Once a poor farmer found a beautiful apple growing on a tree in his fields. The apple was so large, so shiny, and so well shaped that the farmer cried with joy when he saw it. Never had he seen such a beautiful apple on any tree in his country.

The farmer picked the apple and wrapped it in his cloak and brought it to his home. He showed it to his wife and children, and they were as amazed as he was to see such a beautiful apple.

Other farmers who lived in that village heard of the apple and came to the house to see it. They too agreed that it was a wondrous apple. Farmers from distant villages came to see the fruit. They touched it tenderly and exclaimed in loud voices that it was a wonderful apple, shaped to perfection by the hand of God.

After all had admired the apple, the question came — what to do with it? The farmer wished to give it to his favorite daughter. He said to her, "Truly,

this is the only thing that matches you in beauty. On both the fruit and your fair face, the work of God's hand is clear. Take it and eat of it, my beauty."

But the daughter was too modest. She said she was not worthy of such a thing. She urged her father to take the fruit for himself. It was given to him as a sign of God's love and blessings. "It is worthy of a king," the daughter said.

"You are right," the farmer agreed. "Why didn't I think of that myself? Such a fruit is worthy of a king. I will take it to the King. It is the only gift that I, a poor farmer, can give that will be worthy of my King."

The farmer's wife wrapped the apple in the finest cloth she had, and the farmer set out for the royal city. The farmer carried the fruit very carefully in the cloth, and he walked along the road slowly. After many days, he reached the city, but the poor farmer could not get in to see the King. The guards at the palace laughed at him and kept him out.

"The King has thousands of fruit trees," they said. "Surely your fruit can be no more beautiful than that of the King."

The farmer opened the cloth and asked the guards to look. The apple was still as beautiful as the day it had been picked. The farmer would not let any of the guards touch the fruit. Finally they went away to call the commander. The commander admired the apple greatly, although the farmer would not let him touch it. The commander of the guard decided that he would bring the farmer to the chambers of the King.

When the farmer came before the King, he spoke in this way: "Your Majesty, great King, beloved of all of us. I found a most beautiful apple on one of the trees of my field. It was such a wondrously beautiful fruit that men came from miles around to see it. I decided that only our beloved King could deserve such a thing. So I have carried this fruit a great distance from my house. And I wish to give it to you."

The King was greatly moved by the simple love of the farmer. "What would you have from me in return?" the King asked. "Name it, and it is yours."

The farmer was surprised. "I want nothing but to see the joy on your face when you see this that God has made."

The farmer opened his cloth and showed the fruit to the King. "It is surely a work of God's hand," the King agreed. "Such size! Such color! Such a shine! It shines like a bright jewel."

The King called the Queen and all of the family, and they too marveled at the beautiful apple. While the people of the palace were admiring the apple, the poor farmer left the court and started for his home. The King noticed this.

"Where is that farmer?" he asked.

"He has shown me more love with this gift than anyone in the kingdom. Ride after him. Take my best horse, and give it to him. Tell him the horse is from a grateful king who has learned a new lesson in kindness."

The servants rode after the farmer and found him plodding along the road. The farmer was very happy with the gift, which he had not expected. He rode away toward his village.

Word travels fast in a palace. Soon all the people in the royal city learned that the King had given his best horse to a poor farmer — and in exchange for a mere piece of fruit.

A rich merchant of the town heard the story of the King's gift. The merchant began to scheme. He thought, "That poor farmer gave the King a simple apple from a tree. And the King gave him his best horse in exchange. What would the King give me if I gave

him a horse? He might give me his daughter. Or perhaps some valuable jewels!"

The merchant picked the finest horse from his stable and led it up to the gates of the palace. "I have a gift for the King," the merchant told the guards. The guards let the rich merchant in at once.

The merchant went before the King. "I have heard that you have given your own horse to a farmer," the merchant said. "For that reason, I have brought you a fine horse from my stable."

"Thank you very much," the King said.

The merchant moved restlessly, first standing on one foot and then another. The merchant stroked his beard and looked worried. "Did you want something of me?" the King asked. The merchant stared down at the floor and did not meet the King's eyes.

"Ah, I see," the King said. "You have given me a gift. Now you expect something in return. Very well. Wait right here."

The King left the room. The merchant could hardly hide his joy. "It will be the jewels," he thought. "He has gone to get the jewels. I'm sure it will be the jewels."

The King returned carrying something wrapped in a rich cloth. "Take this apple," the King said. "It is most precious to me because it was given by a man who expected nothing in return. But you may have it."

The rich merchant was stunned. When he opened up the cloth he saw the perfection of the apple, but he paid no attention to its beauty. The merchant walked angrily out of the palace. When he was outside, he threw away the fruit. He began to pull out his beard and wail in a loud voice.

The King ordered his guards to drive the merchant from the palace grounds.

"Tell him," the King said, "that a gift is only as good as the heart of the giver. A man should give without expecting a gift in return. Any other gift is worthless."

The King looked at the beautiful horse the merchant had brought him. "The merchant's horse is worthless as a gift," the King said. "As something to ride on, however, it seems to be a very fine horse."

GIVING AND RECEIVING — AN AFRICAN FOLK TALE

1. What events led the farmer to give the gift to the King? What did the farmer say to the King?

2. Why did the King give the farmer his best horse?

3. Why did the merchant give the King a horse? Why did the King give the merchant the apple? What did the merchant think of this gift?

4. Reread what the King said about gifts and givers. Why did the King value the farmer's gift and not the merchant's? How is this tale similar to that of Baucis and Philemon, page 103?

5. Do you agree with the King's statement about gifts and givers? Explain. Can you give some examples of good ways and poor ways to give gifts? Do gifts always have to be valuable material objects? Explain.

WORDS: PREFIXES

When the people in this story saw the apple, they "exclaimed" in loud voices. If we look up the word *exclaim* in the dictionary, we find that it is formed from the Latin word *clamare*, meaning "to cry," and the Latin prefix *ex–*, meaning "out." Thus *exclaim* means "to cry out." A prefix is one or more letters added to the beginning of a word to change its meaning. A prefix can greatly affect a word's meaning. For example, the prefixes *dis–*, *im–*, and *in–* can give an opposite meaning: *connect, disconnect; possible, impossible; secure, insecure.*

How is the meaning of the prefix included in each word below? Name other words containing these prefixes.

Prefix	Meaning	Word
con–	together	conform
pre–	before	predestined
retro–	back	retroactive
sub–	under	submarine

SENTENCES: ADJECTIVE PHRASES AND CLAUSES

Adjective phrases and clauses must stay close to the sentence part they modify. We can see that this is true when we try to put the adjective clause in this sentence in a different position:

"Other farmers *who lived in that village* heard of the apple . . ."

If the clause is put in any other place in the sentence, a kind of nonsense is created.

Here are three sentences from this story which contain adjective clauses or phrases, in italics. What word does each italicized word group modify? What happens to the meaning of each sentence when the modifying word group is moved to other positions in the sentence? Try it and see.

"Farmers *from distant villages* came to see the fruit."

"The guards *at the palace* laughed at him and kept him out."

"The King looked at the beautiful horse *the merchant had brought him.*"

As you see, then, adjective phrases and clauses almost never can be moved away from the word they modify. How do they differ from adverb phrases in this respect (page 106)?

Weep No More, My Lady

JAMES STREET

THE MOONLIGHT SYMPHONY of swamp creatures hushed abruptly, and the dismal bog was as peaceful as unborn time and seemed to brood in its silence. The gaunt man glanced back at the boy and motioned for him to be quiet, but it was too late. Their presence was discovered. A jumbo frog rumbled a warning, and the swamp squirmed into life as its denizens scuttled to safety.

Foxfire [1] was glowing to the west and the bayou was slapping the cypress trees when suddenly a haunting laugh echoed through the wilderness, a strange chuckling yodel ending in a weird "gro-o-o."

The boy's eyes were wide and staring. "That's it, Uncle Jess. Come on! Let's catch it!"

"Uh, oh." The man gripped his shotgun. "That ain't no animal. That's a thing."

They hurried noiselessly in the direction of the sound that Skeeter had been

[1] foxfire: phosphorescent light given off by wood that has been rotted by a fungal growth.

"Weep No More, My Lady" by James Street in *The Saturday Evening Post* of December 6, 1941, copyright 1941 by The Curtis Publishing Company. Reprinted by permission of The Harold Matson Company, Inc.

hearing for several nights. Swamp born and reared, they feared nothing they could shoot or outwit, so they slipped out of the morass and to the side of a ridge. Suddenly, Jesse put out his hand and stopped the child; then he pointed up the slope. The animal, clearly visible in the moonlight, was sitting on its haunches, its head cocked sideways as it chuckled. It was a merry and rather melodious little chuckle.

Skeeter grinned in spite of his surprise, then said, "Sh-h-h. It'll smell us."

Jesse said, "Can't nothing smell that far. Wonder what the durn thing is?" He peered up the ridge, studying the creature. He had no intention of shooting unless attacked, for Jesse Tolliver and his nephew never killed wantonly.

The animal, however, did smell them and whipped her nose into the wind, crouched, and braced. She was about sixteen inches high and weighed about twenty-two pounds. Her coat was red and silky, and there was a blaze of white down her chest and a circle of white around her throat. Her face was wrinkled and sad, like a wise old man's.

Jesse shook his head. "Looks som'n

like a mixture of bloodhound and terrier from here," he whispered. "It beats me —— "

"It's a dog, all right," Skeeter said.

"Can't no dog laugh."

"That dog can." The boy began walking toward the animal, his right hand outstretched. "Heah, heah. I ain't gonna hurt you."

The dog, for she was a dog, cocked her head from one side to the other and watched Skeeter. She was trembling, but she didn't run. And when Skeeter knelt by her, she stopped trembling, for the ways of a boy with a dog are mysterious. He stroked her, and the trim little creature looked up at him and blinked her big hazel eyes. Then she turned over, and Skeeter scratched her. She closed her eyes, stretched, and chuckled, a happy mixture of chortle and yodel. Jesse ambled up, and the dog leaped to her feet and sprang between the boy and the man.

Skeeter calmed her. "That's just Uncle Jess."

Jesse, still bewildered, shook his head again. "I still say that ain't no dog. She don't smell and she don't bark. Ain't natural. And look at her! Licking herself like a cat."

"Well, I'll be a catty wampus," Skeeter said. "Never saw a dog do that before." However, he was quick to defend any mannerism of his friend and said, "She likes to keep herself clean. She's a lady, and I'm gonna name her that, and she's mine 'cause I found her."

"Lady, huh?"

"No, sir. My Lady. If I name her just plain Lady, how folks gonna know she's mine?" He began stroking his dog again. "Gee m'netty, Uncle Jess, I ain't

never had nothing like this before."

"It still don't make sense to me," Jesse said. But he didn't care, for he was happy because the child was happy.

Like most mysteries, there was no mystery at all about My Lady. She was a lady, all right, an aristocratic basenji,[1] one of those strange barkless dogs of Africa. Her ancestors were pets of the Pharaohs, and her line was well established when the now proud races of men were wandering about Europe, begging handouts from nature. A bundle of nerves and muscles, she would fight anything and could scent game up to eighty yards. She had the gait of an antelope and was odorless, washing herself before and after meals. However, the only noises she could make were a piercing cry that sounded almost human and that chuckling little chortle. She could chuckle only when happy, and she had been happy in the woods. Now she was happy again.

As most men judge values, she was worth more than all the possessions of Jesse and his nephew. Several of the dogs had been shipped to New Orleans to avoid the dangerous upper route, thence by motor to a northern kennel. While crossing Mississippi, My Lady had escaped from the station wagon. Her keeper had advertised in several papers, but Jesse and Skeeter never saw papers.

Skeeter said, "Come on, M'Lady. Let's go home."

The dog didn't hesitate, but walked proudly at the boy's side to a cabin on the bank of the bayou. Skeeter crum-

[1] **basenji** (bə·sen'jē): from a Bantu word meaning "bush thing."

bled corn bread, wet it with potlikker,[1] and put it before her. She sniffed the food disdainfully at first, eating it only when she saw the boy fix a bowl for his uncle. She licked herself clean and explored the cabin, sniffing the brush brooms, the piles of wild pecans and hickory nuts, and then the cots. Satisfied at last, she jumped on Skeeter's bed, tucked her nose under her paws, and went to sleep.

"Acts like she owns the place," Jesse said.

"Where you reckon she came from?" The boy slipped his overall straps from his shoulders, flexed his stringy muscles, and yawned.

"Lord knows. Circus maybe." He looked at M'Lady quickly. "Say, maybe she's freak and run off from some show. Bet they'd give us two dollars for her."

Skeeter's face got long. "You don't aim to get rid of her?"

The old man put his shotgun over the mantel and lit his pipe. "Skeets, if you want that thing, I wouldn't get shed of her for a piece of bottom land a mile long. Already plowed and planted."

"I reckoned you wouldn't, 'cause you like me so much. And I know how you like dogs, 'cause I saw you cry when yours got killed. But you can have part of mine."

Jesse sat down and leaned back, blowing smoke into the air to drive away mosquitoes. The boy got a brick and hammer and began cracking nuts, pounding the meat to pulp so his uncle could chew it. Skeeter's yellow hair hadn't been cut for months and was tangled. He had freckles, too. And his

real name was Jonathan. His mother was Jesse's only sister and died when the child was born. No one thereabouts ever knew what happened to his father. Jesse, a leathery, toothless old man with faded blue eyes, took him to bring up and called him Skeeter because he was so little.

In the village, where Jesse seldom visited, folks wondered if he were fit'n to rear a little boy. They considered him shiftless and no-count. Jesse had lived all of his sixty years in the swamp, and his way of life was a torment to folks who believed life must be lived by rules. He earned a few dollars selling jumbo frogs and pelts, but mostly he just paddled around the swamp, watching things and teaching Skeeter about life.

The villagers might have tried to send Skeeter to an orphanage, but for Joe (Cash) Watson, the storekeeper. Cash was a hard man, but fair. He often hunted with Jesse, and the old man had trained Cash's dogs. When there was talk of sending Skeeter away, Cash said, "You ain't gonna do it. You just don't take young'uns away from their folks." And that's all there was to it.

Jesse never coveted the "frills and furbelows[2] of damn-fool folks," and he yearned for only two things — a twenty-gauge shotgun for Skeeter and a set of Roebuckers for himself, as he called store-bought teeth. Cash had promised him the gun and the best false teeth in the catalog for forty-six dollars. Jesse had saved nine dollars and thirty-seven cents.

---

[1] **potlikker:** pot liquor, liquid left in a pot after greens and meat are cooked together.

[2] **furbelows** (fûr′bə·lōz): fussy trimmings (from "fur below").

"Someday I'm gonna get them Roe-buckers," he often told Skeeter. "Then I'm gonna eat me enough roastin' ears to kill a goat. Maybe I can get a set with a couple of gold teeth in 'em. I seen a man once with six gold teeth."

Once Skeeter asked him, "Why don't you get a job and make enough money to buy them Roebuckers?"

"I don't want 'em that bad," Jesse said.

So he was happy for Skeeter to have M'Lady, thinking the dog would sort of make up for the shotgun.

The boy cracked as many nuts as his uncle wanted, then put the hammer away. He was undressing when he glanced over at his dog. "Gosh, Uncle Jess. I'm scared somebody'll come get her."

"I ain't heard of nobody losing no things around here. If'n they had, they'd been to me 'fo' now, beings I know all about dogs and the swamp."

"That's so," Skeeter said. "But you don't reckon she belonged to another fellow like me, do you? I know how I'd feel if I had a dog like her and she got lost."

Jesse said, "She didn't belong to an-other fellow like you. If'n she had, she wouldn't be so happy here."

Skeeter fed M'Lady biscuits and mo-lasses for breakfast, and although the basenji ate it, she still was hungry when she went into the swamp with the boy. He was hoping he could find a bee tree or signs of wild hogs. They were at the edge of a clearing when M'Lady's chokebore [1] nose suddenly tilted and she froze to a flash point,[2] pausing only long enough to get set. Then she dart-ed to the bayou, at least sixty yards away, dived into a clump of reeds, and snatched a water rat. She was eat-

[1] **chokebore** (chŏk′bôr): tapered at the tip.
[2] **flash point:** Hunting dogs are trained to show where game is hiding by holding a position, with body and head pointed toward the game. A flash point is a position held briefly.

ing it when Skeeter ran up.

"Don't do that," he scolded. "Ain't you got no more sense than to run into water after things? A snake or a 'gator might snatch you."

The basenji dropped the rat and tucked her head. She knew the boy was displeased, and when she looked up at him, her eyes were filled, and a woebegone expression was on her face.

Skeeter tried to explain, "I didn't mean to hurt your feelings. Don't cry." He stepped back quickly and stared at her, at the tears in her eyes. "She *is* crying! By John Brown!" Skeeter called her and ran toward the cabin, where Jesse was cutting splinters.

"Uncle Jess! Guess what else my dog can do!"

"Whistle," the old man laughed.

"She can cry! I declare to goodness! Not out loud, but she can cry just the same."

Jesse knew that most dogs will get watery-eyed on occasion, but, not wanting to ridicule M'Lady's accomplishments, asked, "What made her cry?"

"Well, sir, we were walking along and all of a sudden she got a scent and flash-pointed and then . . ." Skeeter remembered something.

"Then what?"

Skeeter sat on the steps. "Uncle Jess," he said slowly, "we must have been fifty or sixty yards from that rat when she smelled it."

"What rat? What's eating you?"

The child told him the story, and Jesse couldn't believe it. For a dog to pick up the scent of a water rat at sixty yards simply isn't credible. Jesse reckoned Skeeter's love for M'Lady had led him to exaggerate.

Skeeter knew Jesse didn't believe the story, so he said, "Come on. I'll show you." He whistled for M'Lady.

The dog came up. "Hey," Jesse said. "That thing knows what a whistle means. Shows she's been around folks." He caught the dog's eye and commanded, "Heel!"

But M'Lady cocked her head quizzically. Then she turned to the boy and chuckled softly. She'd never heard the order before. That was obvious. Her nose came up into the breeze and she wheeled.

Her curved tail suddenly was still and her head was poised.

"Flash pointing," Jesse said. "Well, I'll be a monkey's uncle!"

M'Lady held the strange point only for a second, though, then dashed toward a corn patch about eighty yards from the cabin.

Halfway to the patch, she broke her gait and began creeping. A whir of feathered lightning sounded in the corn, and a covey [1] of quail exploded almost under her nose. She sprang and snatched a bird.

"Partridges!" Jesse's jaw dropped.

The child was as motionless as stone, his face white and his eyes wide in amazement. Finally he found his voice, "She was right here when she smelled them birds. A good eighty yards."

"I know she ain't no dog now," Jesse said. "Can't no dog do that."

"She's fast as greased lightning and ain't scared of nothing." Skeeter still was under the spell of the adventure. "She's a hunting dog from way back."

"She ain't no dog a-tall, I'm telling

[1] **covey** (kuv'ē): small flock.

you. It ain't human." Jesse walked toward M'Lady and told her to fetch the bird, but the dog didn't understand. Instead, she pawed it. "Well," Jesse said. "One thing's certain. She ain't no bird hunter."

"She can do anything," Skeeter said. "Even hunt birds. Maybe I can make a bird dog out'n her. Wouldn't that be som'n?"

"You're batty. Maybe a coon dog, but not a bird dog. I know 'bout dogs."

"Me too," said Skeeter. And he did. He'd seen Jesse train many dogs, even pointers, and had helped him train Big Boy, Cash Watson's prize gun dog.

Jesse eyed Skeeter and read his mind.

"It can't be done, Skeets."

"Maybe not, but I aim to try. Any dog can run coons and rabbits, but it takes a pure D humdinger to hunt birds. Ain't no sin in trying, is it?"

"Naw," Jesse said slowly. "But she'll flush [1] birds."

"I'll learn her not to."

"She won't hold no point. Any dog'll flash point. And she'll hunt rats."

"I'm gonna learn her just to hunt birds. And I'm starting right now," Skeeter said. He started walking away, then turned. "I seen a man once train a razorback hawg to point birds. You know as good as me that if a dog's got pure D hoss sense and a fellow's got bat brains, he can train the dog to hunt birds."

"Wanta bet?" Jesse issued the challenge in an effort to keep Skeeter's enthusiasm and determination at the high-water mark.

[1] flush: drive from cover.

"Yes, sir. If I don't train my dog, then I'll cut all the splinters for a year. If I do, you cut 'em."

"It's a go," Jesse said.

Skeeter ran to the bayou and recovered the rat M'Lady had killed. He tied it round his dog's neck. The basenji was indignant and tried to claw off the hateful burden. Failing, she ran into the house and under a bed, but Skeeter made her come out. M'Lady filled up then, and her face assumed that don't-nobody-love-me look. The boy steeled himself, tapped M'Lady's nose with the rat, and left it around her neck.

"You done whittled out a job for yourself," Jesse said. "If'n you get her trained, you'll lose her in the brush. She's too fast and too little to keep up with."

"I'll bell her," Skeeter said. "I'm gonna learn her ever'thing. I got us a gun dog, Uncle Jess."

The old man sat on the porch and propped against the wall. "Bud, I don't know what that thing is. But you're a thoroughbred. John dog my hide!"

If Skeeter had loved M'Lady one bit less, his patience would have exploded during the ordeal of training the basenji. It takes judgment and infinite patience to train a bird dog properly, but to train a basenji, that'll hunt anything, to concentrate only on quail took something more than discipline and patience. It never could have been done except for that strange affinity between a boy and a dog, and the blind faith of a child.

M'Lady's devotion to Skeeter was so complete that she was anxious to do anything to earn a pat. It wasn't difficult to teach her to heel and follow at Skeeter's feet regardless of the urge to dash away and chase rabbits. The boy used a clothesline as a guide rope and made M'Lady follow him. The first time the dog tried to chase an animal, Skeeter pinched the rope around her neck just a bit and commanded "Heel!" And when she obeyed, Skeeter released the noose. It took M'Lady only a few hours to associate disobedience with disfavor.

The dog learned that when she chased and killed a rat or rabbit, the thing would be tied around her neck. The only things she could hunt without being disciplined were quail. Of course, she often mistook the scent of game chickens for quail and hunted them, but Skeeter punished her by scolding. He never switched his dog, but to M'Lady a harsh word from the boy hurt more than a hickory limb.

Jesse watched the dog's progress and pretended not to be impressed. He never volunteered suggestions. M'Lady learned quickly, but the task of teaching her to point birds seemed hopeless. Skeeter knew she'd never point as pointers do, so he worked out his own system. He taught her to stand motionless when he shouted "Hup!" One day she got a scent of birds, paused and pointed for a moment as most animals will, and was ready to spring away when Skeeter said "Hup!"

M'Lady was confused. Every instinct urged her to chase the birds, but her master had said stand still. She broke, however, and Skeeter scolded her. She pouted at first, then filled up, but the boy ignored her until she obeyed the

next command, then he patted her and she chuckled.

The lessons continued for days and weeks, and slowly and surely M'Lady learned her chores. She learned that the second she smelled birds she must stop and stand still until Skeeter flushed them; that she must not quiver when he shot.

Teaching her to fetch was easy, but teaching her to retrieve dead birds without damaging them was another matter. M'Lady had a hard mouth — that is, she sank her teeth into the birds. Skeeter used one of the oldest hunting tricks of the backwoods to break her.

He got a stick and wrapped it with wire and taught his dog to fetch it. Only once did M'Lady bite hard on the stick, and then the wire hurt her sensitive mouth. Soon she developed a habit of carrying the stick on her tongue and supporting it lightly with her teeth. Skeeter tied quail feathers on the stick, and soon M'Lady's education was complete.

Skeeter led Jesse into a field one day and turned his dog loose. She flashed to a point almost immediately. It was a funny point, and Jesse almost laughed. The dog's curved tail poked up over her back, she spraddled her front legs and sort of squatted, her nose pointing the birds, more than forty yards away. She remained rigid until the boy flushed and shot, then she leaped away, seeking and fetching dead birds.

Jesse was mighty proud. "Well, Skeets, looks like you got yourself a bird hunter."

"Yes, sir," Skeeter said. "And you got yourself a job." He pointed toward the kindling pile.

The swamp was dressing for winter when Cash Watson drove down that day to give his Big Boy a workout in the wild brush.

He fetched Jesse a couple of cans of smoking tobacco and Skeeter a bag of peppermint jawbreakers. He locked his fine pointer in the corncrib for the night and was warming himself in the cabin when he noticed M'Lady for the first time. She was sleeping in front of the fire.

"What's that?" he asked.

"My dog," said Skeeter. "Ain't she a beaut?"

"She sure is," Cash grinned at Jesse. Skeeter went out to the well, and Cash asked his old friend, "What the devil kind of mutt is that?"

"Search me," said Jesse. "Skeets found her in the swamp. I reckon she's got a trace of bloodhound in her and some terrier and a heap of just plain dog."

M'Lady cocked one ear and got up and stretched; then, apparently not liking the company, she turned her tail toward Cash and strutted out, looking for Skeeter.

The men laughed. "Som'n wrong with her throat," Jesse said. "She can't bark. When she tries, she makes a funny sound, sort of a cackling, chuckling yodel. Sounds like she's laughing."

"Well," Cash said, "trust a young'un to love the orner'st dog he can find."

"Wait a minute," Jesse said. "She ain't no-count. She's a bird-hunting fool."

Just then Skeeter entered and Cash jestingly said, "Hear you got yourself a bird dog, son."

The boy clasped his hands behind him and rocked on the balls of his feet as he had seen the men do. "Well, now, I'll tell you, Mr. Cash. M'Lady does ever'thing except tote the gun."

"She must be fair to middling. Why not take her out with Big Boy tomorrow? Do my dog good to hunt in a brace."

"Me and my dog don't want to show Big Boy up. He's a pretty good ol' dog."

"Whoa!" Cash was every inch a bird-dog man and nobody could challenge him without a showdown. Besides, Skeeter was shooting up and should be learning a few things about life. "Any old boiler can pop off steam." Cash winked at Jesse.

"Well, now, sir, if you're itching for a run, I'll just double dog dare you to run your dog against mine. And anybody who'll take a dare will pull up young cotton and push a widow woman's ducks in the water."

Cash admired the boy's confidence. "All right, son, it's a deal. What are the stakes?"

Skeeter started to mention the twenty-gauge gun he wanted, but changed his mind quickly. He reached down and patted M'Lady, then looked up. "If my dog beats yours, then you get them Roebuckers for Uncle Jess."

Jesse's chest suddenly was tight. Cash glanced from the boy to the man, and he, too, was proud of Skeeter. "I wasn't aiming to go that high. But all right. What do I get if I win?"

"I'll cut you ten cords of stove wood."

"And a stack of splinters?"

"Yes, sir."

Cash offered his hand, and Skeeter took it. "It's a race," Cash said. "Jesse will be the judge."

The wind was rustling the sage and there was a nip in the early-morning air when they took the dogs to a clearing and set them down. Skeeter snapped a belt around M'Lady's neck, and, at a word from Jesse, the dogs were released.

Big Boy bounded away and began circling, ranging into the brush. M'Lady tilted her nose into the wind and ripped away toward the sage, her bell tinkling. Cash said, "She sure covers ground." Skeeter made no effort to keep up with her, but waited until he couldn't hear the bell, then ran for a clearing where he had last heard it. And there was M'Lady on a point.

Cash laughed out loud. "That ain't no point, son. That's a squat."

"She's got birds."

"Where?"

Jesse leaned against a tree and watched the fun.

Skeeter pointed toward a clump of sage. "She's pointing birds in that sage."

Cash couldn't restrain his mirth. "Boy, now that's what I call some pointing. Why, Skeeter, it's sixty or seventy yards to that sage."

Just then Big Boy flashed by M'Lady, his head high. He raced to the edge of the sage, caught the wind, then whipped around, freezing to a point. Cash called Jesse's attention to the point.

"That's M'Lady's point," Skeeter said. "She's got the same birds Big Boy has."

Jesse sauntered up. "The boy's right, Cash. I aimed to keep my mouth out'n this race, but M'Lady is pointing them birds. She can catch scents up to eighty yards."

Cash said, "Aw, go on. You're crazy." He walked over and flushed the birds.

Skeeter picked one off and ordered M'Lady to fetch. When she returned with the bird, the boy patted her, and she began chuckling.

Cash really studied her then for the first time. "Hey!" he said suddenly. "A basenji! That's a basenji!"

"A what?" Jesse asked.

"I should have known." Cash was very excited. "That's the dog that was lost by them rich Yankees. I saw about it in the paper." He happened to look at Skeeter then and wished he had cut out his tongue.

The boy's lips were compressed and his face was drawn and white. Jesse had closed his eyes and was rubbing his forehead.

Cash, trying to dismiss the subject, said, "Just 'cause it was in the paper don't make it so. I don't believe that's the same dog, come to think of it."

"Do you aim to tell 'em where the dog is?" Skeeter asked.

Cash looked at Jesse, then at the ground. "It ain't none of my business."

"How 'bout you, Uncle Jess?"

"I ain't telling nobody nothin'."

"I know she's the same dog," Skeeter said. "On account of I just know it. But she's mine now." His voice rose and trembled. "And ain't nobody gonna take her away from me." He ran into the swamp. M'Lady was at his heels.

Cash said, "Durn my lip. I'm sorry, Jesse. If I'd kept my big mouth shut he'd never known the difference."

"It can't be helped, now," Jesse said.

" 'Course she beat Big Boy. Them's the best hunting dogs in the world. And she's worth a mint of money."

They didn't feel up to hunting and returned to the cabin and sat on the porch. Neither had much to say, but kept glancing toward the swamp where Skeeter and M'Lady were walking along the bayou. "Don't you worry," he said tenderly, "ain't nobody gonna bother you."

He sat on a stump and M'Lady put her head on his knee. She wasn't worrying. Nothing could have been more contented than she was.

"I don't care if the sheriff comes down." Skeeter pulled her onto his lap and held her. "I don't give a whoop if the governor comes down. Even the President of the United States! The whole shebang can come, but ain't nobody gonna mess with you."

His words gave him courage, and he felt better, but for only a minute. Then the tug of war between him and his conscience started.

"Once I found a Barlow knife and kept it, and it was all right," he mumbled.

"But this is different."

"Finders, keepers; losers, weepers."

"No, Skeeter."

"Well, I don't care. She's mine."

"Remember what your Uncle Jess said."

"He said a heap of things."

"Yes, but you remember one thing more than the rest. He said, 'Certain things are right and certain things are wrong. And nothing ain't gonna ever change that. When you learn that, then you're fit'n to be a man.' Remember, Skeeter?"

folks know their dog is here."

"If that's how it is——"

"That's how it is," Skeeter said.

The firelight dancing on Jesse's face revealed the old man's dejection, and Skeeter, seeing it, said quickly, "It's best for M'Lady. She's too good for the swamp. They'll give her a good home."

Jesse flinched, and Cash, catching the hurt look in his friend's eyes, said, "Your dog outhunted mine, Skeets. You win them Roebuckers for your uncle."

"I don't want 'em," Jesse said, rather childishly. "I don't care if'n I never eat no roastin' ears." He got up quickly and hurried outside. Cash reckoned he'd better be going and left Skeeter by the fire, rubbing his dog.

Jesse came back in directly and pulled up a chair. Skeeter started to speak, but Jesse spoke first. "I been doing a heap of thinking lately. You're sprouting up. The swamp ain't no place for you."

Skeeter forgot about his dog and faced his uncle, bewildered.

"I reckon you're too good for the swamp too," Jesse said. "I'm aiming to send you into town for a spell. I can make enough to keep you in fit'n clothes and all." He dared not look at the boy.

"Uncle Jess!" Skeeter said reproachfully. "You don't mean that. You're just saying that on account of what I said about M'Lady. I said it just to keep you from feeling so bad about our dog going away. Gee m'netty, Uncle Jess. I ain't ever gonna leave you." He buried his face in his uncle's shoulder. M'Lady put her head on Jesse's knee, and he patted the boy and rubbed the dog.

A feeling of despair and loneliness almost overwhelmed him. He fought off the tears as long as he could, but finally he gave in, and his sobs caused M'Lady to peer into his face and wonder why he was acting that way when she was so happy. He put his arms around her neck and pulled her to him. "My li'l old puppy dog. Poor li'l old puppy dog. But I got to do it."

He sniffed back his tears and got up and walked to the cabin. M'Lady curled up by the fire, and the boy sat down, watching the logs splutter for several minutes. Then he said, almost in a whisper, "Uncle Jess, if you keep som'n that ain't yours, it's the same as stealing, ain't it?"

Cash leaned against the mantel and stared into the fire.

Jesse puffed his pipe slowly. "Son, that's som'n you got to settle with yourself."

Skeeter stood and turned his back to the flames, warming his hands. "Mr. Cash," he said slowly, "when you get back to your store, please let them

"Reckon I'll take them Roebuckers," he said at last. "I been wanting some for a long, long time."

Several days later Cash drove down and told them the man from the kennels was at his store. Skeeter didn't say a word, but called M'Lady and they got in Cash's car. All the way to town, the boy was silent. He held his dog's head in his lap.

The keeper took just one look at M'Lady and said, "That's she, all right. Miss Congo III." He turned to speak to Skeeter, but the boy was walking away. He got a glance at Skeeter's face, however. "I wish you fellows hadn't told me," he muttered. "I hate to take a dog away from a kid."

"He wanted you to know," Cash said.

"Mister" — Jesse closed his left eye and struck his swapping pose — "I'd like to swap you out'n that hound. Now, 'course she ain't much 'count . . ."

The keeper smiled in spite of himself. "If she was mine, I'd give her to the kid. But she's not for sale. The owner wants to breed her and establish her line in this country. And if she was for sale, she'd cost more money than any of us will ever see." He called Skeeter and offered his hand. Skeeter shook it.

"You're a good kid. There's a reward for this dog."

"I don't want no reward." The boy's words tumbled out. "I don't want nothing, except to be left alone. You've got your dog, mister. Take her and go on. Please." He walked away again, fearing he would cry.

Cash said, "I'll take the reward and keep it for him. Some day he'll want it."

Jesse went out to the store porch to be with Skeeter. The keeper handed Cash the money. "It's tough, but the kid'll get over it. The dog never will."

"Is that a fact?"

"Yep. I know the breed. They never forget. That dog'll never laugh again. They never laugh unless they're happy."

He walked to the post where Skeeter had tied M'Lady. He untied the leash and started toward his station wagon. M'Lady braced her front feet and looked around for the boy. Seeing him on the porch, she jerked away from the keeper and ran to her master.

She rubbed against his legs. Skeeter tried to ignore her. The keeper reached for the leash again, and M'Lady crouched, baring her fangs. The keeper shrugged, a helpless gesture.

"Wild elephants couldn't pull that dog away from that boy," he said.

"That's all right, mister." Skeeter unsnapped the leash and tossed it to the keeper. Then he walked to the station wagon, opened the door of a cage, and called, "Heah, M'Lady!" She bounded to him. "Up!" he commanded. She didn't hesitate, but leaped into the cage. The keeper locked the door.

M'Lady, having obeyed a command, pocked her nose between the bars, expecting a pat. The boy rubbed her head. She tried to move closer to him, but the bars held her. She looked quizzically at the bars, then tried to nudge them aside. Then she clawed them. A look of fear suddenly came to her eyes, and she fastened them on Skeeter, wistfully at first, then pleadingly.

She couldn't make a sound, for her unhappiness had sealed her throat. Slowly her eyes filled up.

"Don't cry no more, M'Lady. Ever'thing's gonna be all right." He reached out to pat her, but the station wagon moved off, leaving him standing there in the dust.

Back on the porch, Jesse lit his pipe and said to his friend, "Cash, the boy has lost his dog, and I've lost a boy."

"Aw, Jesse, Skeeter wouldn't leave you."

"That ain't what I mean. He's growed up, Cash. He don't look no older, but he is. He growed up that day in the swamp."

Skeeter walked into the store and Cash followed him. "I've got that reward for you, Jonathan."

It was the first time anyone ever had called him that, and it sounded like man talk.

"And that twenty-gauge is waiting for you," Cash said. "I'm gonna give it to you."

"Thank you, Mr. Cash." The boy bit his lower lip. "But I don't aim to do no more hunting. I don't never want no more dogs."

"Know how you feel. But if you change your mind, the gun's here for you."

Skeeter looked back toward the porch where Jesse was waiting, and said, "Tell you what, though. When you get them Roebuckers, get some with a couple of gold teeth in 'em. Take it out of the reward money."

"Sure, Jonathan."

Jesse joined them, and Skeeter said, "We better be getting back toward the house."

"I'll drive you down," Cash said. "But first I aim to treat you to some lemon pop and sardines."

"That's mighty nice of you," Jesse said, "but we better be gettin' on."

"What's the hurry?" Cash opened the pop.

"It's my time to cut splinters," Jesse said. "That's what I get for betting with a good man."

A GOOD MAN

1. Describe the first meeting of Skeeter and M'Lady.

2. What kind of life did Skeeter and Jesse lead? Why did the village folk disapprove of Jesse?

3. Tell how Skeeter trained M'Lady to be a bird dog. How did Skeeter and M'Lady feel about one another? How did success in a contest lead to tragedy?

4. Reread the passages on page 127 which record Skeeter's tug of war with his conscience. What values held by Skeeter made him decide to return the dog? Where did Skeeter learn his values? People in the village didn't think Jesse lived "by rules." What did they mean?

5. Baucis and Philemon (page 103) were put to a test by the gods. In what way was Skeeter also put to a test? Baucis and Philemon were rewarded for their goodness. Was Skeeter rewarded at all? Is goodness in life usually rewarded as dramatically as it was in the story of Baucis and Philemon? Explain your answers.

6. Midas set his own selfish wishes against the wisdom of the gods. How does Skeeter compare with Midas?

7. Do you think Jesse was "fit'n to rear" Skeeter? Explain. Do you think that Skeeter should have kept M'Lady? Explain. Can you think of any other situations in life that involve this problem of "finders, keepers"?

8. Jesse said, "Cash, the boy has lost his dog, and I've lost a boy." What did he mean by this remark? What decisions in life do young people have to settle all by themselves?

WORDS:
FINDING ROOTS AND PREFIXES

You can learn the meaning of many roots and prefixes by reading the information within brackets in the dictionary. For example, in the first sentence of this story, the author speaks of the "moonlight symphony of swamp creatures." Look up the word *symphony* in a dictionary. Before or after its definition is given, you might find something like this in brackets: <OF *simphonie* <L *symphonia* <Gk. *symphōnia* <*syn*-together + *phōnē* sound. This tells you that this word came down to us from Old French (OF), which came from Latin (L), which came from Greek (Gk.). The Greeks formed the word by putting together the prefix *syn*– for "together" and the word *phōnē* for "sound." Thus, when the author of this story speaks of a "moonlight symphony of swamp creatures," he is talking about all the *sounds* the swamp creatures made *together*.

Look up these words in a large dictionary, and tell what roots and prefixes they are built from: *telegraph*, *biology*, *postscript*, *viaduct*, *export*, *inject*.

COMPOSITION:
DIALOGUE IN NARRATION

The third and fourth paragraphs of "Weep No More, My Lady" consist of a dialogue between Jesse and Skeeter.

"The boy's eyes were wide and staring. 'That's it, Uncle Jess. Come on! Let's catch it!'
" 'Uh, oh.' The man gripped his shotgun. 'That ain't no animal. That's a thing.' "

Did you notice how the author has reproduced the unusual and colorful way his characters use language? The dialogue in this story tells us a great deal about Skeeter and Jesse. We see in this first bit of conversation, for example, that Skeeter is not afraid of strange animals. We also know that Jesse is not well educated, for he uses a slang word like *ain't*.

Study more of the dialogue in this story, and list some of the words and expressions that make it realistic. Which dialogues helped you to understand Skeeter and Jesse better?

Write a short narrative telling about something that happened to you and someone else — perhaps in school or at home or in a strange town. Include in your narrative some dialogue that will tell something about your characters. Before you write your narrative, list some expressions and pronunciations you might use to make your dialogue realistic.

THOUGHTFUL READING:
THE ALL–KNOWING AUTHOR

The author of "Weep No More, My Lady" knows everything about the events in the story. He also knows everything about his characters; not only does he let his readers know what Skeeter and Jesse are thinking, but he also tells what their neighbors are thinking. An author who writes in this way is taking an all-knowing point of view.

Go back over the story and notice when the author takes an all-knowing point of view. Find, for example, the passage in which the author tells the reader about M'Lady's being a basenji — something that Skeeter and Jesse do not know. What other things does the author tell you that the main characters know nothing about? At what points in the story does the author take you right into the minds of the different characters?

THOUGHTS ABOUT WORDS

Our values are often revealed in the words we speak and in the way we interpret the words we hear. Each poem in this group says something about the powerful effect words can have on our lives.

A Word

EMILY DICKINSON

A word is dead
When it is said,
   Some say.
I say it just
Begins to live
   That day.

A Choice of Weapons

PHYLLIS MC GINLEY

Sticks and stones are hard on bones.
Aimed with angry art,
Words can sting like anything.
But silence breaks the heart.

Think As I Think

STEPHEN CRANE

"Think as I think," said a man,
"Or you are abominably wicked;
You are a toad."
And after I had thought of it,
I said, "I will, then, be a toad."

"A Choice of Weapons" from *The Love Letters of Phyllis McGinley*, copyright 1954 by Phyllis McGinley. Originally appeared in *The New Yorker*. Reprinted by permission of The Viking Press, Inc.
"Think As I Think" from *Collected Poems of Stephen Crane*, published 1930. Reprinted by permission of Alfred A. Knopf, Inc.

A Garland of Precepts

PHYLLIS MC GINLEY

Though a seeker since my birth,
Here is all I've learned on earth,
This the gist of what I know:
Give advice and buy a foe.
Random truths are all I find   5
Stuck like burs about my mind.
Salve a blister. Burn a letter.
Do not wash a cashmere sweater.
Tell a tale but seldom twice.
Give a stone before advice.   10

Pressed for rules and verities,
All I recollect are these:
Feed a cold to starve a fever.
Argue with no true believer.
Think-too-long is never-act.   15
Scratch a myth and find a fact.
Stitch in time saves twenty stitches.
Give the rich, to please them, riches.
Give to love your hearth and hall.
But do not give advice at all.   20

WORDS AND VALUES

1. The most important words in Emily Dickinson's poem are *dead* in line 1 and *live* in line 5. What do these words mean in this poem? Give examples of how words can continue to affect a person — either favorably or unfavorably — long after he has heard or read them.

2. Notice the title of Phyllis McGinley's first poem. What "weapons" is she talking about? Which weapon can hurt people most? How did Phyllis McGinley change the old saying ". . . but words can never harm me"? What does the verb *sting* mean in this poem? How might silence be able to hurt someone more than hard words?

3. Why would Stephen Crane, who wrote "Think As I Think," not be influenced by name-calling? Would you mind being called a toad? Why? Why did the poet say in the last line: "I will, then, be a toad"? Which weapon described in Phyllis McGinley's first poem is used by the first speaker in this poem? How do people, like the first speaker in Stephen Crane's poem, try to gain their ends through name-calling? How might they also try to gain their ends by flattery?

4. A precept is a rule of behavior. State in your own words the precepts in Phyllis McGinley's second poem. According to her, what precept (repeated three times) is most important? What does this precept have to do with words?

SENTENCES IN POETRY

Poetry is made up of sentences, just as prose is. In prose, a capital letter is used to signal the beginning of a sentence, but in poetry, a capital letter is also used at the beginning of each line — even though the line may not be a complete sentence. You can tell where a sentence of poetry ends by looking for its end mark — a period, a question mark, or an exclamation point. Look back at the first two poems in this group. Write out the sentences in these two poems, using a capital letter only at the beginning of a sentence. You might want to change the word order of some of these sentences.

"A Garland of Precepts" from *Times Three* by Phyllis McGinley, copyright 1954 by Phyllis McGinley. Originally appeared in *The New Yorker*. Reprinted by permission of The Viking Press, Inc.

Mama and the Graduation Present

KATHRYN FORBES

During the last week that Papa was in the hospital, we rented the big downstairs bedroom to two brothers, Mr. Sam and Mr. George Stanton.

The Stantons worked in the office of the Gas and Electric Company, and they paid a whole month's rent in advance, which was a very good thing for us. They were nice young men, and after dinner every night they would come out to the kitchen to tell Mama how much they enjoyed her cooking.

After they got better acquainted with Miss Durant,[1] they teased her about her "rabbit food" and made bets with each other as to which one of them would be the first to coax her to eat a big, thick steak — medium rare.

Mama was very proud of her three boarders; she listened to their chattering and laughter and said it was going to be fine when we had the hospital bills paid up and the money back to the Aunts. Then we would get more furniture and more boarders. Enough to fill all the chairs in the dining room. The Stanton brothers said they knew two more men from their place who would like to board with us.

On the day that Papa came home from the hospital, it was like a big party. We all stayed home from school, and Mama let Dagmar[2] decorate the table real fancy.

Everything seemed all right again when Papa walked carefully into the kitchen and sat down in the rocking chair. His face was white, and he looked thinner, but his smile was just the same. He had a bandage on his

[1] **Miss Durant:** one of the family's boarders. She ate only raw vegetables.

"Mama and the Graduation Present" from *Mama's Bank Account* by Kathryn Forbes, copyright 1943 by Kathryn Forbes. Reprinted by permission of Harcourt, Brace & World, Inc.

[2] **Dagmar:** Katrin's youngest sister. The other children in the family were Christine, a few years younger than Katrin, and Nels, Katrin's only brother and the oldest child.

head, and he made little jokes about how they shaved off his hair when he wasn't looking.

It was strange having Papa about the house during the day, but it was nice, too. He would be there in the kitchen when I came home from school, and I would tell him all that had happened.

Winford School had become the most important thing in life to me. I was finally friends with the girls, and Carmelita [1] and I were invited to all their parties. Every other Wednesday they came to my house, and we would sit up in my attic, drink chocolate, eat cookies, and make plans about our graduation.

We discussed "High" and vowed that we would stay together all through the next four years. We were the only ones in our class going on to Lowell. Lowell, we told each other loftily, was "academic."

We were enthralled with our superiority. *We* were going to be the first class at Winford to have evening graduation exercises; *we* were having a graduation play; *we* were making our own graduation dresses in sewing class.

And when I was given the second lead in the play — the part of the Grecian boy — I found my own great importance hard to bear. I alone, of all the girls, had to go downtown to the costumer's to rent a wig. A coarse black wig that smelled of disinfectant, but made me feel like Geraldine Farrar. [2] At every opportunity, I would put it on and have Papa listen to my part of the play.

[1] **Carmelita:** Katrin's friend.
[2] **Geraldine Farrar:** a famous opera singer.

Then the girls started talking about graduation presents.

Madeline said that she was getting an onyx ring with a small diamond. Hester was getting a real honest-to-goodness wrist watch. Thyra's family was going to add seven pearls to the necklace they had started for her when she was a baby. Even Carmelita was getting something special; her sister Rose was putting a dollar every payday onto an ivory manicure set.

I was intrigued, and wondered what great surprise my family had in store for me. I talked about it endlessly, hoping for some clue. It would be terrible if my present were not as nice as the rest.

"It is the custom, then," Mama asked, "the giving of gifts when one graduates?"

"My goodness, Mama," I said, "it's practically the most important time in a girl's life — when she graduates."

I had seen a beautiful pink celluloid dresser set at Mr. Schiller's drugstore, and I set my heart upon it. I dropped hint after hint, until Nels took me aside and reminded me that we did not have money for that sort of thing. Had I forgotten that the Aunts and the hospital must be paid up? That just as soon as Papa was well enough, he must do the Beauchamp job [3] for no pay?

"I don't care," I cried recklessly. "I *must* have a graduation present. Why, Nels, think how I will feel if I don't get any. When the girls ask me —— "

Nels got impatient and said he thought I was turning into a spoiled

[3] **Beauchamp job:** Dr. Beauchamp performed an operation on Papa. To help pay for it, Papa would work on the Doctor's house.

brat. And I retorted that since he was a boy, he naturally couldn't be expected to understand certain things.

When Mama and I were alone one day, she asked me how I would like her silver brooch for a graduation present. Mama thought a lot of that brooch — it had been her mother's.

"Mama," I said reasonably, "what in the world would I want an old brooch for?"

"It would be like a — an heirloom, Katrin. It was your grandmother's."

"No, thank you, Mama."

"I could polish it up, Katrin."

I shook my head. "Look, Mama, a graduation present is something like — well, like that beautiful dresser set in Mr. Schiller's window."

There, now, I had told. Surely, with such a hint . . .

Mama looked worried, but she didn't say anything. Just pinned the silver brooch back on her dress.

I was so sure that Mama would find some way to get me the dresser set that I bragged to the girls as if it were a sure thing. I even took them by Schiller's window to admire it. They agreed with me that it was wonderful. There were a comb, a brush, a mirror, a pincushion, a clothes brush, and even something called a hair receiver.

Graduation night was a flurry of excitement.

I didn't forget a single word of my part in the play. Flushed and triumphant, I heard Miss Scanlon say that I was every bit as good as Hester, who had taken elocution lessons for years. And when I went up to the platform for my diploma, the applause for me was long and loud. Of course,

the Aunts and Uncles were all there, and Uncle Ole and Uncle Peter could clap very loud, but I pretended that it was because I was so popular.

And when I got home — there was the pink celluloid dresser set!

Mama and Papa beamed at my delight, but Nels and Christine, I noticed, didn't say anything. I decided that they were jealous, and I felt sorry that they would not join me in my joy.

I carried the box up to my attic and placed the comb and brush carefully on my dresser. It took me a long while to arrange everything to my satisfaction. The mirror, so. The pincushion, here. The hair receiver, there.

Mama let me sleep late the next morning. When I got down for breakfast, she had already gone downtown to do her shopping. Nels was reading the want-ad section of the paper. Since it was vacation, he was going to try to get a job. He read the jobs aloud to Papa, and they discussed each one.

After my breakfast, Christine and I went upstairs to make the beds. I made her wait while I ran up to my attic to look again at my wonderful present. Dagmar came with me, and when she touched the mirror, I scolded her so hard she started to cry.

Christine came up then and wiped Dagmar's tears and sent her down to Papa. She looked at me for a long time.

"Why do you look at me like that, Christine?"

"What do you care? You got what you wanted, didn't you?" She pointed to the dresser set. "Trash," she said, "cheap trash."

"Don't you *dare* talk about my lovely present like that! You're jealous, that's what. I'll tell Mama on you."

"And while you're telling her," Christine said, "ask her what she did with her silver brooch. The one her very own mother gave her. Ask her that."

I looked at Christine with horror. "What? You mean . . . Did Mama . . . ?"

Christine walked away.

I grabbed up the dresser set and ran down the stairs to the kitchen. Papa was drinking his second cup of coffee, and Dagmar was playing with her doll in front of the stove. Nels had left.

"Papa, oh, Papa!" I cried. "Did Mama . . . Christine says . . ." I started to cry then, and Papa had me sit on his lap.

"There now," he said, and patted my shoulder. "There now."

And he dipped a cube of sugar into his coffee and fed it to me. We were not allowed to drink coffee — even with lots of milk in it — until we were considered grown up, but all of us children loved that occasional lump of sugar dipped in coffee.

After my hiccuping and sobbing had stopped, Papa talked to me very seriously. It was like this, he said. I had wanted the graduation present. Mama had wanted my happiness more than she had wanted the silver brooch. So she had traded it to Mr. Schiller for the dresser set.

"But I never wanted her to do that, Papa. If I had known . . . I would never have let her . . ."

"It was what Mama wanted to do, Katrin."

"But she *loved* it so. It was all she had of Grandmother's."

"She always meant it for you, Katrin."

I stood up slowly. I knew what I must do.

And all the way up to Mr. Schiller's drugstore, the graduation present in my arms, I thought of how hard it must have been for Mama to ask Mr. Schiller to take the brooch as payment. It was never easy for Mama to talk to strangers.

Mr. Schiller examined the dresser set with care. He didn't know, he said, about taking it back. After all, a bargain was a bargain, and he had been thinking of giving the brooch to his wife for her birthday next month.

Recklessly, I mortgaged my vacation.

If he would take back the dresser set, if he would give me back the brooch, I would come in and work for him every single day, even Saturdays.

"I'll shine the showcases," I begged. "I'll sweep the floor for you."

Mr. Schiller said that would not be necessary. Since I wanted the brooch back so badly, he would call the deal off. But if I was serious about working during vacation, he might be able to use me.

So I walked out of Mr. Schiller's drugstore not only with Mama's brooch, but also with a job that started the next morning. I felt very proud. The dresser set suddenly seemed a childish and silly thing.

I put the brooch on the table in front of Papa.

He looked at me proudly. "Was it so hard to do, Daughter?"

"Not so hard as I thought." I pinned the brooch on my dress. "I'll wear it always," I said. "I'll keep it forever."

"Mama will be glad, Katrin."

Papa dipped a lump of sugar and held it out to me. I shook my head. "Somehow," I said, "I just don't feel like it, Papa."

"So?" Papa said. "So?"

And he stood up and poured out a cup of coffee and handed it to me.

"For me?" I asked wonderingly.

Papa smiled and nodded. "For my grown-up daughter," he said.

I sat up straight in my chair. And felt very proud as I drank my first cup of coffee.

A GROWN–UP DAUGHTER

1. Why was the graduation present so important to Katrin? What did Nels tell Katrin?

2. What offer did Mama make to Katrin? Why did Katrin not accept this offer?

3. How did the family react when Katrin got her present? What did Christine tell Katrin about Mama's brooch? What did Katrin do then? What was the significance of the first cup of coffee?

4. In this story, how do Mama's values contrast with Katrin's? Why do you think Mama's actions finally influenced Katrin when nothing else seemed to affect her?

5. In what ways is Katrin somewhat like King Midas (page 107)? Did any statement made in "The Gift and the Giver" (page 114) apply to this story? Explain.

6. Which do you think has a greater effect upon young people — the words or the examples of adults? Explain.

SENTENCES:
CONVERSATIONAL STYLE

Kathryn Forbes wrote this first-person narrative in the language and style of a high school girl.

For example, she sometimes makes use of a vague, overworked word like *nice*, saying that the boarders were "nice young men" and that it "was nice" having Papa around the house. She also uses the word *real* informally, saying that Dagmar decorated the table "real fancy."

Sometimes she will use an incomplete sentence, such as the second sentence in this passage.

> "Mama looked worried, but she didn't say anything. Just pinned the silver brooch back on her dress."

Find at least three other incomplete sentences in this story. Notice that most of the sentences in the story have simple, easily understood constructions. Read aloud some of the sentences from the story. Does Kathryn Forbes's style help you to feel that young Katrin herself is telling this story?

THOUGHTFUL READING:
FIRST–PERSON VIEWPOINT

In this story, the main character, Katrin, is supposed to be the author herself. When an author writes from this first-person point of view, she can tell only what her narrator would know, and she can reveal only what her narrator thinks. This first-person point of view creates a realistic tone. When we read a story that is written in the first-person we often forget that the story might be fiction.

Compare the point of view used in this story with that used in "Weep No More, My Lady." Does the narrator of "Mama and the Graduation Present" ever take you into the minds of other characters? Does she ever let you know something that none of the characters know about? In what ways was this story more personal than "Weep No More, My Lady"? Which of these stories seemed more true to you? Explain your answer.

The Countess and the Impossible

RICHARD Y. THURMAN

No ONE in our Utah town knew where the Countess had come from; her carefully precise English indicated that she was not a native American. From the size of her house and staff, we knew that she must be wealthy, but she never entertained, and she made it clear that when she was at home she was completely inaccessible. Only when she stepped outdoors did she become at all a public figure — and then chiefly to the small fry of the town, who lived in awe of her.

The Countess always carried a cane, not only for support but as a means of chastising any youngster she thought needed disciplining. And at one time or another most of the kids in our neighborhood seemed to display that need. By running fast and staying alert I had managed to keep out of her reach. But one day when I was thir-

teen, as I was short-cutting through her hedge, she got close enough to rap my head with her stick. "Ouch!" I yelled, jumping a couple of feet.

"Young man, I want to talk to you," she said. I was expecting a lecture on the evils of trespassing, but as she looked at me, half-smiling, she seemed to change her mind. "Don't you live in that green house with the willow trees, in the next block?"

"Yes, ma'am."

"Do you take care of your lawn? water it? clip it? mow it?"

"Yes, ma'am."

"Good. I've lost my gardener. Be at my house Thursday morning at seven, and don't tell me you have something else to do. I've seen you slouching around on Thursdays."

When the Countess gave an order, it was carried out. I didn't dare not come on that next Thursday. I went over the whole lawn three times with a mower before she was satisfied, and then she had me down on all fours looking for weeds until my knees were as green as the grass. She finally called me up to the porch.

"Well, young man, how much do you want for your day's work?"

"I don't know. Fifty cents maybe."

"Is that what you figure you're worth?"

"Yes'm. About that."

"Very well. Here's the fifty cents you say you're worth, and here's the dollar and a half more that I've earned for you by pushing you. Now I'm going to tell you something about how you and I are going to work together. There are as many ways of mowing a lawn as there are people, and they may be worth anywhere from a penny to five dollars. Let's say that a three-dollar job would be just what you've done today, except that you would do it all by yourself. A four-dollar job would be so perfect that you'd have to be something of a fool to spend that much time on a lawn. A five-dollar lawn is — well, it's

impossible, so we'll forget about that. Now then, each week I'm going to pay you according to your own evaluation of your work."

I left with my two dollars, richer than I remembered being in my whole life and determined that I would get four dollars out of her the next week. But I failed to reach even the three-dollar mark. My will began faltering the second time around her yard.

"Two dollars again, eh? That kind of job puts you right on the edge of being dismissed, young man."

"Yes'm. But I'll do better next week."

And somehow I did. The last time around the lawn I was exhausted, but I found I could spur myself on. In the exhilaration of that new feeling, I had no hesitation in asking the Countess for three dollars.

Each Thursday for the next four or five weeks, I varied between a three- and a three-and-a-half-dollar job. The more I became acquainted with her lawn, places where the ground was

a little high or a little low, places where it needed to be clipped short or left long on the edges to make a more satisfying curve along the garden, the more aware I became of just what a four-dollar lawn would consist of. And each week I would resolve to do just that kind of job. But by the time I had made my three- or three-and-a-half-dollar mark, I was too tired to remember ever having had the ambition to go beyond that point.

"You look like a good, consistent three-fifty man," she would say as she handed me the money.

"I guess so," I would say, too happy at the sight of the money to remember that I had shot for something higher.

"Well, don't feel too bad," she would comfort me. "After all, there are only a handful of people in the world who could do a four-dollar job."

And her words *were* a comfort at first. But then, without my noticing what was happening, her comfort became an irritant that made me resolve to do that four-dollar job, even if it killed me. In the fever of my resolve, I could see myself expiring on her lawn, with the Countess leaning over me, handing me the four dollars with a tear in her eye, and begging my forgiveness for having thought I couldn't do it.

It was in the middle of such a fever, one Thursday night when I was trying to forget that day's defeat and get some sleep, that the truth hit me so hard I sat upright, half-choking in my excitement. It was the *five-dollar* job I had to do, not the four-dollar one! I had to do the job that no one could do because it was impossible.

I was well acquainted with the difficulties ahead. I had the problem, for example, of doing something about the worm mounds in the lawn. The Countess might not even have noticed them yet, they were so small; but in my bare feet, *I* knew about them and had to do something about them. And I *could* go on trimming the garden edges with shears, but I knew that a five-dollar lawn demanded that I line up each edge exactly with a yardstick and then trim it precisely with the edger. And there were other problems that only I and my bare feet knew about.

I started the next Thursday by ironing out the worm mounds with a heavy roller. After two hours of that, I was ready to give up for the day. Nine o'clock in the morning and my will was already gone! It was only by accident that I discovered how to regain it. Sitting under a walnut tree for a few minutes after finishing the rolling, I fell asleep. When I woke up minutes later, the lawn looked so good through my fresh eyes and felt so good under my feet that I was anxious to get on with the job.

I followed this secret for the rest of the day, dozing a few minutes every hour to regain my perspective and replenish my strength. Between naps I mowed four times, two times lengthwise, two times across, until the lawn looked like a green velvet checkerboard. Then I dug around every tree, crumbling the big clods and smoothing the soil with my hand, then finished with the edger, meticulously lining up each stroke so the effect would be perfectly symmetrical. And I carefully trimmed the grass between the

flagstones of the front walk. The shears wore my fingers raw, but the walk never looked better.

Finally about eight o'clock that evening, after I had run home at five for a bite of supper, it was all completed. I was so proud I didn't even feel tired when I went up to her door.

"Well, what is it today?" she asked.

"Five dollars," I said, trying for a little calm and sophistication.

"Five dollars? You mean four dollars, don't you? I told you that a five-dollar lawn isn't possible."

"Yes it is. I just did it."

"Well, young man, the first five-dollar lawn in history certainly deserves some looking around."

We walked about the lawn together in the last light of evening, and even I was quite overcome by the impossibility of what I had done.

"Young man," she said, putting her hand on my shoulder, "what on earth made you do such a crazy, wonderful thing?"

I didn't know why, but even if I had, I couldn't have explained it in the excitement of hearing that I *had* done it.

"I think I know," she continued, "how you felt when this idea came to you of mowing a lawn that I had told you was impossible. It made you very happy when it first came, then a little frightened. Am I right?"

She could see she was right by the startled look on my face.

"I know how you felt because the same thing happens to almost everybody. They feel this sudden burst in them of wanting to do some great thing. They feel a wonderful happiness. But then it passes because they have said, 'No, I can't do that. It's impossible.' Whenever something in you says 'It's impossible,' remember to take a careful look. See if it isn't really God asking you to grow an inch, or a foot, or a mile, that you may come to a fuller life."

She folded my hand around the money. "You've been a great man today. It's not often a man gets paid for a thing like greatness. You're getting paid because you're lucky and I like you. Now run along."

Since that time, some twenty-five years ago, when I have felt myself at an end with nothing before me, suddenly with the appearance of that word "impossible" I have experienced again the unexpected lift, the leap inside me, and known that the only possible way lay through the very middle of the impossible.

A FULLER LIFE

1. What picture does the author first give of the Countess?

2. What did the Countess say on the boy's first day, when he asked for fifty cents? Next time, when he asked for two dollars, what did she tell him?

3. How did the boy get the idea of doing a "five-dollar job"? Tell how he went about doing the impossible.

4. This boy learned the satisfaction of doing a job better than he had ever imagined he could do it. Would he have done the five-dollar job if no one had challenged him? Explain.

5. The Countess said that a man doesn't often get paid for greatness. What do you think she meant by this?

6. The Countess said that meeting "impossible" challenges can help a person come to a fuller life. There are many problems in modern life — both personal and social — that might seem impossible to solve. Can you name any such problems?

WORDS: PREFIXES OF NUMBER

At one point, the Countess was described as "half-smiling." Sometimes we can substitute the prefix *semi–* for the word *half* and make one word instead of two words joined by a hyphen: for example, *semiconscious* instead of *half-conscious; semiannual* instead of *half-yearly.*

Many prefixes in English, like *semi–*, indicate number or quantity. Here are a few of them:

Prefix	*Meaning*
uni–	single
bi–	two
tri–	three
centi–	hundred
milli–	thousand
multi–	many

Think of two words to which each of these prefixes can be added. How does the addition of the prefix indicate a number or quantity? Use a dictionary if necessary.

Can you name any other prefixes that indicate number or quantity?

SENTENCES IN DIALOGUE

At one place in this narrative the Countess asks this:

"Do you take care of your lawn? water it? clip it? mow it?"

Notice that several word groups are incomplete in this quotation. The reader must mentally supply the words "Do you . . ." in the last three questions. If you listen carefully to people speaking, you will notice that they frequently speak in incomplete sentences much like these. Therefore, writers use incomplete sentences in dialogue when they want to imitate ordinary speech.

Examine the rest of the dialogue in this narrative, and notice how often the writer has used incomplete sentences. Read this dialogue aloud. Does it sound authentic?

As the Night the Day

ABIOSEH NICOL

KOJO AND BANDELE walked slowly across the hot, green lawn, holding their science manuals with moist fingers. In the distance they could hear the junior school collecting in the hall of the main school building for singing practice. Nearer, but still far enough, their classmates were strolling toward them. The two reached the science block and entered it. It was a low building set apart from the rest of the high school that sprawled on the hillside of the African savanna. The laboratory was a longish room, and at one end they saw Basu, another boy, looking out of the window, his back turned to them. Mr. Abu, the ferocious laboratory attendant, was not about. The rows of multicolored bottles looked inviting. A Bunsen burner soughed loudly in the heavy weary heat. Where the tip of the light blue triangle of flame ended, a shimmering plastic transparency started. One could see the restless hot air moving in the mi-

nute tornado. The two African boys watched it interestedly.

"They say it is hotter inside the flame than on its surface," Kojo said doubtfully. "I wonder how they know?"

"I think you mean the opposite; let's try it ourselves," Bandele answered.

"How?"

"Let's take the temperature inside."

"All right, here is a thermometer. You do it."

"It says ninety degrees now. I shall take the temperature of the outer flame first, then you can take the inner yellow one."

Bandele held the thermometer gently forward to the flame, and Kojo craned to see. The thin thread of quicksilver shot upward within the stem of the instrument with swift malevolence,[1] and there was a slight crack. The stem had broken. On the bench the small bulbous drops of mercury which had spilled from it shivered with glinting, playful malice and shuddered down to the cement floor, dashing themselves into a thousand

"As the Night the Day" by Abioseh Nicol from *An African Treasury*, edited by Langston Hughes. Originally appeared in *Encounter*. Reprinted by permission of the author, David Higham Associates, Ltd. and *Encounter*.

[1] **malevolence** (mə·lev'ə·lens): spitefulness.

shining pieces, some of which coalesced[1] again and shook gaily as if with silent laughter.

"Oh my gosh!" whispered Kojo hoarsely.

"Shut up!" Bandele said imperiously, in a low voice.

Bandele swept the few drops on the bench into his cupped hand and threw the blob of mercury down the sink. He swept those on the floor under an adjoining cupboard with his bare feet. Then, picking up the broken halves of the thermometer, he tiptoed to the waste bin and dropped them in. He tiptoed back to Kojo, who was standing petrified by the blackboard.

"See no evil, hear no evil, speak no evil," he whispered to Kojo.

It all took place in a few seconds. Then the rest of the class started pouring in, chattering and pushing each other. Basu, who had been at the end of the room with his back turned to them all the time, now turned round and limped laboriously across to join the class, his eyes screwed up as they always were. Basu was clubfooted.

The class ranged itself loosely in a semicircle around the demonstration platform. They were dressed in the school uniform of white shirt and khaki shorts.

Mr. Abu, the laboratory attendant, came in from the adjoining store and briskly cleaned the blackboard. He was a retired African sergeant from the Army Medical Corps and was feared by the boys. If he caught any of them in any petty thieving, he offered them the choice of a hard smack or of being reported to the science masters. Most boys chose the former as they knew the matter would end there, with no protracted interviews and with no entry in the conduct book.

The science master stepped in and stood on his small platform, a tall, thin, dignified Negro with graying hair and silver-rimmed spectacles, badly fitting on his broad nose and always slipping down, making him look avuncular.[2] "Vernier" was his nickname, as he insisted on exact measurement and exact speech "as fine as a vernier scale," he would say, which measured, of course, things in thousandths of a millimeter. Vernier set the experiment for the day and demonstrated it, then retired behind the *Church Times,* which he read seriously in between walking quickly down the aisles of lab benches advising boys. It was a simple heat experiment to show that a dark surface gave out more heat by radiation than a bright surface.

During the class, Vernier was called away to the telephone and Abu was not about. As soon as a posted sentinel announced that he was out of sight, minor pandemonium broke out. Some of the boys raided the store. The wealthier ones swiped rubber tubing to make slingshots and to repair bicycles and helped themselves to chemicals for developing photographic films. The poorer boys were in deadlier earnest and took only things of strict commercial interest which could be sold easily in the market. They emptied stuff into bottles in their pockets. Soda for making soap, salt for cooking, liquid par-

---

[1] **coalesced** (kō′ə·lest′): came together.

[2] **avuncular** (ə·vung′kyə·lər): like an uncle — in other words, like an elderly man.

affin for women's hairdressing, and fine yellow iodoform powder much in demand for sprinkling on sores.

Kojo protested mildly against all this. "Oh, shut up!" a few boys said. Sorie, a huge boy who always wore a fez indoors, commanded respect and some leadership in the class. "Look here, Kojo, you are getting out of hand. What do you think our parents pay taxes and school fees for? For us to enjoy — or to buy a new car every year for Simpson?" The other boys laughed. Simpson was the European headmaster, feared by the small boys, adored by the boys in the middle school, and liked, in a critical fashion, with reservations, by some of the senior boys and African masters. He had a passion for new cars, buying one yearly.

"Come to think of it," Sorie continued to Kojo, "you must take something yourself, then we'll know we are safe." "Yes, you must," the other boys insisted. Kojo gave in and, unwillingly, took a little nitrate for some gunpowder experiments that he was carrying out at home.

"Someone!" the lookout called.

The boys dispersed in a moment. Mr. Abu, the lab attendant, entered and observed the innocent collective expression of the class. He glared round suspiciously. However, Vernier came in then. After asking if anyone was in difficulty, and finding that no one could momentarily think up anything, he retired to his chair and settled down to an article, adjusting his spectacles and thoughtfully sucking an empty tooth socket.

Towards the end of the period, the class collected around Vernier and gave

in their results, which were then discussed. Soon, the class dispersed and started walking back across the hot grass. Kojo and Bandele heaved sighs of relief and joined Sorie's crowd, which was always the largest.

"Come back, all of you, come back!" Mr. Abu's stentorian [1] voice rang out across to them.

They wavered and stopped. Kojo kept walking on in a blind panic. "Stop!" Bandele hissed across. "You fool." He stopped, turned, and joined the returning crowd, closely followed by Bandele. Abu joined Vernier on the platform. The loose semicircle of boys faced them.

"Mr. Abu has just found this in the waste bin," Vernier announced, gray with anger. He held up the two broken halves of the thermometer. "It must be due to someone from this class, as the

---

[1] **stentorian** (sten·tôr′ē·ən): extremely loud.

number of thermometers was checked before being put out."

A little wind gusted in through the window and blew the silence heavily this way and that.

"Who?"

No one answered. Vernier looked round and waited.

"Since no one has owned up, I am afraid I shall have to detain you for an hour after school as punishment," said Vernier.

There was a murmur of dismay and anger. An important soccer house-match was scheduled for that afternoon. Some boys put their hands up and said that they had to play in the match.

"I don't care," Vernier shouted. He felt, in any case, that too much time was devoted to games and not enough to work.

He left Mr. Abu in charge and went off to fetch his things from the main building.

"We shall play 'Bible and Key,'" Abu announced as soon as Vernier had left. Kojo had been afraid of this, and new beads of perspiration sprang from his troubled brow. All the boys knew the details. It was a method of finding out a culprit by divination.[1] A large door-key was placed between the leaves of a Bible at the New Testament passage where Ananias and Sapphira were struck dead before the Apostles for lying, and the Bible was suspended by two bits of string tied to both ends of the key. The combination was held up by someone, and the names of all present were called out in turn. When that

[1] **divination** (div′ə·nā′shən): supernatural means.

of the sinner was called, the Bible was expected to turn round and round violently and to fall.

Now Abu asked for a Bible. Someone produced a copy. He opened the first page and then shook his head and handed it back. "This won't do," he said. "It's a Revised Version; only the genuine Word of God will give us the answer."

An Authorized King James Version was then produced, and he was satisfied. Soon he had the contraption fixed up. He looked round the semicircle from Sorie at one end, through the others, to Bandele, Basu, and Kojo at the other, near the door.

"You seem to have an honest face," he said to Kojo. "Come and hold it." Kojo took the ends of the string gingerly with both hands, trembling slightly.

Abu moved over to the low window and stood at attention, his sharp profile outlined against the red hibiscus flowers, the green trees, and the molten sky. The boys watched anxiously. A black-bodied lizard scurried up a wall and started nodding its pink head with grave impartiality.

Abu fixed his aging, bloodshot eyes on the suspended Bible. He spoke hoarsely and slowly:

Oh Bible, Bible, on a key,
Kindly tell it unto me,
By swinging slowly round and true,
To whom this sinful act is due.

He turned to the boys and barked out their names in a parade-ground voice, beginning with Sorie and working his way round, looking at the Bible after each name.

To Kojo, trembling and shivering as if ice-cold water had been thrown over him, it seemed as if he had lost all power and as if some gigantic being stood behind him holding up his tired, aching elbows. It seemed to him as if the key and Bible had taken on a life of their own, and he watched with fascination the whole combination moving slowly, jerkily, and rhythmically, in short arcs, as if it had acquired a heartbeat.

"Ayo Sogbenri, Sonnir Kargbo, Oji Ndebu." Abu was coming to the end now. "Tommy Longe, Ajayi Cole, Bandele Fagb . . ."

Kojo dropped the Bible. "I am tired," he said in a small scream. "I am tired."

"Yes, he is," Abu agreed, "but we are almost finished; only Bandele and Basu are left."

"Pick up that book, Kojo, and hold it up again." Bandele's voice whipped through the air with cold fury. It sob-ered Kojo, and he picked it up.

"Will you continue please with my name, Mr. Abu?" Bandele asked, turning to the window.

"Go back to your place quickly, Kojo," Abu said. "Vernier is coming. He might be vexed. He is a strongly religious man and so does not believe in the Bible-and-key ceremony."

Kojo slipped back with sick relief, just before Vernier entered.

In the distance the rest of the school was assembling for closing prayers. The class sat and stood around the blackboard and demonstration bench in attitudes of exasperation, resignation, and self-righteous indignation. Kojo's heart was beating so loudly that he was surprised no one else heard it.

Once to every man and nation
Comes the moment to decide.

The closing hymn floated across to them, interrupting the still afternoon.

Kojo got up. He felt now that he must speak the truth or life would be intolerable ever afterwards. Bandele got up swiftly before him. In fact, several things seemed to happen all at the same time. The rest of the class stirred. Vernier looked up from a book review which he had started reading. A butterfly with black and gold wings flew in and sat on the edge of the blackboard, flapping its wings quietly and waiting too.

"Basu was here first before any of the class," Bandele said firmly.

Everyone turned to Basu, who cleared his throat.

"I was just going to say so myself, sir," Basu replied to Vernier's inquiring glance.

"Pity you had not thought of it before," Vernier said, drily. "What were you doing here?"

"I missed the previous class, so I came straight to the lab and waited. I was over there by the window trying to look at the blue sky. I did not break the thermometer, sir."

A few boys tittered. Some looked away. The others muttered. Basu's breath always smelled of onions, but although he could play no games, some boys liked him and were kind to him in a tolerant way.

"Well, if you did not, someone did. We shall continue with the detention."

Vernier noticed Abu standing by. "You need not stay, Mr. Abu," he said to him. "I shall close up. In fact, come with me now, and I shall let you out through the back gate."

He went out with Abu.

When he had left, Sorie turned to Basu and asked mildly:

"You are sure you did not break it?"

"No, I didn't."

"He did it," someone shouted.

"But what about the Bible and key?" Basu protested. "It did not finish. Look at him." He pointed to Bandele.

"I was quite willing for it to go on," said Bandele. "You were the only one left."

Someone threw a book at Basu and said, "Confess!"

Basu backed on to a wall. "I shall call the police if anyone strikes me," he cried fiercely.

"He thinks he can buy the police," a voice called.

"That proves it," someone shouted from the back.

"Yes, he must have done it," the others said, and they started throwing books at Basu. Sorie waved his arm for them to stop, but they did not. Books, corks, boxes of matches rained on Basu. He bent his head and shielded his face with his bent arm.

"I did not do it, I swear I did not do it. Stop it, you fellows," he moaned over and over again. A small cut had appeared on his temple, and he was bleeding. Kojo sat quietly for a while. Then a curious hum started to pass through him, and his hands began to tremble, his armpits to feel curiously wetter. He turned round and picked up a book and flung it with desperate force at Basu, and then another. He felt somehow that there was an awful swelling of guilt which he could only shed by punishing himself through hurting someone. Anger and rage against everything different seized him, because if everything and everyone had been the same, somehow he felt nothing would have been wrong and they would all have been happy. He was carried away now by a torrent which swirled and pounded. He felt that somehow Basu was in the wrong, must be in the wrong, and if he hurt him hard enough, he would convince the others and therefore himself that he had not broken the thermometer and that he had never done anything wrong. He groped for something bulky enough to throw, and picked up the Bible.

"Stop it!" Vernier shouted through the open doorway. "Stop it, you hooligans, you beasts."

They all became quiet and shamefacedly put down what they were going to throw. Basu was crying quietly and hopelessly, his thin body shaking.

"Go home, all of you, go home. I am ashamed of you." His black face shone with anger. "You are an utter disgrace to your nation and to your race."

They crept away, quietly, uneasily, avoiding each other's eyes, like people caught in secret passion.

Vernier went to the first-aid cupboard and started dressing Basu's wounds.

Kojo and Bandele came back and hid behind the door, listening. Bandele insisted that they should.

Vernier put Basu's bandaged head against his waistcoat and dried the boy's tears with his handkerchief, gently patting his shaking shoulders.

"It wouldn't have been so bad if I had done it, sir," he mumbled, "but I did not do it. I swear to God I did not."

"Hush, hush," said Vernier comfortingly.

"Now they will hate me even more," he moaned.

"Hush, hush."

"I don't mind the wounds so much, they will heal."

"Hush, hush."

"They've missed the soccer match and now they will never talk to me again, oh-ee, oh-ee, why have I been so punished?"

"As you grow older," Vernier advised, "you must learn that men are punished not always for what they do, but often for what people think they will do, or for what they are. Remember that and you will find it easier to forgive them. 'To thine own self be true!'" Vernier ended with a flourish, holding up his clenched fist in a mock dramatic gesture, quoting from the

Shakespeare examination book for the year and declaiming to the dripping taps and empty benches and still afternoon, to make Basu laugh.

Basu dried his eyes and smiled wanly and replied, " 'And it must follow as the night the day.' *Hamlet*, Act One, Scene Three, Polonius to Laertes."

"There's a good chap. First class, grade one. I shall give you a lift home."

Kojo and Bandele walked down the red laterite [1] road together, Kojo dispiritedly kicking stones into the gutter.

"The fuss they made over a silly old thermometer," Bandele began.

"I don't know, old man, I don't know," Kojo said impatiently.

They had both been shaken by the scene in the empty lab. A thin, invisible wall of hostility and mistrust was slowly rising between them.

"Basu did not do it, of course," Bandele said.

Kojo stopped dead in his tracks. "Of course he did not do it!" he shouted. "We did it!"

"No need to shout, old man. After all, it was your idea."

"It wasn't," Kojo said furiously. "You suggested we try it."

"Well, you started the argument. Don't be childish." They tramped on silently, raising small clouds of dust with their bare feet.

"I should not take it too much to heart," Bandele continued. "That chap Basu's father hoards foodstuff like rice and palm oil until there is a shortage and then sells them at high prices. The police are watching him."

[1] **laterite** (lat'ər-īt): clay.

"What has that got to do with it?" Kojo asked.

"Don't you see? Basu might quite easily have broken that thermometer. I bet he has done things before that we have all been punished for." Bandele was emphatic.

They walked on steadily down the main road of the town, past the Syrian and Lebanese shops crammed with knickknacks and rolls of cloth, past a large Indian shop with dull red carpets and brass trays displayed in its windows, carefully stepping aside in the narrow road as the British officials sped by in cars to their hill-station bungalows for lunch and siesta.

Kojo reached home at last. He washed his feet and ate his main meal for the day. He sat about heavily and restlessly for some hours. Night soon fell with its usual swiftness, at six, and he finished his homework early and went to bed.

Lying in bed, he rehearsed again what he was determined to do the next day. He would go up to Vernier:

"Sir," he would begin, "I wish to speak with you privately."

"Can it wait?" Vernier would ask.

"No, sir," he would say firmly. "As a matter of fact, it is rather urgent."

Vernier would take him to an empty classroom and say, "What is troubling you, Kojo Ananse?"

"I wish to make a confession, sir. I broke the thermometer yesterday." He had decided he would not name Bandele; it was up to the latter to decide whether he would lead a pure life.

Vernier would adjust his slipping glasses up his nose and think. Then he would say:

"This is a serious matter, Kojo. You realize you should have confessed yesterday."

"Yes, sir, I am very sorry."

"You have done great harm, but better late than never. You will, of course, apologize in front of the class and particularly to Basu, who has shown himself a finer chap than all of you."

"I shall do so, sir."

"Why have you come to me now to apologize? Were you hoping that I would simply forgive you?"

"I was hoping you would, sir. I was hoping you would show your forgiveness by beating me."

Vernier would pull his glasses up his nose again. He would move his tongue inside his mouth reflectively. "I think you are right. Do you feel you deserve six strokes or nine?"

"Nine, sir."

"Bend over!"

Kojo had decided he would not cry, because he was almost a man.

Whack! Whack!

Lying in bed in the dark thinking about it all as it would happen tomorrow, he clenched his teeth in imaginary pain.

Whack! Whack!! Whack!!!

Suddenly, in his room, under his thin cotton sheet, he began to cry. Because he felt the sharp lancing pain already cutting into him. Because of Basu and Simpson and the thermometer. For all the things he wanted to do and be, which would never happen. For all the good men they had told them about. For George Washington, who never told a lie. For Florence Nightingale and David Livingstone. For Kagawa, the Japanese man, for Gandhi, and for

Kwegyir Aggrey, the African. Oh-ee! Oh-ee! Because he knew he would never be as straight and strong and true as the school song said they should be. He saw, for the first time, what this thing would be like, becoming a man. He touched the edge of an inconsolable, eternal grief. Oh-ee! Oh-ee! Always, he felt, always I shall be a disgrace to the nation and the race.

His mother passed by his bedroom door, slowly dragging her slippered feet as she always did. He pushed his face into his wet pillow to stifle his sobs, but she had heard him. She came in and switched on the light.

"What *is* the matter with you, my son?"

He pushed his face further into his pillow.

"Nothing," he said, muffled and choking.

"You have been looking like a sick fowl all afternoon," she continued.

She advanced and put the back of her moist cool fingers against the side of his neck.

"You have got fever," she exclaimed. "I'll get something from the kitchen."

When she had gone out, Kojo dried his tears and turned the dry side of the pillow up. His mother reappeared with a thermometer in one hand and some quinine mixture in the other.

"Oh, take it away, take it away!" he shouted, pointing to her right hand and shutting his eyes tightly.

"All right, all right," she said.

He is a queer boy, she thought, with pride and a little fear, as she watched him drink the clear, bitter fluid.

She then stood by him and held his head against her as he sat up on the low bed, and she stroked his face. She knew he had been crying but did not ask him why, because she was sure he would not tell her. She knew he was learning, first slowly and now quickly, and she would soon cease to be his mother and be only one of the womenfolk in the family. "Such a short time," she thought, "when they are really yours and tell you everything." She sighed and slowly eased his sleeping head down gently.

The next day, Kojo got to school early and set to things briskly. He told Bandele that he was going to confess but would not name him. He half hoped he would join him. But Bandele had said, threateningly, that he had better not mention his name; let him go and be a Boy Scout on his own. The sneer strengthened him, and he went off to the lab. He met Mr. Abu and asked for Vernier. Abu said Vernier was busy, and what was the matter anyhow.

"I broke the thermometer yesterday," Kojo said in a businesslike manner.

Abu put down the glassware he was carrying.

"Well, I never!" he said. "What do you think you will gain by this?"

"I broke it," Kojo repeated.

"Basu broke it," Abu said impatiently. "Sorie got him to confess, and Basu himself came here this morning and told the science master and myself that he knew now that he had knocked the thermometer over by mistake when he came in early yesterday afternoon. He had not turned round to look, but he had definitely heard a tinkle as he walked by. Someone must have picked

it up and put it in the waste bin. The whole matter is settled, the palaver [1] finished."

He tapped a barometer on the wall and, squinting, read the pressure. He turned again to Kojo.

"I should normally have expected him to say so yesterday and save you boys from missing the game. But there you are," he added, shrugging and trying to look reasonable. "You cannot hope for too much from a Syrian boy."

[1] **palaver** (pə·lav′ər): discussion.

SELF–ESTEEM

1. How did the incident in which the thermometer was broken reveal the differences between Kojo and Bandele? What was Basu doing when the thermometer broke? What does the author tell you about Basu?

2. Who were Abu and Vernier? Describe what the students did when these men left the classroom. How did Kojo react to this situation? What kind of person was Sorie? What did he make Kojo do?

3. What did Bandele do just as Kojo was about to confess in front of the detention class? What more do you learn about Basu in this scene? Describe Kojo's feelings as books were thrown at Basu. Why did he want to hurt Basu?

4. Find the scene in which Basu quotes the title of the story. Why did Vernier remind Basu of these words from Shakespeare?

5. Describe how Kojo felt that evening. Reread the paragraph on page 152 beginning "Suddenly, in his room . . ." and explain in your own words why Kojo cried.

6. What happened when Kojo confessed to Abu? How do you think Kojo felt as the story ended?

7. Why do you think Basu confessed?

8. How did the characters in this story show prejudice toward someone who was different from them? What was the effect of their prejudice? Do you think we often dislike people who are "different"?

9. Here is the full sentence from Shakespeare's play *Hamlet,* from which Vernier and Basu quoted:

"This above all: to thine own self be true,
And it must follow, as the night the day,
Thou canst not then be false to any man."

Apply this quotation to other characters in the stories in this unit. Which characters were true to their own values? Which characters refused to recognize what was of real value in their lives?

10. A person's values are often revealed and tested in difficult situations. Can you name any situations in which this is true?

ANALYZING WORD STRUCTURE

If you can recognize some common word prefixes and roots, you will have a head start in figuring out the meanings of new words. The following words, all from "As the Night the Day," might be new to you, but they contain prefixes or roots that have been discussed in previous vocabulary lessons. First look back at the story, and study each word in its context. Then analyze the structure of each word, and see if you can state its meaning. Refer back to previous vocabulary lessons, if necessary.

multicolored (page 144)
semicircle (page 145)
millimeter (page 145)
impartiality (page 147)
intolerable (page 149)
dispiritedly (page 151)

REDUCING LONG SENTENCES

Have you ever noticed that some long sentences that seem complicated are really composed of several short, simple sentences? For example, look at the following sentence, which appears in "As the Night the Day."

"It was a low building set apart from the rest of the high school that sprawled on the hillside of the African savanna."

This long sentence is really composed of three simpler sentences:

It was a low building. The building was set apart from the rest of the high school. The high school sprawled on the hillside of the African savanna.

Below are two more long sentences from this story. Reduce each into several simpler sentences, as was done in the example above.

"Basu, who had been at the end of the room with his back turned to them all the time, now turned round and limped laboriously across to join the class, his eyes screwed up as they always were."

"After asking if anyone was in difficulty, and finding that no one could momentarily think up anything, he returned to his chair and settled down to an article, adjusting his spectacles and thoughtfully sucking an empty tooth socket."

COMPOSITION: A NARRATIVE

This story may have reminded you of some happening in your own school which involved a problem of behavior. Tell the story of such a happening in several paragraphs. Try to apply some of the ideas you learned about composition in this unit. Strive for unity in your paragraphs by omitting unrelated events. Arrange the events of your story in chronological order. If you use dialogue, try to make it realistic by imitating the way your characters would speak.

Narration

The main purpose of a narrative is to tell a story or to tell how certain events occurred. You have already read many narratives, and you will read more in the years to come. What can you do to improve your skill in reading and writing narratives?

Read carefully this narrative passage from the story "As the Night the Day" by Abioseh Nicol.

Bandele held the thermometer gently forward to the flame, and Kojo craned to see. The thin thread of quicksilver shot upward within the stem of the instrument with swift malevolence, and there was a slight crack. The stem had broken. On the bench the small bulbous drops of mercury which had spilled from it shivered with glinting, playful malice and shuddered down to the cement floor, dashing themselves into a thousand shining pieces, some of which coalesced again and shook gaily as if with silent laughter.

"Oh my gosh!" whispered Kojo hoarsely.

"Shut up!" Bandele said imperiously, in a low voice.

Bandele swept the few drops on the bench into his cupped hand and threw the blob of mercury down the sink. He swept those on the floor under an adjoining cupboard with his bare feet. Then, picking up the broken halves of the thermometer, he tiptoed to the waste bin and dropped them in. He tiptoed back to Kojo, who was standing petrified by the blackboard.

"See no evil, hear no evil, speak no evil," he whispered to Kojo.   (pages 144–45)

READING NARRATION

1. *A good reader grasps the main event of a narrative passage almost automatically.* Nearly every narrative passage tells about one main happening. Which statement below best summarizes the main event of the passage from "As the Night the Day"?

   a. Kojo and Bandele broke the thermometer and concealed the crime.
   b. The mercury from the thermometer fell into a thousand pieces.
   c. Bandele dropped the pieces of the thermometer into the waste bin.
   d. Kojo was terrified.

2. *A good reader remembers important supporting details.* Did you recall the important details from this passage? Which of the following details were *not* included?

   a. Bandele held the thermometer to the flame.
   b. Kojo tried to persuade Bandele to confess to the instructor.
   c. Bandele shook with silent laughter when the thermometer broke.
   d. Bandele warned Kojo not to say anything.

Look back at the following narrative passages. What one main event does each passage tell about? List the important supporting details used in each passage.

In "Midas" the two paragraphs on page 109 beginning "Now he was the greatest king . . ." and ending ". . . and take away your gift."

In "Weep No More, My Lady" the eleven paragraphs on page 122 beginning "Skeeter knew Jesse didn't believe the story . . ." and ending "'. . . a hunting dog from way back.' "

WRITING NARRATION

You can quickly and easily tell a friend about something that happened to you — but you probably find it harder to set these events down in writing. Let us see how you can improve your skill in writing narratives.

1. *A narrative should begin in a way that arouses the reader's interest.* Look at the beginnings of some stories in this textbook (for example, pages 42, 320, and 481). Which opening sentences arouse your interest? Why do they do this?

2. *A good, interesting narrative is unified.* When you tell a story aloud and wander off your subject, your listener loses interest. The same is true about a written narrative. Each event should be included because it helps move the action along or reveals something about the characters.

3. *Most narratives are written in chronological order — in the order in which the events occur.* Reread the passage from "As the Night the Day." Are the events set down in the order in which they occurred?

4. *In writing a narrative, it is especially important to include vivid descriptive details.* Such details can hold the reader's attention by making the events seem real and interesting. Reread again the passage from "As the Night the Day." List the ways the author describes the mercury. (For example, he first describes it as a "thin thread of quicksilver.") Try reading this passage without these descriptive details. Is it as realistic and interesting?

5. *A narrative will have additional appeal if it tells how the characters feel and think about various events that occur.* Find a sentence in the model passage that tells how Kojo felt.

Look back at the story "Mama and the Graduation Present" (pages 134–38), and point to passages in which the narrator reveals Katrin's feelings about graduation.

One of the following situations might give you an idea for a narrative of your own.

A student searches for a job.
Someone's dream comes true.
A dog brings home a boy.

Sentence Study. Verbs are important to most writing, but they are very important to a good narrative. Precise, descriptive verbs can lend a feeling of action and movement to a narrative. Notice how good verbs add action to this sentence from the model passage from "As the Night the Day."

"Bandele *swept* the few drops on the bench into his cupped hand and *threw* the blob of mercury down the sink."

Read this sentence again, but substitute the verb *put* for the verbs *swept* and *threw*. Do you get the same sense of movement? What other action verbs can you locate in the model passage from "As the Night the Day"?

In the sentence above, the verbs are compounded. What is their subject?

Combine the following sentences into one sentence by compounding the verbs. Can you replace these rather dull verbs with ones that suggest action?

The spy went across the street. He looked furtively behind him. Then he went into the subway entrance.

ART AND LITERATURE

Sometimes a painter depicts a person or a group of people as if they were frozen in a moment of time. Look closely at the paintings on pages 81–86. Which one makes you most curious? Choose one of these paintings, and then write a brief story telling about the events that you think might have led up to the precise moment of time shown in the picture.

Themes in Literature

Unit 3
Our American Heritage

UNIT 3 Our American Heritage

In this unit are some of America's best-loved stories, poems, and speeches. These selections reveal some of the highest ideals of our nation. Perhaps you will memorize many of the poems and speeches. Some of them could be recited by heart by any child living in America about a hundred years ago.

Salt-Water Tea by Esther Forbes:
> A story about the men — and boys — who helped fan the spirit of freedom in America in the 1770's.

Paul Revere's Ride by Henry Wadsworth Longfellow:
> A poem, recited from generation to generation, about the patriot who warned his countrymen of danger.

The Concord Hymn by Ralph Waldo Emerson:
> A famed poetic tribute to the American farmers who defied the British soldiers.

Old Ironsides by Oliver Wendell Holmes:
> The poem that so aroused public indignation that a great ship was saved from the scrap heap.

The Man Without a Country by Edward Everett Hale:
> The story of a tragic exile, one of the best-loved stories in American literature.

The Drummer Boy of Shiloh by Ray Bradbury:
> The terror and horror of war, as experienced by one young boy, told in unforgettable terms by a contemporary American writer.

The Gettysburg Address by Abraham Lincoln:
> A speech delivered on a shattered American battlefield, called one of the noblest speeches ever given.

O Captain! My Captain! by Walt Whitman:
> A famous poem about the tragic death of a President.

Smoke over the Prairie by Conrad Richter:
> A noted writer's story of bitter conflict as old ways of life in America gave way to new.

Incandescent Genius by C. B. Wall:
> A factual article about the achievements of an amazing American inventor, Thomas Alva Edison.

Sing an Old Song by Eleanor R. Van Zandt:
> A magazine writer's account of America's rich and varied musical heritage.

Salt-Water Tea

FROM *Johnny Tremain*

ESTHER FORBES

Many stories and poems in American literature tell about the difficult days when Americans were trying to throw off the burdensome rule of England. The following story, from a book called *Johnny Tremain,* is based on a true episode in American history — the famous protest made in 1773 by the men of Boston. Esther Forbes tells the story of this protest through the eyes of a fourteen-year-old boy named Johnny Tremain, a printer's apprentice, whose hand had been crippled in an accident. Johnny is an imaginary character, but many of the men who enter the story are real historical people. Esther Forbes has done careful research to give us a sense of the tensions that gripped people in the Revolutionary days in America.

S HIVERING — for the last week in November was bitterly cold — Johnny built up the fire in the attic. From the back window he could see that the roofs of the Afric Queen [1] were white with frost.

---

[1] **the Afric Queen:** an inn near the newspaper shop where Johnny and another boy, Rab, lived and worked.

"Salt-Water Tea" from *Johnny Tremain* by Esther Forbes, copyright 1943 by Esther Forbes Hoskins. Reprinted by permission of Houghton Mifflin Company.

A sharp rat-tat on the shop door below woke Rab.

"What time's it?" he grumbled, as people do who think they are disturbed too early Sunday morning.

"Seven and past. I'll see what's up."

It was Sam Adams himself. When either cold or excited, his palsy increased. His head and hands were shaking. But his strong, seamed face, which always looked cheerful, today looked radiant. Sam Adams was so pleased that Johnny, a little naively, thought he must have word that Parliament had backed down again. The expected tea ships had not sailed.

"Look you, Johnny. I know it's the Lord's Day, but there's a placard I must have printed and posted secretly tonight. The Sons of Liberty [2] will take care of the posting, but Mr. Lorne must see to the printing. Could you run across and ask him to step over? And Rab — where's he?"

Rab was coming down the ladder.

"What's up?" said Rab sleepily.

"The first of the tea ships, the *Dart-*

---

[2] **The Sons of Liberty:** a secret patriotic association, founded in 1764 and made up of colonists who wished to overthrow English rule.

mouth, is entering the harbor. She'll be at Castle Island by nightfall."

"So they dared send them?"

"Yes."

"And the first has come?"

"Yes. God give us strength to resist. That tea cannot be allowed to land."

When Johnny got back with Mr. Lorne, Rab had Mr. Adams' text in his hands, reading it as a printer reads, thinking first of spacing and capitals, not of the meaning.

"I can set that in no time. Two hundred copies? They'll be fairly dry by nightfall."

"Ah, Mr. Lorne," said Adams, shaking hands, "without you printers the cause of liberty would be lost forever."

"Without you" — Mr. Lorne's voice shook with emotion — "there would not have been any belief in liberty to lose. I will, as always, do anything — everything you wish."

"I got word before dawn. It's the *Dartmouth* and she will be as far as Castle Island by nightfall. If that tea is landed — if that tax is paid — everything is lost. The selectmen [1] will meet all day today, and I am calling a mass meeting for tomorrow. This is the placard I will put up."

He took it from Rab's hands and read:

Friends! Brethren! Countrymen! That worst of Plagues, the detested tea shipped for this Port by the East India Company, is now arrived in the Harbor: the hour of destruction, of manly opposition to the machinations of Tyranny, stares you in the Face; every

[1] selectmen: town officers.

Friend to his Country, to Himself, and to Posterity is now called upon to meet at Faneuil [2] Hall, at nine o'clock this day [that, of course, is tomorrow, Monday] at which time the bells will ring to make united and successful resistance to this last, worst, and most destructive measure of Administration.

. . . Boston, Nov. 29, 1773

Then he said quietly: "Up to the last moment — up to the eleventh hour, we will beg the Governor's permission for the ships' return to London with their cargo. We have twenty days."

Johnny knew that by law any cargo that was not unloaded within twenty days might be seized by the customhouse and sold at auction.

"Mr. Lorne, needless to say the Observers [3] will meet tonight. There are *private* decisions to be made before the mass meeting tomorrow at nine."

Johnny pricked up his ears. Ever since he had come to Mr. Lorne's (and Rab said he might be trusted with anything — possibly with men's lives), he had now and then summoned the members of the Observers' Club. They were so close to treason they kept no list of members. Rab made Johnny memorize the twenty-two names. They met in Rab and Johnny's attic.

"Johnny," said Mr. Lorne, anxious and overanxious to please Mr. Adams, "start right out."

[2] Faneuil (fan'yəl).

[3] Observers: in this story, members of the Observers Club, a secret patriotic group that met over the office of the Boston *Observer,* the newspaper published by the printer for whom Johnny Tremain worked.

"No, sir, if you please. Noon will be better. That will give the members time to get home from church. And as usual, Johnny, make no stir. Simply say, 'Mr. So-and-So owes eight shillings for his newspaper.'"

Johnny nodded. That meant the meeting would be tonight at eight o'clock. If he said one pound eight shillings, it would mean the next night at eight. Two pounds, three and six would mean the day after at three-thirty. It gave him a feeling of excitement and pleasure to be even on the fringes of great, secret, dangerous events. . . .

Outside, Johnny could hear shouting, yelling, whistling, and the running of feet. With the coming of night, the Sons of Liberty had gone abroad, tacking up Mr. Adams' placards. Tonight Rab was not out with them, although he had been off once or twice of late helping to frighten the tea consignees [1] out of Boston to the protection of a handful of British soldiers stationed on Castle Island. Johnny was too young to be a "Son." But when the Observers met, the boys always stayed in the room below to run errands for them, and it was always Rab who mixed the fragrant punch with which the meetings ended.

All over Boston was a feeling of excitement. Everyone knew that the *Dartmouth* was but a few miles away. Great events were brewing.

Johnny went to the door to see what the clamor was. A courageous Tory was chasing the men whom he had found tacking a placard on his property. They

[1] **tea consignees:** persons to whom the tea was to be delivered.

had let him chase them thus far to dark Salt Lane and now had turned on him. Such street brawling made Johnny feel sick. He closed the door, sat down beside Rab, and began slicing lemons, oranges, and limes.

"Rab . . ."

"Yes?"

"What will they decide . . . those men upstairs?"

"You heard Sam Adams. If *possible*, the ships will sail home again with their tea. We've got twenty days."

"But if the Governor won't agree?"

"He won't. You don't know Hutchinson. I do. And you saw how happy Sam was this morning? He knows the Governor a lot better than I do."

"And then . . . and what next, Rab?"

Johnny heard blows and oaths from the street outside. His hands shook. He put down the knife so Rab wouldn't know. They were doing something — something awful — to the Tory.

"As soon as we go upstairs with our punch, we'll know. Look at Sam Adams. If he looks as pleased as an old dog fox with a fat pullet in his mouth, we'll know they've agreed to violence if everything else fails. He doesn't care much any more about our patching up our differences with England. He'd just about welcome a war."

"But the King's warships are in the harbor. They'll protect the tea. They'll fight."

"We can fight, too." Rab was putting the last delicate touches to his kettleful of brew, for tonight the punch would be hot. He was grating nutmegs, cautiously sprinkling in cloves, and breaking up cinnamon bark.

"Taste it, Johnny. That Madeira [1] Mr. Hancock brought with him is first class."

But Johnny heard a low moaning in the street, close to the shut door. That Tory, who had been so brave — and foolish — as to follow the Sons of Liberty down a black alley was alone now — was sobbing, not from pain but from humiliation. Johnny declined to taste the punch.

Mr. Lorne called down the ladder.

"Boys, ready with your punch?"

"They made up their minds fast tonight," said Rab. "I rather thought they would."

Johnny carried a handful of pewter cups and the big wooden bowl. Rab followed with two pitchers of his spicy brew.

The attic where the boys commonly slept looked strange enough with those chairs pulled out and arranged for the meeting. John Hancock sat in the moderator's chair. Beside him was Sam Adams leaning toward him, whispering and whispering.

Adams turned his face as Johnny set down the wooden bowl on the baize [2]-covered box before the moderator. Johnny had never seen an old dog fox with a fat pullet in his mouth, but he recognized the expression when he saw it. Rab poured the punch and instantly the tense silence was broken. The men were on their feet, crowding up about the bowl. Rab and Johnny were well known. Here was Paul Revere clinking his cup with Rab and John Hancock.

[1] **Madeira** (mə·dir′ə): sweet wine made in the Portuguese islands of the same name.

[2] **baize** (bāz): fabric usually used for table covers, often dyed green and made to look like felt.

"Here's to December the sixteenth."

"Hear! Hear!"

They drank to that last day, the day on which the tea must be destroyed — unless it was allowed to return to England. And Johnny saw that Sam Adams had carried them all with him. They did not honestly want the tea returned and a peaceful settlement made. They wanted grievances and more grievances . . . well, yes, armed warfare. Things were in such a state they did not honestly believe there could be any permanent, friendly settlement with the mother country. . . .

Sam Adams was standing at the far end of the room. He clapped slightly, and instantly conversation stopped.

"Gentlemen," he said, "tonight we have made our decision — and know the method by which the detested tea can be destroyed if the ships are not allowed to return. Here we have with us two of exactly — ah — the sort of boys or young men we intend to use for our great purpose. Two boys in whom we have implicit trust. If it is the wish of the assembled club members, I suggest we approach them with our proposition tonight . . . enlist their aid. Twenty days will be up before we know. We'd best get on with our plans."

The members once more took their seats, but the pewter cups of punch were passing from hand to hand. Only Will Molineaux was too restless to sit. He was muttering to himself. Ben Church sat alone. He often did. No one really liked him.

All agreed the boys were to be told.

"First," Adams said to the boys, "raise your right hands. Swear by the great name of God Himself never, for as long as you live, to divulge to anyone the secret matters now trusted to you. Do you so swear?"

The boys swore.

"There's no chance — not one — those ships will be allowed to return. The mass meetings that will be held almost daily demanding the return of the tea are to arouse public opinion and to persuade the world we did not turn to violence until every other course had been blocked to us. When the twenty days are up, on the night of the sixteenth of December, those ships are going to be boarded. That tea will be dumped in Boston Harbor. For each ship, the *Dartmouth*, the *Eleanor*, and the brig, the *Beaver*, we will need thirty stout, honest, fearless men and boys. Will you be one, Rab?"

He did not say Rab and Johnny, as the younger boy noticed. Was this because he thought Johnny too cripple-handed for chopping open sea chests — or merely because he knew Rab better, and he was older?

"Of course, sir."

"How many other boys could you find for the night's work? Strong and trustworthy boys — for if one ounce of tea is stolen, the whole thing becomes a robbery — not a protest."

Rab thought.

"Eight or ten tonight, but give me a little time so I can feel about a bit, and I can furnish fifteen or twenty."

"Boys who can keep their mouths shut?"

"Yes."

Paul Revere said, "I can furnish twenty or more from about North Square."

"Not one is to be told in advance just what the work will be, nor who the others are, nor the names of the men who instigated this tea party — that is, the gentlemen gathered here tonight. Simply, as they love their country and liberty and hate tyranny, they are to gather in this shop on the night of December sixteenth, carrying with them such disguises as they can think of, and each armed with an ax or hatchet."

"It will be as you say."

The discussion became more general. Each of these three groups must have a leader, men who could keep discipline.

"I'll go, for one," said Paul Revere.

Doctor Warren warned him. "Look here, Paul, it has been decided this work must be done by apprentices, strangers — little known about Boston. The East India Company may bring suit. If you are recognized —— "

"I'll risk it."

Uncle Lorne was motioning to the boys to leave the conspirators. They did not want to leave, but they did. . . .

Almost every day and sometimes all day, the mass meetings at Old South Church went on. Tempers grew higher and higher. Boston was swept with a passion it had not known since the Boston Massacre three years before. Riding this wild storm were Sam Adams and his trusty henchmen, directing it, building up the anger until, although the matter was not publicly mentioned, they would all see the only thing left for them to do was to destroy the tea.

Sometimes Rab and Johnny went to these meetings. It happened they were there when the sheriff arrived and bade the meeting forthwith to disperse. He said it was lawless and treasonable. This proclamation from Governor Hutchinson was met with howls and hisses. They voted to disobey the order.

Sometimes the boys slipped over to Griffin's Wharf. By the eighth of December, the *Eleanor* had joined the *Dartmouth*. These were strange ships. They had unloaded their cargoes — except the tea. The town of Boston had ordered them not to unload the tea, and the law stated they could not leave until they had unloaded. Nor would the Governor give them a pass to return to England. At Castle Island, the British Colonel Leslie had orders to fire upon them if they attempted to sneak out of the harbor. The *Active* and the *Kingfisher*, British men-of-war, stood by ready to blast them out of the water if they obeyed the town and returned to London with the tea. The ships were held at Griffin's Wharf as though under an enchantment.

Here was none of the usual hustle and bustle. Few of the crew were in sight, but hundreds of spectators gathered every day merely to stare at them. Johnny saw Rotch, the twenty-three-year-old Quaker who owned the *Dartmouth*, running about in despair. The Governor would not let him leave. The town would not let him unload. Between them he was a ruined man. He feared a mob would burn his ship. There was no mob, and night and day armed citizens guarded the ships. They would see to it that no tea was smuggled ashore and that no harm was done to the ships. Back and forth paced the guard. Many of their faces were familiar to Johnny. One day even John Hancock took his turn with a musket on his shoulder, and the next night he saw Paul Revere.

Then on the fifteenth, the third of the tea ships arrived. This was the brig, the *Beaver*.

The next day, the sixteenth, Johnny woke to hear the rain drumming sadly on the roof, and soon enough, once more he heard all the bells of Boston cling-clanging, bidding the inhabitants come once more, and for the last time, to Old South to demand the peaceful return of the ships to England.

By nightfall, when the boys Rab had selected began silently to congregate in the office of the *Observer*, behind locked doors, the rain stopped. Many of them Johnny knew. When they started to assume their disguises, smooch their faces with soot, paint them with red paint, pull on nightcaps, old frocks, torn jackets, and blankets with holes cut for their arms, they began giggling and laughing at each other. Rab could

silence them with one look, however. No one passing outside the shop must guess that toward twenty boys were at that moment dressing themselves as "Indians."

Johnny had taken some pains with his costume. He had sewed for hours on the red blanket Mrs. Lorne had let him cut up, and he had a fine mop of feathers standing upright in the old knitted cap he would wear on his head. But when he started to put on his disguise, Rab said no, wait a minute.

Then Rab divided the boys into three groups. Beside each ship at the wharf they would find a band of men. "You," he said to one group of boys, "will join the boarding party for the *Dartmouth*. You for the *Eleanor*. You for the *Beaver*." Each boy was to speak softly to the leader and say, "Me know you," for that was the countersign. They would know the three leaders because each of them would wear a white handkerchief about the neck and a red string about the right wrist. Then he turned to Johnny.

"You can run faster than any of us.

Somehow get to Old South Church. Mr. Rotch will be back from begging once more the Governor's permission for the ships to sail within a half-hour. Now, Johnny, you are to listen to what Sam Adams says next. Look you, if Mr. Adams then says, 'Now may God help my country,' come back here. Then we will each take off our disguises and go home and say nothing. But if he says, 'This meeting can do nothing more to save the country,' you are to get out of that crowd as fast as you can and, as soon as you get into Cornhill, begin to blow upon this silver whistle. Run as fast as you are able back here to me, and keep on blowing. I'll have boys posted in dark corners, close enough to the church but outside the crowd. Maybe we'll hear you the first time you blow."

About Old South, standing in the streets and inside the church, waiting

for Rotch to return with the very last appeal that could be made to the Governor, was the greatest crowd Boston had ever seen — thousands upon thousands. There was not a chance, not one, that Johnny could ever squirm or wriggle his way inside, but he pushed and shoved until he stood close to one of the doors. Farther than this he could not go — unless he walked on people's heads. It was dark already.

Josiah Quincy's voice rang out from within. "I see the clouds roll and the lightning play, and to that God who rides the whirlwind and directs the storm, I commit my country. . . ."

The words thrilled Johnny, but this was not what he was waiting for, and it was not Sam Adams speaking. He was bothered with only one thing. Quincy had a beautiful carrying voice. It was one thing to hear him and another Sam Adams, who did not speak well at all.

The crowd made way for a chaise. "Rotch is back! Make way for Rotch!" Mr. Rotch passed close to Johnny. He was so young that he looked almost ready to cry. This was proof enough that the Governor had still refused. Such a turmoil followed Rotch's entry, Johnny could not hear any one particular voice. What chance had he of hearing Sam Adams' words? He had his whistle in his hand, but he was so jammed into the crowd about the door that he did not believe he would be able to get his hand to his mouth.

"Silence." That was Quincy again. "Silence, silence. Mr. Adams will speak." Johnny twisted and turned and brought the whistle to his lips.

And suddenly there was silence.

Johnny guessed there were many in that crowd who, like himself, were hanging on those words. Seemingly Mr. Adams was calmly accepting defeat, dismissing the meeting, for now he was saying:

"This meeting can do nothing more to save the country."

Johnny gave his first shrill blast on his whistle, and he heard whistles and cries seemingly in all directions, Indian war whoops and "Boston Harbor a teapot tonight!" "Hurrah for Griffin's Wharf!" "Salt-water tea!" "Hi, Mohawks, get your axes and pay no taxes!"

Johnny was only afraid all would be over before Rab and his henchmen could get to the wharf. Still shrilling on the whistle, he fought and floundered against the tide of the crowd. It was sweeping toward Griffin's Wharf, he struggling to get back to Salt Lane. Now he was afraid the others would have gone on without him. After all, Rab might have decided that Johnny's legs and ears were better than his hands — and deliberately let him do the work that best suited him. Johnny pushed open the door.

Rab was alone. He had Johnny's blanket coat and his ridiculous befeathered knitted cap in his hands.

"Quick!" he said, smooched his face with soot, and drew a red line across his mouth running from ear to ear. Johnny saw Rab's eyes through the mask of soot. They were glowing with that dark excitement he had seen but twice before. His lips were parted. His teeth looked sharp and white as an animal's. In spite of his calm demeanor and calm voice, he was charged and surcharged with a will to action, a readiness to take and enjoy any desperate chance. Rab had come terrifyingly alive.

They flung themselves out of the shop.

"Roundabout!" cried Rab. He meant they would get to the wharf by back alleys.

"Come, follow me. *Now* we're really going to run."

He flew up Salt Lane in the opposite direction from the waterfront. Now they were flinging themselves down back alleys, faster and faster. Once they had a glimpse of a blacksmith shop and other "Indians" clamoring for soot for their faces. Now they were slipping over a back-yard fence, now at last on the waterfront, Sea Street, Flounder Alley. They were running so fast it seemed more like a dream of flying than reality.

The day had started with rain and then there had been clouds, but as they reached Griffin's Wharf the moon, full and white, broke free of the clouds. The three ships, the silent hundreds gathering upon the wharf, all were dipped in the pure white light. The crowds were becoming thousands, and there was not one there but guessed what was to be done, and all approved.

Rab was grunting out of the side of his mouth to a thick-set, active-looking man, who — Johnny would have known anywhere, by his walk and the confident lift of his head — was Mr. Revere. "Me know you."

"Me know you," Johnny repeated this countersign and took his place behind Mr. Revere. The other boys, held up by the crowd, began arriving, and more men and boys. But Johnny guessed that many who were now quietly joining one of those three groups were acting on the spur of the moment, seeing what was up. They had blacked their faces, seized axes, and come along. They were behaving as quietly and were as obedient to their leaders as those who had been so carefully picked for this work of destruction.

There was a boatswain's whistle, and, in silence, one group boarded the *Dartmouth*. The *Eleanor* and the *Beaver* had to be warped[1] in to the wharf. Johnny was close to Mr. Revere's heels. He heard him calling for the captain, promising him, in the jargon everyone talked that night, that not one thing should be damaged on the ship except only the tea, but the captain and all his crew had best stay in the cabin until the work was over.

Captain Hall shrugged and did as he was told, leaving his cabin boy to hand over the keys to the hold. The boy was grinning with pleasure. The "tea party" was not unexpected.

"I'll show you," the boy volunteered, "how to work them hoists. I'll fetch lanterns, mister."

The winches[2] rattled, and the heavy chests began to appear — one hundred and fifty of them. As some men worked in the hold, others broke open the chests and flung the tea into the harbor. But one thing made them unexpected difficulty. The tea inside the chests was wrapped in heavy canvas. The axes went through the wood easily enough — the canvas made endless

---

[1] **warped:** moved into position by hauling on a rope (a *warp*).
[2] **winches:** machines for lifting and pulling, turned by cranks.

trouble. Johnny had never worked so hard in his life. . . .

Not a quarter of a mile away, quite visible in the moonlight, rode the *Active* and the *Kingfisher*. Any moment the tea party might be interrupted by British marines. There was no landing party. Governor Hutchinson had been wise in not sending for their help.

The work on the *Dartmouth* and the *Eleanor* finished about the same time. The *Beaver* took longer, for she had not had time to unload the rest of her cargo, and great care was taken not to injure it. Just as Johnny was about to go over to see if he could help on the *Beaver*, Mr. Revere whispered to him. "Go get brooms. Clean-um deck."

Johnny and a parcel of boys brushed the deck until it was clean as a parlor floor. Then Mr. Revere called the captain to come up and inspect. The tea was utterly gone, but Captain Hall agreed that beyond that there had not been the slightest damage.

It was close upon dawn when the work on all three ships was done. And yet the great, silent audience on the wharf — men, women, and children — had not gone home. As the three groups came off the ships, they formed in fours along the wharf, their axes on their shoulders. Then a hurrah went up and a fife began to play. This was almost the first sound Johnny had heard since the tea party started — except only the crash of axes into sea chests, the squeak of hoists, and a few grunted orders.

He saw Sam Adams standing quietly in the crowd, pretending to be a most innocent bystander. It looked to Johnny as if the dog fox had eaten a couple of fat pullets and had a third in his mouth.

As they started marching back to the center of town, they passed the Coffin House at the head of Griffin's Wharf. A window opened.

"Well, boys," said a voice, so cold one hardly knew whether he spoke in anger or not, "you've had a fine, pleasant evening for your Indian caper, haven't you? But mind . . . you've got to pay the fiddler yet."

It was the British Admiral Montague.

"Come on down here," someone yelled, "and we'll settle that score tonight."

The admiral pulled in his head and slapped down the window.

Johnny and Rab knew, and men like the Observers knew, but best of all Sam Adams knew, that the fiddler would have to be paid. England, unable to find the individuals who had destroyed this valuable property, would punish the whole town of Boston — make every man, woman, and child, Tories and Whigs alike, suffer until this tea was paid for. Nor was she likely to back down on her claim that she might tax the colonists any way she pleased.

Next day, all over Boston, boys and men, some of them with a little paint still showing behind their ears, were so lame they could scarce move their fingers, but none of them — not one — told what it was that had lamed them so. They would stand about and wonder who "those Mohawks" might have been, or what the British Parliament might do next, but never say what they themselves had been doing, for each was sworn to secrecy.

Only Paul Revere showed no signs of the hard physical strain he had been under all the night before. Not long after dawn he had started on horseback for New York and Philadelphia with an account of the Tea Party. He could chop open tea chests all night, and ride all day.

A PROTEST

1. What event brought Sam Adams to the print shop early on Sunday morning? What did he want done? What did the opening events of the story reveal about Sam Adams?

2. Why was the Tory beaten? How did Johnny feel about this incident?

3. What more do you learn about Sam Adams from Rab's conversation with Johnny while the punch was being prepared? How did the members of the Observers' Club feel about America's relations with England? What plan had the Observers made for the tea ships? How was Rab part of this plan?

4. Describe the atmosphere in Boston during the days preceding the sixteenth of December. What assignment did Rab give Johnny on the sixteenth?

5. Why were the men and boys who boarded the British ships dressed as Indians? Describe what happened on the ships. What orders did the men and boys strictly obey?

6. What warning did the British admiral give the Americans?

7. This account of the famous Boston Tea Party is part history and part fiction. The episode of the Boston Tea Party itself, one of the stirring events in American history, is true. What characters in this story are historical people? In what ways did they influence the course of American history? What qualities in these men are admired by Americans today?

8. Which historical figure do you think is portrayed most sympathetically in this

story? How would you describe Miss Forbes's attitude toward Sam Adams? toward the British?

9. By reading historical fiction, you can, in a sense, live through great moments of the past. How would you have acted if you had lived in 1773 and had been an American, like Johnny Tremain? if you had been an Englishman, like Captain Hall? if you had been a shipowner, like Mr. Rotch?

WORDS:
    VARIATIONS AMONG SYNONYMS

Synonyms are words that are similar in meaning. However, synonyms rarely have precisely the same meaning. For example, the words *rebellion, revolution,* and *mutiny* are synonyms, but they are not defined in exactly the same way. They are alike in that they all refer to an organized effort to overthrow a ruling power, but a *rebellion* is an unsuccessful uprising, while a *revolution* is successful, resulting in an actual change in government. A *mutiny,* on the other hand, is an uprising against a military or naval authority. Use the words *rebellion, revolution,* and *mutiny* in sentences to illustrate their distinctive meanings.

Use a dictionary to find how the synonyms *neglect, overlook,* and *ignore* vary in meaning. Use each word in a sentence to illustrate its distinctive meaning.

COMPOSITION: EXPOSITION

You have already examined and written paragraphs of description (which give a word picture of a person, place, or object) and paragraphs of narration (which tell a story or relate events). There is another type of writing, called exposition. The main purpose of exposition is to set forth an explanation, or to present information. Much of the writing in science books, for example, is exposition.

When you write a paragraph that explains something, you will probably introduce your topic in the opening sentence. In the rest of the paragraph you will present specific information about this topic.

Write a paragraph in which you present the specific reasons why the Americans started the Boston Tea Party, as described in this story. Introduce your paragraph with a sentence that states in a general way what you are going to write about.

THOUGHTFUL READING: RECOGNIZING PROPAGANDA

The placard written by Sam Adams is a good example of propaganda. Propaganda tries to persuade people to think and to act in a certain way. One way it does this is by using words that arouse people's feelings. Such words are sometimes referred to as loaded words. Look at the placard:

> "Friends! Brethren! Countrymen! That worst of Plagues, the detested tea shipped for this Port by the East India Company, is now arrived in the Harbor: the hour of destruction, of manly opposition to the machinations of Tyranny, stares you in the Face; every Friend to his Country, to Himself, and to Posterity, is now called upon to meet at Faneuil Hall, at nine o'clock this day, at which time the bells will ring to make united and successful resistance to this last, worst, and most destructive measure of Administration."

By using the words *friends, brethren,* and *countrymen,* Adams wins people to his side almost immediately. Then, he doesn't say just "tea," but the *"worst* of *Plagues,"* *"detested* tea." What other words and phrases in this paragraph would appeal strongly to people's feelings? What does the paragraph suggest about those who do *not* attend the meeting?

Paul Revere's Ride

HENRY WADSWORTH LONGFELLOW

By 1775, feelings between the colonists and the British had become in-increasingly bitter. On the night of April 18, 1775, British soldiers were sent out to raid the Massachusetts towns of Lexington and Concord. But the colonists had been warned, and American farmers, fully armed, met the British soldiers. About eighty years after this event, Longfellow wrote a poem telling the story of how the colonists were warned. His now-famous poem has immortalized the midnight ride of Paul Revere.

Listen, my children, and you shall hear
Of the midnight ride of Paul Revere,
On the eighteenth of April, in seventy-five;
Hardly a man is now alive
Who remembers that famous day and year.   5

He said to his friend, "If the British march
By land or sea from the town tonight,
Hang a lantern aloft in the belfry arch
Of the North Church tower, as a signal light —
One, if by land, and two, if by sea;   10
And I on the opposite shore will be,
Ready to ride and spread the alarm
Through every Middlesex village and farm,
For the country folk to be up and to arm."

Then he said "Good night!" and with muffled oar   15
Silently rowed to the Charlestown shore,
Just as the moon rose over the bay,
Where, swinging wide at her moorings, lay
The *Somerset*, British man-of-war:
A phantom ship, with each mast and spar   20
Across the moon, like a prison bar,
And a huge black hulk, that was magnified
By its own reflection in the tide.

Meanwhile, his friend, through alley and street,
Wanders and watches with eager ears,   25
Till in the silence around him he hears

The muster of men at the barrack door,
The sound of arms, and the tramp of feet,
And the measured tread of the grenadiers
Marching down to their boats on the shore.   30

Then he climbed the tower of the Old North Church
By the wooden stairs, with stealthy tread,
To the belfry chamber overhead,
And startled the pigeons from their perch
On the somber rafters, that round him made   35
Masses and moving shapes of shade —
By the trembling ladder, steep and tall,
To the highest window in the wall,
Where he paused to listen and look down
A moment on the roofs of the town,   40
And the moonlight flowing over all.

Beneath, in the churchyard, lay the dead,
In their night encampment on the hill,
Wrapped in silence so deep and still
That he could hear, like a sentinel's tread,   45
The watchful night wind, as it went
Creeping along from tent to tent,
And seeming to whisper, "All is well!"
A moment only he feels the spell
Of the place and the hour, the secret dread   50
Of the lonely belfry and the dead;
For suddenly all his thoughts are bent
On a shadowy something far away,
Where the river widens to meet the bay —
A line of black, that bends and floats   55
On the rising tide, like a bridge of boats.

Meanwhile, impatient to mount and ride,
Booted and spurred, with a heavy stride
On the opposite shore walked Paul Revere.
Now he patted his horse's side,   60
Now gazed at the landscape far and near,
Then, impetuous, stamped the earth,
And turned and tightened his saddle girth;
But mostly he watched with eager search
The belfry tower of the Old North Church,   65

As it rose above the graves on the hill,
Lonely and spectral and somber and still.
And lo! as he looks, on the belfry's height
A glimmer, and then a gleam of light.
He springs to the saddle, the bridle he turns,   70
But lingers and gazes, till full on his sight
A second lamp in the belfry burns!

A hurry of hoofs in a village street,
A shape in the moonlight, a bulk in the dark,
And beneath, from the pebbles, in passing, a spark   75
Struck out by a steed flying fearless and fleet:
That was all! And yet, through the gloom and the light,
The fate of a nation was riding that night;
And the spark struck out by that steed, in his flight,
Kindled the land into flame with its heat.   80

He has left the village and mounted the steep,
And beneath him, tranquil and broad and deep,

Is the Mystic,° meeting the ocean tides;
And under the alders that skirt its edge,
Now soft on the sand, now loud on the ledge,   85
Is heard the tramp of his steed as he rides.

It was twelve by the village clock,
When he crossed the bridge into Medford town.
He heard the crowing of the cock,
And the barking of the farmer's dog,   90
And felt the damp of the river fog
That rises after the sun goes down.

It was one by the village clock,
When he galloped into Lexington.
He saw the gilded weathercock   95
Swim in the moonlight as he passed,
And the meetinghouse windows, blank and bare,
Gaze at him with a spectral glare,
As if they already stood aghast
At the bloody work they would look upon.   100

It was two by the village clock,
When he came to the bridge in Concord town.
He heard the bleating of the flock,
And the twitter of birds among the trees,
And felt the breath of the morning breeze   105
Blowing over the meadows brown.
And one was safe and asleep in his bed,
Who at the bridge would be first to fall,
Who that day would be lying dead,
Pierced by a British musket ball.   110

You know the rest. In the books you have read
How the British Regulars fired and fled —
How the farmers gave them ball for ball,
From behind each fence and farmyard wall,
Chasing the Redcoats down the lane,   115
Then crossing the fields to emerge again
Under the trees at the turn of the road,
And only pausing to fire and load.

83. **Mystic:** a river flowing into Boston harbor.

So through the night rode Paul Revere;
And so through the night went his cry of alarm   120
To every Middlesex village and farm —
A cry of defiance and not of fear —
A voice in the darkness, a knock at the door,
And a word that shall echo forevermore!
For, borne on the night wind of the past,   125
Through all our history, to the last,
In the hour of darkness and peril and need,
The people will waken and listen to hear
The hurrying hoofbeats of that steed,
And the midnight message of Paul Revere.   130

AN AMERICAN HERO

1. What did Paul Revere say to his friend before he rowed across the bay?

2. How did the friend get his information? Describe his ascent to the tower of the Old North Church. How did Paul Revere behave as he waited for the signal? What signal was given?

3. In lines 77–80, Longfellow uses poetic language to describe the immediate effect of Paul Revere's ride. Explain what these lines mean. What event in American history is referred to in line 80?

4. In lines 125–30, Longfellow describes the long-range effects of the ride. Explain these lines in your own words. Do you think Longfellow was correct?

5. Do Paul Revere's actions in this poem fit his character as it was depicted in "Salt-Water Tea" (page 159)?

6. What other heroes are remembered from the early days in American history? Which heroes or leaders from recent American history would you rank with Paul Revere?

WORDS THAT CREATE ATMOSPHERE

Longfellow wanted you to sense an atmosphere of mystery and danger as Paul Revere and his friend waited for the British to reveal their plans. To help create this atmosphere, Longfellow used words like "*muffled* oar," "*silently* rowed," and "*phantom* ship." What other words in lines 15–56 build up this atmosphere of mystery and danger? The mood of the poem changes in line 57, as the scene switches entirely to Paul Revere waiting on the opposite shore. What words help you to sense the rider's impatience? What words suggest an atmosphere of excitement as Paul Revere sets off on his ride? What words help you to hear the lonely, early-morning sounds that Paul Revere heard?

COMPOSITION: EXPOSITION

In a paragraph of exposition, a writer may present information about an event by giving details which answer the questions *what*, *why*, or *how*. The paragraph may explain *what* was done; it may explain *why* something was done; it may explain *how* something was done. Sometimes, of course, a paragraph may answer all three questions. Write a brief paragraph about Paul Revere's ride, explaining what he did and why and how he did it. Your topic sentence might be: *Paul Revere heroically warned American farmers and villagers that the British were coming.*

The Concord Hymn

RALPH WALDO EMERSON

The first real battle of the Revolutionary War was fought alongside a small bridge in the town of Concord, Massachusetts. There, on April 19, 1775, American farmers forced British soldiers to retreat. A memorial statue was later erected alongside the bridge, and the following poem was written for the dedication ceremonies.

By the rude bridge that arched the flood,
  Their flag to April's breeze unfurled,
Here once the embattled farmers stood,
  And fired the shot heard round the world.

The foe long since in silence slept;   5
  Alike the conqueror silent sleeps;
And Time the ruined bridge has swept
  Down the dark stream which seaward creeps.

On this green bank, by this soft stream,
  We set today a votive stone;
That memory may their deed redeem,
  When, like our sires, our sons are gone.

Spirit, that made those heroes dare
  To die, and leave their children free,
Bid Time and Nature gently spare   15
  The shaft we raise to them and thee.

A DEDICATION

1. What is meant by "flood" in line 1?
2. What happened to the foe, the conqueror, and the bridge?
3. The word *votive* (line 10) can mean "given in devotion." What does "votive stone" refer to? Why was this stone being set?
4. What request is made in the last stanza? To whom is this stanza addressed?
5. Have any other shots been "heard round the world"? What other people died in order to "leave their children free"?

EXAGGERATION FOR EFFECT

In the first stanza of this poem, Emerson says that the farmers fired the shot that was "heard round the world." He said this for effect. How does this statement bring out the importance of this battle? In what ways *were* the farmers' shots "heard round the world"? Writers often use exaggeration for effect. In fact we all use exaggeration in our everyday speech, in expressions like "She wept a bucket of tears," or "He hit the ball a mile." Can you think of other common exaggerations?

Old Ironsides

OLIVER WENDELL HOLMES

The United States Navy became equal to the best in the world as a result of a battle during the War of 1812. In this battle, an American ship named the *Constitution* met a British ship named the *Guerrière*. In thirty minutes, the British ship was a sinking wreck. So slight was the damage done to the *Constitution*, that the ship became known as Old Ironsides. Old Ironsides went on to win more victories, but in 1830 the ship was called unseaworthy and condemned to be scrapped. Holmes, then an unknown poet and only twenty-one years old, wrote the following poem in protest. It so roused public opinion that Old Ironsides was saved.

> Aye, tear her tattered ensign° down!
>   Long has it waved on high,
> And many an eye has danced to see
>   That banner in the sky;
> Beneath it rung the battle shout,   5
>   And burst the cannon's roar —
> The meteor of the ocean air
>   Shall sweep the clouds no more.

1. **ensign** (en'sĭn): flag.

Her decks, once red with heroes' blood,
  Where knelt the vanquished foe,   10
When winds were hurrying o'er the flood,
  And waves were white below,
No more shall feel the victor's tread,
  Or know the conquered knee —
The harpies of the shore shall pluck   15
  The eagle of the sea!

Oh, better that her shattered hulk
  Should sink beneath the wave;
Her thunders shook the mighty deep,
  And there should be her grave;   20
Nail to the mast her holy flag,
  Set every threadbare sail,
And give her to the god of storms,
  The lightning and the gale!

AN APPEAL

1. Which lines from the first two stanzas suggest that great events had happened on the *Constitution?* What does the adjective *tattered* in the first line suggest to you?

2. In the first line the poet seems to be saying, "All right, go ahead and scrap the ship." Does he really mean what he says? How do you know?

3. Can you explain the names the poet gives to the ship in lines 7 and 16?

4. The word *harpies* in line 15 refers to evil, loathesome bird-women in Greek mythology, who snatched away the souls of the dead or stole people's food. Whom is Holmes calling "harpies"?

5. What better end does Holmes suggest for the ship?

6. What historic things or places would you like to see preserved from destruction?

SENTENCES IN POETRY

In order to get certain special effects, poets sometimes reverse the word order of a sentence. Instead of a subject-verb order they may use a verb-subject order, as in line 5 of "Old Ironsides":

          V   S

‖ "Beneath it *rung* the battle *shout*"

Rewrite this line so that the subject precedes the verb. Listed below are two other lines in the poem, in which the poet has placed the verb before the subject.

‖ "And burst the cannon's roar" (line 6)
‖ "Where knelt the vanquished foe" (line 10)

Rewrite each of these lines so that the subject precedes the verb. What happens to the rhyme and rhythm of the poem when these rewritten lines are used in place of the originals?

The American Heritage in Painting

At first, settlers in the American colonies were so busy just building new homes and communities that they had almost no time left over to cultivate the arts. By the middle of the eighteenth century, however, wealthy landowners and merchants in Boston and other prosperous towns had money to spend on portraits of themselves and their families, as well as on costly furnishings for their homes. Gradually, native artists found it possible to make a living at their work. One of these was the portrait painter John Singleton Copley. Another was the silversmith Paul Revere. Each of them came from a humble Boston background, but the fine quality of their work soon made them known throughout New England.

In 1766, nine years before Paul Revere was to make his famous ride from Charlestown to Lexington, he sat for his portrait by Copley (PLATE 1). According to custom, Revere should have posed in a formal attitude, wearing a fine coat and waistcoat, but Copley posed him instead in his shirtsleeves, at work in his shop. On the table in front of Revere are the tools he used to engrave designs on fine silver, such as the teapot he holds in his hand. Yet notice that in spite of Revere's informal pose, nothing in the composition has been left to chance. Copley arranged every detail with the utmost care.

On the eve of the Revolutionary War, Copley left the colonies to study abroad, eventually settling permanently in London. There he met another American artist named Benjamin West, who had been living in England since 1763 and had been appointed historical painter to King George III in 1772. West was very hospitable to many visiting American artists, often giving them technical training and allowing them the use of his studio. One of his students during the early 1780's was John Trumbull of Connecticut, who had served as an American officer in the early years of the Revolutionary War. After peace had been signed between England and the new United States, West and Thomas Jefferson urged Trumbull to depict the great battle scenes of the war as historical records. In West's studio, Trumbull painted *The Battle of Bunker's Hill* (PLATES 2 and 3), the first of a series he was to work on for a number of years. To make his pictures historically accurate, Trumbull journeyed through Europe and America, painting portrait sketches of many of the people who had been present at the various battles. Quite consciously, he set about to create an "American heritage" by glorifying in dramatic stagelike scenes the bravery of the citizens who had fought in the Revolution.

The peace that followed the Revolution and continued into the first half of the nineteenth century created an atmosphere for settling and working the land. Two artists of this period, William Sidney Mount and George Caleb Bingham, painted subjects which reflect the everyday life of farmers and other working people. Mount, who spent most of his life on Long Island, built a studio on wheels which he drove about the countryside in search of subjects for his pictures. Bingham, on the other hand, looked for his subjects along the Missouri and Mississippi rivers, among the frontier settlements he had known as a boy.

Sometimes Mount and Bingham chose very similar subjects. In both Mount's *Raffling for the Goose* (PLATE 4) and Bingham's *Shooting for the Beef* (PLATE 5) country folk are competing for a prize — in one by gambling, in the other through marksmanship. The composition of Mount's picture is relatively simple: light and shadow, as well as the grouping of figures, converge at the center of the picture. The shelf in the background seems unimportant, as if put there only to fill up empty space. The composition of Bingham's *Shooting for the Beef*, however, is quite subtle and complex. The main weight is on the extreme left side. Yet the balance is restored because of the way Bingham has made the action of the picture sweep toward the right, following the aim of the marksman toward his target. And notice how prominently the trees and man in the distance are silhouetted against the open sky.

During the early nineteenth century many artists were self-taught. Some of these we refer to as "primitives" because of the naive character of their work. The most famous of these painters was Edward Hicks, who earned his living as a sign painter and Quaker preacher, but who in his spare time painted historical and Biblical landscapes. *The Peaceable Kingdom* (PLATE 6), a picture which he painted in many versions, is one of his most delightful fantasies.

PLATE 1. JOHN SINGLETON COPLEY (American, 1738–1815): *Paul Revere*. About 1765–70. Oil on canvas, 34⅞ x 28½ inches. (Courtesy, Museum of Fine Arts, Boston, Gift of the Revere family)

PLATE 2. JOHN TRUMBULL (American, 1756–1843): *The Battle of Bunker's Hill*. 1786. Oil on canvas, 25 x 34 inches. (Yale University Art Gallery, New Haven, Connecticut)

PLATE 3. Detail from PLATE 2.

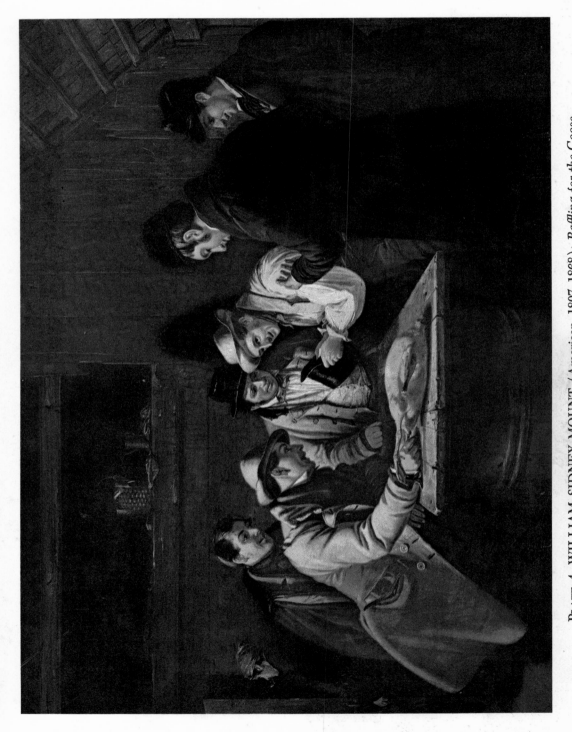

PLATE 4. WILLIAM SIDNEY MOUNT (American, 1807–1868): *Raffling for the Goose.* 1837. Oil on wood, 17 x 23⅝ inches. (The Metropolitan Museum of Art, New York, Gift of John D. Crimmins, 1897)

184

PLATE 5. GEORGE CALEB BINGHAM (American, 1811–1879): *Shooting for the Beef.* 1850. Oil on canvas, 33½ x 49¾ inches. (The Brooklyn Museum, Brooklyn, New York)

PLATE 6. EDWARD HICKS (American, 1780–1849): *The Peaceable Kingdom*. About 1833. Oil on canvas, 17¼ x 23½ inches. (Worcester Art Museum, Worcester, Massachusetts)

The Man Without a Country

EDWARD EVERETT HALE

One of the most famous American stories about patriotism is this fictional story about the tragic ordeal of Philip Nolan.

I SUPPOSE THAT very few readers of the New York *Herald* of August 13, 1863, observed in an obscure corner, among the "Deaths," the announcement:

NOLAN. Died on board the U.S. Corvette *Levant*, Lat. 2° 11′ S., Long. 131° W., on May 11, PHILIP NOLAN.

Hundreds of readers would have paused at that announcement, if it had read thus: "DIED, MAY 11, THE MAN WITHOUT A COUNTRY." For it was as "The Man Without a Country" that poor Philip Nolan had generally been known by the officers who had him in charge during some fifty years, as, indeed, by all the men who sailed under them.

There can now be no possible harm in telling this poor creature's story. Reason enough there has been till now for very strict secrecy, the secrecy of honor itself, among the gentlemen of the navy who have had Nolan in charge. And certainly it speaks well for the profession and the personal honor of its members that to the press this man's story has been wholly unknown — and, I think, to the country at large also. This I do know, that no naval officer has mentioned Nolan in his report of a cruise.

But, there is no need for secrecy any longer. Now the poor creature is dead, it seems to me worthwhile to tell a little of his story, by way of showing young Americans of today what it is to be "A Man Without a Country."

NOLAN'S FATAL WISH

Philip Nolan was as fine a young officer as there was in the "Legion of the West," as the Western division of our army was then called. When Aaron Burr [1] made his first dashing expedition down to New Orleans in 1805, he met this gay, bright, young fellow. Burr marked him, talked to him, walked with him, took him a day or two's voyage in his flatboat, and, in short, fascinated him. For the next year, barrack life was very tame to poor Nolan. He occasionally availed himself of the permission the great man had given him to write to him. Long, stilted letters the poor boy wrote and rewrote and copied. But never a line did he have in reply. The other boys in the garrison sneered at him, because he lost the fun which they found in shooting or rowing while he was working away on these grand letters to his grand friend. But before long, the young fellow had his revenge. For this time His Excellency, Honorable Aaron Burr, appeared again under a very different aspect. There were rumors that he had an army behind him and an empire before him. At that time the youngsters all envied him. Burr had not been talking twenty minutes with the commander before he asked him to send for Lieutenant Nolan. Then, after a little talk, he asked Nolan if he could show him something of the great river and the plans for the new post. He asked Nolan to take him out in his skiff to show him a canebrake or a cottonwood tree, as he said — really to win him over; and by the time the sail was over, Nolan was enlisted body and soul. From that time, though he did not yet know it, he lived as a man without a country.

What Burr meant to do I know no more than you. It is none of our business just now. Only, when the grand catastrophe came, Burr's treason trial at Richmond, Fort Adams [2] got up a string of courts-martial on the officers there. One and another of the colonels and majors were tried, and, to fill out the list, little Nolan, against whom there was evidence enough that he was sick of the service, had been willing to be false to it, and would have obeyed any order to march anywhere had the order been signed, "By command of his Exc. A. Burr." The courts dragged on. The big flies [3] escaped — rightly for all I know. Nolan was proved guilty enough, yet you and I would never have heard of him but that, when the president of the court asked him at the close whether he wished to say anything to show that he had always been faithful to the United States, he cried out in a fit of frenzy:

"Damn the United States! I wish I may never hear of the United States again!"

NOLAN'S PUNISHMENT

I suppose he did not know how the words shocked old Colonel Morgan, who was holding the court. Half the officers who sat in it had served through the Revolution, and their lives had been risked for the very idea which he cursed in his madness. He, on his part, had grown up in the West of those days. He had been educated

---

[1] **Aaron Burr** (1756–1836): a prominent figure in his day, at one time suspected of plotting to set up an empire in the Southwest.

[2] **Fort Adams**: Nolan was stationed at Fort Adams.

[3] **the big flies**: Burr and the other important men who may have plotted with him.

on a plantation where the finest company was a Spanish officer or a French merchant from Orleans. His education had been perfected in commercial expeditions to Veracruz,[1] and I think he told me his father once hired an Englishman to be a private tutor for a winter on the plantation. He had spent half his youth with an older brother, hunting horses in Texas; and to him *United States* was scarcely a reality. I do not excuse Nolan; I only explain to the reader why he damned his country and wished he might never hear her name again.

From that moment, September 23, 1807, till the day he died, May 11, 1863, he never heard her name again. For that half-century and more, he was a man without a country.

Old Morgan, as I said, was terribly shocked. If Nolan had compared George Washington to Benedict Arnold, or had cried, "God save King George," Morgan would not have felt worse. He called the court into his private room and returned in fifteen minutes, with a face like a sheet, to say:

"Prisoner, hear the sentence of the court! The court decides, subject to the approval of the President, that you never hear the name of the United States again."

Nolan laughed. But nobody else laughed. Old Morgan was too solemn, and the whole room was hushed dead as night for a minute. Even Nolan lost his swagger in a moment. Then Morgan added:

"Mr. Marshal, take the prisoner to

Orleans, in an armed boat, and deliver him to the naval commander there."

The marshal gave his orders and the prisoner was taken out of court.

"Mr. Marshal," continued old Morgan, "see that no one mentions the United States to the prisoner. Mr. Marshal, make my respects to Lieutenant Mitchell at Orleans, and request him to order that no one shall mention the United States to the prisoner while he is on board ship. You will receive your written orders from the officer on duty here this evening. The court is adjourned."

Before the *Nautilus* [2] got round from New Orleans to the northern Atlantic coast with the prisoner on board, the sentence had been approved by the President, and he was a man without a country.

The plan then adopted was substantially the same which was necessarily

---

[1] **Veracruz** (ver'ə·krōōz'): a Gulf seaport in Mexico.

[2] *Nautilus:* naval ship to which Nolan was delivered.

followed ever after. The Secretary of the Navy was requested to put Nolan on board a government vessel bound on a long cruise, and to direct that he should be only so far confined there as to make it certain that he never saw or heard of the country. We had few long cruises then, and I do not know certainly what his first cruise was. But the commander to whom he was entrusted regulated the etiquette and the precautions of the affair, and according to his scheme they were carried out till Nolan died.

When I was second officer of the *Intrepid,* some thirty years after, I saw the original paper of instructions. I have been sorry ever since that I did not copy the whole of it. It ran, however, much in this way:

Washington [with a date, which must have been late in 1807]
Sir:
You will receive from Lieutenant Neale the person of Philip Nolan, late a lieutenant in the United States Army.

This person on trial by court-martial expressed, with an oath, the wish that he might "never hear of the United States again."

The court sentenced him to have his wish fulfilled.

For the present, the execution of the order is entrusted by the President to this department.

You will take the prisoner on board your ship, and keep him there with such precautions as shall prevent his escape.

You will provide him with such quarters, rations, and clothing as would be proper for an officer of his late rank, if he were a passenger on your vessel on the business of his government.

The gentlemen on board will make any arrangements agreeable to themselves regarding his society. He is to be exposed to no indignity of any kind, nor is he ever unnecessarily to be reminded that he is a prisoner.

But under no circumstances is he ever to hear of his country or to see any information regarding it; and you will especially caution all the officers under your command to take care that this rule, in which his punishment is involved, shall not be broken.

It is the intention of the government that he shall never again see the country which he has disowned. Before the end of your cruise, you will receive orders which will give effect to this intention.

Respectfully yours,
W. SOUTHARD,
for the Secretary of the Navy

The rule adopted on board the ships on which I have met "The Man Without a Country" was, I think, transmitted from the beginning. No mess [1] liked to have him permanently, because his presence cut off all talk of home or of the prospect of return, of politics or letters, of peace or of war — cut off more than half the talk men liked to have at sea. But it was always thought too hard that he should never meet the rest of us, except to touch hats, and we finally sank into one sys-

---

[1] **mess:** the naval term for a group of men who eat their meals together.

tem. He was not permitted to talk with the men unless an officer was by. With officers he had unrestrained intercourse, as far as they and he chose. But he grew shy, though he had favorites: I was one. Then the captain always asked him to dinner on Monday. Every mess in succession took up the invitation in its turn. According to the size of the ship, you had him at your mess more or less often at dinner. His breakfast he ate in his own stateroom. Whatever else he ate or drank, he ate or drank alone. Sometimes, when the marines or sailors had any special jollification, they were permitted to invite Plain Buttons, as they called him. Then Nolan was sent with some officer, and the men were forbidden to speak of home while he was there. I believe the theory was that the sight of his punishment did them good. They called him Plain Buttons, because, while he always chose to wear a regulation army uniform, he was not permitted to wear the army button, for the reason that it bore either the initials or the insignia of the country he had disowned.

THE READING

I remember, soon after I joined the Navy, I was on shore with some of the older officers from our ship, and some of the gentlemen fell to talking about Nolan, and someone told the system which was adopted from the first about his books and other reading. As he was almost never permitted to go on shore, even though the vessel lay in port for months, his time at the best hung heavy. Everybody was permitted to lend him books, if they were not published in America and made no allusion to it. These were common enough in the old days. He had almost all the foreign papers that came into the ship, sooner or later; only somebody must go over them first, and cut out any advertisement or stray paragraph that referred to America. This was a little cruel sometimes, when the back of what was cut out might be innocent. Right in the midst of one of Napoleon's battles, poor Nolan would find a great hole, because on the back of the page of that paper there had been an advertisement of a packet [1] for New York, or a scrap from the President's message. This was the first time I ever heard of this plan. I remember it, because poor Phillips, who was of the party, told a story of something which happened at the Cape of Good Hope on Nolan's first voyage. They had touched at the Cape, paid their respects to the English admiral and the fleet, and then Phillips had borrowed a lot of English books from an officer. Among them was *The Lay of the Last Minstrel*,[2] which they had all of them heard of, but which most of them had never seen. I think it could not have been published long. Well, nobody thought there could be any risk of anything national in that. So Nolan was permitted to join the circle one afternoon when a lot of them sat on deck smoking and reading aloud. In his turn, Nolan took the book and read

[1] **packet:** packet boat, a ship that travels between ports, carrying mail, goods, and passengers.
[2] *The Lay of the Last Minstrel:* a long poem by Sir Walter Scott (1771–1832).

to the others; and he read very well, as I know. Nobody in the circle knew a line of the poem, only it was all magic and chivalry, and was ten thousand years ago. Poor Nolan read steadily through the fifth canto, stopped a minute and drank something, and then began, without a thought of what was coming:

Breathes there the man with soul so
    dead,
Who never to himself hath said . . .

It seems impossible to us that anybody ever heard this for the first time; but all these fellows did then, and poor Nolan himself went on, still unconsciously or mechanically:

This is my own, my native land!

Then they all saw that something was to pay; but he expected to get through, I suppose, turned a little pale, but plunged on:

Whose heart hath ne'er within him
    burned,
As home his footsteps he hath turned
From wandering on a foreign strand!
If such there breathe, go, mark him
    well . . .

By this time, the men were all beside themselves, wishing there was any way to make him turn over two pages; but he had not quite presence of mind for that; he gagged a little, colored crimson, and staggered on:

For him no minstrel raptures swell;
High though his titles, proud his
    name,
Boundless his wealth as wish can
    claim;

Despite these titles, power, and
    pelf,[1]
The wretch, concentered all in
    self . . .

Here the poor fellow choked, could not go on, but started up, swung the book into the sea, vanished into his stateroom, "And by Jove," said Phillips, "we did not see him for two months again. And I had to make up some story to that English surgeon why I did not return his Walter Scott to him."

That story shows about the time when Nolan's braggadocio[2] must have broken down. At first, they said, he took a very high tone, considered his imprisonment a mere farce, affected to enjoy the voyage, and all that; but Phillips said that after he came out of his stateroom he never was the same man again. He never read aloud again, unless it was the Bible or Shakespeare, or something else he was sure of. But it was not that merely. He never entered in with the other young men exactly as a companion again. He was always shy afterward, when I knew him — very seldom spoke unless he was spoken to, except to a very few friends. He lighted up occasionally, but generally he had the nervous, tired look of a heart-wounded man.

THE BALL

When Captain Shaw was coming home, rather to the surprise of everybody they made one of the Windward

---

[1] **pelf:** wealth.
[2] **braggadocio** (brag'ə·dō'shē·ō): swaggering pose; here, pretense that he did not mind his punishment.

Islands,[1] and lay off and on for nearly a week. The boys said the officers were sick of salt-junk,[2] and meant to have turtle soup before they came home. But after several days, the *Warren* came to the same rendezvous; they exchanged signals; she told them she was outward-bound, perhaps to the Mediterranean, and took poor Nolan and his traps[3] on the boat to try his second cruise. He looked very blank when he was told to get ready to join her. He had known enough of the signs of the sky to know that till that moment he was going "home." But this was a distinct evidence of something he had not thought of, perhaps — that there was no going home for him, even to a prison. And this was the first of some twenty such transfers, which brought him sooner or later into half our best vessels, but which kept him all his life at least some hundred miles from the country he had hoped he might never hear of again.

It may have been on that second cruise — it was once when he was up the Mediterranean — that Mrs. Graff, the celebrated Southern beauty of those days, danced with him. The ship had been lying a long time in the Bay of Naples, and the officers were very intimate in the English fleet, and there had been great festivities, and our men thought they must give a great ball on board the ship. They wanted to use Nolan's stateroom for something, and they hated to do it without asking him to the ball; so the captain said they might ask him, if they would be re-

sponsible that he did not talk with the wrong people, "who would give him intelligence."[4] So the dance went on. For ladies they had the family of the American consul, one or two travelers who had adventured so far, and a nice bevy of English girls and matrons.

Well, different officers relieved each other in standing and talking with Nolan in a friendly way, so as to be sure that nobody else spoke to him. The dancing went on with spirit, and after a while even the fellows who took this honorary guard of Nolan ceased to fear any trouble.

As the dancing went on, Nolan and our fellows all got at ease, as I said — so much, that it seemed quite natural for him to bow to that splendid Mrs. Graff, and say, "I hope you have not forgotten me, Miss Rutledge. Shall I have the honor of dancing?"

He did it so quickly that Fellows, who was with him, could not hinder him. She laughed and said, "I am not Miss Rutledge any longer, Mr. Nolan; but I will dance all the same." She nodded to Fellows, as if to say he must leave Mr. Nolan to her, and led Nolan off to the place where the dance was forming.

Nolan thought he had got his chance. He had known her at Philadelphia. He said boldly — a little pale, she said, as she told me the story years after — "And what do you hear from home, Mrs. Graff?"

And that splendid creature looked *through* him. Jove! How she *must* have looked through him!

"Home! Mr. Nolan! I thought you

---

[1] **Windward Islands:** in the West Indies.
[2] **salt-junk:** salted meat.
[3] **traps:** luggage.

[4] **intelligence:** here, information about his country.

were the man who never wanted to hear of home again!" — and she walked directly up the deck to her husband and left poor Nolan alone. He did not dance again.

THE BATTLE

A happier story than either of these I have told is of the war.[1] That came along soon after. I have heard this affair told in three or four ways — and, indeed, it may have happened more than once. In one of the great frigate duels with the English, in which the Navy was really baptized, it happened that a round shot [2] from the enemy entered one of our ports [3] square, and

---

¹ **the war:** the War of 1812, between the United States and England.

² **round shot:** cannon ball.

³ **ports:** here, openings in the side of the ship for cannons.

took right down the officer of the gun himself and almost every man of the gun's crew. Now you may say what you choose about courage, but that is not a nice thing to see. But, as the men who were not killed picked themselves up, and as they and the surgeon's people were carrying off the bodies, there appeared Nolan, in his shirt-sleeves, with the rammer in his hand, and, just as if he had been the officer, told them off with authority — who should go to the cockpit with the wounded men, who should stay with him — perfectly cheery, and with that way which makes men feel sure all is right and is going to be right. And he finished loading the gun with his own hands, aimed it, and bade the men fire. And there he stayed, captain of that gun, keeping those fellows in spirits, till the enemy struck [4] — sitting on the carriage while the gun was cooling, though he was exposed all the time, showing them easier ways to handle heavy shot, making the raw hands laugh at their own blunders, and when the gun cooled again, getting it loaded and fired twice as often as any other gun on the ship. The captain walked forward by way of encouraging the men, and Nolan touched his hat and said, "I am showing them how we do this in the artillery, sir."

And this is the part of the story where all the legends agree; the commodore said, "I see you are, and I thank you, sir; and I shall never forget this day, sir, and you never shall, sir."

After the whole thing was over, and the commodore had the Englishman's

---

⁴ **struck:** from the phrase "struck their colors," that is, hauled down their flag to admit defeat.

sword,[1] in the midst of the state and ceremony of the quarter-deck, he said, "Where is Mr. Nolan? Ask Mr. Nolan to come here."

And when Nolan came, he said, "Mr. Nolan, we are all very grateful to you today; you are one of us today; you will be named in the dispatches."

And then the old man took off his own sword of ceremony, gave it to Nolan, and made him put it on. The man who told me this saw it. Nolan cried like a baby, and well he might. He had not worn a sword since that infernal day at Fort Adams. But always afterward on occasions of ceremony he wore that quaint old sword of the commodore.

The captain did mention him in the dispatches. It was always said he asked that Nolan might be pardoned. He wrote a special letter to the Secretary of War, but nothing ever came of it.

All that was nearly fifty years ago. If Nolan was thirty then, he must have been near eighty when he died. He looked sixty when he was forty. But he never seemed to me to change a hair afterward. As I imagine his life, from what I have seen and heard of it, he must have been in every sea, and yet almost never on land. Till he grew very old, he went aloft a great deal. He always kept up his exercise, and I never heard that he was ill. If any other man was ill, he was the kindest nurse in the world; and he knew more than half the surgeons do. Then if anybody was sick or died, or if the captain wanted him to, or on any other occa-

sion, he was always ready to read prayers. I have said that he read beautifully.

THE SLAVES

My own acquaintance with Philip Nolan began six or eight years after the English war, on my first voyage after I was appointed a midshipman. From the time I joined, I believe I thought Nolan was a sort of lay chaplain — a chaplain with a blue coat. I never asked about him. Everything in the ship was strange to me. I knew it was green to ask questions, and I suppose I thought there was a Plain Buttons on every ship. We had him to dine in our mess once a week, and the caution was given that on that day nothing was to be said about home. But if they had told us not to say anything about the planet Mars or the Book of Deuteronomy, I should not have asked why; there were a great many things which seemed to me to have as little reason. I first came to understand anything about "The Man Without a Country" one day when we overhauled a dirty little schooner which had slaves[2] on board. An officer named Vaughan was sent to take charge of her, and, after a few minutes, he sent back his boat to ask that someone might be sent who could speak Portuguese. None of the officers did; and just as the captain was sending forward to ask if any of the people could, Nolan stepped out and said he should be glad to interpret, if the cap-

[1] **Englishman's sword:** In those days a defeated commander gave up his sword to the victor.

[2] **slaves:** In 1808 the United States made it illegal to bring slaves into the country. In 1842 America and England agreed to patrol the African coast with ships to prevent any more men and women from being sent abroad as slaves.

tain wished, as he understood the language. The captain thanked him, fitted out another boat with him, and in this boat it was my luck to go.

When we got there, it was such a scene as you seldom see — and never want to. Nastiness beyond account, and chaos ran loose in the midst of the nastiness. There were not a great many of the Negroes. By way of making what there were understand that they were free, Vaughan had had their handcuffs and anklecuffs knocked off. The Negroes were, most of them, out of the hold and swarming all around the dirty deck, with a central throng surrounding Vaughan and addressing him in every dialect.

As we came on deck, Vaughan looked down from a hogshead,[1] which he had mounted in desperation, and said, "Is there anybody who can make these wretches understand something?"

Nolan said he could speak Portuguese, and one or two fine-looking Krumen[2] who had worked for the Portuguese on the coast were dragged out.

"Tell them they are free," said Vaughan.

Nolan explained it in such Portuguese as the Krumen could understand, and they in turn to such of the Negroes as could understand them. Then there was a yell of delight, clenching of fists, leaping and dancing, and kissing of Nolan's feet by way of spontaneous celebration of the occasion.

"Tell them," said Vaughan, well

pleased, "that I will take them all to Cape Palmas."[3]

This did not answer so well. Cape Palmas was practically as far from the homes of most of them as New Orleans or Rio de Janeiro was; that is, they would be eternally separated from home there. And their interpreters, as we could understand, instantly said, "*Ah, non Palmas*" and began to protest loudly. Vaughan was rather disappointed at this result of his liberality, and he asked Nolan eagerly what they said. The drops stood on poor Nolan's white forehead, as he hushed the men down, and said, "He says, 'Not Palmas.' He says, 'Take us home; take us to our own country; take us to our own house; take us to our own children and our own women.' He says he has an old father and mother who will die if they do not see him. And this one says that he left his people all sick, and paddled down to Fernando to beg the white doctor to come and help them, and that these devils caught him in the bay just in sight of home, and that he has never seen anybody from home since then. And this one says," choked out Nolan, "that he has not heard a word from his home in six months."

Vaughan always said Nolan grew gray himself while he struggled through this interpretation. I, who did not understand anything of the passion involved in it, saw that the very elements were melting with fervent heat and that something was to pay some-

---

[1] hogshead: large cask.
[2] Krumen (krōō′men): members of a tribe of northern Africa.

[3] Cape Palmas: a point on the southern border of Liberia, on the western coast of Africa — about two thousand miles from the part of northern Africa which was the Negroes' home.

where. Even the Negroes themselves stopped howling as they saw Nolan's agony and Vaughan's almost equal agony of sympathy. As quick as he could get words, Vaughan said, "Tell them yes, yes, yes; tell them they shall go to the Mountains of the Moon, if they will. If I sail the schooner through the Great White Desert, they shall go home!"

And after some fashion, Nolan said so. And then they all fell to kissing him again and wanted to rub his nose with theirs.

But he could not stand it long; and getting Vaughan to say he might go back, he beckoned me down into our boat. As we started back he said to me: "Youngster, let that show you what it is to be without a family, without a home, and without a country. If you are ever tempted to say a word or to do a thing that shall put a bar between you and your family, your home, and your country, pray God in His mercy to take you that instant home to His own heaven. Think of your home, boy; write and send and talk about it. Let it be nearer and nearer to your thought the farther you have to travel from it, and rush back to it when you are free, as that poor slave is doing now. And for your country, boy," and the words rattled in his throat, "and for that flag," and he pointed to the ship, "never dream a dream but of serving her as she bids you, though the service carry you through a thousand hells. No matter what happens to you, no matter who flatters you or who abuses you, never look at another flag, never let a night pass but you pray God to bless the flag. Remember, boy, that behind all these men you have to do with, behind officers, and government, and people even, there is the Country herself, your Country, and that you belong to her as you belong to your own mother. Stand by her, boy, as you would stand by your mother!"

I was frightened to death by his calm, hard passion; but I blundered out that I would, by all that was holy, and that I had never thought of doing anything else. He hardly seemed to hear me; but he did, almost in a whisper, say, "Oh, if anybody had said so to me when I was of your age!"

I think it was this half-confidence of his, which I never abused, that afterward made us great friends. He was very kind to me. Often he sat up, or even got up, at night, to walk the deck with me when it was my watch. He explained to me a great deal of my mathematics, and I owe him my taste for mathematics. He lent me books and helped me about my reading. He never referred so directly to his story again; but from one and another officer, I have learned, in thirty years, what I am telling.

NOLAN'S REPENTANCE

After that cruise I never saw Nolan again. The other men tell me that in those fifteen years he aged very fast, but he was still the same gentle, uncomplaining, silent sufferer that he ever was, bearing as best he could his self-appointed punishment. And now it seems that the dear old fellow is dead. He has found a home at last, and a country.

Since writing this, and while considering whether or not I would print it, as a warning to the young Nolans of today of what it is to throw away a country, I have received from Danforth, who is on board the *Levant,* a letter which gives an account of Nolan's last hours. It removes all my doubts about telling this story.

Here is the letter:

Dear Fred,

I try to find heart and life to tell you that it is all over with dear old Nolan. I have been with him on this voyage more than I ever was, and I can understand wholly now the way in which you used to speak of the dear old fellow. I could see that he was not strong, but I had no idea the end was so near. The doctor has been watching him very carefully, and yesterday morning he came to me and told me that Nolan was not so well and had not left his stateroom — a thing I never remember before. He had let the doctor come and see him as he lay there — the first time the doctor had been in the stateroom — and he said he

should like to see me. Do you remember the mysteries we boys used to invent about his room in the old *Intrepid* days? Well, I went in, and there, to be sure, the poor fellow lay in his berth, smiling pleasantly as he gave me his hand but looking very frail. I could not help a glance round, which showed me what a little shrine he had made of the box he was lying in. The Stars and Stripes were draped up above and around a picture of Washington, and he had painted a majestic eagle, with lightnings blazing from his beak and his foot just clasping the whole globe, which his wings overshadowed. The dear old boy saw my glance, and said, with a sad smile, "Here, you see, I have a country!" Then he pointed to the foot of his bed, where I had not seen before a great map of the United States, as he had drawn it from memory, and which he had there to look upon as he lay. Quaint, queer old names were on it, in large letters: "Indiana Territory," "Mississippi Territory," and "Louisiana Ter-

ritory," as I suppose our fathers learned such things: but the old fellow had patched in Texas, too; he had carried his western boundary all the way to the Pacific, but on that shore he had defined nothing.

"O Captain," he said, "I know I am dying. I cannot get home. Surely you will tell me something now? . . . Stop! Stop! . . . Do not speak till I say what I am sure you know, that there is not in this ship, that there is not in America — God bless her! — a more loyal man than I. There cannot be a man who loves the old flag as I do, or prays for it as I do, or hopes for it as I do. There are thirty-four stars in it now, Danforth. I thank God for that, though I do not know what their names are. There has never been one taken away; I thank God for that. I know by that that there has never been any successful Burr. O Danforth, Danforth," he sighed out, "how like a wretched night's dream a boy's idea of personal fame or of separate sovereignty seems, when one looks back on it after such a life as mine! But tell me — tell me something — tell me everything, Danforth, before I die!"

I swear to you that I felt like a monster because I had not told him everything before. "Mr. Nolan," said I, "I will tell you everything you ask about. Only, where shall I begin?"

Oh, the blessed smile that crept over his white face! He pressed my hand and said, "God bless you! Tell me their names," he said, and he pointed to the stars on the flag. "The last I know is Ohio. My father lived in Kentucky. But I have guessed

Michigan, and Indiana, and Mississippi — that is where Fort Adams was — they make twenty. But where are your other fourteen? You have not cut up any of the old ones, I hope?"

Well, that was not a bad text, and I told him the names in as good order as I could, and he bade me take down his beautiful map and draw them in as I best could with my pencil. He was wild with delight about Texas, told me how his cousin died there; he had marked a gold cross near where he supposed his grave was; and he had guessed at Texas. Then he was delighted as he saw California and Oregon — that, he said, he had suspected partly, because he had never been permitted to land on that shore, though the ships were there so much. Then he asked about the old war — told me the story of his serving the gun the day we took the *Java*. Then he settled down more quietly, and very happily, to hear me tell in an hour the history of fifty years.

How I wish it had been somebody who knew something! But I did as well as I could. I told him of the English war. I told him of Fulton and the steamboat beginning. I told him about old Scott,[1] and Jackson,[2] told him all I could think of about the Mississippi, and New Orleans, and Texas, and his own old Kentucky.

I tell you, it was a hard thing to

---

[1] **Scott:** General Winfield Scott, in command in the War of 1812 and the Mexican War.
[2] **Jackson:** Andrew Jackson, who won the battle of New Orleans and was later President.

condense the history of half a century into that talk with a sick man. And I do not now know what I told him — of emigration and the means of it — of steamboats, and railroads, and telegraphs — of inventions, and books, and literature — of the colleges, and West Point, and the Naval School, but with the queerest interruptions that ever you heard. You see it was Robinson Crusoe asking all the accumulated questions of fifty-six years!

I remember he asked, all of a sudden, who was President now; and when I told him, he asked if Old Abe was General Benjamin Lincoln's son. He said he met old General Lincoln, when he was quite a boy himself, at some Indian treaty. I said no, that Old Abe was a Kentuckian like himself, but I could not tell him of what family; he had worked up from the ranks. "Good for him!" cried Nolan; "I am glad of that." Then I got talking about my visit to Washington. I told him everything I could think of that would show the grandeur of his country and its prosperity.

And he drank it in and enjoyed it as I cannot tell you. He grew more and more silent, yet I never thought he was tired or faint. I gave him a glass of water, but he just wet his lips, and told me not to go away. Then he asked me to bring the Presbyterian *Book of Public Prayer* which lay there, and said, with a smile, that it would open at the right place — and so it did. There was his double red mark down the page; and I knelt down and read, and he repeated with me:

> For ourselves and our country, O gracious God, we thank Thee, that, notwithstanding our manifold transgressions of Thy Holy laws, Thou hast continued to us Thy marvelous kindness . . .

and so to the end of that thanksgiving. Then he turned to the end of the same book, and I read the words more familiar to me:

> Most heartily we beseech Thee with Thy favor to behold and bless Thy servant, the President of the United States, and all others in authority.

"Danforth," said he, "I have repeated those prayers night and morning — it is now fifty-five years." And then he said he would go to sleep. He bent me down over him and kissed me; and he said, "Look in my Bible, Captain, when I am gone." And I went away.

But I had no thought it was the end. I thought he was tired and would sleep. I knew he was happy, and I wanted him to be alone.

But in an hour, when the doctor went in gently, he found Nolan had breathed his life away with a smile.

We looked in his Bible, and there was a slip of paper at the place where he had marked the text:

> They desire a country, even a heavenly: where God is not ashamed to be called their God: for He hath prepared for them a city.

On this slip of paper he had written this:

> Bury me in the sea; it has been my home, and I love it. But will not

someone set up a stone for my memory, that my disgrace may not be more than I ought to bear? Say on it:

In Memory of
Philip Nolan
Lieutenant in the Army
of the United States

HE LOVED HIS COUNTRY
AS NO OTHER MAN HAS LOVED HER;
BUT NO MAN DESERVED LESS
AT HER HANDS.

PATRIOTISM

1. What facts does the author give about Nolan's early life in order to explain his lack of patriotism? Describe the conspiracy into which the young man was drawn. What terrible wish did Nolan express in the courtroom?

2. Tell in detail how Nolan's punishment was carried out. Relate the incidents of the reading, the ball, the battle, and the slaves. Show how Nolan's behavior during these incidents revealed his feelings toward his country. Which incident seemed hardest for him to bear?

3. What did the objects in Nolan's room reveal about his feelings for his country? What did Nolan reveal about himself in his epitaph?

4. Early in the story, the author states his purpose in writing it. Find the sentence in which he tells you his purpose. In what ways is this story a lesson in patriotism?

5. Read the passage from *The Lay of the Last Minstrel* (page 192). Which lines express the theme of this story? State briefly what you consider this theme to be. Do you agree with it? Why?

6. Nolan had never heard of many main events of American history. Try to imagine some of the details that Captain Danforth told him about wars, emigration, inventions, books, and other events. Why do you think Captain Danforth finally told Nolan all he wanted to know about his country?

WORDS: LATIN AND GREEK ROOTS

The roots of many of our words go back thousands of years, to words of older languages. For example, in our word *territory* we find part of the Latin word *terra*, which means "earth" or "land." A territory is a geographical area or body of land; it can also be an area of land over which a government has jurisdiction. In our word *geography* we find the Greek word *gē*, which also means "earth." Geography is the science that describes the earth's surface. These two word roots, *terra* and *gē*, both meaning "earth" or "land," are found in many English words. For example, each of the following words is based on one of these roots: *terrain, terrace, terra cotta, geology, geometry*. Use a dictionary, if necessary, to see if "earth" or "land" is a part of the meaning of each of these words.

COMPOSITION:
SUPPORTING AN OPINION

In writing, as in speaking, your statements of opinion are made more forceful when you present clear, logical reasons to support them.

Here are two questions that have been asked many times of readers of "The Man Without a Country":

Do you think Nolan deserved his punishment?

Do you think such a punishment would be given to Nolan today?

Choose one of these questions, and decide how you would answer it. Then, in a paragraph, give at least two reasons explaining why you feel this way. Be sure to state your opinion in the introductory sentence.

The Drummer Boy of Shiloh

RAY BRADBURY

In 1861, the states of our still-young nation became involved in a bitter four-year war. The following short story tells about a boy who was probably like the thousands of youngsters who fought on each side in that war. The story is set in Tennessee. The time is the night before the terrible battle that has come to be known as the Battle of Shiloh.

IN THE APRIL NIGHT, more than once, blossoms fell from the orchard trees and lighted with rustling taps on the drumhead. At midnight a peach stone, left miraculously on a branch through winter, flicked by a bird, fell swift and unseen; it struck once, like panic, and jerked the boy upright. In silence he listened to his own heart ruffle away, away — at last gone from his ears and back in his chest again.

After that he turned the drum on its side, where its great lunar face peered at him whenever he opened his eyes.

His face, alert or at rest, was solemn. It was a solemn time and a solemn night for a boy just turned fourteen in the peach orchard near Owl Creek, not far from the church at Shiloh.

". . . thirty-one . . . thirty-two . . . thirty-three." Unable to see, he stopped counting.

Beyond the thirty-three familiar shadows, forty thousand men, exhausted by nervous expectation and unable to sleep for romantic dreams of battles yet unfought, lay crazily askew in their uniforms. A mile farther on, another army was strewn helter-skelter, turning slowly, basting themselves with the thought of what they would do when the time came — a leap, a yell, a blind plunge their strategy, raw youth their protection and benediction.

Now and again the boy heard a vast wind come up that gently stirred the air. But he knew what it was — the army here, the army there, whispering to itself in the dark. Some men talking to others, others murmuring to themselves, and all so quiet it was like a natural element arisen from South or North with the motion of the earth toward dawn.

What the men whispered the boy could only guess, and he guessed that it was "Me, I'm the one, I'm the one of all the rest who won't die. I'll live through it. I'll go home. The band will play. And I'll be there to hear it."

"Yes," thought the boy, *"that's all very well for them, they can give as good as they get!"*

For with the careless bones of the young men, harvested by night and bindled [1] around campfires, were the similarly strewn steel bones of their rifles with bayonets fixed like eternal lightning lost in the orchard grass.

"Me," thought the boy, *"I got only a drum, two sticks to beat it, and no shield."*

There wasn't a man-boy on this ground tonight who did not have a shield he cast, riveted, or carved himself on his way to his first attack, compounded of remote but nonetheless firm and fiery family devotion, flag-blown patriotism, and cocksure immortality, strengthened by the touchstone of very real gunpowder, ramrod, Minié ball,[2] and flint. But without these last, the boy felt his family move yet farther off in the dark, as if one of those great prairie-burning trains had chanted them away, never to return — leaving him with this drum, which was worse

---

[1] **bindled** (bin'dəld): bound or tied together.
[2] **Minié** (min'ē-ā) **ball**: a type of rifle bullet.

than a toy in the game to be played tomorrow or someday much too soon.

The boy turned on his side. A moth brushed his face, but it was peach blossom. A peach blossom flicked him, but it was a moth. Nothing stayed put. Nothing had a name. Nothing was as it once was.

If he stayed very still when the dawn came up and the soldiers put on their bravery with their caps, perhaps they might go away, the war with them, and not notice him lying small here, no more than a toy himself.

"Well, by thunder now," said a voice. The boy shut his eyes to hide inside himself, but it was too late. Someone, walking by in the night, stood over him. "Well," said the voice quietly, "here's a soldier crying *before* the fight. Good. Get it over. Won't be time once it all starts."

And the voice was about to move on when the boy, startled, touched the drum at his elbow. The man above, hearing this, stopped. The boy could feel his eyes, sense him slowly bending near. A hand must have come down out of the night, for there was a little *rat-tat* as the fingernails brushed and the man's breath fanned the boy's face.

"Why, it's the drummer boy, isn't it?"

The boy nodded, not knowing if his nod was seen. "Sir, is that you?" he said.

"I assume it is." The man's knees cracked as he bent still closer. He smelled as all fathers should smell, of salt-sweat, tobacco, horse and boot leather, and the earth he walked upon. He had many eyes. No, not eyes, brass buttons that watched the boy.

He could only be, and was, the general. "What's your name, boy?" he asked.

"Joby, sir," whispered the boy, starting to sit up.

"All right, Joby, don't stir." A hand pressed his chest gently, and the boy relaxed. "How long you been with us, Joby?"

"Three weeks, sir."

"Run off from home or join legitimate, boy?"

Silence.

"Darn-fool question," said the general. "Do you shave yet, boy? Even more of a fool. There's your cheek, fell right off the tree overhead. And the others here, not much older. Raw, raw, darn raw, the lot of you. You ready for tomorrow or the next day, Joby?"

"I think so, sir."

"You want to cry some more, go on ahead. I did the same last night."

"You, sir?"

"God's truth. Thinking of everything ahead. Both sides figuring the other side will just give up, and soon, and the war done in weeks and us all home. Well, that's not how it's going to be. And maybe that's why I cried."

"Yes, sir," said Joby.

The general must have taken out a cigar now, for the dark was suddenly filled with the Indian smell of tobacco — unlighted yet, but chewed as the man thought what next to say.

"It's going to be a crazy time," said the general. "Counting both sides, there's a hundred thousand men — give or take a few thousand — out there tonight, not one as can spit a sparrow off a tree or knows a horse clod from a Minié ball. Stand up, bare the breast, ask to be a target, thank them, and sit down, that's us, that's them. We should turn tail and train four months; they should do the same. But here we are, taken with spring fever and thinking it blood lust, taking our sulphur with cannons instead of with molasses, as it should be — going to be a hero, going to live forever. And I can see all them over there nodding agreement, save the other way around. It's wrong, boy, it's wrong as a head put on hindside front and a man marching backward through life. Sometime this week more innocents will get shot out of pure Cherokee enthusiasm than ever got shot before. Oil Creek was full of boys splashing around in the noonday sun just a few hours ago. I fear it will be full of boys again, just floating, at sundown tomorrow, not caring where the current takes them."

The general stopped and made a little pile of winter leaves and twigs in

1. Describe the setting of this story. What details in the opening paragraphs make you aware of the silence of the night?

2. How did the boy feel about his position in the army? What sentences express the confusion in Joby's mind?

3. What feeling about the coming battle did the general share with the boy? According to the general, what did the young soldiers have to learn? How did the general say that the drummer boy could help the army?

4. What effect does the author create by not telling the reader whether the boy was in the Northern or Southern army?

5. What do you think happened to the drummer boy the next day?

6. About how many years separate the events in this story from the events in which Johnny Tremain participated? Discuss the ways the two boys took part in these different historic events. Which story did you prefer: "Salt-Water Tea" or "The

people or angry geese often make. Can you think of any other words, like *hiss*, that imitate sounds?

By using "sound words," a writer can make us hear things as we read. For example, Ray Bradbury uses the word *murmuring* on page 203. Say *murmur* aloud. Do you hear the low, indistinct sound of talk?

Can you locate the words in the first paragraph of this story which imitate sounds? Read the paragraph aloud. Can you hear the sounds that Joby heard on that April night?

FIGURATIVE LANGUAGE

In the second paragraph of this story, Ray Bradbury talks about Joby's drum: ". . . its great lunar face peered at him whenever he opened his eyes." Ray Bradbury has used language figuratively here because he is comparing the drum to the face of the moon looking at Joby.

In the fifth paragraph, the sleeping sol-

Soldiers, not much older than the drummer boy in this story, look over a muddy and dismal campsite during a lull in the war.

the dark, as if he might at any moment strike fire to them to see his way through the coming days when the sun might not show its face because of what was happening here and just beyond.

The boy watched the hand stirring the leaves and opened his lips to say something, but did not say it. The general heard the boy's breath and spoke himself.

"Why am I telling you this? That's what you wanted to ask, eh? Well, when you got a bunch of wild horses on a loose rein somewhere, somehow you got to bring order, rein them in. These lads, fresh out of the milkshed,

don't know what I know; and I can't tell them — men actually die in war. So each is his own army. I got to make one army of them. And for that, boy, I need you."

"Me!" The boy's lips barely twitched.

"You, boy," said the general quietly. "You are the heart of the army. Think about that. You are the heart of the army. Listen to me, now."

And lying there, Joby listened. And the general spoke. If he, Joby, beat slow tomorrow, the heart would beat slow in the men. They would lag by the wayside. They would drowse in the fields on their muskets. They would sleep forever after that — in those same

The Gettysburg Address

ABRAHAM LINCOLN

In 1863, in the midst of the war, a ceremony was held to dedicate the Soldiers' National Cemetery at Gettysburg. At the end of the ceremony, President Lincoln rose to say a few words. The President had a high-pitched voice, and many people in the crowd could not hear him. It was later, when the speech was published, that Americans began to realize that the Gettysburg Address was one of the greatest speeches of all time.

FOUR SCORE and seven years ago our fathers brought forth on this continent a new nation, conceived in liberty, and dedicated to the proposition that all men are created equal.

Now we are engaged in a great civil war, testing whether that nation, or any nation so conceived and so dedicated, can long endure. We are met on a great battlefield of that war. We have come to dedicate a portion of that field as a final resting place for those who here gave their lives that that nation might live. It is altogether fitting and proper that we should do this.

But, in a larger sense, we cannot dedicate — we cannot consecrate — we cannot hallow this ground. The brave men, living and dead, who struggled here, have consecrated it far above our poor power to add or detract. The world will little note nor long remember what we say here, but it can never forget what they did here. It is for us the living, rather, to be dedicated here to the unfinished work which they who fought here have thus far so nobly advanced. It is rather for us to be here dedicated to the great task remaining before us — that from these honored dead we take increased devotion to that cause for which they gave the last full measure of devotion; that we here highly resolve that these dead shall not have died in vain; that this nation, under God, shall have a new birth of freedom; and that government of the people, by the people, for the people, shall not perish from the earth.

Crowds watch a regiment parade up a Gettysburg street. A few hours later they heard Lincoln speak.

ENDURING WORDS

1. What important event in American history was Lincoln referring to in the first sentence?

2. In the first paragraph, how did Lincoln state the purposes for which this nation was founded? Explain in your own words what Lincoln meant.

3. In the second paragraph, what did Lincoln say was the reason for which the soldiers had died?

4. In the third paragraph, what tasks did Lincoln set for the living? What does he mean by "unfinished work"?

5. Why do you think this speech has endured? In what ways does this speech apply to Americans of today?

6. "The world will little note nor long remember what we say here . . ." said Lincoln in the third paragraph of this speech. How has Lincoln been proved wrong? What does this statement tell you about Lincoln?

7. What "enduring words" have been uttered by other American statesmen?

THOUGHTFUL READING: LOOKING BACK

Reread the first two sentences of "The Gettysburg Address." What nation did Lincoln mean in the second sentence by "that nation"? If you had read carefully, you would know that Lincoln was referring back to a long phrase from the first sentence: "a new nation, conceived in liberty, and dedicated to the proposition that all men are created equal."

When you find the words *this, that,* and *those* (and *who* and *which*) in a sentence, you must be sure you know to which words or word groups the writer is referring. Here are the next three sentences from "The Gettysburg Address." What words do the italicized words refer back to?

"We are met on a great battlefield of *that war*. We have come to dedicate a portion of *that field* as a final resting place for those who here gave their lives that *that nation* might live. It is altogether fitting and proper that we should do *this*."

O Captain! My Captain!

WALT WHITMAN

A nation, like a person, must go through times of tragedy and grief. In 1865 the terrible War Between the States was drawing to a close. War-weary people were beginning to feel some relief, but their relief was mixed with sadness when the news came that President Lincoln had been assassinated. Walt Whitman, a famous American poet who was living during this time, expressed the nation's mixed feelings in this famous poem.

O Captain! my Captain! our fearful trip is done,
The ship has weathered every rack,° the prize we sought is won,
The port is near, the bells I hear, the people all exulting,
While follow eyes the steady keel, the vessel grim and daring;
        But O heart! heart! heart! 5
          O the bleeding drops of red,
            Where on the deck my Captain lies,
            Fallen cold and dead.

O Captain! my Captain! rise up and hear the bells;
Rise up — for you the flag is flung — for you the bugle trills, 10
For you bouquets and ribboned wreaths — for you the shores a-crowding,
For you they call, the swaying mass, their eager faces turning;
        Here Captain! dear father!
          This arm beneath your head!
            It is some dream that on the deck 15
            You've fallen cold and dead.

My Captain does not answer, his lips are pale and still,
My father does not feel my arm, he has no pulse nor will,
The ship is anchored safe and sound, its voyage closed and done,
From fearful trip the victor ship comes in with object won; 20
        Exult O shores! and ring O bells!
          But I with mournful tread
            Walk the deck my Captain lies,
            Fallen cold and dead.

2. **rack:** strain, as from storms.

from Fort Dodge to Old Pueblo as Gant's Mansion, a squat palace of adobe standing on the San Blas [1] plain, and to see again the wide hall trooping with a grave procession of princely territorial governors and hook-nosed judges, of Indian agents like blue-eyed foxes, of brass-buttoned Army officers, Federal officials, Mexican dons and *ricos*,[2] and the hungry, grunting chiefs of the Utes, the Apaches, and the Navajos.

But even then a cloud no bigger than your hand was beginning to cast a shadow over those adobe walls that stood thick enough to entomb horses. The smoke of the native cedar is blue

several hours from ten days among his sheep in the Canyon Bonito country. I had seen his dust-covered buggy pull up to the store, both horses lathered to the mane, as always when my father held the lines. I found him gone from the store, and I looked for him in his wholesale warehouses sprawling nearby, each a kind of Ali Baba cave with barred windows, dim and odorous and heaped with boxes, fat hogsheads,[3] bulging bales, mountains of plump sacks, grain bins, piles of hides to the roof, monstrous sacks of unwashed wool, and poisonous-looking copper ingots.[4]

He wasn't there, and I went in turn

Following the assassination, Lincoln's body was placed on a train and taken to Illinois for burial. Above, the flag-draped funeral train stops at Philadelphia. The portrait below was signed by Lincoln himself.

THE PRESIDENT'S DEATH

1. Throughout this poem, Whitman draws many comparisons. He compares Lincoln to a captain who has steered a ship through a fearful trip. What was this "fearful trip"? What does the "ship" stand for in the poem? What kinds of strains had the "ship" weathered? What was the "prize" that had been sought? What was the "port"?

2. Find the phrases that describe how people felt toward Lincoln at the war's end. In what ways are the last four lines of the second stanza more personal than the last lines of the first stanza?

3. What lines in the poem show that Whitman felt more like grieving than rejoicing?

4. To what other times in America's history might this poem be applied? When have similar circumstances or similar emotions prevailed?

comfortable moment stood in the door-way.

A fire of pinyon [1] logs blazed in the bedroom fireplace, and on the floor with his back to it sat Guero,[2] the Mes-calero Apache chief, huge and greasy, with the eyes, nose, and talons of an eagle, his red blanket thrown back from his shoulders, and, bared in his rawhide belt, a long American trade knife and the forbidden revolver.

And coolly talking to him from a white bowl on the floor, washing him-self from a second bowl on the marble top of the washstand, unclothed, un-armed, and unconcerned, stood my fa-ther — a powerful naked figure, not tall, but herculean, in a black beard that twisted and stood out from his chin and cheeks like fine wire. And I noticed that the same stubborn, black, invinci-ble growth curled from his chest and the hard cylinders of his legs.

So far, he had not even glanced at the open door, and now he looked up with some impatience.

"Come in, come in!" he barked, and I stepped hastily into the room, dimly realizing that he had not known who was knocking, that it might have been one of the Mexican women servants with, perhaps, the governor and his lady behind her, but that my father did not care. His unforgettable eyes fixed themselves upon me. "You know Chief Guero," he commanded sternly. "Go up, shake hands, and ask him in Span-ish about his family."

When my father had pulled on clean linen and fresh black broadcloth, he summed up his long talk to Guero:

---

[1] **pinyon**: pine.
[2] **Guero** (ger'ō).

"Tell your people this: Tell them there is no danger from the railroad. It will bring no white people here to take away your rights. It makes big prom-ises. It talks big words. Today it boasts. Tomorrow it is forgotten."

He left Guero sitting on the earthen floor of the office, bent voraciously over a huge bowl of steaming mutton stew.

"Now," he said to me in the hall, "you say your mother wants to see me?" For a moment or two as he stood there, he reminded me of the male blackbirds I had often seen in the tules,[3] drawing in their brilliant-scarlet shoulder straps and soberly ruffling their feathers until their strut and sheen had vanished and they looked subdued and brown. Then I accompanied him in si-lence to my mother's door. He knocked and, without waiting for an answer, formally entered.

"Nettie!" He bowed gravely, and in that single word still in my ear I can detect greeting, irony, dignity, indul-gence, and uncomfortable expectation of what was to come.

My mother made no answer except the further clamp of her lip and the faint, unaccustomed rose in her cheeks. She motioned me to come and sit be-side her, which I did, painfully con-scious that it was an ignoble role I was to play, like the favorite child in *Ten Nights in a Barroom,* by whom the re-generation of the father was to be made.

My mother's quarters, which she sel-dom left, seemed perpetually com-pressed with a stale and heavy air, the musty scent of Eastern carpets, stuffed chests and wardrobes, soaps, medi-

---

[3] **tules** (tōō'lēz): bulrushes.

cines, and moth balls, all very distasteful to a boy. But today I felt that the sluggish air had been charged with sharp and potent currents. And when I looked at the golden-brown shawl which hung like a vestment about my mother's shoulders, there was almost the play of lightning upon it.

"Must I speak of it?" my mother began bitterly. "I should think you'd confess it yourself with shame!"

No step was audible outside the door, but the latch lifted and drew our eyes. Slowly the door opened. It was Juliana. I can see her today, framed in that massive doorway with the light like a nimbus [1] behind her, quiet, gravefaced, a girlish figure in her full skirts and snug bodice, both of them dovecolored, and over the latter the gold chain and heart-shaped locket in which I knew she carried the picture of her father.

"John is here. Can't I stay?" she asked, and closed the door. With the hushed step of a young woman late to church, she crossed the room to a chair, and the appeal in her eyes, as for a moment she glanced up at my father, might almost have been at God.

My mother's eyes burned with maternal satisfaction at Juliana's presence.

"People are saying," she went on scathingly to my father, "that Mr. Rutherford has disappeared like other enemies of the high-handed interests in this territory."

I fancied I saw a hidden stain through the beard on my father's cheeks, and my mind traveled with a sort of horror to Vance Rutherford, tall, fine-looking, and gentlemanly, whom Juliana had met at the Coddoms' in Capitan.[2] Up until the last ten days, he had kept driving to the mansion in a livery rig to pay her attentions, and I had wondered what had become of his narrow-brimmed hat and the invariable desert marigold in his buttonhole.

"People say many things, Nettie; many things," my father said.

"Is he dead?" my mother demanded in a blunt voice, and I saw the locket hang motionless for a moment on Juliana's breast.

"No-o," my father said blandly. "Not that I know of." And the locket resumed its silent rise and fall.

"Then you warned him to leave the territory?" my mother accused.

"I may have" — my father lifted a square hand — "seen that he heard certain discreet things."

"You had nothing against him, Frank Gant, except that he's chief engineer for the railroad!" my mother challenged hotly. "Where can you find another young man in such a high position? Do you want your daughter to marry a cowboy or a buffalo hunter, who rides and kills and gambles and soaks himself in the whisky you sell like coffee and sugar over your counters?"

My father prudently said nothing. The color gathered in my mother's face.

"You're prejudiced against the railroad! I say thank God for the railroad. It's the finest thing that could happen to this lawless land. It will bring schools and churches."

---

[1] **nimbus:** halo.

[2] **Capitan** (căp·ē·tän').

"They're not building it to bring schools and churches," my father reminded mildly. "They're building it to make it pay. They want to lay down eight hundred miles west and south in the territory. It's to cost eighteen thousand dollars a mile or more. That's fourteen million dollars." He ran his hand over his unruly black beard. "Fourteen million dollars when we already have trails that cost nothing and freighters who've built up their trains to more than five thousand steers and mules."

"Steers and mules!" My mother's eyes were blazing. "Have steers and mules ever civilized this country? How many shooting scrapes does the Capitan *Enterprise* print every week? Murders, they should be called — cold-blooded murders! And that doesn't count the lynchings and the men who disappear and the women and children scalped by your friends the Apaches! Is it any wonder that good people refuse to come to this barbarous country?"

My father looked very humble.

"Aren't you confusing it, Nettie, with farming country like Kansas?" he asked. "That's a new country. This is old. White people have been here for hundreds of years, but they never got very far with farming. I've heard you say yourself it's only a desert. But this young promoter, Rutherford" — I saw Juliana's eyelashes quiver — "wants to spend fourteen million dollars to give the desert a railroad. He tells our towns to go in debt with bonds and buy railroad stock with the money. He tells them the railroad will some day be one of the biggest in the country."

I saw that my mother was staggered despite herself by the unanswerable facts and figures. She leaned forward appealingly.

"When one of your Mexican herders' relatives gets into trouble, Frank, you always feel sorry and help him out. Can't you feel sorry for an American who isn't much more than a boy, who works for the railroad company and believes what the higher officials tell him?"

"No," my father said slowly, and it was the first hardness I had heard in his voice since he had entered the room. I saw that he had straightened. "I have sympathy, Nettie, for a man who knows he is gambling and loses, and for a man who knows he may get hung for stealing a horse and steals it. But I have none for anyone who throws away other people's hard-earned money, who's gullible enough to swallow a wild dream like a fourteen-million-dollar railroad on the desert." He looked straight at my mother and went on, drawing in his bearded lips with great force: "Such a waster will never become a member of my house — not while I'm alive!"

There were streaks of chalk in my mother's cheeks, but what is hard to forget is Juliana. Quiet, the locket still moving gently on her dove-colored bodice, she sat on her chair, and her face was no paler than when she had come in. But the eyes that stared at my father were the eyes of a dead person. I was aware of my mother laying her ringed fingers, as if for divine strength, on the gilded covers of the thick family Bible that lay on the table beside her.

"God will punish you, Frank Gant!" she said.

Now that he had taken his position,

my father had become his old self
again, firm, robust, Atlantean,[1] almost
like a Nubian lion [2] in his black beard
and broadcloth, standing there with
such living power that I felt that words,
shafts, bullets, and even the hand of
God must glance off from him.

"Perhaps Julie feels badly now," he
went on confidently, "but she'll get
over it till I get back. My early clip [3]
has started to move east, and I'm leaving for St. Louis in the morning to
sell it."

The plains had deepened in grass to
my pony's knees before my father returned. He always remembered me
from the St. Louis shops, with some-

[1] **Atlantean:** looking like Atlas, the mythical
hero who supported the sky on his shoulders.
[2] **Nubian lion:** African lion, one having a
black mane.
[3] **clip:** wool clipped from sheep.

thing not easily obtainable in his store
— a boy's light rifle or silver spurs. Usually his gifts for Juliana were slighter
— a sterling napkin ring engraved with
her name, a golden-leather album with
the photographs of President and Mrs.
Hayes in front, and once a mahogany
lap secretary. I know that secretly he
was very fond of her, but she was only
a girl — an heir who would never carry
on his name; or smoke heavy cigars
while making contracts with Kansas
City jobbers or colonels of the quarter-
master's department; or drive a buggy
over a region half as large as New England, overseeing the lambing of a vast
number of ewes and sleeping among
the herders in all kinds of spring
weather.

But no one could predict my father.
When, hale, lusty, and radiating vitality, he left the mansion for the store,
after greeting us on his return far
ahead of his mule train, Trinidad
brought in two canvas valises from the
boot of a new buggy.

There were, I remember, taffetas and
alpacas for my mother, but most of it,
I glimpsed at once, was for Juliana.
My mother held them up to her, one
after the other, but all I can recall are
a blue velvet riding dress with an extraordinarily long skirt and a black,
lathlike sheath dress, a style none of us
had ever seen before, and in which,
my mother promptly declared, no self-
respecting girl would show her figure
or could walk across the room if she
did.

When I ran to the store with my
new silver-mounted bridle, which was
on the bottom of the second valise, my
father glanced at me sharply.

"What did Juliana say?" he questioned. "Did she try on the dresses?"

I felt a faint chill up my spine, but one look at his eyes convinced me that I must tell the truth. No one today has eyes like his, blue-green above his black beard, leaping at times with a gusto that would stop at nothing, burning again with a deadly green flame, and, as quickly, freezing to blue ice.

"I don't reckon she was feeling good, Papa," I stammered. "She just went to her room and didn't say anything."

Al Sleeper, the head clerk, turned quickly to rearrange the wooden boot boxes that stood in a pile on the floor, and the faces of the listening men stiffened as if someone had suddenly brushed them all with varnish. But my father's face did not change, neither then nor day after day when I saw him look up with a steeled expression to see what Juliana was wearing, only to find her monotonously, almost disrespectfully, in the dove-colored gray.

Something had happened to Juliana. There was a spring in a *cañada* [1] of the San Blas plain that the Mexicans called El Olvidado.[2] The grass was never so green as there, with a fringe of tules and red-winged blackbirds and the living water welling up cool and clear. My pony and I had often drunk there. But the last year something strange had come to the place. The tules were still there and the red-winged blackbirds, and the grass still looked green, but there was no water to drink.

It was like that with Juliana. She had the same clear skin and straight white path running back along the center of her smoothly parted, dark hair, and the heart-shaped locket still stirred to her breathing, but something clear and living had vanished. Her custom-made sidesaddle gathered gritty plains dust in the harness room, and her cream-colored buckskin mare grew wild on the range. Most of the time she spent quietly in her room, and when I came in, she would be sitting on the edge of her bed, a two-month-old copy of the New York *Ledger* or *Saturday Night* in her fingers, but her eyes would be gazing over the top of the pages and out of the deep window to the plain that already, in August, was a gray, imprisoning sea.

People in the territory were not different from people anywhere else, and I knew they were talking. Whenever Juliana was called into my mother's rooms to greet visitors, I saw them exchange guarded glances. And when she crossed to the store to match yarn for my mother's tireless bone needles — seeing almost no one, walking with open eyes like one asleep — customers watched her furtively, and Mexican women murmured sympathetically, "*Pobrecita*," [3] after she had gone. My father never murmured in his life, and his full-charged, indomitable figure remained as always, but more than once when my mother was not looking, I watched him glance characteristically at Juliana. And although his bearded face remained adamant, I fancied I could see a kind of Spartan pain afterwards in his eyes.

[1] *cañada* (cä·nyä′dä): a Spanish word meaning "valley."

[2] **El Olvidado** (el ôl·vē·dä′dō): a Spanish name meaning a place of forgetfulness.

[3] *Pobrecita* (pō·brä·sē′tä): a Spanish word meaning "poor little thing."

Looking back now, I can understand perfectly, and everything falls into its place like the letters of the alphabet. But I was only a boy on my pony that day in Capitan when lawyer Henry Coddom asked me to come into his house. In the parlor a man was pacing up and down, and, even in that dim room so soon after the bright sunlight, I saw at once that it was Vance Rutherford, tall, perhaps a little older, his cheekbones faintly haggard, a fresh desert marigold as always in the buttonhole of his high Eastern coat, and the familiar far-away look in his eyes, which to me had never seemed to belong to the long, fighting lines of his face.

I stiffened at the sight of him, but Vance Rutherford bowed in his impersonal, gentlemanly manner.

"Good morning, Johnnie," he said gravely, and asked me to sit down on the black horsehair sofa, where, for a time, like a pair of grown men, we spoke formally on trivial subjects, none of which touched the railroad or my family.

"Johnnie," he said quietly after a little, "will you take a letter to your sister and not let anyone else see it?"

He did not try to urge me. I thought of Juliana walking with mute eyes around the mansion, and I told myself that I didn't like to be the one to keep a letter from her.

"I don't care," I said, meaning I would do it, and he brought it out, and, without either of us saying another word, I slipped it into a pocket.

The letter burned like a live coal all the way back on the saddle to Gant's, and I felt relieved that my father was in the Merino Valley and that I did not have to smuggle the letter past him. All afternoon I watched the men shovel the new crop of barley and corn into the dusty warehouse bins, and, when I put my saddle and bridle away in the harness room in the last golden, stabbing rays of the sun, I found, with surprise, that Juliana's sidesaddle was missing. She did not come to the table for supper, and when I heard the long, doleful bugle of a prairie wolf after nightfall, I went to my mother.

"It's all right, John," she said, and I think she knew about the letter then.

"Someone will see Juliana home, or she'll stay all night at the Hudspeths'."

It was during the heavy hours of the night that I was awakened by the feel of a kiss on my cheek. I twisted my head on the bolster, and there was Juliana with a lighted candlestick in her hand. She didn't say a word, just stood there looking down at me, and there was in her face a shining something I had never seen before. It wasn't altogether real — the late hour, her illuminated figure against the blackness of the huge room, the strange luminosity in her eyes, and her appearance in the stunning blue velvet riding dress my father had brought her. I had the singular impression that it was a dream, but when I reached out to see if I could touch her, she squeezed my fingers, and I found her hand substantial and throbbing with warmth.

I thought it strange that she was not at breakfast, and when I looked into her room, the smoothness of the bright, quilted counterpane told me that her bed had not been slept in. Lupita and Piedad,[1] two of the Mexican servants, professed to know nothing about it, but I knew, by the impassive restraint in which they moved away, that a feeling of excitement pervaded the house. And as I passed my mother's open door, I saw her wiping her eyes.

That afternoon my father drove home in time for supper. His beard was roan[2] from the trail, and his eyes glinted through it like pieces of turquoise in the dust. As a rule, my mother took her meals in her rooms, where she ate in

---

[1] **Piedad** (pyä′däd).
[2] **roan** (rōn): reddish brown mixed with white.

lone state from a massive silver tray covered with hammered dots. And I felt the keen import tonight when her full taffeta skirts came rustling to the dining room.

I think my father sensed it, too. Twice I saw him glance deliberately at the empty chair standing with such silent power at the table. And before he spoke, his bearded lips tightened.

"Where's Juliana?" he asked, and the brown face of Lupita, the table girl, grew thin with emotion. But my mother's eyes burned with a triumphant light across the table.

"She's gone!" she told him, as if she had waited long for this moment. "She was married to Vance Rutherford at the Coddoms' last evening. They're halfway to Kansas by now."

I did not dare look at my father. Sitting there with my dark antelope steak smoking on the plate before me, I suddenly knew why Juliana had come in during the night to kiss me. And for a long, vivid moment I could see her in her blue velvet and Vance Rutherford with a fresh desert marigold in his buttonhole sitting close together in the bridal coach as they swept northeast across the territory, followed by a golden whirlwind of earthy cloud. And now, hours after they had left, it was as if I could still see their dust lying over the plain in the calm October sunlight like a long, motionless finger pointing out to my father the direction in which they had gone.

Every second I expected to hear him push back his chair and call for Trinidad to hitch Prince and Custer, his fastest buggy team. When at last I looked up, he had regained his indomitable control. But his face was like the faint grayness of winter snow through the heavy growth of black spruce on lone, powerful Mount Jeddo.

He did not speak during the rest of the supper. Lupita tiptoed around the table. The meal lasted interminably. For all of my father's lack of hunger, he did not allow himself to eat a mouthful less than customary. When he rose to go to the store, which always stayed open till ten o'clock, he must have been aware that every clerk and customer would by this time probably know. His beard and shoulders up, the deep smoldering fire in his eyes warning everyone he met, he walked steadily across the trail in the dusk.

Juliana wrote to my mother, letters filled with bright pictures of her new life. She and Vance lived in a beautiful brick house with a marble doorstep in Kansas City. She had bought a stunning maroon cheviot suit[1] with pearl buttons and a bonnet with plumes to match. Every Sunday morning she and Vance attended church, and already at weekday breakfast she knew the day's news of the world. Her letters closed: "Give my dearest love to Papa and Johnnie. Your affectionate daughter, Juliana." But if my mother ever ventured to give it, I never heard her.

All winter I did not mention her name to my father and never heard him speak it. I doubted if he ever would. When, sometimes, I would see him walking silently and rigidly about the place, it was as if he were trying by sheer force of will to erase her ghostlike presence from our hall and

rooms, from the aisles of the store, and even from the territory. By the following spring it almost seemed as if she might never have been there. But once my mother read aloud from the *Enterprise* that Mr. and Mrs. Henry Coddom had been to Kansas City, and when she came to the words: "they called on Mrs. Vance Rutherford, the former Juliana Gant," something wrenched open in my mind, and Juliana was back in the mansion with us as real as she had ever been in the flesh.

It was only in this way she came that windy day in April when the dust was flying in yellow sheets across the plain. A private coach had stopped at our feed corral to buy grain for the horses. Someone walked into the mansion courtyard, and old Piedad came hurrying back through the hall with a kind of consternation on her wrinkled face. Rather curiously, I went to the door and, for a moment, had the feeling that Juliana had come. It was Vance Rutherford, a little heavier and more mature, his face solid and squarer, with a reddish mustache and a marigold as always in his buttonhole.

I stood uncomfortably in the doorway, not knowing quite what to do or say, but Piedad had gone on to my mother's rooms, and now my mother came with loud sibilations of taffeta skirts, seized both of Vance Rutherford's hands in hers, kissed him as if he were my brother, and poured out a dozen questions about Juliana.

"Juliana's fine," he said. "She wanted to come along, but I'm on business." His face sobered. "I've got to see Mr. Gant in the store and then hurry back, but I promised to see you first, so I

---

[1] **cheviot** (shev′ē·ət) **suit:** suit made of heavy twill cloth.

could tell her how you all looked."

At the mention of my father, the bright, birdlike glint came into my mother's eyes. I saw that she itched to know the cause of his visit, but he did not offer to tell her, and when he left for the store, she feverishly insisted that I go along, as if my companionship might in some mysterious brotherly manner ingratiate him into my father's good graces.

It was the last place in the world that I wanted to be at the moment, and I kicked grimly at every bone and horn I met in the dust to the wide store-steps. Through the open door I could see my father standing in a circle of respectfully listening men, his back and clasped hands to the cold, fat-bellied, unblackened stove. Then I stepped discreetly aside to let Vance Rutherford enter first.

It could not have been possible for more than a few of our customers to know Vance Rutherford by sight; yet when he stepped past the pile of carriage blankets at the door, something was in the air of the big store room that wasn't there before. Ike Roehl, halfway up a stepladder, soundlessly dropped an armful of ladies' zephyrs[1] to the counter. Over by the sugar barrels, a clerk and customer stopped talking. In the silence that followed, I could hear the windows rattling and the fine sand sifting across the small panes. And suspended on their nails along the ceiling, the rows of wooden buckets kept swinging silently in the draft.

"Could I see you a few minutes in

[1] **zephyrs** (zef′ərz): garments made of light material, such as shawls and sweaters.

your office, Mr. Gant?" Vance Rutherford asked.

I expected to see rushing into my father's face that volcanic violence from which I had often watched men shrink. Instead, he seemed to be seized by some strange perversity. Not long before, he had come in from overseeing the loading of fleeces on one of his eastbound wagon trains. The rolling brim of his hat was gray with dust. Wisps of wool clung to his broadcloth and buttons. And now he stood with his chin half-sunken on his chest and his eyes half-closed, as if warding off someone he intensely disliked, with a kind of ponderous lethargy.

"Anything you have to say, you can say it here," he rumbled.

Vance Rutherford stood very straight, but I saw him bite his lip.

"I wanted to talk to you in private, sir," he flushed, "so you'd be free to act as you thought best in the matter." He waited a few moments. "If you force me to make it public property, I'll do it." He waited again, and when my father made neither movement nor further expression, his face grew longer and harder, and I saw that it had not lost any of its fighting lines. "The railroad is coming into the territory, sir!" he announced tensely. "We're starting to lay track across the line in May."

None of the listening men moved so much as a finger, but I could feel a wave of something electric sweep over the room. Only my father seemed immune from it. He still stood like a dozing buffalo bull, only partly aware of what might be going on around him.

"You're coming as far as Capitan?" he grunted.

"We'll have trains running into Capitan in a year," Vance Rutherford promised.

My father lifted his massive head, and I saw his deep smoldering eyes.

"You still have railroad stock for sale?"

"We have, Mr. Gant," the younger man said simply. "It takes money to build a railroad."

"I understand," my father rumbled on, "that you figure on spending millions in the territory?"

"Millions!" Vance Rutherford agreed. "But it will all come back to us, once we're in operation." He leaned forward earnestly. "Mr. Gant, you've been a pioneer in this country. You've had to deal with savages and outlaws, but those days are nearly over. The territory is on the threshold of prosperity. A flood of people are coming with the railroad. Schools and churches will spring up everywhere. It's going to be an empire, the southwestern empire, sir. I can see the railroad a few years from now hauling train after train of passengers and rich freight all the vast distance from the Mississippi to the Pacific!"

I was fascinated by his eloquence. There was something magically convincing in his voice and enthusiasm, and, for the moment, I could actually see a railroad train sweeping triumphantly across our San Blas plain, and the Indians and Mexicans fleeing from it in terror. And, looking into the staring eyes of grizzled old teamsters, I believed they could see it too.

Vance Rutherford seemed to feel his power. He went on appealingly:

"Mr. Gant, you're one of the biggest freighters in the country. You know your business, and, if you do, you must know that the day of mule and bull trains is past. You've seen what happened along the Santa Fe Trail in Kansas. You know what will happen to the wagon business in this territory as soon as we have trains running into Capitan. Don't you agree, sir, that it's good business for a freighter to sell his wagons and mules while there's a demand and to put his money into the railroad?"

I heard a sound like a deep mutter that could be no longer withheld, and, before I looked, I knew that my father had thrown up his massive head and was standing there, rude and immovable, his shaggy beard throwing off defiance, and green fire like the dog star in his eyes.

"No!" he bellowed, and I heard the tinware on the shelves murmur his decree after him. "My only interest in your stock, young man, was to find out whether I could trust you and your fourteen-million-dollar-railroad officials to horse feed when they came through!"

I saw Al Sleeper open his mouth in a soundless laugh and a rancher from the Tres Ritos [1] bring one hand down silently on his denim thigh. The spell of the railroad was irreparably broken. Customers and loafers nudged one another, and Vance Rutherford looked as if he had been struck across the face. His temples twitched, but he stood his ground.

"I think, Mr. Gant," he said, with a great effort at dignity, "if the railroad ever asks it, your feed corral would be justified in extending credit."

[1] **Tres Ritos** (träs rē′tōs).

I expected him to go, but for a long moment the two men continued to face each other, both iron-willed and unyielding — one, young in years, gentlemanly, with a flower in his buttonhole; the other, older, powerful, with streaks of wool and dust on his clothing; one of the new age; one of the old. Then the younger man turned silently and went out.

News of the coming of the railroad spread like a gold strike through the territory. Stories reached the store by stage and wagon train, by buckboard and carriage. The railroad was awarding contracts for grading, ties, bridge timbers, and telegraph poles. The railroad contractors were buying herds of horses and mules. The railroad was blasting tunnels through the San Dimas [1] Mountains. The railroad was crossing the mountains on the old wagon trail. All summer and fall, the railroad expected to lay from one to two miles of track a day.

By Christmas the byword among the teamsters returning from the iron rails was "Look out for the locomotive!" They reported the sleepy old Mexican village of La Luz [2] booming since the railroad had arrived. The Capitan *Enterprise* announced with pride that Baldwin's was building a new, huge, eighty-ton locomotive for use in the territory and that it would be "in charge of men fully competent to handle the monster." And it added that Vance Rutherford, engineer for the railroad, had promised lawyer Henry Coddom that he was pushing construction with every resource at his command and that

trains would be running into Capitan by the Fourth of July.

In the very next issue of the *Enterprise,* Capitan stores advertised in tall type that no new merchandise would come from the East until it arrived more cheaply and safely by steam train. My mother had always abhorred the trail, its clouds of dust, the shouts and curses of its drivers, the crack of whips and report of linchpins,[3] and the snail-like drag of long files of chained steers. Ever since I could remember, she had shut it out with heavy brown hangings. But now she began to draw them back and sit at her knitting where she could see, at last, traffic slowly but steadily fading like late afternoon on the old trail. It seemed to give her a satisfaction, as if the railroad were just over the rise, ruthlessly pushing the creaking freight wagons out of the way.

I knew that every vanished wagon and silent wheel was a secret growing cancer in the heart of my father. He never alluded to it, but when I rode along in his buggy to Capitan, I could see the steely glitter in his eyes at sight of the copper ingots, which his trains formerly freighted to Kansas, piling up in great mounds at the proposed site of the new depot. And his eyes looked straight ahead when we passed teams unloading wool and hides into adobe warehouses that had sprung up like molehills where Henry Coddom had sold the railroad a tract of land for the new Capitan town site and which, already, people were calling Newtown.

---

[1] **San Dimas** (sän dē'mäs).
[2] **La Luz** (lä lōos).

[3] **linchpins:** pins that keep wheels in place. They squeak as the wheels turn.

There was actually no more railroad to be seen in Capitan than out on the sand hills, but every day now rigs began passing our store on their way to Capitan to trade. Cowboys nightly celebrated the railroad by shooting up the town. There was talk of the *Enterprise* becoming a daily after the telegraph had arrived. I saw where Strome Brothers had torn down their old wooden hitching rack and set up individual posts with citified snap chains. And the *Enterprise* boasted that there wasn't a vacant house in the town.

Up to this time I had never seen a railroad in my young life, and it seemed that our store and trail were being blighted by some mysterious and invisible weapon in Vance Rutherford's hand. This morning I noticed my father throw up his head to gaze at the northeast. When I looked, there it hung like a black dust cloud over the green of the prairie, the railroad at last. And as my father stared at the smoke funneling up persistently on the distant horizon, I saw the same wild defiance come into his bearded face as had that day at his sheep camp along the Rio Cedro [1] when we had watched a Comanche or Kiowa smoke signal from the hills.

Every morning after this, the smoke was there, and I came to think of it as the powerful black breath of Vance Rutherford, moving steadily, silently, inexorably southwest toward Capitan. Now it passed the red mesa, and now for a few days it changed rugged Mount Jeddo into an active volcano. And one day when it had reached some

[1] **Rio Cedro** (rē′ō sä′drō).

miles abreast of us, I could not resist galloping my pony secretly across the plain to a grassy swell from which I could see a whole bank being sliced away like cake. The prairie there seemed to boil with men and teams, with wagons, plows, and drags. The air was filled with the flash of moving picks and shovels and the ring of iron hammers. And creeping back and forward in the background, hissing, some-

times outshrieking any mountain lion, glided one of Vance Rutherford's tamed iron monsters.

I was only a boy, but I could tell, as I rode thoughtfully homeward, that in this thing my mother called civilization there was no quarter, no compromise, no pity. It was not like your grazing pony that, after tiring you for an hour, would let you catch it, or like a wagon train that welcomed you with a blanket, food, and the red warmth of a campfire. This was something of another kidney, of another and newer age.

After that initial challenging scrutiny, I never saw my father acknowledge the black smoke's presence. When he entered the store, the subject changed. Only once I heard him refer again to the railroad. A passenger on the halted stage boasted that a Mississippi-Pacific train had done twenty-five miles an hour crossing the plains. My father turned with heavy deliberation and stared him into confusion.

"Sir, I can do as much with one of my Kentucky buggy teams!" he scorned. "And if the trail is uphill, I have gold to wager that I can soundly whip your train!"

But some hours after the stage had gone, I saw him silent and solitary behind our warehouse, pacing measuredly around what none of us had ever seen before — a corral of his stilled freight wagons. Mute, deserted, and depressing, they stood there, an unforgettable reminder of what had been. And late that evening when my mother sent me to take the St. Louis paper back to his office, I don't think he knew I was there, for I heard from his bedroom deep incredible sounds, like a man praying, which instantly riveted me to the floor. I couldn't understand a word he said, but the shock of hearing my strong father give way like that in secret shook me to my foundations.

Next morning at breakfast he was staunch and powerful as always, and I told myself that I must have been mistaken. And that afternoon I felt sure of it. I was counting twenty-, ten-, and five-dollar gold pieces, silver dollars, halves, and quarters — there was nothing smaller — on his battered desk in the mansion office, when through the window I saw lawyer Henry Coddom climb determinedly out of his phaeton [1] in the courtyard. The two men had not met since Juliana had been married in the Coddom parlor, and now, with Henry Coddom appointed attorney for the railroad in the territory, I could feel the clouds gather and thicken. When Piedad brought the visitor to the office door, he asked to speak with my father in private, and I was sent away.

Twenty minutes later Henry Coddom came out like a cuffed schoolboy, hat in his hand, his face crimson. And when my father stepped into the hall to order me back to my counting, there were still pitchforks in his eyes, and I had never seen him more absolute and unconquerable. Then he became aware of my mother standing in the doorway to her rooms, color in her quilted cheeks and a newspaper in her hand.

"Nettie" — he inclined his head.

"Frank!" she begged him. "You didn't throw away your invitation?"

"Invitation?" His uncompromising eyes bored her.

"It's in the *Enterprise!*" my mother went on feverishly. "They're running the first train into Capitan the Fourth of July. The whole territory's going to celebrate. They expect crowds from every county. The Governor and judges and politicos and all the big men of the territory will get on the train at La Luz and ride into Capitan. The

[1] **phaeton** (fā′ə·tən): a light horse-drawn carriage.

Governor of Kansas and his wife will be on the train, and a Kansas band. They've telegraphed an invitation to President Hayes."

Granite had come into my father's face.

"I got no invitation," he answered harshly. "Henry Coddom came to tell me the railroad wants to build to California." His eyes blazed. "They want eighty miles of my land. They want to build through the Canyon Bonito. They want to blacken my grass, plow trains through my sheep, dump squatters along the Bonito all the way from Big Flat to Gant's Valley."

I am not sure that my mother heard him.

"Frank," she went on desperately, "it's to be the biggest thing that ever happened in the territory. The railroad's giving a banquet at the Wooton House. There'll be dancing till morning. And all the railroad officials and their wives will be there!"

It was almost as if my mother had mentioned Vance Rutherford and Juliana by name. With a titanic effort to control himself, my father turned without a word into the mansion office. And all the time my fingers kept building up fat piles of white and yellow coins, I could feel the raw emotion working in him. And from the next issue of the *Enterprise* we found that the railroad company was daring to drag him soon, like some petty thief or cattle rustler, into court in Bonito County, half of whose vast spaces he owned, to show why eighty miles of his choicest river pasture land should not be condemned for the railroad right of way.

For days afterward he remained around home, silent and implacable, waiting for the case to be called. And when I saw the dull fire leaping in his eyes, I knew he was forging the bolts of lightning he would let loose in that small adobe courtroom at Bonito. Of course Mr. Stryker, his lawyer, would be with him, but it was my father who would dominate the court.

"No judge in this territory," Al Sleeper declared, "can look Frank Gant in the eye and turn over his land to Henry Coddom and a Kansas railroad."

For weeks my father waited while the railroad pushed its mailed arm into Capitan, while June grew closer to July, and Juliana's cream-colored mare had a second colt that Juliana had never seen. And all the time I could see in my mother's eyes the hope that the case had not yet been called in Judge Tatum's court at Bonito because he and Vance Rutherford expected to come to my father privately and settle the differences out of court in time to get him to the celebration. I knew that if anybody could reason with my father, it was Judge Tatum, whom I had often seen slouched in the mansion office, an extraordinarily long figure with a face like a sorrel horse, his long legs up on the battered desk, a thick tumbler and a jug of my father's whisky beside him, and my father laughing indulgently through his beard at what the Judge was saying.

Then all hope of my father's going to the celebration faded from my mother's eyes. One of his old herders, Gil Jaramillo, arrived in the mansion courtyard on a spent horse. Tall and cadaverous, his eyes rolling with the mad light of so many men who spend their lives with the sheep, he called out, "*Amo!*" [1] with excitement as soon as he was at the door. And when my father had come into the hall, he stammered out in Spanish that the Cross V's, whose cattle ranch adjoined my father's Rio Cedro pastures, were warring on his sheep, driving some of them into the river, scattering the rest to be preyed upon by coyotes and wolves, and badly beating up the *caporal* [2] and herders.

I expected to see the anger flame on my father's face. Instead, it grew calmer than for weeks, as if news of violence and bloodshed were almost a welcome relief from this petty waiting for a summons to court. Within the hour he drove off for the Rio Cedro, sitting his buggy like a king, Trinidad brown and solid beside him, and a change of horses galloping through the dust behind. And long after he had gone, I could see him in my mind, whipping his team across a region half as wide as France, the goats leaping with flying beards from in front of the horses, the cedar branches whipping the buggy from both sides of the narrow trail, himself staying the night in some humble *placita* [3] and, if there was a bed in the village, sleeping in it, and finally matching his strength against his enemies, who had always been putty in his hands.

I was glad he had gone that evening when the deputy from Bonito County arrived apologetically with the summons. But the gray glance of Al Sleeper held a queer light, and under his mustache, jutting out from his face like the waterfall of a roily [4] mountain stream, his mouth looked forbidding. He spoke to my mother and early next morning sent the summons with a Mexican rider after my father, but I knew it was like a desert finch trying to catch an eagle.

The mansion seemed like a convent with my father gone. Our native villagers kept asking if we were not to ride with the Governor on the bunting-trimmed train. I told them we didn't like crowds, that we had plenty of bunting in the mansion, and that we intended to wait until there was room in Capitan to breathe. They nodded solemnly, polite Mexicans that they were, but they knew as well as I why we weren't going.

And now from morning till night the migration toward Capitan began passing our door — American ranchers and miners in the saddle, in buggy and buckboard; officers' families from Fort Gates in Army ambulances with the side curtains rolled up for air; but mostly natives who had never seen the iron horse — Mexican families in heavy wagons, in a few private carriages, and in endless saddles; Ute Indians decked with bright ribbons, their bony ponies packed for trade; and aloof Navajos in red calicos and blue velvets and clinking silver.

By noon of the Fourth all had passed. The last trip the stage would ever make by our door took place about one, the westbound coach

[1] *Amo* (ä′mō): a Spanish word meaning "master."

[2] *caporal* (cä·pō·räl′): a Spanish word meaning "chief."

[3] *placita* (plä·sē′tä): a Spanish word meaning "small village."

[4] **roily**: muddy.

crowded with passengers. It threw off our leather bag of mail, but failed to stop. And after it had gone and the trail lay quiet again, I suddenly realized that it looked different from what I had ever seen it, old, tired, abandoned, almost like the ruins of an ancient *camino* [1] winding desolately over the plain.

About two o'clock I glimpsed a distant smudge of dust to the northeast, a smudge that swirled rapidly nearer, and finally I could make out our bay team plunging wearily toward home, my father driving and Trinidad still beside him, but only one horse galloping behind. My father swerved the foaming, bulging-eyed team into the mansion courtyard. As I slipped back into the hall, he said something to Trinidad, who at once drove away. Then I saw through my mother's doorway that she had stiffened in her chair and bent her face defensively over her knitting.

My father scarcely tossed a glance at me as he came in, haggard and grim, his hat, beard, and broadcloth layered with dust. He halted in the center of the hall, from where his eyes could flash turbulently into my mother's room.

"Was Stryker here to see me?"

My mother's rigid needles kept moving.

"Yesterday, Frank," she answered.

"Well?" he breathed heavily.

"Judge Tatum appointed commissioners to condemn the land." My mother's lips were tight bands. "He told Mr. Stryker that no individual

[1] *camino* (cä-mē'nō): a Spanish word meaning "road."

could stand in the way of progress and the railroad."

My father hadn't moved. My mother tried to leave the subject: "Did you settle the trouble with the Cross V's?"

"There was," my father answered harshly, "no trouble to settle."

"What do you mean?" For the first time she looked up at him.

"I mean," my father said, and now that he had started, the words poured out in a wild torrent, "that progress isn't above using the tricks of a blackleg gambler!" The green lightning had leaped from his eyes, and at each successive sentence the bolt seemed to hurl itself again, as I had often watched it in a distant cloud, traversing over and over the same forked path. "There wasn't any sheep war. Nobody had beaten a herder. I didn't find a ewe touched. Somebody paid Gil Jaramillo to come here. They bribed him to lie to me. They had me drive hundreds of miles in a buggy and kill one of my best horses to keep me away from Judge Tatum's court!" Then he turned and went into his office.

I thought I could hear him moving about in his bedroom. There was a purr of wheels in the courtyard, and through the pane at the side of the door I saw Trinidad drive up in the red-wheeled buggy without a top.

My father came out almost immediately. He had changed his clothes, but the dust still clung to his beard and eyebrows. In his hand was the blacksnake whip with which he had once whipped a herder for the arch crime of deserting his sheep, and I saw that the lash was still caked with dried particles of red.

"Frank!" my mother cried. She had run to her doorway. "Where are you going?"

He paid her utterly no attention. I don't think he knew she was there.

"Frank!" she screamed after him. "Whoever bribed Gil Jaramillo, it wasn't Vance Rutherford or the railroad! They wouldn't stoop to a thing like that!"

He went on out of the door. Never had I seen my mother move so rapidly. Her full skirts seemed to whisper in terror as they glided over the floor. Her hands seized my shoulder.

"Get him to take you with him!" she begged me. "He never does those violent things when you're along!" She pushed me out of the doorway, and I saw the sun glinting on the sleek flanks of the dancing Kentucky team.

I ran to the right side, where the springs had already deeply settled.

"I want to go along, Papa!" I shouted at him.

He looked down at me.

"You're sure you want to go along?" he asked, and at his mad eyes a chill ran down my spine, but I nodded. He told the impassive Trinidad to step out, and I climbed in beside him. Prince and Custer were crazy to be off. They had not been driven for days. One hand of my father pulled them back, rearing.

"Easy, boys," he said through his teeth and beard. "We'll have plenty time when we get there."

Crouching on the cushion, I told myself I couldn't see how trouble could happen on a day like this. The sky was a blue bowl, and I could smell the freshness of last night's shower in the bunch grass all around us. Horned larks flushed in front of the horses. A road runner clowned at us, his crest and long tail rising and falling comically. But I did not laugh. Ahead, like a bed of mushrooms sprung up on the prairie, I could see the buildings of Capitan.

Halfway across the prairie something ran shining through the grass — the twin iron bands of the railroad. From here to Capitan they had built straight as an arrow, close beside the trail, as if

to ridicule the earthy ruts, crude windings, and arroyo [1] dips of the sprawling old overland route. Here the railroad cut insolently over the trail, and the light buggy pitched on the rough planks of the crossing, but my father gave no sign that the railroad was there — not even when a wailing cry drifted over the prairie behind us and I knew without turning my head that the horizon must be stormy with smoke.

Within a mile or two the rails only a few yards from the trail were crackling. Our Kentucky buggy horses had grown uneasy and were trying to throw frightened looks over their shoulders, but my father held their heads with an iron hand. Twisting in my seat, I could see the afternoon sun sparkling on something that moved behind us, pursuing us, not galloping up and down like a buffalo, but gliding through the grass like a snake. The bulging smokestack was as high as the neck of a camel, the boiler as big as the belly of a horse, and below it a cowcatcher, long and pointed like Judge Tatum's nose, ran on its own pony wheels. A man rode in the cab, which was as high off the ground as a buggy, and behind him streamed the coaches of the territory's celebration train.

I could hear a brass band in the cars now. It was playing "Dixie." Everything on the train was gaiety as it pulled beside us. Red, white, and blue bunting fluttered from headlight, smokestack, and whistle. The bell rang triumphantly. The small pony wheels spun. The black-and-gold driving shafts shot backward and forward. Faces pressed at the small, square windows, and on the open platforms of the short, boxlike coaches a few male passengers stood holding to iron railings and brake wheels. But for all the attention my father gave it, the train might not have been there.

So far the railroad and train had been slightly downhill. Now the train reached the foot of the steady prairie grade up to Capitan. The engine began to puff valiantly, and a cloud of cinders came flying back into our faces. Suddenly I realized that, although my father still sat like a bearded statue beside me, his thewlike [2] fingers had let out some slack on the lines, and the long-denied horses were leaping.

I told myself it couldn't be a race, because my father wasn't racing. He just sat there deaf and unapproachable, but now I know that of all the matches between horseflesh and the iron horse that were to follow on the same rude course, this was the most intense and deadly in earnest. Heads began to appear out of the open car windows. Passengers waved, jeered, and challenged. But the train no longer was moving faster than the buggy.

Suddenly something inside of me seemed to stand still. Peering round my father, I had caught a glimpse of a face at a car window. It was more of a lady's face than I had remembered, but the eyes under the nodding plumes were unchanged. They were fixed on my father with a look that I shall never forget, almost the look they had given him that day she had

[1] **arroyo** (ə·roi′ō): gully.

[2] **thewlike:** muscular.

tiptoed into my mother's room two years before, a straining look of appeal that might almost have been at God. Only a matter of thirty or forty feet separated her from my father, but it might as well have been the width of Kansas. He did not turn. The horses raced on, and when I looked again, all I could see in the glass was the blurred reflection of prairie sky, and the face of Juliana had gone.

I had to keep bracing myself on the rocking cushion. The train beside us rode smoothly enough, almost contemptuously, over its new roadbed, but the buggy plunged from rut to pitch hole, and yet, window by window and now coach by coach, the buggy was gaining. Directly ahead I could make out a dense frieze of men's hats and ladies' parasols around the new depot. Nearer, on both sides of the railroad, the green plain blossomed with visiting tents and camp wagons. And now the trail just in front of us began to teem with American, Mexican, and Indian spectators, who fell back whooping and shooting as we tore by.

I can still see Prince and Custer running, their heads outstretched, their manes wildly flinging, and at every jump the fine muscles on their hips appearing and disappearing like so many fingered hands. With both horses bent into shying half arcs, we breasted the laboring engine, passed it, left its bright flutter of bunting definitely behind us. And I told myself exultantly that my father had whipped the celebration train, humbled the railroad in front of half the territory. Then I saw ahead where the trail swerved sharply, and remembered that we had another

crossing in store.

There was no necessity for my father to take it. He might have turned off the trail on the unfenced prairie. But my father never turned off the trail for anything, God or the devil, cruelty or mercy; so long as it lay squarely in his path, he knew no other justice. Leaning far to the side for the curve, he snatched the whip from its socket and the buggy reeled on two wheels for the crossing.

Through the din of the train I could hear the band playing magnificently. It sounded like "Columbia, the Gem of the Ocean." High above it shrieked the voice of the engine whistling down brakes for the station. It seemed far enough away when it started, grew steadily louder, louder, till the sound seemed to split my ear. I saw my father drop the reins and felt him swing me up in his arms. There was a sound like chair legs crashing, and the blurred earth, engine, and the white faces of the engineer and frontier crowd turned over like the markings on a grindstone.

It wasn't exactly a pain in my back. I felt benumbed, as if an arrow pinned me down. My eyes seemed to be ground shut with dust and sand, and when I forced them open, I could see nothing but the dude hats of men who had come from the train and the gaily trimmed bonnets of the ladies, all swimming around me in a kind of leisurely whirlwind.

Only one of the bonnets looked familiar. It was very near, fashioned with drooping plumes, and I knew that somewhere I had seen it before.

A portly man in a long coat with a velvet collar thrust a flask to my lips.

I sputtered and strangled, but when I could breathe again, I felt better.

"Where's my father?" I asked them. They all just stood there looking at me. I twisted my head and saw Vance Rutherford. He was close to me, a flower in his buttonhole, comforting Juliana, who was bitterly crying. When I closed my eyes I could still see my father sitting in the buggy beside me, aloof, powerful, absolute, his black beard turned stubbornly in the wind, the reins in his thewlike fingers. All these men from the train looked white and soft in comparison. They couldn't, I told myself, whip the bloody back of a herder who had broken the trust to his sheep. I wanted my father. One bark from his bearded lips, and most of this crowd would scurry like prairie dogs.

"Where'd he go?" I cried, and struggled to sit up. Vance Rutherford and the portly man helped me. The crowd fell back slightly. All I could see between tailored trousers and gaily flounced dresses were the iron bands of the railroad running triumphantly westward and glinting like mottled silver in the sun.

CHANGE AND CONFLICT

1. What memories of the narrator reveal the vastness and variety of his father's enterprises?

2. How are the contrasts and conflicts between the narrator's mother and father quickly drawn? Is their conflict over the railroad, over Juliana and Vance Rutherford, or over some other unmentioned factor? Explain.

3. Why did the father so dislike Vance Rutherford and the railroad? How did these two men differ from one another?

4. Describe the scene in the store when Vance Rutherford told about the railroad's coming. What effect did this news have upon the territory? Why was the father summoned to court? What trick kept him out of court? Who do you think played this trick on him?

5. Describe the father's last act of defiance against the railroad. What caused the accident at the crossing? Who do you think finally won the contest? Why?

6. What does the word *smoke* in the title of this story refer to?

7. One of the legacies left to us by the Old West is a strong desire for personal freedom and an admiration for man's courage. In what ways does the personality of the father in this story represent the spirit of the Old West?

8. As our country developed, the Old West changed. What spirit in America does Vance Rutherford represent? Were Vance Rutherford and the father in this story alike in any ways? Explain. Did any other people in this unit resemble Vance Rutherford or the father?

9. How do you feel about the father in this story? about the mother? Do you think the narrator sympathized more with the father or with the mother and Vance Rutherford? Explain.

10. In what other ways have people had their lives disrupted by technology or by other changes? In what ways are our lives likely to be changed in the future? How do you think people should meet these changes?

WORDS FROM SPANISH

Conrad Richter uses several Spanish words to tell this story about the Southwest, a territory bordering on Spanish-speaking Mexico. Most of the Spanish words in the story are footnoted, but a few are not. These words are so common that you probably do not realize you are speaking Spanish when you use them. For example, *Santa Fe* comes from two Spanish words — *santa,* "holy," and *fe,* "faith." Many other words used in this country reflect the Spanish influence on our language. In a dictionary or encyclopedia, look up the following words. How do they reflect the Spanish influence on our language?

guerrilla	San Francisco
corral	Los Angeles
canyon	Colorado
adobe	Sierra Nevada

SENTENCES: COMBINING IDEAS

Conrad Richter uses many long and detailed sentences in this story. Here is one of these sentences. Notice how an interesting sentence has been built around one subject and verb (in italics).

> "And coolly talking to him from a white bowl on the floor, washing himself from a second bowl on the marble top of the washstand, unclothed, unarmed, and unconcerned, *stood* my *father* — a powerful naked figure, not tall, but herculean, in a black beard that twisted and stood out from his chin and cheeks like fine wire."

Here is how these ideas might have been expressed in separate sentences.

My father was coolly talking to him. My father was talking to him from a white bowl. The bowl was on the floor. My father was washing himself from a second bowl. The second bowl was on the washstand. The washstand had a marble top. My father was unclothed. He was unarmed. He was unconcerned. He was a powerful naked figure. He was not tall. He was herculean. He had a black beard. The beard twisted. The beard stood out from his chin and cheeks. The beard looked like fine wire.

Look at the paragraph on page 212 beginning "And today I would give a great deal . . ." This paragraph is composed of one detailed sentence. Can you locate its subject and verb? To see how many ideas are skillfully combined in this one long sentence, put these thoughts into separate short sentences.

COMPOSITION:
SUPPORTING A TOPIC STATEMENT

You will often be asked to write a paragraph or composition in which you make a general statement about some story, poem, or play you have read. When you write such a paragraph or composition, you should refer to details from the selection itself which support what you are saying. For example, suppose you are writing a paragraph around this general statement: *The mother in the story "Smoke over the Prairie" despised the West.* In your paragraph, you would elaborate on at least these three facts from the story.

(1) The mother seldom left her room, which was furnished in an Eastern style.

(2) She hated the noise and dust of the wagons and the oxen trains.

(3) She wanted her daughter to marry an ambitious Easterner, not a cowboy or hunter.

Below are two other statements that might be made about this story. Write a paragraph in support of one of these statements. Refer to at least three specific details from the story which support the statement you have chosen. Before you write your paragraph, make a list of the supporting details you will use.

The father loved Juliana and was upset over her elopement, though he fought to conceal his feelings.

The boy who tells the story indicates that he wished the railroad had not destroyed his father's empire.

Incandescent Genius

C. B. WALL

Technology was beginning to flower as America approached the twentieth century. During the next decades, the country would be transformed, as imaginative men produced a series of amazing, practical inventions: the telephone, the airplane, the electric light, the automobile. This article tells about the American who has been called the greatest inventor of them all.

HE HAS BEEN DEAD now for over twenty-five years, yet he is part of our lives in a thousand ways.

As we watch television, listen to the radio, send a telegram, pound a typewriter, talk on the telephone, go to the movies, play a phonograph record, or switch on an electric light, we are in debt to his genius.

His name? Thomas Alva Edison.

If all the American success stories were rolled into one, the result could barely describe the life of Thomas Alva Edison. Even in an age of giants — for giants strode America in the late nineteenth and early twentieth centuries — he was an outsize and legendary figure.

Thomas Edison was born in Milan, Ohio, in 1847, the sixth child of Samuel Edison, who operated a small lumber mill. From the moment he began to toddle he was an unusual youngster. One spring evening, when he was five, his parents found him in a neighbor's barn, squatting patiently on a nest of duck eggs. He had been there for at least ten hours and was blue with cold, but he protested bitterly as the elders bundled him home.

"I can hatch 'em. I know I can hatch 'em," he said.

When he was seven, the family moved to Port Huron, Michigan, where Edison began what was probably the briefest formal education in history. At the end of two months the teacher had a talk with his mother:

"I'm sorry, but your boy seems definitely backward. He simply doesn't want to learn."

"Nonsense!" Nancy Edison exploded. "Tom's a brilliant boy — I'll teach him myself."

She was an unusual woman, and her son had an unusual education. After teaching him to read and write, she let him follow his own interests.

Gradually the farmhouse cellar became a laboratory stocked with hundreds of jars and bottles. Young Edison was particularly fascinated by a description of Samuel Morse's recent invention. He puzzled over the construction of wet batteries, the rigging of telegraph lines, the design of instruments, the Morse code.

By the time he was twelve, the youngster decided to strike out for financial independence. His laboratory needed expensive materials, and he was buying new science books as fast as they appeared. So the inventor went into business. He persuaded the Grand Trunk Railway to let him have the newspaper and candy concession on its new daily train between Port Huron and Detroit.

In Detroit the young news butcher [1] was soon spending his spare time in the reading rooms of the Young Men's Society. He had already learned to read rapidly and could skim through several average-size volumes in an evening, retaining the important facts in a prodigious memory which seemed to operate like a high-speed camera.

The Grand Trunk project prospered, and within three years he had expanded it, hired newsboys for other trains, and set up a fresh fruit and vegetable business.

In the baggage car, young Edison had set up a chemical laboratory in which he conducted experiments outlined in his scientific readings. One

[1] **news butcher:** person who sells items like magazines, newspapers, and candy on trains.

Edison in his laboratory. It is doubtful that either ever looked this tidy.

afternoon, as the train lurched over a rough stretch of track, a jar of highly combustible material broke on the floor, igniting newspapers and other flammable odds and ends. After the train crew had brought the flames under control, Edison and his paraphernalia were dumped at the first crossroad. That was the end of his career on the Grand Trunk system.

It was also the beginning of a new career. While still a news butcher, Edison had risked his life to snatch a three-year-old boy from the path of a train approaching the Mount Clemens stop. In his gratitude, the child's father, who was the Mount Clemens telegrapher, offered to teach Edison telegraphy. The young man practiced eighteen hours a day.

All copy in that pre-typewriter day was handwritten. Characteristically, Edison began experimenting with various methods of handwriting in a search for the speediest and most legible form. He finally struck on a printlike, vertical script with characters as sharply formed as steel engraving and as legible as newspaper type. After months of practice, he achieved a speed of fifty-five words a minute, which was faster than any operator could send.

For a skilled telegrapher, employment was no problem, and Edison soon commanded a top salary of $125 a month. His skill was all the more extraordinary because of his deafness. Only the vibration of the clicking instruments enabled him to hear messages.

Long before his eighteenth birthday Edison was quite deaf. During his Grand Trunk days, a brakeman, trying to help him climb aboard a moving train, had pulled him through the baggage-car door by his ears. As a result Edison's auditory nerves had been irreparably damaged.

Wherever he went — to the theater, to the dinner table, on the job — he invariably carried a pocket notebook in which he jotted down drawings and notes for experiments. He wore cracked, run-down shoes, seedy, ink-stained clothes, a disreputable slouch hat, and in the coldest winters refused to spend money for an overcoat, preferring to splurge his entire pay check on scientific books and experimental apparatus.

Sometimes his intense interest in telegraphic theory was held against him. One of the projects in his notebook was that of sending two messages in opposite directions simultaneously over the same wire. One day, while working for Western Union in Memphis, he tried to explain his theory to the Western Union chief there, a General Coleman. The chief was indignant.

"Look here, Edison," Coleman roared, "any fool ought to know that a wire can't be worked both ways at the same time!" He promptly fired Edison as an irresponsible character.

The young scientist's technical proficiency as an operator was tested to the utmost when he applied for a job in Boston. After one look at Edison, with his untrimmed mane falling over a threadbare coat, his socks showing through the cracks in his battered shoes, the Western Union operators in Boston decided to send him back to the haystacks. On his first trial night on the job, they arranged to have the fastest sender in New York crackle through press messages at his highest speed.

As Edison sat down at the desk they gathered around, grinning at one another. The New York operator started out at a normal pace and then gradually increased it, abbreviating long words which the receiver had to transcribe in longhand. Without faltering, the applicant covered page after page with his precise script. There were no mistakes. Each sheet looked as though it had come off the press. The grind continued for four incredible hours.

Finally Edison nonchalantly opened his key and clicked: "Send with the other foot."

The Boston boys gave up. After examining Edison's faultless copy, the Western Union superintendent said, "He is as good an operator as I ever met."

It was in a Boston bookstore that Edison found his first complete set of the works of the British scientist Michael Faraday. He had already begun his lifetime schedule, which allowed him only four hours' sleep out of twenty-four, but that night he didn't close his eyes at all. At breakfast he was still reading Faraday.

"Aren't you going to eat?" his roommate asked.

Edison looked up briefly. "Not now," he said. "I've got too much to do, and life is pretty short."

Working nights as a press-wire operator, he spent the rest of his hours in a Boston machine shop, carrying out experiments which were already beginning to fill countless notebooks. (At his death, Edison had filled more than 2,500.)

Deciding a change of scenery might bring a change of luck, he left Boston for New York.

He borrowed the money for passage on the night boat from Boston, and arrived in the big city without a cent. Through an ex-Boston telegrapher he found lodging in the boiler room of the Gold Exchange.[1] His cot was next to the master transmitter, which sent out fluctuating gold prices to the Exchange and three hundred brokerage houses. Edison spent two evenings studying the complicated mechanism, dreaming up improvements.

On his third morning in the metropolis, just as he was going out to resume his job hunt, chaos broke loose on the floor of the Exchange. The master transmitter had creaked to a halt. Brokers on the floor and in hundreds of offices were without the day's opening prices on gold and scores of commodities. Messenger boys streamed in from the financial district. The operators, unable to find the trouble, were panic stricken.

Edison clumped back down to the basement, took one look at the transmitter.

"Contact spring broken," he pointed out calmly to the manager. "It's fallen between the gears."

The manager regarded the cool gray-blue eyes, the crumpled suit that had been slept in night after night, the

---

[1] **Gold Exchange:** At this time gold was freely bought and sold in the United States, like other commodities. In New York, commerce in gold was carried on in the Gold Exchange.

straggly unbarbered hair that fell from the brim of the battered felt hat.

"Can you fix it?"

Edison pushed back his hat and went to work. Within two hours the transmitter was clicking smoothly. Edison was hired on the spot as mechanical superintendent at the incredible salary of $300 a month.

But, as usual, he was far from content with a payroll job — no matter what the figure. Soon he and two friends rented shop quarters in Jersey City and set themselves up as electrical engineers, specializing in stock tickers and private telegraph facilities. The concern had been in business for less than six months when General Marshall Lefferts of the Gold and Stock Telegraph Company offered to buy them out for $15,000. They accepted. Within months the young inventor had designed the Edison Universal Printer — the basic features of which are still in use today. It was much simpler and far more reliable than the automatic printers then in use among brokerage houses, and General Lefferts was highly enthusiastic.

One morning he called the inventor into his office. "How much do you want for your printer?" he asked.

Edison first thought of asking $3,000. Could he dare ask $5,000?

"I don't know, General," he answered at last, "but would you care to make me an offer?"

"All right. How about $40,000?"

In the first months of 1870, Edison put his capital to work by opening his own manufacturing shop in Newark.

Although he was then only twenty-three, Edison was known as "the Old Man" to his employees. There was an odd, raffish [1] maturity about him. Heavy-set, with sharp gray-blue eyes beneath heavy brows and an extraordinarily broad forehead, he shuffled around his shop in rumpled, grease-stained clothes, looking more like a wayward tramp than a rising young manufacturer. One applicant who inspected the place and then decided not to work for Edison said later, "It struck me that everyone in the shop — including the boss — acted sort of crazy."

He paid top wages, but he demanded the same single-minded devotion to a job which he displayed himself. He despised a clock-watcher and installed half a dozen clocks around the shop — all set at different times.

Although Samuel Morse invented the telegraph there is no doubt that Edison so completely revolutionized it that Morse himself would barely have recognized it. He invented the duplex (sending two messages in opposite directions over the same wire at the same time) and also the diplex (two messages in the same direction).

On Christmas Day of 1871, Edison married Mary Stilwell of Newark, a charming eighteen-year-old girl who taught in the Newark Sunday School and worked in one of his shops. A few hours after the ceremony, he excused himself from the wedding party and hustled back to the shop "for a few minutes." About midnight his best man found him up to his ears in experiments.

"You'd better come home, Tom," he advised.

[1] **raffish** (raf'ish): not quite respectable looking.

"I've got an awful lot of work to do," Edison replied.

"But you just got married today," the other pointed out reproachfully, "and Mary's waiting to go to Boston on her honeymoon."

Edison gradually emerged from his cocoon of concentration and banged his desk. "That's right!" he cried. "I did get married today!"

Despite this unpromising start, the marriage was a happy and rewarding one.

Edison felt that rents in Newark were too high, and in 1876 he broke ground for a new laboratory, at Menlo Park, New Jersey, twenty-five miles from New York. That Menlo Park laboratory, every detail of which he designed himself, was soon to become world famous.

The year it was built, Western Union pressed Edison to improve the telephone, which Alexander Graham Bell had just patented, and on which Edison had already done considerable experimental work.

"Bell may have been the first to invent the telephone," an observer wrote, "but it was Edison who made it possible to hear something on it."

It was Edison's invention of the phonograph, however, which first stamped him as a genius in the public mind.

The first machine that talked can be attributed to Edison's acute powers of observation and deduction rather than to any set series of experiments. He was tinkering one summer day of 1877 with his "automatic telegraph repeater," designed to record telegraph messages on chemically treated paper.

This instrument had a metal point which passed in and out of a series of indentations on a whirling paper disk. By accident, Edison set the disk to spinning at high speed. He noticed a whining sound which seemed to rise and fall in direct relation to the indentations on the disk. Fascinated, he lowered the speed, then tried it again at high speed, this time substituting a small diaphragm with a pin attached for the repeater's metal point. The volume of the strange sound was much greater.

At midnight he went to his desk and began a crude sketch. It specified a metal cylinder with spiral grooves, mounted on a long shaft in such a way that it could be spun by a crank. A wooden telephone-transmitter case, fitted with a diaphragm with a blunt pin in its center, was to be attached to a metal arm.

Next morning he called in one of his men, an expert Swiss craftsman named John Kruesi, who had a knack for translating Edison's roughest sketches into finished machines.

"What's it for, boss?" he asked. "Don't seem to make sense."

Edison, who liked a touch of mystery, waved him away with his cigar. "You'll see when you bring it back. I think you'll be surprised."

When the Swiss brought the finished gadget to Edison, a curious group gathered around.

"All right, boss," said Kruesi, "there she is. Now, what's she for?"

Edison shifted his cigar in his mouth. "This machine must talk, Kruesi. Think it will?"

Kruesi was startled. The others

stopped smiling. One of the men behind Edison tapped his brow significantly and shook his head. The Old Man had always been a trifle on the queer side. Was he now definitely breaking from overwork?

There was pity on their faces as they watched the serious, young Old Man carefully wrap a sheet of tinfoil around the cylinder. At the first turn of the crank, the pinpoint ripped across the foil. The screeching sound jarred the nerves of the watchers. And Edison's intent look frightened them.

He patiently replaced the torn foil with another sheet, this time firmly fastening the ends together with glue. He placed the needle at the starting position, picked up the long mouthpiece, and began turning the crank, reciting in a loud voice:

Mary had a little lamb,
Its fleece was white as snow . . .

When he finished the verse, Edison calmly replaced the needle at the starting point, and again began turning the crank.

Suddenly his voice began eerily arising from the spinning cylinder.

Mary had a little lamb . . .

Except for the echoing voice, the room was quite silent. The workmen, their hearts pounding, their palms sweating, literally held their breath. Even Edison was a little frightened. The miracle of the phonograph's birth had been achieved.

The imagination of people everywhere was captured by this unearthly machine that could actually store and reproduce the human voice. Millions of words about the inventor were cabled all over the world. The name of Thomas Edison became perhaps better known than that of any other living man. He was then thirty-one. His shy mannerisms, colorful speech, sloppy dress, and complete lack of pretension appealed to the press. He was interviewed on every possible subject, and fantastic stories circulated about him. Through a chance newspaper caption he became known as "The Wizard of Menlo Park," a man who could produce miracles at will. This name, which pictured an effortless sorcery, always irritated Edison. As his son, Charles Edison, former Secretary of the Navy and Governor of New Jersey, remarked wryly: "No man ever worked harder to be a wizard."

In his early thirties, with one hundred and fifty-seven patents already to his credit and seventy-eight pending in Washington, Edison followed a fantastic, steady work pattern. Embarked on a "campaign" — his phrase for intensive research — he frequently kept going for three or four days and nights before allowing himself to go to bed. He had, however, a remarkable facility for taking restorative cat naps. "Even amid the most exciting work," a friend once observed, "the Old Man could turn a switch, relax completely, and fall asleep. Fifteen minutes later he'd wake up — a new man."

In 1878 Edison began work on the incandescent light. He started, as usual, by making an exhaustive review of what others had done, reading every available scientific paper. He then squared away for his "campaign." It was to prove stupendous. Of the

2500 three-hundred-page notebooks preserved today by the Edison Foundation, more than two hundred are concerned with electric-light experiments. These notes were the basis for one of the most astonishing feats of inventive and industrial pioneering ever performed in American history.

In five years' time, although electrical engineering was then in its infancy and everything had to be worked out almost from scratch, Edison built a full-blown prototype[1] of the electric-lighting industry and established it as a practical public utility. He not only developed the electric light, as well as generators, dynamos, meters, and techniques of installation, but in order to give electricity its first large-scale test he also wired a square mile of New York City. It was a breathtaking accomplishment. Back of it was an infinitely painstaking and systematic approach to the problem. Charles F. Kettering has said, "To my mind, Edison's greatest 'invention' was organized research."

When Edison first tackled incandescent lighting, he entered a virtually unexplored scientific plateau.

In his search for a more effective light, Edison first tried winding platinum wire around the stem of an ordinary clay pipe. He noticed that after the platinum had been heated several times by electric current it became much harder and could stand higher temperatures. Apparently, heating expelled gases from the platinum, causing it to become more dense. Reasoning that still more gases could be driven out in a vacuum, and that the platinum would become still harder and give more intense light, he tried passing a current through it while its glass enclosure was connected to the vacuum pump. The light was amazingly brighter.

Edison thereupon turned to the problem of maintaining a lasting vacuum in a lamp. Since no suitable glass-forming machine then existed, he hired a skilled glass blower who laboriously shaped the first experimental bulbs by hand and sealed them off while they were still connected to the vacuum pump.

The vacuum theory was proved, but Edison finally decided that a platinum filament was too complicated and expensive, and that it consumed too much energy for the light it gave. He proceeded to try — and discard — other rare metals: rhodium, ruthenium, titanium, zirconium, barium. All proved unsatisfactory.

One midnight as he sat in his laboratory the answer came to him. Since heavy carbon burners had not stood up, why not try a slender carbonized filament which was almost threadlike? Pursuing this thought, Edison turned from platinum, rarest of metals, to one of man's homeliest commodities — cotton sewing thread.

The experiments were maddening. Edison ordered sewing threads to be packed with powdered carbon, baked in earthenware crucibles, then slowly cooled. One after another the delicate threads, less than $\frac{1}{64}$ of an inch in diameter, crumbled in various stages of the process. But at last a carbonized filament was installed in a lamp under

[1] **prototype:** model.

vacuum. When the current was turned on it began to glow with a steady, brilliant light. Edison and his workers barely breathed. It worked, but how long could this unbelievably delicate filament continue to burn?

Two hours crept by . . . three . . . six . . . ten. As the brave glow held steady against the dawn, Edison threw himself down on a cot for his first sleep in more than sixty hours. Assistants took over. From all over the laboratory and machine shops workers came to watch. As the hours piled up into the thirties, keyed-up workmen grinned, pounded each other happily. After forty hours, Edison characteristically began experimenting with increased voltage. The overloaded filament finally flared and burned out.

Edison next tried filaments of carbonized cardboard. They were even more successful. The life of the lamp was gradually increased to one hundred and seventy hours. A public demonstration on New Year's Eve of 1879, when all of Menlo Park was brilliantly lighted with the new lamps, drew three thousand people. The spectacle created a profound impression. Immediately thereafter gas stocks hit a new low.

But Edison knew he must have something tougher, more enduring than a cardboard filament if the electric lamp were to be commercially successful. One morning his roving eyes rested on a palm-leaf fan, and he noticed the thin strips of bamboo which bound its outer edges. At once he had the bamboo shredded into filaments and carbonized. It proved far superior to anything yet tried.

That experiment began a worldwide search for the best variety of bamboo. Altogether Edison tested some six thousand varieties of plant and vegetable fibers before selecting a bamboo grown especially for him in Japan. The carbonized bamboo filament was used for more than ten years, being supplanted first by "squirted cellulose," and then by tungsten, which is in use today.

Edison had realized that if his light were to be practical for home illumination, each lamp must be able to be switched on and off independently. Arc lights then burned "in series" — current flowed through *all* the lamps. If one lamp went out, all the others failed, as do certain types of Christmas-tree lights today. He had therefore perfected a "multiple circuit" which allowed each lamp to burn independently, and had developed a satisfactory generator to produce steady current.

Edison was now ready to build a test lighting system for that crucial square mile in lower New York. Newspapers hooted when he outlined his plans for putting wires underground in conduits. New York streets were then a maze of telegraph and telephone wires overhead. Who ever heard of putting electric wires underground! Didn't the man know they might get wet and leak, and electrocute pedestrians right and left? Edison calmly went ahead with his plans, perfecting new types of insulation to do the job.

Building the first electric-lighting system was, Edison later said, "the greatest adventure of my life." He threw everything into the gamble: his reputation, his money, the faith of his friends, the trust of the public. Realizing that he would have to make his product cheaper and more efficient than gas — for the powerful gas trust then had a monopoly on lighting — he made the installations for prospective electric customers without charge, and asked no deposit on the meter. The user would pay the metered charge only if the lighting system worked satisfactorily. Edison personally guaranteed the bills would be lower than those for gas!

As the time for the first test approached, the eyes of the whole world were fastened on that single square mile of downtown New York. Great things were expected and stock in the Edison Company had soared from $100 to $3,500 a share. If Edison failed, it would be the most publicized failure in history.

On Monday, September 4, 1882, the new lighting system was pronounced ready. In the powerhouse, firemen stoked the glowing coals, steam hissed up from the boilers into the engines of the mighty jumbo generators. Faster and faster the dynamos whirred. Edison reached for the master switch to send the mysterious force surging over eighty thousand lineal feet of underground wiring. He was, he admitted later, sobered by the "great responsibility of turning a mighty power loose under the streets and buildings of New York." But there was no hitch. When he pulled the switch, the windows of the downtown district suddenly sprang to life.

"It was a light," wrote the New York Times, "that a man could use for hours without the consciousness of having any artificial light about him. Soft, mellow, and grateful to the eye, it seemed almost like daylight . . . without a particle of flicker and with scarcely any heat to make the head ache."

Edison's great gamble had been vindicated.

In his thirties, his genius flared in a dozen directions. Even during his struggle for a practical electric light, he had taken a few days out to perfect and patent a method of preserving fruit under vacuum. And his notebooks of that period carried sketches of what is now known as the helicopter — which Edison was later to advocate as the safest, most useful form of air transport.

At Menlo Park he had started operation of the country's first passenger electric railway. He had sketched plans for a cotton harvester, an electric sewing machine, an electric elevator, a new kind of snow-removal machine.

In his ever-restless ranging, it is startling to observe how near he came to breaking through the barrier of the unknown and into the age of present-day electronics. As early as 1875 he discovered a unique electrical phenomenon which he called "etheric force" (later recognized as being caused by electric waves in free space). He experimented with it, then was diverted to other quests. He gave his findings to Marconi at a time when that scientist was racing with others to perfect the wireless. Marconi was lastingly grateful for Edison's help.

Without realizing it, Edison discovered the radio rectifier tube. He had invented the microphone as a by-product

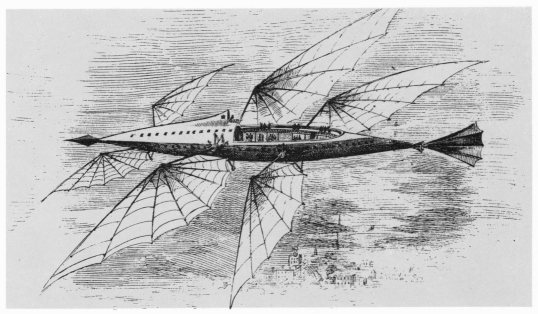

Edison was always ahead of his time, and by 1880 he had designed an airplane. The wings of this model were made of silk, though Edison had preferred feathers.

of his work on the telephone transmitter, and now he was on the very threshold of high-frequency radio transmission. Yet he turned away to other things, allowing other men to develop his discoveries.

One drowsy summer afternoon in 1887, a friend brought Edison a whimsical gift. It was "The Wheel of Life," a simple mechanical toy. One peeped through a slot, spun the wheel, and a series of pictures sprang into action, giving the illusion of motion. The device was familiar to millions of Americans.

Edison chuckled as he spun the wheel and watched the antics of a dancing bear. Presently his laughter faded, and he regarded the gadget with a speculative eye. Why, he wondered, wouldn't it be possible to obtain action

pictures in just this very way — a series of tiny photographs reproduced at great speed?

Slumping back in his chair, he drew out his ever-present notebook and began sketching. These casual sketches were Edison's first work on the motion-picture camera that was to change the face of the entertainment world and create a multi-million-dollar industry.

In 1889 Edison actually showed a talking picture in his laboratory, synchronizing the film with a phonograph. So all-embracing were his basic patents that the film industry paid him royalties for many years. Edison was the first of the film tycoons.

In the late 1890's and early 1900's he also took a fling at producing. He built a large, oblong building, covered inside and outside with black tarpaper.

Revolving on a turntable device, it moved with the sun, allowing every possible moment of daylight to shine through its slid-back roof.

In his new role, Edison was all over the place, writing comical sketches, directing the actors, grinding the cameras, repairing them when they broke down. He enjoyed it all hugely. His first productions were fairly crude — Jim Corbett boxing a few rounds, an Italian organ grinder cavorting with a mischievous monkey, and the like — but they packed the nickelodeons.[1] Later he built a $100,000 glass studio in Bronx Park and made several full-length pictures.

Once the movie industry was well launched, however, Edison turned to other challenges. Experimenting with Roentgen's newly discovered X ray, he developed the fluoroscope, which he gave, unpatented, to the medical profession. Concurrently he also developed the first fluorescent electric lamp.

Although none of Edison's later inventions were as spectacular to the public eye as were his phonograph, movies and electric light, his prodigality in turning out solidly useful inventions was to continue all his life. So homely and apparently commonplace were many of his creations that people wondered why no one had thought of them before.

Around the turn of the century he brought out his Ediphone dictating machine and began his search for a better storage battery. It took him ten years to find the satisfactory combination — nickel, iron, alkaline — but he

finally evolved a product which still solves the power problem in scores of industries.

"If Edison's experiments, investigations, and work on the storage battery were all he had ever done," an industrial engineer once said, "I should say he was not only a notable inventor but also a great man."

The years rolled on, but the Old Man refused to recognize their passage. In his sixties his work week remained as long as ever, and it irked him when reporters began interviewing him on his birthdays.

But the yearly interviews produced arresting copy. What was the secret of his success? "The ability to stick to things." What was genius? "Two percent inspiration and ninety-eight percent perspiration."

Each night, he told reporters, he wrote on slips of paper the tasks for the day ahead, and then carried them to completion. "If everyone would try it," he said, "it would surprise them to see how much could be accomplished in a day."

He believed intense brainwork was the real secret of health and longevity. He had little use for physical exercise. "The only use for my body," he observed, "is to carry my brain around."

He found recreation in changing his work pattern. After weeks on one problem, he would turn to another, and then to another. He always had at least half a dozen projects on the fire. He read continuously and voluminously, with a photographic memory.

Edison was nearly seventy when America entered the first World War, but at the request of Secretary of the

[1] **nickelodeons:** motion-picture theaters that charged a nickel admission.

Navy Josephus Daniels he became president of the Naval Consulting Board. He developed an apparatus to detect torpedoes, underwater search-lights for submarines, turbine-powered projectiles, and submarine stabilizers. For these and other wartime inventions — more than forty altogether — he won the Distinguished Service Medal.

No matter how hard the driving pace of his working day, Edison never lost his relish for humor. For nearly half a century, famous men from all over the world sent him their latest jokes. Edison spread out the jokes and chortled over them before beginning the day's work. Often, an associate recalls, his laugh was "a roar you could hear all over the place."

At seventy-five, Edison cut his working day to sixteen hours. At eighty he brought out his first long-playing phonograph record. For thirty-eight cents the buyer received forty minutes of music.

"I have enough ideas," he told interviewers, "to keep the laboratories busy for years."

Up to the very week of his death Edison continued the process of self-education which began on the day his mother took him out of school at seven. Even on his deathbed, he was an avid reader of books on a wide variety of subjects. Three days before he died he was busily making plans for future experiments.

His curiosity was the despair of his physicians. He inquired into the whys and wherefores of his own sickness and kept his own chart of his condition. He argued with them over medicines and drugs. Blood tests intrigued him, and he insisted on examining the slides and microscopes. Death never had a more wide-eyed, observant victim.

Edison began his last Great Exploration on October 18, 1931, at the age of eighty-four. On the night of his funeral, in response to President Hoover's proclamation, the lights all over America were turned off for a full minute in tribute to the man who had lighted them fifty-two years before. By a dramatic coincidence the date was the anniversary of the lighting of the first successful lamp in Menlo Park.

INVENTIVE GENIUS

1. How did Edison's education differ from that of most American boys?

2. How did Edison show his inventive genius in becoming an outstanding telegraph operator?

3. In what ways did Edison's experience at the brokerage office show that he could apply himself to practical problems?

4. How did the methods used by Edison to invent the phonograph illustrate his powers of observation and deduction? How did this invention affect Edison's reputation with the public?

5. Describe Edison's use of notebooks. How did he use his "notebook method" in creating a practical incandescent light?

6. What chance event led to Edison's invention of movies?

7. What do you think of Edison's secrets of success and long life (page 246)?

8. Edison might be thought of as the embodiment of American inventive genius. Make a list of Edison's discoveries and inventions that are important in American life today.

9. Tell how Edison was truly self-educated. How might this method of education have affected his adult life? Why is it

important for everyone to be an independent learner? If Edison were a boy today, do you think his lack of formal education would restrict him in years to come? Why?

10. Edison called one of his projects "the greatest adventure of my life." How do you think such an attitude toward work could affect a person's life?

11. Edison once said that genius is two percent inspiration and ninety-eight percent perspiration. What did he mean? Do you think he was right? Why?

COINING WORDS

At one time phonographs were known as "Edisons." Whenever a new invention is created, a word must be coined to name it. The word *phonograph*, for example, was made from two Greek roots; *phono* comes from a Greek word meaning "sound," and *graph* comes from a Greek word meaning "to write." Since a phonograph records, or "writes," sounds, this seems like a good name for the invention.

Each of the following words was coined to name an invention. They are all built from a Greek word *tele*, meaning "far off," or "operating at a distance." Explain why each word is appropriate for the invention it names: *telegraph, telephone, television, telegram, Telstar.*

COMPOUND SENTENCES

A compound sentence is one that has two main clauses — two complete subject-verb patterns. You can think of each clause of a compound sentence as a sentence in itself. Here is a compound sentence from "Incandescent Genius."

> "The Grand Trunk project prospered, and within three years he had expanded it, hired newsboys for other trains, and set up a fresh fruit and vegetable business."

Notice that the second pattern has one subject and three verbs, and that each verb has an object. Can you name the key words that make up the two patterns of this sentence?

Here are four short sentences. Can you combine them into a single sentence with compound parts, imitating the pattern of the sentence quoted above?

> Edison represents the American inventive genius. His imagination has lighted our homes. It has given us the phonograph. It has provided us with motion pictures.

COMPOSITION: AN ANECDOTE

At one place in this account of Edison's life, the author wants to tell his readers that Edison's inventive mind often got him into trouble. To make this point emphatic, he relates a story, or anecdote, explaining how Edison's suggestions once got him fired. Note that the main topic of this passage is stated in the first sentence (in italics).

> *"Sometimes his intense interest in telegraphic theory was held against him.* One of the projects in his notebook was that of sending two messages in opposite directions simultaneously over the same wire. One day, while working for Western Union in Memphis, he tried to explain his theory to the Western Union chief there, a General Coleman. The chief was indignant.

> " 'Look here, Edison,' Coleman roared, 'any fool ought to know that a wire can't be worked both ways at the same time!' He promptly fired Edison as an irresponsible character."

Tell a brief anecdote that will explain something about a friend, a member of your family, or even a character in literature. Open your composition with a topic sentence.

Sing an Old Song

ELEANOR R. VAN ZANDT

Millions of ordinary people worked and struggled to build this country. These men and women, whose individual names will never be known, have left us a priceless legacy of music.

THE SIDEWALK outside New York's Town Hall was crowded with concertgoers. They were mostly young people, including many teen-agers. Many pushed toward the box office hopefully, only to be told that the concert was sold out. Those who had planned ahead and had already bought tickets poured through the doors and filled the auditorium and part of the stage.

Finally, the lights dimmed, and onto the stage walked the girl they had come to hear, a black-haired girl of Irish-Mexican parentage. She wore a red blouse and full red-and-white peasant skirt and carried a guitar. When the applause died, she began to sing in a rich, clear, soprano voice. The songs told of love, bravery, and sorrow. They had been created and sung by people who lived many years ago in remote places, but they found a warm reception in that audience of city dwellers.

So it is all over the country today. Americans are rediscovering the charm of their own folk music. They find it in concert halls and on the "Top Forty"; they find it in the self-conscious amateur gatherings in Greenwich Village (home of the "citybillies," as they are called); and they find it in the performances of obscure and untrained singers whose recordings are collected by devotees of "pure" folk music.

The passion for folk songs is most deeply rooted in college students. It is they, primarily, who swarm into Newport, Rhode Island, in the summer for the annual three-day folk festival, some having hitchhiked all the way across the country. For hours they listen to the "greats" of folk music, pleading for encores until the small hours of the morning. For this audience, the end of the concert is not the end of the music. Breaking into groups, they head for the beach, remove their own instruments from their cases, and sing and play songs until dawn. These informal folk-singing sessions, called "hootenannies," are rapidly increasing in popularity on college campuses.

What, exactly, is the fascination of the folk song? Why do people nourished on lush Hollywood orchestrations and the subtle wanderings of modern jazz flock to Town Hall to hear a girl with a guitar sing about a kind-hearted outlaw named Pretty Boy Floyd? The answer lies partly in the very simplicity and straightforwardness of these songs. The tune and the words tell the story and express the singer's feelings; there's a refreshing lack of frosting.

More important, folk songs express the heritage of a people. "Their first function," says Alan Lomax, a well-known authority on folk music, "is to produce a feeling of security for the listener by voicing the particular quality of a land and the life of its people." It's not surprising that in these times of insecurity and of mechanized living, people like to listen nostalgically to the simple songs of more primitive times. Few of the sandaled, bearded folk-participants in a college "hoot" would really care to change places with the work-burdened pioneers of whom they sing; but in theory the idea is attractive and the songs a pleasant escape from the pace of modern society.

Furthermore, folk songs evoke certain basic emotions that do not change over the years. Customs die out; events fade into history. We no longer cross the plains in covered wagons, but we know what it is to be homesick and afraid, as these travelers often were. And so their songs have meaning for us as human beings who can share their feelings.

There is no such thing as "pure" American folk music. Our folk songs are a blending of many patterns, rhythms, and harmonies. As people came to the new continent, they brought their favorite songs with them. Sometimes they changed the words a little to suit their new environment. They wanted to sing about the experiences they had, and so they made up new words as they pleased. Some of the songs from the Old World were deemed too frivolous by our Puritan forefathers and were either dropped entirely or altered to their taste.

Of course, they were not content with singing only the old songs. New ones arose out of new situations, and as time went on there emerged distinctly American forms like the Negro spiritual, the blues, and the Western song. Often, even these were based on much older melodies. Everywhere, people sang their own versions of the songs and passed them down to their children. As they traveled around, the songs took new forms, and the music of one area influenced that of another.

It is often supposed that New England was such a strait-laced area back in the old days that songs had virtually no chance to develop. This isn't true. The Puritans expressed themselves musically through their psalms and hymns and avoided secular songs. But there were plenty of other New Englanders who enjoyed the good old songs; and it is in this area that we find the greatest number of English ballads, brought there by a constant stream of immigrants.

There were fighting songs, too — largely Irish ones, introduced by the Irish mercenaries who fought bravely in the Indian wars and for the Colonists in the Revolutionary War. Their spirited tunes found their way into several subsequent wars, a familiar example being "When Johnny Comes Marching Home," a favorite of Civil War days.

Out on the sea, American sailors made their contribution to our musical heritage. The sea chantey was not original with them; records indicate that European seamen centuries earlier had sung and shouted as they worked. American sailors followed this practice, and occasionally they brought forth some truly beautiful music, such as the lovely "Shenandoah."

O Shenandoah, I love your daughter,
  Away, you rolling river;
For her I've crossed the rolling
  water;
  Away, we're bound away,
  Across the wide Missouri.

Farther south, in colonial days, people of English and Scotch-Irish descent were settling in the backwoods, up in the Appalachian Mountains of Kentucky, Tennessee, Virginia, and North Carolina. Keeping to themselves, remote from the slave-holding plantation society, they created a unique culture and a unique music. Today, this area is famous for its hillbilly songs and fast-moving square dances.

Pioneers traveling over the Cumberland Gap found the new country fertile and rich with game and fish. They held some pretty wild celebrations there and danced many a jig. Sometimes they danced to the music of a fiddle, the most common musical instrument in those times; but if there was no fiddle, they "made do" with "mouth music" — rhymed verses which matched the rhythm of the tunes and served to guide the dancers' feet. Among many of the mountain people, dancing was forbidden by religion, and so they turned to singing games, played to such lively tunes as "The Paw Paw Patch" and "Jubilee."

The mountaineers, like the New England settlers, still sang the old ballads from England, Scotland, and Ireland. The women, especially, enjoyed these ballads, with their often mournful account of the course of true love. Burdened as they were with the tasks of keeping house and rearing children under primitive conditions, they liked to sing about women who rebelled at conventions, or of blighted romance. "Barbara Allen" was one of their favorites. They also liked such wistful love lyrics as "Old Smokey" (popular a few years ago) and the beautiful "Black Is the Color."

Black is the color of my true love's
  hair;
Her cheeks are like some rosy fair,
The prettiest eyes and the neatest
  hands;
I love the ground whereon she
  stands.

In the lowlands, on the plantations, another kind of distinctly Southern music was evolving. Since they had first been brought to the New World as slaves, the Negroes had found release from their troubles in singing and dancing. In Africa, each tribe had had its own songs for each different occasion and emotion. In North America, however, the tribes were mingled, so that they lost their individual character. But they didn't stop singing. Rapidly, they picked up European forms of music and European harmony. In fact, they used harmony much more than the white people did in their folk singing, which was mostly solo with an occasional unison chorus. Generally, in Negro songs the music was more important than the words. They would take a few lines and repeat them over and over with many variations.

The Negro songs were very functional. There were songs for working in the fields and around the house, songs for dancing, and spirituals to console them with the thought of a better life after death. These spirituals are truly original American folk music. The slaves were encouraged by their masters to hold religious meetings. On these occasions they demonstrated their creative ability and their enthusiastic response to the Gospel. Some of their songs were slow and conveyed their weariness with life; but others rang with joy, like the ever-popular "When the Saints Go Marching In."

Besides their spirituals, the Negroes contributed many catchy, singable work songs, ballads, and — of course — the "blues," which have had such a strong influence upon American popular and even serious music. The familiar story of "Frankie and Johnny" is among the well-known Negro ballads, as are the numerous versions of "John Henry" and "Casey Jones." The blues emerged from the feelings of homesickness experienced by both Negroes and whites who moved from place to place. After emancipation, many a Negro felt a bit like the boll weevil in the song who was "lookin' for a home, just a-lookin' for a home." One famous blues song was composed by a Louisiana convict called Lead Belly. Its name: "Irene" — a hit song of 1950.

Another great American song tradition is that of the West, where a true blending of Northern and Southern music took place. Texas cowboys carried the Southern backwoods songs into Northern territory, and many Northern ballads were sung with a Southern accent. Most of those who settled the West were adventurers, and their songs reflect their easy-going virility. The Gold Rush gave birth to many new songs and reworked versions of the old ones. A ballad, "Sweet Betsy," tells the story of a woman's trip to California with the Forty-niners. Outlaws inspired many of the songs, one of the most famous being "Jesse James," which recounts the betrayal of Jesse by one of his men.

When the price of beef rose sharply after the War Between the States, Texas discovered it had a "gold mine" in the cattle roaming over the land. This marked the beginning of the era of the cowboy — and of his songs. At night while they rounded up the cattle, the cowboys sang ballads like "The Old Chisolm Trail" and "The Night-Herding Song." They sang to keep awake, and also to let their coworkers know where they were, so they would not get lost from each other and possibly trampled to death. It was a lonely life, and this feeling of loneliness pervades most of the cowboy songs.

The breadth of the American folk music is tremendous. It has a voice for all emotions; it captures the lives and customs of all its people; its roots extend back to other lands and distant times. In our collective heritage it stands as a prized possession.

PRIDE IN OUR HERITAGE

1. According to Alan Lomax, what is the first function of folk songs and to what basic emotions do folk songs appeal?

2. Explain how American folk songs came into being. How did various peoples contribute to American folk music?

3. How did the Negro folk music differ from other forms of American folk music? What form of Negro folk music does the author consider truly American?

4. Describe the contribution made by the West to American folk music.

5. The last sentence in the article talks about our "collective" American heritage. What does the word *collective* mean here? Think back over the other selections in this unit; what other possessions make up the American heritage? What attitudes make up our heritage?

SHORTENED WORD FORMS

People now talk about going to a "hoot"; they have shortened the word *hootenanny* and have thus made up a new word. A living language is always changing, and new words are often developed when people imaginatively shorten a long word. Below are four shortened word forms commonly used today. What longer word is each short word made from?

math	hi-fi
ad	vet
photo	sub

Can you think of any other words that have been made by shortening a longer word?

COMPOSITION:
SUPPORTING A TOPIC STATEMENT

Here is a paragraph from "Sing an Old Song." The first sentence, in italics, states the topic of the paragraph.

> *The passion for folk songs is most deeply rooted in college students.* It is they, primarily, who swarm into Newport, Rhode Island, in the summer for the annual three-day folk festival, some having hitchhiked all the way across the country. For hours they listen to the 'greats' of folk music, pleading for encores until the small hours of the morning. For this audience, the end of the concert is not the end of the music. Breaking into groups, they head for the beach, remove their own instruments from their cases, and sing and play songs until dawn. These informal folk-singing sessions, called 'hootenannies,' are rapidly increasing in popularity on college campuses.

An expository paragraph often begins, as this one does, with a topic sentence. The rest of the paragraph then gives details to support the topic. List the factual details which this writer has used. Have these details convinced you that the passion for folk music is most deeply rooted in college students?

Write a paragraph in which you use factual details to support a topic statement. You might want to use one of the following topic statements. Perhaps you'll want to use facts that will disprove the statement.

The most popular songs in America are sad songs.

Television is often educational.

The characters in most stories and novels are realistic.

Exposition

In the first two units, you studied two kinds of writing — description and narration. In this unit, you studied another kind of writing — exposition. The main purpose of exposition is to explain something, to present certain information or ideas. History and science books, for example, use a great deal of expository writing.

Read closely these two expository paragraphs from "Sing an Old Song" by Eleanor R. Van Zandt.

There is no such thing as "pure" American folk music. Our folk songs are a blending of many patterns, rhythms, and harmonies. As people came to the new continent, they brought their favorite songs with them. Sometimes they changed the words a little to suit their new environment. They wanted to sing about the experiences they had, and so they made up new words as they pleased. Some of the songs from the Old World were deemed too frivolous by our Puritan forefathers and were either dropped entirely or altered to their taste.

Of course, they were not content with singing only the old songs. New ones arose out of new situations, and as time went on there emerged distinctly American forms like the Negro spiritual, the blues, and the Western song. Often, even these were based on much older melodies. Everywhere, people sang their own versions of the songs and passed them down to their children. As they traveled around, the songs took new forms, and the music of one area influenced that of another.

(page 250)

READING EXPOSITION

1. *When you read informative writing, look for topic statements.* In such statements, the writer will tell you in a general way what he is going to discuss. A topic sentence may appear anywhere in a paragraph, though it is usually placed at the beginning or at the end. In the first paragraph in the model passage, the opening sentence states the topic. What sentence states the topic to be discussed in the second paragraph?

2. *In reading an expository paragraph, take note of the specific facts or examples used to support the topic statement.* Can you name the specific facts that support the topic statements in the model paragraphs?

3. *When you are reading to get information about something, be sure that you understand just how each detail in a passage relates to the topio and to other details.* In the model passage, can you explain how the second statement in the first paragraph is related to the topic statement? Many writers use transitional expressions to help you see how certain statements are linked or related to one another. Can you name the words that the frequently-repeated pronoun *they* (in the first model paragraph) refers to? What transitional expression links the second paragraph to the first one? Can you explain why this word was used? What words does *they* in the opening sentence of the second paragraph refer to?

4. *To be a good reader, you should understand how each paragraph in an informative article is logically related to paragraphs that come before and after it.*

Read the two model paragraphs in their context. How do they relate to paragraphs coming before and after them?

5. *Finally, you should learn to evaluate what you read.* Sometimes you may feel that the writer of an informative article has not been clear, or that he has not been convincing, or that he has been inaccurate. How would you evaluate these two model paragraphs?

WRITING EXPOSITION

The next time you explain something in writing — whether it be giving sewing directions or explaining the causes of the Trojan War — keep the following points in mind:

1. *Have each paragraph deal with one main topic.* Clearly state this main topic in a sentence at the beginning or end of the paragraph.

2. *Develop and support the main topic with specific facts, examples, or reasons.* Choose your supporting details carefully; make sure they are strong and forceful.

3. *Present the supporting details in clear, logical order.* One thought should lead easily into the next. Try rearranging the sentences in the first model paragraph. Do your rearrangements muddle or improve the paragraph?

4. *Weed out details that do not relate to your main topic.* Look back at the model paragraphs. Can you locate any details that destroy their unity?

Write a paragraph in which you give specific details (either facts, reasons, or examples) to support one of these topic statements.

Thomas Edison was an inventive genius.
Some people never change.
My philosophy of life is simple.
A sandwich must be made with imagination.
Here is how pig latin works.

Sentence Study. A skillful writer varies the lengths of sentences. He knows that a paragraph made up entirely of long sentences can be monotonous or difficult to read. Look back at the model paragraphs. Do you find variety in sentence length? Read these paragraphs aloud. Do they read smoothly? Where are compound structures located in these paragraphs? Where are the short simple sentences?

The following paragraph reads awkwardly. Try to make it more readable by staggering the length of its sentences. Which sentences should you combine? Which sentences are better left short?

Myths tell exciting stories about gods. They also tell about heroes. They also tell about monsters. Sometimes myths give imaginary explanations of a natural happening. The natural happening puzzled ancient people. Thunder is explained in a myth. So is the change of seasons. We use words from mythology today. *Panic* is from mythology. So is *typhoon. Panic* comes from the name Pan. Pan was a god. Pan put sudden fear into people. Typhon was a monster. He had a hundred heads. The heads had black tongues. The heads could roar. They could hiss. They could talk. Typhon lived beneath the earth.

ART AND LITERATURE

Select two of the paintings on pages 181–86, and explain clearly how they are alike or different. Organize your composition with care; you may choose to discuss one painting at a time or discuss both paintings point by point.

You might compare or contrast the paintings in regard to their color, subject matter, and realism. You might also compare or contrast the mood that each painting evokes in you. Do you have different feelings when you look at them?

PART TWO

Langston Hughes

T. S. Eliot

Forms of Literature

Unit 4
Stories

UNIT 4 Stories

A writer works with words, the same words that we use every day. With words, a writer hopes to do what a musician hopes to do when he composes a symphony and what a painter hopes to do when he paints a picture. All artists wish to express or communicate something to other people. The writer, working with words, tries to express in an artistic way man's experiences. He may choose to express himself in one of several literary forms: stories, poems, plays, essays.

Throughout the ages, men have been telling stories. In this book you have already read some myths of ancient Greece and Rome, some folk tales from other lands, and some legends from medieval times. Although storytelling itself is very old, it has been only within the last hundred years that the short story has become a distinct form of literature. Today we think of the short story as having plot, characterization, and theme.

In this unit you will read four outstanding short stories.

The Legend of Sleepy Hollow by Washington Irving:
A superstitious schoolteacher, a fickle girl, a bold joker, and a mysterious headless horseman are the main characters in this ghost story, told by one of America's first writers.

The Ransom of Red Chief by O. Henry:
One of America's funniest stories is this one about a pair of tough kidnapers and their amazing victim. O. Henry is one of America's most famous short-story writers, and this tale of two misguided criminals is one of his best.

The Red-headed League by Sir Arthur Conan Doyle:
Conan Doyle's stories are so realistic that many people think there really was a detective named Sherlock Holmes. In this story, the master detective coolly goes about solving a crime before it is even committed.

The Apprentice by Dorothy Canfield:
A famous contemporary writer tells a story with a strong theme — about an ordinary girl who realizes with sudden horror what it means to be an adult.

The Legend of Sleepy Hollow

WASHINGTON IRVING

In the bosom of one of those spacious coves which indent the eastern shore of the Hudson, at that broad expansion of the river named by the ancient Dutch navigators the Tappan Zee, there lies a small market town or rural port, which by some is called Greensburgh, but which is more generally and properly known by the name of Tarrytown. This name was given, we are told, in former days by the good housewives of the adjacent country, from the tendency of their husbands to linger about the village tavern on market days. Not far from this village, perhaps about two miles, there is a little valley among high hills, which is one of the quietest places in the whole world. A small brook glides through it, with just murmur enough to lull one to repose; and the occasional whistle of a quail, or tapping of a woodpecker, is almost the only sound that ever breaks in upon the uniform tranquillity.

I recollect that, when a stripling,[1] my first exploit in squirrel shooting was in a grove of tall walnut trees, which shades one side of the valley. I had wandered into it at noontime, when all nature is peculiarly quiet, and was startled by the roar of my own gun as it broke the Sabbath stillness around and was prolonged and reverberated by the angry echoes. If ever I should wish for a retreat, whither I might steal from the world and its distractions and dream quietly away the remnant of a troubled life, I know of none more promising than this little valley.

From the listless repose of the place and the peculiar character of its inhabitants, who are descendants from the original Dutch settlers, this sequestered[2] glen has long been known by the name of Sleepy Hollow, and its rustic lads are called the Sleepy Hollow Boys throughout all the neighboring country. A drowsy, dreamy influence seems to hang over the land and to pervade the very atmosphere. Some say that the place was bewitched by a high German doctor during the early days of the settlement; others, that an old Indian chief, the prophet or wizard of his tribe,

---

[1] **stripling:** mere youth.

[2] **sequestered** (si·kwes′tərd): secluded.

held his powwows there before the country was discovered by Master Hendrick Hudson. Certain it is, the place still continues under the sway of some witching power that holds a spell over the minds of the good people, causing them to walk in a continual reverie. They are given to all kinds of marvelous beliefs, are subject to trances and visions, and frequently see strange sights and hear music and voices in the air. The whole neighborhood abounds with local tales, haunted spots, and twilight superstitions. Stars shoot and meteors glare oftener across the valley than in any other part of the country, and the nightmare, with her whole ninefold,[1] seems to make it the favorite scene of her gambols.

The dominant spirit, however, that haunts this enchanted region and seems to be commander-in-chief of all the powers of the air, is the apparition of a figure on horseback without a head. It is said by some to be the ghost of a Hessian trooper, whose head had been carried away by a cannon ball, in some nameless battle during the Revolutionary War, and who is ever and anon seen by the country folk, hurrying along in the gloom of night, as if on the wings of the wind. His haunts are not confined to the valley, but extend at times to the adjacent roads, and especially to the vicinity of a church at no great distance. Indeed, certain historians of those parts, who have been careful in collecting the floating facts concerning this specter, allege that the body of the trooper having been buried in the churchyard, the ghost rides forth to the scene of battle in nightly quest of his head; and that the rushing speed with which he sometimes passes along the Hollow, like a midnight blast, is owing to his being late and in a hurry to get back to the churchyard before daybreak.

Such is the general purport of this legendary superstition, which has furnished materials for many a wild story in that region of shadows; and the specter is known at all the country firesides by the name of the Headless Horseman of Sleepy Hollow.

It is remarkable that the visionary propensity[2] I have mentioned is not confined to the native inhabitants of the valley, but is unconsciously imbibed by everyone who resides there for a time. However wide awake they may have been before they entered that sleepy region, they are sure, in a little time, to inhale the witching influence of the air, and they begin to grow imaginative, to dream dreams, and to see apparitions.

In this by-place of nature, there abode, in a remote period of American history, a worthy fellow of the name of Ichabod Crane, who sojourned, or, as he expressed it, "tarried," in Sleepy Hollow for the purpose of instructing the children of the vicinity. He was a native of Connecticut. The name of Crane was not inapplicable to his person. He was tall, but exceedingly lank, with narrow shoulders, long arms and legs, hands that dangled a mile out of his sleeves, feet that might have served for shovels,

---

[1] **nightmare . . . ninefold:** In old times, the word *nightmare* was often used to refer to an evil hag, attended by nine other spirits, who suffocated people in their sleep.

[2] **propensity** (prə·pen′sə·tē): inclination.

books. It was most ingeniously secured at vacant hours by a branch twisted in the handle of the door, and stakes set against the window shutters, so that though a thief might get in with perfect ease, he would find some embarrassment in getting out. The schoolhouse stood in a rather lonely but pleasant situation, just at the foot of a woody hill, with a brook running close by and a formidable birch tree growing at one end of it. From hence, the low murmur of his pupils' voices, conning over their lessons, might be heard on a drowsy summer's day, like the hum of a beehive, interrupted now and then by the authoritative voice of the master, in the tone of menace or command, or, perhaps, by the appalling sound of the birch as he urged some tardy loiterer along the flowery path of knowledge. Truth to say, he was a conscientious man and ever bore in mind the golden maxim, "Spare the rod and spoil the child." Ichabod Crane's scholars certainly were not spoiled.

I would not have it imagined, however, that he was one of those cruel tyrants of the school who joy in the suffering of their subjects. On the contrary, he administered justice with discrimination rather than severity, taking the burden off the backs of the weak and laying it on those of the strong. Your mere puny stripling that winced at the least flourish of the rod was passed by with indulgence; but the claims of justice were satisfied by inflicting a double portion on some little, tough, wrong-headed, broad-skirted Dutch urchin who sulked and swelled and grew dogged and sullen beneath the birch. All this he called doing his

and his whole frame most loosely hung together. His head was small and flat at top, with huge ears, large green glassy eyes, and a long snipe nose, so that it looked like a weathercock perched upon his spindle neck to tell which way the wind blew. To have seen him striding along the profile of a hill on a windy day, with his clothes bagging and fluttering about him, one might have mistaken him for the spirit of famine descending upon the earth or some scarecrow eloped from a cornfield.

His schoolhouse was a low building of one large room, rudely constructed of logs, the windows partly glazed and partly patched with leaves of old copy-

duty by their parents, and he never inflicted a chastisement without following it by the assurance, so consoling to the smarting urchin, that he would remember it and thank him for it the longest day he had to live.

When school hours were over, he was even the companion and playmate of the larger boys, and on holiday afternoons he would convoy some of the smaller ones home, who happened to have pretty sisters, or good housewives for mothers, noted for the comforts of the cupboard. Indeed it behooved him to keep on good terms with his pupils. The revenue arising from his school was small and would have been scarcely sufficient to furnish him with daily bread, for he was a huge feeder and, though lank, had the dilating powers of an anaconda.[1] But to help out his maintenance, he was, according to country custom in those parts, boarded and lodged at the houses of the farmers whose children he instructed. With these he lived successively a week at a time, thus going the rounds of the neighborhood with all his worldly effects tied up in a cotton handkerchief.

That all this might not be too hard on the purses of his rustic patrons, who are apt to consider the costs of schooling a grievous burden and schoolmasters as mere drones, he had various ways of rendering himself both useful and agreeable. He assisted the farmers occasionally in the lighter labors of their farms, helped to make hay, mended the fences, took the horses to water, drove the cows from pasture, and cut wood for the winter fire. He laid aside, too, all the dominant dignity and absolute sway with which he lorded it in his little empire, the school, and became wonderfully gentle and ingratiating. He found favor in the eyes of the mothers by petting the children, particularly the youngest, and he would sit with a child on one knee and rock a cradle with his foot for whole hours together.

In addition to his other vocations, he was the singing master of the neighborhood and picked up many bright shillings by instructing the young folks in psalmody.[2] It was a matter of no little vanity to him, on Sundays, to take his station in front of the church gallery with a band of chosen singers, where, in his own mind, he completely carried away the palm from the parson. Certain it is, his voice resounded far above all the rest of the congregation; and there are peculiar quavers still to be heard in that church, and which may even be heard half a mile off, quite to the opposite side of the millpond, on a still Sunday morning, and which are said to be legitimately descended from the nose of Ichabod Crane. Thus, by diverse little makeshifts, the worthy pedagogue got on tolerably enough, and was thought, by all who understood nothing of the labor of headwork, to have a wonderfully easy life of it.

The schoolmaster is generally a man of some importance in the female circle of a rural neighborhood, being considered a kind of idle gentlemanlike personage, of vastly superior taste and

[1] **dilating . . . anaconda:** An anaconda is a large snake. Many exaggerated stories are told about its ability to expand (or *dilate*) itself in order to swallow large animals.

[2] **psalmody** (sä′mə·dē): psalm singing.

accomplishments to the rough country swains, and, indeed, inferior in learning only to the parson. His appearance, therefore, is apt to occasion some little stir at the tea table of a farmhouse, and the addition of an extra dish of cakes or sweetmeats, or, perhaps, the parade of a silver teapot. Our man of letters, therefore, was peculiarly happy in the smiles of all the country damsels. How he would figure among them in the churchyard between services on Sundays, gathering grapes for them from the wild vines that overran the surrounding trees, reciting for their amusement all the epitaphs of the tombstones, or sauntering with a whole bevy of them along the banks of the adjacent millpond, while the more bashful country bumpkins hung sheepishly back, envying his superior elegance and address.[1]

From his half-itinerant life, also, he was a kind of traveling gazette, carrying the whole budget of local gossip from house to house, so that his appearance was always greeted with satisfaction. He was, moreover, esteemed by the women as a man of great learning, for he had read several books quite through and was a perfect master of Cotton Mather's *History of New England Witchcraft,* in which, by the way, he most firmly and potently believed.

He was, in fact, an odd mixture of small shrewdness and simple credulity.[2] His appetite for the marvelous and his powers of digesting it were equally extraordinary, and both had been increased by his residence in this spell-bound region. No tale was too gross or monstrous for his capacious swallow. It was often his delight, after his school was dismissed in the afternoon, to stretch himself on the rich bed of clover bordering the little brook that whimpered by his schoolhouse, and there con over old Mather's direful tales until the gathering dusk of the evening made the printed page a mere mist before his eyes. Then, as he wended his way by swamp and stream and awful woodland to the farmhouse where he happened to be quartered, every sound of nature at that witching hour fluttered his excited imagination: the moan of the whippoorwill from the hillside; the boding cry of the tree toad, that harbinger of storm; the dreary hooting of the screech owl; or the sudden rustling in the thicket of birds, frightened from their roost. The fireflies, too, which sparkled most vividly in the darkest places, now and then startled him, as one of uncommon brightness would stream across his path; and if, by chance, a huge blockhead of a beetle came winging his blundering flight against him, the poor varlet was ready to give up the ghost, with the idea that he was struck with a witch's token. His only resource on such occasions, either to drown thought or drive away evil spirits, was to sing psalm tunes; and the good people of Sleepy Hollow, as they sat by their doors of an evening, were often filled with awe at hearing his nasal melody floating from the distant hill or along the dusky road.

Another of his sources of fearful pleasure was to pass long winter evenings with the old Dutch wives as they sat spinning by the fire, with a row of

[1] **address:** manner of speaking.
[2] **credulity** (krə·dōō′lə·tē): readiness to believe on slight evidence; gullibility.

apples roasting and spluttering along the hearth, and to listen to their marvelous tales of ghosts and goblins, and haunted fields, and haunted brooks, and haunted bridges, and haunted houses, and particularly of the headless horseman, or Galloping Hessian of the Hollow, as they sometimes called him. He would delight them equally by his anecdotes of witchcraft and of the direful omens and portentous sights and sounds in the air, which prevailed in the earlier times of Connecticut, and would frighten them woefully with speculations upon comets and shooting stars and with the alarming fact that the world did absolutely turn round and that they were half the time topsy-turvy!

But if there was a pleasure in all this, while snugly cuddling in the chimney corner of a chamber that was all of a ruddy glow from the crackling wood fire, and where, of course, no specter dared to show his face, it was dearly purchased by the terrors of his subsequent walk homeward. What fearful shapes and shadows beset his path amidst the dim and ghastly glare of a snowy night! With what wistful look did he eye every trembling ray of light streaming across the waste fields from some distant window! How often was he appalled by some shrub covered with snow, which, like a sheeted specter, beset his very path! How often did he shrink with curdling awe at the sound of his own steps on the frosty crust beneath his feet and dread to look over his shoulder, lest he should behold some uncouth being tramping close behind him! And how often was he thrown into complete dismay by some

rushing blast, howling among the trees, in the idea that it was the Galloping Hessian on one of his nightly scourings! [1]

All these, however, were mere terrors of the night, phantoms of the mind that walk in darkness; and though he had seen many specters in his time and had been more than once beset by Satan in diverse shapes, in his lonely walks, yet daylight put an end to all these evils. He would have passed a pleasant life of it, if his path had not been crossed by a being that causes more perplexity to mortal man than ghosts, goblins, and the whole race of witches put together, and that was — a woman.

Among the musical disciples who assembled one evening each week to receive his instructions in psalmody was Katrina Van Tassel, the daughter and only child of a substantial Dutch farmer. She was a blooming lass of fresh eighteen, plump as a partridge, ripe and melting and rosy cheeked as one of her father's peaches, and universally famed, not merely for her beauty, but for her vast expectations. [2] She was, withal, a little of a coquette, as might be perceived even in her dress, which was a mixture of ancient and modern fashions, as most suited to set off her charms. She wore the ornaments of pure yellow gold that her great-great-grandmother had brought over from Holland, the tempting stomacher of the olden time, and a provokingly short petticoat to display the prettiest foot and ankle in the country round.

[1] **scourings:** swift rides, in this case, in search of his head.
[2] **expectations:** of wealth. Katrina would inherit her father's money and land.

Ichabod Crane had a soft and foolish heart toward the sex; and it is not to be wondered at that so tempting a morsel soon found favor in his eyes, more especially after he had visited her in her paternal mansion. Old Baltus Van Tassel was a perfect picture of a thriving, contented, liberal-hearted farmer. He seldom, it is true, sent either his eyes or his thoughts beyond the boundaries of his own farm, but within those everything was snug, happy, and well conditioned. He was satisfied with his wealth, but not proud of it; and he prided himself upon the hearty abundance rather than the style in which he lived. His stronghold was situated on the banks of the Hudson, in one of those green, sheltered, fertile nooks in which the Dutch farmers are so fond of nestling. A great elm tree spread its broad branches over it. At the foot of the tree bubbled up a spring of the softest and sweetest water, in a little well formed of a barrel. The spring then stole sparkling away through the grass to a neighboring brook that bubbled along among alders and dwarf willows. Close by the farmhouse was a vast barn, which might have served for a church, every window and crevice of which seemed bursting forth with the treasures of the farm. The flail was busily resounding within it from morning till night; swallows and martins skimmed twittering about the eaves; and rows of pigeons, some with one eye turned up, as if watching the weather, some with their heads under their wings or buried in their bosoms, and others swelling and cooing and bowing about their dames, were enjoying the sunshine on the roof. Sleek unwieldy porkers were grunting in the repose and abundance of their pens, from which sallied forth, now and then, troops of sucking pigs, as if to snuff the air. A stately squadron of snowy geese was riding in an adjoining pond, convoying whole fleets of ducks. Regiments of turkeys were gobbling through the farmyard, and guinea fowls fretting about it, like ill-tempered housewives, with their peevish discontented cry. Before the barn door strutted the gallant cock, clapping his burnished wings and crowing in the pride and gladness of his heart — sometimes tearing up the earth with his feet and then generously calling his ever-hungry family of wives and children to enjoy the rich morsel which he had discovered.

The pedagogue's mouth watered as he looked upon this sumptuous promise of luxurious winter fare. In his devouring mind's eye he pictured to himself every roasting pig running about with a pudding in his belly and an apple in his mouth; the pigeons were snugly put to bed in a comfortable pie, and tucked in with a coverlet of crust; the geese were swimming in their own gravy; and the ducks were pairing cosily in dishes, like snug married couples, with a decent competency of onion sauce. In the porkers he saw carved out the future sleek side of bacon and juicy relishing ham; not a turkey but he beheld daintily trussed up, with its gizzard under its wing and, perhaps, a necklace of savory sausages; and even bright chanticleer [1] himself lay sprawling on his back, in a sidedish, with uplifted claws.

---

[1] **chanticleer:** another name for a rooster.

As the enraptured Ichabod fancied all this, and as he rolled his great green eyes over the fat meadowlands, the rich fields of wheat, of rye, of buckwheat, and of Indian corn, and the orchard burdened with ruddy fruit, which surrounded the warm tenement of Van Tassel, his heart yearned after the damsel who was to inherit these domains, and his imagination expanded with the idea how they might be readily turned into cash, and the money invested in immense tracts of wild land and shingle palaces in the wilderness. Nay, his busy fancy already realized his hopes and presented to him the blooming Katrina with a whole family of children, mounted on the top of a wagon loaded with household trumpery,[1] with pots and kettles dangling beneath; and he beheld himself bestriding a pacing mare, with a colt at her heels, setting out for Kentucky, Tennessee, or the Lord knows where.

When he entered the house, the conquest of his heart was complete. It was one of those spacious farmhouses with high-ridged but lowly sloping roofs, built in the style handed down from the first Dutch settlers, the low projecting eaves forming a piazza[2] along the front, capable of being closed up in bad weather. Under this were hung flails, harnesses, various utensils of husbandry, and nets for fishing in the neighboring river. Benches were built along the sides for summer use, and a great spinning wheel at one end and a churn at the other showed the various uses to which this important porch might be devoted. From this piazza the wondering Ichabod entered the hall, which formed the center of the mansion and the place of usual residence. Here, rows of resplendent pewter, ranged on a long dresser, dazzled his eyes. In one corner stood a huge bag of wool ready to be spun, in another, a quantity of linsey-woolsey[3] just from the loom; ears of Indian corn and strings of dried apples and peaches hung in gay festoons along the walls, mingled with the gaud of red peppers. A door left ajar

[1] **trumpery:** showy but worthless finery.

[2] **piazza:** porch.
[3] **linsey-woolsey:** coarse cloth made of wool and either linen or cotton.

gave him a peep into the best parlor, where the claw-footed chairs and dark mahogany tables shone like mirrors; andirons, with their accompanying shovel and tongs, glistened from their covert of asparagus tops; mock oranges and conch shells decorated the mantelpiece, and strings of various colored birds' eggs were suspended above it; a great ostrich egg was hung from the center of the room; and a corner cupboard, knowingly left open, displayed immense treasures of old silver and well-mended china.

From the moment Ichabod laid his eyes upon these regions of delight, the peace of his mind was at an end, and his only study was how to gain the affections of the peerless daughter of Van Tassel. In this enterprise, however, he had more real difficulties than generally fell to the lot of a knight errant of yore, who seldom had anything but giants, enchanters, fiery dragons, and such easily conquered adversaries to contend with, and who had to make his way merely through gates of iron and brass and walls of adamant [1] to the castle keep, where the lady of his heart was confined; all of which he achieved as easily as a man would carve his way to the center of a Christmas pie, and then the lady gave him her hand as a matter of course. Ichabod, on the contrary, had to win his way to the heart of a country coquette, beset with a labyrinth of whims and caprices that were forever presenting new difficulties and impediments; and he had to encounter a host of fearful adversaries of real flesh and blood — the numerous rustic

admirers who beset every portal to her heart, keeping a watchful and angry eye upon each other, but ready to fly out in the common cause against any new competitor.

Among these the most formidable was a burly, roaring, roistering blade, of the name of Abraham, or, according to the Dutch abbreviation, Brom Van Brunt, the hero of the country round, which rang with his feats of strength and hardihood. He was broad shouldered and double-jointed, with short, curly, black hair, and a bluff but not unpleasant countenance, having a mingled air of fun and arrogance. From his herculean frame and great powers of limb, he had received the nickname of Brom Bones, by which he was universally known. He was famed for great knowledge and skill in horsemanship. He was foremost at all races and cock-fights; and, with the ascendancy which bodily strength acquires in rustic life, was the umpire in all disputes, setting his hat on one side and giving his decisions with an air and tone admitting of no gainsay or appeal. He was always ready for either a fight or a frolic; but had more mischief than ill will in his composition; and, with all his overbearing roughness, there was a strong dash of waggish good humor at bottom. He had three or four boon companions, who regarded him as their model, and at the head of whom he scoured the country, attending every scene of feud or merriment for miles round. In cold weather he was distinguished by a fur cap, surmounted with a flaunting fox's tail; and when the folks at a country gathering descried this well-known crest at a distance,

---

[1] **adamant:** a very hard mineral.

whisking about among a squad of hard riders, they always stood by for a squall. Sometimes his crew would be heard dashing along past the farmhouses at midnight, with whoop and halloo; and the old dames, startled out of their sleep, would listen for a moment till the hurry-scurry had clattered by, and then exclaim, "Ay, there goes Brom Bones and his gang!" The neighbors looked upon him with a mixture of awe, admiration, and good will; and when any madcap prank or rustic brawl occurred in the vicinity, they always shook their heads and warranted Brom Bones was at the bottom of it.

This harum-scarum hero had for some time singled out the blooming Katrina for the object of his gallantries; and though his amorous toyings were something like the gentle caresses and endearments of a bear, yet it was whispered that she did not altogether discourage his hopes. Certain it is, his advances were signals for rival candidates to retire. When his horse was seen tied to Van Tassel's paling on a Sunday night, a sure sign that his master was courting within, all other suitors passed by in despair and carried the war into other quarters.

Such was the formidable rival with whom Ichabod Crane had to contend, and, considering all things, a stouter man than he would have shrunk from the competition, and a wiser man would have despaired. He had, however, a happy mixture of pliability and perseverance in his nature; he was in form and spirit like a supplejack [1]: yielding, but tough; though he bent,

[1] **supplejack:** a tough but flexible climbing vine.

he never broke; and though he bowed beneath the slightest pressure, yet, the moment it was away — jerk! he was as erect and carried his head as high as ever.

To have taken the field openly against his rival would have been madness, for he was not a man to be thwarted in his amours. Ichabod, therefore, made his advances in a quiet and gently insinuating manner. Under cover of his character of singing master, he had made frequent visits at the farmhouse — not that he had anything to fear from the meddlesome interference of parents, which is so often a stumbling block in the path of lovers. Balt Van Tassel was an easy, indulgent soul; he loved his daughter better even than his pipe and, like a reasonable man and an excellent father, let her have her way in everything. His notable little wife, too, had enough to do to attend to her housekeeping and manage her poultry; for, as she sagely observed, ducks and geese are foolish things and must be looked after, but girls can take care of themselves. Thus while the busy dame bustled about the house, or plied her spinning wheel at one end of the piazza, honest Balt would sit smoking his evening pipe at the other. In the meantime, Ichabod would carry on his suit with the daughter by the side of the spring under the great elm, or sauntering along in the twilight — that hour so favorable to the lover's eloquence.

I profess not to know how women's hearts are wooed and won. To me they have always been matters of riddle and admiration. Some seem to have but one vulnerable point or door of access, while others have a thousand avenues and may be captured in a thousand different ways. It is a great triumph of skill to gain the former, but a still greater proof of generalship to maintain possession of the latter, for the man must battle for his fortress at every door and window. He who wins a thousand common hearts is therefore entitled to some renown, but he who keeps undisputed sway over the heart of a coquette is indeed a hero. Certain it is, this was not the case with the redoubtable [1] Brom Bones, and from the moment Ichabod Crane made his advances, the interests of the former evidently declined. His horse was no longer seen tied at the palings on Sunday nights, and a deadly feud gradually arose between him and the schoolmaster of Sleepy Hollow.

Brom, who had a degree of rough chivalry in his nature, would fain have carried matters to open warfare, and have settled their pretensions to the lady according to the mode of those simple reasoners, the knights errant of yore — by single combat. But Ichabod was too conscious of the superior might of his adversary to enter the lists against him. He had overheard a boast of Bones, that he would "double the schoolmaster up, and lay him on a shelf of his own schoolhouse," and he was too wary to give him an opportunity. There was something extremely provoking in this obstinately pacific system; it left Brom no alternative but to draw upon the funds of rustic waggery in his disposition and to play boorish practical jokes upon his rival. Ichabod

became the object of whimsical persecution to Bones and his gang of rough riders. They harried his hitherto peaceful domains, smoked out his singing school by stopping up the chimney, broke into the schoolhouse at night, in spite of its formidable fastenings of branch and window stakes, and turned everything topsy-turvy, so that the poor schoolmaster began to think all the witches in the country held their meetings there. But what was still more annoying, Brom took opportunities of turning him into ridicule in the presence of his mistress, and he had a scoundrel dog whom he taught to whine in the most ludicrous manner and introduced as a rival of Ichabod's to instruct her in psalmody.

In this way matters went on for some time, without producing any material effect on the relative situation of the contending powers. On a fine autumnal afternoon, Ichabod, in pensive mood, sat enthroned on the lofty stool whence he usually watched all the concerns of his little literary realm. In his hand he swayed a ruler, that scepter of despotic power; the birch of justice reposed on three nails behind the throne, a constant terror to evildoers; while on the desk before him might be seen various contraband [2] articles and prohibited weapons, detected upon the persons of idle urchins, such as half-munched apples, popguns, whirligigs, fly cages, and whole legions of rampant little paper gamecocks. Apparently there had been some appalling act of justice recently inflicted, for his scholars were all busily intent upon their books or slyly whis-

---

[1] **redoubtable** (ri·dou′tə·bəl): causing fear and respect.

[2] **contraband**: illegal.

pering behind them with one eye kept upon the master; and a kind of buzzing stillness reigned throughout the schoolroom. It was suddenly interrupted by the appearance of a man who came clattering up to the school door with an invitation to Ichabod to attend a merry-making to be held that evening at Mynheer Van Tassel's.

All was now bustle and hubbub in the late, quiet schoolroom. The scholars were hurried through their lessons without stopping at trifles; those who were nimble skipped over half with impunity,[1] and those who were tardy had a smart application now and then in the rear to quicken their speed or help them over a tall word. Books were flung aside without being put away on the shelves, inkstands were overturned, benches thrown down, and the whole school was turned loose an hour before the usual time, bursting forth like a legion of young imps, yelping and racketing about the green in joy at their early emancipation.

The gallant Ichabod now spent at least an extra half hour at his toilet, brushing and furbishing up his best and indeed only suit of rusty black and arranging his looks by a bit of broken looking glass that hung up in the schoolhouse. That he might make his appearance before his mistress in the true style of a cavalier, he borrowed a horse from the farmer with whom he was living, a choleric[2] old Dutchman of the name of Hans Van Ripper, and, thus gallantly mounted, he issued forth like a knight errant in quest of adven-

tures. But it is proper that I should, in the true spirit of romantic story, give some account of the looks and equipments of my hero and his steed. The animal he bestrode was a broken-down plow horse that had outlived almost everything but his viciousness. He was gaunt and shaggy, with a ewe neck[3] and a head like a hammer; his rusty mane and tail were tangled and knotted with burrs; one eye had lost its pupil and was glaring and spectral; but the other had the gleam of a genuine devil in it. Still he must have had fire and mettle[4] in his day, if we may judge from the name he bore of Gunpowder. He had, in fact, been a favorite steed of his master's, the choleric Van Ripper, who was a furious rider and had infused, very probably, some of his own spirit into the animal; for, old and broken-down as he looked, there was more of the lurking devil in him than in any young filly in the country.

Ichabod was a suitable figure for such a steed. He rode with short stirrups, which brought his knees nearly up to the pommel of the saddle; his sharp elbows stuck out like a grasshopper's; he carried his whip perpendicularly in his hand, like a scepter, and as his horse jogged on, the motion of his arms was not unlike the flapping of a pair of wings. A small wool hat rested on the top of his nose, for so his scanty strip of forehead might be called; and the skirts of his black coat fluttered out almost to the horse's tail. Such was the appearance of Ichabod and his steed as they shambled out of the gate of Hans

---

[1] **impunity** (im·pyoō′nə·tē): freedom from punishment.
[2] **choleric** (kol′ər·ik): easily angered.

[3] **a ewe neck**: a neck that is thin and bent backwards.
[4] **mettle**: spirit.

Van Ripper, and it was altogether such an apparition as is seldom to be met with in broad daylight.

It was, as I have said, a fine autumnal day; the sky was clear and serene, and nature wore that rich and golden livery which we always associate with abundance. The forests had put on their sober brown and yellow, while some trees of the tenderer kind had been nipped by the frosts into brilliant dyes of orange, purple, and scarlet. Streaming files of wild ducks began to make their appearance high in the air; the bark of the squirrel might be heard from the groves of beech and hickory nuts, and the pensive whistle of the quail at intervals from the neighboring stubble field.

As Ichabod jogged slowly on his way, his eye, ever open to every symptom of culinary [1] abundance, ranged with delight over the treasures of jolly autumn. On all sides he beheld vast stores of apples: some hanging in oppressive opulence on the trees; some gathered into baskets and barrels for the market; others heaped up in rich piles for the cider press. Farther on he beheld great fields of Indian corn, with its golden ears peeping from their leafy coverts and holding out the promise of cakes and hasty pudding, and the yellow pumpkins lying beneath them, turning up their fair round bellies to the sun and giving ample prospects of the most luxurious of pies; and anon he passed the fragrant buckwheat fields, breathing the odor of the beehive, and as he beheld them, soft anticipations stole over his mind of dainty slapjacks, well-buttered and garnished with honey by the delicate little dimpled hand of Katrina Van Tassel.

Thus feeding his mind with many sweet thoughts, he journeyed along the sides of a range of hills which look out upon some of the goodliest scenes of the mighty Hudson. The sun gradually wheeled his broad disk down into the west. The wide bosom of the Tappan Zee lay motionless and glossy. A few amber clouds floated in the sky without a breath of air to move them. The horizon was of a fine golden tint, changing gradually into a pure apple-green, and from that into the deep blue of the midheaven. A slanting ray lingered on the woody crests of the precipices that overhang some parts of the river, giving greater depth to the dark-gray and purple of their rocky sides. A sloop was loitering in the distance, dropping slowly down with the tide, her sail hanging uselessly against the mast; and as the reflection of the sky gleamed along the still water, it seemed as if the vessel were suspended in the air.

It was toward evening that Ichabod arrived at the castle of the Heer Van Tassel, which he found thronged with the pride and flower of the adjacent country: old farmers, a spare leathern-faced race in homespun coats and breeches, blue stockings, huge shoes, and magnificent pewter buckles; their brisk, withered little dames, in close, crimped caps, long-waisted short-gowns, homespun petticoats, with scissors and pincushions and gay calico pockets hanging on the outside; buxom lasses, almost as old-fashioned as their mothers, excepting where a straw hat, a fine ribbon, or perhaps a white frock,

---

[1] **culinary** (kyōō′lə·ner′ē): pertaining to food.

gave symptoms of city innovation; the sons, in short square-skirted coats with rows of stupendous brass buttons, and their hair generally pigtailed in the fashion of the times.

Brom Bones, however, was the hero of the scene, having come to the gathering on his favorite steed, Daredevil, a creature, like himself, full of mettle and mischief, and which no one but himself could manage. He was, in fact, noted for preferring vicious animals, given to all kinds of tricks, which kept the rider in constant risk of his neck, for he held a tractable [1] well-broken horse as unworthy of a lad of spirit.

Fain would I pause to dwell upon the world of charms that burst upon the enraptured gaze of my hero as he entered the state parlor of Van Tassel's mansion — not those of the bevy of buxom lasses, with their luxurious display of red and white, but the ample charms of a genuine Dutch country tea table, in the sumptuous time of autumn. Such heaped-up platters of cakes of various and almost indescribable kinds, known only to experienced Dutch housewives! There were the doughty [2] doughnut, the tenderer oly-koek, [3] and the crisp and crumbling cruller, sweet cakes and short cakes, ginger cakes and honey cakes, and the whole family of cakes. And then there were apple pies and peach pies and pumpkin pies; besides slices of ham and smoked beef; and, moreover, delectable dishes of preserved plums and peaches and pears and quinces; not to mention broiled shad and roasted chick-

ens; together with bowls of milk and cream, all mingled higgledy-piggledy, pretty much as I have enumerated them, with the motherly teapot sending up its clouds of vapor from the midst. Heaven bless the mark! I want breath and time to discuss this banquet as it deserves, and am too eager to get on with my story. Happily, Ichabod Crane was not in so great a hurry as his historian, but did ample justice to every dainty.

He was a kind and thankful creature, whose heart dilated in proportion as his skin was filled with good cheer and whose spirits rose with eating as some men's do with drink. He could not help, too, rolling his large eyes round him as he ate and chuckling with the possibility that he might one day be lord of all this scene of almost unimaginable luxury and splendor. Then, he thought, how soon he'd turn his back upon the old schoolhouse, snap his fingers in the face of Hans Van Ripper, and every other niggardly [4] patron, and kick any itinerant pedagogue out-of-doors that should dare to call him comrade!

Old Baltus Van Tassel moved about among his guests, with a face dilated with content and good humor, round and jolly as the harvest moon. His hospitable attentions were brief, but expressive, being confined to a shake of the hand, a slap on the shoulder, a loud laugh, and a pressing invitation to fall to and help themselves.

And now the sound of the music from the common room, or hall, summoned to the dance. The musician was an old gray-headed man who had been

---

[1] **tractable:** manageable.
[2] **doughty** (dou'tĕ): brave.
[3] **olykoek** (ôl'i·kook): a type of doughnut.

[4] **niggardly:** stingy.

the itinerant orchestra of the neighborhood for more than half a century. His instrument was as old and battered as himself. The greater part of the time he scraped on two or three strings, accompanying every movement of the bow with a motion of the head; bowing almost to the ground, and stamping with his foot whenever a fresh couple were to start.

Ichabod prided himself upon his dancing as much as upon his vocal powers. Not a limb, not a fiber about him was idle; and to have seen his loosely hung frame in full motion, and clattering about the room, you would have thought Saint Vitus himself, that blessed patron of the dance, was figuring before you in person. How could the flogger of urchins be otherwise than animated and joyous? The lady of his heart was his partner in the dance and was smiling graciously in reply to all his amorous oglings, while Brom

Bones, sorely smitten with love and jealousy, sat brooding by himself in one corner.

When the dance was at an end, Ichabod was attracted to a knot of the sager folks, who, with old Van Tassel, sat smoking at one end of the piazza, gossiping over former times and drawing out long stories about the war.

This neighborhood, at the time of which I am speaking, was one of those highly favored places which abound with chronicle and great men. The British and American line had run near it during the war; it had, therefore, been the scene of marauding, and infested with refugees, cowboys, and all kinds of border chivalry. Just sufficient time had elapsed to enable each storyteller to dress up his tale with a little becoming fiction and, in the indistinctness of his recollection, to make himself the hero of every exploit.

There was the story of a large blue-bearded Dutchman who had nearly taken a British frigate with an old iron nine-pounder, only that his gun burst at the sixth discharge. And there was another old gentleman who, in the Battle of White Plains, parried a musket ball with a small sword, insomuch that he absolutely felt it whiz round the blade and glance off at the hilt, in proof of which he was ready at any time to show the sword with the hilt a little bent. There were several more that had been equally great in the field, not one of whom but was persuaded that he had a considerable hand in bringing the war to a happy conclusion.

But all these were nothing to the tales of ghosts and apparitions that followed. The neighborhood is rich in legendary treasures of the kind. The immediate cause of the prevalence of supernatural stories in these parts was doubtless owing to the vicinity of Sleepy Hollow. There was a contagion in the very air that blew from that haunted region; it breathed forth an atmosphere of dreams and fancies infecting all the land. Several of the Sleepy Hollow people were present at Van Tassel's, and, as usual, were doling out their wild and wonderful legends. Many dismal tales were told about funeral trains and mourning cries and wailings heard and seen about the great tree where the unfortunate Major André [1] was taken, and which stood in the neighborhood. Some mention was made also of the woman in white who haunted the dark glen at Raven Rock and was often heard to shriek on winter nights before a storm, having

[1] **Major André:** a British officer, hanged as a spy in 1780, during the Revolutionary War.

perished there in the snow. The chief part of the stories, however, turned upon the favorite specter of Sleepy Hollow, the headless horseman, who had been heard several times of late patrolling the country, and who, it was said, tethered his horse nightly among the graves in the churchyard.

The sequestered situation of this church seems always to have made it a favorite haunt of troubled spirits. It stands on a knoll, surrounded by locust trees and lofty elms, from among which its decent whitewashed walls shine modestly forth. A gentle slope descends from it to a silver sheet of water, bordered by high trees, between which peeps may be caught at the blue hills of the Hudson. To look upon its grass-grown yard, where the sunbeams seem to sleep so quietly, one would think that there at least the dead might rest in peace. On one side of the church extends a wide, woody dell, along which a large brook raves among broken rocks and trunks of fallen trees. Over a deep part of the stream, not far from the church, a wooden bridge had been built. The road that led to it and the bridge itself were thickly shaded by overhanging trees, which cast a gloom about it even in the daytime, but occasioned a fearful darkness at night. This was one of the favorite haunts of the headless horseman and the place where he was most frequently encountered. The tale was told of how old Brouwer, a most heretical disbeliever in ghosts, met the horseman returning from his foray into Sleepy Hollow and was obliged to get up behind him; how they galloped over bush and brake, over hill and swamp, until they reached the bridge, when the horseman suddenly turned into a skeleton, threw old Brouwer into the brook, and sprang away over the treetops with a clap of thunder.

This story was immediately matched by a thrice marvelous adventure of Brom Bones, who made light of the Galloping Hessian as an errant jockey. He affirmed that, on returning one night from the neighboring village of Sing Sing, he had been overtaken by this midnight trooper; that he had offered to race with him for a bowl of punch, and should have won it too, for Daredevil beat the goblin horse all hollow, but, just as they came to the church bridge, the Hessian bolted and vanished in a flash of fire.

All these tales, told in that drowsy undertone with which men talk in the dark, the countenances of the listeners only now and then receiving a casual gleam from the glare of a pipe, sank deep in the mind of Ichabod. He repaid them in kind with large extracts from his invaluable author, Cotton Mather, and added many marvelous events that had taken place in his native state of Connecticut and fearful sights which he had seen in his nightly walks about Sleepy Hollow.

The revel now gradually broke up. The old farmers gathered together their families in their wagons and were heard for some time rattling along the hollow roads and over the distant hills. Some of the damsels mounted behind their favorite swains, and their light-hearted laughter, mingling with the clatter of hoofs, echoed along the silent woodlands, sounding fainter and fainter until they gradually died away —

and the late scene of noise and frolic was all silent and deserted. Ichabod only lingered behind, according to the custom of country lovers, to have a *tête-à-tête* [1] with the heiress, fully convinced that he was now on the highroad to success. What passed at this interview I will not pretend to say, for in fact I do not know. Something, however, I fear me, must have gone wrong, for he certainly sallied forth, after no very great interval, with an air quite desolate and chapfallen. Oh, these women! these women! Could that girl have been playing off any of her coquettish tricks? Was her encouragement of the poor pedagogue all a mere sham to secure her conquest of his rival? Heaven only knows, not I! Let it suffice to say, Ichabod stole forth with the air of one who had been sacking a hen roost rather than a fair lady's heart. Without looking to the right or left to notice the scene of rural wealth on which he had so often gloated, he went straight to the stable and, with several hearty cuffs and kicks, roused his steed most uncourteously from the comfortable quarters in which he was soundly sleeping, dreaming of mountains of corn and oats and whole valleys of timothy and clover.

It was the very witching time of night that Ichabod, heavy-hearted and crestfallen, pursued his travel homewards, along the sides of the lofty hills which rise above Tarrytown and which he had traversed so cheerily in the afternoon. The hour was as dismal as himself. Far below him, the Tappan Zee spread its dusky and indistinct

[1] *tête-à-tête* (tāt′ə·tāt′): private chat.

waste of waters, with here and there the tall mast of a sloop riding quietly at anchor under the land. In the dead hush of midnight he could even hear the barking of the watchdog from the opposite shore of the Hudson, but it was so vague and faint as only to give an idea of his distance from this faithful companion of man. Now and then, too, the long-drawn crowing of a cock, accidentally awakened, would sound far, far off, from some farmhouse away among the hills — but it was like a dreaming sound in his ear. No signs of life occurred near him, but occasionally the melancholy chirp of a cricket or, perhaps, the guttural twang of a bullfrog from a neighboring marsh, as if sleeping uncomfortably and turning suddenly in his bed.

All the stories of ghosts and goblins that he had heard in the afternoon now came crowding upon his recollection. The night grew darker and darker; the stars seemed to sink deeper in the sky, and driving clouds occasionally hid them from his sight. He had never felt so lonely and dismal. He was, moreover, approaching the very place where many of the scenes of the ghost stories had been laid. In the center of the road stood an enormous tulip tree that towered like a giant above all the other trees of the neighborhood and formed a kind of landmark. Its limbs were gnarled and fantastic, large enough to form trunks for ordinary trees, twisting down almost to the earth and rising again into the air. It was connected with the tragical story of the unfortunate André, who had been taken prisoner nearby, and was universally known by the name of Major André's Tree. The common people regarded it with a mixture of respect and superstition, partly out of sympathy for the fate of its ill-starred namesake, and partly from the tales of strange sights and doleful lamentations told concerning it.

As Ichabod approached this fearful tree, he began to whistle; he thought his whistle was answered — it was but a blast sweeping sharply through the dry branches. As he approached a little nearer, he thought he saw something white hanging in the midst of the tree; he paused and ceased whistling — but on looking more narrowly, perceived that it was a place where the tree had been scathed by lightning and the white wood laid bare. Suddenly he heard a groan; his teeth chattered and his knees smote against the saddle — it was but the rubbing of one huge bough upon another as they were swayed about by the breeze. He passed the tree in safety, but new perils lay before him.

About two hundred yards from the tree, a small brook crossed the road and ran into a marshy and thickly wooded glen, known by the name of Wiley's Swamp. A few rough logs laid side by side served for a bridge over this stream. On that side of the road where the brook entered the wood, a group of oaks and chestnuts, matted thick with wild grape vines, threw a cavernous gloom over it. To pass this bridge was the severest trial. It was at this identical spot that the unfortunate André was captured, and under the covert of those chestnuts and vines were concealed the sturdy yeomen who surprised him. This has ever since been considered a haunted stream, and fearful are the feelings of the schoolboy who has to pass it alone after dark.

As he approached the stream, his heart began to thump; he summoned up, however, all his resolution, gave his horse half a score of kicks in the ribs, and attempted to dash briskly across the bridge; but instead of starting forward, the perverse old animal made a lateral movement and ran broadside against the fence. Ichabod, whose fears increased with the delay, jerked the reins on the other side and kicked lustily with the opposite foot. It was all in vain; his steed started, it is true, but it was only to plunge to the opposite side of the road into a thicket of brambles and alder bushes. The schoolmaster now bestowed both whip and heel upon the starveling ribs of old Gunpowder, who dashed forward, snuffling and snorting, but came to a stand just by the bridge with a suddenness that nearly sent his rider sprawling over his head. Just at this moment, a splashy step by the side of the bridge caught the sensitive ear of Ichabod. In the dark shadow of the grove, on the margin of the brook, he beheld something huge, misshapen, black, and towering. It stirred not, but seemed gathered up in a gloom, like some gigantic monster ready to spring upon the traveler.

The hair of the frightened pedagogue rose upon his head with terror. What was to be done? To turn and fly was now too late; and besides, what chance was there of escaping ghost or goblin, if such it was, which could ride upon the wings of the wind? Summoning up, therefore, a show of courage, he demanded in stammering accents,

"Who are you?" He received no reply. He repeated his demand in a still more agitated voice. Still there was no answer. Once more he cudgeled the sides of the inflexible Gunpowder, and, shutting his eyes, broke forth with involuntary fervor into a psalm tune. Just then the shadowy object of alarm put itself in motion and, with a scramble and a bound, stood at once in the middle of the road. Though the night was dark and dismal, yet the form of the unknown might now in some degree be ascertained. He appeared to be a horseman of large dimensions and mounted on a black horse of powerful frame. He made no offer of molestation or sociability, but kept aloof on one side of the road, jogging along on the blind side of old Gunpowder, who had now got over his fright and waywardness.

Ichabod, who had no relish for this strange midnight companion, and who bethought himself of the adventure of Brom Bones with the Galloping Hessian, now quickened his steed in hopes of leaving him behind. The stranger, however, quickened his horse to an equal pace. Ichabod pulled up and fell into a walk, thinking to lag behind — the other did the same. His heart began to sink within him; he endeavored to resume his psalm tune, but his parched tongue cleaved to the roof of his mouth, and he could not utter a stave.[1] There was something in the moody and dogged silence of this persistent companion that was mysterious and appalling. It was soon fearfully accounted for. On mounting a rising ground, which brought the figure of

[1] **stave:** here, a measure of music.

his fellow traveler in relief against the sky, gigantic in height and muffled in a cloak, Ichabod was horror struck on perceiving that he was headless! But his horror was still more increased on observing that the head, which should have rested on his shoulders, was carried before him on the pommel of the saddle. His terror rose to desperation; he rained a shower of kicks and blows upon Gunpowder, hoping, by a sudden movement, to give his companion the slip — but the specter started full jump with him. Away then they dashed through thick and thin, stones flying and sparks flashing at every bound. Ichabod's flimsy garments fluttered in the air as he stretched his long, lank body away over his horse's head, in the eagerness of his flight.

They had now reached the road which turns off to Sleepy Hollow; but Gunpowder, who seemed possessed with a demon, instead of keeping up it, made an opposite turn and plunged headlong downhill to the left. This road leads through a sandy hollow, shaded by trees for about a quarter of

a mile, where it crosses the bridge famous in goblin story, and just beyond swells the green knoll on which stands the whitewashed church.

As yet the panic of the steed had given his unskillful rider an apparent advantage in the chase; but just as he had got halfway through the hollow, the girths of the saddle gave way, and he felt it slipping from under him. He seized it by the pommel and endeavored to hold it firm, but in vain, and had just time to save himself by clasping old Gunpowder round the neck, when the saddle fell to the earth, and he heard it trampled underfoot by his pursuer. For a moment the terror of Hans Van Ripper's wrath passed across his mind — for it was his Sunday saddle; but this was no time for petty fears. The goblin was hard on his haunches, and (unskillful rider that he was!) he had much ado to maintain his seat, sometimes slipping on one side, sometimes on another, and sometimes jolted on the high ridge of his horse's backbone with a violence that he feared would cleave him asunder.

An opening in the trees now cheered him with the hopes that the church bridge was at hand. The wavering reflection of a silver star in the bosom of the brook told him that he was not mistaken. He saw the walls of the church dimly glaring under the trees beyond. He recollected the place where Brom Bones's ghostly competitor had disappeared. "If I can but reach that bridge," thought Ichabod, "I am safe." Just then he heard the black steed panting and blowing close behind him; he even fancied that he felt its hot breath. Another convulsive kick in the ribs, and old Gunpowder sprang upon the bridge; he thundered over the resounding planks; he gained the opposite side; and now Ichabod cast a look behind to see if his pursuer should vanish, according to rule, in a flash of fire and brimstone. Just then he saw the goblin rising in his stirrups and in the very act of hurling his head at him. Ichabod endeavored to dodge the horrible missile, but too late. It encountered his cranium with a tremendous crash — he was tumbled headlong into the dust, and Gunpowder, the black steed, and the goblin rider passed by like a whirlwind.

The next morning the old horse was found without his saddle and with the bridle under his feet, soberly cropping the grass at his master's gate. Ichabod did not make his appearance at breakfast — dinner hour came, but no Ichabod. The boys assembled at the schoolhouse and strolled idly about the banks of the brook, but no schoolmaster. Hans Van Ripper now began to feel some uneasiness about the fate of poor Ichabod and his saddle. An inquiry was set on foot, and after diligent investigation they came upon his traces. In one part of the road leading to the church was found the saddle, trampled in the dirt; the tracks of horses' hoofs, deeply dented in the road and evidently at furious speed, were traced to the bridge, beyond which, on the bank of a broad part of the brook where the water ran deep and black, was found the hat of the unfortunate Ichabod, and close beside it a shattered pumpkin.

The brook was searched, but the body of the schoolmaster was not to be discovered. Hans Van Ripper, as executor of his estate, examined the bundle which contained all his worldly effects. They consisted of two shirts and a half; two neckties; a pair or two of worsted stockings; an old pair of corduroy knee breeches; a rusty razor; a book of psalm tunes, full of dogs' ears; and a broken pitchpipe. As to the books and furniture of the schoolhouse, they belonged to the community, excepting Cotton Mather's *History of New England Witchcraft*, the *New England Almanac*, and a book of dreams and fortunetelling in which there was a sheet of paper much scribbled and blotted in several fruitless attempts to make a copy of verses in honor of the heiress Van Tassel. These magic books and the poetic scrawl were forthwith consigned to the flames by Hans Van Ripper, who from that time forward determined to send his children no more to school, observing that he never knew any good to come of reading and writing. Whatever money the schoolmaster possessed, and he had received his quarter's pay but a day or two before, he must have had about his person at the time of his disappearance.

The mysterious event caused much speculation at the church on the following Sunday. Knots of gazers and gossips were collected in the churchyard, at the bridge, and at the spot where the hat and pumpkin had been found. The stories of Brouwer and of Bones and a whole budget of others were called to mind; and when they had diligently considered them all and compared them with the symptoms of the present case, they shook their heads and came to the conclusion that Ichabod had been carried off by the Galloping Hessian. As he was a bachelor and in nobody's debt, nobody troubled his head any more about him. The school was removed to a different quarter of the hollow, and another pedagogue reigned in his stead.

It is true that an old farmer who had been down to New York on a visit several years after and from whom this account of the ghostly adventure was received, brought home the intelligence that Ichabod Crane was still alive; that he had left the neighborhood, partly through fear of the goblin and Hans Van Ripper and partly in mortification at having been suddenly dismissed by the heiress; that he had changed his quarters to a distant part of the country, had kept school and studied law at the same time, had been admitted to the bar, had turned politician, electioneered, written for the newspapers, and finally had been made a justice of the Ten Pound Court.[1] Brom Bones too, who shortly after his rival's disappearance conducted the blooming Katrina in triumph to the altar, was observed to look exceedingly knowing whenever the story of Ichabod was related, and always burst into a hearty laugh at the mention of the pumpkin, which led some to suspect that he knew more about the matter than he chose to tell.

The old country wives, however, who are the best judges of these matters, maintain to this day that Ichabod was spirited away by supernatural means, and it is a favorite story often told about the neighborhood round the winter evening fire. The bridge became more than ever an object of superstitious awe, and that may be the reason why the road has been altered of late years, so as to approach the church by the border of the millpond. The schoolhouse, being deserted, soon fell to decay and was reported to be haunted by the ghost of the unfortunate pedagogue; and the plowboy, loitering homeward of a still summer evening, has often fancied Ichabod's voice at a distance, chanting a melancholy psalm tune among the tranquil solitudes of Sleepy Hollow.

---

[1] **Ten Pound Court:** a court that could try minor cases and impose fines only up to ten pounds. A pound is a British unit of money, worth about five dollars at that time.

ELEMENTS IN A SHORT STORY

Characterization. People are the center and the heart of fiction. A writer must create characters that his readers will see as real individuals. How does he do this?

1. *The writer tells what a character looks like.* Find the paragraph at the beginning of the story which describes Ichabod. What details help you to picture him? To what different things is Ichabod compared? What is humorous about Ichabod's appearance?

2. *The character is placed in a setting.* Reread the paragraph describing Ichabod's school. How was it different from the Van Tassel house?

3. *The character's behavior is described.* How did Ichabod act toward his pupils? How did he spend his time after school? What do his actions tell you about him?

4. *The character's thoughts and reactions, his likes and dislikes, are revealed.* What does Ichabod's "appetite for the marvelous" tell you about him? How did he react to the sounds of the night? What did you find out about his taste in music? Why did Ichabod like Katrina and the Van Tassel farm? Describe his weakness for gossiping.

5. *The author adds another dimension to his main character by telling how other characters in the story react to him.* What did the ladies in the vicinity think of Ichabod? What did Brom Bones think of him? What do you think Katrina really thought about Ichabod?

6. *Other characters are developed, some in contrast to the main character.* What kind of character was Ichabod's rival? How did Brom Bones play upon Ichabod's weakness? How does Ichabod contrast with Brom Bones? Do you think there is a hero in this story? If so, who is it?

Suspense. In a short story, we usually find forces working against the main character's wishes. As the story goes on, the reader wonders what is going to happen and how things will turn out for the hero.

7. What did Ichabod desire? What forces worked against him? At what points in the story did you begin to feel suspense? Was your curiosity entirely satisfied by the end of the story? Explain your answer.

8. Irving shared Ichabod's feelings and thoughts with us. Do you think the suspense in the story would have been less if we were taken into the minds of other characters as well? Explain.

Effect. A short story writer strives to produce a strong effect on his reader. Sometimes he wants to amuse his reader, sometimes to terrify him, sometimes to surprise him. Sometimes a writer wants to make a serious point in his story.

9. Do you think Irving had a serious purpose in telling this story, or do you think he chiefly wanted to entertain and amuse us? How would you describe Irving's attitude toward the characters and events in this story — was he being deadly serious, or do you think he was smiling as he told about Ichabod and the ghost? Point to passages of the story to support your answers.

10. Many people find Irving's descriptive passages especially pleasant to read. Find in this story at least one passage in which Irving describes (a) the countryside; (b) the farmhouses; (c) the people and their dress. What kind of atmosphere is created by these passages? Do you feel that these descriptions give you a view of country life as it was lived in earlier days?

SENTENCES: DESCRIPTIVE WORDS

Washington Irving lived in the nineteenth century, a time when many writers used long, detailed sentences. Irving's sentences are usually built up with many descriptive words. A long sentence from "The Legend of Sleepy Hollow" is quoted on the next page. If we took away most of the descriptive words from this long sentence, we would have the following brief statement: *Every sound fluttered his imagination.* But look at how Irving expanded this short sentence into a detailed one. The descriptive words or word groups are in brackets.

"[Then], [as he wended his way by swamp and stream and awful woodland to the farmhouse where he happened to be quartered], *every sound* [of nature] [at that witching hour] *fluttered his* [excited] *imagination:* [the moan of the whippoorwill from the hillside]; [the boding cry of the tree toad, that harbinger of storm]; [the dreary hooting of the screech owl]; [or the sudden rustling in the thicket of birds, frightened from their roost]."

Below is another long, well-constructed sentence from the story. If you cut away the descriptive words from this sentence, what basic brief statement are you left with? What interesting descriptive details are added by all the other words in this sentence?

"He would delight them equally by his anecdotes of witchcraft and of the direful omens and portentous sights and sounds in the air, which prevailed in the earlier times of Connecticut, and would frighten them woefully with speculations upon comets and shooting stars and with the alarming fact that the world did absolutely turn round and that they were half the time topsy-turvy!"

COMPOSITION: SPECIFIC DETAILS IN
    DESCRIPTION

In this paragraph from "The Legend of Sleepy Hollow," Irving describes what Ichabod sees in the Van Tassel house.

"When he entered the house, the conquest of his heart was complete. It was one of those spacious farmhouses with high-ridged but lowly sloping roofs, built in the style handed down from the first Dutch settlers, the low projecting eaves forming a piazza along the front, capable of being closed up in bad weather. Under this were hung flails, harnesses, various utensils of husbandry, and nets for fishing in the neighboring river. Benches were built along the sides for summer use, and a great spinning wheel at one end and a churn at the other showed the various uses to which this important porch might be devoted. From this piazza the wondering Ichabod entered the hall, which formed the center of the mansion and the place of usual residence. Here, rows of resplendent pewter, ranged on a long dresser, dazzled his eyes. In one corner stood a huge bag of wool ready to be spun, in another, a quantity of linsey-woolsey just from the loom; ears of Indian corn and strings of dried apples and peaches hung in gay festoons along the walls, mingled with the gaud of red peppers. A door left ajar gave him a peep into the best parlor, where the claw-footed chairs and dark mahogany tables shone like mirrors; andirons, with their accompanying shovel and tongs, glistened from their covert of asparagus tops; mock oranges and conch shells decorated the mantelpiece, and strings of various colored birds' eggs were suspended above it; a great ostrich egg was hung from the center of the room; and a corner cupboard, knowingly left open, displayed immense treasures of old silver and well-mended china."

Irving's sense of detail was remarkable. List all the nouns he uses to name precisely what met Ichabod's eyes as he looked around the house. Which adjectives helped you to see even more vividly some of these objects? Which verbs did you think were especially descriptive?

Write a paragraph in which you describe a place in detail. Perhaps you can describe what you see in your house at holiday time, or you might describe a display in a store. Try to be precise in naming what you see.

The Ransom of Red Chief

O. HENRY

IT LOOKED LIKE a good thing: but wait till I tell you. We were down South, in Alabama — Bill Driscoll and myself — when this kidnaping idea struck us. It was, as Bill afterward expressed it, "during a moment of temporary mental apparition";[1] but we didn't find that out till later.

There was a town down there, as flat as a flannel cake, and called Summit, of course. It contained inhabitants of as undeleterious[2] and self-satisfied a class of peasantry as ever clustered around a Maypole.

Bill and me had a joint capital of about six hundred dollars, and we needed just two thousand dollars more to pull off a fraudulent town-lot scheme in western Illinois with. We talked it over on the front steps of the hotel. Philoprogenitiveness,[3] says we, is strong in semirural communities; therefore,

and for other reasons, a kidnaping project ought to do better there than in the radius of newspapers that send reporters out in plain clothes to stir up talk about such things. We knew that Summit couldn't get after us with anything stronger than constables and, maybe, some lackadaisical bloodhounds and a diatribe[4] or two in the *Weekly Farmers' Budget*. So, it looked good.

We selected for our victim the only child of a prominent citizen named Ebenezer Dorset. The father was respectable and tight, a mortgage fancier and a stern, upright collection-plate passer and forecloser. The kid was a boy of ten, with bas-relief[5] freckles, and hair the color of the cover of the magazine you buy at the newsstand when you want to catch a train. Bill and me figured that Ebenezer would melt down for a ransom of two thousand dollars to a cent. But wait till I tell you.

About two miles from Summit was a little mountain, covered with a dense

---

[1] **apparition** (ap'ə·rish'ən): Bill means *aberration* (ab'ə·rā'shən), a lapse from sanity.

[2] **undeleterious** (un·del'ə·tir'ē·əs): harmless.

[3] **Philoprogenitiveness** (fil'ə·prō·jen'ə·tiv·nis): love of parents for their children.

[4] **diatribe** (dī'ə·trīb): here, a bitter article.

[5] **bas-relief** (bä' ri·lēf'): raised slightly from the background, like some kinds of wall sculpture.

cedar brake. On the rear elevation of this mountain was a cave. There we stored provisions.

One evening after sundown, we drove in a buggy past old Dorset's house. The kid was in the street, throwing rocks at a kitten on the opposite fence.

"Hey, little boy!" says Bill. "Would you like to have a bag of candy and a nice ride?"

The boy catches Bill neatly in the eye with a piece of brick.

"That will cost the old man an extra five hundred dollars," says Bill, climbing over the wheel.

That boy put up a fight like a welterweight cinnamon bear; but, at last, we got him down in the bottom of the buggy and drove away. We took him up to the cave, and I hitched the horse in the cedar brake. After dark I drove the buggy to the little village, three miles away, where we had hired it, and walked back to the mountain.

Bill was pasting court plaster over the scratches and bruises on his features. There was a fire burning behind the big rock at the entrance of the cave, and the boy was watching a pot of boiling coffee, with two buzzard tail feathers stuck in his red hair. He points a stick at me when I come up, and says:

"Ha! cursèd paleface, do you dare to enter the camp of Red Chief, the terror of the plains?"

"He's all right now," says Bill, rolling up his trousers and examining some bruises on his shins. "We're playing Indian. We're making Buffalo Bill's show look like magic-lantern views of Palestine in the town hall. I'm Old Hank the Trapper, Red Chief's captive, and I'm to be scalped at daybreak. By Geronimo! That kid can kick hard!"

Yes, sir, that boy seemed to be having the time of his life. The fun of camping out in a cave had made him forget that he was a captive himself. He immediately christened me Snake-Eye the Spy, and announced that, when his braves returned from the war-path, I was to be broiled at the stake at the rising of the sun.

Then we had supper; and he filled his mouth full of bacon and bread and gravy, and began to talk. He made a during-dinner speech something like this:

"I like this fine. I never camped out before; but I had a pet possum once, and I was nine last birthday. I hate to go to school. Rats ate up sixteen of Jimmy Talbot's aunt's speckled hen's eggs. Are there any real Indians in these woods? I want some more gravy. Does the trees moving make the wind blow? We had five puppies. What makes your nose so red, Hank? My father has lots of money. Are the stars hot? I whipped Ed Walker twice, Saturday. I don't like girls. You dassent catch toads unless with a string. Do oxen make any noise? Why are oranges round? Have you got beds to sleep on in this cave? Amos Murray has got six toes. A parrot can talk, but a monkey or a fish can't. How many does it take to make twelve?"

Every few minutes he would remember that he was a pesky redskin and pick up his stick rifle and tiptoe to the mouth of the cave to rubber for the scouts of the hated paleface. Now and then he would let out a war whoop that made Old Hank the Trapper shiver.

That boy had Bill terrorized from the start.

"Red Chief," says I to the kid, "would you like to go home?"

"Aw, what for?" says he. "I don't have any fun at home. I hate to go to school. I like to camp out. You won't take me back home again, Snake-Eye, will you?"

"Not right away," says I. "We'll stay here in the cave a while."

"All right!" says he. "That'll be fine. I never had such fun in all my life."

We went to bed about eleven o'clock. We spread down some wide blankets and quilts and put Red Chief between us. We weren't afraid he'd run away. He kept us awake for three hours, jumping up and reaching for his rifle and screeching: "Hist! pard," in mine and Bill's ears, as the fancied crackle of a twig or the rustle of a leaf revealed to his young imagination the stealthy approach of the outlaw band. At last, I fell into a troubled sleep and dreamed that I had been kidnaped and chained to a tree by a ferocious pirate with red hair.

Just at daybreak, I was awakened by a series of awful screams from Bill. They weren't yells, or howls, or shouts, or whoops, or yawps, such as you'd expect from a manly set of vocal organs — they were simply indecent, terrifying, humiliating screams, such as women emit when they see ghosts or caterpillars. It's an awful thing to hear a strong, desperate, fat man scream incontinently [1] in a cave at daybreak.

I jumped up to see what the matter was. Red Chief was sitting on Bill's chest, with one hand twined in Bill's hair. In the other he had the sharp case knife we used for slicing bacon, and he was industriously and realistically trying to take Bill's scalp, according to the sentence that had been pronounced upon him the evening before.

I got the knife away from the kid and made him lie down again. But, from that moment, Bill's spirit was broken. He laid down on his side of the bed, but he never closed an eye again in sleep as long as that boy was with

[1] **incontinently**: uncontrollably.

us. I dozed off for a while, but along toward sunup I remembered that Red Chief had said I was to be burned at the stake at the rising of the sun. I wasn't nervous or afraid; but I sat up and lit my pipe and leaned against a rock.

"What you getting up so soon for, Sam?" asked Bill.

"Me?" says I. "Oh, I got a kind of a pain in my shoulder. I thought sitting up would rest it."

"You're a liar!" says Bill. "You're afraid. You was to be burned at sunrise, and you was afraid he'd do it. And he would, too, if he could find a match. Ain't it awful, Sam? Do you think anybody will pay out money to get a little imp like that back home?"

"Sure," said I. "A rowdy kid like that is just the kind that parents dote on. Now, you and the Chief get up and cook breakfast, while I go up on the top of this mountain and reconnoiter."

I went up on the peak of the little mountain and ran my eye over the contiguous [1] vicinity. Over toward Summit I expected to see the sturdy yeomanry of the village, armed with scythes and pitchforks, beating the countryside for the dastardly kidnapers. But what I saw was a peaceful landscape dotted with one man plowing with a dun mule. Nobody was dragging the creek; no couriers dashed hither and yon, bringing tidings of no news to the distracted parents. There was a sylvan [2] attitude of somnolent [3] sleepiness pervading that section of the external outward surface of Alabama that lay ex-

posed to my view. "Perhaps," says I to myself, "it has not yet been discovered that the wolves have borne away the tender lambkin from the fold. Heaven help the wolves!" says I, and I went down the mountain to breakfast.

When I got to the cave, I found Bill backed up against the side of it, breathing hard, and the boy threatening to smash him with a rock half as big as a coconut.

"He put a red-hot boiled potato down my back," explained Bill, "and then mashed it with his foot; and I boxed his ears. Have you got a gun about you, Sam?"

I took the rock away from the boy and kind of patched up the argument. "I'll fix you," says the kid to Bill. "No man ever yet struck the Red Chief but what he got paid for it. You better beware!"

After breakfast the kid takes a piece of leather with strings wrapped around it out of his pocket and goes outside the cave unwinding it.

"What's he up to now?" says Bill anxiously. "You don't think he'll run away, do you, Sam?"

"No fear of it," says I. "He don't seem to be much of a homebody. But we've got to fix up some plan about the ransom. There don't seem to be much excitement around Summit on account of his disappearance, but maybe they haven't realized yet that he's gone. His folks may think he's spending the night with Aunt Jane or one of the neighbors. Anyhow, he'll be missed today. Tonight we must get a message to his father demanding the two thousand dollars for his return."

Just then we heard a kind of war

---

[1] **contiguous** (kən·tig′yŏŏ·əs): nearby.
[2] **sylvan**: woodsy.
[3] **somnolent** (som′nə·lənt): drowsy.

whoop, such as David might have emitted when he knocked out the champion Goliath. It was a sling that Red Chief had pulled out of his pocket, and he was whirling it around his head.

I dodged and heard a heavy thud and a kind of a sigh from Bill, like a horse gives out when you take his saddle off. A rock the size of an egg had caught Bill just behind his left ear. He loosened himself all over and fell in the fire across the frying pan of hot water for washing the dishes. I dragged him out and poured cold water on his head for half an hour.

By and by, Bill sits up and feels behind his ear and says: "Sam, do you know who my favorite Biblical character is?"

"Take it easy," says I. "You'll come to your senses presently."

"King Herod," [1] says he. "You won't go away and leave me here alone, will you, Sam?"

I went out and caught that boy and shook him until his freckles rattled.

"If you don't behave," says I, "I'll take you straight home. Now, are you going to be good or not?"

"I was only funning," says he sullenly. "I didn't meant to hurt Old Hank. But what did he hit me for? I'll behave, Snake-Eye, if you won't send me home, and if you'll let me play the Black Scout today."

"I don't know the game," says I. "That's for you and Mr. Bill to decide. He's your playmate for the day. I'm going away for a while, on business. Now,

you come in and make friends with him and say you are sorry for hurting him, or home you go, at once."

I made him and Bill shake hands, and then I took Bill aside and told him I was going to Poplar Cove, a little village three miles from the cave, and find out what I could about how the kidnaping had been regarded in Summit. Also, I thought it best to send a peremptory [2] letter to old man Dorset that day, demanding the ransom and dictating how it should be paid.

"You know, Sam," says Bill, "I've stood by you without batting an eye in earthquakes, fire, and flood — in poker games, dynamite outrages, police raids, train robberies, and cyclones. I never lost my nerve yet till we kidnaped that two-legged skyrocket of a kid. He's got me going. You won't leave me long with him, will you, Sam?"

"I'll be back some time this afternoon," says I. "You must keep the boy amused and quiet till I return. And now we'll write the letter to old Dorset."

Bill and I got paper and pencil and worked on the letter while Red Chief, with a blanket wrapped around him, strutted up and down, guarding the mouth of the cave. Bill begged me tearfully to make the ransom fifteen hundred dollars instead of two thousand. "I ain't attempting," says he, "to decry the celebrated moral aspect of parental affection, but we're dealing with humans, and it ain't human for anybody to give up two thousand dollars for that forty-pound chunk of freckled wildcat. I'm willing to take a chance at fifteen hun-

[1] **King Herod:** the king who, according to the Bible story, ordered the killing of all male children under two in Bethlehem in an effort to slay the infant Jesus.

[2] **peremptory** (pə·remp'tər·ē): decisive.

dred dollars. You can charge the difference up to me."

So, to relieve Bill, I acceded, and we collaborated a letter that ran this way:

Ebenezer Dorset, Esq.:

We have your boy concealed in a place far from Summit. It is useless for you or the most skillful detectives to attempt to find him. Absolutely, the only terms on which you can have him restored to you are these: We demand fifteen hundred dollars in large bills for his return; the money to be left at midnight tonight at the same spot and in the same box as your reply — as hereinafter described. If you agree to these terms, send your answer in writing by a solitary messenger tonight at half-past eight o'clock. After crossing Owl Creek, on the road to Poplar Cove, there are three large trees about a hundred yards apart, close to the fence of the wheat field on the right-hand side. At the bottom of the fence post, opposite the third tree, will be found a small pasteboard box.

The messenger will place the answer in this box and return immediately to Summit.

If you attempt any treachery or fail to comply with our demand as stated, you will never see your boy again.

If you pay the money as demanded, he will be returned to you safe and well within three hours. These terms are final, and if you do not accede to them, no further communication will be attempted.

Two Desperate Men

I addressed this letter to Dorset and put it in my pocket. As I was about to start, the kid comes up to me and says:

"Aw, Snake-Eye, you said I could play the Black Scout while you was gone."

"Play it, of course," says I. "Mr. Bill will play with you. What kind of a game is it?"

"I'm the Black Scout," says Red Chief, "and I have to ride to the stockade to warn the settlers that the Indians are coming. I'm tired of playing Indian myself. I want to be the Black Scout."

"All right," says I. "It sounds harmless to me. I guess Mr. Bill will help you foil the pesky savages."

"What am I to do?" asks Bill, looking at the kid suspiciously.

"You are the hoss," says Black Scout. "Get down on your hands and knees. How can I ride to the stockade without a hoss?"

"You'd better keep him interested," said I, "till we get the scheme going. Loosen up."

Bill gets down on his all fours, and a look comes in his eye like a rabbit's when you catch it in a trap.

"How far is it to the stockade, kid?" he asks, in a husky manner of voice.

"Ninety miles," says the Black Scout. "And you have to hump yourself to get there on time. Whoa, now!" The Black Scout jumps on Bill's back and digs his heels in his side.

"For heaven's sake," says Bill, "hurry back, Sam, as soon as you can. I wish we hadn't made the ransom more than a thousand. Say, you quit kicking me or I'll get up and warm you good."

I walked over to Poplar Cove and

sat round the post office and store talking with the chaw-bacons that came in to trade. One whiskerando says that he hears Summit is all upset on account of Elder Ebenezer Dorset's boy having been lost or stolen. That was all I wanted to know. I bought some smoking tobacco, referred casually to the price of black-eyed peas, posted my letter surreptitiously,[1] and came away. The postmaster said the mail carrier would come by in an hour to take the mail on to Summit.

When I got back to the cave, Bill and the boy were not to be found. I explored the vicinity of the cave and risked a yodel or two, but there was no response.

So I lighted my pipe and sat down on a mossy bank to await developments.

In about half an hour I heard the bushes rustle, and Bill wabbled out into the little glade in front of the cave. Behind him was the kid, stepping softly like a scout, with a broad grin on his face. Bill stopped, took off his hat, and wiped his face with a red handkerchief. The kid stopped about eight feet behind him.

"Sam," says Bill, "I suppose you'll think I'm a renegade, but I couldn't help it. I'm a grown person with masculine proclivities[2] and habits of self-defense, but there is a time when all systems of egotism and predominances fail. The boy is gone. I have sent him home. All is off. There was martyrs in old times," goes on Bill, "that suffered death rather than give up the particular graft they enjoyed. None of 'em ever was subjugated to such supernatural tortures as I have been. I tried to be faithful to our articles of depredation,[3] but there came a limit."

"What's the trouble, Bill?" I asks him.

"I was rode," says Bill, "the ninety miles to the stockade, not barring an inch. Then, when the settlers was rescued, I was given oats. Sand ain't a palatable substitute. And then, for an

---

[1] **surreptitiously** (sûr′əp·tish′əs·lē): stealthily.

[2] **proclivities** (prō·kliv′ə·tēz): tendencies.
[3] **depredation** (dep′rə·dā′shən): robbery.

hour I had to try to explain to him why there was nothin' in holes, how a road can run both ways, and what makes the grass green. I tell you, Sam, a human can only stand so much. I takes him by the neck of his clothes and drags him down the mountain. On the way, he kicks my legs black-and-blue from the knees down; and I've got to have two or three bites on my thumb and hand cauterized.

"But he's gone" — continues Bill — "gone home. I showed him the road to Summit and kicked him about eight feet nearer there at one kick. I'm sorry we lose the ransom, but it was either that or Bill Driscoll to the madhouse."

Bill is puffing and blowing, but there is a look of ineffable peace and growing content on his rose-pink features.

"Bill," says I, "there isn't any heart disease in your family, is there?"

"No," says Bill, "nothing chronic except malaria and accidents. Why?"

"Then you might turn around," says I, "and have a look behind you."

Bill turns and sees the boy, and loses his complexion and sits down plump on the ground and begins to pluck aimlessly at grass and little sticks. For an hour I was afraid for his mind. And then I told him that my scheme was to put the whole job through immediately and that we would get the ransom and be off with it by midnight if old Dorset fell in with our proposition. So Bill braced up enough to give the kid a weak sort of a smile and a promise to play the Russian in a Japanese war with him as soon as he felt a little better.

I had a scheme for collecting that ransom without danger of being caught

by counterplots that ought to commend itself to professional kidnapers. The tree under which the answer was to be left — and the money later on — was close to the road fence with big, bare fields on all sides. If a gang of constables should be watching for anyone to come for the note, they could see him a long way off crossing the fields or in the road. But no, siree! At half-past eight I was up in that tree, as well-hidden as a tree toad, waiting for the messenger to arrive.

Exactly on time, a half-grown boy rides up the road on a bicycle, locates the pasteboard box at the foot of the fence post, slips a folded piece of paper into it, and pedals away again back toward Summit.

I waited an hour and then concluded the thing was square. I slid down the tree, got the note, slipped along the fence till I struck the woods, and was back at the cave in another half an hour. I opened the note, got near the lantern, and read it to Bill. It was written with a pen in a crabbed hand, and the sum and substance of it was this:

Two Desperate Men:

Gentlemen, I received your letter today by post, in regard to the ransom you ask for the return of my son. I think you are a little high in your demands, and I hereby make you a counterproposition, which I am inclined to believe you will accept. You bring Johnny home and pay me two hundred and fifty dollars in cash, and I agree to take him off your hands. You had better come at night, for the neighbors believe he is lost, and I couldn't be responsible for what they would do to anybody they saw bringing him back.

Very respectfully,
EBENEZER DORSET

"Great pirates of Penzance!" says I; "of all the impudent — "

But I glanced at Bill and hesitated. He had the most appealing look in his eyes I ever saw on the face of a dumb or a talking brute.

"Sam," says he, "what's two hundred and fifty dollars, after all? We've got the money. One more night of this kid will send me to a bed in Bedlam.[1] Besides being a thorough gentleman, I think Mr. Dorset is a spendthrift for making us such a liberal offer. You ain't going to let the chance go, are you?"

"Tell you the truth, Bill," says I, "this little he ewe lamb has somewhat got on my nerves, too. We'll take him home, pay the ransom, and make our getaway."

[1] **Bedlam:** once a hospital for the insane.

We took him home that night. We got him to go by telling him that his father had bought a silver-mounted rifle and a pair of moccasins for him and that we were going to hunt bears the next day.

It was just twelve o'clock when we knocked at Ebenezer's front door. Just at the moment when I should have been abstracting the fifteen hundred dollars from the box under the tree, according to the original proposition, Bill was counting out two hundred and fifty dollars into Dorset's hand.

When the kid found out we were going to leave him at home, he started up a howl like a calliope[2] and fastened himself as tight as a leech to Bill's leg. His father peeled him away gradually, like a porous plaster.

"How long can you hold him?" asks Bill.

"I'm not as strong as I used to be," says old Dorset, "but I think I can promise you ten minutes."

"Enough," says Bill. "In ten minutes I shall cross the Central, Southern, and Middle-Western states and be legging it trippingly for the Canadian border."

And, as dark as it was, and as fat as Bill was, and as good a runner as I am, he was a good mile and a half out of Summit before I could catch up with him.

[2] **calliope** (kə·lī′ə·pē): a mechanical organ with a shrill whistling sound. Sam probably pronounced it kal′ē·ōp.

ELEMENTS IN A SHORT STORY

Plot. The way in which the sequence of events is worked out in a short story is called the plot. A short story begins with a situation, in which the author reveals the conflict of the story. From this situation the plot starts to move. Complications develop and continue until the turning point, or climax, is reached, and this quickly leads to the conclusion of the story.

1. What was the initial situation in "The Ransom of Red Chief"? What action of the criminals started the plot going? What actions of Red Chief complicated things for the "heroes"? What reaction of Red Chief's father further complicated things and resulted in the climax of the story? What action quickly followed the climax and concluded the story?

Foreshadowing. In working out his plot, an author often gives his reader hints of what is to come. This is known as foreshadowing.

2. In what ways were the unusual developments of the kidnaping foreshadowed in the first paragraph?

3. How did O. Henry foreshadow the future behavior of Red Chief when the boy was introduced in the story? How did Red Chief's actions during the first night foreshadow trouble?

4. When did you get the first hint that the ransom demand might not be met? Trace the steady, humorous decline in the ransom demand.

Irony. O. Henry is known for the funny ironic twists in the plots of his stories. For example, in "The Ransom of Red Chief" we read about two desperate kidnapers who are, in reality, afraid of a little boy. A situation like this — one in which the truth is exactly the opposite of what would be ordinarily expected — is ironic.

5. What other situations in the plot of this story are ironic — that is, exactly the reverse of what would be expected?

6. How are the characterizations ironic: how were Sam's and Bill's actions not suitable to tough, desperate men?

Point of View. The author's decision about who is to narrate his story is an important one. O. Henry tells this story as though one of the main characters is relating it.

7. Did O. Henry choose the best point of view for the effect he wanted? What would the story have been like if it had been told from the father's point of view?

WORDS: HUMOROUS EFFECTS

O. Henry was a "collector" of elaborate and unusual words, and in this story he has Sam, and sometimes Bill, use some of these elaborate words. In fact, it sometimes seems as if Sam, especially, did not use a short, simple word if a longer, fancier word were available. But we realize that Sam and Bill are not well educated because they make several mistakes in English, and occasionally use the wrong "fancy" word. By having men like Sam and Bill use long words, O. Henry gives another humorous twist to his story.

Here are three sentences in which Sam uses elaborate words:

"It contained inhabitants of as *undeleterious* and self-satisfied a class of *peasantry* as ever clustered around a Maypole."

"*Philoprogenitiveness*, says we, is strong in *semirural communities*."

"There was a *sylvan* attitude of *somnolent* sleepiness *pervading* that section of Alabama that *lay exposed to my view*."

If some of the italicized words above are not defined in a footnote, look them up in a dictionary to see what they mean. What simpler words might you have expected a man like Sam to use in place of each italicized word?

Can you locate at least four errors in English or in word pronunciation which make the criminals' use of elaborate words even more humorous?

MASTERPIECES OF ART

How Painters Express Action

Painted pictures do not move, but painters can create illusions of action on a still surface. To show us a little dog and his master walking across a picture (PLATE 1), the twentieth-century Italian painter Giacomo Balla used a method familiar to everyone who has looked at comics. He repeated the shapes of the moving feet and leash as they would appear in many positions at many moments of the walk. The leash swings, the dog wags his tail, and you can almost hear the patter of his feet and the heavier, slower tread of his master.

Balla's method is a modern one. Paolo Uccello, who lived some five hundred years earlier, used other methods to celebrate a military victory of his fellow Florentines over an army from Milan (PLATE 2). First, by placing broken lances and a dead soldier so that they slant back toward the hills, he made a space for figures to move in. There in the distance, tiny Milanese soldiers are retreating out of the top of the picture. Into this broad space-illusion, the Florentine army advances like a parade, horses rearing and banners waving, toward a dramatic hand-to-hand combat between two knights at the right. The losing Milanese knight faces the whole army, and it almost seems that he stops them from marching out of the picture.

The precise dark and light pattern of horses, hoofs, and spears makes a rhythmic beat, like martial music, and sets a slow and orderly pace for the action. The Florentine commander points his baton forward. Spears and flagstaffs repeat his gesture, and the knight who strikes the enemy seems to have the strength of the whole army behind him. All together they make the falling sword-blow the mightiest action in the picture.

Peter Paul Rubens, when he painted Henry IV at the Battle of Ivry (PLATE 3), preferred swifter and more violent action. In this painting the two armies flow together like surging waves and meet with a shock at the center. The French king, Henry IV, leads his troops from the right in a smooth flying wedge, his horse pointing upward, the lances downward. These two diagonal movements meet, and the adversary's rearing white steed throws his master. Notice that the body of a dead warrior on the ground at the right is arranged on a diagonal slant that repeats the lancers' thrusting action. Dead as he is, his position in the picture seems to help the advancing army along.

In battle scenes, opposing armies must move toward each other. But in a horse race, all the movement is in one direction, so a painter has a different problem to solve in keeping his picture balanced. Two nine-teenth-century French painters, Géricault and Manet, found two different solutions to this problem. Géricault stretched his four horses across the canvas so that they run *across* our field of vision (PLATE 4). All the horses' bodies and legs are in the same extended position, and they fly like arrows, graceful, sleek, and low to the ground. Although a galloping horse never looks like this, the illusion of speed is helped by this untrue posture. Géricault has included one still, vertical marker to contrast with the action of the horses. Is the picture less interesting if you cover up this post? Try it.

Manet chose to let the horses thunder down the track straight at us (PLATE 5). This way we cannot see their long sides stretching in the direction of their movement. Manet, however, has made the *track* move. Its slanting, diagonal edges zoom off in the opposite direction, and we seem to see the ground slipping rapidly back under the horses' hoofs. Looked at another way, the track seems to open up toward us, and the group of horses and jockeys appears to explode before our eyes.

Diagonal lines create both space and action in pictures. Vertical and horizontal lines tend to keep the surface flat and still. The modern American painter John Marin has skillfully combined some of these possibilities in his picture of a busy New York street crossing (PLATE 6). Almost nowhere is there a horizontal line. Buildings surge outward at both sides behind a milling crowd which moves in all directions. Buildings and even people are made of diagonal lines meeting at sharp angles. But the vertical skyscrapers and the vivid, vertical traffic light pin down this restless composition and keep it from pulling itself apart.

Why do painters like to put action in their pictures? It is more than the desire to represent stories of people in action. What moves seems alive. If a painter can bring a dead surface to life, he is working miracles and doing his job well.

PLATE 1. GIACOMO BALLA (Italian, 1874–1958): *Dog on a Leash*. 1912. Oil on canvas, 35⅝ x 43¼ inches. (Courtesy of George F. Goodyear and the Buffalo Fine Arts Academy)

PLATE 2. PAOLO UCCELLO (Florentine, 1397–1475): *Battle of San Romano.* About 1456. Tempera on wood panel, 71¾ x 125 inches. (Reproduced by courtesy of the Trustees, The National Gallery, London)

296

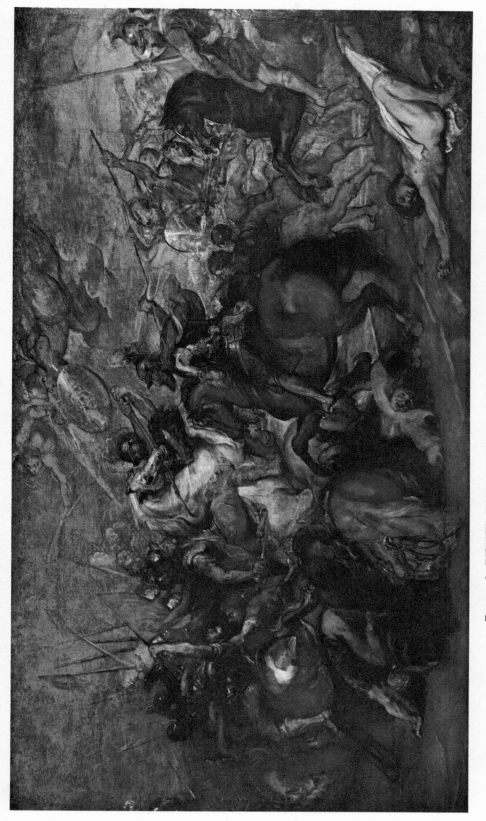

PLATE 3. PETER PAUL RUBENS (Flemish, 1577–1640): *Henry IV at the Battle of Ivry*. Between 1628–31. Oil on canvas, 144 x 273 inches. (Uffizi, Florence)

PLATE 4. THÉODORE GÉRICAULT (French, 1791–1824): *The Derby at Epsom.* 1821. Oil on canvas, 35 x 47 inches. (The Louvre, Paris)

PLATE 5. ÉDOUARD MANET (French, 1832–1883): *The Races at Longchamp.* 1864. Oil on canvas, 17¼ x 33¾ inches. (Courtesy of The Art Institute of Chicago, Potter Palmer Collection)

PLATE 6. JOHN MARIN (American, 1870–1953): *Fifth Avenue at Forty-second Street.* 1933. Oil on canvas, 28 x 36½ inches. (The Phillips Collection, Washington, D.C.)

The Red-headed League

SIR ARTHUR CONAN DOYLE

I HAD CALLED upon my friend, Mr. Sherlock Holmes, one day in the autumn of last year and found him in deep conversation with a very stout, florid-faced, elderly gentleman with fiery red hair. With an apology for my intrusion, I was about to withdraw when Holmes pulled me abruptly into the room and closed the door behind me.

"You could not possibly have come at a better time, my dear Watson," he said, cordially.

"I was afraid that you were engaged."

"So I am. Very much so."

"Then I can wait in the next room."

"Not at all. This gentleman, Mr. Wilson, has been my partner and helper in many of my most successful cases, and I have no doubt that he will be of the utmost use to me in yours also."

The stout gentleman half-rose from his chair and gave a bob of greeting, with a quick little questioning glance from his small, fat-encircled eyes.

"Try the settee," said Holmes, relapsing into his armchair and putting his fingertips together, as was his custom when in judicial moods. "I know, my dear Watson, that you share my love of all that is bizarre and outside the conventions and humdrum routine of everyday life. You have shown your relish for it by the enthusiasm which has prompted you to chronicle and, if you will excuse my saying so, somewhat to embellish so many of my own little adventures."

"Your cases have indeed been of the greatest interest to me," I observed.

"You will remember that I remarked the other day, just before we went into the very simple problem presented by Miss Mary Sutherland, that for strange effects and extraordinary combinations we must go to life itself, which is always far more daring than any effort of the imagination."

"A proposition which I took the liberty of doubting."

"You did, Doctor, but none the less you must come round to my view, for otherwise I shall keep on piling fact upon fact on you, until your reason breaks down under them and acknowledges me to be right. Now, Mr. Jabez Wilson here has been good enough to call upon me this morning and to begin a narrative which promises to be one of the most singular that I have listened to for some time. You have heard me remark that the strangest and most unique things are very often connected not with the larger but with the smaller crimes and occasionally, indeed, where there is room for doubt whether any positive crime has been committed. As far as I have heard, it is impossible for me to say whether the present case is an instance of crime or not, but the course of events is certainly among the most singular that I have ever listened to. Perhaps, Mr. Wilson, you would have the great kindness to recommence your narrative. I ask you, not merely because my friend Dr. Watson has not heard the opening part, but also because the peculiar nature of the story makes me anxious to have every possible detail from your lips. As a rule, when I have heard some slight indication of the course of events, I am able to guide myself by the thousands of other similar cases which occur to my memory. In the present instance, I am forced to admit that the facts are, to the best of my belief, unique."

The portly client puffed out his chest with an appearance of some little pride, and pulled a dirty and wrinkled newspaper from the inside pocket of his greatcoat. As he glanced down the advertisement column, with his head thrust forward and the paper flattened out upon his knees, I took a good look at the man, and endeavored, after the fashion of my companion, to read the indications which might be presented by his dress or appearance.

I did not gain very much, however, by my inspection. Our visitor bore every mark of being an average, commonplace British tradesman, obese, pompous, and slow. He wore rather baggy, gray shepherd's-check trousers, a not overclean black frock coat, unbuttoned in the front, and a drab waistcoat with a heavy, brassy Albert chain and a square pierced bit of metal dangling down as an ornament. A frayed top hat and a faded brown overcoat with a wrinkled velvet collar lay upon a chair beside him. Altogether, look as I would, there was nothing remarkable about the man, save his blazing red head and the expression of extreme chagrin[1] and discontent upon his features.

Sherlock Holmes's quick eye took in my occupation, and he shook his head with a smile as he noticed my questioning glances. "Beyond the obvious facts that he has at some time done manual labor, that he takes snuff, that he is a Freemason, that he has been in China, and that he has done a considerable amount of writing lately, I can deduce nothing else."

Mr. Jabez Wilson started up in his chair, with his forefinger upon the paper, but his eyes upon my companion.

"How, in the name of good fortune, did you know all that, Mr. Holmes?" he asked. "How did you know, for example, that I did manual labor? It's as true as gospel, for I began as a ship's carpenter."

"Your hands, my dear sir. Your right

---

[1] **chagrin** (shə·grin'): mortification.

hand is quite a size larger than your left. You have worked with it, and the muscles are more developed."

"Well, the snuff, then, and the Freemasonry?"

"I won't insult your intelligence by telling you how I read that, especially as, rather against the strict rules of your order, you use an arc-and-compass breastpin."

"Ah, of course, I forgot that. But the writing?"

"What else can be indicated by that right cuff so very shiny for five inches, and the left one with the smooth patch near the elbow where you rest it upon the desk?"

"Well, but China?"

"The fish that you have tattooed immediately above your right wrist could only have been done in China. I have made a small study of tattoo marks, and have even contributed to the literature of the subject. That trick of staining the fish's scales of a delicate pink is quite peculiar to China. When, in addition, I see a Chinese coin hanging from your watch chain, the matter becomes even more simple."

Mr. Jabez Wilson laughed heavily. "Well, I never!" said he. "I thought at first that you had done something clever, but I see that there was nothing in it, after all."

"I begin to think, Watson," said Holmes, "that I make a mistake in explaining. *Omne ignotum pro magnifico*,[1] you know, and my poor little reputation, such as it is, will suffer shipwreck if I am so candid. Can you not find the advertisement, Mr. Wilson?"

"Yes, I have got it now," he answered, with his thick, red finger plant-

---

[1] *Omne ignotum pro magnifico:* a Latin saying, meaning "Everything unknown passes for miraculous."

ed halfway down the column. "Here it is. This is what began it all. You just read it for yourself, sir."

I took the paper from him, and read as follows:

To the Red-headed League

On account of the bequest of the late Ezekiah Hopkins, of Lebanon, Pa., U.S.A., there is now another vacancy open which entitles a member of the League to a salary of £4[1] a week for purely nominal services. All red-headed men who are sound in body and mind and above the age of twenty-one years are eligible. Apply in person on Monday at eleven o'clock to Duncan Ross, at the offices of the League, 7 Pope's Court, Fleet Street.

"What on earth does this mean?" I ejaculated, after I had twice read over the extraordinary announcement.

Holmes chuckled, and wriggled in his chair, as was his habit when in high spirits. "It is a little off the beaten track, isn't it?" said he. "And now, Mr. Wilson, off you go at scratch, and tell us all about yourself, your household, and the effect which this advertisement had upon your fortunes. You will first make a note, Doctor, of the paper and the date."

"It is the *Morning Chronicle*, of August 9, 1890. Just two months ago."

"Very good. Now, Mr. Wilson?"

"Well, it is just as I have been telling you, Mr. Sherlock Holmes," said Jabez Wilson, mopping his forehead. "I have

---

[1] £4: four pounds. The symbol £ stands for "pound," an English monetary unit, equal to about $2.80 today.

a small pawnbroker's business at Coburg Square, near the city. It's not a very large affair, and of late years it has not done more than just give me a living. I used to be able to keep two assistants, but now I only keep one; and I would have a job to pay him, but that he is willing to come for half wages, so as to learn the business."

"What is the name of this obliging youth?" asked Sherlock Holmes.

"His name is Vincent Spaulding, and he's not such a youth, either. It's hard to say his age. I should not wish a smarter assistant, Mr. Holmes; and I know very well that he could better himself and earn twice what I am able to give him. But, after all, if he is satisfied, why should I put ideas in his head?"

"Why, indeed? You seem most fortunate in having an employee who comes under the full market price. It is not a common experience among employers in this age. I don't know that your assistant is not as remarkable as your advertisement."

"Oh, he has his faults, too," said Mr. Wilson. "Never was such a fellow for photography. Snapping away with a camera when he ought to be improving his mind, and then diving down into the cellar like a rabbit into its hole to develop his pictures. That is his main fault; but, on the whole, he's a good worker. There's no vice in him."

"He is still with you, I presume?"

"Yes, sir. He and a girl of fourteen, who does a bit of simple cooking and keeps the place clean — that's all I have in the house, for I am a widower and never had any family. We live very quietly, sir, the three of us; and we keep a roof over our heads and pay our debts, if we do nothing more.

"The first thing that put us out was that advertisement. Spaulding, he came down into the office just this day eight weeks with this very paper in his hand, and he says:

"'I wish to the Lord, Mr. Wilson, that I was a red-headed man.'

"'Why that?' I asks.

"'Why,' says he, 'here's another vacancy on the League of the Red-headed Men. It's worth quite a little fortune to any man who gets it, and I understand that there are more vacancies than there are men, so that the trustees are at their wits' end what to do with the money. If my hair would only change color, here's a nice little crib all ready for me to step into.'

"'Why, what is it, then?' I asked. You see, Mr. Holmes, I am a very stay-at-home man, and, as my business came to me instead of my having to go to it, I was often weeks on end without putting my foot over the door mat. In that way I didn't know much of what was going on outside, and I was always glad of a bit of news.

"'Have you never heard of the League of the Red-headed Men?' he asked, with his eyes open.

"'Never.'

"'Why, I wonder at that, for you are eligible yourself for one of the vacancies.'

"'And what are they worth?' I asked.

"'Oh, merely a couple of hundred a year, but the work is slight, and it need not interfere very much with one's other occupations.'

"Well, you can easily think that that made me prick up my ears, for the business has not been overgood for some years, and an extra couple of hundred would have been very handy.

"'Tell me all about it,' said I.

"'Well,' said he, showing me the advertisement, 'you can see for yourself that the League has a vacancy, and there is the address where you should apply for particulars. As far as I can make out, the League was founded by an American millionaire, Ezekiah Hopkins, who was very peculiar in his ways. He was himself red headed, and he had a great sympathy for all red-headed men; so, when he died, it was found that he had left his enormous fortune in the hands of trustees, with instructions to apply the interest to the providing of easy berths to men whose hair is of that color. From all I hear, it is splendid pay and very little to do.'

"'But,' said I, 'there would be millions of red-headed men who would apply.'

"'Not so many as you might think,' he answered. 'You see it is really confined to Londoners, and to grown men. This American had started from London when he was young, and he wanted to do the old town a good turn. Then, again, I have heard it is no use your applying if your hair is light red or dark red or anything but real bright, blazing, fiery red. Now, if you cared to apply, Mr. Wilson, you would just walk in; but perhaps it would hardly be worth your while to put yourself out of the way for the sake of a few hundred pounds.'

"Now, it is a fact, gentlemen, as you may see for yourselves, that my hair is of a very full and rich tint, so that it seemed to me that if there was to be any competition in the matter, I stood as good a chance as any man that I had ever met. Vincent Spaulding seemed to know so much about it that I thought he might prove useful, so I just ordered him to put up the shutters for the day, and to come right away with me. He was very willing to have a holiday, so we shut the business up and started off for the address that was given us in the advertisement.

"I never hope to see such a sight as that again, Mr. Holmes. From north, south, east, and west, every man who had a shade of red in his hair had tramped into the city to answer the advertisement. Fleet Street was choked with red-headed folk, and Pope's Court looked like a coster's [1] orange barrow. I should not have thought there were so many in the whole country as were brought together by that single advertisement. Every shade of color they were — straw, lemon, orange, brick, Irish-setter, liver, clay; but, as Spaulding said, there were not many who had the real vivid flame-colored tint. When I saw how many were waiting I would have given it up in despair; but Spaulding would not hear of it. How he did it I could not imagine, but he pushed and pulled and butted until he got me through the crowd and right up to the steps which led to the office. There was a double stream upon the stairs, some going up in hope, and some coming back dejected; but we wedged in as well as we could and soon found ourselves in the office."

"Your experience has been a most entertaining one," remarked Holmes, as

his client paused and refreshed his memory with a huge pinch of snuff. "Pray continue your very interesting statement."

"There was nothing in the office but a couple of wooden chairs and a deal table, behind which sat a small man, with a head that was even redder than mine. He said a few words to each candidate as he came up, and then he always managed to find some fault in them which would disqualify them. Getting a vacancy did not seem to be such a very easy matter, after all. However, when our turn came, the little man was much more favorable to me than to any of the others, and he closed the door as we entered, so that he might have a private word with us.

" 'This is Mr. Jabez Wilson,' said my assistant, 'and he is willing to fill a vacancy in the league.'

" 'And he is admirably suited for it,' the other answered. 'He has every requirement. I cannot recall when I have seen anything so fine.' He took a step backward, cocked his head on one side, and gazed at my hair until I felt quite bashful. Then suddenly he plunged forward, wrung my hand, and congratulated me warmly on my success.

" 'It would be injustice to hesitate,' said he. 'You will, however, I am sure, excuse me for taking an obvious precaution.' With that he seized my hair in both his hands and tugged until I yelled with the pain. 'There is water in your eyes,' said he, as he released me. 'I perceive that all is as it should be. But we have to be careful, for we have twice been deceived by wigs and once by paint. I could tell you tales of cobbler's wax which would disgust you

[1] **coster's:** street vendor's.

with human nature.' He stepped over to the window, and shouted through it at the top of his voice that the vacancy was filled. A groan of disappointment came up from below, and the folk all trooped away in different directions, until there was not a red head to be seen except my own and that of the manager.

" 'My name,' said he, 'is Mr. Duncan Ross, and I am myself one of the pensioners upon the fund left by our noble benefactor. Are you a married man, Mr. Wilson? Have you a family?'

"I answered that I had not. His face fell immediately.

" 'Dear me!' he said, gravely, 'that is very serious indeed! I am sorry to hear you say that. The fund was, of course, for the propagation and spread of the red heads as well as for their maintenance. It is exceedingly unfortunate that you should be a bachelor.'

"My face lengthened at this, Mr. Holmes, for I thought that I was not to have the vacancy after all; but, after thinking it over for a few minutes, he said that it would be all right.

" 'In the case of another,' said he, 'the objection might be fatal, but we must stretch a point in favor of a man with such a head of hair as yours. When shall you be able to enter upon your new duties?'

" 'Well, it is a little awkward, for I have a business already,' said I.

" 'Oh, never mind about that, Mr. Wilson!' said Vincent Spaulding. 'I shall be able to look after that for you.'

" 'What would be the hours?' I asked.

" 'Ten to two.'

"Now a pawnbroker's business is mostly done of an evening, Mr. Holmes, especially Thursday and Friday evenings, which are just before pay day; so it would suit me very well to earn a little in the mornings. Besides, I knew that my assistant was a good man, and that he would see to anything that turned up.

" 'That would suit me very well,' said I. 'And the pay?'

" 'Is £4 a week.'

" 'And the work?'

" 'Is purely nominal.'

" 'What do you call purely nominal?'

" 'Well, you have to be in the office, or at least in the building, the whole time. If you leave, you forfeit your whole position forever. The will is very clear upon that point. You don't comply with the conditions if you budge from the office during that time.'

" 'It's only four hours a day, and I should not think of leaving,' said I.

" 'No excuse will avail,' said Mr. Duncan Ross; 'neither sickness nor business nor anything else. There you must stay, or you lose your billet.'

" 'And the work?'

" 'Is to copy out the *Encyclopædia Britannica*. There is the first volume of it in that press. You must find your own ink, pens, and blotting paper, but we provide this table and chair. Will you be ready tomorrow?'

" 'Certainly,' I answered.

" 'Then, good-bye, Mr. Jabez Wilson, and let me congratulate you once more on the important position which you have been fortunate enough to gain.' He bowed me out of the room, and I went home with my assistant, hardly knowing what to say or do, I was so pleased at my own good fortune.

"Well, I thought over the matter all

day, and by evening I was in low spirits again; for I had quite persuaded myself that the whole affair must be some great hoax or fraud, though what its object might be I could not imagine. It seemed altogether past belief that any one could make such a will, or that they would pay such a sum for doing anything so simple as copying out the *Encyclopædia Britannica*. Vincent Spaulding did what he could to cheer me up, but by bedtime I had reasoned myself out of the whole thing. However, in the morning I determined to have a look at it anyhow, so I bought a penny bottle of ink, and with a quill pen and seven sheets of foolscap,[1] I started off for Pope's Court.

"Well, to my surprise and delight, everything was as right as possible. The table was set out ready for me, and Mr. Duncan Ross was there to see that I got fairly to work. He started me off upon the letter *A*, and then he left me; but he would drop in from time to time to see that all was right with me. At two o'clock he bade me good-day, complimented me upon the amount that I had written, and locked the door to the office after me.

[1] **foolscap:** writing paper measuring about 13½ × 17 inches.

"This went on day after day, Mr. Holmes, and on Saturday the manager came in and planked down four golden sovereigns for my week's work. It was the same next week, and the same the week after. Every morning I was there at ten, and every afternoon I left at two. By degrees Mr. Duncan Ross took to coming in only once of a morning, and then, after a time, he did not come in at all. Still, of course, I never dared to leave the room for an instant, for I was not sure when he might come, and the billet was such a good one and suited me so well that I would not risk the loss of it.

"Eight weeks passed away like this, and I had written about Abbots and Archery and Armor and Architecture and Attica, and hoped with diligence that I might get on to the *B*'s before very long. It cost me something in foolscap, and I had pretty nearly filled a shelf with my writings. And then suddenly the whole business came to an end."

"To an end?"

"Yes, sir. And no later than this morning. I went to my work as usual at ten o'clock, but the door was shut and locked, with a little square of cardboard hammered on to the middle of the panel with a tack. Here it is, and you can read for yourself."

He held up a piece of white cardboard about the size of a sheet of note paper. It read in this fashion:

The Red-headed League
Is
Dissolved
October 9, 1890

Sherlock Holmes and I surveyed this curt announcement and the rueful face behind it, until the comical side of the affair so completely overtopped every other consideration that we both burst out into a roar of laughter.

"I cannot see that there is anything very funny," cried our client, flushing up to the roots of his flaming head. "If you can do nothing better than laugh at me, I can go elsewhere."

"No, no," cried Holmes, shoving him back into the chair from which he had half risen. "I really wouldn't miss your case for the world. It is most refreshingly unusual. But there is, if you will excuse my saying so, something just a little funny about it. Pray what steps did you take when you found the card upon the door?"

"I was staggered, sir. I did not know what to do. Then I called at the offices round, but none of them seemed to know anything about it. Finally, I went to the landlord, who is an accountant living on the ground floor, and I asked him if he could tell me what had become of the Red-headed League. He said that he had never heard of any such body. Then I asked him who Mr. Duncan Ross was. He answered that the name was new to him.

"'Well,' said I, 'the gentleman at Number 4.'

"'What, the red-headed man?'

"'Yes.'

"'Oh,' said he, 'his name was William Morris. He was a solicitor and was using my room as a temporary convenience until his new premises were ready. He moved out yesterday.'

"'Where could I find him?'

"'Oh, at his new offices. He did tell me the address. Yes, 17 King Edward Street, near St. Paul's.'

"I started off, Mr. Holmes, but when I got to that address it was a factory of artificial kneecaps, and no one in it had ever heard of either Mr. William Morris or Mr. Duncan Ross."

"And what did you do then?" asked Holmes.

"I went home to Saxe-Coburg Square, and I took the advice of my assistant. But he could not help me in any way. He could only say that if I waited I should hear by post. But that was not quite good enough, Mr. Holmes. I did not wish to lose such a place without a struggle, so, as I had heard that you were good enough to give advice to poor folk who were in need of it, I came right away to you."

"And you did very wisely," said Holmes. "Your case is an exceedingly remarkable one, and I shall be happy to look into it. From what you have told me, I think that it is possible that graver issues hang from it than might at first sight appear."

"Grave enough!" said Mr. Jabez Wilson. "Why, I have lost four pound a week."

"As far as you are personally concerned," remarked Holmes, "I do not see that you have any grievance against this extraordinary league. On the contrary, you are, as I understand, richer by some £30, to say nothing of the minute knowledge which you have gained on every subject which comes under the letter A. You have lost nothing by them."

"No, sir. But I want to find out about them and who they are and what their object was in playing this prank — if it was a prank — upon me. It was a pretty expensive joke for them, for it cost them two and thirty pounds."

"We shall endeavor to clear up these points for you. And, first, one or two questions, Mr. Wilson. This assistant of yours who first called your attention to the advertisement — how long had he been with you?"

"About a month then."

"How did he come?"

"In answer to an advertisement."

"Was he the only applicant?"

"No, I had a dozen."

"Why did you pick him?"

"Because he was handy and would come cheap."

"At half wages, in fact."

"Yes."

"What is he like, this Vincent Spaulding?"

"Small, stout-built, very quick in his ways, no hair on his face, though he's not short of thirty. Has a white splash of acid upon his forehead."

Holmes sat up in his chair in considerable excitement. "I thought as much," said he. "Have you ever observed that his ears are pierced for earrings?"

"Yes, sir. He told me that a gypsy had done it for him when he was a lad."

"Hum!" said Holmes, sinking back in deep thought. "He is still with you?"

"Oh yes, sir; I have only just left him."

"And has your business been attended to in your absence?"

"Nothing to complain of, sir. There's never very much to do of a morning."

"That will do, Mr. Wilson. I shall be happy to give you an opinion upon the subject in the course of a day or two. Today is Saturday, and I hope that by Monday we may come to a conclusion."

"Well, Watson," said Holmes, when our visitor had left us, "what do you make of it all?"

"I make nothing of it," I answered frankly. "It is a most mysterious business."

"As a rule," said Holmes, "the more bizarre a thing is the less mysterious it proves to be. It is your commonplace, featureless crimes which are really puzzling, just as a commonplace face is the most difficult to identify. But I must be prompt over this matter."

"What are you going to do, then?" I asked.

"To smoke," he answered. "It is quite a three-pipe problem, and I beg that you won't speak to me for fifty minutes." He curled himself up in his chair, with his thin knees drawn up to his hawklike nose, and there he sat with his eyes closed and his black clay pipe thrusting out like the bill of some strange bird. I had come to the conclusion that he had dropped asleep, and indeed was nodding myself, when he suddenly sprang out of his chair with the gesture of a man who has made up his mind, and put his pipe down upon the mantelpiece.

"Sarasate [1] plays at the St. James's Hall this afternoon," he remarked. "What do you think, Watson? Could your patients spare you for a few hours?"

"I have nothing to do today. My practice is never very absorbing."

"Then put on your hat and come. I am going through the city first, and we can have some lunch on the way. I ob-

---

[1] **Sarasate** (sä′rä·sä′tä): Pablo de Sarasate (1844–1908), a Spanish violinist and composer.

serve that there is a good deal of German music on the program, which is rather more to my taste than Italian or French. It is introspective, and I want to introspect. Come along!"

We traveled by the underground as far as Aldersgate, and a short walk took us to Saxe-Coburg Square, the scene of the singular story which we had listened to in the morning. It was a poky, little, shabby-genteel place, where four lines of dingy two-storied brick houses looked out into a small railed-in enclosure where a lawn of weedy grass and a few clumps of faded laurel bushes made a hard fight against a smoke-laden and uncongenial atmosphere. Three gilt balls and a brown board with JABEZ WILSON in white letters, upon a corner house, announced the place where our red-headed client carried on his business. Sherlock Holmes stopped in front of it with his head on one side and looked it all over, with his eyes shining brightly between puckered lids. Then he walked slowly up the street, and then down again to the corner, still looking keenly at the houses. Finally he returned to the pawnbroker's, and, having thumped vigorously upon the pavement with his stick two or three times, he went up to the door and knocked. It was instantly opened by a bright-looking, clean-shaven young fellow, who asked him to step in.

"Thank you," said Holmes, "I only wished to ask you how you would go from here to the Strand."

"Third right, fourth left," answered the assistant, promptly, closing the door.

"Smart fellow, that," observed Holmes, as we walked away. "He is, in my judgment, the fourth smartest man in London, and for daring I am not sure that he has not a claim to be third. I have known something of him before."

"Evidently," said I, "Mr. Wilson's assistant counts for a good deal in this mystery of the Red-headed League. I am sure that you inquired your way merely in order that you might see him."

"Not him."

"What then?"

"The knees of his trousers."

"And what did you see?"

"What I expected to see."

"Why did you beat the pavement?"

"My dear Doctor, this is a time for observation, not for talk. We are spies in an enemy's country. We know something of Saxe-Coburg Square. Let us now explore the parts which lie behind it."

The road in which we found ourselves as we turned round the corner from the retired Saxe-Coburg Square presented as great a contrast to it as the front of a picture does to the back. It was one of the main arteries which convey the traffic of the city to the north and west. The roadway was blocked with the immense stream of commerce flowing in a double tide inward and outward, while the footpaths were black with the hurrying swarm of pedestrians. It was difficult to realize as we looked at the line of fine shops and stately business premises that they really abutted on the other side upon the faded and stagnant square which we had just quitted.

"Let me see," said Holmes, standing

at the corner, and glancing along the line, "I should like just to remember the order of the houses here. It is a hobby of mine to have an exact knowledge of London. There is Mortimer's, the tobacconist, the little newspaper shop, the Coburg branch of the City and Suburban Bank, the Vegetarian Restaurant, and McFarlane's carriage-building depot. That carries us right on to the other block. And now, Doctor, we've done our work, so it's time we had some play. A sandwich and a cup of coffee, and then off to violin land, where all is sweetness and delicacy and harmony, and there are no red-headed clients to vex us with their conundrums." [1]

My friend was an enthusiastic musician, being himself not only a very capable performer, but a composer of no ordinary merit. All the afternoon he sat in the stalls, wrapped in the most perfect happiness, gently waving his long, thin fingers in time to the music, while his gently smiling face and his languid, dreamy eyes were as unlike those of Holmes the sleuthhound, Holmes the relentless, keen-witted, ready-handed criminal agent, as it was possible to conceive. In his singular character the dual nature alternately asserted itself, and his extreme exactness and astuteness represented, as I have often thought, the reaction against the poetic and contemplative mood which occasionally predominated in him. The swing of his nature took him from extreme languor to devouring energy; and, as I knew well, he was never so truly formidable as when, for days on end, he had been lounging in his

armchair amid his improvisations and his black-letter editions.[2] Then it was that the lust of the chase would suddenly come upon him and that his brilliant reasoning power would rise to the level of intuition, until those who were unacquainted with his methods would look askance at him as on a man whose knowledge was not that of other mortals. When I saw him that afternoon so enwrapped in the music at St. James's Hall, I felt that an evil time might be coming upon those whom he had set himself to hunt down.

"You want to go home, no doubt, Doctor," he remarked, as we emerged.

"Yes, it would be as well."

"And I have some business to do which will take some hours. This business at Coburg Square is serious."

"Why serious?"

"A considerable crime is in contemplation. I have every reason to believe that we shall be in time to stop it. But today being Saturday rather complicates matters. I shall want your help tonight."

"At what time?"

"Ten will be early enough."

"I shall be at Baker Street at ten."

"Very well. And, I say, Doctor, there may be some little danger, so kindly put your army revolver in your pocket." He waved his hand, turned on his heel, and disappeared in an instant among the crowd.

I trust that I am not more dense than my neighbors, but I was always oppressed with a sense of my own stu-

---

[1] **conundrums** (kə·nun′drəms): problems.

[2] **improvisations . . . black-letter editions:** Here, improvisations are musical compositions performed without a score. Black-letter editions are old books printed in a certain kind of type.

pidity in my dealings with Sherlock Holmes. Here I had heard what he had heard, I had seen what he had seen, and yet from his words it was evident that he saw clearly not only what had happened but what was about to happen, while to me the whole business was confused and grotesque. As I drove home to my house in Kensington, I thought over it all, from the extraordinary story of the red-headed copier of the encyclopedia down to the visit to Saxe-Coburg Square and the ominous words with which he had parted from me. What was this nocturnal expedition, and why should I go armed? Where were we going, and what were we to do? I had the hint from Holmes that the smooth-faced pawnbroker's assistant was a formidable man — a man who might play a deep game. I tried to puzzle it out, but gave it up in despair and set the matter aside until night should bring an explanation.

It was a quarter past nine when I started from home and made my way across the Park, and so through Oxford Street to Baker Street. Two hansoms were standing at the door, and, as I entered the passage, I heard the sound of voices from above. On entering his room I found Holmes in animated conversation with two men, one of whom I recognized as Peter Jones, the official police agent, while the other was a long, thin, sad-faced man, with a very shiny hat and oppressively respectable frock coat.

"Ha! our party is complete," said Holmes, buttoning up his pea jacket and taking his heavy hunting crop from the rack. "Watson, I think you know Mr. Jones, of Scotland Yard? Let me introduce you to Mr. Merryweather, who is to be our companion in tonight's adventure."

"We're hunting in couples again, Doctor, you see," said Jones, in his consequential way. "Our friend here is a wonderful man for starting a chase. All he wants is an old dog to help him to do the running down."

"I hope a wild goose may not prove to be the end of our chase," observed Mr. Merryweather, gloomily.

"You may place considerable confidence in Mr. Holmes, sir," said the police agent, loftily. "He has his own little methods, which are, if he won't mind my saying so, just a little too theoretical and fantastic, but he has the makings of a detective in him. It is not too much to say that once or twice, as in that business of the Sholto murder and the Agra treasure, he has been more nearly correct than the official force."

"Oh, if you say so, Mr. Jones, it is all right," said the stranger, with deference. "Still, I confess that I miss my rubber.[1] It is the first Saturday night for seven-and-twenty years that I have not had my rubber."

"I think you will find," said Sherlock Holmes, "that you will play for a higher stake tonight than you have ever done yet, and that the play will be more exciting. For you, Mr. Merryweather, the stake will be some £30,000; and for you, Jones, it will be the man upon whom you wish to lay your hands."

"John Clay, the murderer, thief, smasher, and forger. He's a young man,

---

[1] **rubber:** a term used in card games, especially bridge and whist, indicating that a team has won two games.

Mr. Merryweather, but he is at the head of his profession, and I would rather have my bracelets on him than on any criminal in London. He's a remarkable man, is young John Clay. His grandfather was a royal duke, and he himself has been to Eton and Oxford. His brain is as cunning as his fingers, and though we meet signs of him at every turn, we never know where to find the man himself. He'll crack a crib in Scotland one week and be raising money to build an orphanage in Cornwall the next. I've been on his track for years and have never set eyes on him yet."

"I hope that I may have the pleasure of introducing you tonight. I've had one or two little turns also with Mr. John Clay, and I agree with you that he is at the head of his profession. It is past ten, however, and quite time that we started. If you two will take the first hansom, Watson and I will follow in the second."

Sherlock Holmes was not very communicative during the long drive, and lay back in the cab humming the tunes which he had heard in the afternoon. We rattled through an endless labyrinth of gas-lit streets until we emerged into Farringdon Street.

"We are close there now," my friend remarked. "This fellow Merryweather is a bank director and personally interested in the matter. I thought it as well to have Jones with us also. He is not a bad fellow, though an absolute imbecile in his profession. He has one positive virtue. He is as brave as a bulldog, and as tenacious as a lobster if he gets his claws upon any one. Here we are, and they are waiting for us."

We had reached the same crowded thoroughfare in which we had found ourselves in the morning. Our cabs were dismissed, and, following the guidance of Mr. Merryweather, we passed down a narrow passage and through a side door that he opened for us. Within there was a small corridor, that ended in a very massive iron gate. This also was opened, and led down a flight of winding stone steps that terminated at another formidable gate. Mr. Merryweather stopped to light a lantern and then conducted us down a dark, earth-smelling passage and so, after opening a third door, into a huge vault or cellar that was piled all round with crates and massive boxes.

"You are not very vulnerable from above," Holmes remarked, as he held up the lantern and gazed about him.

"Nor from below," said Mr. Merryweather, striking his stick upon the flags which lined the floor. "Why, dear me, it sounds quite hollow!" he remarked, looking up in surprise.

"I must really ask you to be a little more quiet," said Holmes, severely. "You have already imperiled the whole success of our expedition. Might I beg that you would have the goodness to sit down upon one of those boxes and not to interfere?"

The solemn Mr. Merryweather perched himself upon a crate, with a very injured expression upon his face, while Holmes fell upon his knees upon the floor and, with the lantern and a magnifying lens, began to examine minutely the cracks between the stones. A few seconds sufficed to satisfy him, for he sprang to his feet again and put his glass in his pocket.

"We have at least an hour before us,"

he remarked; "for they can hardly take any steps until the good pawnbroker is safely in bed. Then they will not lose a minute, for the sooner they do their work the longer time they will have for their escape. We are at present, Doctor — as no doubt you have divined — in the cellar of the city branch of one of the principal London banks. Mr. Merryweather is the chairman of directors, and he will explain to you that there are reasons why the more daring criminals of London should take a considerable interest in this cellar at present."

"It is our French gold," whispered the director. "We have had several warnings that an attempt might be made upon it."

"Your French gold?"

"Yes. We had occasion some months ago to strengthen our resources, and borrowed, for that purpose, 30,000 napoleons [1] from the Bank of France. It has become known that we have never had occasion to unpack the money, and that it is still lying in our cellar. The crate upon which I sit contains 2000 napoleons packed between layers of lead foil. Our reserve of bullion [2] is much larger at present than is usually kept in a single branch office, and the directors have had misgivings upon the subject."

"Which were very well justified," observed Holmes. "And now it is time that we arranged our little plans. I expect that within an hour matters will come to a head. In the meantime, Mr. Merryweather, we must put the screen over that dark lantern."

"And sit in the dark?"

"I am afraid so. I had brought a pack of cards in my pocket, and I thought that, as we were a *partie carrée*,[3] you might have your rubber after all. But I see that the enemy's preparations have gone so far that we cannot risk the presence of a light. And, first of all, we must choose our positions. These are daring men, and though we shall take them at a disadvantage, they may do us some harm unless we are careful. I shall stand behind this crate, and do you conceal yourselves behind those. Then, when I flash a light upon them, close in swiftly. If they fire, Watson, have no compunction about shooting them down."

I placed my revolver, cocked, upon the top of the wooden case behind which I crouched. Holmes shot the slide across the front of his lantern, and left us in pitch darkness — such an absolute darkness as I have never before experienced. The smell of hot metal remained to assure us that the light

[1] **napoleons:** formerly, gold coins of France.

[2] **bullion** (bŏŏl'yən): gold, or silver, in the form of bars.

[3] *partie carrée* (pàr·tē cá·rā′): That is, there were four of them in the group.

was still there, ready to flash out at a moment's notice. To me, with my nerves worked up to a pitch of expectancy, there was something depressing and subduing in the sudden gloom and in the cold, dank air of the vault.

"They have but one retreat," whispered Holmes. "That is back through the house into Saxe-Coburg Square. I hope that you have done what I asked you, Jones?"

"I have an inspector and two officers waiting at the front door."

"Then we have stopped all the holes. And now we must be silent and wait."

What a time it seemed! From comparing notes afterwards it was but an hour and a quarter, yet it appeared to me that the night must have almost gone and the dawn must be breaking above us. My limbs were weary and stiff, for I feared to change my position; yet my nerves were worked up to the highest pitch of tension, and my hearing was so acute that I could not only hear the gentle breathing of my companions, but I could also distinguish the deeper, heavier in-breath of the bulky Jones from the thin, sighing note of the bank director. From my position, I could look over the case in the direction of the floor. Suddenly my eyes caught the glint of a light.

At first it was but a lurid spark upon the stone pavement. Then it lengthened out until it became a yellow line, and then, without any warning or sound, a gash seemed to open and a hand appeared; a white, almost womanly hand, which felt about in the center of the little area of light. For a minute or more the hand, with its writhing fingers, protruded out of the floor. Then it was withdrawn as suddenly as it appeared, and all was dark again save the single lurid spark which marked a chink between the stones.

Its disappearance, however, was but momentary. With a rending, tearing sound, one of the broad, white stones turned over upon its side, and left a square, gaping hole, through which streamed the light of a lantern. Over the edge there peeped a clean-cut, boyish face, which looked keenly about it, and then, with a hand on either side of the aperture,[1] drew itself shoulder high and waist high, until one knee rested upon the edge. In another instant he stood at the side of the hole, and was hauling after him a companion, lithe and small like himself, with a pale face and a shock of very red hair.

"It's all clear," he whispered. "Have you the chisel and the bags? Great Scott! Jump, Archie, jump, and I'll swing for it!"

Sherlock Holmes had sprung out and seized the intruder by the collar. The other dived down the hole, and I heard the sound of rending cloth as Jones clutched at his skirts. The light flashed upon the barrel of a revolver, but Holmes's hunting crop came down on the man's wrist, and the pistol clinked upon the stone floor.

"It's no use, John Clay," said Holmes, blandly. "You have no chance at all."

"So I see," the other answered, with the utmost coolness. "I fancy that my pal is all right, though I see you have got his coattails."

---

[1] aperture (ap′ər·chŏŏr): opening.

"There are three men waiting for him at the door," said Holmes.

"Oh, indeed! You seem to have done the thing very completely, I must compliment you."

"And I you," Holmes answered. "Your red-headed idea was very new and effective."

"You'll see your pal again presently," said Jones. "He's quicker at climbing down holes than I am. Just hold out while I fix the derbies." [1]

"I beg that you will not touch me with your filthy hands," remarked our prisoner, as the handcuffs clattered upon his wrists. "You may not be aware that I have royal blood in my veins. Have the goodness, also, when you address me always to say 'sir' and 'please.'"

"All right," said Jones, with a stare and a snigger. "Well, would you please, sir, march upstairs, where we can get a cab to carry your highness to the police station?"

"That is better," said John Clay, serenely. He made a sweeping bow to the three of us and walked quietly off in the custody of the detective.

"Really, Mr. Holmes," said Mr. Merryweather, as we followed them from the cellar, "I do not know how the bank can thank you or repay you. There is no doubt that you have detected and defeated in the most complete manner one of the most determined attempts at bank robbery that have ever come within my experience."

"I have had one or two little scores of my own to settle with Mr. John Clay," said Holmes. "I have been at some small expense over this matter, which I shall expect the bank to refund, but beyond that I am amply repaid by having had an experience that is in many ways unique and by hearing the very remarkable narrative of the Red-headed League."

"You see, Watson," he explained, in the early hours of the morning, as we sat over a glass of whisky and soda in Baker Street, "it was perfectly obvious from the first that the only possible object of this rather fantastic business of the advertisement of the League, and the copying of the encyclopedia, must be to get this not overbright pawnbroker out of the way for a number of hours every day. It was a curious way of managing it, but, really, it would be difficult to suggest a better. The method was no doubt suggested to Clay's ingenious mind by the color of his accomplice's hair. The £4 a week was a lure which must draw him, and what was it to them, who were playing for thousands? They put in the advertisement, one rogue has the temporary office, the other rogue incites the man to apply for it, and together they manage to secure his absence every morning in the week. From the time that I heard of the assistant having come for half wages, it was obvious to me that he had some strong motive for securing the situation."

"But how could you guess what the motive was?"

"Had there been women in the house, I should have suspected a mere vulgar intrigue. That, however, was out of the question. The man's business was a small one, and there was noth-

[1] derbies: a British term for "handcuffs."

ing in his house which could account for such elaborate preparations and such an expenditure as they were at. It must, then, be something out of the house. What could it be? I thought of the assistant's fondness for photography and his trick of vanishing into the cellar. The cellar! There was the end of this tangled clue. Then I made inquiries as to this mysterious assistant, and found that I had to deal with one of the coolest and most daring criminals in London. He was doing something in the cellar — something which took many hours a day for months on end. What could it be, once more? I could think of nothing save that he was running a tunnel to some other building.

"So far I had got when we went to visit the scene of action. I surprised you by beating upon the pavement with my stick. I was ascertaining whether the cellar stretched out in front or behind. It was not in front. Then I rang the bell, and, as I hoped, the assistant answered it. We have had some skirmishes, but we had never set eyes upon each other before. I hardly looked at his face. His knees were what I wished to see. You must yourself have remarked how worn, wrinkled, and stained they were. They spoke of those hours of burrowing. The only remaining point was what they were burrowing for. I walked round the corner, saw that the City and Suburban Bank abutted on our friend's premises, and felt that I had solved my problem. When you drove home after the concert I called upon Scotland Yard and upon the chairman of the bank directors, with the result that you have seen."

"And how could you tell that they would make their attempt tonight?" I asked.

"Well, when they closed their league offices that was a sign that they cared no longer about Mr. Jabez Wilson's presence — in other words, that they had completed their tunnel. But it was essential that they should use it soon, as it might be discovered, or the bullion might be removed. Saturday would suit them better than any other day, as it would give them two days for their escape. For all these reasons, I expected them to come tonight."

"You reasoned it out beautifully," I exclaimed, in unfeigned admiration. "It is so long a chain, and yet every link rings true."

"It saved me from ennui,"[1] he answered, yawning. "Alas! I already feel it closing in upon me. My life is spent in one long effort to escape from the commonplaces of existence. These little problems help me to do so."

"And you are a benefactor of the race," said I.

He shrugged his shoulders. "Well, perhaps, after all, it is of some little use," he remarked. "*L'homme c'est rien — l'œuvre c'est tout*, as Gustave Flaubert wrote to George Sand."[2]

[1] **ennui** (än'wē): boredom.
[2] *"L'homme . . . . George Sand"*: literally, "Man is nothing, work is everything." Flaubert and Sand were writers of the nineteenth century.

THE DETECTIVE STORY

Plot. In almost every short story we find conflict and suspense. In a detective story, the conflict is between the detective, who wants to catch the criminal, and the criminal, who wants to escape detection. The reader feels suspense because he wants to know who will win the struggle. If you have ever read a detective story, you know that usually you will try to match wits with the detective — to see if you can use the clues to solve the mystery before the story ends.

1. This detective story has a twist to it — the mystery was solved before the crime had been committed. Did you guess what the crime might be? What explanations of the mystery were not made until the story's end?

2. What was the opening situation of the story? What event brought Jabez Wilson to Holmes?

3. At what point in the story do you think the climax, or turning point, occurred? What was the outcome of the conflict of the story? Did the outcome surprise you at all? Why?

4. Point out clues that foreshadowed parts of the outcome. Did you often feel like Watson in your battle of wits with Holmes? How? Were Holmes's deductions logical? Do you think that, in reality, anyone could have arrived at these deductions? Why?

Characterization. In most detective stories, the reader is supposed to side with the detective. The detective is usually a man of superior intelligence, with a great fund of knowledge. Often the detective and the police are not on the best of terms. The criminal, of course, must be clever enough to compete with the detective, or there would be no suspense to grip the reader's interest.

5. In what ways did Holmes show superior intelligence? Give examples of his powers of deduction. What did Watson think of Holmes's ability as a detective?

What did the Scotland Yard man think? What did you learn of Holmes's taste in music? How would you describe the character of Sherlock Holmes? of Watson?

6. What was clever about the criminal? What was unappealing about him? What mistakes led to his downfall?

7. For years, the detective story has been a popular form of literature, and Sir Arthur Conan Doyle has been one of the most famous of all detective-story writers. Think of other detective stories you have read, or of motion pictures or television shows about detectives. What do they have in common with this story?

8. Many people think that Sherlock Holmes is the embodiment of the perfect detective. What do you think?

WORDS: FORMAL LANGUAGE

Dr. Watson and Sherlock Holmes, two British gentlemen of the nineteenth century, often use words that are as elaborate and stiff as their personalities. For example, here is a sentence spoken by Sherlock Holmes: " 'A considerable crime is in contemplation.' " A more casual character might have said, "A serious crime is being planned," or even, "A big crime is in the works."

Here are four more sentences spoken by Watson or Holmes. Notice the formal words (in italics). What words would less formal, less pompous characters probably have used in their places?

" 'Perhaps, Mr. Wilson, you would have the great kindness to *recommence* your *narrative*.' "

" 'What on earth does this mean?' I *ejaculated* . . .' "

" 'We shall *endeavor* to clear up these points for you.' "

" 'If they fire, Watson, *have no compunction about* shooting them down.' "

The Apprentice

DOROTHY CANFIELD

THE DAY had been one of the unbearable ones, when every sound had set her teeth on edge like chalk creaking on a blackboard, when every word her father or mother said to her or did not say to her seemed an intentional injustice. And of course it would happen, as the fitting end to such a day, that just as the sun went down back of the mountain and the long twilight began, she noticed that Rollie was not around.

Tense with exasperation at what her mother would say, she began to call him in a carefully casual tone — she would simply explode if Mother got going — "Here, Rollie! He-ere, boy! Want to go for a walk, Rollie?" Whistling to him cheerfully, her heart full of wrath at the way the world treated her, she made the rounds of his haunts: the corner of the woodshed, where he liked to curl up on the wool of Father's discarded old sweater; the hay barn; the cow barn; the sunny spot on the side porch. No Rollie.

Perhaps he had sneaked upstairs to lie on her bed, where he was not supposed to go — not that *she* would have minded! That rule was a part of

Mother's fussiness, part, too, of Mother's bossiness. It was *her* bed, wasn't it? But was she allowed the say-so about it? Not on your life. They *said* she could have things the way she wanted in her own room, now she was in her teens, but . . . Her heart burned at unfairness as she took the stairs stormily, two steps at a time, her pigtails flopping up and down on her back. If Rollie was there, she was just going to let him stay there, and Mother could say what she wanted to.

But he was not there. The bedspread and pillow were crumpled, but that was where she had flung herself down to cry that afternoon. Every nerve in her had been twanging discordantly, but she couldn't cry. She could only lie there, her hands doubled up hard, furious that she had nothing to cry about. Not really. She was too big to cry just over Father's having said to her, severely, "I told you if I let you take the chess set, you were to put it away when you got through with it. One of the pawns was on the floor of our bedroom this morning. I stepped on it. If I'd had my shoes on, I'd have broken it."

Well, he *had* told her that. And he hadn't said she mustn't ever take the set again. No, the instant she thought about that, she knew she couldn't cry about it. She could be, and was, in a rage about the way Father kept on talking long after she'd got his point: "It's not that I care so much about the chess set. It's because if you don't learn how to take care of things, you yourself will suffer for it. You'll forget or neglect something that will be really important for *you*. We *have* to try to teach you to be responsible for what you've said you'll take care of. If we . . ." on and on.

She stood there, dry-eyed, by the bed that Rollie had not crumpled, and thought, *"I hope Mother sees the spread and says something about Rollie — I just hope she does."*

She heard her mother coming down the hall, and hastily shut her door. She had a right to shut the door to her own room, hadn't she? She had *some* rights, she supposed, even if she was only thirteen and the youngest child. If her mother opened it to say, "What are you doing in here that you don't want me to see?" she'd say — she'd just say —

But her mother did not open the door. Her feet went steadily on along the hall, and then, carefully, slowly, down the stairs. She probably had an armful of winter things she was bringing down from the attic. She was probably thinking that a tall, thirteen-year-old daughter was big enough to help with a chore like that. But she wouldn't *say* anything. She would just get out that insulting look of a grownup silently putting up with a crazy, unreasonable kid. She had worn that expression all day; it was too much to be endured.

Up in her bedroom behind her closed door, the thirteen-year-old stamped her foot in a gust of uncontrollable rage, none the less savage and heartshaking because it was mysterious to her.

But she had not located Rollie. She would be cut into little pieces before she would let her father and mother know she had lost sight of him, forgotten about him. They would not scold her, she knew. They would do worse; they would look at her. And in their silence she would hear, droning on reproachfully, what they had said when she had been begging to keep for her own the sweet, woolly collie puppy in her arms.

How warm he had felt! Astonishing how warm and alive a puppy was compared with a doll! She had never liked her dolls much after she had held Rollie, feeling him warm against her breast, warm and wriggling, bursting with life, reaching up to lick her face. He had loved her from that first instant. As he felt her arms around him, his liquid, beautiful eyes had melted in trusting sweetness. And they did now, whenever he looked at her. Her dog was the only creature in the world who *really* loved her, she thought passionately.

And back then, at the very minute when, as a darling baby dog, he was beginning to love her, her father and mother were saying, so cold, so reasonable — gosh, how she *hated* reasonableness! — "Now, Peg, remember that, living where we do, with sheep on the farms around us, it is a serious responsibility to have a collie dog. If you keep him, you've got to be the one to take care of him. You'll have to be the one to train him to stay at home. We're too busy with you children to start bringing up a puppy, too."

Rollie, nestling in her arms, let one hind leg drop awkwardly. It must be uncomfortable. She looked down at him tenderly, tucked his leg up under him, and gave him a hug. He laughed up in her face — he really did laugh, his mouth stretched wide in a cheerful grin. Now he was snug in a warm little ball.

Her parents were saying, "If you want him, you can have him. But you must be responsible for him. If he gets to running sheep, he'll just have to be shot, you know that."

They had not said, aloud, "Like the Wilsons' collie." They never mentioned that awfulness — her racing unsuspectingly down across the fields just at the horrible moment when Mr. Wilson shot his collie, caught in the very act of killing sheep. They probably thought that if they never spoke about it, she would forget it — *forget* the crack of that rifle and the collapse of the great beautiful dog! Forget the red, red blood spurting from the hole in his head. She hadn't forgotten. She never would. She knew as well as they did how important it was to train a collie puppy about sheep. They didn't have to rub it in like that. They always rubbed everything in. She had told them, fervently, indignantly, that of *course* she would take care of him, be responsible for him, teach him to stay at home. Of course. Of course. *She* understood!

And now, when he was six months old, tall, rangy, powerful, standing up far above her knee, nearly to her waist, she didn't know where he was. But of course he must be somewhere around. He always was. She composed her face to look natural and went downstairs to search the house. He was probably asleep somewhere. She looked every room over carefully. Her mother was nowhere visible. It was safe to call him again, to give the special piercing whistle which always brought him racing to her, the white-feathered plume of his tail waving in elation that she wanted him.

But he did not answer. She stood still on the front porch to think.

Could he have gone up to their special place in the edge of the field where the three young pines, their branches growing close to the ground, made a triangular, walled-in space, completely hidden from the world? Sometimes he went up there with her, and when she lay down on the dried grass to dream, he too lay down quietly, his head on his paws, his beautiful eyes fixed adoringly on her. He entered into her every mood. If she wanted to be quiet, all right, he did too. It didn't seem as though he would have gone alone there. Still . . . She loped up the steep slope of the field rather fast, beginning to be anxious.

No, he was not there. She stood irresolutely in the roofless, green-walled, triangular hide-out, wondering what to do next.

Then, before she knew what thought had come into her mind, its emotional impact knocked her down. At least her knees crumpled under her. The Wilsons had, last Wednesday, brought their sheep down from the far upper pasture to the home farm! They were — she herself had seen them on her way to school, and like an idiot had not thought of Rollie — on the river meadow.

She was off like a racer at the crack of the starting pistol, her long, strong legs stretched in great leaps, her pigtails flying. She took the short cut, regardless of the brambles. Their thorn-spiked, wiry stems tore at her flesh, but she did not care. She welcomed the pain. It was something she was doing for Rollie, for her Rollie.

She was in the pine woods now, rushing down the steep, stony path, tripping over roots, half falling, catching herself just in time, not slackening her speed. She burst out on the open knoll above the river meadow, calling wildly, "Rollie, here, Rollie, here, boy! Here! Here!" She tried to whistle, but she was crying too hard to pucker her lips.

There was nobody to see or hear her. Twilight was falling over the bare, grassy knoll. The sunless evening wind slid down the mountain like an invisible river, engulfing her in cold Her teeth began to chatter. "Here, Rollie, here, boy, here!" She strained her eyes to look down into the meadow to see if the sheep were there. She could not be sure. She stopped calling him as she would a dog, and called out his name despairingly, as if he were her child, "Rollie! Oh, *Rollie*, where are you?"

The tears ran down her cheeks in streams. She sobbed loudly, terribly; she did not try to control herself, since there was no one to hear. "Hou! Hou! Hou!" she sobbed, her face contorted grotesquely. "Oh, Rollie! Rollie! Rollie!" She had wanted something to cry about. Oh, how terribly now she had something to cry about.

She saw him as clearly as if he were there beside her, his muzzle and gaping mouth all smeared with the betraying blood (like the Wilsons' collie). "But he didn't *know* it was wrong!" she screamed like a wild creature. "Nobody *told* him it was wrong. It was my fault. I should have taken better care of him. I will now. I will!"

But no matter how she screamed, she could not make herself heard. In the cold gathering darkness, she saw him stand, poor, guiltless victim of his ignorance, who should have been protected from his own nature, his beautiful soft eyes looking at her with love, his splendid plumed tail waving gently. "It was my fault. I promised I would bring him up. I should have *made* him stay at home. I was responsible for him. It was my fault."

But she could not make his executioners hear her. The shot rang out. Rollie sank down, his beautiful liquid eyes glazed, the blood spurting from the hole in his head — like the Wilsons' collie. She gave a wild shriek, long, soul-satisfying, frantic. It was the scream — at sudden, unendurable tragedy — of a mature, full-blooded woman. It drained dry the girl of thirteen. She came to herself. She was standing on the knoll, trembling and quaking with cold, the darkness closing in on her.

Her breath had given out. For once in her life she had wept all the tears there were in her body. Her hands were so stiff with cold she could scarcely close them. How her nose was running! Simply streaming down her upper lip. And she had no handkerchief. She lifted her skirt, fumbled for her slip, stooped, blew her nose on it, wiped her eyes, drew a long quavering breath — and heard something! Far off in the distance, a faint sound, like a dog's muffled bark.

She whirled on her heels and bent her head to listen. The sound did not come from the meadow below the knoll. It came from back of her, from the Wilson's maple grove higher up. She held her breath. Yes, it came from there. She began to run again, but now she was not sobbing. She was silent, absorbed in her effort to cover ground. If she could only live to get there, to see if it really were Rollie. She ran steadily till she came to the fence, and went over this in a great plunge. Her skirt caught on a nail. She impatiently pulled at it, not hearing or not heeding the long sibilant tear as it came loose. She was in the dusky maple woods, stumbling over the rocks as she ran. As she tore on up the slope, she knew it was Rollie's bark.

She stopped short and leaned weakly against a tree, sick with the breathlessness of her straining lungs, sick in the reaction of relief, sick with anger at Rollie, who had been here having a wonderful time while she had been dying, just dying in terror about him.

For she could now not only hear that it was Rollie's bark, she could hear, in the dog language she knew as well as he, what he was saying in those excited yips: that he had run a woodchuck into a hole in the tumbled stone wall, that he almost had him, that the intoxicating wild-animal smell was as close to him — almost — as if he had his

jaws on his quarry. Yip! Woof! Yip! Yip!

The wild, joyful quality of the dog talk enraged the girl. She was trembling in exhaustion, in indignation. So that was where he had been, when she was killing herself trying to take care of him. Plenty near enough to hear her calling and whistling to him, if he had paid attention. Just so set on having his foolish good time, he never thought to listen for her call.

She stooped to pick up a stout stick. She would teach him! It was time he had something to make him remember to listen. She started forward.

But she stopped, stood thinking. One of the things to remember about collies — everybody knew that — was their sensitiveness. A collie who had been beaten was never "right" again. His spirit was broken. "Anything but a broken-spirited collie," the farmers often said. They were no good after that.

She threw down her stick. Anyhow, she thought, he was too young to know, really, that he had done wrong. He was still only a puppy. Like all puppies, he got perfectly crazy over wild-animal smells. Probably he really and truly hadn't heard her calling and whistling.

All the same, all the same — she stared intently into the twilight — he couldn't be let to grow up just as he wanted to. She would have to make him understand that he mustn't go off this way by himself. He must be trained to know how to do what a good dog does — not because *she* wanted him to, but for his own sake.

She walked on now steady, purposeful, gathering her inner strength together, Olympian in her understanding of the full meaning of the event.

When he heard his own special young god approaching, he turned delightedly and ran to meet her, panting, his tongue hanging out. His eyes shone. He jumped up on her in an ecstasy of welcome and licked her face.

But she pushed him away. Her face and voice were grave. "No, Rollie, *no!*" she said severely. "You're *bad.* You know you're not to go off in the woods without me! You are — a — *bad* — dog."

He was horrified, stricken into misery. He stood facing her, frozen, the gladness going out of his eyes, the erect waving plume of his tail slowly lowering to slinking, guilty dejection.

"I know you were all wrapped up in that woodchuck. But that's no excuse. You *could* have heard me calling you,

whistling for you, if you'd paid attention," she went on. "You've got to learn, and I've got to teach you."

With a shudder of misery, he lay down, his tail stretched out limp on the ground, his head flat on his paws, his ears drooping — ears ringing with doomsday awfulness of the voice he so loved and revered. He must have been utterly wicked. He trembled and turned his head away from her august [1] look of blame, groveling in remorse for whatever mysterious sin he had committed.

She sat down by him, as miserable as he. "I don't *want* to scold you. But I have to! I have to bring you up right, or you'll get shot, Rollie. You *mustn't* go away from the house without me, do you hear, *never!*"

Catching, with his sharp ears yearning for her approval, a faint overtone

[1] **august:** stately, imposing.

of relenting affection in her voice, he lifted his eyes to her, humbly, soft in imploring fondness.

"Oh, Rollie!" she said, stooping low over him. "I *do* love you. I do. But I *have* to bring you up. I'm responsible for you, don't you see?"

He did not see. Hearing sternness or something else he did not recognize in the beloved voice, he shut his eyes tight in sorrow and made a little whimpering lament in his throat.

She had never heard him cry before. It was too much. She sat down by him and drew his head to her, rocking him in her arms, soothing him with inarticulate small murmurs.

He leaped in her arms and wriggled happily as he had when he was a baby; he reached up to lick her face as he had then. But he was no baby now. He was half as big as she, a great, warm, pulsing, living armful of love. She clasped him closely. Her heart was brimming full, but calmed, quiet. The blood flowed in equable gentleness all over her body. She was deliciously warm. Her nose was still running a little. She sniffed and wiped it on her sleeve.

It was almost dark now. "We'll be late to supper, Rollie," she said responsibly. Pushing him gently off, she stood up. "Home, Rollie, home!"

Here was a command he could understand. At once he trotted along the path toward home. His plumed tail, held high, waved cheerfully. His short dog memory had dropped into oblivion the suffering just back of him.

Her human memory was longer. His prancing gait was as carefree as a young child's. Plodding heavily like a serious adult, she trod behind him. Her very shoulders seemed bowed by what she had lived through. She felt, she thought, like an old, old woman of thirty. But it was all right now. She knew she had made an impression on him.

When they came out into the open pasture, Rollie ran back to get her to play with him. He leaped around her in circles, barking in cheerful yawps, jumping up on her, inviting her to run a race with him, to throw him a stick, to come alive.

His high spirits were ridiculous — but infectious. She gave one little leap to match his. Rollie pretended that this was a threat to him, planted his forepaws low and barked loudly at her, laughing between yips. He was so funny, she thought, when he grinned that way. She laughed back and gave another mock-threatening leap at him. Radiant that his sky was once more clear, he sprang high on his spring-steel muscles in an explosion of happiness, and bounded in circles around her.

Following him, not noting in the dusk where she was going, she felt the grassy slope drop steeply. Oh, yes, she knew where she was. They had come to the rolling-down hill just back of the house. All the kids rolled down there, even the little ones, because it was soft grass without a stone. She had rolled down that slope a million times — years and years ago, when she was a kid herself. It was fun. She remembered well the whirling dizziness of the descent, all the world turning over and over crazily. And the delicious giddy staggering when you first stood up, the earth still spinning under your feet.

"All right, Rollie, let's go," she cried, and flung herself down in the rolling position, her arms straight up over her head.

Rollie had never seen this skylarking before. It threw him into almost hysterical amusement. He capered around the rapidly rolling figure, half scared, mystified, enchanted.

His wild frolicsome barking might have come from her own throat, so accurately did it sound the way she felt — crazy, foolish, like a little kid no more than five years old, the age she had been when she had last rolled down that hill.

At the bottom she sprang up, on muscles as steel-strong as Rollie's. She staggered a little and laughed aloud.

The living-room windows were just before them. How yellow lighted windows looked when you were in the darkness going home! How nice and yellow! Maybe Mother had waffles for supper. She was a swell cook, Mother was, and she certainly gave her family all the breaks when it came to meals.

"Home, Rollie, home!" She burst open the door to the living room. "Hi, Mom, what you got for supper?"

From the kitchen her mother announced coolly, "I hate to break the news to you, but it's waffles."

"Oh, *Mom!*" she shouted in ecstasy.

Her mother could not see her. She did not need to. "For goodness' sakes, go and wash," she called.

In the long mirror across the room she saw herself, her hair hanging wild, her long bare legs scratched, her broadly smiling face dirt-streaked, her torn skirt dangling, her dog laughing up at her. Gosh, was it a relief to feel your own age, just exactly thirteen years old!

A STORY WITH A THEME

Though many stories, like the first three in this unit, can be read purely for entertainment, some short stories can also be read on a second, deeper level. In such stories an author wants to express an idea that concerns him.

1. Think about the title of this story. What is an apprentice? Who was the apprentice in the story? In what ways is this an appropriate title for the story? How does the title help to emphasize the theme or idea underlying the story?

2. On page 323, Peg screamed in horror as she realized that Rollie might be shot. The author then says this: "It was the scream — at sudden, unendurable tragedy — of a mature, full-blooded woman. It drained dry the girl of thirteen." Indirectly, the author is saying that something had happened to Peg. What was it?

3. Why was Peg enraged at Rollie when she found him? In what ways had Peg's actions become just like those she had resented in her parents? How was Rollie like Peg herself? Do you think Peg recognized these similarities? Explain.

4. Although Peg had just had a powerful and sobering experience, she reverted to a childhood action when she got to the rolling-down hill. Why do you think she did this?

5. Reread the last paragraphs of the story. Does the author say directly that Peg has a different attitude toward her mother? Do you think Peg had changed?

6. After answering the previous questions and thinking about the story, state in your own words what you think the author is saying.

7. One of the pleasures of literature is that it can help us to understand ourselves and other people. Do you think this story described feelings which are universal to mankind? How would this story help you to understand people better?

8. Are people always, in some respects, "apprentices" in life? Explain.

SENTENCES: LIVELY MODIFIERS

Dorothy Canfield has put extra life and action into this story by frequently using the *–ing* form of a verb as a modifier. This form of the verb is often called the present participle. For example, we read about a *running* dog, *flying* pigtails, and a *gaping* mouth. Often, such *–ing* words introduce a whole phrase which is used as a modifier. Here is a sentence from the story in which *–ing* phrases are used as modifiers. The phrases are in brackets, and the present participles are in italics.

"She was in the pine woods now, [*rushing* down the steep, stony path], [*tripping* over roots], [half *falling*], [*catching* herself just in time], [not *slackening* her speed]."

The *–ing* phrases in this sentence all describe Peg, and refer to the pronoun *she*.

Which words in the following sentences are described by the phrases in brackets?

"She was standing on the knoll, [*trembling* and *quaking* with cold], the darkness [*closing* in on her]."

"She had never liked her dolls much after she had held Rollie, [*feeling* him warm against her breast], [warm and *wriggling*], [*bursting* with life], [*reaching* up to lick her face]."

COMPOSITION:
CHARACTER DESCRIPTION

Dorothy Canfield has created a memorable picture of a thirteen-year-old girl. Peg becomes very real to us, not because her looks are described in any detail, but because her thoughts and feelings are described so well. Here, for example, is a passage describing how Peg feels as the story opens.

"Tense with exasperation at what her mother would say, she began to call him in a carefully casual tone — she would simply explode if Mother got going — 'Here, Rollie! He-ere, boy! Want to go for a walk, Rollie?' Whistling to him cheerfully, her heart full of wrath at the way the world treated her, she made the rounds of his haunts . . ."

In the next paragraph, we are taken right into Peg's mind and told what she is thinking.

"Perhaps he had sneaked upstairs to lie on her bed, where he was not supposed to go — not that *she* would have minded! That rule was a part of Mother's fussiness, part, too, of Mother's bossiness. It was *her* bed, wasn't it? But was she allowed the say-so about it? Not on your life. They *said* she could have things the way she wanted in her own room, now she was in her teens, but . . . Her heart burned at unfairness as she took the stairs stormily two steps at a time, her pigtails flopping up and down on her back. If Rollie was there, she was just going to let him stay there, and Mother could say what she wanted to."

Which details in these passages do you think described Peg's feelings most vividly?

Write a paragraph or two in which you take the reader into a character's mind and reveal his thoughts and feelings. Perhaps you will want to look into your own mind. Here are some sentences that might help you to start such a paragraph.

The day had been one of those happy ones.

During the last hours, I felt desperate.

Talking to her, he was strangely shy.

Stories

You have already spent some time studying the techniques of narration in the second unit. Here you will learn more about narrative writing, particularly about some techniques used in the form of literature called the short story.

Read closely this narrative passage from "The Ransom of Red Chief" by O. Henry.

I got the knife away from the kid and made him lie down again. But, from that moment, Bill's spirit was broken. He laid down on his side of the bed, but he never closed an eye again in sleep as long as that boy was with us. I dozed off for a while, but along toward sunup I remembered that Red Chief had said I was to be burned at the stake at the rising of the sun. I wasn't nervous or afraid, but I sat up and lit my pipe and leaned against a rock.

"What you getting up so soon for, Sam?" asked Bill.

"Me?" says I. "Oh, I got a kind of a pain in my shoulder. I thought sitting up would rest it."

"You're a liar!" says Bill. "You're afraid. You was to be burned at sunrise, and you was afraid he'd do it. And he would, too, if he could find a match. Ain't it awful, Sam? Do you think anybody will pay out money to get a little imp like that back home?" (pages 285–86)

READING A STORY

1. *When you read a story, note who the narrator is.* Some stories are told by an "I," in the first person. Who is the "I" telling the story about Red Chief? Is the narrator involved in the story, or is he just a recorder of the events?

Some stories are told in the third person; in these stories, the narrator doesn't enter into the action.

Look back at "The Legend of Sleepy Hollow," "The Red-headed League," and "The Apprentice." How far do you have to read before you know who the narrator of each story is? Does the narrator of any of these stories enter into its action?

2. *Note that the writer of a story chooses a particular point of view in order to create a certain effect.* A story told in the first person, for example, is sometimes more realistic or immediate than one told in the third person. Compare the first sentence below, written by O. Henry, with the second one:

"I wasn't nervous or afraid, but I sat up and lit my pipe and leaned against a rock."

Sam wasn't nervous or afraid, but he sat up and lit his pipe and leaned against a rock.

The first sentence is from the first paragraph of the model passage. Rewrite this paragraph from the third person point of view. Which point of view do you prefer? Why?

Look back at "The Apprentice." Would this story have differed in effect had it been narrated by Peg's mother? Try rewriting the third paragraph of this story from Peg's mother's viewpoint.

3. *Note the details the story writer uses to tell you about the time and the setting and the mood of the story.* Often these details are provided in the opening sentences

of a story. For example, here are the two sentences which open a famous story, "The Fall of the House of Usher" by Edgar Allan Poe. Read them carefully.

> During the whole of a dull, dark, and soundless day in the autumn of the year, when the clouds hung oppressively low in the heavens, I had been passing alone, on horseback, through a singularly dreary tract of country, and at length found myself, as the shades of the evening drew on, within view of the melancholy House of Usher. I know not how it was — but, with the first glimpse of the building, a sense of insufferable gloom pervaded my spirit . . .

This passage is rich in detail. Without looking back, see if you can answer these questions. (Check yourself later.)

- a. The setting of the story is (a dreary countryside, a deserted town, a rainy seashore).
- b. The time of day is (midnight, evening, morning).
- c. The time of year is (winter, autumn, late summer).
- d. The narrator's mood is (cheery, curious, gloomy).

Look back at the stories on pages 118, 202, and 283. How far do you have to read before you find details setting the time, place, and mood of each story?

WRITING STORIES

Professional writers who give advice to young writers usually tell them to start off by writing about what they know best. Your best stories will probably be those based on your own experiences. Why, do you think, is this generally true?

As you write, keep in mind the following points, in addition to those on page 156.

1. *Choose a point of view.* Will the narrator be in the action or outside?

2. *Use realistic and natural dialogue.* What makes the dialogue in the model passage sound natural?

3. *Fill in your narrative with descriptive details.* In your opening sentences, locate the time and setting and set the mood of your story.

Write a brief story about the first time you did something (for example, the first time you saw someone famous, or the first time you traveled by train or plane).

Perhaps you prefer to use your imagination. If so, write a brief story about fictional events, maybe one of these:

The Time They Outlawed Books
A Day in the Life of a Cave Man
The City That Grew Too Big

Sentence Study. One way to show that two or more ideas are roughly equal in importance is to write a compound sentence. The ideas in a compound sentence are usually joined by *and* (to add an idea); *but* or *yet* (to contrast one idea with another); or *or* (to join alternative ideas).

In the first paragraph of the model passage by O. Henry, there are three sentences made up of contrasting ideas, joined by *but*. Find these sentences. Could other connective words have been used?

Look at Poe's sentences. How many different ideas are combined in these structures? What words are used to connect these ideas?

ART AND LITERATURE

From pages 295–300, choose a painting that you feel depicts action particularly well. Then write a brief story around the scene in the painting. Use action verbs to describe the movement in the painting.

Forms of Literature

Unit 5
Plays

UNIT 5 Plays

In two plays in this unit are these dramatic episodes.

Episode One

"BLANCHE. . . . Why are you here? What is the meaning of all this?

DENIS. God knows! I find myself a prisoner in a house of mad people. . . .

BLANCHE. Then how did you come here?

DENIS. By accident. I was driven within by a street brawl . . . Now it is my turn to ask questions. Why are *you* in this predicament? I cannot believe that anyone so innocent — so lovely — has brought dishonor to her family."

From **The Sire de Maletroit's Door** by Robert Louis Stevenson

Episode Two

"KING. What you are trying to say in the fewest words possible is that my daughter is not beautiful.

CHANCELLOR. Her beauty is certainly elusive, Your Majesty.

KING. It is. It has eluded you, it has eluded me, it has eluded everybody who has seen her. It even eluded the Court Painter. His last words were, 'Well, I did my best.' . . .

CHANCELLOR. It is unfortunate, Your Majesty, but there it is. One just cannot understand how it can have occurred."

From **The Ugly Duckling** by A. A. Milne

As you read on to discover what becomes of Denis and Blanche and how the homely princess fools everyone, remember that you are reading a form of literature that is centuries old. Twenty-five hundred years ago, the citizens of Greece would gather outdoors on a rocky hillside to watch plays enacted. Today we see plays on television and in the legitimate theater, or in the form of movies. But the appeal of drama is still the same. Today, as centuries ago, people respond with fascination when a good story comes alive before their eyes.

The Sire de Maletroit's Door

ROBERT LOUIS STEVENSON

Adapted for Television by
Reginald Denham and Mary Orr

Characters

DENIS OF BEAULIEU (pronounced byōō'lē, like an English name), *a handsome, aristocratic English soldier of twenty-five, an expert swordsman*

SIRE DE MALETROIT, *a venerable French aristocrat of sixty-five. He has gray hair and a neatly trimmed white beard and mustache. In spite of a benign smile, there is something sinister in his eyes. Like most well-born Frenchmen of his day, he speaks English practically without an accent.*

BLANCHE DE MALETROIT, *his niece, a*

* Sire de Maletroit's (sēr də mȧl·ā·trwȧz').

beautiful French girl of seventeen. She too has been taught to speak English, and has only a trace of an accent.

PRIEST, *Maletroit's private chaplain, well fed and worldly*

INNKEEPER, *a stout French peasant. He speaks English with an accent.*

BURGUNDIAN SOLDIERS (six), *from the region of France called Burgundy*

PIKEMEN (four), *Maletroit's armed retainers*

CHORISTERS, *unseen boy singers*

[*Fade in camera on a photograph or etching of the medieval walled city of Carcassonne,[1] France. Superim-*

[1] **Carcassonne** (kȧr·kȧ·sôn'): a city in southern France. The town in which this play is set resembles Carcassonne.

*pose and rotate over the picture, the
following:*

FRANCE: 1428

HENRY THE FIFTH HAD WON THE
BATTLE OF AGINCOURT.[1] A LARGE
PART OF FRANCE HAD BEEN CON-
QUERED BY THE BRITISH. THE
TROOPS OF BURGUNDY AND ENGLAND
RULED SIDE BY SIDE UNDER AN UN-
EASY TRUCE.

*Dissolve to a painting of Joan of Arc
in full armor. Superimpose:*

HOWEVER, THIS STATE OF ARMED
NEUTRALITY WAS TO BE SHORT-
LIVED. A YEAR LATER, JOAN OF ARC
WOULD DON HER ARMOR AND DRIVE
THE HATED ENGLISH BACK ACROSS
THE CHANNEL.

*Dissolve to two banners flying in the
breeze — the oriflamme [2] of France
and the cross of St. George of England. Superimpose:*

BUT THAT IS TO ANTICIPATE HIS-
TORY: THE ORIFLAMME OF FRANCE
AND THE CROSS OF ST. GEORGE OF
ENGLAND STILL FLUTTERED OVER
THE CITADEL OF THE WALLED TOWN
OF CHÂTEAU LANDONNE [3] DURING
THE NIGHT THIS STRANGE, ROMANTIC
TALE TOOK PLACE.

*Dissolve to a tavern sign. On it is
painted a black horse and under-*
neath it the words LE CHEVAL NOIR.[4]
*Dissolve to interior of the tavern. All
that need be seen is a corner of the
room.* DENIS OF BEAULIEU, *a young
English aristocrat, is sprawling nonchalantly in a large oak armchair. In
front of him is a table on which is a
stone flagon and a half-filled glass.
He is a soldier. His coat of chain mail
shimmers in the flickering firelight.
His sword and belt hang over the
back of his chair. He wears spurs. He
is young, handsome, and, at the moment, the picture of boredom. He
drains off the glass, then raps on the
table.*]

DENIS. Landlord! . . . Landlord! . . .

[*A fat French* INNKEEPER *comes into
camera. He has bristling mustachios
and speaks good English with an accent.*]

INNKEEPER. Monsieur?

DENIS. Your cellar boasts an excellent
cordial. Where was it brewed?

INNKEEPER. At the abbey of Fécamp.[5] The Benedictine monks distill
it.

DENIS. I must take a sample back
with me to England when my mission
is accomplished. Can you secure me a
cask?

INNKEEPER. With ease, monsieur.

DENIS. Good! . . . Just the same,
this priests' potion does not compensate for the lack of company. How
does a stranger allay boredom in your
benighted town?

---

[1] **Agincourt** (aj'in·kôrt): a village in northern France. King Henry the Fifth of England
won a victory over the French there in 1415,
during the Hundred Years' War.

[2] **oriflamme** (or'ə·flam): a red silk banner,
the battle flag of the early French kings, as the
cross of St. George was the battle flag of the
English kings.

[3] **Château Landonne** (shä·tō' län·dôn').

[4] **Le Cheval Noir** (lə shə·vàl nwàr'): The
Black Horse.

[5] **Fécamp** (fā·kän').

INNKEEPER. Pardon, monsieur, but if the stranger is English — and wise — he will retire safely to his bed. It is dangerous to be on the streets of Château Landonne, alone, after curfew.

DENIS. Pox on you, man! France and England are no longer at war — and I am here on safe conduct.

INNKEEPER. What use are safe-conduct papers in the dark? It is only the kings who have made this peace, not their subjects. I regret, monsieur, but there is little love between my people and yours. Every night the Burgundian soldiers, drunk with wine, roam the by-ways. They search for trouble — trouble in the shape of an English accent with a sword.

DENIS (*rising scornfully*). You insult me, landlord. Do you think I cannot defend myself? Do you think I fear your Burgundians? One Englishman is worth a half a dozen of those tattered mercenaries.[1] King Harry proved that on the field of Agincourt.

INNKEEPER (*groveling*). Pardon — I didn't mean to offend, monsieur. I had one thought alone — your safety.

DENIS (*softening*). I am obliged for your concern. Nevertheless, I intend to venture forth tonight. Otherwise I shall drown myself in that sticky Benedictine brew. . . . Tell me, mine host, where can a gentleman find a game of cards?

INNKEEPER. The English officers are billeted at the southwest corner of the town — at the Auberge Normande,[2] below the keep.[3] Doubtlessly, they would furnish you with a game.

DENIS. I devoutly hope so! Now give me my sword! (*The* INNKEEPER *does so and helps him to buckle it on.*) How does one reach this hostelry?

INNKEEPER. Walk a thousand roods [4] due east, then turn north by the walls of the Sire de Maletroit's château. You cannot fail to recognize it, even in the

[1] **mercenaries:** soldiers who hire themselves out as fighters; here, a term of scorn.

[2] **Auberge Normande** (ō·berzh′ nôr·mänd′): an inn.

[3] **keep:** castle or fortress.

[4] **a thousand roods:** about three or four miles.

dark. You will see the round stern of a chapel on the opposite corner. The Auberge lies at the end of this lane.

[*They walk toward the door.* DENIS *puts on his cloak and hat.*]

DENIS (*the typical patronizing aristocrat*). You speak English uncommonly well — for a snail-eating Frenchie.

INNKEEPER (*bowing low*). Monsieur is too gracious! . . . My father taught me your language. This has been a hundred years' war between our countries, monsieur. (*With a meaningful smile*) English soldiers have come to this inn — and gone — many times.

[DENIS *looks at him and laughs good-humoredly. He opens the door and departs.*]

[*Dissolve to outside of the Sire de Maletroit's château. Long shot. What we see is an L-shaped stone wall. In the short part of the L is an imposing Norman door, heavily carved in massive oak. The Maletroit coat of arms is on a large shield over the door. There is a striking gargoyle over the shield.*

The long arm of the L is supported by three projecting buttresses. The corners formed by these supports are in complete darkness. But the wall itself and the cobblestone street in front of it are streaked with moonlight.

Three drunken BURGUNDIAN SOLDIERS, *coming from the direction in which the door stands, stagger along the streets. They wear steel helmets and breastplates, and are armed with swords. They are singing a French marching song of the period. They*

stop, pass a flagon around, and assuage their thirst from it. Then they draw their swords, wave them wildly toward the heavens, and curse the English.*]

BURGUNDIAN SOLDIERS (*together*). *A bas, les anglais!* [1] . . . etc., etc.!

[*They drink again, then link arms and stagger out of the picture. A moment or so later,* DENIS *comes along the lane from the same direction. He walks warily, obviously keeping his eye on the drunken men ahead of him. Suddenly their singing, which has been growing fainter, crescendos again, indicating that they have wheeled around and are returning his way.*

Seeing that he will come face to face with these men if he pursues his present route, DENIS *darts into the shadow of the center buttress and flattens himself against the wall. Except for a faint gleam on his chain mail, he is completely hidden from sight.*

The three BURGUNDIAN SOLDIERS *return. They pass where* DENIS *is concealed. Inadvertently, he shifts his position. His sword clatters against the stone wall. The* BURGUNDIAN SOLDIERS *hesitate, turn, and stare into the shadows.*]

BURGUNDIAN SOLDIER. *Qui v'là?* [2] . . .

[*He lurches into the shadows and drags* DENIS *into the light.* DENIS *immediately whips out his sword.*]

[1] *A bas, les anglais!* (ä·bä′ lä·zän·glä′): Down with the English!
[2] *Qui v'là?* (kē v'lä′): Who goes there?

DENIS. Filthy French offal![1] Out of my way! . . .

BURGUNDIAN SOLDIER. *Parbleu! Un anglais![2]*

[*The three* BURGUNDIAN SOLDIERS *draw their swords and scream a volley of oaths at* DENIS. *Then they hurl themselves upon him.* DENIS *takes on the three, confident that his superior, and sober, swordsmanship will see him through. He overcomes the first two after a hard but brief exchange of swords. They writhe on the ground, severely wounded. The third one proves to be a better swordsman and gives* DENIS *considerable difficulty.*

The clank of steel is heard by other BURGUNDIAN SOLDIERS *in the neighborhood. Three more dash to the scene. They immediately whip out their swords and enter the fray.* DENIS *is now tiring, outnumbered, and in danger of being killed. He is forced to take the defensive. He retreats down the street in the direction of the door. The* BURGUNDIAN SOLDIERS *follow, lunging at him the while.* DENIS *finds himself against the door. It gives under his weight. Just as the leading* BURGUNDIAN SOLDIER *is about to deliver him a fatal blow,* DENIS *kicks the door further open, slips behind it, and slams it in his foe's face.*

The BURGUNDIAN SOLDIERS *curse, then batter on the door wildly. They find it will not budge. Eventually they give up, return to their wounded comrades, who are groaning on the cobblestones, and carry them off.*]

[*Cut to a small enclosed stone porch of the Sire de Maletroit's château. On one side of it is the Maletroit door. Facing this door is a little staircase leading up to another door. It is bare of any furniture or trappings.* DENIS *is leaning against the door he has entered, breathing heavily and listening intently. He hears the* BURGUNDIAN SOLDIERS *batter on the other side of the door. Their voices eventually recede, and there is silence.*

DENIS *wipes the blood from his sword with his kerchief and returns it to its scabbard. Satisfied that it will now be safe to regain the street, he tries to find the latch to the door. To his amazement, there is neither latch nor handle nor bolt. Suddenly, while he is occupied in trying to pry it open in some fashion, the other door, the one at the top of the stairs, creaks ajar very slightly. He turns swiftly and draws his sword again, but there is no person to be seen. All that meets his eye is a faint edge of light outlining the door. Very cautiously, he tiptoes up the stairs, then slowly opens this door.*]

[*Cut to the grand hall in the Sire de Maletroit's château. This is a large pentagonal room — obviously part of a five-sided turret — with walls of polished stone. Various banners, tapestries, and standards adorn them. Across one corner is a large chimney piece carved with the arms of the Maletroits. Oaken love seats face each other beneath it. There is a large window looking down into a*

---

[1] offal: garbage.
[2] *Parbleu! Un anglais!* (pàr·bluh′ uh·näṅ·glä′): By Heaven! An Englishman! (The pronunciation of this expression only approximates the way a Frenchman would say it.)

courtyard. In the wall on the op-
posite side of the room there is an
arras covering a Norman archway
to a chapel. When this tapestry is
pulled aside, it is only necessary to
see a suggestion of an altar, and a
tiny stained glass window. A low,
tiny oak door is beside the mantel-
piece leading to an anteroom. The
door through which DENIS *has en-*
tered is not seen until a moment or
two later. There is an imposing oak
table in the center of the hall and a
high armchair behind it. The table is
littered with parchments, quill pens,
an inkwell, and a receptacle for
holding sand to sprinkle on parch-
ment as a blotter. A small earthen-
ware bowl holds a gay bunch of ca-
mellias.

The camera moves around the room,
then finally rests on the SIRE DE
MALETROIT *himself. He is standing*
by a large wooden bird cage that is
hanging from a bracket on the wall.
In it there is a small falcon. He is
feeding the bird shreds of meat. The
SIRE DE MALETROIT *is a venerable-*
looking old man. His white beard
and mustache are neatly trimmed.
Only an almost comically evil look
in his eyes betrays something
greedy, maybe brutal, in his nature.
Camera on DENIS. *He is standing inside*
the door. Seeing no one more alarm-
ing than an apparently harmless old
man, he sheathes his sword.]

DENIS. Your pardon, Sire, for this intrusion.

MALETROIT. Pray step in. I have been
expecting you all the evening.

DENIS (*much puzzled*). You have
been what, Sire?

MALETROIT. I will explain further,
when I have finished feeding Merlin
his supper. A bird of unique spirit. My
constant companion. One of nature's
better efforts. His body an arrow —
death in his wings. (*He closes one eye
and cocks his head to one side.*) As in
your sword, young man.

DENIS. You saw that skirmish outside
your walls?

[*Close shot of* MALETROIT. *He covers
Merlin's cage with a cloth. He then
moves over to* DENIS. *He rubs his
frail hands together in relish.*]

MALETROIT. I can never resist a good
fight. I heard the clash of steel and
watched from a turret window. You
are a brave man. Your swordsmanship
was better than I would have expected
from a fop of an Englishman.

[DENIS *moves his hand swiftly to his
sword. He half draws it, then
sheathes it again.*]

DENIS. Only your venerable gray
hairs, Sire, prevent my avenging that
insult.

[MALETROIT *cackles malevolently.*]

MALETROIT. Tut, tut! We are hot
tempered, are we not? Pray be seated.
Cool your heels, together with your
head. I had no intention to anger you.
Put yourself entirely at your ease. We
shall arrange our affairs in good time.

DENIS. Sire, I guess you to be the
Master of Maletroit.

MALETROIT (*sarcastically*). How
clever of you!

DENIS. Then there can be nothing to
settle between us. We are strangers.

This is merely a chance encounter. I found myself against your door. It happened to be open. I sought temporary refuge behind it. When I wanted to re-enter the street, it remained fast.

MALETROIT (*with a benign smile*). Ah, yes! My door! An excellent example of French ingenuity, eh? By your own admission you were anxious to avoid my acquaintance. (*Nodding his head wisely*) Well, what of that? We old ones look for such reluctance now and then. But when it touches our honor, we cast about until we find some way of overcoming it. You arrived uninvited — but you are welcome. (*With a sly wink*) Very welcome!

DENIS. You persist in error, Sire. How can any affairs of mine touch your honor? This is my first night in your countryside. I was on my way to the Auberge Normande for a game of cards with some of my King's officers. I had already passed your abode when I was forced to retreat by those Burgundian scum.

MALETROIT (*unbelievingly*). Indeed?

DENIS. I am not accustomed to having my word doubted, Sire. (*He stands proudly.*) I am the elder son of Sir Roland of Beaulieu. Our rich acres stretch from the Port of Southampton to the Forest of Brockenhurst. The land was a grant to my grandsire from Edward the Third, for valor at the Battle of Crécy.[1]

MALETROIT. A happy surprise! It is some satisfaction to know that your pocket is well lined.

[1] **Crécy** (krā'sē'): a village in northern France, scene of an English victory over the French in 1346, during the Hundred Years' War.

DENIS (*thoroughly aroused*). Sire, you persist in making a fool of me. I waste my time conversing with a lunatic. There is no power under God that will make me stay here any longer. If I cannot make my way out in a peaceful fashion, I will hack a hole in your door with my sword.

[DENIS *draws his sword and walks toward the entrance by which he came.*]

MALETROIT (*in a sudden harsh voice*). Sit down — Nephew.

DENIS (*wheeling around — amazed*). Nephew?! . . .

[*The old man shakes with silent laughter as* DENIS *continues to stare at him.*]

MALETROIT. You rogue! Do you fancy that when I made my little contrivance for the door I stopped short with that?

[*The old man claps his hands. Camera moves swiftly to the door to the vestibule. Four armored* PIKEMEN (*men carrying large spears with diamond-shaped points*) *appear and stand awaiting orders from* MALETROIT.]

MALETROIT (*suavely*). Now, my dear Nephew, if you wish to remain a free young buck, agreeably conversing with an old — lunatic (*Chuckling at this sally*), sit as I command, in peace, and God be with you.

DENIS (*slowly*). Do you mean — I'm a prisoner?

MALETROIT (*with a wave of his delicate hand*). I leave that conclusion to your natural wits — not that they are plentiful in English heads.

[DENIS *controls his boiling indignation and sits.* MALETROIT *shakes with laughter again.*]

DENIS. What do you want of me?

MALETROIT (*in utter scorn*). As if you did not know! . . . (*He turns to the* PIKEMEN *at the door.*) Wait by the outer door. This man is not to leave without my permission.

[*The* PIKEMEN *depart.* MALETROIT *crosses to the arras covering the arch to the chapel and pulls the tapestry aside.*]

MALETROIT (*calling inside*). Father, I wish to speak with you.

[*After a moment, a tall, robed* PRIEST *comes forth.*]

PRIEST. Yes, messire.

MALETROIT (*with a twisted smile — pointing to* DENIS). Behold! The young gallant has arrived! Indeed, so anxious was he to steal the prize from under my roof that he literally fought his way in.

· PRIEST (*looking* DENIS *over*). I am relieved, Sire. I had expected someone much less presentable.

[*They cease staring at* DENIS.]

MALETROIT. And how is my niece? In a better frame of spirit?

PRIEST. More resigned, messire.

MALETROIT (*sneering*). The Lord help her, she is hard to please! What more would she have than a likely stripling of her own choosing?

PRIEST. A young damsel is prone to blushes, messire. And the situation *is* unusual.

MALETROIT. Heaven knows it was none of *my* making. *She* began this dance, and she shall finish it. . . .

Bring her hither. (*Again with a sneer*) And bid her dry those foolish tears. . . .

[*The* PRIEST *bows and goes behind the arras.* MALETROIT *crosses to* DENIS.]

MALETROIT. Come, come, monsieur, Paris should not look so sourly when he meets his Helen.[1]

[*Camera on the arras. The* PRIEST *returns, leading by the hand a singularly beautiful young girl of seventeen,* BLANCHE DE MALETROIT. *She is considerably distressed. Her face is deathly pale. Her eyes betray that she has been crying for hours. She appears with extreme reluctance. Her eyes are cast downward; she stands staring at the floor. She is attired as a bride in the costume of the period.*
Close shot of DENIS. *He rises slowly, deeply struck by her beauty and tragic appearance.*
Close shot of MALETROIT.]

MALETROIT (*softly — insinuatingly*). Blanche — I have brought a friend to see you. Come forward, my little chick, and give him your pretty hand. It is good to be modest, but necessary to be polite. (*Sharply*) Come, my niece! . . .

[*Close shot of* BLANCHE. *Very slowly she leaves the* PRIEST *and moves to* DENIS. *Camera rolls back as she moves. She still cannot bring herself to raise her eyes. She stares at his feet, trembling.* DENIS *is staring breathlessly at her.*

[1] **Paris . . . Helen:** According to Greek legend, the goddess of love promised Paris that if he would judge her the most beautiful of the goddesses, she would give him the most beautiful woman in the world, Helen.

Camera on BLANCHE. *She has now raised her head and is staring at* DENIS. *Her eyes meet his. Shame gives place to horror and terror in her looks. With a piercing scream, she covers her face with her hands and sinks to the floor.*

Change angle. MALETROIT *comes quickly to her side, kneels, and raises her to her feet. She gazes at him piteously.*]

BLANCHE. My Uncle, this is not the man! . . .

[MALETROIT'S *lips curl in an unbelieving smile.*]

BLANCHE (*frantically*). I tell you, Uncle, this is not the man.

MALETROIT (*chirping agreeably*). Of course not! I had expected you to say that. Just as you pretended you did not know his name.

BLANCHE. You must believe me. I have never seen this person until this moment — never so much as set my eyes upon him. And I never wish to see him again. (*She turns to* DENIS.) Monsieur, if you are a gentleman, you will bear me out. Have I ever seen you? Have you ever seen me — before this dreadful hour?

DENIS. You are correct! I have never seen you before — such is my bad fortune. . . . Sire de Maletroit, this is the first time that I have met your engaging niece. I will swear it — (*Pointing to the arras*) on that altar — if you so desire.

BLANCHE (*with a profound sigh of relief*). Thank you, monsieur. You have earned my eternal gratitude.

[*Close shot of* MALETROIT *and the* PRIEST. *They exchange a look.*]

MALETROIT. Distressing, is it not, Father?

PRIEST. Alas, yes, messire! (*With a beatific smile*) But the barrier is not insurmountable.

MALETROIT. My point of view, exactly. I had little acquaintance with my poor late wife before I wedded her. Impromptu marriages are sometimes the best in the long run.

[DENIS *comes into the picture belligerently.*]

DENIS. Sire, you are proposing to marry me to your niece? Would you ignore my voice in such a matter?

MALETROIT. Not entirely. I will give you a few moments of leisure to make up for lost time — before we proceed with the ceremony.

[MALETROIT *proceeds toward the little door by the mantelpiece, the* PRIEST *toward the chapel.* BLANCHE *rushes frantically after her uncle, flings herself on the ground, and clutches him by the knees.*]

BLANCHE. Sire — Uncle — have pity on me! I declare before God I will stab myself rather than be forced on that young man. My heart rebels against it. God forbids such marriages. You dishonor your gray hairs. You ——

MALETROIT (*breaking in harshly*). Witness this talk about dishonor! It is you yourself, Blanche, who have besmirched the name of Maletroit. You have forfeited your right to question my designs.

BLANCHE. But I have done nothing — nothing! . . .

MALETROIT. Had your father been alive, I doubt if he would have agreed with you. His was the hand of iron. He would have turned you from his doors.

You may bless your stars you now have only to deal with a hand of velvet, mademoiselle.

[MALETROIT *caresses her hair with his thin hand.* BLANCHE *flinches.*]

BLANCHE. Any woman in the world would prefer death to such a marriage.

[MALETROIT *takes* BLANCHE *sternly by the shoulders and lifts her to her feet again.*]

MALETROIT. I have finished arguing with you, Blanche. After your scandalous behavior, it is my duty to get you married without delay. Out of pure kindness of heart, I have tried to find your own gallant for you. I still believe I have succeeded. If I have failed, I care not one jackstraw. So I recommend you make yourself agreeable to this young man. If you do not, your next groom may not be so — presentable. When either one of you decides to admit your duplicity, knock on this door. I shall be waiting in my anteroom.

[MALETROIT *goes, shutting the door behind him. Change angle. The* PRIEST *is standing by the arras.* BLANCHE *goes to him in supplication.*]

BLANCHE. Can you not help me, Father?

PRIEST. My child, your duty is clear. You must obey your uncle.

[*At this moment, in the distance, some* CHORISTERS *can be heard chanting a plainsong in Latin.*]

PRIEST. Listen! The choristers are practicing your nuptial hymn. . . .

[*The* PRIEST *goes. There is an embarrassed silence.* BLANCHE *hangs her head again. After a moment,* DENIS *crosses to her slowly.*]

DENIS. Mademoiselle, it grieves me to see you so distressed.

BLANCHE (*flashing him a look of disdain*). I can scarcely believe that — seeing your presence has added to my woes. Why are you here? What is the meaning of all this?

DENIS. God knows! I find myself a prisoner in a house of mad people. As to everything else, I am completely in the dark.

BLANCHE. Then how did you come here?

DENIS. By accident. I was driven within during a street brawl that was none of my seeking. (*He goes a little closer to her.*) Now it is my turn to ask questions. Why are *you* in this predicament? I cannot believe that anyone so innocent — so lovely — has brought dishonor to her family.

BLANCHE (*with a grateful look*). That is true. My uncle wrongs me. At the worst I have been a little — unmaidenly.

DENIS. Tell me. You can trust me.

BLANCHE (*searching his eyes*). I believe I can. I have been without father and mother, monsieur — oh, for as long as I can recollect. Indeed, I have been lonely and unhappy for most of my life — until three months ago! . . . Tell me, monsieur, is it wrong to smile? If so, then I am much to blame.

DENIS. How can I tell whether it is wrong? Alas, I have never seen your smile.

[BLANCHE *tries to favor* DENIS *with one, but it is only a pathetic flicker.*]

BLANCHE. It was in church. A young captain — an Englishman like yourself

— began to stand near me every Sunday. I could see that I pleased him. He smiled at me. I smiled back. I was so touched that anyone should like me.

DENIS (*with an understanding grin*). And then one day he secretly passed you a note.

BLANCHE (*in innocent surprise*). Yes. You know him? He has told you?

DENIS. No. But I have known young men like him. It has been done before. And it will be done again, as long as there are beautiful damsels — like you — to inspire such an action.

BLANCHE (*gravely*). You are very wise in the ways of the world, monsieur! . . .

DENIS. It does not take wisdom to know how to court a chaperoned maiden. That springs from instinct! . . . May I ask what was in the note?

BLANCHE. He asked me to leave the wall door open, so that we might speak together upon the stairs.

DENIS. And did you?

BLANCHE. No. I knew my uncle trusted me. . . . This officer has since besieged me with notes with the same request. I have always ignored them.

DENIS. Then you have never so much as even spoken to this man?

BLANCHE. Alas, no!

[DENIS *looks at the door behind which* MALETROIT *left and takes a pace or two about the floor.*]

DENIS. Your uncle is a disgrace to mankind. (DENIS *comes to* BLANCHE'S *side again.*) How did he find out?

BLANCHE. That I do not know. He is very shrewd. This morning when we came from Mass, he took my hand in his, forced it open, and read my little billet.[1] He gave it back to me with great politeness.

DENIS. Did it contain another request to leave the door open — this evening?

BLANCHE. Yes. I fear that is what has been the downfall of us. . . . My uncle kept me strictly in my room all day. Then he ordered me to dress myself in this, as you see me — my mother's bridal gown!

DENIS. How does it happen that he does not know your young man's name?

BLANCHE (*after a slight hesitation*). He never told it to me. The notes were signed — (*Shyly*) "One who worships from afar." Even if he *had* disclosed his name, I would not have told my uncle, for how could I know whether the gentleman would be willing to take me for a wife. He might have been trifling with me.

DENIS. I understand! Everything now is clear! . . . Mademoiselle, you have honored me with your confidence. It remains for me to prove it that I am not unworthy of the honor. We will call your uncle.

[DENIS *moves over to the little door. He raps on it sharply.*]

DENIS (*calling*). Sire de Maletroit, my interview with your niece is at an end.

[MALETROIT *reenters.*]

DENIS (*assuming his most confident manner*). Sire — I believe it is customary for a man to have some say in the ordering of his marriage. Therefore, let me tell you, I will be no party to forcing my hand on this lady. Had she offered herself freely to me, I should

---

[1] **billet** (bil'it) (archaic): brief note.

have been proud to accept. (*He turns to* BLANCHE *and looks at her with growing admiration.*) For, unlike yourself, I judge her to be as good as she is beautiful. However, things being as they are, I am reluctantly forced to refuse her hand.

[*Close-up of* BLANCHE *as she reacts to his statement. Her eyes shine with gratitude.*
Close shot of MALETROIT. *His smile grows.*]

MALETROIT. I am afraid, Monsieur de Beaulieu, you do not understand the choice I am offering you. . . . Follow me to this window. . . .

[*Change angle.* MALETROIT *crosses to the window followed by* DENIS. MALETROIT *flings it wide open and points.*]

Observe, monsieur, there is an iron ring in the upper masonry; and reeved through [1] it, a very stout rope.

[*Close-up of a hangman's noose dangling from a buttress above the window.*]

MALETROIT'S VOICE. Now, mark my words! If you persist in refusing to marry my beautiful niece, I shall have you hanged by this rope at sunrise.

[*Close shot of* BLANCHE. *She gasps in horror as she puts her hands to her cheeks.*]

DENIS (*aghast*). You would not dare! . . .

MALETROIT. You know little of what a Maletroit does, or does not, dare — particularly where an Englishman is concerned. Not that your death is my *primary* desire. Indeed, the picture of your spurs (*Looking down at* DENIS's *legs*) dangling in the breeze below my windows would be middling distasteful to me and would mar the view of my beautiful garden.

DENIS. But this is sheer murder! Even a lowly peasant is given a trial.

MALETROIT. Not murder — expiation! The erasing of a stain! The honor of my house has been compromised. I believe you to be the guilty person. Furthermore, even if you were one of my own countrymen — if you sprang from Charlemagne [2] himself — you cannot refuse the hand of a Maletroit with impunity.[3]

DENIS. Neither can you hang a Beaulieu! . . . (*He draws his sword.*) If you or any of your minions [4] attempt to lay a hand on me, I will drench this floor with blood.

MALETROIT (*laughing scornfully*). Put up your sword! Hot-headed nonsense! Would you fight the world? . . . You have seen my pikemen. They still stand behind that door. Others await my summons in the anteroom, there. (*He points to the little door.*) Still another band stands at arms in the chapel. They are all eager to make mincemeat of you. . . .

[*Close shot of* BLANCHE]

BLANCHE. Uncle, will you permit me to speak with this gentleman? I would not ——

MALETROIT (*in a voice of doom*). Silence, girl! I am doing the speaking!

---

[1] **reeved through**: passed through.

[2] **Charlemagne** (shär′lə·mān) (742?–814): ruler of an empire which later became France; a great French hero.

[3] **impunity** (im·pyōo′nə·tē): freedom from punishment.

[4] **minions** (min′yənz): slavish followers.

And these are my final words on this subject. (*He moves over to his desk, where he picks up the hourglass.*) Monsieur de Beaulieu — look well on this hourglass! When these sands have run three times from top to bottom, it will be daybreak. Three hours of life are always three hours. Even the course of history has been changed in shorter time. Three little hours! I give them to you — for reflection. A wife may be a millstone round the neck — but not so deadly a one as yonder noose. (*He hobbles to the little door and turns.*) Besides, my niece appears to have something still to say to you. Do not disfigure your last moments by a want of courtesy.

[MALETROIT *goes. Camera on* BLANCHE. *She looks after her uncle, then goes over to* DENIS *in desperation.*]

BLANCHE. Monsieur, you shall not die! You shall marry me after all.

DENIS. Do you think I stand in that much fear of death?

BLANCHE. Oh, no, no! I do not believe you to be a coward! It is for my own peace of spirit that I offer myself. I could not have it on my conscience that you were slain for such a scruple.

DENIS. Mademoiselle, you do not perceive the core of the problem. What you offer — in pity, I must refuse — in pride. In this impulsive moment of generosity, you forget what you owe to another.

BLANCHE. But I must do something to help you.

DENIS. Believe me, mademoiselle, there is no young man in England, or France, who would not be glad to die in doing you a service.

BLANCHE. Must someone die — because I smiled?

[BLANCHE *suddenly bursts into tears, walks away from him, flings herself into her uncle's chair behind the desk, and buries her head in her arms. After a moment, she speaks through her tears.*]

BLANCHE. If my uncle persists in carrying out his threat, I will hide myself from the world.

[*Camera on* DENIS. *He stands looking down on her for a moment. Her sobs distress him considerably. As they continue, he turns quietly away and walks over to the window, where he stares at the noose.*

Close-up of BLANCHE. *After a moment, camera moves from her to the hourglass on the desk beside her. The sands are trickling slowly from the upper part to the lower. Fade out.*]

[*Fade in. Camera is still on the hourglass. The sands have run out. The hand of* DENIS *comes into camera and turns the hourglass over. The sands begin to trickle again.* DENIS *is standing, staring down at* BLANCHE, *who is still sobbing. He puts his hand gently on her shoulder.*]

DENIS. Mademoiselle — an hour has passed, and you still weep. Will you not reflect on the little time I have before me? Spare me the sight of your distress.

[BLANCHE *manages to stop sobbing and looks up at him.*]

BLANCHE. I am very selfish, monsieur. I will try to be brave — for your sake. (*She shivers.*) I am cold! . . . Shall we not sit by the fire? (*They go* to the fireplace, to the love seats.) Seat yourself opposite me, monsieur. (DENIS does so.) Put it in my power to do something more for you than weep. If — if you are determined to die — have you no family to whom I could carry your farewells?

DENIS (shaking his head). My father fell in battle. My mother has married again and has a young family to tend. My only brother, Neville de Beaulieu, will inherit my estates. (Bitterly) If I am not in error, that will amply compensate him for my passing. (She hangs her head again.) Do not look so sad, mademoiselle! What is life but a little vapor that passeth away?

BLANCHE. Have you no friends?

DENIS. But few. And once I am beneath the sod I shall have none.

BLANCHE. You are wrong, monsieur. You forget Blanche de Maletroit. She will think of you until she, too, is in her grave.

DENIS. You have a sweet nature, mademoiselle, and estimate my little service beyond its worth.

BLANCHE. It is not that! I say so because you are the noblest man I have ever met.

DENIS (mockingly). Have you met so many?

BLANCHE (with her first smile). You are pleased to tease me, monsieur.

DENIS. I had hoped to make you smile — and I succeeded.

BLANCHE (blushing shyly and changing the subject). Let us talk of things other than my unfortunate smile, which led us into our sad predicament. . . . What brought you to France — and this ill-fated town?

DENIS (slapping his thigh). By the

Lord Harry — you remind me of my mission. I had forgotten it in the presence of your distress — and your beauty. (He stands and unbuckles a pouch from his belt.) I am a courier from the Master of the English Fleet. (Pointing to pouch) In this is a sealed missive to the Governor of Calais.[1] My country needs more ships to expand her trade to the Indies. . . . Is it in your power to have it delivered?

BLANCHE (holding out her hand). I promise it shall reach its destination.

[He gives it to her.]

DENIS. Thank you, mademoiselle.

[He continues to gaze at her in frank admiration. She returns his look for a moment, then lowers her eyes.]

BLANCHE (talking to cover her embarrassment). Monsieur — tell me something of your island. Though I have been taught to speak your tongue, I have never been beyond the walled gates of this town.

DENIS (in quiet rapture). England! Where shall I begin? . . . In the springtime? . . . I wish you could see our countryside in the spring! The meadows yellow with daffodils. The sky-blue hyacinths carpeting the woods. The banks of primroses. . . . And our lazy streams — the Test River that flows through my land, drenched in the morning mist. The still herons roosting like purple sentinels in the willows. (His voice gradually fades.) . . . Near the castle of Beaulieu is a vast forest of stalwart oaks rich in deer — that same forest where King William

[1] **Calais** (kal'ā): a port city of northern France.

the Red was slain by an arrow as he . . . (*Picture fades out with his voice.*)

[*Fade in.* DENIS *is still talking, but he is now seated beside* BLANCHE, *holding her hand. She is looking up at him with wide adoring eyes and listening with rapt attention.*]

DENIS. . . . and for that small feat, the King awarded me an additional twenty thousand acres. I assure you it was undeserved. It was the luck of battle.

BLANCHE. I cannot believe that, monsieur. Do not forget, I have seen a sample of your courage.

[*This remark brings them back to a state of reality. There is a momentary silence.* DENIS *looks down and they both realize that he is holding her hand. She tries to withdraw it, but he does not let go.*]

DENIS. Mademoiselle, forgive my chattering tongue and my idle boasts. I have babbled shamelessly of my country, my thoughts, and my deeds in battle. How I must have wearied you! Why did you not stop me?

BLANCHE. Because I was enchanted by your every word! Never has a night passed so quickly. (*She points to the hourglass.*) Why, look — the hourglass!

[*Cut to close-up of the hourglass. The sands have run out.*]

BLANCHE. We forgot to turn it. We do not even know what o'clock it is.

DENIS. It is late enough! . . . Too late.

[BLANCHE *rises as if she would go to the hourglass to turn it upside down again.* DENIS *jumps quickly to his feet*

and detains her by putting his arm around her shoulder.]

DENIS. No, Blanche! Let it lie. (*Something arresting in his voice and manner causes* BLANCHE *to turn back to* DENIS.) There are moments when time stands still; you cannot measure their length by sand.

[*Close-up of* BLANCHE. *Her face becomes gradually transfigured by love.*]

BLANCHE. Then, while the clock waits, let me tell you something I became aware of, whilst you held my hand. It is only right that you should go to your death, knowing . . . When I asked you to marry me, it was not only because I respected and admired you. It was because — I loved you. From the first moment you took my part against my uncle, I loved you.

DENIS (*deeply moved*). Blanche! Blanche! You know I would never force myself on you without your free consent. But since you ——

BLANCHE (*breaking in*). No, hear me out! Although I have revealed the secret of my heart, I cannot forget your first sentiments toward me. Nor can I forgive them. You chose the noose rather than my hand. So, if you have it in mind to go back on your word, know this! I would no more marry you now than I would my uncle's groom. I, too, have pride.

[*After a pause,* DENIS *sighs deeply. His spirits seem to droop. He points to the window.*]

DENIS. Look! The dawn is creeping in! Any moment now your uncle will be here. . . . (*He takes her gently by*

the shoulders and looks into her eyes.)
Blanche — can you not read my eyes?
You must also know by now that I too
love you. Are we to lose each other because we are both tangled in pride?

BLANCHE. But it is impossible. There
is another reason why I cannot wed
you. I — I lied to you.

[DENIS *jealously tightens his grip on her
shoulders.*]

DENIS. Don't tell me that, after all,
you *did* meet that impertinent sender
of notes?

BLANCHE. No, no! But I lied when I
said I did not know his name. I sent
my serving maid to the Auberge Normande to seek it out. It was — Percy of
Warbecke.

[*His jealousy evaporates as suddenly
as it came.*]

DENIS. Little goose, is that all?
BLANCHE. You do not despise me?
DENIS. For being feminine? Of course
not! Besides, it is so easy to blot his
name from our memory.

[*Without waiting for her permission,
he kisses her on the lips. There is a
discreet cough behind them.*
Camera on MALETROIT *and the* PRIEST
standing at the anteroom door. MALE-
TROIT *is smiling and rubbing his
hands.*]

MALETROIT. A touching scene! Are
you kissing farewell or sealing a betrothal?

[DENIS *and* BLANCHE *break apart.*]

DENIS (*with an elaborate bow*). Sire
— we have decided to accede to your
wishes.

[*The* PRIEST *and* MALETROIT *exchange
satisfied glances. The* PRIEST *goes
quickly toward the chapel.*]

DENIS. Furthermore, I owe you an
apology, Sire. I *was* the man — all the
time. (*Camera moves in to a very close
shot as* DENIS *bends to kiss* BLANCHE
again. He whispers into her ear.) Now
we are equal in lies.

[*The sound of the bridal chant floats
into the room. Fade out.*]

THE PLOT OF THE PLAY

Presenting the Characters and the Setting.
You can learn a great deal about a play
during its opening minutes. In the very
first part of the play, the setting (the time
and place) is made clear, and the main
characters are introduced.

1. Some lengthy stage directions describe what should be shown on the television screen as this play opens. What did
these directions tell you about the setting
of *The Sire de Maletroit's Door?* What
different pictures would you see on the
television screen as the play begins?

2. What did you learn about Denis
when you first saw him, before he spoke?
What did his dialogue with the innkeeper
tell you about him? Did you like Denis?
Why?

3. What impression did you get of the
Sire de Maletroit when he first appeared
in the play? How did his second speech
add a sinister note to the scene?

4. The mysteries deepened when
Blanche was led in. What was strange and
dramatic about her first appearance? How
did she contrast with her uncle? Did you
like her? Why?

Developing the Conflict. When all the
characters are presented, we learn more
about their conflict or problem. Usually,

we find that a conflict exists because someone wants something which he cannot get without a great struggle.

5. What were the conflicts in this play? What was the main character's problem?

6. Why did the Sire de Maletroit devise such a drastic punishment for his niece? How were his actions made more understandable by what we know about the times?

7. Blanche's offer to marry Denis would have solved his problem. Why did Denis refuse her? How did the stubborn pride of these characters cause further complications in the plot?

8. What effect did the playwright create by having the camera focus on the hourglass?

Reaching the Climax. The climax of a play comes when the action reaches a turning point, when suspense is at its peak, when the hero might either get what he wants or be defeated.

9. At what moment in this play do you think the climax occurred? Explain your answer.

Resolving the Conflict. As soon as the climax is reached, the action is directed toward resolving the conflict. When the conflict is resolved by having the hero lose out, we call the play a tragedy.

10. How was the main conflict resolved? What caused events to turn out this way?

11. Who do you think was the "hero" of this play? Did the hero triumph at the end? Explain. Do you think there was a villain? If so, who was he? Was anyone defeated in the end?

STAGE DIRECTIONS

The theater has a whole vocabulary of its own, and in the stage directions for a play, you will often find many technical terms. For example, the first words in the stage directions of *The Sire de Maletroit's Door* are "fade in." In television, these words direct the cameraman to bring a picture gradually into view on the screen. Below are some other television terms from this play. Notice that they are all combinations of ordinary words. Do you know what each word would mean to the director of a television play?

long shot
cut to
close shot
fade out
superimpose over
dissolve to

SENTENCES: PITCH, STRESS, PAUSES

The way an actor speaks his lines can determine the way the audience interprets the play. When an actor rehearses his part, he decides where he will pitch his voice high or low, he decides which words he will stress, and he decides where he will use pauses.

Choose four dramatic speeches from *The Sire de Maletroit's Door*. How do you think they should be read? Where would you raise or lower the pitch of your voice? Which words would you stress? Where would you make dramatic pauses?

COMPOSITION: PRESENTING AN OPINION

After you have read a selection of literature, you are often asked, "What did you think of it?" That is, you are asked to give an opinion. In one paragraph, give your opinion of *The Sire de Maletroit's Door*, explaining fully one or more reasons why you liked or disliked the play. Be sure to refer to passages of the play when you are explaining your opinion.

The Happy Journey to Trenton and Camden

THORNTON WILDER

Characters

THE STAGE MANAGER

MA KIRBY

ARTHUR KIRBY

CAROLINE KIRBY

ELMER KIRBY (PA)

BEULAH

No scenery is required for this play.
Perhaps a few dusty flats [1] *may be seen*
leaning against the brick wall at the
back of the stage.

The five members of the Kirby fam-
ily and THE STAGE MANAGER *compose*
the cast. THE STAGE MANAGER *not only*
moves forward and withdraws the few
properties that are required, but he
reads from a typescript the lines of all
the minor characters. He reads them
clearly, but with little attempt at char-
acterization, scarcely troubling himself
to alter his voice, even when he re-
sponds in the person of a child or a
woman.

[*As the curtain rises,* THE STAGE MAN-
AGER *is leaning lazily against the pro-*
scenium pillar [2] *at the audience's left.*
ARTHUR *is playing marbles in the cen-*
ter of the stage. CAROLINE *is at the re-*
mote back, right, talking to some girls
who are invisible to us. MA KIRBY *is*
anxiously putting on her hat before
an imaginary mirror.]

MA. Where's your pa? Why isn't he
here? I declare we'll never get started.

ARTHUR. Ma, where's my hat? I guess
I don't go if I can't find my hat.

MA. Go out into the hall and see if
it isn't there. Where's Caroline gone to
now, the plagued child?

ARTHUR. She's out waitin' in the
street talkin' to the Jones girls. — I just
looked in the hall a thousand times,
Ma, and it isn't there. (*He spits for*
good luck before a difficult shot and

mutters.) Come on, baby.

MA. Go and look again, I say. Look
carefully.

[ARTHUR *rises, runs to the right, turns*
around swiftly, returns to his game,
flinging himself on the floor with a
terrible impact, and starts shooting
an aggie.]

ARTHUR. No. Ma, it's not there.

MA (*serenely*). Well, you don't leave
Newark without that hat, make up your
mind to that. I don't go no journeys
with a hoodlum.

ARTHUR. Aw, Ma!

[MA *comes down to the footlights and*
talks toward the audience as through
a window.]

MA. Oh, Mrs. Schwartz!

THE STAGE MANAGER (*consulting his*
script). Here I am, Mrs. Kirby. Are you
going yet?

MA. I guess we're going in just a minute. How's the baby?

THE STAGE MANAGER. She's all right
now. We slapped her on the back and
she spat it up.

MA. Isn't that fine! — Well now, if
you'll be good enough to give the cat
a saucer of milk in the morning and the
evening, Mrs. Schwartz, I'll be ever so
grateful to you. — Oh, good afternoon,
Mrs. Hobmeyer!

THE STAGE MANAGER. Good afternoon, Mrs. Kirby. I hear you're going
away.

MA (*modestly*). Oh, just for three
days, Mrs. Hobmeyer, to see my married daughter, Beulah, in Camden. Elmer's got his vacation week from the
laundry early this year, and he's just
the best driver in the world.

[CAROLINE *comes "into the house" and stands by her mother.*]

THE STAGE MANAGER. Is the whole family going?

MA. Yes, all four of us that's here. The change ought to be good for the children. My married daughter was downright sick a while ago —— .

THE STAGE MANAGER. Tchk — tchk — tchk! Yes. I remember you tellin' us.

MA. And I just want to go down and see the child. I ain't seen her since then. I just won't rest easy in my mind without I see her. (*To* CAROLINE) Can't you say good afternoon to Mrs. Hobmeyer?

CAROLINE (*blushes and lowers her eyes and says woodenly*). Good afternoon, Mrs. Hobmeyer.

THE STAGE MANAGER. Good afternoon, dear. — Well, I'll wait and beat these rugs until after you're gone, because I don't want to choke you. I hope you have a good time and find everything all right.

MA. Thank you, Mrs. Hobmeyer, I hope I will. — Well, I guess that milk for the cat is all, Mrs. Schwartz, if you're sure you don't mind. If anything should come up, the key to the back door is hanging by the icebox.

ARTHUR and CAROLINE. Ma! Not so loud. Everybody can hear yuh.

MA. Stop pullin' my dress, children. (*In a loud whisper*) The key to the back door I'll leave hangin' by the icebox, and I'll leave the screen door unhooked.

THE STAGE MANAGER. Now have a good trip, dear, and give my love to Loolie.

MA. I will, and thank you a thousand times. (*She returns "into the room."*)

What can be keeping your pa?

ARTHUR. I can't find my hat, Ma.

[*Enter* ELMER *holding a hat.*]

ELMER. Here's Arthur's hat. He musta left it in the car Sunday.

MA. That's a mercy. Now we can start. — Caroline Kirby, what you done to your cheeks?

CAROLINE (*defiant, abashed*). Nothin'.

MA. If you've put anything on 'em, I'll slap you.

CAROLINE. No, Ma, of course I haven't. (*Hanging her head*) I just rubbed'm to make'm red. All the girls do that at high school when they're goin' places.

MA. Such silliness I never saw. Elmer, what kep' you?

ELMER (*always even-voiced and always looking out a little anxiously through his spectacles*). I just went to the garage and had Charlie give a last look at it, Kate.

MA. I'm glad you did. I wouldn't like to have no breakdown miles from anywhere. Now we can start. Arthur, put those marbles away. Anybody'd think you didn't want to go on a journey to look at yuh.

[*They go out through the "hall," take short steps that denote going downstairs, and find themselves in the street.*]

ELMER. Here, you boys, you keep away from that car.

MA. Those Sullivan boys put their heads into everything.

[THE STAGE MANAGER *has moved forward four chairs and a low platform.*

This is the automobile. It is in the center of the stage and faces the audience. The platform slightly raises the two chairs in the rear. PA's *hands hold an imaginary steering wheel, and he continually shifts gears.* CAROLINE *sits beside him.* ARTHUR *is behind him and* MA *behind* CAROLINE.]

CAROLINE (*self-consciously*). Good-bye, Mildred. Good-bye, Helen.

THE STAGE MANAGER. Good-bye, Caroline. Good-bye, Mrs. Kirby. I hope y' have a good time.

MA. Good-bye girls.

THE STAGE MANAGER. Good-bye, Kate. The car looks fine.

MA (*looking upward toward a window*). Oh, good-bye, Emma! (*Modestly*) We think it's the best little Chevrolet in the world. — Oh, good-bye, Mrs. Adler!

THE STAGE MANAGER. What, are you going away, Mrs. Kirby?

MA. Just for three days, Mrs. Adler, to see my married daughter in Camden.

THE STAGE MANAGER. Have a good time.

[*Now* MA, CAROLINE, *and* THE STAGE MANAGER *break out into a tremendous chorus of good-byes. The whole street is saying good-bye.* ARTHUR *takes out his peashooter and lets fly happily into the air. There is a lurch or two, and they are off.*]

ARTHUR (*in sudden fright*). Pa! Pa! Don't go by the school. Mr. Biedenbach might see us!

MA. I don't care if he does see us. I guess I can take my children out of school for one day without having to hide down back streets about it. (EL-

MER *nods to a passer-by.* MA *asks without sharpness:*) Who was that you spoke to, Elmer?

ELMER. That was the fellow who arranges our banquets down to the lodge, Kate.

MA. Is he the one who had to buy four hundred steaks? (PA *nods.*) I declare, I'm glad I'm not him.

ELMER. The air's getting better already. Take deep breaths, children.

[*They inhale noisily.*]

ARTHUR. Gee, it's almost open fields already. "Weber and Heilbronner Suits for Well-dressed Men." Ma, can I have one of them someday?

MA. If you graduate with good marks, perhaps your father'll let you have one for graduation.

CAROLINE (*whining*). Oh, Pa! Do we have to wait while that whole funeral goes by?

[PA *takes off his hat.* MA *cranes forward with absorbed curiosity.*]

MA. Take off your hat, Arthur. Look at your father.— Why, Elmer, I do believe that's a lodge brother of yours. See the banner? I suppose this is the Elizabeth branch. (ELMER *nods.* MA *sighs.*) Tchk — tchk — tchk. (*They all lean forward and watch the funeral in silence, growing momentarily more solemnized. After a pause,* MA *continues almost dreamily.*) Well, we haven't forgotten the one that we went on, have we? We haven't forgotten our good Harold. He gave his life for his country, we mustn't forget that. (*She passes her finger from the corner of her eye across her cheek. There is another pause.*) Well, we'll all hold up the traffic for a few minutes someday.

ARTHUR and CAROLINE (*very uncomfortably*). Ma!

MA (*without self-pity*). Well I'm "ready," children. I hope everybody in this car is "ready." (*She puts her hand on* PA's *shoulder.*) And I pray to go first, Elmer. Yes. (PA *touches her hand.*)

ARTHUR and CAROLINE. Ma, everybody's looking at you. Everybody's laughing at you.

MA. Oh, hold your tongues! I don't care what a lot of silly people in Elizabeth, New Jersey, think of me.— Now we can go on. That's the last.

[*There is another lurch, and the car goes on.*]

CAROLINE. "Fit-rite Suspenders. The Working Man's Choice." Pa, why do they spell *rite* that way?

ELMER. So that it'll make you stop and ask about it, missy.

CAROLINE. Papa, you're teasing me.— Ma, why do they say "Three Hundred Rooms Three Hundred Baths?"

ARTHUR. "Miller's Spaghetti: The Family's Favorite Dish." Ma, why don't you ever have spaghetti?

MA. Go along, you'd never eat it.

ARTHUR. Ma, I like it now.

CAROLINE (*with a gesture*). Yum-yum. It looks wonderful up there. Ma, make some when we get home?

MA (*dryly*). "The management is always happy to receive suggestions. We aim to please."

[*The whole family finds this exquisitely funny.* ARTHUR *and* CAROLINE *scream with laughter. Even* ELMER *smiles.* MA *remains modest.*]

ELMER. Well, I guess no one's complaining, Kate. Everybody knows you're a good cook.

MA. I don't know whether I'm a good cook or not, but I know I've had practice. At least I've cooked three meals a day for twenty-five years.

ARTHUR. Aw, Ma, you went out to eat once in a while.

MA. Yes. That made it a leap year.

[*This joke is no less successful than its predecessor. When the laughter dies down,* CAROLINE *turns around in an ecstasy of well-being and kneels on the cushions.*]

CAROLINE. Ma, I love going out in the country like this. Let's do it often, Ma.

MA. Goodness, smell that air, will you! It's got the whole ocean in it.— Elmer, drive careful over that bridge. This must be New Brunswick we're coming to.

ARTHUR (*jealous of his mother's successes*). Ma, when is the next comfort station?

MA (*unruffled*). You don't want one. You just said that to be awful.

CAROLINE (*shrilly*). Yes, he did, Ma. He's terrible. He says that kind of thing right out in school, and I want to sink through the floor, Ma. He's terrible.

MA. Oh, don't get so excited about nothing, Miss Proper! I guess we're all yewman beings in this car, at least as far as I know. And Arthur, you try and be a gentleman.— Elmer, don't run over that collie dog. (*She follows the dog with her eyes.*) Looked kinda peaked to me. Needs a good honest bowl of leavings. Pretty dog, too. (*Her eyes fall on a billboard.*) That's a pretty advertisement for Chesterfield cigarettes, isn't it? Looks like Beulah, a little.

ARTHUR. Ma?

MA. Yes.

ARTHUR (*"route" rhyming with "out"*). Can't I take a paper route with the *Newark Daily Post?*

MA. No, you cannot. No, sir. I hear they make the paper boys get up at four-thirty in the morning. No son of mine is going to get up at four-thirty every morning, not if it's to make a million dollars. Your *Saturday Evening Post* route on Thursday mornings is enough.

ARTHUR. Aw, Ma.

MA. No, sir. No son of mine is going to get up at four-thirty and miss the sleep God meant him to have.

ARTHUR (*sullenly*). Hhm! Ma's always talking about God. I guess she got a letter from him this morning.

[MA *rises, outraged.*]

MA. Elmer, stop that automobile this minute. I don't go another step with anybody that says things like that. Arthur, you can get out of this car. Elmer, you give him another dollar bill. He can go back to Newark by himself. I don't want him.

ARTHUR. What did I say? There wasn't anything terrible about that.

ELMER. I didn't hear what he said, Kate.

MA. God has done a lot of things for me, and I won't have Him made fun of by anybody. Go away. Go away from me.

CAROLINE. Aw Ma — don't spoil the ride.

MA. No.

ELMER. We might as well go on, Kate,

since we've got started. I'll talk to the boy tonight.

MA (*slowly conceding*). All right, if you say so, Elmer. But I won't sit beside him. Caroline, you come and sit by me.

ARTHUR (*frightened*). Aw, Ma, that wasn't so terrible.

MA. I don't want to talk about it. I hope your father washes your mouth out with soap and water. Where'd we all be if I started talking about God like that, I'd like to know! We'd be in the speakeasies and night clubs and places like that, that's where we'd be. — All right, Elmer, you can go on now.

CAROLINE. What did he say, Ma? I didn't hear what he said.

MA. I don't want to talk about it.

[*They drive on in silence for a moment, the shocked silence after a scandal.*]

ELMER. I'm going to stop and give the car a little water, I guess.

MA. All right, Elmer. You know best.

ELMER (*to a garage hand*). Could I have a little water in the radiator — to make sure?

THE STAGE MANAGER. (*In this scene alone he lays aside his script and enters into a role seriously.*) You sure can. (*He punches the tires.*) Air all right? Do you need any oil or gas?

ELMER. No, I think not. I just got fixed up in Newark.

MA. We're on the right road for Camden, are we?

THE STAGE MANAGER. Yes, keep straight ahead. You can't miss it. You'll be in Trenton in a few minutes. (*He carefully pours some water into the hood.*) Camden's a great town, lady, believe me.

MA. My daughter likes it fine — my married daughter.

THE STAGE MANAGER. Ye'? It's a great burg all right. I guess I think so because I was born near there.

MA. Well, well. Your folks still live there?

THE STAGE MANAGER. No, my old man sold the farm, and they built a factory on it. So the folks moved to Philadelphia.

MA. My married daughter Beulah lives there because her husband works in the telephone company. — Stop pokin' me, Caroline! — We're all going down to see her for a few days.

THE STAGE MANAGER. Ye'?

MA. She's been sick, you see, and I just felt I had to go and see her. My husband and my boy are going to stay at the YMCA. I hear they've got a dormitory on the top floor that's real clean and comfortable. Had you ever been there?

THE STAGE MANAGER. No. I'm Knights of Columbus myself.

MA. Oh.

THE STAGE MANAGER. I used to play basketball at the Y, though. It looked all right to me. (*He has been standing with one foot on the rung of* MA'*s chair. They have taken a great fancy to one another. He reluctantly shakes himself out of it and pretends to examine the car again, whistling.*) Well, I guess you're all set now, lady. I hope you have a good trip; you can't miss it.

EVERYBODY. Thanks. Thanks a lot. Good luck to you.

[*They all jolt and lurch.*]

MA (*with a sigh*). The world's full of nice people. That's what I call a nice young man.

CAROLINE (*earnestly*). Ma, you oughtn't to tell 'm all everything about yourself.

MA. Well, Caroline, you do your way, and I'll do mine. — He looked kinda thin to me. I'd like to feed him up for a few days. His mother lives in Philadelphia, and I expect he eats at dreadful places.

CAROLINE. I'm hungry. Pa, there's a hot-dog stand. K'n I have one?

ELMER. We'll all have one, eh, Kate? We had such an early lunch.

MA. Just as you think best, Elmer.

ELMER. Arthur, here's half a dollar. — Run over and see what they have. Not too much mustard, either.

[ARTHUR *descends from the car and goes off-stage, right.* MA *and* CAROLINE *get out and walk a bit.*]

MA. What's that flower over there? — I'll take some of those to Beulah.

CAROLINE. It's just a weed, Ma.

MA. I like it. — My, look at the sky, wouldya! I'm glad I was born in New Jersey. I've always said it was the best state in the Union. Every state has something no other state has got.

[*They stroll about humming. Presently* ARTHUR *returns with his hands full of imaginary hot dogs, which he distributes. He is still very much cast down by the recent scandal. He finally approaches his mother.*]

ARTHUR (*falteringly*). Ma, I'm sorry for what I said. (*He bursts into tears and puts his forehead against her elbow.*)

MA. There. There. We all say wicked things at times. I know you didn't mean it like it sounded. (*He weeps still more violently than before.*) Why, now, now! I forgive you, Arthur, and tonight before you go to bed you . . . (*She whispers.*) You're a good boy at heart, Arthur, and we all know it. (CAROLINE *starts to cry, too.* MA *is suddenly joyously alive and happy.*) Sakes alive, it's too nice a day for us all to be cryin'. Come now, get in. You go up in front with your father, Caroline. Ma wants to sit with her beau. I never saw such children. Your hot dogs are all getting wet. Now chew them fine, everybody. — All right, Elmer, forward march. — Caroline, whatever are you doing?

CAROLINE. I'm spitting out the leather, Ma.

MA. Then say, "Excuse me."

CAROLINE. Excuse me, please.

MA. What's this place? Arthur, did you see the post office?

ARTHUR. It said "Lawrenceville."

MA. Hhm. School kinda nice. I wonder what that big yellow house set back was. — Now it's beginning to be Trenton.

CAROLINE. Papa, it was near here that George Washington crossed the Delaware. It was near Trenton, Mamma. He was first in war and first in peace and first in the hearts of his countrymen.

MA (*surveying the passing world, serene and didactic* [1]). Well, the thing I like about him best was that he never told a lie. (*The children are duly cast down. There is a pause.*) There's a sunset for you. There's nothing like a good sunset.

ARTHUR. There's an Ohio license in

---

[1] **didactic:** inclined to instruct or teach.

front of us. Ma, have you ever been to Ohio?

MA. No.

[*A dreamy silence descends upon them.* CAROLINE *sits closer to* PA. MA *puts her arm around* ARTHUR.]

ARTHUR. Ma, what a lotta people there are in the world, Ma. There must be thousands and thousands in the United States. Ma, how many are there?

MA. I don't know. Ask your father.

ARTHUR. Pa, how many are there?

ELMER. There are a hundred and twenty-six million, Kate.

MA (*giving a pressure about* ARTHUR's *shoulder*). And they all like to drive out in the evening with their children beside'm. (*Another pause.*) Why doesn't somebody sing something? Arthur, you're always singing something; what's the matter with you?

ARTHUR. All right. What'll we sing? (*He sketches.*)

> In the Blue Ridge Mountains
>   of Virginia,
> On the trail of the lonesome
>   pine . . .

No, I don't like that any more. Let's do:

> I been workin' on de railroad
> All de liblong day.
> I been workin' on de railroad
> Just to pass de time away.

[CAROLINE *joins in at once. Finally even* MA *is singing. Even* PA *is singing.* MA *suddenly jumps up with a wild cry.*]

MA. Elmer, that signpost said Camden, I saw it.

ELMER. All right, Kate, if you're sure.

[*There is much shifting of gears, backing, and jolting.*]

MA. Yes, there it is. Camden — five miles. Dear old Beulah. — Now, children, you be good and quiet during dinner. She's just got out of bed after a big sorta operation, and we must all move around kinda quiet. First you drop me and Caroline at the door and just say hello, and then you menfolk go over to the YMCA and come back for dinner in about an hour.

CAROLINE (*shutting her eyes and pressing her fists passionately against her nose*). I see the first star. Everybody make a wish.

> Star light, star bright,
> First star I seen tonight.
> I wish I may, I wish I might
> Have the wish I wish tonight.

(*Then solemnly*) Pins. Mamma, you say "needles." (*She interlocks little fingers with her mother.*)

MA. Needles.

CAROLINE. Shakespeare. Ma, you say "Longfellow."

MA. Longfellow.

CAROLINE. Now it's a secret and I can't tell it to anybody. Ma, you make a wish.

MA (*with almost grim humor*). No, I can make wishes without waiting for no star. And I can tell my wishes right out loud, too. Do you want to hear them?

CAROLINE (*resignedly*). No, Ma, we know'm already. We've heard'm. (*She hangs her head affectedly on her left shoulder and speaks with unmalicious mimicry.*) You want me to be a good girl, and you want Arthur to be honest-in-word-and-deed.

MA (*majestically*). Yes. So mind yourself.

ELMER. Caroline, take out that letter from Beulah in my coat pocket by you and read aloud the places I marked with red pencil.

CAROLINE (*working*). "A few blocks after you pass the two big oil tanks on your left —— "

EVERYBODY (*pointing backward*). There they are!

CAROLINE. "—— you come to a corner where there's an A & P store on the left and a firehouse kitty-corner to it—— (*They all jubilantly identify these landmarks.*) ——turn right, go two blocks, and our house is Weyerhauser Street, Number 471."

MA. It's an even nicer street than they used to live in. And right handy to an A & P.

CAROLINE (*whispering*). Ma, it's better than our street. It's richer than our street. — Ma, isn't Beulah richer than we are?

MA (*looking at her with a firm and glassy eye*). Mind yourself, missy. I don't want to hear anybody talking about rich or not rich when I'm around. If people aren't nice I don't care how rich they are. I live in the best street in the world because my husband and children live there. (*She glares impressively at* CAROLINE *a moment to let this lesson sink in, then looks up, sees* BEULAH *and waves.*) There's Beulah standing on the steps lookin' for us.

[BEULAH *has appeared and is waving.*]

EVERYBODY. Hello, Beulah.— Hello.

[*Presently, they are all getting out of the car.* BEULAH *kisses* PA *long and affectionately.*]

BEULAH. Hello, Papa. Good old Papa. You look tired, Pa. — Hello, Mamma. — Lookit how Arthur and Caroline are growing!

MA. They're bursting all their clothes! — Yes, your pa needs a rest. Thank heaven his vacation has come just now. We'll feed him up and let him sleep late. Pa has a present for you, Loolie. He would go and buy it.

BEULAH. Why, Pa, you're terrible to go and buy anything for me. Isn't he terrible?

MA. Well, it's a secret. You can open it at dinner.

ELMER. Where's Horace, Loolie?

BEULAH. He was kep' over a little at the office. He'll be here any minute. He's crazy to see you all.

MA. All right. You men go over to the Y and come back in about an hour.

[As ELMER *returns to the wheel*, BEU-LAH *stands out in the street beside him.*]

BEULAH. Go straight along, Pa, you can't miss it. It just stares at yuh. (*She puts her arm around his neck and rubs her nose against his temple.*) Crazy old Pa, goin' buyin' things! It's me that ought to be buyin' things for you, Pa.

ELMER. Oh no! There's only one Loo-lie in the world.

BEULAH (*whispering, as her eyes fill with tears*). Are you glad I'm still alive, Pa? (*She kisses him abruptly and goes back to the house steps.* THE STAGE MAN-AGER *removes the automobile with the help of* ELMER *and* ARTHUR, *who go off waving their good-byes.*) Well, come on upstairs, Ma, and take off your things. Caroline, there's a surprise for you in the back yard.

CAROLINE. Rabbits?

BEULAH. No.

CAROLINE. Chickins?

BEULAH. No. Go and see. (CAROLINE *runs off-stage.* BEULAH *and* MA *gradu-ally go upstairs.*) There are two new puppies. You be thinking over whether you can keep one in Newark.

MA. I guess we can. It's a nice house, Beulah. You just got a *lovely* home.

BEULAH. When I got back from the hospital, Horace had moved everything into it, and there wasn't anything for me to do.

MA. It's lovely.

[THE STAGE MANAGER *pushes out a bed from the left. Its foot is toward the right.* BEULAH *sits on it, testing the springs.*]

BEULAH. I think you'll find the bed comfortable, Ma.

MA (*taking off her hat*). Oh, I could sleep on a heapa shoes, Loolie! I don't have no trouble sleepin'. (*She sits down beside her.*) Now let me look at my girl. Well, well, when I last saw you, you didn't know me. You kep' say-ing, "When's Mamma comin'? When's Mamma comin'?" But the doctor sent me away.

BEULAH (*puts her head on her moth-er's shoulder and weeps*). It was awful, Mamma. It was awful. She didn't even live a few minutes, Mamma. It was aw-ful.

MA (*looking far away*). God thought best, dear. God thought best. We don't understand why. We just go on, honey, doin' our business. (*Then, almost abruptly, passing the back of her hand across her cheek*) Well, now, what are we giving the men to eat tonight?

BEULAH. There's a chicken in the oven.

MA. What time didya put it in?

BEULAH (*restraining her*). Aw, Ma, don't go yet. I like to sit here with you this way. You always get the fidgets when we try and pet yuh, Mamma.

MA (*ruefully, laughing*). Yes, it's kinda foolish. I'm just an old Newark bag o' bones. (*She glances at the backs of her hands.*)

BEULAH (*indignantly*). Why, Ma, you're good-lookin'! We always said you were good-lookin'. — And besides, you're the best ma we could ever have.

MA. (*uncomfortably*). Well, I hope you like me. There's nothin' like being liked by your family. — Now I'm going downstairs to look at the chicken. You stretch out here for a minute and shut your eyes. — Have you got everything laid in for breakfast before the shops close?

BEULAH. Oh, you know! Ham and eggs.

[*They both laugh.*]

MA. I declare I never could understand what men see in ham and eggs. I think they're horrible. — What time did you put the chicken in?

BEULAH. Five o'clock.

MA. Well, now, you shut your eyes for ten minutes. (BEULAH *stretches out and shuts her eyes.* MA *descends the stairs absent-mindedly singing.*)

There were ninety and nine that
    safely lay
In the shelter of the fold,
But one was out on the hills away,
Far off from the gates of gold. . . .

[*And the curtain falls.*]

A CHARACTER PLAY

Characterization. The characters in Thornton Wilder's plays are ordinary people — men and women much like ourselves. We watch these characters as they encounter not world-shaking events but the sad and joyful happenings of everyday life. Thornton Wilder wants us to think as we watch his characters: he wants us to see beneath our commonplace experiences, to gain deeper insight into things we usually take for granted.

1. In a sense, this is Ma's play. How did Ma, when we first met her, help set the mood for the play? What did you learn about her as the play progressed? If Ma had been a different kind of person, would the play have had the same effect on you? Explain.

2. How are these characters like people you know? How do they differ from characters in *The Sire de Maletroit's Door*?

3. Why do you think the author had The Stage Manager take the parts of the minor characters in the play?

Setting. In some plays, the setting is so important that it is hard to image the action happening in a different place or time.

4. This play began in Newark and ended in Camden, small cities in New Jersey. Name some of the sights that interested the Kirbys as they drove to Camden. Would this play have had the same effect if it had been set in a huge city?

5. The play takes place in the 1920's. Would a "journey" from one city to another in one state be such an event today? Why?

Conflict. The conflict in this play is not dramatic; it is simply between the "happy journey" and anything that might keep it from being happy.

6. What small disagreements between the characters were revealed before the journey began?

7. What was the first occurrence that interrupted the "happy journey" and created conflict? How did the billboards and Ma bring the family back to "happiness"?

8. What "scandal" committed by Arthur next created a conflict in the "happy journey"? Were you prepared for Ma's reaction to Arthur's words? Explain. What did Elmer do to change the situation? How did Arthur and Ma patch things up?

Theme. In this play, Thornton Wilder expresses an idea about life, and so the play has what we call a theme. To decide what this theme is, ask yourself the following questions.

9. What might the journey symbolize, or stand for? What might Wilder be saying about people — especially families — who make this journey? What might he be saying about happiness on this journey?

STAGE DIRECTIONS

When you read a play, you must put your imagination and your intelligence to work. You should picture what movements the characters are making. You should decide what the characters are like by thinking carefully about what they say and how they say it. You should even try to imagine what the characters look like and what they are wearing. Stage directions can help you do all these things.

For example, here is Ma's fourth speech. Previous stage directions have told us that Ma is putting on a hat. Notice that these stage directions, in parentheses, tell us further that she is speaking serenely.

"MA (*serenely*). Well, you don't leave Newark without that hat, make up your mind to that. I don't go no journeys with a hoodlum."

What movements do you picture Ma making when she says these lines? What does "serenely" tell about Ma? What different idea would we have of Ma if we were told that she spoke these lines "angrily" or "in a nagging way"?

Here is Elmer's second speech. Ma has just asked him what has kept him with the car.

"ELMER (*always even-voiced and always looking out a little anxiously through his spectacles*). I just went to the garage and had Charlie give a last look at it, Kate."

What do you picture Elmer doing as he says this speech? What different ideas would you have of Elmer if you had been told that he spoke "impatiently" or "stupidly"?

Reread the first four pages of this play, up to the time when the Kirbys drive off. Pay special attention to the stage directions. What actions do you picture the characters making? What do you think the characters are wearing? What do you think they look like? What do you learn about the characters from examining what they say and how they say it?

COMPOSITION:
PRESENTING A CONTRAST

When you read several selections of literature, you often will want to compare one selection with another. For example, you might have noticed that the play *The Happy Journey* is more true to life than the other play you read in this unit, *The Sire de Maletroit's Door*. To make a contrast, it may help to make two lists. In one list, name the ways in which you think *The Happy Journey* is true to life; in the other list, name ways in which you feel *The Sire de Maletroit's Door* is not like real life. Then you are ready to write a paragraph in which you present the contrasts. State your opinion about the plays in your first sentence. Then show the specific ways in which the plays contrast, using the points in the lists you have made.

The Ugly Duckling

A. A. MILNE

Characters

KING
CHANCELLOR
QUEEN
PRINCESS CAMILLA
DULCIBELLA, *waiting maid to Princess Camilla*
PRINCE SIMON
CARLO, *attendant to Prince Simon*
VOICE, *an announcer*

SETTING. *The Throne Room of the palace, a room of many doors, or, if preferred, curtain openings, simply furnished with three thrones for Their Majesties and Her Royal Highness the* PRINCESS CAMILLA — *in other words, with three handsome chairs. At each side is a long seat, reserved, as it might be, for His Majesty's Council (if any), but useful, as today, for other purposes.*

The KING *is asleep on his throne, with a handkerchief over his face. He is a king of any country from any storybook, in whatever costume you please. But he should be wearing his crown.*

The Ugly Duckling by A. A. Milne, copyright 1941 by A. A. Milne. Reprinted by permission of the author's estate.

VOICE (*announcing*). His Excellency, the Chancellor!

[*The* CHANCELLOR, *an elderly man in horn-rimmed spectacles, enters bowing. The* KING *wakes up with a start and removes the handkerchief from his face.*]

KING (*with simple dignity*). I was thinking.

CHANCELLOR (*bowing*). Never, Your Majesty, was greater need for thought than now.

KING. That's what I was thinking. (*He struggles into a more dignified position.*) Well, what is it? More trouble?

CHANCELLOR. What we might call the old trouble, Your Majesty.

KING. It's what I was saying last night to the Queen. "Uneasy lies the head that wears a crown," was how I put it.

CHANCELLOR. A profound and original thought, which may well go down to posterity.

KING. You mean it may go down well with posterity. I hope so. Remind me to tell you some time of another little thing I said to Her Majesty: something about a fierce light beating on a throne.

Posterity would like that, too. Well, what is it?

CHANCELLOR. It is in the matter of Her Royal Highness' wedding.

KING. Oh . . . yes.

CHANCELLOR. As Your Majesty is aware, the young Prince Simon arrives today to seek Her Royal Highness' hand in marriage. He has been traveling in distant lands and, as I understand, has not . . . er . . . has not ——

KING. You mean he hasn't heard anything.

CHANCELLOR. It is a little difficult to put this tactfully, your Majesty.

KING. Do your best, and I will tell you afterwards how you got on.

CHANCELLOR. Let me put it this way. The Prince Simon will naturally assume that Her Royal Highness has the customary — so customary as to be, in my own poor opinion, slightly monotonous — has what one might call the inevitable — so inevitable as to be, in my opinion again, almost mechanical — will assume, that she has the, as *I* think of it, faultily faultless, icily regular, splendidly ——

KING. What you are trying to say in the fewest words possible is that my daughter is not beautiful.

CHANCELLOR. Her beauty is certainly elusive, Your Majesty.

KING. It is. It has eluded you, it has eluded me, it has eluded everybody who has seen her. It even eluded the Court Painter. His last words were, "Well, I did my best." His successor is now painting the view across the water meadows from the West Turret. He says that his doctor has advised him to keep to landscape.

CHANCELLOR. It is unfortate, Your Majesty, but there it is. One just cannot understand how it could have occurred.

KING. You don't think she takes after *me*, at all? You don't detect a likeness?

CHANCELLOR. Most certainly not, Your Majesty.

KING. Good. . . . Your predecessor did.

CHANCELLOR. I have often wondered what happened to my predecessor.

KING. Well, now you know.

[*There is a short silence.*]

CHANCELLOR. Looking at the bright side, although Her Royal Highness is not, strictly speaking, beautiful

KING. Not, truthfully speaking, beautiful . . .

CHANCELLOR. Yet she has great beauty of character.

KING. My dear Chancellor, we are not considering Her Royal Highness' character, but her chances of getting married. You observe that there is a distinction.

CHANCELLOR. Yes, Your Majesty.

KING. Look at it from the suitor's point of view. If a girl is beautiful, it is easy to assume that she has, tucked away inside her, an equally beautiful character. But it is impossible to assume that an unattractive girl, however elevated in character, has, tucked away inside her, an equally beautiful face. That is, so to speak, not where you want it — tucked away.

CHANCELLOR. Quite so, Your Majesty.

KING. This doesn't, of course, alter the fact that the Princess Camilla is quite the nicest person in the kingdom.

CHANCELLOR (*enthusiastically*). She is indeed, Your Majesty. (*Hurriedly*) With the exception, I need hardly say, of Your Majesty — and Her Majesty.

KING. Your exceptions are tolerated for their loyalty and condemned for their extreme fatuity.[1]

CHANCELLOR. Thank you, Your Majesty.

KING. As an adjective for your King, the word *nice* is ill chosen. As an adjective for Her Majesty, it is . . . ill chosen.

[*At this moment the* QUEEN *comes in. The* KING *rises. The* CHANCELLOR *puts himself at right angles.*]

QUEEN (*briskly*). Ah. Talking about Camilla? (*She sits down.*)

KING (*returning to his throne*). As always, my dear, you are right.

QUEEN (*to* CHANCELLOR). This fellow, Simon — what's he like?

CHANCELLOR. Nobody has seen him, Your Majesty.

QUEEN. How old is he?

CHANCELLOR. Five-and-twenty, I understand.

QUEEN. In twenty-five years he must

---

[1] **fatuity** (fə·tōo'ə·tē): foolishness.

have been seen by somebody.

KING (*to the* CHANCELLOR). Just a fleeting glimpse?

CHANCELLOR. I meant, Your Majesty, that no detailed report of him has reached this country, save that he has the usual personal advantages and qualities expected of a prince and has been traveling in distant and dangerous lands.

QUEEN. Ah! Nothing gone wrong with his eyes? Sunstroke or anything?

CHANCELLOR. Not that I am aware of, Your Majesty. At the same time, as I was venturing to say to His Majesty, Her Royal Highness' character and disposition are so outstandingly ——

QUEEN. Stuff and nonsense. You remember what happened when we had the Tournament of Love last year.

CHANCELLOR. I was not myself present, Your Majesty. I had not then the honor of — I was abroad, and never heard the full story.

QUEEN. No; it was the other fool. They all rode up to Camilla to pay their homage — it was the first time they had seen her. The heralds blew their trumpets and announced that she would marry whichever prince was left master of the field when all but one had been unhorsed. The trumpets were blown again, they charged enthusiastically into the fight, and —— (*The* KING *looks nonchalantly at the ceiling and whistles a few bars.*) Don't do that.

KING. I'm sorry, my dear.

QUEEN (*to* CHANCELLOR). And what happened? They all simultaneously fell off their horses and assumed a posture of defeat.

KING. One of them was not quite so quick as the others. I was very quick.

I proclaimed him the victor.

QUEEN. At the Feast of Betrothal held that night ——

KING. We were all very quick.

QUEEN. —— the Chancellor announced that by the laws of the country the successful suitor had to pass a further test. He had to give the correct answer to a riddle.

CHANCELLOR. Such undoubtedly is the fact, Your Majesty.

KING. There are times for announcing facts, and times for looking at things in a broad-minded way. Please remember that, Chancellor.

CHANCELLOR. Yes, Your Majesty.

QUEEN. I invented the riddle myself. Quite an easy one. What is it that has four legs and barks like a dog? The answer is, "a dog."

KING (*to* CHANCELLOR). You see that?

CHANCELLOR. Yes, Your Majesty.

KING. It isn't difficult.

QUEEN. He, however, seemed to find it so. He said an eagle. Then he said a serpent; a very high mountain with slippery sides; two peacocks; a moonlight night; the day after tomorrow ——

KING. Nobody could accuse him of not trying.

QUEEN. *I* did.

KING. I *should* have said that nobody could fail to recognize in his attitude an appearance of doggedness.

QUEEN. Finally he said death. I nudged the King ——

KING. Accepting the word *nudge* for the moment, I rubbed my ankle with one hand, clapped him on the shoulder with the other, and congratulated him on the correct answer. He disappeared under the table, and, person-ally, I never saw him again.

QUEEN. His body was found in the moat next morning.

CHANCELLOR. But what was he doing in the moat, Your Majesty?

KING. Bobbing about. Try not to ask needless questions.

CHANCELLOR. It all seems so strange.

QUEEN. What does?

CHANCELLOR. That Her Royal Highness, alone of all the princesses one has ever heard of, should lack that invariable attribute of royalty, supreme beauty.

QUEEN (*to the* KING). That was your Great-Aunt Malkin. She came to the christening. You know what she said.

KING. It was cryptic.[1] Great-Aunt Malkin's besetting weakness. She came to *my* christening — she was one hundred and one then, and that was fifty-one years ago. (*To the* CHANCELLOR) How old would that make her?

CHANCELLOR. One hundred and fifty-two, Your Majesty.

KING (*after thought*). About that, yes. She promised me that when I grew up I should have all the happiness which my wife deserved. It struck me at the time — well, when I say "at the time," I was only a week old — but it did strike me as soon as anything could strike me — I mean of that nature . . . well, work it out for yourself, Chancellor. It opens up a most interesting field of speculation. Though naturally I have not liked to go into it at all deeply with Her Majesty.

QUEEN. I never heard anything less cryptic. She was wishing you extreme happiness.

---

[1] **cryptic** (krip′tik): puzzling.

KING. I don't think she was *wishing* me anything. However.

CHANCELLOR (*to the* QUEEN). But what, Your Majesty, did she wish Her Royal Highness?

QUEEN. Her other godmother — on my side — had promised her the dazzling beauty for which all the women in my family are famous. (*She pauses, and the* KING *snaps his fingers surreptitiously*[1] *in the direction of the* CHANCELLOR.)

CHANCELLOR (*hurriedly*). Indeed, yes, Your Majesty. (*The* KING *relaxes.*)

QUEEN. And Great-Aunt Malkin said . . . (*To the* KING) What were the words?

KING.

I give you with this kiss
A wedding-day surprise.
Where ignorance is bliss
'Tis folly to be wise.

I thought the last two lines rather neat. But what it *meant* ——

QUEEN. We can all see what it meant. She was given beauty — and where is it? Great-Aunt Malkin took it away from her. The wedding-day surprise is that there will never be a wedding day.

KING. Young men being what they are, my dear, it would be much more surprising if there *were* a wedding day. So how ——

[*The* PRINCESS *comes in. She is young, happy, healthy, but not beautiful. Or let us say that by some trick of make-up or arrangement of hair she seems plain to us, unlike the princesses of the storybooks.*]

[1] **surreptitiously** (sûr′əp·ti′shəs·lē): secretly, in a concealed way.

PRINCESS (*to the* KING). Hallo, darling! (*Seeing the others*) Oh, I say! Affairs of state? Sorry.

KING (*holding out his hand*). Don't go, Camilla.

[*The* PRINCESS *takes the hand of the* KING.]

CHANCELLOR. Shall I withdraw, Your Majesty?

QUEEN. You are aware, Camilla, that Prince Simon arrives today?

PRINCESS. He has arrived. They're just letting down the drawbridge.

KING (*jumping up*). Arrived! I must ——

PRINCESS. Darling, you know what the drawbridge is like. It takes at *least* half an hour to let it down.

KING (*sitting down*. It wants oil. (*To the* CHANCELLOR) Have *you* been grudging it oil?

PRINCESS. It wants a new drawbridge, darling.

CHANCELLOR. Have I Your Majesty's permission ——

KING. Yes, yes.

[*The* CHANCELLOR *bows and goes out.*]

QUEEN. You've told him, of course? It's the only chance.

KING. Er . . . no. I was just going to, when ——

QUEEN. Then I'd better. (*She goes to the door.*) You can explain to the girl; I'll have her sent to you. You've told Camilla?

KING. Er . . . no. I was just going to, when ——

QUEEN. Then you'd better tell her now.

KING. My dear, are you sure ——

QUEEN. It's the only chance left. (*Dramatically, to heaven*) My daughter!

[*The* QUEEN *goes out. There is a little silence when she is gone.*]

KING. Camilla, I want to talk seriously to you about marriage.

PRINCESS. Yes, Father.

KING. It is time that you learned some of the facts of life.

PRINCESS. Yes, Father.

KING. Now the great fact about marriage is that once you're married you live happy ever after. All our history books affirm this.

PRINCESS. And your own experience too, darling.

KING (*with dignity*). Let us confine ourselves to history for the moment.

PRINCESS. Yes, Father.

KING. Of course, there *may* be an ex-

ception here and there, which, as it were, proves the rule; just as — oh, well, never mind.

PRINCESS (*smiling*). Go on, darling. You were going to say that an exception here and there proves the rule that all princesses are beautiful.

KING. Well — leave that for the moment. The point is that it doesn't matter *how* you marry, or *who* you marry, as long as you *get* married. Because you'll be happy ever after in any case. Do you follow me so far?

PRINCESS. Yes, Father.

KING. Well, your mother and I have a little plan ——

PRINCESS. Was that it, going out of the door just now?

KING. Er . . . yes. It concerns your waiting maid.

PRINCESS. Darling, I have several.

KING. Only one that leaps to the eye, so to speak. The one with the . . . well, with everything.

PRINCESS. Dulcibella?

KING. That's the one. It is our little plan that at the first meeting she should pass herself off as the Princess — a harmless ruse, of which you will find frequent record in the history books — and allure Prince Simon to his . . . that is to say, bring him up to the . . . In other words, the wedding will take place immediately afterwards, and as quietly as possible . . . well, naturally in view of the fact that your Aunt Malkin is one hundred and fifty-two; and since you will be wearing the family bridal veil — which is no doubt how the custom arose — the surprise after the ceremony will be his. Are you following me at all? Your attention seems to be wandering.

PRINCESS. I was wondering why you needed to tell me.

KING. Just a precautionary measure, in case you happened to meet the Prince or his attendant before the ceremony; in which case, of course, you would pass yourself off as the maid ——

PRINCESS. A harmless ruse, of which, also, you will find frequent record in the history books.

KING. Exactly. But the occasion need not arise.

VOICE (*announcing*). The woman Dulcibella!

KING. Ah! (*To the* PRINCESS) Now, Camilla, if you will just retire to your own apartments, I will come to you there when we are ready for the actual ceremony. (*He leads her out as he is talking; and as he returns calls out.*) Come in, my dear! (DULCIBELLA *comes in. She is beautiful, but dumb.*) Now don't be frightened, there is nothing to be frightened about. Has Her Majesty told you what you have to do?

DULCIBELLA. Y-yes, Your Majesty.

KING. Well now, let's see how well you can do it. You are sitting here, we will say. (*He leads her to a seat.*) Now imagine that I am Prince Simon. (*He curls his mustache and puts his stomach in. She giggles.*) You are the beautiful Princess Camilla whom he has never seen. (*She giggles again.*) This is a serious moment in your life, and you will find that a giggle will not be helpful. (*He goes to the door.*) I am announced: "His Royal Highness Prince Simon!" That's me being announced. Remember what I said about giggling. You should have a far-away look upon the face. (*She does her best.*) Farther away than that. (*She tries again.*) No, that's too far. You are sitting there, thinking beautiful thoughts — in maiden meditation, fancy free, as I remember saying to Her Majesty once — speaking of somebody else — fancy free, but with the mouth definitely shut — that's better. I advance and fall upon one knee. (*He does so.*) You extend your hand graciously — *graciously;*

you're not trying to push him in the face — that's better, and I raise it to my lips — so — and I kiss it (*He kisses it warmly.*) . . . no, perhaps not so ardently as that, more like this (*He kisses it again.*), and I say, "Your Royal Highness, this is the most . . . er . . . Your Royal Highness, I shall ever be . . . no . . . Your Royal Highness, it is the proudest . . ." Well, the point is that *he* will say it, and it will be something complimentary, and then he will take your hand in both of his and press it to his heart. (*He does so.*) And then — what do *you* say?

DULCIBELLA. Coo!

KING. No, *not* "coo."

DULCIBELLA. Never had anyone do *that* to me before.

KING. That also strikes the wrong note. What you want to say is, "Oh, Prince Simon!" . . . Say it.

DULCIBELLA (*loudly*). Oh, Prince Simon!

KING. No, no. You don't need to shout until he has said "What?" two or three times. Always consider the possibility that he *isn't* deaf. Softly, and giving the words a dying fall, letting them play around his head like a flight of doves.

DULCIBELLA (*still a little overloud*). O-o-o-o-h, Prinsimon!

KING. Keep the idea in your mind of a flight of *doves* rather than a flight of panic-stricken elephants, and you will be all right. Now I'm going to get up, and you must, as it were, *waft* me into a seat by your side. (*She starts wafting.*) *Not* rescuing a drowning man, that's another idea altogether, useful at times, but at the moment inappropriate. Wafting. Prince Simon will put the necessary muscles into play — all you

require to do is to indicate by a gracious movement of the hand the seat you require him to take. Now! (*He gets up, a little stiffly, and sits next to her.*) That was better. Well, here we are. Now, I think you give me a look: something, let us say, halfway between breathless adoration and regal dignity, touched, as it were, with good comradeship. Now try that. (*She gives him a vacant look of bewilderment.*) Frankly, that didn't quite get it. There was just a little something missing. An absence, as it were, of all the qualities I asked for, and in their place an odd resemblance to an unsatisfied fish. Let us try to get at it another way. Dulcibella, have you a young man of your own?

DULCIBELLA (*eagerly, seizing his hand*). Oo, yes, he's ever so smart, he's an archer, well not as you might say a real archer, he works in the armory, but old Bottlenose, *you* know who I mean, the Captain of the Guard, says the very next man they ever has to shoot, my Eg shall take his place, knowing Father and how it is with Eg and me, and me being maid to Her Royal Highness and can't marry me till he's a real soldier, but ever so loving, and funny like, the things he says, I said to him once, "Eg," I said ——

KING (*getting up*). I rather fancy, Dulcibella, that if you think of Eg all the time, *say* as little as possible, and, when thinking of Eg, see that the mouth is not more than partially open, you will do very well. I will show you where you are to sit and wait for His Royal Highness. (*He leads her out. On the way he is saying*) Now remember — *waft — waft* — not *hoick*.

[PRINCE SIMON *wanders in from the back unannounced. He is a very ordinary-looking young man in rather dusty clothes. He gives a deep sigh of relief as he sinks into the throne of the* KING. . . . CAMILLA, *a new and strangely beautiful* CAMILLA, *comes in.*]

PRINCESS (*surprised*). Well!

PRINCE. Oh, hallo!

PRINCESS. Ought you?

PRINCE (*getting up*). Do sit down, won't you?

PRINCESS. Who are you, and how did you get here?

PRINCE. Well, that's rather a long story. Couldn't we sit down? You could sit here if you liked, but it isn't very comfortable.

PRINCESS. That is the King's throne.

PRINCE. Oh, is that what it is?

PRINCESS. Thrones are not meant to be comfortable.

PRINCE. Well, I don't know if they're meant to be, but they certainly aren't.

PRINCESS. Why were you sitting on the King's throne, and who are you?

PRINCE. My name is Carlo.

PRINCESS. Mine is Dulcibella.

PRINCE. Good. And now couldn't we sit down?

PRINCESS (*sitting down on the long seat to the left of the throne, and, as it were, wafting him to a place next to her*). You may sit here, if you like. Why are you so tired?

[*The* PRINCE *sits down.*]

PRINCE. I've been taking very strenuous exercise.

PRINCESS. Is that part of the long story?

PRINCE. It is.

PRINCESS (*settling herself*). I love stories.

PRINCE. This isn't a story really. You see, I'm attendant on Prince Simon, who is visiting here.

PRINCESS. Oh? I'm attendant on Her Royal Highness.

PRINCE. Then you know what he's here for.

PRINCESS. Yes.

PRINCE. She's very beautiful, I hear.

PRINCESS. Did you hear that? Where have you been lately?

PRINCE. Traveling in distant lands — with Prince Simon.

PRINCESS. Ah! All the same, I don't understand. Is Prince Simon in the palace now? The drawbridge *can't* be down yet!

PRINCE. I don't suppose it is. *And* what a noise it makes coming down!

PRINCESS. Isn't it terrible?

PRINCE. I couldn't stand it any more. I just had to get away. That's why I'm here.

PRINCESS. But how?

PRINCE. Well, there's only one way, isn't there? That beech tree, and then a swing and a grab for the battlements, and don't ask me to remember it all . . . (*He shudders.*)

PRINCESS. You mean you came across the moat by that beech tree?

PRINCE. Yes. I got so tired of hanging about.

PRINCESS. But it's terribly dangerous!

PRINCE. That's why I'm so exhausted. Nervous shock. (*He lies back and breathes loudly.*)

PRINCESS. Of course, it's different for *me.*

PRINCE (*sitting up*). Say that again. I must have got it wrong.

PRINCESS. It's different for me, because I'm used to it. Besides, I'm so much lighter.

PRINCE. You don't mean that *you* ——

PRINCESS. Oh yes, often.

PRINCE. And I thought I was a brave man! At least, I didn't until five minutes ago, and now I don't again.

PRINCESS. Oh, but you are! And I think it's wonderful to do it straight off the first time.

PRINCE. Well, *you* did.

PRINCESS. Oh no, not the first time. When I was a child.

PRINCE. You mean that you crashed?

PRINCESS. Well, you only fall into the moat.

PRINCE. Only! Can you *swim?*

PRINCESS. Of course.

PRINCE. So you swam to the castle walls, and yelled for help, and they fished you out and walloped you. And next day you tried again. Well, if *that* isn't pluck ——

PRINCESS. Of course I didn't. I swam back, and did it at once; I mean I tried again at once. It wasn't until the third time that I actually did it. You see, I was afraid I might lose my nerve.

PRINCE. Afraid she might lose her nerve!

PRINCESS. There's a way of getting over from this side, too; a tree grows out from the wall and you jump into another tree — I don't think it's quite so easy.

PRINCE. Not quite so easy. Good. You must show me.

PRINCESS. Oh, I will.

PRINCE. Perhaps it might be as well if you taught me how to swim first. I've often heard about swimming, but never ——

PRINCESS. You can't swim?

PRINCE. No. Don't look so surprised. There are a lot of other things that I can't do. I'll tell you about them as soon as you have a couple of years to spare.

PRINCESS. You can't swim and yet you crossed by the beech tree! And you're *ever* so much heavier than I am! Now who's brave?

PRINCE (*getting up*). You keep talking about how light you are. I must see if there's anything in it. Stand up! (*She stands obediently and he picks her up.*) You're right, Dulcibella. I could hold you here forever. (*Looking at her*) You're very lovely. Do you know how lovely you are?

PRINCESS. Yes. (*She laughs suddenly and happily.*)

PRINCE. Why do you laugh?

PRINCESS. Aren't you tired of holding me?

PRINCE. Frankly, yes. I exaggerated when I said I could hold you forever. When you've been hanging by the arms for ten minutes over a very deep moat, wondering if it's too late to learn how to swim . . . (*He puts her down.*) What I meant was that I should *like* to

hold you forever. Why did you laugh?

PRINCESS. Oh, well, it was a little private joke of mine.

PRINCE. If it comes to that, I've got a private joke too. Let's exchange them.

PRINCESS. Mine's very private. One other woman in the whole world knows, and that's all.

PRINCE. Mine's just as private. One other man knows, and that's all.

PRINCESS. What fun. I love secrets. . . . Well, here's mine. When I was born, one of my godmothers promised that I should be very beautiful.

PRINCE. How right she was.

PRINCESS. But the other one said this:

> I give you with this kiss
> A wedding-day surprise.
> Where ignorance is bliss
> 'Tis folly to be wise.

And nobody knew what it meant. And I grew up very plain. And then, when I was about ten, I met my godmother in the forest one day. It was my tenth birthday. Nobody knows this — except you.

PRINCE. Except us.

PRINCESS. Except us. And she told me what her gift meant. It meant that I *was* beautiful — but everybody else was to go on being ignorant and thinking me plain, until my wedding day. Because, she said, she didn't want me to grow up spoiled and willful and vain, as I should have done if everybody had always been saying how beautiful I was; and the best thing in the world, she said, was to be quite sure of yourself, but not to expect admiration from other people. So ever since then my mirror has told me I'm beautiful, and everybody else thinks me ugly, and I get a lot of fun out of it.

PRINCE. Well, seeing that Dulcibella is the result, I can only say that your godmother was very, very wise.

PRINCESS. And now tell me *your* secret.

PRINCE. It isn't such a pretty one. You see, Prince Simon was going to woo Princess Camilla, and he'd heard that she was beautiful and haughty and imperious — all *you* would have been if your godmother hadn't been so wise. And being a very ordinary-looking fellow himself, he was afraid she wouldn't think much of him, so he suggested to one of his attendants, a man called Carlo, of extremely attractive appearance, that *he* should pretend to be the Prince and win the Princess's hand; and then at the last moment they would change places ——

PRINCESS. How would they do that?

PRINCE. The Prince was going to have been married in full armor — with his visor down.

PRINCESS (*laughing happily*). Oh, what fun!

PRINCE. Neat, isn't it?

PRINCESS (*laughing*). Oh, very . . . very . . . very.

PRINCE. Neat, but not so terribly *funny*. Why do you keep laughing?

PRINCESS. Well, that's another secret.

PRINCE. If it comes to that, *I've* got another one up my sleeve. Shall we exchange again?

PRINCESS. All right. You go first this time.

PRINCE. Very well. . . . I am not Carlo. (*Standing up and speaking dramatically*) I am Simon! — *ow!* (*He sits

down and rubs his leg violently.*)

PRINCESS (*alarmed*). What is it?

PRINCE. Cramp. (*In a mild voice, still rubbing*) I was saying that I was Prince Simon.

PRINCESS. Shall I rub it for you? (*She rubs.*)

PRINCE (*still hopefully*). I am Simon.

PRINCESS. Is that better?

PRINCE (*despairingly*). I am Simon.

PRINCESS. I know.

PRINCE. How did you know?

PRINCESS. Well, you told me.

PRINCE. But oughtn't you to swoon or something?

PRINCESS. Why? History records many similar ruses.

PRINCE (*amazed*). Is that so? I've never read history. I thought I was being profoundly original.

PRINCESS. Oh, no! Now I'll tell you *my* secret. For reasons very much like your own, the Princess Camilla, who is held to be extremely plain, feared to meet Prince Simon. Is the drawbridge down yet?

PRINCE. Do your people give a faint, surprised cheer every time it gets down?

PRINCESS. Naturally.

PRINCE. Then it came down about three minutes ago.

PRINCESS. Ah! Then at this very moment your man Carlo is declaring his passionate love for my maid, Dulcibella. That, I think, is funny. (*So does the* PRINCE. *He laughs heartily.*) Dulcibella, by the way, is in love with a man she calls Eg, so I hope Carlo isn't getting carried away.

PRINCE. Carlo is married to a girl he calls "the little woman," so Eg has nothing to fear.

PRINCESS. By the way, I don't know if you heard, but I said, or as good as said, that I am the Princess Camilla.

PRINCE. I wasn't surprised. History, of which I read a great deal, records many similar ruses.

PRINCESS. (*laughing*). Simon!

PRINCE (*laughing*). Camilla! (*He stands up.*) May I try holding you again? (*She nods. He takes her in his arms and kisses her.*) Sweetheart!

PRINCESS. You see, when you lifted me up before, you said, "You're very lovely," and my godmother said that the first person to whom I would seem lovely was the man I should marry; so I knew then that you were Simon and I should marry you.

PRINCE. I knew directly I saw you that I should marry you, even if you were Dulcibella. By the way, which of you *am* I marrying?

PRINCESS. When she lifts her veil, it will be Camilla. (*Voices are heard outside.*) Until then it will be Dulcibella.

PRINCE (*in a whisper*). Then good-bye, Camilla, until you lift your veil.

PRINCESS. Good-bye, Simon, until you raise your visor.

[*The* KING *and* QUEEN *come in arm-in-arm, followed by* CARLO *and* DULCI-BELLA, *also arm-in-arm. The* CHAN-CELLOR *precedes them, walking backwards, at a loyal angle.*]

PRINCE (*supporting the* CHANCELLOR *as an accident seems inevitable*). Careful!

[*The* CHANCELLOR *turns indignantly.*]

KING. Who and what is this? More accurately who and what are all these?

CARLO. My attendant, Carlo, Your Majesty. He will, with Your Majesty's permission, prepare me for the ceremony.

[*The* PRINCE *bows.*]

KING. Of course, of course!

QUEEN (*to* DULCIBELLA). Your maid, Dulcibella, is it not, my love? (DULCI-BELLA *nods violently.*) I thought so. (*To* CARLO) *She* will prepare Her Royal Highness.

[*The* PRINCESS *curtsies.*]

KING. Ah, yes. Yes. *Most* important.

PRINCESS (*curtsying*). I beg your pardon, Your Majesty, if I've done wrong, but I found the gentleman wandering ——

KING (*crossing to her*). Quite right, my dear, quite right. (*He pinches her cheek and takes advantage of this kingly gesture to speak in a loud whisper.*) We've pulled it off!

[*They sit down: the* KING *and* QUEEN *on their thrones,* DULCIBELLA *on the* PRINCESS's *throne.* CARLO *stands behind* DULCIBELLA, *the* CHANCELLOR *on the right of the* QUEEN, *and the* PRINCE *and* PRINCESS *behind the long seat on the left.*]

CHANCELLOR (*consulting documents*). H'r'm! Have I Your Majesty's authority to put the final test to His Royal Highness?

QUEEN (*whispering to the* KING). Is this safe?

KING (*whispering*). Perfectly, my dear. I told him the answer a minute ago. (*Over his shoulder to* CARLO) Don't forget. *Dog.* (*Aloud*) Proceed, Your Excellency. It is my desire that the affairs of my country should ever be conducted in a strictly constitutional manner.

CHANCELLOR (*oratorically*). By the constitution of the country, a suitor to Her Royal Highness' hand cannot be deemed successful until he has given the correct answer to a riddle. (*Conversationally*) The last suitor answered incorrectly, and thus failed to win his bride.

KING. By a coincidence he fell into the moat.

CHANCELLOR (*to* CARLO). I have now to ask Your Royal Highness if you are prepared for the ordeal?

CARLO (*cheerfully*). Absolutely.

CHANCELLOR. I may mention, as a matter possibly of some slight historical interest to our visitor, that by the constitution of the country, the same riddle is not allowed to be asked on two successive occasions.

KING (*startled*). What's that?

CHANCELLOR. This one, it is interesting to recall, was propounded exactly a century ago, and we must take it as a fortunate omen that it was well and truly solved.

KING (*to the* QUEEN). I may want my sword directly.

CHANCELLOR. The riddle is this. What is it that has four legs and mews like a cat?

CARLO (*promptly*). A dog.

KING (*still more promptly*). Bravo, bravo!

[*He claps loudly and nudges the* QUEEN, *who claps too.*]

CHANCELLOR (*peering at his documents*). According to the records of the occasion to which I referred, the correct answer would seem to be ——

PRINCESS (*to* PRINCE). Say something, quick!

CHANCELLOR. —— not dog, but ——

PRINCE. Your Majesty, have I permission to speak? Naturally His Royal Highness could not think of justifying himself on such an occasion, but I think that with Your Majesty's gracious permission, I could ——

KING. Certainly, certainly.

PRINCE. In our country, we have an animal to which we have given the name "dog," or, in the local dialect of the more mountainous districts, "doggie." It sits by the fireside and purrs.

CARLO. That's right. It purrs like anything.

PRINCE. When it needs milk, which is its staple food, it mews.

CARLO (*enthusiastically*). Mews like nobody's business.

PRINCE. It also has four legs.

CARLO. One at each corner.

PRINCE. In some countries, I understand, this animal is called a "cat." In one distant country to which His Royal Highness and I penetrated, it was called by the very curious name of "hippopotamus."

CARLO. That's right. (*To the* PRINCE) Do you remember that ginger-colored hippopotamus which used to climb onto my shoulder and lick my ear?

PRINCE. I shall never forget it, sir. (*To the* KING) So you see, Your Majesty ——

KING. Thank you. I think that makes it perfectly clear. (*Firmly to the* CHANCELLOR) You are about to agree?

CHANCELLOR. Undoubtedly, Your Majesty. May I be the first to congratulate His Royal Highness on solving the riddle so accurately?

KING. You may be the first to see that all is in order for an immediate wedding.

CHANCELLOR. Thank you, Your Majesty.

[*The* CHANCELLOR *bows and withdraws. The* KING *rises, as do the* QUEEN *and* DULCIBELLA.]

KING (*to* CARLO). Doubtless, Prince Simon, you will wish to retire and prepare yourself for the ceremony.

CARLO. Thank you, sir.

PRINCE. Have I Your Majesty's permission to attend His Royal Highness? It is the custom of his country for princes of the royal blood to be married in full armor, a matter which requires a certain adjustment ——

KING. Of course, of course. (CARLO *bows to the* KING *and* QUEEN *and goes out. As the* PRINCE *is about to follow, the* KING *stops him.*) Young man, you have a quality of quickness which I admire. It is my pleasure to reward it in any way which commends itself to you.

PRINCE. Your Majesty is ever gracious. May I ask for my reward *after* the ceremony?

[*The* PRINCE *catches the eye of the* PRINCESS, *and they give each other a secret smile.*]

KING. Certainly.

[*The* PRINCE *bows and goes out.*]

KING (*to* DULCIBELLA). Now young woman, make yourself scarce. You have done your work excellently, and we will see that you and your . . . What was his name?

DULCIBELLA. Eg, Your Majesty.

KING. . . . that you and your Eg are not forgotten.

DULCIBELLA. Coo!

[DULCIBELLA *curtsies and goes out.*]

PRINCESS (*calling*). Wait for me, Dulcibella!

KING (*to* QUEEN). Well, my dear, we may congratulate ourselves. As I remember saying to somebody once, "You have not lost a daughter, you have gained a son." How does he strike you?

QUEEN. Stupid.

KING. They made a very handsome pair, I thought, he and Dulcibella.

QUEEN. Both stupid.

KING. I said nothing about stupidity. What I *said* was that they were both extremely handsome. That is the important thing. (*Struck by a sudden idea*) Or isn't it?

QUEEN. What do you think of Prince Simon, Camilla?

PRINCESS. I adore him. We shall be so happy together.

KING. Well, of course you will. I told you so. Happy ever after.

QUEEN. Run along now and get ready.

PRINCESS. Yes, Mother.

[*The* PRINCESS *throws a kiss to the* KING *and* QUEEN *and goes out.*]

KING (*anxiously*). My dear, have we been wrong about Camilla all this time? It seemed to me that she wasn't looking *quite* so plain as usual just now. Did *you* notice anything?

QUEEN (*carelessly*). Just the excitement of the marriage.

KING (*relieved*). Ah, yes, that would account for it.

[*Curtain.*]

A COMEDY

Characterization. Some types of characters are found in one comedy after another. For example, you have probably seen television shows or movies which feature such stock characters as the beautiful but dumb girl, the domineering wife, or the henpecked husband. Stock characters like these have been used by dramatists down through the centuries — and they have always made audiences laugh.

1. What funny pose was the King seen in as the curtain rose? The Chancellor entered wearing horn-rimmed glasses. Would you expect a storybook character from olden times to be wearing horn-rimmed glasses? Why? In what ways did the King turn out to be unkinglike?

2. What did we learn about the Princess at the opening of the play? What fantastic information about previous suitors was added after the Queen entered? What kind of person was the Queen? How did she treat the King?

3. How was additional comedy provided in Dulcibella's scenes?

4. Have you ever seen comic characters like the King, Queen, and Dulcibella in movies or on television? Explain.

Plot. The plot of a comedy is often full of unexpected and funny entanglements. The problems of the hero and heroine are often solved by an unbelievable twist of events.

5. What complicated plan had been devised by the King and Queen to fool Prince Simon? What secrets were exchanged by Camilla and Simon? What complications were added to the plot in this scene?

6. The climax of the plot occurred when the "prince" was tested. By what ridiculous means did Simon save the day?

Theme. This play is a satire; that is, it makes us laugh at certain kinds of people and their ways of thinking.

7. The title of this play is also the title of a famous fairy tale by Hans Christian Anderson. As you probably recall, the ugly duckling in that story turned into a beautiful swan. In what ways was this play like that fairy tale? What ideas about beauty is Milne making fun of in this play?

8. Do people in real life scheme in the ways the King and Queen did? Did Milne make you laugh at these people?

9. What did the Princess's godmother say was the "best thing in the world"? Do you agree? Why?

Interpretation. A satirical comedy such as this one is difficult to present. The actors must seem to be very serious, but all the time they are really "spoofing" certain kinds of people.

10. One of the funniest scenes in the play is the scene that the King plays with Dulcibella. How do you think the King should act during this scene? How should he say his lines? How can Dulcibella use facial expressions to add to the humor?

COMPOSITION:
PRESENTING AN ARGUMENT

Suppose your class is discussing which of the three plays in this unit should be presented in a school assembly. You yourself have decided which one would be best. Write a paragraph to the class, giving your reasons for choosing one play over the other two.

A paragraph that makes an argument is almost like a paragraph that gives an opinion (page 350). In an argument, however, your purpose is to convince your readers that you are right and to win them over to your way of thinking. In writing this paragraph, therefore, use reasons that will convince your readers that your choice is the best one.

Dialogue

The playwright tells his story with dialogue, and a play, of course, is meant to be seen and heard. When you read a play, you must use your imagination to try to make up for the fact that you are not watching people act out the story on a stage.

There are devices built right into the play itself that help you do this. For example, read carefully this dramatic passage from *The Happy Journey to Trenton and Camden* by Thornton Wilder.

CAROLINE (*whining*). Oh, Pa! Do we have to wait while that whole funeral goes by?

[PA *takes off his hat.* MA *cranes forward with absorbed curiosity.*]

MA. Take off your hat, Arthur. Look at your father. — Why, Elmer, I do believe that's a lodge brother of yours. See the banner? I suppose this is the Elizabeth branch. (ELMER *nods.* MA *sighs.*) Tchk — tchk — tchk. (*They all lean forward and watch the funeral in silence, growing momentarily more solemnized. After a pause,* MA *continues almost dreamily.*) Well, we haven't forgotten the one that we went on, have we? We haven't forgotten our good Harold. He gave his life for his country, we mustn't forget that. (*She passes her finger from the corner of her eye across her cheek. There is another pause.*) Well, we'll all hold up the traffic for a few minutes someday.

ARTHUR and CAROLINE (*very uncomfortably*). Ma!

MA (*without self-pity*). Well I'm "ready" children. I hope everybody in this car is "ready." (*She puts her hand on* PA's *shoulder.*) And I pray to go first, Elmer. Yes. (PA *touches her hand.*)

ARTHUR and CAROLINE. Ma, everybody's looking at you. Everybody's laughing at you.

MA. Oh, hold your tongues! I don't care what a lot of silly people in Elizabeth, New Jersey, think of me. — Now we can go on. That's the last.

[*There is another lurch, and the car goes on.*] (pages 354–55)

READING A PLAY

1. *Note the stage directions telling how certain speeches are to be delivered.* Thornton Wilder has described how certain lines should be spoken — "whining," "almost dreamily," "very uncomfortably," "without self-pity." Read these speeches aloud, in ways that express these different feelings. Can Ma's "almost dreamily" speech be read in more than one way? Compare your reading of this speech with those of your classmates.

Look at the speeches for which the author has not given stage directions. In what tone of voice do you imagine Ma would say the speech that begins "Take off your hat, Arthur"? How would the children say "Ma, everybody's looking at you"? Write stage directions to describe how these speeches should be spoken.

2. *Read carefully the stage directions telling what the actors should be doing on the stage.* Find such directions in the model passage and act them out. What do these actions tell you about the characters?

3. *Use imagination in reading a play.* The actors on a stage, of course, do much more than just what is described in stage directions. The reader of a play has to fill in many details for himself. Tell what you think the actors would be doing as the last two speeches in the model passage are being spoken.

Look back at the scene in which Denis first encounters Maletroit in *The Sire de Maletroit's Door* (pages 338–39). What do the stage directions tell you about the characters in this scene? If you were playing Maletroit, what facial expressions would you use? How would you speak your first lines? At what point would you use your voice to give Denis an indication of your evil intentions? Name the different emotions expressed by Denis in this scene. Do stage directions specify all of them?

Look back at *The Ugly Duckling*, at the scene between Dulcibella and the King (pages 369–70). To picture everything going on in this hilarious scene, you must let the dialogue, as well as the stage directions, help you. Find the stage directions that tell exactly what the King and Dulcibella are doing. Then look closely at the King's speech beginning in column two on page 369. What words tell you Dulcibella has just let her mouth hang open? Find other words in the dialogue which indicate something is happening on the stage. What other actions do you picture these two characters going through in this scene?

WRITING DIALOGUE

Playwrights write dialogue to suit their characters.

Read aloud the two speeches that follow. Which would be spoken by Denis, the English aristocrat in *The Sire de Maletroit's Door*? Which sounds like a "tough guy" in a television show? Point to the words and expressions that account for the differences in these speeches.

> Sire, you persist in making a fool of me. I waste my time conversing with a lunatic. There is no power under God that will make me stay here any longer.

> Mister, yer makin' a fool o' me. I'm wastin' my time talkin' to a nut. There's no power under God'll make me stay here any longer.

Read aloud the following speech from *The Happy Journey to Trenton and Camden*. Note how the italicized words are written to imitate slurred sounds.

BEULAH. Go straight along, Pa, you can't miss it. It just stares at *yuh*. . . . Crazy old Pa, *goin'· buyin'* things! It's me that ought to be *buyin'* things for you, Pa.

(page 360)

Rewrite this speech to imitate the way an English aristocrat like Denis would say it. Would this type of dialogue suit the character of Beulah?

Write a dramatic conversation. Choose a fairly simple situation, but one that has some conflict. For example, you might write about a boy or girl asking an adult for permission to do something. Try to make each character, through his speech, stand out as a distinct person.

ART AND LITERATURE

Did you ever wonder what the people in a painting might be saying to one another? Choose one of the paintings in the art insert (pages 295–300) and write a short conversation that might be taking place there. In stage directions, describe the people's voices and movements.

Forms of Literature

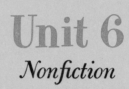

Unit 6
Nonfiction

UNIT 6 Nonfiction

The term nonfiction includes many kinds of writing. Nonfiction can be an editorial in a newspaper. It can be an informational article in a magazine, an essay, or a biography. It can even be a letter. But nonfiction cannot be a poem, a play, a short story, or a novel.

In nonfiction, an author's personality often shines through the writing. Style is usually important in nonfiction. It may be serious, formal, clever, funny, or even flip. We read nonfiction to be entertained as well as to be informed. We also read it — as we read all kinds of literature — in order to enter, briefly and partially, into the minds and hearts of people.

In this unit you will sample several kinds of nonfiction, with topics ranging from baseball to outer space.

Your Change by Robert Benchley:
> A humorous essay about the terrors that overwhelm one of America's funniest writers when he faces a cashier.

Mary White by William Allen White:
> An editorial written in 1921 by a famous newspaperman, about the death of his young daughter.

George Washington Carver by Florence Crannell Means:
> Selected incidents from a biography of the desperately poor boy from Missouri who became a scientific wizard.

First Pitch by Robert Creamer:
> An essay to whet your appetite for spring . . . and baseball.

An Old-fashioned Iowa Christmas by Paul Engle:
> A noted writer and teacher's fond recollection of a treasured family custom.

From Spring to Summer by Edwin Way Teale:
> A great naturalist's journal, recording his observations and personal thoughts on the quiet, awesome coming of spring.

Where's Everybody? by Arthur C. Clarke:
> An article in which a noted British scientist asks a disturbing question about our "neighbors" in outer space.

Your Change

ROBERT BENCHLEY

It MAY BE that my fingers were frozen when I was a very small child and have never quite thawed out, or it may be that I just become panicky at having a man look at me through a little window, but, whatever the cause, I am physically unable to pick up change which has been shoved out at me by a man at a ticket booth.

I can scoop up change like lightning from a store counter, and in the morning it is the work of only a split second for me to gather up the pocket money I have left on the bureau the night before (possibly because there is so little of it), but let me stand in front of a ticket window in a theater lobby or a railroad station, with a line of people behind me, and a boy with a magnet could pick up a mound of iron filings one by one quicker than it takes me to garner twenty cents in change.

People in front of me seem to have no trouble. Even women with gloves on do a better job of it than I do. I see my predecessors sweep up their change with one swoop, and I say to myself: "Come now, Benchley! Be a man! You can do it, too!" And then I buy my ticket, pass in my bill, and, when the rattle of the change sounds on the marble slab, everything goes black in front of my eyes, my fingers grow numb, and I pick and claw at each individual coin like a canary. Sometimes I will get a dime almost up into the air high enough to get a grip on it, and then, crazed with success, lose my hold — and off it rolls into the money drawer or onto the floor. I would sometimes suspect that the man at the window has put some sort of stickum on my particular coins, were it not for the fact that they roll so easily once I have lost my grip.

By this time the man behind me has

pushed up to the window and ordered his ticket, shoving his money past me in an unpleasant manner. I frantically draw my pile of change over to my side of the window and there, in ignominious [1] panic, scrape it off into my hand, or rather partly into one hand, partly down into the front of my overcoat, and partly onto the floor. Often I dash off without waiting to pick it all up, rather than subject myself to the scorn of the people behind me. I suppose that I leave thousands and thousands of dollars a year on ticket counters and surrounding floors. I must leave them *somewhere*. I haven't got them now.

I do not know how to combat this weakness. I have thought of just handing my money, taking the ticket, and then dashing off with a cheery: "The rest is for you!" to the man. I have tried saying to myself, as I stood in line: "Why should you be afraid of a man behind bars like that? He is probably just as afraid of you." (This is not true and I know it.) I have tried pushing my whole hand under the bars and holding it open for him to drop the change into, but then I find that, as I close my fist on it, I am unable to get my hand out again.

I think the only way out for me is just not to try to buy tickets except at a ticket agency.

[1] **ignominious** (ig′nə·min′ē·əs): humiliating.

A HUMOROUS ESSAY

The Author's Purpose. In reading an essay, we should first decide what the author's purpose is. One way we can judge the essay is in terms of whether or not the author accomplishes his purpose.

1. Do you think Benchley's purpose in writing this essay was to inform, convince, or entertain? Do you think he accomplished his purpose? Explain.

2. What common human weaknesses did Benchley make fun of?

Style. One way in which writers can make us laugh is by using humorous exaggeration. Here Benchley talked about a minor situation as if it were very serious.

3. How does the first sentence set a humorous tone for the essay?

4. What exaggerations did Benchley use to make his little frustrations at the ticket window seem funny? How did he make himself seem bumbling and foolish? What incidents do you think he invented? What comic pictures does he put in your mind?

The Reader's Reaction. We can react to an essay in various ways. We may laugh or become angry or become stimulated to think or act in a certain way.

5. Did you find this essay amusing? Did it remind you of times when you yourself became flustered because people were watching you? Did it remind you of any ordinary routines in life that others find simple but that you find difficult?

SENTENCES: THE WORD *BUT*

But is a little word, but it can signal an important shift in meaning. Look back at the second paragraph of this essay; it is composed of only one long sentence. The first half tells how *easy* it is for Benchley to pick up change at some times, and the second half tells how *hard* it is in front of a ticket window. The word *but*, placed between the two halves of this sentence, signals that the second half is going to be the opposite of what came before.

Make up three sentences using *but* to signal a shift in meaning.

Mary White

WILLIAM ALLEN WHITE

THE Associated Press reports carrying the news of Mary White's death declared that it came as the result of a fall from a horse. How she would have hooted at that! She never fell from a horse in her life. Horses have fallen on her and with her — "I'm always trying to hold 'em in my lap," she used to say. But she was proud of few things, and one was that she could ride anything that had four legs and hair. Her death resulted not from a fall, but from a blow on the head which fractured her skull, and the blow came from the limb of an overhanging tree on the parking.

The last hour of her life was typical of its happiness. She came home from a day's work at school, topped off by a hard grind with the copy on the high school annual, and felt that a ride would refresh her. She climbed into her khakis, chattering to her mother about the work she was doing, and hurried to get her horse and be out on the dirt roads for the country air and the radiant green fields of the spring. As she rode through the town at an easy gallop, she kept waving at passers-by. She knew everyone in town. For a decade the little figure with the long pigtail and the red hair ribbon has been familiar on the streets of Emporia, and she got in the way of speaking to those who nodded at her. Walking the horse, she passed the Kerrs in front of the normal library,[1] and waved at them; passed another friend a few hundred feet farther on and waved at her. The horse was walking; and as she turned into north Merchant Street she took off her cowboy hat, and the horse swung into a lope. She passed the Tripletts and waved her cowboy hat at them, still moving gaily north on Merchant Street. A *Gazette* carrier passed — a high school boy friend — and she waved at him, but with her bridle hand; the horse veered quickly, plunged into the parking where the low-hanging limb faced her, and, while she still looked back waving, the blow came. But she did not fall from the horse; she slipped off, dazed a bit, staggered, and fell in a faint. She never quite recovered consciousness.

But she did not fall from the horse,

"Mary White" by William Allen White in *The Emporia Gazette* of May 17, 1921. Reprinted by permission of W. L. White.

[1] **normal library:** In those days (1920's), schools that prepared people to teach were called "normal schools."

neither was she riding fast. A year or so ago she used to go like the wind. But that habit was broken, and she used the horse to get into the open, to get fresh, hard exercise, and to work off a certain surplus energy that welled up in her and needed a physical outlet. That need has been in her heart for years. It was back of the impulse that kept the dauntless, little brown-clad figure on the streets and country roads of this community and that built into a strong, muscular body what had been a frail and sickly frame during the first years of her life. But the riding gave her more than a body. It released a gay and hardy soul. She was the happiest thing in the world. And she was happy because she was enlarging her horizon. She came to know all sorts and conditions of men. Charley O'Brien, the traffic cop, was one of her best friends. W. L. Holtz, the Latin teacher, was another. Tom O'Connor, farmer-politician, and Reverend John H. J. Rice, preacher and police judge, and Frank Beach, music master, were her special friends, and all the girls, black and white, above the track and below the track, in Pepville and Stringtown, were among her acquaintances. And she brought home riotous stories of her adventures. She loved to rollick; persiflage [1] was her natural expression at home. Her humor was a continual bubble of joy. She seemed to think in hyperbole and metaphor.[2] She was mis-

chievous without malice, as full of faults as an old shoe. No angel was Mary White, but an easy girl to live with, for she never nursed a grouch five minutes in her life.

With all her eagerness for the out-of-doors, she loved books. On her table when she left her room were a book by Conrad, one by Galsworthy, *Creative Chemistry* by E. E. Slosson, and a Kipling book. She read Mark Twain, Dickens, and Kipling before she was ten — all of their writings. Wells and Arnold Bennett particularly amused and diverted her. She was entered as a student in Wellesley for 1922; was assistant editor of the high school annual this year, and in line for election to the editorship of the annual next year. She was a member of the executive committee of the high-school YWCA.

Within the last two years she had begun to be moved by an ambition to draw. She began as most children do by scribbling funny pictures in her school books. She bought cartoon magazines and took a course — rather casually, naturally, for she was, after all, a child with no strong purposes — and this year she tasted the first fruits of success by having her pictures accepted by the high school annual. But the thrill of delight she got when Mr. Ecord, of the normal annual, asked her to do the cartooning for that book this spring was too beautiful for words. She fell to her work with all her enthusiastic heart. Her drawings were accepted, and her pride — always repressed by a lively sense of the ridiculousness of the figure she was cutting — was a really gorgeous thing to see. No successful artist ever drank a deeper draft of satisfac-

---

[1] **persiflage** (pûr′sə-fläzh): a light flippant way of talking.
[2] **hyperbole** (hī-pûr′bə-lē) **and metaphor:** A hyperbole is an exaggeration used for effect, such as "I'm so hungry I could eat a horse." A metaphor is a comparison, such as "Joe is a lamb."

tion than she took from the little fame her work was getting among her school-fellows. In her glory, she almost forgot her horse — but never her car.

For she used the car as a jitney bus. It was her social life. She never had a "party" in all her nearly seventeen years — wouldn't have one; but she never drove a block in the car in her life that she didn't begin to fill the car with pick-ups! Everybody rode with Mary White — white and black, old and young, rich and poor, men and women. She liked nothing better than to fill the car full of long-legged high school boys and an occasional girl, and parade the town. She never had a "date," nor went to a dance, except once with her brother, Bill, and the "boy proposition" didn't interest her — yet. But young people — great, spring-breaking, varnish-cracking, fender-bending, door-sagging carloads of "kids" — gave her great pleasure. Her zests were keen. But the most fun she ever had in her life was acting as chairman of the committee that got up the big turkey dinner for the poor folks at the county home; scores of pies, gallons of slaw, jam, cakes, preserves, oranges, and a wilderness of turkey were loaded in the car and taken to the county home And, being of a practical turn of mind, she risked her own Christmas dinner by staying to see that the poor folks actually got it all. Not that she was a cynic; she just disliked to tempt folks. While there she found a blind colored man, very old, who could do nothing but make rag rugs, and she rustled up from her school friends rags enough to keep him busy for a season. The last engagement she tried to make was to take the guests at the county

home out for a car ride.

The poor she had always with her, and was glad of it. She hungered and thirsted for righteousness; and was the most impious creature in the world. She joined the Congregational Church without consulting her parents; not particularly for her soul's good. She never had a thrill of piety in her life, and would have hooted at a "testimony." But even as a little child she felt the church was an agency for helping people to more of life's abundance, and she wanted to help. She never wanted help for herself. Clothes meant little to her. It was a fight to get a new rig on her, but eventually a harder fight to get it off. She never wore a jewel and had no ring but her high school class ring, and she never asked for anything but a wrist watch. She refused to have her hair up, though she was nearly seventeen. "Mother," she protested, "you don't know how much I get by with, in my braided pigtails, that I could not with my hair up." Above every other passion of her life was her passion not to grow up, to be a child. The tomboy in her, which was big, seemed to loathe to be put away forever in skirts. She was a Peter Pan, who refused to grow up.

Her funeral yesterday at the Congregational Church was as she would have wished it: no singing, no flowers save the big bunch of red roses from her brother Bill's Harvard classmen — heavens, how proud that would have made her! — and the red roses from the *Gazette* force, in vases at her head and feet. A short prayer, Paul's beautiful essay on love, from the thirteenth chapter of First Corinthians, some re-

William A. White, whose honest, intelligent columns were read all over the country.

marks about her democratic spirit by her friend, John H. J. Rice, pastor and police judge, which she would have deprecated [1] if she could, a prayer sent down for her by her friend, Carl Nau, and opening the service the slow, poignant movement from Beethoven's "Moonlight Sonata," which she loved, and closing the service a cutting from the joyously melancholy first movement of Tchaikovsky's "Symphonie Pathétique," which she liked to hear, in certain moods, on the phonograph, then the Lord's Prayer by her friends in the high school.

That was all.

For her pallbearers only her friends were chosen: her Latin teacher, W. L. Holtz; her high school principal, Rice Brown; her doctor, Frank Foncannon;

[1] deprecated (dep′ra·kāt·ed): disapproved of.

her friend, W. W. Finney; her pal at the *Gazette* office, Walter Hughes; and her brother Bill. It would have made her smile to know that her friend, Charley O'Brien, the traffic cop, had been transferred from Sixth and Commercial to the corner near the church to direct her friends who came to bid her good-bye.

A rift in the clouds in a gray day threw a shaft of sunlight upon her coffin as her nervous, energetic little body sank to its last sleep. But the soul of her, the glowing, gorgeous, fervent soul of her, surely was flaming in eager joy upon some other dawn.

AN EDITORIAL

The Author's Purpose. Mary's father, William Allen White, was the editor of a newspaper in Emporia, Kansas. He wrote this essay as an editorial for the paper the day after Mary's funeral.

1. Editorials often are written in appreciation of prominent citizens. Why do you think Mr. White wrote an editorial about his own daughter? What do you think Mr. White's purpose was in writing this editorial? Do you think he accomplished it?

Tone. Tone refers to the writer's attitude or feeling toward his subject. Some editorials are light in tone. Most editorial writers, however, treat their subjects seriously.

2. How would you describe Mr. White's attitude toward his daughter and toward her death? Would you say that the tone of this essay was sad, affectionate, or bitter? Explain your answer.

The Reader's Reaction. Usually, an editorial writer wants to arouse certain feeling in his readers.

3. Describe the feelings you had after you read this editorial about Mary White.

4. Did Mary seem like a real person to you? Do you think Mr. White was a good father? Did he understand Mary? Explain.

COMPOSITION:
UNITY IN A PARAGRAPH

The fifth paragraph of this essay tells about Mary's interest in drawing. The topic of this paragraph is stated in the first sentence.

"Within the last two years she had begun to be moved by an ambition to draw. She began as most children do by scribbling funny pictures in her school books. She bought cartoon magazines and took a course — rather casually, naturally, for she was, after all, a child with no strong purposes — and this year she tasted the first fruits of success by having her pictures accepted by the high school annual. But the thrill of de-

light she got when Mr. Ecord, of the normal annual, asked her to do the cartooning for that book this spring was too beautiful for words. She fell to her work with all her enthusiastic heart. Her drawings were accepted, and her pride — always repressed by a lively sense of the ridiculousness of the figure she was cutting — was a really gorgeous thing to see. No successful artist ever drank a deeper draft of satisfaction than she took from the little fame her work was getting among her schoolfellows. In her glory, she almost forgot her horse — but never her car."

Is there any sentence in this paragraph that does not add some detail about Mary's interest in drawing? When a paragraph holds to one topic, we say it has unity.

Write a paragraph telling about an interest that you, a member of your family, or a friend has. Open your paragraph with a sentence that states what this interest is, and make your paragraph unified.

FIGURES OF SPEECH

At one point this writer says that Mary was "as full of faults as an old shoe." He could have said simply: "She was not perfect." But notice how much more effective the other phrase is. Figures of speech, or comparisons, like this one are often used to create vivid descriptions.

Here are three other sentences from this editorial which make use of figures of speech. Can you locate the figures of speech? What does each one mean?

"Her humor was a continual bubble of joy."

"The tomboy in her . . . seemed to loathe to be put away forever in skirts."

"She was a Peter Pan, who refused to grow up."

George Washington Carver

FLORENCE CRANNELL MEANS

George Washington Carver was born a slave in Missouri in 1864. Fighting against poverty and prejudice, he managed to prepare himself for college. He graduated from Iowa State College in Ames, and for a while he taught there after graduation. When he had acquired a Master's degree, the young scientist was offered a position at Tuskegee Institute in Alabama.

Booker T. Washington, the great Negro educator and reformer, had founded Tuskegee in 1881 as an industrial and vocational school for Negro boys. When Dr. Washington invited Carver to serve on his faculty, the school was still struggling for its existence. But Carver decided to leave Iowa and go to Tuskegee, and he did so with these words: "It has always been the one great ideal of my life to be of the greatest good to the greatest number of 'my people,' and to this end I have been preparing myself for these many years." So in 1896, George Washington Carver began his astonishing life at Tuskegee.

The selection that follows, taken from a biography of George Washington Carver, tells something about the scientist's career at Tuskegee Institute.

A GROUP of students were sitting on the steps of the first men's dormitory, barnlike old Porter Hall, when a one-horse dray [1] drove up from the railway station at Chehaw, five miles away. In the dray, astride a tin-covered trunk, sat a striking young man. He was tall and thin. His gray suit was skimpy, so that his long hands dangled below his cuffs, and his well-blacked work shoes were just as noticeable below his trousers. His nose was a proud high beak, but the mouth, half-hidden by a well-kept mustache, was gentle, and the eyes, which ruled the whole face, were smiling ones. The pink rose in his lapel completed his unusual appearance.

[1] **dray:** cart.

From *Carver's George* by Florence Crannell Means. Reprinted by permission of Houghton Mifflin Company.

The students were even more astonished at him when he spoke, for his voice was unusually high and soft. "Young men," he asked, "where may I find Mr. Washington's office?"

One of the boys asked what class the newcomer was expecting to enter at Tuskegee.

"Young man," Mr. Carver answered, "Mr. Washington has asked me to come here as one of his instructors."

Still more amazed, the boys pointed out the office. As Mr. Carver went on, one of them muttered, "Well, this is one time I think B. T. has made a mistake."

That first day, Tuskegee impressed Mr. Carver as little as Mr. Carver impressed Tuskegee. After tidy, fertile Ames, this campus shocked him. It was crisscrossed by great gullies, torn in the red, yellow, gray, and purple Alabama soil. The country round Tuskegee seemed blighted, with its unpainted, shackly cabins and general air of poverty. The people looked crude, untidy, sick. They were sick. Many of them were weak with pellagra, a disease caused by their poor diet of corn meal and pork.

At once Professor Carver saw one reason for the poverty and sickness. This district, like the rest of the South, was drained by the one-crop system. For years cotton had sucked the earth dry of food, and yearly the fields were burned over to prepare them for the next planting. Thus they lost even the little food they might have got if the old stalks had been plowed under. Besides, the cotton was planted up to the very doors of the tenant farmers. They had no place for even the small gardens that would have given them fresh green vegetables.

First this misery and waste saddened Professor Carver, and next it excited him like a challenge. And as he talked over the conditions with his new chief, he was strengthened by the feeling that they were two men with one goal: the uplifting of their race.

The first thing needed for teaching science was a laboratory. The building was there, but it was empty, and there was no money to buy the usual costly apparatus.

"We'll make what we need," the new professor told his thirteen pupils.

"What out of?" they asked blankly.

"Out of things we'll find," their teacher replied.

He led them on a scavenger hunt to school and town dumps. They knocked at back doors, asking for leaky kettles, discarded jars, old rubber. Some pupils snickered, and some sulked, but they all went, since Professor Carver led the way.

As soon as they had gathered a good assortment of junk, Professor Carver set to work with it. He showed his class how jars and bottles could be cut down into retorts [1] and beakers, and how useful a cracked cup could be as a mortar. He made an alcohol lamp out of an ink bottle, and pipettes from reeds which he gathered in the swamp. An old tin shingle with different-sized holes punched in it became a grater. The wild bamboo was made to order for their needs. He cut a square opening between each two joints, slipped in a

---

[1] **retorts:** vessels in which substances are distilled or decomposed by heat.

piece of glass for a window, and had a display case for various types of soil.

Even while outfitting his laboratory, Professor Carver was working on the soil problem to help the wretched neighborhood farmers. In this purpose his chief agreed with him, but he urged Professor Carver not to neglect the campus wells; the cattle, which gave little milk; the poultry; the proposed orchard; the repair of the school wagons.

Professor Carver felt that his greatest duty was to the farmers, and he put it first, often to Mr. Washington's impatience. Professor Carver brought in samples of soil from the neighborhood farms and analyzed them to find what could be added to better them, and what crops they would best grow. He found all the soils poor, ranging from coarse sand to sandy or clayey loam.

He planned to have bulletins printed in the school shop and given to the farmers. These bulletins would explain how anyone could improve the harmful pork and corn meal diet by cooking the greens that grew free along every roadside. The bulletins would tell how to prepare the greens so that they not only would prevent pellagra, but would be tasty as well. They would also tell in simple words about the soil's need for food, and how to feed it.

There was an obstacle. Few of the farmers could read. For those who could not, Professor Carver "wrote" a different kind of bulletin, twenty acres across. He and his class tilled a field and showed what could be done with soil so poor that the school strawberry patch yielded only a cupful of berries a day.

He had found one place on the campus where vegetation throve. On the dump where he had gathered laboratory equipment, pumpkin vines grew and bore fine pumpkins. Thinking of these, Professor Carver concluded that any kind of decaying matter was food for hungry soil — not only animal manure and vegetable waste. He set his students to making compost heaps. Grumbling, they piled up all sorts of rubbish, covered it with leaves, and left it to decay. That was for the future, for tomorrow.

For today, Professor Carver requested a two-horse plow. Everyone laughed at the demand, for plowing was still done the old way in Macon County — with a simple plow drawn by a single ox or horse. However, the professor got his plow and broke the ground thoroughly. Then he had his class bring swamp muck and barnyard manure and spread them over the red, yellow, and purple earth. Finally, he had them plant the acre in cowpeas. They laughed again at the small crop he harvested after all his trouble. Professor Carver cheerfully cooked the despised cowpeas and served them to his boys, who were astonished to find them good.

Next the professor planted sweet potatoes on the same ground, and, after the sweet potatoes, cotton of a strain he had been working on. The first year the Institute farm lost $16.25. The second year it earned $4.00, the third, $75 an acre from two crops of sweet potatoes. When, from an acre of the worthless ground, Professor Carver harvested the unheard-of crop of a five-hundred-pound bale of cotton, people stopped laughing. Maybe there was something in the man's wild ideas, after all.

By this time Professor Carver needed equipment which he could not find on the dump. He decided to use what he had and to make out of it what he wanted. He had music! In striped trousers and frock coat, he made a concert tour of the South — "Professor Carver at the piano." From this journey and from his growing acquaintance with the region round Tuskegee, Professor Carver gained new vision into the needs of southern farmers.

Professor Carver was fitting into his new setting. Some of it he could fit to himself instead. In his second year he landscaped the campus. He had it graded and terraced, and he planted Bermuda grass to cloak it with green. He set trees and shrubs and swift-growing honeysuckle and wisteria to cover the steep banks.

Other things about Tuskegee were as unlike Ames as the campus was. As he searched fields, woods, and roadsides for plants, the townspeople often spoke kindly to him. The colored people soon came to know him. Puzzlingly different from anyone they had met before, they found him able to help them when they tramped to the Institute to tell him their troubles. Soon they were calling him "Doctor." Even when he cured them, some still puzzled about him. Others had no feelings except gratitude and admiration, and they welcomed him eagerly when he came to sit awhile in their cabins, noticing their needs and suggesting helpful changes.

Though the Institute found the new teacher hard to understand, they soon learned to like him. He became popular even with those who did not guess his worth. Here, as at Ames, his dining table was the gayest in the room. It was his idea to celebrate the birthdays of everyone at the table, and for each he painted cards and planned something special. When three of them had birthdays the same month he protested, "We want a party every month. After this we'll ask everyone his birth date before we let him join us."

He loved to joke. He enjoyed tussling with "his boys," and would give them a good paddling when the fun ran high. This was the first time he had been in a community made up of his own people, and while he missed his wide circle of friends in the North, this easy sociability had charm.

He believed he was not meant to have home and family, yet home life was dear to him. For years he had Thanksgiving dinner regularly with the family of a fellow professor. Dr. Carver was quietly happy when a child of this family was named after him, and he mourned the stillness in the house when one after another the children went out into the world.

After a few years Mr. Washington offered Dr. Carver an increase in his fifteen-hundred-dollar salary. Dr. Carver refused it. What use had he for money? He had all God's universe to draw on for his needs. He believed that God had made a world that would supply His children's every want, if only they would take the trouble to use it. He therefore felt small need of money, that man-made medium of exchange.

His indifference bothered the Institute treasurer. Dr. Carver upset the bookkeeping by failing to cash his salary checks. Once when asked to give to a worthy cause, Dr. Carver explained that he had no money. Then a thought struck him, and he rummaged in his crowded desk. "This might help," he added, "and this, and this." He handed the astonished caller forgotten salary checks amounting to several hundred dollars.

During his first ten years at Tuskegee Dr. Carver busily experimented with soil improvement, with sweet potatoes, cowpeas, velvet beans, and cotton, and with grains which might be profitable to the South. He also had courses to teach and practical matters to attend to in addition to the research, in which he was so brilliant.

After fifteen years, the Department of Agricultural Research was established at Tuskegee, with Dr. Carver in complete charge. The new position was supposed to relieve him of all teaching, but students begged for classes with him and would not be refused. For many more years he continued to teach a limited number. Loving young people and seeing their possibilities, he was able to inspire as well as instruct them. After he became Director of Research, the news of his discoveries spread abroad more generally. He was asked to address churches, clubs, and other organizations far and wide, and to take his exhibits to fairs and conventions.

It was Dr. Carver's experiments with peanuts that brought him his first wide fame.

He had always tried to improve conditions on southern farms. He disliked the one-crop system, with nothing but cotton planted. King Cotton destroyed soil, plantation owners, and tenant farmers by taking all the nutriment from the ground where it grew. Yet Dr. Carver felt that the time for cotton's overthrow had not yet come. Farmers could not be made to believe that other crops would serve them better. Therefore, he compromised, perfecting more profitable kinds of cotton by crossing valuable long-staple cotton with the sturdier short-staple. One bush would bear two hundred and seventy-five huge bolls, without use of commercial fertilizer.

Agriculturalists began to seek him out. The Colonial Secretary of the German Empire spent days at Tuskegee consulting him, and an Australian took the remarkable new seed to his government, which introduced it in Australia. Distant farmers sent him specimens of their soil and well water for analysis. He always answered with thoughtful advice. A group of pecan growers, their groves dying of an unknown disease, sought Dr. Carver's help. His suggested treatment saved them from ruin — but Dr. Carver politely returned the check they sent him.

At last the day he had expected came, when King Cotton's throne tottered. For years the boll weevil had been marching northward from Mexico like an army, boring into the cotton bolls and destroying the cotton be-

Carver in his laboratory, where he produced hundreds of synthetic products.

fore it could ripen. No one could prevent the destruction, but Dr. Carver believed he could rebuild after they had torn down, at the same time helping to end the one-crop system. There were crops that would grow well in Alabama's poor soil and at the same time feed it instead of draining it as cotton did. Among these were the velvet bean, good for stock feed, and the soy bean, with its hundred uses, almost unnoticed then, except by Dr. Carver.

Dr. Carver knew people as well as plants. He knew it would take many years to coax them to plant unfamiliar crops. So he proposed a plant as familiar as an old shoe, the peanut. Every garden had a peanut patch, for everyone liked peanuts, though nobody thought them important.

The plant has unusual ways. When the flower withers, the stem lengthens and bends, pushing the seed pod into the ground to ripen. Like other members of the pea family, it has queer roots. These roots bear small swellings or tubercles, containing bacterialike matter which has the ability to take nitrogen from the air and hold it in a form the plants can use. For this reason such plants are good to grow in orchards or between the rows of fields in poor soil. Either by the decay of their roots or by the plowing under of the plants, they enrich the earth.

When the boll weevil arrived, Dr. Carver stood ready to defend Macon County, Alabama. His weapon was a peanut.

He told the farmers to plow up their infected cotton and destroy it. They must spray the ground where it had grown, let it stand idle for a month, and plant peanuts on it. After fifteen years, the farmers had learned to respect Dr. Carver's judgment, and many of them did as he said. The first result was deep trouble for Dr. Carver.

The peanut harvest was the largest in the history of Alabama, and there was no market for it. Peanuts were sold at the circus, with popcorn and pink lemonade, and a few were made into the novelty spread, peanut butter. But the demand was small and was supplied by imports from the Orient. The problem was first brought to Dr. Carver by a widow who had followed his suggestion and now had a large useless crop on her hands. Dr. Carver was deeply concerned, feeling that he had given advice without looking far enough ahead.

However, it was his habit to make use of his misfortunes. First he went out after a supply of peanuts. Then he drew guards over his sweater sleeves, put on his flour-sack apron, and went to work.

He shelled a double handful of peanuts, laying the hulls aside for further experiment, and ground the nuts fine. Then he heated part of them and put them in a cotton bag and under a press, which he screwed down till it had extracted all the oil it could.

The cake that remained looked dry, but Dr. Carver knew that it retained some oil. Long fingers flying, he added a solvent which released the last bit of the oil. It was wonderful stuff, as he had long known. Most of the animal fats had a gelatinous membrane around each oil particle, but this had none. Therefore, it was much easier to break down its fat globules.

From some of the ground peanuts, he had extracted a fluid that looked like creamy Jersey milk. It not only looked like milk, but analysis showed it to be milk, even though no cow, goat, or other animal grew on its family tree. What was more, a small glassful of shelled peanuts produced a pint. And if he was not mistaken, it had every value that cow's milk had, except for calcium, which it possessed in smaller proportion. All the lines of the Doctor's face curved upward in grateful satisfaction as he set it to one side.

The dry cake he put into another vessel, together with water and an enzyme, one of those mysterious digestive substances which animal bodies manufacture. This he set at a heat which would hold it at body temperature, so that the proteins should be separated from other elements.

He had absent-mindedly turned on the lights and continued with his work, dimly aware from time to time that voices grumbled and coaxed outside his locked door. When the doorknob rattled sharply he only muttered under his breath.

The artificial process of digestion was reasonably rapid. In a few hours he could tell that the peanut was rich in protein. It would take a much longer series of experiments to sort out the different kinds of amino acids that made up the protein. He must be sure that there were at least sixteen, so that it would fill all nutritional requirements.

Suddenly he was so tired that he paused in his work. His windowpanes were completely black, and all noises had seeped away, leaving a great silence. He glanced at his watch and murmured, "Well, I declare!" Strange how the hours had raced past.

The gray light of morning had drained the brightness from his electric bulbs when he inspected the beaker where he had poured his peanut milk the evening before. He chuckled. A rich coating of cream covered it. He skimmed off the cream and noted with pleasure that the milk showed no separation or curdling. Deftly he whipped the cream and chuckled anew. Sweet and fresh though it was, it formed a tiny lump of good butter. When he had time, he would see what kind of cheese this vegetable milk would make. Now he must proceed with the isolating and identifying of the other elements of the peanut.

All that day he worked, sometimes making no reply at all to the urgent voices at the door. For two days and two nights he went on asking what the peanut was and what it was for. At last he emerged, gray and shaking with weariness but serenely joyful.

He had sorted out the contents of the tight little package that was the peanut. He had found water, fats, oils, gums, resins, sugars, starches, pectins, pentosans, and proteins. He had recombined these elements at different heats and under different pressures, and had worked out twenty usable products from them. The biggest possible peanut harvest could be used with profit.

Even then he did not stop asking. He went on rearranging the substances — making what he wanted out of what he had — until he had discovered over three hundred useful peanut products.

Among the three hundred products were the "rich Jersey milk" drinks, including instant coffee, Worcestershire and other sauces, flour, mixed pickles, salve, bleach, face cream, shaving cream, wallboard, synthetic rubber, linoleum. He sent samples of the face cream to several ladies, and while most of them were delighted, one protested that it was fattening her face.

In his home economics classes, he taught ways to prepare peanuts for the table. As a climax, he had his girls serve Mr. Washington and other guests a five course peanut luncheon. The menu was soup, mock chicken, peanuts creamed as a vegetable, bread, ice cream, cookies, coffee, and candy. The only item that did not contain peanuts was the salad, of pepper grass, sheep sorrel, and chicory.

Meanwhile, the peanut milk proved an unquestionable blessing. The great Indian leader, Gandhi, found it a healthful food, along with the soybean formula Dr. Carver worked out for him. In Africa the milk saved lives. If an African mother died when her child was born, the child also died. Or if the mother lived but could not nurse her baby, there was no way to raise it. That was because wild animals and tsetse flies prevent the keeping of cows. Now the missionaries fed starving babies on Dr. Carver's peanut milk, and they grew plump and strong.

The peanut milk proved well suited to cheesemaking, also. While it takes a hundred pounds of cow's milk to make ten pounds of cheese, only thirty-three pounds of peanut milk are required.

By 1921 the peanut industry had become so important that the tariff on peanuts also became important. Almost half the supply was shipped from China and Japan, and the duty was only three-eighths of a cent a pound on the unshelled, and three-fourths of a cent on the shelled. American growers felt that four and five cents duty was needed to cover the difference in cost between Oriental and American labor. So the Peanut Grower's Association asked "the Tuskegee man" to show the possibilities of the peanut to the Ways and Means Committee of the House of Representatives.

George Washington Carver went to Washington. He had a wooden box in which he carried twenty-five or thirty specimens of his peanut exhibit. This case he always packed and lugged himself. Arriving in the Washington railway station, he found no one to meet him and asked a redcap to help him to a cab with his box. The redcap was friendly but busy. "Sorry, grandpop," he said, "but I'm supposed to pick up some great scientist from Alabama and take him to the Capitol."

Dr. Carver doubtless chuckled inwardly, but he was too stubborn to explain the mistake. Finally he found a taxi that could take him and his box, and they started out. He had time for sightseeing on the way, and the driver, though amused, was good-natured. At his fare's request, he drove through the botanical gardens and stopped when asked. Dr. Carver had caught sight of a rare shrub infected with a dangerous disease. Before he could be stopped, he was breaking off sick branches, clucking to himself. When an official had been called, Dr. Carver pointed out the evidence of disease, told the

official that it must have come into this country in plants from Far Eastern jungles, and explained how to wipe it out. The Washington botanist gave grateful attention.

When Dr. Carver reached the House of Representatives, he sat quietly in the rear and listened to endless fussing and reading of briefs. He was uneasy over having to talk to so disorderly a crowd. Besides, it was almost four o'clock, and four o'clock was closing time.

At last peanuts came on the docket, and the Virginia-Carolina Co-operative Peanut Exchange attested that a "protective tariff on peanuts was the only thing that could save the sandy-land farmers from ruin." George Washington Carver's name was called, and he lugged his heavy case to the platform. Representatives sprawled yawning in their seats and then straightened to gape at the elderly Negro slowly mounting the steps.

"Your time has been cut to ten minutes," the chairman said.

He had come all this way for ten minutes. Many speakers would have protested indignantly. Dr. Carver had always said, "Make what you want out of what you have." Now he had ten minutes, an audience of bored men, his array of peanut products, and his self-control, wit, and gentle fun-making. With these he went to work.

His clear, silvery voice pierced the stale air like a bird song, and sleepy lawmakers stopped their yawns in the middle. "I've been asked to tell about the extension of the peanut," Dr. Carver began, "but we'll have to hurry if we are to extend it, because in ten minutes you will tell me to stop."

With practiced speed he unpacked his products. He held up a chocolate candy and popped it into his mouth with a joke about having to enjoy it for them. They stopped yawning. This was a good show after hours of dull debate.

First he told them that the peanut and the sweet potato were twin brothers. If all other foods were taken away, these twins would give man everything needed for healthful diet. He showed a syrup made from sweet potato and used with peanuts to make a candy bar. He showed them stock feed, ice cream ready to freeze, linoleum. When he had them fascinated, he remarked meekly that his ten minutes were up. They insisted on his having more time.

So, keeping them amused with jokes, he went on. He showed peanut milk, covered with thick cream, and cereal coffee, whose flavor he had enriched by repeated roastings. He showed buttermilk, and evaporated milk such as had saved the African babies. He showed face cream, meat substitutes, wood dyes. His ten minutes stretched to an hour and three-quarters, and his whole audience was wide awake and asking interested questions.

When one Representative scoffingly asked what Dr. Carver knew about tariffs, Dr. Carver jokingly retorted, "This is all the tariff means: to shut the other fellow out."

That was all he said about it, but after seeing his exhibition the committee wrote into the pending bill the best tariff rate the American peanut growers had ever had.

As a result of all this development, the peanut crop gradually worked up to a value second only to that of cotton, and the one-crop system was ended. An interesting example of the change is Dothan, Alabama, the "capital of the peanut belt." The peanut boosted the town's population from a thousand or less to twenty-one thousand, its main industry being the extraction of peanut oil for butter, salad dressing, and other products.

Maxwell County actually put up a monument to the boll weevil, because that pest had forced them to stop raising cotton and start raising peanuts. To use a slang expression, the peanut business is no longer "peanuts." A few years ago statistics showed that it was bringing Southern growers about fifty-five million dollars a year, and bringing the peanut industry about two hundred million. All those millions have flowed indirectly from Dr. Carver's little workshop. Small wonder he was called the Peanut Wizard.

BIOGRAPHY

The Author's Purpose. In reading a biography, you should notice the details of the subject's life that the author has chosen to tell about. Because a biographer must be selective, he sometimes reveals his purpose through the details he chooses.

1. What examples did the biographer give to show how Carver personally helped other people? What anecdote illustrated Carver's attitude toward money? What were we told about Carver's success as a teacher? How did the biographer let us know that Carver was humble? What details were included to tell us that Carver's research helped people all over the

world? What incident illustrated Carver's sense of humor?

2. Has the biographer selected only good things to tell about Carver? Cite passages from the selection to support your answer.

3. In your opinion, did the author write this biography to give information about Carver's discoveries or to give an appealing picture of a famous man? Explain.

Tone. The author of a biography has an opinion of the person he is writing about, and this opinion affects the tone of his writing. The tone of a biography may be light, but it is usually serious, and either generally approving or disapproving.

4. Did this biographer like Carver? What is her attitude toward Carver's achievements?

The Reader's Reaction

5. Do you think that this biography presented a realistic picture of George Washington Carver? Explain.

6. What parts of this account interested you most? Did you get any new ideas from this account, or were any of your attitudes changed as a result of it? Explain.

WORD FORMS

The author says that farmers sent Carver soil specimens for *analysis*. When you learn the meaning of the noun *analysis*, you should also know the verb *analyze*, and perhaps the adjective *analytic*. Can you use *analysis, analyze,* and *analytic* in sentences?

Compare the meanings of the nouns *analysis* and *synthesis*. What form does *synthesis* take when it is used as a verb? as an adjective? Use the noun, verb, and adjective forms of *synthesis* in sentences.

Here are three other nouns which can be made into verbs and adjectives by making slight changes in their spelling. Can

you name the verb and adjective forms of each of these nouns?

paralysis   hypnosis   emphasis

COMPOSITION: SPECIFIC DETAILS

The topic of a paragraph is often stated in the opening sentence. The other sentences in the paragraph then supply specific details to support this general topic statement.

For example, here is a paragraph from the biography of Carver. Note that the author has used specific details to develop her topic, which she states in the first sentence.

"As soon as they had gathered a good assortment of junk, Professor Carver set to work with it. He showed his class how jars and bottles could be cut down into retorts and beakers, and how useful a cracked cup could be as a mortar. He made an alcohol lamp out of an ink bottle, and pipettes from reeds which he gathered in the swamp. An old tin shingle with different-sized holes punched in it became a grater. The wild bamboo was made to order for their needs. He cut a square opening between each two joints, slipped in a piece of glass for a window, and had a display case for various types of soil."

This paragraph uses specific details to tell how Carver transformed "junk" into laboratory equipment. List these items of junk and tell what they were used for.

Write a topic sentence stating in a general way how some procedure is performed. Perhaps you will want to use one of the sentences below. Follow up your topic sentence with at least three other sentences that add some detailed, specific information.

An assortment of ingredients is needed to make a stew (pie, pizza).

Getting ready for a trip is a tiring job.

MASTERPIECES OF ART

Movement and Rhythm in Painting

"Still life" is what artists call pictures of familiar objects like those in PLATES 1, 2, and 3. Though these objects are indeed still, the pictures are in a way "lively." Juan Sánchez Cotán, a painter of seventeenth-century Spain, shows us in PLATE 1 fresh fruits and vegetables so realistically rendered that they may make us hungry. No doubt it was the artist, and not the cook, who placed them in such an odd arrangement. A line drawn from each object to the next would make a slow curve from the upper left to the lower right corner. Even though a curved line is not visible, we imagine it as our eyes move from quince to cabbage to melon to cucumber. The nearly equal spaces between the objects make them appear as accents of an even, rhythmic beat. Repetitions at regular intervals create rhythmic patterns that suggest motion, as in music or dancing.

In *Still Life with Ginger Jar and Eggplants* (PLATE 2), Paul Cézanne has placed his rounded fruits and jars in a huddle, as though the heaving waves of a sea of drapery had tossed them together. The precariously slanting dish of pears seems ready to slide down the path of a point of white, with a wave chasing it from behind. But since your eye jumps quickly from the yellow pears to the yellower lemon, this fate is averted. You continue up and around from lemon to melon to green jar to bottle to eggplants. There is a suspenseful pause — then a drop to the silhouetted dark pear and back to the sliding plate. A fat, stable ginger jar, however, sits calmly in the center, governing the surrounding movement like the sun in our solar system.

Georges Braque's still life titled *Musical Forms with the Words* Fête *and* Journ (PLATE 3) is actually a picture of a violin, sheet music, a folded newspaper, a wine glass, and a pipe. But the artist has shown us these objects in parts, seen from different angles and distances, and he has assembled them into one larger "object" that contains them all.

401

Planes like sheets of glass pass through one another, forces push and pull, and the whole "object" threatens to shake apart. Yet distributed all over it is a lively pattern of straight edges, angles, parts of circles, and trembling texture strokes of brush or charcoal that keep your eyes racing back and forth and up and down. Finally, however, the almost vertical lines triumph with a steady vibration like the sound of the violin strings which are seen in the middle of this still life.

In painting landscapes, artists do not have the wind's movement to enliven their still canvasses. In *The Mill at Wijk-bij-Duurstede* (PLATE 4), the Dutch painter Jacob van Ruisdael left the sailboat becalmed, but he made the windmill churn the air simply by placing its sails in diagonal positions. (Imagine them vertical and horizontal, and note the difference it would make.) The clouds also form diagonal patterns, and interlocking wedges of land and sea make a zigzag line that moves our eye toward the horizon. But what seems to move most is the light. As the clouds loom toward us, sunlight filters through them, advancing around the curving shape of the mill, flickering on the red roof, and creating bands of light and shadow across earth and sea.

Vincent van Gogh, also a Dutch painter, painted a picture called *Cypresses* (PLATE 5) in which nothing is at rest. A wavelike convulsion has taken hold of the cypress trees and has spread like fire through the grass, the mountains, the clouds, and even the sky. It is as though all the things in the picture are made of the same substance: that substance is *paint*. The paint is applied in continually repeating waves, no matter what object is represented. Van Gogh saw in the flamelike shapes of a cypress tree the forces that make the world go around, and he caused this movement to pervade the whole world of his picture.

Georges Seurat's landscape *The Bridge at Courbevoie* (PLATE 6) presents us with a paradox: the scene appears hushed and still, yet the composition is alive with rhythmic movement. Upright, parallel masts and their reflections march sedately across the picture. The river bank rushes swiftly down, but two silent figures act like brakes on its headlong movement. The dark tree abruptly changes these rhythms to rising curves which spray out at the top. There you are left floating gently with a flight of birds and the lilting swing of pointed sail and curving smoke. And all through the picture runs a tremor made by the tiny color spots of Seurat's brush strokes, which seem to remind us that all things are made of atoms in motion.

Since it is the artist who creates the "motion" in his paintings, he can control it however he likes.

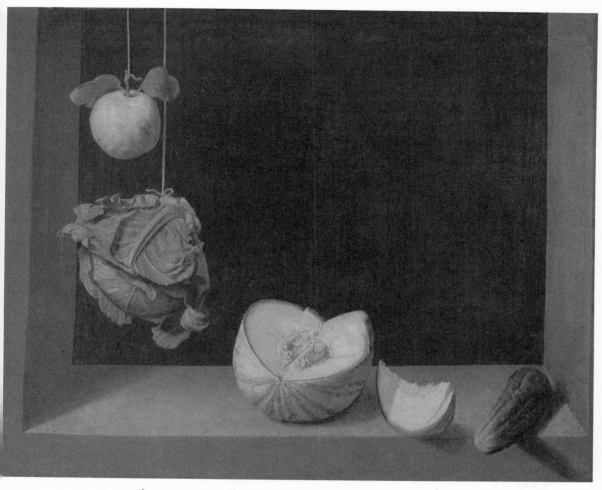

PLATE 1. JUAN SÁNCHEZ COTÁN (Spanish, 1561–1627): *Still Life: Quince, Cabbage, Melon and Cucumber.* About 1602. Oil on canvas, 26½ x 32¾ inches. (Collection of the Fine Arts Society of San Diego, Gift of the Misses Anne R. and Amy Putnam, 1945)

PLATE 2. PAUL CEZANNE (French, 1839–1906): *Still Life with Ginger Jar and Eggplants.* About 1890–94. Oil on canvas, 28½ x 36¼ inches. (The Metropolitan Museum of Art, New York, Bequest of Stephen C. Clark, 1960)

PLATE 3. GEORGES BRAQUE (French, 1882–1964): *Musical Forms with the Words Fête and* Journ. 1913. Oil, pencil, and charcoal on canvas, 36¼ x 23½ inches. (Philadelphia Museum of Art, The Louise and Walter Arensberg Collection)

PLATE 4. JACOB VAN RUISDAEL (Dutch, 1628/29–1682): *The Mill at Wijk-bij-Duur-stede*. About 1676. Oil on canvas, 32¾ x 39¾ inches. (Rijksmuseum, Amsterdam)

PLATE 5. VINCENT VAN GOGH (Dutch, 1853–1890): *Cypresses*. 1889. Oil on canvas, 36¾ x 29⅛ inches. (The Metropolitan Museum of Art, New York, Rogers Fund, 1949)

PLATE 6. GEORGES SEURAT (French, 1859–1891): *The Bridge at Courbevoie*. 1886.
Oil on canvas, 18 x 21½ inches. (Courtauld Institute Galleries, London)

First Pitch

ROBERT CREAMER

Tʜᴇ Aᴍᴇʀɪᴄᴀɴ sᴘʀɪɴɢ is very much like spring anywhere — lively green fingers of things poking their way up through the dull and barren ground; the sudden surprise of tulips; the great, quiet explosion of apple blossoms.

These are, in one form or another, universals. But the American spring has something else, too — an element that is rich with the same awakening spirit of rebirth, life lived again. The boy, sensing the working of the earth, says to his friend: "It smells like baseball." The father picks up the son's baseball glove and tries it on, working his hand into it, punching it a couple of times.

The gardener rests, letting the sun warm his back, and thinks of the lush summer ahead. The boy and the man think of pitchers and batters, a sharp base hit, an outfielder running, the crowds, the cry of the vendor, the taste of the frankfurter.

The green grass grows, the tulip burns with color, the blossoms gently stroke the air. The ball, the bat, the glove, and the hard (at first), then muddy (for a while) diamond seem to grow, too, as dormant skills are slowly aroused in the small boy, the young man, the professional.

The sun crosses the equator on its journey north. At that moment, say the precisionists, it is spring. But in America (and perhaps wherever baseball is played) there is another moment. One day a major league pitcher, standing in the center of the formal garden of the infield, working in union with his teammates but isolated from them, takes a deep breath, grasps the slick new baseball, winds up, and throws to the opposing batsman. It is the first pitch of the new season.

Then, in America, it is spring. □

"First Pitch" from *The Spectacle of Sport* by Robert Creamer, published by Prentice-Hall, Inc., © 1957 by Time, Inc. Reprinted by permission of *Sports Illustrated*.

An Old-fashioned Iowa Christmas

PAUL ENGLE

"There are no such arrivals any more . . ."
(Detail from painting on page 412.)

Every Christmas should begin with the sound of bells, and when I was a child mine always did. But they were sleigh bells, not church bells, for we lived in a part of Cedar Rapids, Iowa, where there were no churches. My bells were on my father's team of horses as he drove up to our horse-headed hitching post with the bobsled that would take us to celebrate Christmas on the family farm ten miles out in the country. My father would bring the team down Fifth Avenue at a smart trot, flicking his whip over the horses' rumps and making the bells double their light, thin jangling over the snow.

There are no such departures any more: the whole family piling into the bobsled with a foot of golden oat straw to lie in and heavy buffalo robes to lie under, the horses stamping the soft

snow, and at every motion of their hoofs the bells jingling, jingling.

There are no streets like those any more: the snow sensibly left on the road for the sake of sleighs and easy travel. We could hop off and ride the heavy runners as they made their hissing, tearing sound over the packed snow. And along the streets we met other horses, so that we moved from one set of bells to another. There would be an occasional brass-mounted automobile laboring on its narrow tires and as often as not pulled up the slippery hills by a horse, and we would pass it with a triumphant shout for an awkward nuisance which was obviously not here to stay.

The country road ran through a landscape of little hills and shallow valleys and heavy groves of timber. The great moment was when we left the road and turned up the long lane on the farm. Near the low house on the hill, with oaks on one side and apple trees on the other, my father would stand up, flourish his whip, and bring the bobsled right up to the door of the house with a burst of speed.

There are no such arrivals any more: the harness bells ringing and clashing like faraway steeples, the horses whinnying at the horses in the barn and receiving a great, trumpeting whinny in reply, the dogs leaping into the bobsled and burrowing under the buffalo robes, a squawking from the hen house, a yelling of "Whoa, whoa," at the excited horses, boy and girl cousins howling around the bobsled, and the descent into the snow with the Christmas basket carried by my mother.

While my mother and sisters went into the house, the team was unhitched and taken to the barn to be covered with blankets and given a little grain. That winter odor of a barn is a wonderfully complex one, rich and warm and utterly unlike the smell of the same barn in summer: the body heat of many animals weighing a thousand pounds and more; pigs in one corner making their dark, brown-sounding grunts; milk cattle still nuzzling the manger for wisps of hay; horses eying the newcomers; oats, hay, and straw, tangy still with the live August sunlight; the sharp odor of leather harness rubbed with neat's-foot oil [1] to keep it supple; the molasses-sweet odor of ensilage [2] in the silo where the fodder was almost fermenting. It is a smell from strong and living things, and my father always said it

was the secret of health, that it scoured out a man's lungs. He would stand there, breathing deeply, one hand on a horse's rump, watching the steam come out from under the blankets as the team cooled down from their rapid trot up the lane. It gave him a better appetite, he argued, than plain fresh air, which was thin and had no body to it.

A barn with cattle and horses is the place to begin Christmas; after all, that's where the original event happened, and that same smell was the first air that the Christ Child breathed.

By the time we reached the house, my mother and sisters were wearing aprons and busying themselves in the kitchen, as red-faced as the women who had been there all morning. The kitchen was the biggest room in the house, and all family life save sleeping went on there. My uncle even had a couch along one wall where he napped and where the children lay when they were ill. The kitchen range was a tremendous black and gleaming one called a Smoke Eater, with pans bubbling over the holes above the fire box and a reservoir of hot water at the side, lined with dull copper, from which my uncle would dip a basin of water and shave above the sink, turning his lathered face now and then to drop a remark into the women's talk, waving his straight-edged razor, as if it were a threat, to make them believe him. My job was to go to the woodpile out back to split the chunks of oak and hickory and keep the fire burning.

It was a handmade Christmas. The tree came from down in the grove, and on it were many paper ornaments

[1] **neat's-foot oil:** oil made by boiling the bones and feet of cattle.

[2] **ensilage** (en′sə·lij): fermented animal feed (fodder).

made by my cousins, as well as beautiful ones brought from the Black Forest,[1] where the family had originally lived. There were popcorn balls, paper horns with homemade candy, and apples from the orchard. The gifts tended to be hand-knit socks or wool ties or fancy crocheted "yokes" for nightgowns, tatted collars for blouses, doilies with fancy flower patterns for tables, and tidies for chairs. Once I received a brilliantly polished cow horn with a cavalryman crudely but bravely carved on it. And there would

[1] **the Black Forest:** a region in Germany.

usually be a cornhusk doll, perhaps with a prune or walnut for a face, and a gay dress of an old corset-cover scrap with its ribbons still bright. And there were real candles burning with real flames, every guest sniffing the air for the smell of scorching pine needles.

There are no dinners like that any more: every item from the farm itself, with no deep freezer, no car for driving into town for packaged food. The pies had been baked the day before, pumpkin, apple, and mince; as we ate them, we could look out the window and see the cornfield where the pumpkins grew, the trees from

Scenes from an old-fashioned New England Christmas, titled "Out for the Christmas Trees," painted by Grandma Moses. (Copyright Grandma Moses Properties, Inc. Courtesy Galerie St. Etienne, New York.)

which the apples were picked. The bread had been baked that morning, heating up the oven for the meat, and as my aunt hurried by I could smell in her apron that freshest of all odors with which the human nose is honored — bread straight from the oven. There would be a huge brown crock of beans with smoked pork from the hog butchered every November.

There would be every form of preserve: wild grape from the vines in the grove, crab-apple jelly, wild blackberry and tame raspberry, strawberry from the bed in the garden, sweet and sour pickles with dill from the edge of the lane where it grew wild, pickles from the rind of the same watermelon we had cooled in the tank at the milk house and eaten on a hot September afternoon.

Cut into the slope of the hill behind the house, with a little door of its own, was the vegetable cellar, from which came carrots, turnips, cabbages, potatoes, squash. And of course there was the traditional sauerkraut, with flecks of caraway seed. I remember one Christmas Day when a ten-gallon crock of it in the basement, with a stone weighting down the lid, had blown up, driving the stone against the floor of the parlor.

All the meat was from the home place, too. Most useful of all was the goose — the very one which had chased me the summer before, hissing and darting out its bill at the end of its curving neck like a feathered snake. Here was the universal bird of an older Christmas: its down was plucked, washed, and hung in bags in the barn to be put into pillows; its awkward

"The trees came from down in the grove . . ." (Detail from painting on page 412.)

body was roasted until the skin was crisp as a fine paper; and the grease from its carcass was melted down, a little camphor added, and rubbed on the chests of coughing children. We ate, slept on, and wore that goose.

And of course the trimmings were from the farm, too: the hickory-nut cake made with nuts gathered in the grove after the first frost and hulled out by my cousins with yellowed hands; the black-walnut cookies, sweeter than any taste; the fudge with butternuts crowding it. In the mornings we would be given a hammer, a flatiron, and a bowl of nuts to crack and pick out for the homemade ice cream.

All families had their special Christmas food. Ours was called Dutch bread, made from a dough halfway between bread and cake, stuffed with citron and every sort of nut from the farm — hazel, black walnut, hickory, butternut. A little round one was always baked for me in a baking-soda can, and my last act on Christmas Eve was to put it by the tree so that Santa

Claus would find it and have a snack —
after all, he'd come a long, cold way
to our house. And every Christmas
morning, he would have eaten it. My
aunt made the same Dutch bread and
we smeared over it the same butter
she had been churning from their own
Jersey milk that same morning.

To eat in the same room where food
is cooked — that is the way to thank
the Lord for His abundance. The long
table, with its different levels where
additions had been made for the small
fry, ran the length of the kitchen. The
air was heavy with odors, not only of
food on plates but of the act of cooking itself along with the metallic smell
of heated iron from the hard-working
Smoke Eater, and the whole stove offered us its yet uneaten prospects of
more goose and untouched pies. To
see the giblet gravy made and poured
into a gravy boat is the surest way to
overeat its swimming richness.

The warning for Christmas dinner
was always an order to go to the milk
house for cream, where we skimmed
from the cooling pans of fresh milk the
cream which had the same golden
color as the flanks of the Jersey cows
which had given it. The last deed before eating was grinding the coffee
beans in the little mill, adding that
exotic odor to the more native ones of
goose and spiced pumpkin pie. Then
all would sit at the table and my uncle
would ask the grace, sometimes in
German, but later, for the benefit of us
ignorant children, in English:

Come, Lord Jesus, be our guest,
Share this food that you have
    blessed.

"The country road ran through a landscape of little hills . . ." (Detail from
painting on page 412.)

My aunt kept a turmoil of food circulating, and to refuse any of it was
somehow to violate the elevated nature
of the day. To consume the length and
breadth of that meal was to suffer!
But we all faced the ordeal with courage. Uncle Ben would let out his belt —
a fancy Western belt with steer heads
and silver buckle —with a snap and a
sigh. The women managed better by
always getting up from the table and
trotting to the kitchen sink or the
Smoke Eater or outdoors for some item
left in the cold. The men sat there,
grimly enduring the glory of their ap-
petites.

After dinner, late in the afternoon,
the women would make despairing gestures toward the dirty dishes and scoop
up hot water from the reservoir at the
side of the range. The men would go
to the barn and look after the live-
stock. My older cousin would take his
new .22 rifle and stalk out across the
pasture with the remark, "I saw that
fox just now, looking for his Christmas
goose." Or sleds would be dragged

out and we would slide in a long snake, feet hooked into the sled behind, down the hill and across the westward sloping fields into the sunset. Bones would be thrown to dogs, suet tied in the oak trees for the juncos and winter-defying chickadees, a saucer of skimmed milk set out for the cats, daintily and disgustedly picking their padded feet through the snow, and crumbs scattered on a bird feeder where already the crimson cardinals would be dropping out of the sky like blood. Then back to the house for a final warming-up before leaving.

There was usually a song around the tree before we were all bundled up, many thanks all around for gifts, the basket as loaded as when it came, more so, for leftover food had been piled in it. My father and uncle would have brought up the team from the barn and hooked them into the double shafts of the bobsled, and we would all go out into the freezing air of early evening.

And now those bells again as the horses, impatient from their long standing in the barn, stamped and shook their harness, my father holding them back with a soft clucking in his throat and a hard pull on the reins. The smell of wood smoke flavoring the air in our noses, the cousins shivering with cold, "Good-bye, good-bye," called out by everyone, and the bobsled would move off, creaking over the frost-brittle snow. All of us, my mother included, would dig down in the straw and pull the buffalo robes up to our chins. As the horses settled into a steady trot, the bells gently chiming in their rhythmical beat, we would fall half asleep, the hiss of the runners comforting. As we looked up at the night sky through half-closed eyelids, the constant bounce and swerve of the runners would seem to shake the little stars as if they would fall into our laps. But that one great star in the East never wavered. Nothing could shake it from the sky as we drifted home on Christmas.

A FAMILIAR ESSAY

The Author's Purpose. An essay such as this, in which the author reveals his personal thoughts and feelings, is sometimes called a *familiar* essay.

1. What effect do you think Paul Engle wanted this essay to have on the reader? Did he succeed? Explain.

2. What is the meaning of such statements as "There are no such departures any more . . ." (page 410)? What other things did Paul Engle mention that aren't "any more"? In what ways was Paul Engle showing us how old-fashioned Christmases contrast with holidays celebrated today?

3. Refer to parts of the essay to show that Paul Engle was pointing out that family spirit was an important part of Christmas.

Organization. Every well-written essay must have a plan. Note the careful organization of Paul Engle's essay.

4. In this essay, Paul Engle described about ten aspects of an old-fashioned Christmas, beginning with the departure to the farm and ending with the ride home. List these events. Are they arranged in chronological order?

5. Another feature of this essay is that Paul Engle consistently supplies details about each event. For example, look at the nine paragraphs about the Christmas dinner. What specific details are given about (a) the source of the food, (b) the preserves, (c) the vegetables, (d) the meat,

(e) the trimmings, (f) the Dutch bread, (g) the kitchen, and (h) the last-minute activities?

The Reader's Reaction

6. Some people think that life was better in the past. What is your opinion? What did you think of this old-fashioned Christmas? Were there any aspects of this old-fashioned Christmas which you would like to find in today's holiday celebrations? In what ways do you think your own holiday celebrations are as good as the one described by Paul Engle?

LONG SENTENCES

In this essay Paul Engle uses many details to tell us what he recalls about old-fashioned Christmases, and several of his sentences are very long. Here is the long sentence used to describe the kitchen range.

> "The kitchen range was a tremendous black and gleaming one called a Smoke Eater, with pans bubbling over the holes above the fire box and a reservoir of hot water at the side, lined with dull copper, from which my uncle would dip a basin of water and shave above the sink, turning his lathered face now and then to drop a remark into the women's talk, waving his straight-edged razor, as if it were a threat, to make them believe him."

There are many ideas embedded in this long sentence. Were you aware of them all? To find these separate ideas, reduce this sentence to several short, simple statements. The first complete idea we can get from this long sentence, for example, is as follows:

The kitchen range was tremendous.

Continue listing the separate ideas embedded in this long sentence. Can you find other long sentences in this essay which contain many separate ideas?

COMPOSITION: SPECIFIC DETAILS

Engle tells us that Christmas in his boyhood was "handmade." Then, in a paragraph, he gives at least a dozen specific ways in which they were "handmade." Here is the paragraph. Notice that the topic is stated in the first sentence.

> "It was a handmade Christmas. The tree came from down in the grove, and on it were many paper ornaments made by my cousins, as well as beautiful ones brought from the Black Forest, where the family had originally lived. There were popcorn balls, paper horns with homemade candy, and apples from the orchard. The gifts tended to be hand-knit socks or wool ties or fancy crocheted "yokes" for nightgowns, tatted collars for blouses, doilies with fancy flower patterns for tables, and tidies for chairs. Once I received a brilliantly polished cow horn with a cavalryman crudely but bravely carved on it. And there would usually be a cornhusk doll, perhaps with a prune or walnut for a face, and a gay dress of an old corset-cover scrap with its ribbons still bright. And there were real candles burning with real flames, every guest sniffing the air for the smell of scorching pine needles."

List at least twelve ways in which this Christmas was handmade. Notice that Engle doesn't give us bare details. He makes his details very specific. For example, he tells us that the cow horn not only was handmade, but also was "brilliantly polished" and had a "cavalryman crudely but bravely carved on it." What specific details does he give about the doll?

Write a paragraph in which you follow up a general statement with some specific descriptive details. You might want to use one of these topic sentences.

To me, the city means people.

Surfing is a sport of thrills.

From Spring to Summer

EDWIN WAY TEALE

March 20.

IT IS OFFICIALLY spring! But what an anticlimax! Gust-driven rain is slashing the trees under a sullen sky; the air is raw and chill. I recall Henry van Dyke's [1] observation that the first day of spring and the first spring day are not always the same thing.

To me spring was marked this year by the return of the male redwing blackbirds, who came back with a rush a month ago. Almost overnight the drear stretches of our winter swamp were filled with life. Everywhere, with scarlet epaulets flashing, the blackbirds have been singing and darting about, chasing each other, shooting up like rockets, whirling like pinwheels. It is a kind of Oklahoma land rush.[2] Before the females arrive, each male stakes out a homestead and then, with spectacu-

lar acrobatics, defends and holds as much of the territory as possible.

The air rings with their wild xylophone calling. It is an exultant, jubilant call, a fitting voice for a season of flowing sap and awakening life.

March 24.

The time of baby squirrels is at hand. Each year around this time I see gray squirrels stripping off the dry bark of cedar limbs and carrying it away to their nesting holes. And now I also see them carrying bits of newspapers.

I wonder if there is some untaught wisdom that leads the squirrels to the cedar tree and makes them prefer newsprint to other paper. Cedar protects clothes from moths, and newspapers are sometimes used for the same purpose. Do they also help keep a squirrel's nest free from vermin?

March 26.

At sunset I walk along the swamp path. Only a few weeks ago the frozen earth appeared hard and dead, yet

[1] **Henry van Dyke** (1852–1933): a noted American clergyman and writer.
[2] **Oklahoma land rush:** On April 22, 1889, at an appointed hour, approximately fifty thousand home-seekers rushed into the Oklahoma territory to set out claims on land.

now I see the beginning of a flood of life that nothing can halt.

Because growth in plants is a gradual thing, we often overlook the power that is contained in the rising shoot and expanding seed. I once saw peas, planted in a flowerpot, lift and thrust aside a heavy sheet of plate glass laid over the top. Another time, when peas and water were tightly sealed in thick glass bottles, the germinating seeds developed pressures sufficient to shatter the glass. An explosion, in slow motion, had occurred within the bottles.

March 28.

In the breeding season the starlings' mimicking of other birds reaches its peak. One male has been sitting in my silver maple today giving the calls of such varied species as the crow, catbird, meadow lark, and killdeer, and even the quacking of a flying mallard duck. Also, a neighborhood child has been blowing a shrill police whistle, and now the starling imitates that sound, too — a little softer but unmistakable.

March 31.

As I walked up through the old orchard late this afternoon I looked back and caught the different shades of green in new grass clumps and young leaves, all suddenly brilliant in the sun, which had just emerged from behind a cloud. In the same way, the peculiar illumination before a summer thunderstorm brings out special details and alters a whole landscape. As I stood there, an old saying took on added meaning: "to see it in a *new* light."

April 4.

A long soaking rain before daybreak, and earthworms are stranded everywhere on the inhospitable cement of sidewalks, in imminent danger of early birds or drying sun. So my morning walk is slowed by stops to put earthworms back on the ground where they belong. People probably wonder what treasure I am finding when they see me stoop so often.

And, in a way, I am dealing in treasure. A silver fox may sell for hundreds of dollars; a race horse may be insured for a quarter of a million. Yet the world's most valuable animal is the earthworm — a humble burrower, nature's plowman!

April 15.

At 6:30 this morning I watched a velvet-coated bumblebee begin hunting for a nest site. I see her investigate every possible opening near a pile of moldering fence rails. Zigzagging, hovering, alighting, she peers into a rusting tin can in the weeds, explores under a maple root, in a knothole. She investigates the region around my shoe, and then along a bit of board lying in the grass. She will continue searching for hours and days, and may consider thousands of sites before she decides where to establish her nest. She is the founder of an insect city, and the fate of her colony depends to a great extent upon the wisdom of her choice.

April 21.

Just before I start for a walk in the misty dawn this morning, the radio is filling the air waves with the troubles of the world. But out-of-doors the news is good. All of nature is a going concern. The business of spring is prospering. I stand for a long time beside the swamp stream in a fairyland setting of low-lying mist, glowing and tinted with the pink of the sunrise. Such a sight sets us to rights again. For the disturbed mind, the still beauty of the dawn is nature's finest balm.

April 22.

This is the time of robins bewitched. People write me letters about robins that peck endlessly at shiny hubcaps, that spend their days fluttering against windowpanes and pecking at the glass. Have the birds gone crazy? What ails them?

Wherever robins are nesting, the same thing is taking place. Males are defending their nesting territories. Catching sight of his own reflection in a window or a shiny metal surface, the male robin dashes to drive the intruder away. He may battle this phantom rival for days on end.

Only windows with darkened rooms behind them, turning the glass into a mirror, attract the birds. Merely turn on a light in the room or hang a white cloth in the window and the bird's reflection will disappear. The robin imagines it has vanquished its rival and, in high good spirits, returns to the normal life of a redbreast in the spring.

April 29.

Rain in the night, and this morning the fallen white petals of the pear trees lie scattered across my path like confetti. Mingled with the gray rain has been the green rain of descending maple flowers as well. They dot the sidewalks and form yellow-green windrows [1] at the edges of the puddles. Leaf fall in the autumn and flower fall in the spring!

May 2.

Someone dumped the limbs and trunk of a willow tree beside the road, and they have been lying there a good part of the winter. Today I noticed that innumerable sprouts have pushed out all along the length of one of the discarded logs. The sight recalled the experience of a man I know who left rustic willow chairs out in his yard all winter. In the spring he discovered that every chair had taken root!

May 18.

Through my glasses, I watched a female redwing working at a cattail stem floating in the water, stripping away

---

[1] **windrows:** wind-swept lines, as of dry leaves or dust.

fibers for her nest. But fibers and other time-honored construction materials are being supplemented these days with a surprising number of modern odds and ends. Near here, a wood thrush made use of torn-up bus tickets; another wood thrush, nesting near a refreshment stand in an Indiana park, collected discarded pop-bottle straws. Small nails, carried from a building project to a birdhouse, formed the steel nest of a house wren, while a redstart made its nest entirely of insulating material.

May 24.

All along the shallow eastern edge of Milburn Pond the sunfish have been scraping away the silt to provide bare, clean patches of gravel for spawning — a sign that the water's temperature has risen to 68 degrees. Over each of these scoured patches was a guardian fish that rushed toward every interloper. Where two patches overlapped, the guardians kept rushing back and forth in a seesaw battle. The fury of the attacker waned quickly as it advanced into the defender's territory, while its courage seemed to mount when it was pursued into its own. Thus they continued as long as I remained at the pond.

All the defenders were males. They build the nest, guard it, fertilize the eggs — often laid by several females — and defend the young that hatch there among the pebbles.

June 1.

Outside a little after five on this first morning of June. The machinery of nature, with its winds and dews and dawns and morning mists, produces poetry as well as seasons and growth and change. The functioning of nature's cogs [1] has created dewdrops and veils of luminous mist caught among the cattails. Before the work of the day, taste the poetry of the day!

As I crossed the hillside, a small patch of dry, yellow grass caught my eye. Carefully I pulled aside the grass and the soft gray blanket of fur I found beneath, and exposed the little ears of a nestful of baby cottontails. Just as carefully, I replaced the fur coverlet and the grass. In a little while, now, I will see rabbits hopping about my hillside.

June 4.

One of the gray squirrels that shares our yard is using a crutch. It injured a hind leg somehow and, although it gets about on three legs fairly well, when I throw it a peanut it is unable to sit up to eat it. So the crippled squirrel carries its nut to a branch that fell from a dying maple and braces itself against that. Thus supported, it can eat its nut sitting up, in the traditional squirrel fashion.

June 12.

To the sea moor at sunset, to witness again one of the most ancient dramas of the earth: the coming of the king crabs to the shallows to fertilize and leave their eggs. This is the great annual event in the lives of these "horsefoots," as the baymen call them. They are among the oldest dwellers in the

---

[1] **nature's cogs:** *Cog* refers to a part of a machine. In this paragraph, the author is comparing nature to a machine.

sea, creatures that have lived on and on after some of their early contemporaries have become fossils.

Moment by moment the water creeps ahead as the tide runs in. Shadowy at first, the crabs appear from the murky water. Farther and farther they push up into the shallows to deposit the translucent little globes of their eggs. These events, as I watch them in the twilight of this June day, are the same as they were a hundred million years before the dinosaurs. In an unbroken chain they link the Atomic Age with the primeval world.

June 14.

Who can doubt that it "feels good" to the turtle to sun itself on a log; that it "feels good" to the flicker to rap its bill on hollow wood; that it "feels good" to the muskrat to dive into water? Pleasure and pain, comfort and discomfort, these are the push and pull of instinct.

June 19.

Glistening globes of white, each about the size of a pea, shine out from the grass tangles of the hillside this morning. Each mass of froth, like beaten egg white, is produced by a tiny immature insect inside, using a mechanism unknown elsewhere in all of nature. For upward of ten million years these insects, commonly known as froghoppers, have literally been saving their lives by blowing bubbles. Safe within its little foam castle, the insect lies moist and hidden, sucking sap from the grass stem. Later it develops wings and flies away, a nondescript brownish little bug that is rarely noticed. Its

great achievement, its claim to fame, is this shining house of foam that is produced during its earliest days.

June 21.

This is the hinge day of the seasons. Today the yearly tide of light reaches its flood. Tomorrow it will begin the long rollback to the dark days of December. I heard robins singing this morning shortly after four, Daylight Saving Time, and they are still singing at nine o'clock at night. A robin uses up all the daylight, even on this longest day of the year.

In the later sunset of this final day of spring, my wife and I walk to the bay. As we stand there, in the quiet of the evening and with the smell of the sea all around us, a faint mist forms in the air. Twilight here is doubly impressive for we are face to face with twin mysteries — the mystery of the sea and the mystery of the night.

Thus ends another spring — rich in the small everyday events of the earth as all springs are for those who find delight in simple things. The institutions of men alter and disintegrate. But in the endless repetitions of nature — in the recurrence of spring, in the coming of new birds to sing the ancient songs, in the continuity of life and the web of the living — here we find the solid foundation that underlies at once the past, the present, and the future.

A PERSONAL JOURNAL

The Author's Purpose. A diary or journal is usually kept for the writer himself, but here we have a journal that the author has shared with thousands of readers. As you answer these questions, try to decide why a writer might publish his journal.

1. In the last sentence of the first entry, how is the season of spring described?

2. What question did the author ask about the "untaught wisdom" of the squirrels? What information did he give about the power of growing plants? What fact did he give about the value of the earthworm? What opinion did he give on April 21?

3. What did Teale mean by the "poetry of the day," in his June 1 entry? On June 12, what link did he observe between the Atomic age and the primeval world?

4. What personal thoughts did Teale share with us in the concluding entry?

Tone. Reading Teale's journal is like having an intimate talk with the writer. Teale reveals much of himself in these entries.

5. Find entries to show that Teale is a sensitive person, especially aware of beauty. Find entries to show that he respects the lives of small creatures. How did he show that he has trained his powers of observation?

The Reader's Reaction

6. What information about nature did you get from this essay? Which ideas from these entries do you think are worth remembering?

7. Which signs of spring not mentioned in the journal have you yourself noticed?

WORDS: THE PREFIX *TRANS–*

Teale describes the eggs of the crab as "translucent little globes." The word *translucent* contains a very common and useful Latin prefix, *trans–*, meaning "through, across, beyond, or on the other side of." The root of *translucent* comes from the Latin word *lucere*, meaning "to shine." Thus the eggs let the "light" shine "through." Compare the meaning of *trans-*

lucent with *transparent*. Then look in a dictionary to find the great number of other words containing the prefix *trans–*.

COMPOSITION:
A SUMMARIZING SENTENCE

Here is Teale's entry for June 19. The first sentence tells us that he is going to talk about some "glistening globes of white" that he saw on the grass.

"Glistening globes of white, each about the size of a pea, shine out from the grass tangles of the hillside this morning. Each mass of froth, like beaten egg white, is produced by a tiny immature insect inside, using a mechanism unknown elsewhere in all of nature. For upward of ten million years these insects, commonly known as froghoppers, have literally been saving their lives by blowing bubbles. Safe within its little foam castle, the insect lies moist and hidden, sucking sap from the grass stem. Later it develops wings and flies away, a nondescript brownish little bug that is rarely noticed. Its great achievement, its claim to fame, is this shining house of foam that is produced during its earliest days."

The last sentence is a good summary of the paragraph. From what you learned in this paragraph, tell why the "shining house of foam" is the great achievement of the froghopper.

Not all paragraphs of explanation have summarizing sentences, but many writers use such sentences to emphasize the main point of the paragraph.

Write a paragraph about some natural phenomenon that you have observed — such as the growth of a child or the falling of snow. Open your paragraph with a sentence that states the topic. Try to end the paragraph with a sentence that summarizes your main point.

Where's Everybody?

ARTHUR C. CLARKE

At this moment of time, there is a centuries-old question which presses more and more urgently for an answer. In almost any astronomy book you will find a chapter devoted to the subject: "Is there life on other worlds?" — the answer given depending upon the optimism of the author and the period in which he is writing (for there are fashions in astronomy as in everything else).

Today that question needs to be reframed and brought up to date. There must be very few astronomers now who are conceited enough to suppose that only Earth is the abode of life, or even that it is the only home of intelligence. Assuming this to be the case, we have an interesting problem on our hands. How are we to explain the peculiar behavior of the other intelligent races which share our universe?

What peculiar behavior, Holmes? [1]

---

[1] **Holmes:** the detective in Sir Arthur Conan Doyle's famous stories. Dr. Watson, Holmes' companion, frequently questions the detective in this way. (See the story on page 301.)

Assuming that such races exist, they have done absolutely nothing about us.

Precisely, my dear Watson . . .

Having stated the problem, let's look at it scientifically and dispassionately [2] as we can. It falls into three distinct sections — astronomical, biological, and technical — and we'll deal with them in that order.

On a clear, moonless night the sky seems so packed with stars that it is hard to believe that they could ever be counted. Yet in reality the unaided eye can see only a couple of thousand stars at any one time: even a small telescope shows millions, and the photographic plate billions. All those stars are suns, many of them larger than ours, most of them smaller. Unfortunately, there is no way in which we can tell if any of them possess planets, except in cases so unusual that only a couple of examples are known.

However, even these examples are enough to suggest that planets are not as rare as they were once thought to be; it may in fact turn out that most stars have small, cold bodies circling

---

[2] **dispassionately:** calmly and objectively.

them. And if no more than one in a hundred does, that would still be some *billion* planetary systems in our galaxy alone.

By the laws of probability, we should expect at least one planet capable of supporting life to exist within ten light-years [1] of Earth. (The nearest star, Proxima Centauri, is just over four light-years away; ten light-years is the approximate distance of the brightest star, Sirius.) On the cosmic scale, such distances are trivial. Our galaxy — the island universe of which the sun is a not particularly outstanding member — is about a hundred thousand light-years from end to end. And the remotest of the myriads of other galaxies we have so far detected lies more than a billion light-years away (6,000,000,000,000,-000,000,000 miles, if anyone prefers it that way).

Given a suitable planet, the next question is this: "Will life evolve upon it?" It used to be thought that life was a very improbable phenomenon, requiring such a fantastic chain of events for it to come about that it would occur only on a very, very few planets — perhaps, indeed, only upon Earth.

Quite recently it has been shown that surprisingly complicated chemicals are produced by purely natural forces — such as lightning and ultraviolet rays — acting on the substances which might be found in the primitive seas and atmosphere of many planets. Some of these chemicals are the basic building blocks of living organisms, and biolo-gists have been able to construct rather convincing schemes to show how, in the lengths of time available, life could arise from these nonliving materials. In a few hundred million years, even most unlikely events are bound to happen, and one of the things that nature possesses in large quantities is time.

It seems, therefore, that life is virtually certain to arise wherever conditions are at all favorable. That is a lesson we might have learned from a study of our own planet. There is hardly a spot on Earth, from the highest mountains to the ultimate depths of the sea, which some creature has not been able to conquer by suitable adaptation. Life may be found frozen eleven months out of twelve in the Antarctic wastes — or flourishing a few degrees below boiling point in sulfur springs.

Yet even if life is common throughout the universe, intelligence may still be rare. There are millions of different types of living creatures on Earth, but only one with the power of abstract thought — and he hasn't been around for very long. Just how late man has appeared on the cosmic stage can best be realized by this analogy, borrowed, with improvements, from Sir James Jeans.[2]

Let the height of the Empire State Building represent the age of Earth; on this scale, a foot is about two million years. Now (if the wind will let you) stand an average-sized book upright on the TV tower. It won't look very conspicuous from ground level — but its

---

[1] **light-years:** units of measurement, each equal to the distance traveled by light in one year. One light-year is about six trillion miles.

[2] **Sir James Jeans** (1877–1946): a British mathematician.

few inches of height correspond roughly to the entire existence of *Homo sapiens*.[1]

Now place a slightly worn dime on top of the book. The thickness of the coin corresponds to the whole of man's civilization, right back to the building of the first cities. And if you want to represent the era of modern science and technology — *that* is about as thick as a postage stamp.

The postage stamp on the top of the Empire State Building is a picture we should bear in mind; it shows how extremely unlikely it is that, on any particular world, intelligence should exist at this moment *at our precise level of development*. Even assuming that evolution takes similar roads on all suitable planets, only upon one world in millions could we expect to find a civilization that had discovered steam power a couple of centuries ago, and which now dreams of the conquest of space as it passes into its atomic age.

No — it is far more likely that if oth-er intelligent races exist, the vast majority of them will be at stages of development corresponding to points millions of years in our past — or in our future. The latter, indeed, seems more likely, for our own history is so short that we must surely be among the youngest peoples in the universe.

This leads us to an inescapable conclusion. Scattered around us in space, at distances which may not be more than a few scores of light-years, there must be not a few civilizations far in advance of ours — and there may be dozens of them. Which brings us back to our opening question: *if* they are so advanced, why haven't they come here?

At this point, I have to pause briefly to deal with the hordes of flying saucer believers who have appeared on the horizon, waving affidavits and smudgy photographs. To dispose of them would need another article a good deal longer than this one, not all of it printable. I'll merely state my views on this agitated subject, without giving the reasons that have led me to them after several years of thought, reading, interviewing, and

[1] *Homo sapiens* (hō'mō sā'pē·ənz): the race of man capable of abstract thought. (*Homo* and *sapiens* are Latin for "man" and "wise.")

No one is seen on the lonely surface of the moon, as recreated here by an artist. Notice the earth glowing in the distance. (Courtesy American Museum — Hayden Planetarium.)

personal observations. I think there may be "Unidentified Flying Objects" which are exactly what their name implies, and which may turn out to be quite interesting and exciting when we discover their cause. At the same time I am pretty sure that they're not — repeat *not* — spaceships. If they were, many consequences would have arisen. If I'm wrong, that still proves the main point of my thesis, so I can't lose anyway.

Assuming, therefore, that during modern times there have been no visitors from space, we have to look for an explanation. It may well be argued (and indeed has been by many eminent scientists) that our apparent isolation can be explained very simply. Travel from planet to planet inside the solar system may be possible in the relatively near future, so that we shall visit neighboring worlds such as Mars and Venus. But travel to the planets of other suns — *interstellar* travel — may be totally impossible because of the sheer distances involved. On this theory, the universe may be full of intelligent races, but they must forever exist in total ignorance of each other, quarantined by space itself.

This is a serious and plausible argument, and must be dealt with before we proceed any further. First of all, let us get clearly into our minds the important — the fundamental — distinction between the distances of interplanetary space, which our children will be challenging, and the immensely greater distances which separate us from the stars.

Planetary distances are about a million-fold greater than those of ordinary, everyday life. For example: Venus at its closest, 26 million miles; Mars, at its closest, 35 million miles. The stars, however, are about a million times farther away still (*e.g.*, Proxima Centauri, 25 million million miles). When we get to the remotest planet, therefore, we will be little nearer the stars than we are today.

But distance itself means nothing; all that really matters is the length of time any particular journey requires. In the last hundred years we have seen the world shrink beyond the wildest imagination of our forefathers. Jules Verne [1] was laughed at when he dared to suggest that one might circumnavigate Earth in eighty days, but now it has been done in two — and the IGY [2] satellites, the harbingers [3] of the Space age, will go around the globe in almost as many minutes as Philéas Fogg required days.[4]

This steady increase in speed shows no sign of slackening; indeed, the development of the jet and the rocket gave the curve an even steeper upward trend. We already know how long the first interplanetary journeys will take, with the fuels and techniques that exist

---

[1] **Jules Verne** (1828–1905): the first novelist of science fiction, best known for his adventure story *Around the World in Eighty Days*, in which a character named Philéas Fogg travels around the world in eighty days.

[2] **IGY:** International Geophysical Year (July 1, 1957 to December 31, 1958), a time in which scientists from sixty-six nations participated in an intensive study of the planet Earth.

[3] **harbingers:** heralds, those who announce the coming of something.

[4] This article was written in 1957. Notice that all of these events have since taken place, and many earlier speed records have been broken. The first satellite of the IGY, for example, was launched on October 4, 1957.

today. Mars and Venus are both much less than a year's flight away with chemical fuels; as *atomic* propulsion becomes available, the journeys will be measured in weeks and ultimately in days. This state of affairs will arise nearer the beginning of the next century than its end.

It is partly because interplanetary travel must become possible quite early in the history of a technically-minded race, that I think it most unlikely that there is intelligent life elsewhere in the solar system. It is much more likely that we have missed the Martians by a few million years, and that the Venusians may miss us by even more.

So we must look beyond the sun's other planets for life — at least intelligent life, for there are good grounds for thinking that there is vegetation on Mars — and pin our hopes upon the distant stars. Can we — or any other race — ever hope to attain such velocities that the interstellar gulfs will be bridged in reasonably short periods of time?

I'll go out on a limb by saying that this is one question that we *can* answer, even today. And the answer is "Yes, but —"

To put the matter in the right perspective, let's look at the entire gamut of speed — past, present, and future. The past can be dealt with very briefly; from the dawn of history until the beginning of the nineteenth century, no man had ever traveled much faster than 10 m.p.h.

There are men still alive who can remember when 100 m.p.h. was reached; 1,000 m.p.h. was attained — and doubled — only recently. Manned flight at 10,000 m.p.h. will be achieved in the 1960's; unmanned rockets have already passed this speed, and the satellites will far exceed it.

You'll notice that we are going up in steps of ten. Each jump seemed enormous when it was made — and nothing much to boast about when it had become history. The next surge forward — to 100,000 m.p.h. — will take place when atomic energy is harnessed to rocket propulsion, and today's chemical fuels join the wax candles and kerosene lamps in the museums.

A not-very-efficient atomic propulsion system, such as might reasonably be developed around the turn of this century, would enable us to attain speed in the 1,000,000 m.p.h. category. This would mean Mars in less than two days — and Venus in one (though starting and stopping would extend these times somewhat!).

A million miles an hour is such a nice, round figure that one is tempted to see what impression it would make on interstellar distances — since it certainly deflates interplanetary ones. The result is startling; even the very nearest of the stars would be almost 3,000 years away.

We want a few more zeros on our speedometer. What about 10,000,000 m.p.h.? Well, there's no theoretical reason why it should be impossible in the frictionless vacuum of space. The atom contains enough energy, if we are smart enough to apply it in the right way. And when a thing is possible in theory, it's usually done in practice sooner or later. So — Proxima Centauri in only 300 years.

100,000,000 m.p.h.? Yes, even that's

still not asking too much of atomic energy. However, we'll need to learn a few new tricks, such as the *total* conversion of matter into energy, not the annihilation of the miserable fraction of a percent which is all that our present atomic devices achieve. That would take us to the nearest star in thirty years; still too long, but the figures are beginning to look reasonable at last. One more jump and we're nearly there.

1,000,000,000 m.p.h.? I'm sorry — no. A new factor has come into the picture. On our way to that extra zero, we've passed the speed limit of the universe. It happens to be 670,000,000 m.p.h. and is a limit that's rigorously enforced. It is the velocity of light — more usually quoted as 186,000 miles per second.

If the Theory of Relativity is correct — and the evidence of the past years indicates that it is — nothing can ever surpass this speed, and it would require an infinite amount of energy merely to reach it. Why this should be so is a complicated story which I have no intention of going into here; all that matters at the moment is that the velocity of light is not just an arbitrary figure, but is bound up with the very structure of the universe. Even if you could, in theory, exceed it, you wouldn't be in our space and time any longer; you'd be somewhere else — if there is somewhere else.

The velocity of light, therefore, appears to set a limit to the speed with which any object can move through space. That speed may be approached more and more closely as propulsion systems improve, but it can never be reached, still less exceeded. If this is the case, time of travel between even the closest star systems can never be less than four or five years; between *inhabited* star systems, in our fairly crowded corner of the galaxy, we might not be far out if we fix the lower limit of travel as ten years.

This is a good deal longer than we would like, especially as the return trip still has to be considered. But can anyone seriously argue that it is an absolute insuperable [1] objection to interstellar flight? Of course not; as soon as the propulsion problems were solved, there would be members even of our ephemeral [2] species who would be prepared to devote a quarter of their lives to the supreme adventure of contacting new races, new civilizations on the other side of the stellar abyss.

Recent progress in medical science may be of assistance here. Suspended animation — the deliberate production of a trancelike state in which the subject is unaware of the progress of time — is no longer a fantasy. It can be induced for short periods by drugs or cold, and it does not require much imagination to suppose that what the dormouse [3] can do, men may also be able to achieve. The distances between the stars will no longer seem so terrifying if we can sleep our way across them.

In any event, there is no need to assume that exploring vessels designed to cross interstellar space would carry living crews; it is much more likely that the first ones would not. All the rockets we have so far launched beyond the at-

---

[1] **insuperable:** not able to be overcome.

[2] **ephemeral** (i·fem′ər·əl): short-lived.

[3] **dormouse:** a member of the rodent family, like a squirrel. The dormouse hibernates during the cold weeks of winter.

mosphere carried recording instruments; spaceships which set out on journeys of indefinite duration and uncertain goal would be purely automatic, controlled by elaborate electronic brains which had been conditioned to perform one task — to gather all the information they could, and to bring it safely home. Since we will be able to build such robot scouts ourselves in the near future, other races must have had them for ages, and sooner or later they will come sniffing around Earth.

Sooner or later. That, perhaps, is the crux of the whole matter. Visitors from space may have landed on our planets dozens — hundreds — of times during the long, empty ages while man was still a dream of the distant future. Indeed, they could have landed on 90 percent of Earth as recently as two or three hundred years ago — and we would never have heard of it. If one searches through old newspapers and local records one can find large numbers of curious incidents that could be interpreted as visitations from space. That stimulating if eccentric writer Charles Fort made a collection of such occurrences in his book *Lo!*, and one is inclined to give them more weight than any comparable modern reports for the simple reason that they happened long before anyone had ever thought of space travel. Yet at the same time, one cannot take them *too* seriously because before scientific education was widespread, even the commonest celestial phenomena — meteors, comets, auroras, and so on — gave rise to the most incredible stories. As they still do, in fact.

Going further back in time, it has been suggested that some of the legends and myths of prehistory, perhaps even the weird entities [1] of many pagan religions, may have been inspired by glimpses of beings from other worlds. But this is pure and unprofitable speculation — unprofitable for the reason that it can never be proved or disproved, but only argued endlessly.

Do we have to wait ten years or a thousand years before the next ship calls? Or if none has ever called before, when will Earth's billions of years of isolation be ended? It may be that our first meeting with alien intelligences is already far nearer to us in time than Columbus' landing in the New World.

One would like to think that we will be the discoverers, not the discovered. Yet perhaps, when we leave the snug little confines of the solar system, we may meet a bored reception committee that greets us with the words: "Taken your time, haven't you? Welcome to the Galactic Federation; here's the book of rules."

Or — and this is the most depressing thought of all — perhaps we have already been blacklisted. It provides a very simple, and horribly plausible, explanation for our apparent lack of visitors to date.

The neighbors may already know everything about us; who can blame them, therefore, if they've kept a few light-years away?

[1] **entities:** here, gods.

AN ARTICLE FOR DISCUSSION

The Author's Purpose. Arthur Clarke, a famous British scientist, frequently writes stimulating articles and stories for a nonscientific audience.

1. Clarke states the purpose of this essay in his opening paragraph. What old question did he say needs to be brought up to date? How did he answer the old question? What problem did he propose to discuss in this essay?

Organization and Development. After Clarke states the purpose of his article, he tells you that his discussion will fall into three sections: astronomical, biological, and technical.

2. What *astronomical* facts should we know when we discuss life in other worlds?

3. From a *biological* point of view, what are the chances that life exists in other worlds? What are Clarke's theories on the level of development of life in other worlds?

4. Discuss the *technical* aspects of man's ever being able to visit planets in other solar systems.

5. Why did Clarke call this essay "Where's Everybody?"

The Reader's Reaction. In this essay, Clarke seems interested in provoking a reaction from the reader.

6. What did you think of Clarke's reasoning and of his conclusions? Did you find them believable? Why? Did you think his thoughts were presented clearly? Explain.

7. What does Clarke suggest in the last paragraph? What do you think of this viewpoint?

8. Do you think that man should strive to explore space, or do you think such ventures are a waste of resources? Explain.

WORDS: SPACE–AGE LANGUAGE

It is interesting to look closely at some of the new space-age words to see how they came to be made up. The word *cos-monaut*, for example, is a space-age word coming from two Greek words, *kosmos*, meaning "universe," and *nautilos* meaning "sailor." A cosmonaut, then, is a "sailor of the universe." Here are some other space-age words. What does each word mean? Use a dictionary or encyclopedia to figure out how each word came to be made up.

retrorockets	satellite
atomic energy	astronaut
sputnik	lox

CRITICAL READING

Some interesting and exciting questions have been raised in this essay, but for many of these questions, science, as yet, has no answers. Clarke has suggested some answers, but, though he has backed them up with good reasons, you must remember that these answers are still one scientist's opinions.

Here are some statements from this article. Which statements are facts (those that can be checked and proved to be true), and which statements are opinions of the author?

"The nearest star, Proxima Centauri, is just over four light-years away. . . ." (See page 424.)

"It is partly because interplanetary travel must become possible quite early in the history of a technically-minded race, that I think it most unlikely that there is intelligent life elsewhere in the solar system." (See page 427.)

"Since we will be able to build such robot scouts ourselves in the near future, other races must have had them for ages, and sooner or later they will come sniffing around Earth." (See page 429.)

Can you find any other statements in this article which are statements of opinion, not of fact? If so, where?

Nonfiction

READING AN ESSAY

In an essay, a writer attempts to express his thoughts and ideas about some topic. The following paragraphs are from the start of an essay called "An Old-fashioned Iowa Christmas," by Paul Engle. In this essay, the writer expresses his thoughts about a cherished custom of his boyhood.

Every Christmas should begin with the sound of bells, and when I was a child mine always did. But they were sleigh bells, not church bells, for we lived in a part of Cedar Rapids, Iowa, where there were no churches. My bells were on my father's team of horses as he drove up to our horse-headed hitching post with the bobsled that would take us to celebrate Christmas on the family farm ten miles out in the country. My father would bring the team down Fifth Avenue at a smart trot, flicking his whip over the horses' rumps and making the bells double their light, thin jangling over the snow.

There are no such departures any more: the whole family piling into the bobsled with a foot of golden oat straw to lie in and heavy buffalo robes to lie under, the horses stamping the soft snow, and at every motion of their hoofs the bells jingling, jingling.   (page 410)

When you read an essay, keep in mind the following suggestions.

1. *Read for the author's purpose.* When you begin an essay, you should look for clues that will tell you the author's purpose. Will the essay be packed with new information and require a great deal of thought to read? Will it be light in tone and entertaining and relaxing to read? Does the writer want to change your way of thinking? Reread the first two sentences of the model passage. What clues are you given there about the author's purpose? How would you describe the author's purpose in writing this essay?

Look back now and reread the first two sentences of "Your Change" (page 383) and of "Where's Everybody?" (page 423). What clues are you given there about the authors' purposes? Describe the different purposes of these two essays.

2. *Recognize topic statements.* In writing an essay, an author frequently makes certain general topic statements. Look for such key topic statements, in which the writer states his ideas or opinions or feelings. In what sentence do you find a general statement of topic in the model passage?

Look back at "Mary White," at the paragraph on pages 387–88 beginning "Her funeral yesterday . . ." What topic statement can you locate in this paragraph?

3. *Note supporting details.* Because it often deals with ideas, an essay is usually full of details. Such details are important because they help to develop the writer's ideas. List the specific details included in the paragraphs of the model passage. What are you told about the bells? What do you find out about the departure?

Look back at the essay "First Pitch" (page 409). List the specific details used in the opening paragraph to support the statement that spring in America is much like spring anywhere. Would this opening paragraph have been as effective if the author had concluded the paragraph after the word *anywhere?*

4. *Learn to evaluate conclusions.* Many times the writer of an essay will come to some conclusion, to some judgment or general opinion about his topic. Sometimes the writer will state his conclusions directly, perhaps at the opening or the end of his article. But at other times he may leave the conclusion up to you, for you to work out yourself. Did Paul Engle come to any conclusions about the Christmases of his boyhood? Did he state these conclusions anywhere or did you have to work them out for yourself? Do you agree with his conclusions? Why?

Look back again at the essay "Where's Everybody?" (page 423). The author used a question as the title of this essay. This should have clued you to look for an answer to the question in the essay itself. How does the author answer this question? Point to specific sentences that, provide this answer. Do you agree with this answer? Why?

5. *Try to sense the author's personality.* The essays you have read in this unit differ from other kinds of factual writing. Do you know why? How do the two essays on the coming of spring (pages 409 and 417), for example, differ from a straight scientific account of how spring arrives, such as you might find in your science book? The answer is that the authors who wrote the essays in this unit wrote not only with their minds but also with their feelings. When we read "First Pitch" and "From Spring to Summer," for example, we share each writer's emotions as well as his knowledge. What personal feelings for his family does Paul Engle communicate to you in the model passage?

Look back at "From Spring to Summer," at the entry for June 12, on pages 420–21. What personal thoughts does the author reveal to you in this entry?

EXPRESSING AN OPINION

When you express an opinion, you want to convince other people that your ideas and thoughts are good ones. In everyday conversation, you almost automatically give convincing reasons to show people why you think the way you do. Here are two fundamental suggestions for you to follow when you have to support an opinion in writing.

1. *State your opinion in a clear sentence at the opening of your paragraph.*

2. *Use forceful and specific details to support or explain or illustrate this statement.*

Write an essay in which you express your opinion about something. Perhaps you have an opinion about one of the following quotations, taken from selections in this unit. Do you agree with the quotation?

"'Make what you want out of what you have.'" (See page 398.)

"For the disturbed mind, the still beauty of the dawn is nature's finest balm." (See page 419.)

"Every Christmas should begin with the sound of bells . . ." (See page 410.)

ART AND LITERATURE

Some people say that the most enjoyable essay is an informal one, in which the writer relaxes with his reader while he shares a point of view about something.

Write a brief, informal essay (about two or three paragraphs), sharing your viewpoint toward one of the paintings on pages 403–08. Your essay might be funny or serious, depending on your mood. Can you tell your reader how you felt or what you thought about as you looked at the painting? How did the painting affect you later?

Forms of Literature

Unit 7
Poems

UNIT 7 Poems

"What is poetry? Who knows?" A poet herself once pondered this question. (See page 449 for her answer.) Though many people have tried to define it, no one can really tell you what poetry is. We can only make some statements about poetry. All poetry has rhythm, for example. It may or may not have rhyme. Poetry can be serious, or it can be gay. It can describe beautiful flowers or a dreary city street. It can sing a song of contentment, or it can blast a noisy protest. Read aloud the ways that some of the poets in this unit have expressed themselves.

"Once upon a midnight dreary, while I pondered, weak
　　and weary,
Over many a quaint and curious volume of forgotten
　　lore —
While I nodded, nearly napping, suddenly there came a
　　tapping,
As of someone gently rapping, rapping at my chamber
　　door."

From **The Raven** by Edgar Allan Poe

"I wandered lonely as a cloud
That floats on high o'er vales and hills,
When all at once I saw a crowd,
A host, of golden daffodils"

From **The Daffodils** by William Wordsworth

"what if a dawn of a doom of a dream
bites this universe in two,
peels forever out of his grave
and sprinkles nowhere with me and you?"

From **what if a much of a which of a wind**
by E. E. Cummings

You will probably like some of the poems in this unit and dislike others. Those you like you will find hard to forget. The American poet Robert Frost said that we could read good poems a hundred times and they would still keep fresh. These are the poems which never lose meaning for us.

HUMOROUS VERSE

Most people enjoy a bit of fun. And since good humorous verse uses some of the same techniques used in serious poetry, a study of light verse can be a good and enjoyable prelude to a study of poetry.

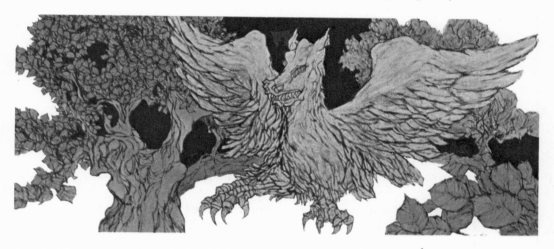

Jabberwocky

LEWIS CARROLL

'Twas brillig, and the slithy toves
   Did gyre and gimble in the wabe;
All mimsy were the borogoves,
   And the mome raths outgrabe.

"Beware the Jabberwock, my son!   5
   The jaws that bite, the claws that
      catch!
Beware the Jubjub bird and shun
   The frumious Bandersnatch!"

He took his vorpal sword in hand:
   Long time the manxome foe he
      sought —   10
So rested he by the Tumtum tree,
   And stood awhile in thought.

And as in uffish thought he stood,
   The Jabberwock, with eyes of flame,
Came whiffling through the tulgey
    wood,   15
   And burbled as it came!

One, two! One, two! And through and
    through
The vorpal blade went snicker-snack!
He left it dead, and with its head
   He went galumphing back.   20

"And hast thou slain the Jabberwock?
   Come to my arms, my beamish boy!
A frabjous day! Callooh! Callay!"
   He chortled in his joy.

'Twas brillig, and the slithy toves   25
   Did gyre and gimble in the wabe;
All mimsy were the borogoves,
   And the mome raths outgrabe.

Casey at the Bat

ERNEST LAWRENCE THAYER

The outlook wasn't brilliant for the Mudville nine that day;
The score stood four to two, with but one inning more to play;
And so, when Cooney died at first, and Burrows did the same,
A sickly silence fell upon the patrons of the game.

A straggling few got up to go in deep despair. The rest   5
Clung to the hope which springs eternal in the human breast;
They thought, if only Casey could but get a whack, at that,
They'd put up even money now, with Casey at the bat.

But Flynn preceded Casey, as did also Jimmy Blake,
And the former was a pudding, and the latter was a fake;   10
So upon that stricken multitude grim melancholy sat,
For there seemed but little chance of Casey's getting to the bat.

But Flynn let drive a single, to the wonderment of all,
And Blake, the much-despised, tore the cover off the ball;
And when the dust had lifted, and they saw what had occurred,   15
There was Jimmy safe on second, and Flynn a-hugging third.

Then from the gladdened multitude went up a joyous yell;
It bounded from the mountaintop, and rattled in the dell;
It struck upon the hillside, and recoiled upon the flat;
For Casey, mighty Casey, was advancing to the bat.   20

There was ease in Casey's manner as he stepped into his place;
There was pride in Casey's bearing, and a smile on Casey's face;
And when, responding to the cheers, he lightly doffed his hat,
No stranger in the crowd could doubt 'twas Casey at the bat.

Ten thousand eyes were on him as he rubbed his hands with dirt;   25
Five thousand tongues applauded when he wiped them on his shirt;
Then while the writhing pitcher ground the ball into his hip,
Defiance gleamed in Casey's eye, a sneer curled Casey's lip.

And now the leather-covered sphere came hurtling through the air,
And Casy stood a-watching it in haughty grandeur there;   30
Close by the sturdy batsman the ball unheeded sped.
"That ain't my style," said Casey. "Strike one," the umpire said.

From the benches, black with people, there went up a muffled roar,
Like the beating of the storm waves on a stern and distant shore;
"Kill him! Kill the umpire!" shouted someone on the stand;   35
And it's likely they'd have killed him had not Casey raised his hand.

With a smile of Christian charity great Casey's visage shone;
He stilled the rising tumult; he bade the game go on;
He signaled to the pitcher, and once more the spheroid flew;
But Casey still ignored it, and the umpire said, "Strike two."   40

"Fraud!" cried the maddened thousands, and the echo answered,
      "Fraud!"
But a scornful look from Casey, and the audience was awed;
They saw his face grow stern and cold, they saw his muscles strain,
And they knew that Casey wouldn't let that ball go by again.

The sneer is gone from Casey's lips, his teeth are clenched in hate,   45
He pounds with cruel violence his bat upon the plate;
And now the pitcher holds the ball, and now he lets it go,
And now the air is shattered by the force of Casey's blow.

Oh! somewhere in this favored land the sun is shining bright;
The band is playing somewhere, and somewhere hearts are light;   50
And somewhere men are laughing, and somewhere children shout,
But there is no joy in Mudville — mighty Casey has struck out!

PRIVATE ZOO

OGDEN NASH

The Panther

The panther is like a leopard,
Except it hasn't been peppered.
Should you behold a panther crouch,
Prepare to say Ouch.
Better yet, if called by a panther,
Don't anther.

The Porcupine

Any hound a porcupine nudges
Can't be blamed for harboring grudges.
I know one hound that laughed all winter
At a porcupine that sat on a splinter.

The Eel

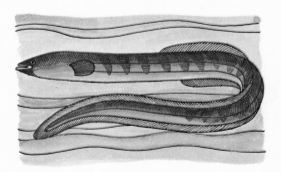

I don't mind eels
Except as meals.
And the way they feels.

The Termite

Some primal termite knocked on wood
And tasted it, and found it good,
And that is why your Cousin May
Fell through the parlor floor today.

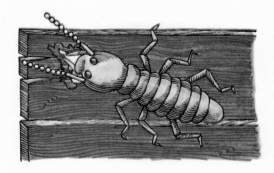

The Naming of Cats

T. S. ELIOT

The Naming of Cats is a difficult matter,
   It isn't just one of your holiday games;
You may think at first I'm as mad as a hatter
When I tell you, a cat must have THREE DIFFERENT NAMES.
First of all, there's the name that the family use daily,   5
   Such as Peter, Augustus, Alonzo, or James,
Such as Victor or Jonathan, George or Bill Bailey —
   All of them sensible everyday names.
There are fancier names if you think they sound sweeter,
   Some for the gentlemen, some for the dames: 10
Such as Plato, Admetus, Electra, Demeter —
   But all of them sensible everyday names.
But I tell you, a cat needs a name that's particular,
   A name that's peculiar, and more dignified,
Else how can he keep up his tail perpendicular,   15
   Or spread out his whiskers, or cherish his pride?
Of names of this kind, I can give you a quorum,
   Such as Munkustrap, Quaxo, or Coricopat,
Such as Bombalurina, or else Jellylorum —
   Names that never belong to more than one cat.   20
But above and beyond there's still one name left over,
   And that is the name that you never will guess;
The name that no human research can discover —
   But THE CAT HIMSELF KNOWS, and will never confess.
When you notice a cat in profound meditation,   25
   The reason, I tell you, is always the same:
His mind is engaged in a rapt contemplation
   Of the thought, of the thought, of the thought of his name:
     His ineffable effable°
     Effanineffable   30
Deep and inscrutable singular Name.

---

29. **ineffable effable:** *Ineffable* means "unutterable," "too overpowering for words."
Effable is an old-fashioned word, meaning the opposite of *ineffable*.

The Content of the Poems

1. In *Through the Looking Glass* (the story from which "Jabberwocky" is taken) a character named Alice reads the poem and says in bewilderment: "It seems very pretty, but it's *rather* hard to understand. Somehow it seems to fill my head with ideas — only I don't exactly know what they are. However, *somebody* killed *something:* that's clear, at any rate." What do *you* think happens in "Jabberwocky"?

2. Tell the sorrowful story of "Casey at the Bat."

3. What did Ogden Nash have to say about each of the different animals in "Private Zoo"?

4. According to Eliot, what three different kinds of names does a cat need? What did Eliot say a cat in "profound meditation" is thinking of?

Style

5. Lewis Carroll made up some famous nonsensical words in the poem "Jabberwocky." One of his nonsensical words, *chortle,* has since found its way into everyday use and is even included in the dictionary. Carroll said that *chortle* is a combination of *chuckle* and *snort.* How does your dictionary define it? Carroll has helped us to interpret some of his other funny made-up words. If you listen to them carefully, you will find that other words, like *chortle,* are combinations of ordinary words. Say these words aloud: *slithy, burbled, galumphing.* What ordinary words do you think are combined in them? Other words in "Jabberwocky" sound like one ordinary English word. For example, *brillig,* according to Carroll, means four o'clock in the afternoon when we begin to *broil* things for dinner. Say the words *jabberwocky* and *uffish* aloud.

What words do they sound like? Can you guess the meanings of the other nonsense words in this poem?

6. In "Casey at the Bat," the poet's language creates an amusing effect. Here, high-flown, elegant-sounding language was used on an ordinary subject — a ball game played in a town called Mudville. What fancy words and phrases describe Casey and the baseball game? How would a sports announcer describe this baseball game?

7. What did you think of T. S. Eliot's choices of names for cats? How did Eliot play with words in the last three lines?

Rhythm and Rhyme. As you have probably noticed, poetry *sounds* different from prose. This is because the poet uses language in a special way. Poets arrange their words in lines, and they usually make sure that each line has a certain number of stressed syllables. Poets also frequently repeat sounds. When end sounds are repeated, we say that the poem rhymes.

8. Read aloud the first stanza of "Casey at the Bat." Do the lines beat out in a regular, almost singsong rhythm? Do any lines in this poem not show this regular rhythm? Read aloud the other poems in this group. Do all of these poems beat out in a strong rhythm?

9. What funny unexpected words were paired in rhyme in Ogden Nash's verses? Did the other poems in this group also rhyme? Were any of these rhymes funny?

Total Effect

10. Do you think that any of these stories or observations would have been as funny had they been written in prose, not in verse? Why?

11. Which of these humorous poems did you enjoy the most? the least? Explain your answers.

NARRATIVE POEMS

Poems that tell stories may be the oldest forms of literature. Like any story, a narrative poem usually has interesting characters and exciting conflicts, but a narrative poem can be even more appealing than a prose story because it uses sound in a special way.

Two famous narrative poems follow. In "Lochinvar," by the British poet Sir Walter Scott, you will find a romantic hero and lilting lines. In "The Raven," by the American poet Edgar Allan Poe, you will read one of literature's strangest stories of mystery and terror.

Lochinvar

SIR WALTER SCOTT

Oh, young Lochinvar is come out of the west,
Through all the wide Border° his steed was the best;
And, save his good broadsword, he weapons had none,
He rode all unarmed, and he rode all alone.
So faithful in love, and so dauntless in war,   5
There never was knight like the young Lochinvar.

He stayed not for brake,° and he stopped not for stone,
He swam the Eske River where ford there was none;
But ere he alighted at Netherby gate,
The bride had consented, the gallant came late: 10
For a laggard in love, and a dastard in war,
Was to wed the fair Ellen of brave Lochinvar.

So boldly he entered the Netherby Hall,
Among bridesmen, and kinsmen, and brothers, and all.
Then spoke the bride's father, his hand on his sword   15
(For the poor craven bridegroom said never a word),
"Oh, come ye in peace here, or come ye in war,
Or to dance at our bridal, young Lord Lochinvar?"

2. **Border:** border country between Scotland and England.   7. **brake:** a dense growth of bushes.

"I long wooed your daughter, my suit you denied —
Love swells like the Solway,° but ebbs like its tide —   20
And now I am come, with this lost love of mine,
To lead but one measure, drink one cup of wine.
There are maidens in Scotland more lovely by far,
That would gladly be bride to the young Lochinvar."

The bride kissed the goblet; the knight took it up;   25
He quaffed off the wine, and he threw down the cup.
She looked down to blush, and she looked up to sigh,
With a smile on her lips, and a tear in her eye.
He took her soft hand, ere her mother could bar —
"Now tread we a measure!" said young Lochinvar.   30

So stately his form, and so lovely her face,
That never a hall such a galliard° did grace;
While her mother did fret, and her father did fume,
And the bridegroom stood dangling his bonnet and plume,
And the bridesmaidens whispered, " 'Twere better by far,   35
To have matched our fair cousin with young Lochinvar."

20. **Solway** (sol′wā): an inlet between England and Scotland. 32. **galliard**
(gal′yərd): lively sixteenth-century dance.

One touch to her hand, and one word to her ear,
When they reached the hall door, and the charger stood near,
So light to the croup° the fair lady he swung,
So light to the saddle before her he sprung!   40
"She is won! we are gone, over bank, brush, and scaur;°
They'll have fleet steeds that follow," quoth young Lochinvar.

There was mounting 'mong Græmes of the Netherby clan;
Forsters, Fenwicks, and Musgraves, they rode and they ran.
There was racing and chasing on Cannobie Lee,°   45
But the lost bride of Netherby ne'er did they see.
So daring in love, and so dauntless in war,
Have ye e'er heard of gallant like young Lochinvar?

---

39. **croup** (kroop): horse's back, behind the saddle. 41. **scaur** (skär): rock.
45. **Cannobie Lee:** the name of a· field.

A LOVE STORY

The Content of the Poem

1. Which words in the first two stanzas describe the setting of this tale?

2. Find the lines that describe the main characters.

3. How does Lochinvar differ from the bridegroom?

4. What lines suggest that part of the story has started before the poem opens? Summarize what you think probably occurred before the action of this poem begins.

5. What trick did Lochinvar play on the bride's parents?

6. What do the reactions of the bride (lines 27–28) tell you about her feelings for Lochinvar?

7. What action is described in lines 43–45? How does the story end?

The Language of the Poem

8. Point out some words in the poem which are not commonly used today. What words might be used today in place of these words?

9. Poets, like other writers, often transpose the word order in sentences. For example, line 3 says ". . . he weapons had none." The regular word order would be *he had no weapons*. What happens to the rhythm when you try to fit this into the poem? Show how the poet changed word order in the following lines:

". . . where ford there was none" (line 8)

" 'Now tread we a measure . . .'" (line 30)

"So light to the croup the fair lady he swung" (line 39)

"So light to the saddle before her he sprung" (line 40)

"But the lost bride of Netherby ne'er did they see" (line 46)

COMPOSITION: A SUMMARY

One kind of composition that you may often be asked to write is a summary of a poem or story. The questions above, under content, will help guide you in writing such a summary of "Lochinvar."

Conclude your composition by giving your reaction to the story.

The Raven

EDGAR ALLAN POE

Once upon a midnight dreary, while I pondered, weak and weary,
Over many a quaint and curious volume of forgotten lore —
While I nodded, nearly napping, suddenly there came a tapping,
As of someone gently rapping, rapping at my chamber door.
" 'Tis some visitor," I muttered, "tapping at my chamber door —   5
                         Only this and nothing more."

Ah, distinctly I remember it was in the bleak December,
And each separate dying ember wrought its ghost upon the floor.
Eagerly I wished the morrow; vainly I had sought to borrow
From my books surcease° of sorrow — sorrow for the lost Lenore —   10
For the rare and radiant maiden whom the angels name Lenore —
                         Nameless *here* forevermore.

And the silken, sad, uncertain rustling of each purple curtain
Thrilled me — filled me with fantastic terrors never felt before;
So that now, to still the beating of my heart, I stood repeating,   15
" 'Tis some visitor entreating entrance at my chamber door,
Some late visitor entreating entrance at my chamber door;
                         That it is and nothing more."

Presently my soul grew stronger; hesitating then no longer,
"Sir," said I, "or Madam, truly your forgiveness I implore;   20
But the fact is I was napping, and so gently you came rapping,
And so faintly you came tapping, tapping at my chamber door,
That I scarce was sure I heard you" — here I opened wide the door —
                         Darkness there and nothing more.

Deep into that darkness peering, long I stood there wondering, fearing,
Doubting, dreaming dreams no mortal ever dared to dream before;   26
But the silence was unbroken, and the stillness gave no token,
And the only word there spoken was the whispered word, "Lenore!"
This I whispered, and an echo murmured back the word "Lenore!" —
                         Merely this and nothing more.

10. **surcease:** end.

Back into the chamber turning, all my soul within me burning,   31
Soon again I heard a tapping somewhat louder than before.
"Surely," said I, "surely that is something at my window lattice;
Let me see, then, what thereat is, and this mystery explore;
Let my heart be still a moment and this mystery explore —   35
                           'Tis the wind and nothing more."

Open here I flung the shutter, when, with many a flirt and flutter,
In there stepped a stately Raven of the saintly days of yore.
Not the least obeisance° made he; not a minute stopped or stayed he,
But with mien° of lord or lady perched above my chamber door —   40
Perched upon a bust of Pallas° just above my chamber door —
                          Perched, and sat, and nothing more.

Then this ebony bird beguiling my sad fancy into smiling
By the grave and stern decorum of the countenance it wore,
"Though thy crest be shorn and shaven, thou," I said, "art sure no
    craven,   45

39. **obeisance** (ō·bā′səns): bow or curtsy. 40. **mien** (mēn): manner or bearing.
41. **Pallas** (pal′əs): Pallas Athena, Greek goddess of wisdom.

Ghastly grim and ancient Raven wandering from the nightly shore —
Tell me what thy lordly name is on the Night's Plutonian shore!"°
                       Quoth the Raven, "Nevermore."

Much I marveled this ungainly fowl to hear discourse so plainly,
Though its answer little meaning — little relevancy bore;   50
For we cannot help agreeing that no living human being
Ever yet was blessed with seeing bird above his chamber door —
Bird or beast upon the sculptured bust above his chamber door,
                     With such name as "Nevermore."

But the Raven, sitting lonely on the placid bust, spoke only   55
That one word, as if his soul in that one word he did outpour.
Nothing further then he uttered, not a feather then he fluttered,
Till I scarcely more than muttered, "Other friends have flown before —
On the morrow *he* will leave me, as my Hopes have flown before."
                   Then the bird said, "Nevermore."

Startled at the stillness broken by reply so aptly spoken,   61
"Doubtless," said I, "what it utters is its only stock and store,
Caught from some unhappy master whom unmerciful Disaster
Followed fast and followed faster till his songs one burden bore —
Till the dirges of his Hope that melancholy burden bore   65
                   Of 'Never — nevermore.' "

But the Raven still beguiling all my fancy into smiling,
Straight I wheeled a cushioned seat in front of bird and bust and door;
Then, upon the velvet sinking, I betook myself to linking
Fancy unto fancy, thinking what this ominous bird of yore —   70
What this grim, ungainly, ghastly, gaunt, and ominous bird of yore
                 Meant in croaking, "Nevermore."

This I sat engaged in guessing, but no syllable expressing
To the fowl, whose fiery eyes now burned into my bosom's core;
This and more I sat divining, with my head at ease reclining   75
On the cushion's velvet lining that the lamplight gloated o'er,
But whose velvet violet lining with the lamplight gloating o'er
               She shall press, ah, nevermore!

47. **Night's Plutonian shore**: the shore of the river leading to the region of the dead.
Pluto, in Greek and Roman mythology, ruled the underworld.

Then, methought, the air grew denser, perfumed from an unseen censer°
Swung by seraphim° whose footfalls tinkled on the tufted floor.   80
"Wretch," I cried, "thy God hath lent thee — by these angels he hath sent thee
Respite° — respite and nepenthe° from thy memories of Lenore!
Quaff, oh, quaff this kind nepenthe, and forget this lost Lenore!"
                         Quoth the Raven, "Nevermore."

"Prophet!" said I, "thing of evil! prophet still, if bird or devil!   85
Whether Tempter sent, or whether tempest tossed thee here ashore,
Desolate yet all undaunted, on this desert land enchanted —
On this home by Horror haunted — tell me truly, I implore —
Is there — *is* there balm in Gilead?° — tell me — tell me, I implore!"
                         Quoth the Raven, "Nevermore."

"Prophet!" said I, "thing of evil! prophet still, if bird or devil!   91
By that heaven that bends above us, by that God we both adore,
Tell this soul with sorrow laden if, within the distant Aidenn,°
It shall clasp a sainted maiden whom the angels name Lenore —
Clasp a rare and radiant maiden whom the angels name Lenore!"   95
                         Quoth the Raven, "Nevermore."

"Be that word our sign of parting, bird or fiend!" I shrieked, upstarting —
"Get thee back into the tempest and the Night's Plutonian shore!
Leave no black plume as a token of that lie thy soul hath spoken!
Leave my loneliness unbroken! Quit the bust above my door!   100
Take thy beak from out my heart, and take thy form from off my door!"
                         Quoth the Raven, "Nevermore."

And the Raven, never flitting, still is sitting, still is sitting
On the pallid bust of Pallas just above my chamber door;
And his eyes have all the seeming of a demon's that is dreaming,   105
And the lamplight o'er him streaming throws his shadow on the floor;
And my soul from out that shadow that lies floating on the floor
                       Shall be lifted — nevermore!

79. **censer:** a container in which incense is burned.   80. **seraphim** (ser′ə·fim): angels.
82. **respite** (res′pit): an interval of rest.   **nepenthe** (ni·pen′thē): a drug thought to
relieve sorrow.   89. **balm** (bäm) **in Gilead** (gil′ē·əd): balm is a soothing ointment;
Gilead was a region of ancient Palestine, where such a balm was made.   93. **Aidenn**
(ā′din): Eden, or Paradise.

The Content of the Poem

1. What is the setting of the story? What had the narrator been doing before the Raven tapped? In what mood and condition was the narrator when he first heard the tapping? Find the lines that tell how the narrator felt when he first heard the tapping sound.

2. Lenore is first mentioned in line 10. Who was she? What had happened to her?

3. What hope and fear might have been in the narrator's mind as he whispered "Lenore!" in line 28?

4. What questions did the narrator ask the Raven? How did the Raven answer? What was the narrator's first attitude toward the Raven? How did his mood change as the story continued? What told you that the narrator thought the Raven might have come from hell? Whom was the narrator addressing in lines 81–83?

5. In line 101, the speaker cried to the Raven: "Take thy beak from out my heart . . ." What did he mean?

6. What is the conclusion of this story of horror? Are you left with questions?

The Words in the Poem. Poets are interested in the effects of words. Some words can greatly influence our imaginations and emotions. We say that such words have strong connotations, or suggestive meanings. For example, in "The Raven" the words *midnight* and *dreary* suggest to us the loneliness and gloom of the night on which these events took place.

7. List the words which Poe used to describe the narrator of the poem and the Raven. What effects do they have on your emotions? What vivid pictures do they put into your mind?

The Sounds in the Poem. Poe once said that a poem should not appeal chiefly to the mind or reason. When Poe wrote a poem like "The Raven," he was not interested in developing a plot or story. Poetry, according to Poe, should give us pleasure and excite us. It should appeal to our sense of beauty. Much of the excitement and beauty of Poe's poetry comes from its sounds.

8. How many lines in each stanza of "The Raven" end with the sound *ôr?* What name in the poem does this sound constantly remind you of?

9. In the first stanza, the words *tapping* and *rapping* remind us of the Raven's beak pecking at the window. Can you find any other sounds in this poem that remind you of certain noises?

10. The term alliteration refers to the repetition of an initial word sound within one line. Poe used alliteration in line 1 when he said "weak and weary." Point to the other uses of alliteration in this poem.

11. In line 1, the words *dreary* and *weary* rhyme. Read aloud other words within a line that rhyme.

The Deeper Meaning of the Poem

12. Do you think the Raven really was there? What might the Raven stand for, or symbolize? What lines suggest that the narrator might be insane?

You saw how Poe used words to create a mood of mystery and terror. This same technique can be used in prose.

Write a paragraph describing some setting or some situation. Your purpose will be to create a mood. Use words that will make your reader feel this mood very strongly. Here are some ideas:

Face-to-Face with a Martian
A Perfect Hour
No Lights!

LYRIC POEMS

When a poet writes to express personal thoughts and feelings, he is writing lyric poetry. Most of the poems that follow are arranged in groups. The titles of these groups reveal some of the things you can look for in lyric poetry: "Pictures in Poetry," "Experiences in Poetry," "Deeper Meanings in Poetry," and "Different Views in Poetry."

Although people have been reading and writing poetry for centuries, no one has yet been able to define exactly what poetry is. Carl Sandburg said that it is the art "which gathers the beautiful into words." And the poet Eleanor Farjeon, in her poem "Poetry," put it this way:

What is poetry? Who knows?
Not the rose, but the scent of the rose;
Not the sky, but the light in the sky;
Not the fly, but the gleam of the fly;
Not the sea, but the sound of the sea;
Not myself, but what makes me
See, hear, and feel something that prose
Cannot, and what it is, who knows?

A group of Japanese poems will introduce you to lyric poetry. In each of these brief poems a poet has used language to capture a fleeting moment of beauty.

Five Japanese Poems

1

A spark in the sun,
this tiny flower has roots
deep in the cool earth.

2

The tight string broke and
the loose kite fell fluttering,
losing its spirit.

"Poetry" from *Poems for Children* by Eleanor Farjeon, copyright 1938 by Eleanor Farjeon. Reprinted by permission of J. B. Lippincott Company.
Nos. 1 and 2 from *Cricket Songs: Japanese Haiku*, translated by Harry Behn, © 1964 by Harry Behn. Reprinted by permission of Harcourt, Brace & World, Inc.

3

An old silent pond . . .
A frog jumps into the pond,
splash! Silence again.

4

Scattered petals lie
on rice-seedling waters; bright
is the starlit sky.

5

A child stretched forth
A tiny hand
Between the slats of the window
To feel the spring rain.

A SINGLE MOMENT

1. Like many lyrics, these poems create little pictures. Describe the picture you are shown in each poem.

2. Poets often notice how one thing in the world resembles something else. What is the petal-scattered water, in the fourth poem, compared to? In the last poem, a child stretches out for the rain. In what ways is this child like a flower?

3. Some of these poets have placed contrasting images, or pictures, side by side with one another. What contrasting images do you see in the first three poems?

4. Like many poets, the poets who wrote these poems felt deeply about nature. Show that all but one of these poems mentions something in nature.

5. Like most poems, these use words that make us see, smell, feel, or hear things in the world. Point out words in these poems that appeal to your senses.

COMPOSITION: A POEM

Try writing some brief poems, such as the ones you have just read. Do not worry about using complete sentences. Concentrate on finding concrete, ordinary words which will capture, to your satisfaction, a fleeting moment or a feeling.

Here are several possible first lines, but it would be better to begin with your own.

See the falling star
The evening comes
Oh! Ride the wild waves

No. 3 from *Cricket Songs: Japanese Haiku,* translated by Harry Behn, © 1964 by Harry Behn. Reprinted by permission of Harcourt, Brace & World, Inc.
No. 4 from *An Introduction to Haiku* by Harold G. Henderson, copyright © 1958 by Harold G. Henderson. Reprinted by permission of Doubleday & Company, Inc.
No. 5 from *The Year of My Life,* translated by Nobuyuki Yuasa. Reprinted by permission of University of California Press.

PICTURES IN POETRY

Often a poet has been so moved by a scene that he wants to picture it in words. Fog, a river, a summer day, a winter evening, and a bird in the snow — these are five different scenes that have impressed poets. You will read about them in these lyrics.

Fog

CARL SANDBURG

The fog comes
on little cat feet.

It sits looking
over harbor and city
on silent haunches
and then moves on.

The River Is a Piece of Sky

JOHN CIARDI

From the top of a bridge
The river below
Is a piece of sky —
    Until you throw
    A penny in   5
    Or a cockleshell
    Or a pebble or two
    Or a bicycle bell
    Or a cobblestone
    Or a fat man's cane —   10
And then you can see
It's a river again.

The difference you'll see
When you drop your penny:
The river has splashes,   15
The sky hasn't any.

The Lonely Street

WILLIAM   CARLOS   WILLIAMS

School is over. It is too hot
to walk at ease. At ease
in light frocks they walk the streets
to while the time away.
They have grown tall. They hold   5
pink flames in their right hands.
In white from head to foot,
with sidelong, idle look —
in yellow, floating stuff,
black sash and stockings —   10
touching their avid mouths
with pink sugar on a stick —
like a carnation each holds in her hand —
they mount the lonely street.

Prelude I: The Winter Evening

T.   S.   ELIOT

The winter evening settles down
With smell of steaks in passageways.
Six o'clock.
The burnt-out ends of smoky days.
And now a gusty shower wraps   5
The grimy scraps
Of withered leaves about your feet
And newspapers from vacant lots;
The showers beat
On broken blinds and chimney pots,   10
And at the corner of the street
A lonely cab-horse steams and stamps.
And then the lighting of the lamps.

A Widow Bird

PERCY BYSSHE SHELLEY

A widow bird sat mourning for her love
    Upon a wintry bough;
The frozen wind crept on above,
    The freezing stream below.

There was no leaf upon the forest bare,
    No flower upon the ground,
And little motion in the air
    Except the mill-wheel's sound.

PICTURES

The Content of the Poems

1. What is the subject of Sandburg's poem: fog or cats? What does "it" in line 3 refer to?

2. According to Ciardi, when do we know that the river is not a piece of sky?

3. In "The Lonely Street," who thinks it is too hot to be on the street? Whom does "they" in line 5 refer to? What are "they" wearing and eating?

4. What kind of place is described in T. S. Eliot's poem? What time of day is it? What is the weather like?

5. Describe the widow bird's surroundings. Why did Shelley call the bird a "widow"?

The Language of the Poems. One way a poet expresses comparisons is through personification. Personification simply means that something inanimate is talked about as if it had human or living qualities. Personification is used in everyday language, too, when we say things like "The thunder growled."

6. How has Sandburg used personification in "Fog"? What do you think he meant in saying that the fog comes in "on little cat feet"? In what ways does fog "sit"? What other living things could fog be compared to?

7. What comparison did Ciardi make in his poem? In what different ways is this a good comparison?

8. What comparisons did Williams make in lines 5–6 and 12–13?

The Poets' Attitudes. Often the words used by a poet can tell us how he feels about his subject.

9. From the way Sandburg described fog, would you say that he liked it? How might someone else feel about fog?

10. What effect did Williams achieve by calling the street "lonely"? Would the effect have been the same had he described it as "quiet"? What do you think the poet's mood was as he looked on this scene? Try to justify your answer by citing lines in the poem.

11. In his poem, Eliot used words like *burnt-out, smoky, grimy, withered, vacant, broken, lonely.* What is the total effect of these words? Do you think Eliot wanted you to like the scene he has described?

12. Point to words in "A Widow Bird" that give an impression of cold and bleakness. How do you think the poet felt as he looked at the bird?

EXPERIENCES IN POETRY

Poets, like other people, feel deeply, but a poet has a deep desire to express his feelings and to share them with other people. In each lyric that follows, you will read about how a poet has responded to a particular experience in his life.

The Daffodils

WILLIAM WORDSWORTH

I wandered lonely as a cloud
That floats on high o'er vales and hills,
When all at once I saw a crowd,
A host, of golden daffodils,
Beside the lake, beneath the trees,   5
Fluttering and dancing in the breeze.

Continuous as the stars that shine
And twinkle on the milky way,
They stretched in never-ending line
Along the margin of a bay: 10
Ten thousand saw I at a glance,
Tossing their heads in sprightly dance.

The waves beside them danced: but they
Outdid the sparkling waves in glee.
A poet could not but be gay,   15
In such a jocund° company.
I gazed — and gazed — but little thought
What wealth the show to me had brought.

For oft, when on my couch I lie
In vacant or in pensive mood,   20
They flash upon that inward eye
Which is the bliss of solitude;
And then my heart with pleasure fills,
And dances with the daffodils.

16. **jocund** (jŏk′ənd): merry.

The Hearth Fire

JOHN GREENLEAF WHITTIER

We piled, with care, our nightly stack
Of wood against the chimney back —
The oaken log, green, huge, and thick,
And on its top the stout backstick;
The knotty forestick laid apart,   5
And filled between with curious art
The ragged brush; then, hovering near,
We watched the first red blaze appear,
Heard the sharp crackle, caught the gleam
On whitewashed wall and sagging beam,   10
Until the old, rude-furnished room
Burst, flowerlike, into rosy bloom. . . .

Shut in from all the world without,
We sat the clean-winged° hearth about,
Content to let the north wind roar   15
In baffled rage at pane and door,
While the red logs before us beat
The frost line back with tropic heat;
And ever, when a louder blast
Shook beam and rafter as it passed,   20
The merrier up its roaring draft
The great throat of the chimney laughed.
The house dog on his paws outspread
Laid to the fire his drowsy head;
The cat's dark silhouette on the wall   25
A couchant° tiger's seemed to fall;
And, for the winter fireside meet,°
Between the andirons' straddling feet,
The mug of cider simmered slow,
The apples sputtered in a row,   30
And, close at hand, the basket stood
With nuts from brown October's wood.

What matter how the night behaved?
What matter how the north wind raved?
Blow high, blow low, not all its snow   35
Could quench our hearth fire's ruddy glow.

14. **clean-winged:** A turkey wing was used to sweep the hearth. 26. **couchant**
(kou'chənt): lying down. 27. **meet:** well-suited.

Jean

ROBERT BURNS

Of a' the airts° the wind can blaw
   I dearly like the west,
For there the bonnie lassie lives,
   The lassie I lo'e best:
There wild woods grow, and rivers row,°   5
   And mony a hill between;
But day and night my fancy's flight
   Is ever wi' my Jean.

I see her in the dewy flowers,
   I see her sweet and fair: 10
I hear her in the tunefu' birds,
   I hear her charm the air:
There's not a bonnie flower that springs
   By fountain, shaw,° or green,
There's not a bonnie bird that sings   15
   But minds me o' my Jean.

1. **airts:** directions.   5. **row:** roll.   14. **shaw:** grove.

Crossing a Creek

HERBERT CLARK JOHNSON

He who has rolled his pants up to his knee
And walked a lowland creek from bank to bank
Has mixed his pulse with that of land and sea.
And though, in after days, he cross his streams
By bridge or log, he'll always feel its beat
Against his body, even in his dreams.

"Crossing a Creek" by Herbert Clark Johnson in *Opportunity* Magazine of November 1940. Reprinted by permission of the National Urban League.

The Wise Old Apple Tree in Spring

ROBERT HILLYER

The wise old apple tree in spring,
Though split and hollow, makes a crown
Of such fantastic blossoming
We cannot let them cut it down.
It bears no fruit, but honeybees   5
Prefer it to the other trees.

The orchard man chalks his mark
And says, "This empty shell must go."
We nod and rub it off the bark
As soon as he goes down the row.   10
Each spring he looks bewildered. "Queer,
I thought I marked this thing last year."

Ten orchard men have come and gone
Since first I saw my grandfather
Slyly erase it. I'm the one   15
To do it now. As I defer
The showy veteran's removal
My grandson nods his full approval.

Like mine, my fellow ancient's roots
Are deep in the last century   20
From which our memories send shoots
For all our grandchildren to see
How spring, inviting bloom and rhyme,
Defeats the orchard men of time.

High Flight

PILOT-OFFICER JOHN GILLESPIE MAGEE, JR., RCAF

Oh, I have slipped the surly bonds of earth,
And danced the skies on laughter-silvered wings;
Sunward I've climbed and joined the tumbling mirth
Of sun-split clouds — and done a hundred things
You have not dreamed of — wheeled and soared and swung   5
High in the sunlit silence. Hov'ring there,
I've chased the shouting wind along and flung
My eager craft through footless halls of air.
Up, up the long delirious, burning blue
I've topped the wind-swept heights with easy grace,   10
Where never lark, or even eagle, flew;
And, while with silent, lifting mind I've trod
The high untrespassed sanctity of space,
Put out my hand, and touched the face of God.

Exiled

EDNA ST. VINCENT MILLAY

Searching my heart for its true sorrow,
   This is the thing I find to be:
That I am weary of words and people,
   Sick of the city, wanting the sea;

Wanting the sticky, salty sweetness   5
   Of the strong wind and shattered spray;
Wanting the loud sound and the soft sound
   Of the big surf that breaks all day.

Always before about my dooryard,
   Marking the reach of the winter sea,   10
Rooted in sand and dragging driftwood,
   Straggled the purple wild sweetpea;

"High Flight" by Pilot-Officer John Gillespie Magee, Jr., RCAF, in the *New York Herald Tribune* of February 8, 1942. Reprinted by permission of the publishers and Mrs. John G. Magee.
"Exiled" from *Collected Poems* by Edna St. Vincent Millay, Harper & Row, Publishers, copyright 1921, 1948 by Edna St. Vincent Millay. Reprinted by permission of Norma Millay Ellis.

Always I climbed the wave at morning,
  Shook the sand from my shoes at night,
That now am caught beneath great buildings,   15
  Stricken with noise, confused with light.

If I could hear the green piles° groaning
  Under the windy wooden piers,
See once again the bobbing barrels,
  And the black sticks that fence the weirs,°   20

If I could see the weedy mussels
  Crusting the wrecked and rotting hulls,
Hear once again the hungry crying
  Overhead, of the wheeling gulls,

Feel once again the shanty straining   25
  Under the turning of the tide,
Fear once again the rising freshet,°
  Dread the bell in the fog outside —

I should be happy — that was happy
  All day long on the coast of Maine!   30
I have a need to hold and handle
  Shells and anchors and ships again!

I should be happy, that am happy
  Never at all since I came here.
I am too long away from water.   35
  I have a need of water near.

17. **piles**: posts supporting a pier. 20. **weirs** (wirz): enclosures to keep fish in.
27. **freshet**: sudden rise of water.

The Content and Meaning of the Poems

1. In "Daffodils," what was the poet's mood as he walked? What effect did the sight of the daffodils later have on him? What is a "vacant" mood? What do you think "that inward eye" is?

2. "The Hearth Fire" is from a long poem called *Snowbound*. What effect did the fire have upon the room and upon the people who were snowbound?

3. Why did Robert Burns like the west wind? What things reminded him of Jean?

4. What simple experience did Johnson talk about in his poem? What does "its" in line 5 refer to? According to the poet, what is the effect of this experience?

5. Is the narrator of "The Wise Old Apple Tree in Spring" a young or an old man? How do you know? To whom or what does "showy veteran" in line 17 refer? Why was the old tree saved each year? Does the poet indicate that the tree will continue to be saved? How did the tree remind the poet of himself? What is the poet saying in lines 23–24?

6. Why do you think the writer of "High Flight" used the adjective *surly* to describe the "bonds of earth"? What is a "lifting" mind, line 12? What do you think the last line of the poem means?

7. What was the mood of the poet as she wrote "Exiled"? What things about the city bothered Edna St. Vincent Millay? What did she miss about the seashore?

The Language of the Poems

8. Just as Carl Sandburg personified fog by talking about it as if it were a cat (page 451), so Wordsworth personified daffodils by talking about them as if they were dancers. Find the words that compare the flowers to dancers.

9. How did Whittier use personification in lines 21–22 of "The Hearth Fire"?

10. In what ways did Robert Hillyer personify the old apple tree? In what ways was this tree "wise"?

Rhythm, Rhyme, and Sounds in the Poems. As you have seen, the language of poetry is different from the language of prose. The difference is partly in the way poets use images and comparisons. But an even bigger difference is in the way poets use rhythm, rhyme, and other sounds. In most poetry, each line is written so that the voice will rise and fall in a regular rhythmic pattern. If you read "The Daffodils" aloud, you might have noticed the regular pattern of stressed (´) and unstressed (˘) syllables in each line of the poem.

"I wandered lonely as a cloud
That floats on high o'er vales and hills,
When all at once I saw a crowd,
A host, of golden daffodils"

Notice, too, that the rhyme of these lines forms a pattern. The sounds of the first and third lines rhyme, and those of the second and fourth lines rhyme. In addition to rhyme and rhythm, poets often use words for sound effects. For example, a series of *s* sounds can remind us of the wind, and a series of hard *t* sounds or *p* sounds can remind us of tapping or galloping.

11. Look back at any two poems in this grouping. Read them aloud. Does your voice rise and fall in a regular rhythmic beat? How are these poems rhymed? Do the rhyming sounds recur in a regular pattern?

12. Look back at "The Hearth Fire." How do the words in lines 19–22 remind you of wind? What sound effects are suggested by the words in line 9? in lines 29–30? in line 35?

DEEPER MEANINGS IN POETRY

A poem can say more than it appears to say. A poem's content may be fairly easy to see, but you should be alert to clues that might lead to deeper meaning. As you think about the lyrics that follow, you might even find that sometimes the situation described in the poem is not really the subject of the poem at all.

The Dark Hills

EDWIN ARLINGTON ROBINSON

Dark hills at evening in the west,
Where sunset hovers like a sound
Of golden horns that sang to rest
Old bones of warriors under ground,
Far now from all the bannered ways
Where flash the legions of the sun,
You fade — as if the last of days
Were fading, and all wars were done.

Last Week in October

THOMAS HARDY

The trees are undressing, and fling in many places —
On the gray road, the roof, the window sill —
Their radiant robes and ribbons and yellow laces;
A leaf each second so is flung at will,
Here, there, another and another, still and still.   5

A spider's web has caught one while downcoming,
That stays there dangling when the rest pass on;
Like a suspended criminal hangs he, mumming°
In golden garb, while one yet green, high yon,
Trembles, as fearing such a fate for himself anon.   10

8. **mumming:** acting. A mummer is a person who performs in colorful costume.

what if a much of a which of a wind

E. E. CUMMINGS

what if a much of a which of a wind
gives the truth to summer's lie;
bloodies with dizzying leaves the sun
and yanks immortal stars awry?°
Blow king to beggar and queen to seem   5
(blow friend to fiend: blow space to time)
— when skies are hanged and oceans drowned,
the single secret will still be man

what if a keen of a lean wind flays
screaming hills with sleet and snow: 10
strangles valleys by ropes of thing
and stifles forests in white ago?
Blow hope to terror; blow seeing to blind
(blow pity to envy and soul to mind)
— whose hearts are mountains, roots are trees,   15
it's they shall cry hello to the spring

what if a dawn of a doom of a dream
bites this universe in two,
peels forever out of his grave
and sprinkles nowhere with me and you?   20
Blow soon to never and never to twice
(blow life to isn't: blow death to was)
— all nothing's only our hugest home;
the most who die, the more we live

4. **awry** (ə·rī′): out of place.

"what if a much of a which of a wind" from *Poems 1923–1954* by E. E. Cummings. Reprinted by permission of Harcourt, Brace & World, Inc.

Kid in the Park

LANGSTON HUGHES

Lonely little question mark
on a bench in the park:

See the people passing by?
See the airplanes in the sky?

See the birds   5
flying home
before
dark?

Home's just around
the corner   10
there —
but not really
anywhere.

DEEPER MEANING

1. In "The Dark Hills," the poet saw hills dark against the setting sun. In what ways is a sunset like the lingering echo of horns (lines 2–3)? The poet says that the dark hills seem far away from "all the bannered ways where flash the legions of the sun" (lines 5–6). What do you think this means? In line 7 he says to the hills: "You fade . . ." Why do the hills seem to be fading? What does Robinson say to the hills in the last two lines? Have you ever watched a sunset and thought that it looked like the end of time?

2. What picture is presented in the first stanza of "Last Week in October"? What does "one" in line 6 refer to? What does "that" in line 7 refer to? Why was the green leaf trembling? To the poet, what might be represented by the dead golden leaf caught in the web? What might the living green leaf represent, or symbolize? Do you think Hardy was interested only in describing a leaf fall in this poem, or did he have something else on his mind?

3. E. E. Cummings did strange things with words and with English grammar. By listening to the poem read aloud, however, you should be able to figure out some of its puzzling lines. In the first stanza, the poet speaks of a wind blowing things out of place. What is "summer's lie," in line 2? What does this entire line mean? Name some of the other things that might be changed by the wind. If such things ever happen, what, according to line 8, would still be the greatest miracle, or "single secret"?

4. In the second stanza of his poem, Cummings speaks of a terrible winter storm that might do awful things to the world. Name some of the things that might happen to the world and to man as a result of such a storm. What do you think Cummings means by "ropes of thing" in line 11? What could "white ago" be, in line 12? According to lines 15–16, who would survive such a terrible, violent winter storm?

5. What possibility does Cummings talk about in the third stanza? What might make you think that he could have been describing a terrible, destructive weapon, such as a bomb? What is the poet's answer to such a possibility (lines 23–24)?

6. Is Cummings talking about wind in this poem or is he saying something about mankind? Explain.

7. Why do you think Langston Hughes calls the child in the park a "lonely little question mark"? Why do you think the last two lines are in italics? What effect did these lines have on you?

DIFFERENT VIEWS IN POETRY

Two poets can look at the same subject in different ways. The next two lyrics are about trains, but the poets see the trains through different eyes and with different feelings.

Night Journey

THEODORE ROETHKE

Now as the train bears west,
Its rhythm rocks the earth,
And from my Pullman berth
I stare into the night
While others take their rest.   5
Bridges of iron lace,
A suddenness of trees,
A lap of mountain mist
All cross my line of sight,
Then a bleak wasted place,   10
And a lake below my knees.
Full on my neck I feel
The straining at a curve;
My muscles move with steel;
I wake in every nerve.   15
I watch a beacon swing
From dark to blazing bright;
We thunder through ravines
And gullies washed with light.
Beyond the mountain pass   20
Mist deepens on the pane;
We rush into a rain
That rattles double glass.
Wheels shake the roadbed stone;
The pistons jerk and shove;   25
I stay up half the night
To see the land I love.

I Like to See It Lap the Miles

EMILY DICKINSON

I like to see it lap the miles,
And lick the valleys up,
And stop to feed itself at tanks;
And then, prodigious,° step

Around a pile of mountains,   5
And, supercilious,° peer
In shanties by the sides of roads;
And then a quarry pare

To fit its sides, and crawl between,
Complaining all the while   10
In horrid, hooting stanza;
Then chase itself down hill

And neigh like Boanerges;°
Then, punctual as a star,
Stop — docile and omnipotent —   15
At its own stable door.

---

4. **prodigious** (prə·dij′əs): enormous. 6. **supercilious** (sōō′pər·sil′ē·əs): haughty.
12. **Boanerges** (bō′ə·nûr′jēz): a noisy or thunderous orator. In the Bible (Mark 3:17),
Boanerges was the name that Jesus Christ gave the sons of Zebedee.

TWO TRAINS

The Content of the Poems

1. Where was Theodore Roethke's train going? What did the poet see and feel and hear on the train? What does he mean by a "suddenness" of trees (line 7)?

2. Trace the route of the train described by Emily Dickinson. What animal is the train compared to? List the verbs which tell what this "animal" does on its route. Miss Dickinson used the words *prodigious, supercilious, complaining, punctual, docile,* and *omnipotent* to describe the train.

What does each word mean? How can a train be all these things at once? Is the word *train* ever mentioned in this poem?

The Poets' Purposes

3. What mood does Theodore Roethke want you to get from his poem? Read his poem aloud. Can you feel the speed and the rocking rhythm of a train in the beat of the lines? Did he like this train ride?

4. What picture of a train do you think Emily Dickinson wants to give you? How do you think she felt about the train? What is the mood of this poem?

Poetry

Ever since man first began to use words, he has been expressing himself by using language in a way that we call poetry. No one can tell you exactly how to read poetry, but the following suggestions might help you develop your own techniques for reading poetry with more understanding.

READING POETRY

1. *Read the complete thought.* When you read a poem, do not make the mistake, as so many people do, of reading in lines only. A line of poetry is not necessarily a complete thought or sentence. The end of a complete thought in a poem is usually indicated by a period or a semicolon. Sometimes these punctuation marks will come in the middle of a line of poetry; sometimes you will have to read several lines before a thought is completed. Read aloud the following lines of poetry, from "The Lonely Street" by William Carlos Williams. Where should you stop completely? What do you do when you come to a comma?

School is over. It is too hot
to walk at ease. At ease
in light frocks they walk the streets
to while the time away.   (page 452)

Look back at page 465 and read aloud "I Like to See It Lap the Miles." Where should you make complete stops? Where should you pause?

2. *Be aware of inverted word order.* Some people complain that poetry is hard to read because the words do not make sense. Poets, like other writers, oc-casionally seem to say things "backward," that is, in an order different from what we would use in ordinary conversation. Look at the word order of this sentence from "Lochinvar" by Sir Walter Scott.

He swam the Eske River where ford
   there was none   (page 441)

The normal word order of this sentence would be this:

He swam the Eske River where there was no ford.

Look back at "The Raven." Put lines 25 and 49 in more normal order.

3. *Look for figurative language.* You use figurative language every day, whenever you say things like "He ran like lightning" or "The wind moaned" or "She is a doll." Figurative language is a language of comparison. It never is completely, literally true. (She isn't really a doll; she just looks like one.)

Here is a figure of speech from "The Hearth Fire" by John Greenleaf Whittier.

And ever, when a louder blast
Shook beam and rafter as it passed,
The merrier up its roaring draft
The great throat of the chimney laughed.
            (page 455)

In prose, Whittier might have said this:

Whenever a particularly strong gust of wind came along, shaking beams and rafters, the draft from the chimney increased the roaring of the fire.

What image, or picture, does Whittier's

figure of speech put in your mind? Does the prose statement do the same thing?

Here is another example of figurative language, from "Prelude I: The Winter Evening" by T. S. Eliot. Suppose this line had been written in prose. How might it be expressed? What is being compared in this figure of speech?

> The burnt-out ends of smoky days
> (page 452)

Look back at "Fog," page 451. What comparison is essential to this poem?

4. *Paraphrase difficult lines.* A paraphrase or a rewording of the poem cannot "take the place" of the poem itself. In fact, even a careful paraphrase sometimes cannot summarize all that a poem says, for part of the appeal of poetry is that it expresses thoughts and feelings that just cannot be put into the kind of language we use every day. Paraphrasing a poem, however, can often help you to understand some difficult lines of a poem.

Here is a paraphrase of one of the poems in this unit. Which one is it? (Does the paraphrase really express what is said in line 3 of the poem?)

A boy who has rolled his pants up to his knees and walked barefoot through a creek has experienced a great closeness to the earth. Even when he is a man and crosses creeks on bridges or logs, he will remember this boyhood experience.

Look back at the following pages and paraphrase the lines given below.

"The Raven," lines 103–08, page 447
"Prelude I: The Winter Evening," the entire poem, page 452
"The Daffodils," lines 19–24, page 454

5. *Ask yourself what the poet is saying.* After you have found the sentences, figured out the inverted word order, under-stood the figures of speech, and perhaps paraphrased parts of the poem—what does it all mean? Ask yourself this question when you have finished your first slow reading of a poem. Then reread the poem again. Try these techniques with the poem "The Wise Old Apple Tree in Spring," page 457.

WRITING POETRY

You will appreciate the poet's craft when you try to write a poem yourself. Some people—not everyone—have the gift of writing poetry easily. But everyone has the ability to write something poetic. To find a subject for a short poem, think back to some experience, scene, thought, or person that provoked emotion in you. Then keep these points in mind:

1. *As you begin writing poetry, do not worry about formal rhyme schemes and regular patterns of rhythm.* Try imitating the style of the Japanese poems on pages 449–50, of "Fog" on page 451, and of "The Lonely Street" on page 452.

2. *Say things in a fresh, new way.* Avoid overused comparisons, such as "red as a rose" or "as black as night."

ART AND LITERATURE

Poet Emily Dickinson once said that a book was like a ship that could take her lands away. A painting is like a ship, too. It can transport you anywhere—it can show you sights you could never see in your own limited world. Just as with reading a book, you never have to pay a toll when you travel with a painting.

Select three paintings from any group in this book—paintings that carried you away somewhere. Write a short poem about each painting, expressing what the painting did for you, what you felt as you looked at it, and how it affected you later.

PART THREE

Mark Twain

Robert Frost

A Close Look
at Four Authors

Unit 8

UNIT 8 A Close Look at Four Authors

A stage master in a window of the Shakespeare Memorial Museum in Stratford-on-Avon.

By way of introducing the writers in this unit, here are some things they have said about themselves or their work:

Mark Twain

"I was always told that I was a sickly and precarious and tiresome and uncertain child and lived mainly on medicines . . . I asked my mother about this in her old age — she was in her eighty-eighth year — and said:

" 'I suppose that . . . you were uneasy about me?'

" 'Yes . . .'

" 'Afraid I wouldn't live?'

"After a reflective pause — ostensibly to think out the facts — 'No — afraid you would.' "

Robert Frost

"Someone asked the question, 'What's grandma reading the Bible so much for lately?' 'She's cramming for her finals.' I wish I had said that, you know, that's the kind of thing you covet, you wish you'd said. And have you ever had . . . little thoughts like that, or big thoughts . . . ? Have you ever dared write them down . . . so that you yourself, not your teachers, could try them a year afterwards, see if they have gone empty or gone ridiculous?"

James Thurber

"A professor of mine once said that if a thing cannot stand laughter, it is not a good thing; and we must not lose in this country the uses of laughter."

William Shakespeare

"Not marble, nor the gilded monuments
Of princes, shall outlive this powerful rhyme."

From *The Autobiography of Mark Twain*, edited by Charles Neider. Reprinted by permission of Harper & Row, Publishers.
From interviews with Robert Frost filmed for the National Educational Television and Radio Corporation.

MARK TWAIN
1835–1910

Mark Twain was only eighteen when he left the little Missouri town of Hannibal and struck out on his own to see the world. One day, on a trip down the Mississippi on his way to Brazil, he apprenticed himself to a steamboat pilot. So greatly did he love the Mississippi that he stayed there until the War Between the North and the South brought river traffic almost to a standstill.

The young adventurer's start in writing came when he went West. He found no gold in the Western mines, but he did find success as a newspaper writer. Here he began to sign his articles not with his real name, Samuel Clemens, but with the name "Mark Twain." He took his penname from the cry of the steamboat men, "By the mark, twain!" — meaning that by their measure (mark) they had found that the river was two (twain) fathoms deep.

Twain's first big opportunity came when he persuaded a San Francisco newspaper to send him as a correspondent with a group of tourists bound for Europe and the Holy Land. His writings about this trip were published as a humorous book called *Innocents Abroad*, which quickly became a best seller. Twain's books from then on were eagerly bought by the American public. Mark Twain drew upon his boyhood memories for some of his greatest and most popular writings — among them the novel *The Adventures of Tom Sawyer*. The sequel to this, *The Adventures of Huckleberry Finn*, is considered Twain's greatest work and a masterpiece.

Like most great humorists, Mark Twain was a serious thinker and a critic of society, a writer who used laughter to help people see themselves more honestly.

Boyhood Reminiscences

FROM *The Autobiography of Mark Twain*

During his last years, Mark Twain dictated the story of his life. In the following passages, he recalls some incidents from his boyhood which he later used in *The Adventures of Tom Sawyer*. Twain's rambling recollections of a happy boyhood give us an unmatched record of what it was like to grow up in the near-West of America in the mid-nineteenth century.

MY SCHOOL DAYS began when I was four years and a half old. There were no public schools in Missouri in those early days, but there were two private schools — terms twenty-five cents per week per pupil and collect it if you can. Mrs. Horr taught the children in a small log house at the southern end of Main Street. Mr. Sam Cross taught the young people of larger growth in a frame schoolhouse on the hill. I was sent to Mrs. Horr's school, and I remember my first day in that little log house with perfect clearness after these sixty-five years and upwards — at least I remember an episode of that first day. I broke one of the rules and was warned not to do it again and was told that the penalty for a second breach was a whipping. I presently broke the rule again and Mrs. Horr told me to go out and find a switch and fetch it. I was glad she appointed me, for I believed I could select a switch suitable to the occasion with more judiciousness than anybody else.

In the mud I found a cooper's [1] shaving of the old-time pattern, oak, two inches broad, a quarter of an inch thick, and rising in a shallow curve at one end. There were nice new shavings of the same breed close by, but I took this one, although it was rotten. I carried it to Mrs. Horr, presented it, and stood before her in an attitude of meekness and resignation which seemed to me calculated to win favor and sympathy, but it did not happen. She divided a long look of strong disapproval equally between me and the shaving; then she called me by my entire name, Samuel Langhorne Clemens (probably the first time I had ever heard it all strung together in one procession), and said she was

[1] **cooper's:** barrelmaker's.

ashamed of me. I was to learn later that when a teacher calls a boy by his entire name it means trouble. She said she would try and appoint a boy with a better judgment than mine in the matter of switches, and it saddens me yet to remember how many faces lighted up with the hope of getting that appointment. Jim Dunlap got it and when he returned with the switch of his choice I recognized that he was an expert.

Mrs. Horr was a New England lady of middle age with New England ways and principles, and she always opened school with prayer and a chapter from the New Testament; also, she explained the chapter with a brief talk. In one of these talks she dwelt upon the text, "Ask and ye shall receive," and said that whosoever prayed for a thing with earnestness and strong desire need not doubt that his prayer would be answered.

I was so forcibly struck by this information and so gratified by the opportunities which it offered that this was probably the first time I had heard of it. I thought I would give it a trial. I believed in Mrs. Horr thoroughly, and I had no doubts as to the result. I prayed for gingerbread. Margaret Kooneman, who was the baker's daughter, brought a slab of gingerbread to school every morning. She had always kept it out of sight before, but when I finished my prayer and glanced up, there it was in easy reach, and she was looking the other way. In all my life I believe I never enjoyed an answer to prayer more than I enjoyed that one; and I was a convert, too. I had no end of wants and they had always

remained unsatisfied up to that time, but I meant to supply them and extend them now that I had found out how to do it.

But this dream was like almost all the other dreams we indulge in in life — there was nothing in it. I did as much praying during the next two or three days as anyone in that town, I suppose, and I was very sincere and earnest about it too, but nothing came of it. I found that not even the most powerful prayer was competent to lift that gingerbread again.

My mother had a good deal of trouble with me, but I think she enjoyed it. She had none at all with my brother· Henry, who was two years younger than I, and I think that the unbroken monotony of his goodness and truthfulness and obedience would have been a burden to her but for the relief and variety which I furnished in the other direction. I was a tonic. I was valuable to her. I never thought of it before, but now I see it. I never knew Henry to do a vicious thing toward me or toward anyone else — but he frequently did righteous ones that cost me as heavily. It was his duty to report me, when I needed reporting and neglected to do it myself, and he was very faithful in discharging that duty. He is Sid in *Tom Sawyer*. But Sid was not Henry. Henry was a very much finer and better boy than ever Sid was.

It was Henry who called my mother's attention to the fact that the thread with which she had sewed my collar together to keep me from going in swimming had changed color. My mother would not have discovered it but for that, and she was manifestly piqued [1] when she recognized that that prominent bit of circumstantial evidence had escaped her sharp eye. That detail probably added a detail to my punishment. It is human. We generally visit our shortcomings on somebody else when there is a possible excuse for it — but no matter. I took it out of Henry. There is always compensation for such as are unjustly used. I often took it out of him — sometimes as an advance payment for something which I hadn't yet done. These were occasions when the opportunity was too strong a temptation, and I had to draw on the future. I did not need to copy this idea from my mother and probably didn't. It is most likely that I invented it for myself. Still, she wrought upon that principle upon occasion.

If the incident of the broken sugar bowl is in *Tom Sawyer* — I don't remember whether it is or not — that is an example of it. Henry never stole sugar. He took it openly from the bowl. His mother knew he wouldn't take sugar when she wasn't looking, but she had her doubts about me. Not exactly doubts, either. She knew very well I *would*. One day when she was not present, Henry took sugar from her prized and precious old-English sugar bowl, which was an heirloom in the family — and he managed to break the bowl. It was the first time I had ever had a chance to tell anything on him, and I was inexpressibly glad. I told him I was going to tell on him, but

he was not disturbed. When my mother came in and saw the bowl lying on the floor in fragments she was speechless for a minute. I allowed that silence to work; I judged it would increase the effect. I was waiting for her to ask, "Who did that?" — so that I could fetch out my news. But it was an error of calculation. When she got through with her silence, she didn't ask anything about it — she merely gave me a crack on the skull with her thimble, which I felt all the way down to my heels. Then I broke out with my injured innocence, expecting to make her very sorry that she had punished the wrong one. I expected her to go something remorseful and pathetic. I told her that I was not the one — it was Henry. But there was no upheaval. She said, without emotion: "It's all right. It isn't any matter. You deserve it for something that you are going to do that I shan't hear about."

There was a stairway outside the house, which led up to the rear part of the second story. One day Henry was sent on an errand, and he took a tin bucket along. I knew he would have to ascend those stairs, so I went up and locked the door on the inside and came down into the garden, which had been newly plowed and was rich in choice, firm clods of black mold. I gathered a generous equipment of these and ambushed him. I waited till he had climbed the stairs and was near the landing and couldn't escape. Then I bombarded him with clods, which he warded off with his tin bucket the best he could, but without much success, for I was a good marksman. The clods smashing against the weather-

[1] **piqued** (pēkt): irritated.

boarding fetched my mother out to see what was the matter, and I tried to explain that I was amusing Henry. Both of them were after me in a minute, but I knew the way over that high board fence and escaped for that time. After an hour or two, when I ventured back, there was no one around, and I thought the incident was closed. But it was not so. Henry was ambushing me. With an unusually competent aim for him, he landed a stone on the side of my head, which raised a bump there which felt like the Matterhorn. I carried it to my mother straightway for sympathy, but she was not strongly moved. It seemed to be her idea that incidents like this would eventually reform me if I harvested enough of them. So the matter was only educational. I had had a sterner view of it than that before.

It was not right to give the cat the Pain Killer; I realize it now. I would not repeat it in these days. But in those "Tom Sawyer" days it was a great and sincere satisfaction to me to see Peter [1] perform under its influence — and if actions *do* speak as loud as words, he took as much interest in it as I did. It was a most detestable medicine, Perry Davis's Pain Killer.

Those were the cholera [2] days of '49. The people along the Mississippi were paralyzed with fright. Those who could run away did it. And many died of fright in the flight. Fright killed three persons where the cholera killed one. Those who couldn't flee kept themselves drenched with cholera preventives, and my mother chose Perry Davis's Pain Killer for me. She was not distressed about herself. She avoided that kind of preventive. But she made me promise to take a teaspoonful of Pain Killer every day. Originally it was my intention to keep the promise, but at that time I didn't know as much about Pain Killer as I knew after my first experiment with it. She didn't

---

[1] **Peter:** the cat.
[2] **cholera** (kol'ər·ə): a serious intestinal disease, contagious and sometimes fatal.

watch Henry's bottle — she could trust Henry. But she marked my bottle with a pencil on the label every day, and examined it to see if the teaspoonful had been removed. The floor was not carpeted. It had cracks in it, and I fed the Pain Killer to the cracks with very good results — no cholera occurred down below.

It was upon one of these occasions that that friendly cat came waving his tail and supplicating for Pain Killer — which he got — and then went into those hysterics which ended with his colliding with all the furniture in the room and finally going out of the open window and carrying the flowerpots with him, just in time for my mother to arrive and look over her glasses in petrified astonishment and say, "What in the world is the matter with Peter?"

I don't remember what my explanation was, but if it is recorded in that book,[1] it may not be the right one.

Whenever my conduct was of such exaggerated impropriety that my mother's extemporary punishments were inadequate, she saved the matter up for Sunday and made me go to church Sunday night — which was a penalty sometimes bearable, perhaps, but as a rule it was not, and I avoided it for the sake of my constitution. She would never believe that I had been to church until she had applied her test. She made me tell her what the text [2] was. That was a simple matter — caused me no trouble. I didn't have to go to church to get a text. I selected one for

myself. This worked very well until one time when my text and the one furnished by a neighbor, who had been to church, didn't tally. After that my mother took other methods. I don't know what they were now.

In those days men and boys wore rather long cloaks in the wintertime. They were black and were lined with very bright and showy Scotch plaids. One winter's night when I was starting to church to square a crime of some kind committed during the week, I hid my cloak near the gate and went off and played with the other boys until church was over. Then I returned home. But in the dark I put the cloak on wrong side out, entered the room, threw the cloak aside, and then stood the usual examination. I got along very well until the temperature of the church was mentioned. My mother said, "It must have been impossible to keep warm there on such a night."

I didn't see the art of that remark and was foolish enough to explain that I wore my cloak all the time I was in church. She asked if I kept it on from church to home, too. I didn't see the bearing of that remark. I said that that was what I had done. She said: "You wore it with that red Scotch plaid outside and glaring? Didn't that attract any attention?"

Of course to continue such a dialogue would have been tedious and unprofitable, and I let it go and took the consequences.

That was about 1849, when I was fourteen years old. We were still living in Hannibal, on the banks of the Mississippi, in the new "frame" house built

---

[1] **that book:** *The Adventures of Tom Sawyer.*
[2] **text:** the passage of the Bible which the minister read at the service.

by my father five years before. That is, some of us lived in the new part, the rest in the old part back of it and attached to it. In the autumn, my sister gave a party and invited all the marriageable young people of the village. I was too young for this society and was too bashful to mingle with young ladies, anyway, therefore I was not invited — at least not for the whole evening. Ten minutes of it was to be my whole share. I was to do the part of a bear in a small fairy play. I was to be disguised all over in some close-fitting brown hairy stuff proper for a bear. About half past ten I was told to go to my room and put on this disguise and be ready in half an hour. I started but changed my mind, for I wanted to practice a little and that room was very small. I crossed over to the large unoccupied house on the corner of Main Street, unaware that a dozen of the young people were also going there to dress for their parts. I took the little boy Sandy with me and we selected a roomy and empty chamber on the second floor. We entered it talking and this gave a couple of half-dressed young ladies an opportunity to take refuge behind a screen undiscovered. Their gowns and things were hanging on hooks behind the door but I did not see them; it was Sandy that shut the door but all his heart was in the theatricals and he was as unlikely to notice them as I was myself.

That was a rickety screen with many holes in it, but as I did not know there were girls behind it, I was not disturbed by that detail. If I had known, I could not have undressed in the flood of cruel moonlight that was pouring in at the curtainless windows; I should have died of shame. Untroubled by apprehensions, I stripped to the skin and began my practice. I was full of ambition; I was determined to make a hit; I was burning to establish a reputation as a bear and get further engagements; so I threw myself into my work with an abandon that promised great things. I capered back and forth from one end of the room to the other on all fours, Sandy applauding with enthusiasm. I walked upright and growled and snapped and snarled. I stood on my head; I flung handsprings. I danced a lubberly dance with my paws bent and my imaginary snout sniffing from side

to side. I did everything a bear could do and many things which no bear could ever do and no bear with any dignity would want to do, anyway; and of course I never suspected that I was making a spectacle of myself to anyone but Sandy. At last, standing on my head, I paused in that attitude to take a minute's rest. There was a moment's silence, then Sandy spoke up with excited interest and said:

"Sam, has you ever seed a dried herring?"

"No. What is that?"

"It's a fish."

"Well, what of it? Anything peculiar about it?"

"You bet you dey is. *Dey* eats 'em innards and all!"

There was a smothered burst of feminine snickers from behind the screen! All the strength went out of me and I toppled forward like an undermined tower and brought the screen down with my weight, burying the young ladies under it. In their fright they discharged a couple of piercing screams — and possibly others — but I did not wait to count. I snatched my clothes and fled to the dark hall below, Sandy following. I was dressed in half a minute and out the back way. I swore Sandy to eternal silence; then we went away and hid until the party was over. The ambition was all out of me. I could not have faced that giddy company after my adventure, for there would be two performers there who knew my secret and would be privately laughing at me all the time. I was searched for but not found, and the bear had to be played by a young gentleman in his civilized clothes. The house was still and everybody asleep when I finally ventured home. I was very heavy-hearted and full of a bitter sense of disgrace. Pinned to my pillow I found a slip of paper which bore a line which did not lighten my heart, but only made my face burn. It was written in a laboriously disguised hand and these were its mocking terms:

You probably couldn't have played bear but you played bare very well — oh, very, *very* well!

We think boys are rude, unsensitive animals, but it is not so in all cases. Each boy has one or two sensitive spots, and if you can find out where they are located, you have only to touch them and you can scorch him as with fire. I suffered miserably over that episode. I expected that the facts would be all over the village in the morning, but it was not so. The secret remained confined to the two girls and Sandy and me. That was some appeasement of my pain, but it was far from sufficient — the main trouble remained: I was under four mocking eyes and it might as well have been a thousand, for I suspected all girls' eyes of being the ones I so dreaded. During several weeks I could not look any young lady in the face; I dropped my eyes in confusion when any one of them smiled upon me and gave me greeting; I said to myself, "That is one of them," and got quickly away. Of course I was meeting the right girls everywhere, but if they ever let slip any betraying sign, I was not bright enough to catch it. When I left Hannibal four years later the secret was still a secret; I had never guessed those girls out and was no longer hoping or expecting to do it.

One of the dearest and prettiest girls in the village at the time of my mishap was one whom I will call Mary Wilson, because that was not her name. She was twenty years old; she was dainty and sweet, peach-blooming and exquisite, gracious and lovely in character. I stood in awe of her, for she seemed to me to be made out of angel clay and rightfully unapproachable by just any unholy ordinary kind of boy like me. I probably never suspected *her*. But . . .

The scene changes to Calcutta — forty-seven years later. It was in 1896. I arrived there on a lecturing trip. As I entered the hotel a vision passed out of it, clothed in the glory of the Indian sunshine — the Mary Wilson of my long-vanished boyhood! It was a startling thing. Before I could recover from the pleasant shock and speak to her she was gone. I thought maybe I had seen an apparition but it was not so, she was flesh. She was the granddaughter of the other Mary. The other Mary, now a widow, was upstairs and presently sent for me. She was old and gray haired but she looked young and was very handsome. We sat down and talked. We steeped our thirsty souls in the reviving wine of the past, the pathetic past, the beautiful past, the dear and lamented past; we uttered the names that had been silent upon our lips for fifty years, and it was as if they were made of music; with reverent hands we unburied our dead, the mates of our youth, and caressed them with our speech; we searched the dusty chambers of our memories and dragged forth incident after incident,

episode after episode, folly after folly, and laughed such good laughs over them, with the tears running down; and finally Mary said, suddenly, and without any leading up:

"Tell me! What is the special peculiarity of dried herrings?"

It seemed a strange question at such a hallowed time as this — and so inconsequential, too. I was a little shocked. And yet I was aware of a stir of some kind away back in the deeps of my memory somewhere. It set me to musing — thinking — searching. Dried herrings? Dried herrings? The peculiarity of dri . . . I glanced up. Her face was grave, but there was a dim and shadowy twinkle in her eye which —— All of a sudden I knew, and far away down in the hoary [1] past I heard a remembered voice murmur, "Dey eats 'em innards and all!"

"At — last! I've found one of you, anyway! Who was the other girl?"

But she drew the line there. She wouldn't tell me.

[1] **hoary**: ancient.

STORIES ABOUT HIMSELF

In his autobiography, Mark Twain often looks at himself with a sense of humor. He reveals his own weaknesses and errors, but he also helps us to take a fresh look at ourselves.

1. What happened to Twain on his first day at school? How did he take literally his teacher's talk about prayer?

2. What did Twain say that the incident of the broken sugar bowl illustrates? How did the cholera scare affect him? What humorous mistake did he make on a Sunday night?

3. How do the words *bear* and *bare* figure in an episode in his youth?

4. Mark Twain excelled in laughing at himself. What action backfired on him during his first day at school? How was the bear story a joke on Twain?

5. Most authors use their personal experiences as source material for their writing, and Mark Twain was no exception. What kind of character did his brother Henry become in *The Adventures of Tom Sawyer*? What true incidents did he use in that same book?

6. In telling these anecdotes about his life, Mark Twain often revealed his thoughts about the world and the people in it. For example, when telling about his praying for gingerbread, he said, "But this dream was like almost all the other dreams we indulge in in life — there was nothing in it." What other statements of opinion and philosophy did Mark Twain reveal in telling about his brother Henry? in telling the incident of the bare bear? What do you think of these statements?

7. How do you think Twain felt about his brother? What do you think he was indirectly saying about his mother?

WORDS: MEANING FROM CONTEXT

When you read Mark Twain, you should try to figure out the meanings of some of the difficult words from their contexts. For example, Twain said on page 472 that his teacher gave him "a long look of strong disapprobation." You may have guessed that the word *disapprobation* means "disapproval" or "condemnation," since you knew that the teacher did not like the switch which Twain had selected.

Go back and read the following italicized words in their contexts. Can you guess their meanings? Check your guesses in a dictionary.

". . . I believed I could select a switch suitable to the occasion with more *judiciousness* than anybody else." (See page 472.)

"Whenever my conduct was of such exaggerated *impropriety* that my mother's *extemporary* punishments were inadequate . . ." (See page 476.)

"That was some *appeasement* of my pain, but it was far from sufficient . . ." (See page 478.)

SHORT AND LONG SENTENCES

Mark Twain varied the lengths of his sentences. Some are short and direct like these four sentences:

"Those were the cholera days of '49. The people along the Mississippi were paralyzed with fright. Those who could run away did it. And many died of fright in the flight."

To show that you, too, can vary sentence length, combine these four short sentences into one or two long sentences.

Some of Twain's sentences are as long as an average paragraph, such as the sentence on page 476 beginning "It was upon one of these occasions . . ." Reduce this paragraph-length sentence to four short sentences.

COMPOSITION:
   A HUMOROUS ANECDOTE

This selection from Twain's autobiography was made up of several humorous anecdotes about his boyhood days. These anecdotes are told in an easy narrative style, just as Mark Twain might have related them from a lecture platform. Think of an incident from your own life that you would incorporate in your autobiography — perhaps something humorous. Try to write it as you would tell it to the class.

Cub Pilot on the Mississippi

The Mississippi River had a powerful effect on Mark Twain. You know that he took his famous penname from the cry of the rivermen. He also wrote an entire book about life on the great river in the 1850's. In this book, Twain captured the glamour of the now-gone days of the river steamboats.

WHEN I WAS A BOY, there was but one permanent ambition among my comrades in our village on the west bank of the Mississippi River. That was to be a steamboatman. When a circus came and went, it left us all burning to become clowns; the first minstrel show that ever came to our section left us all suffering to try that kind of life; now and then we had a hope that, if we lived and were good, God would permit us to be pirates. These ambitions faded out, each in its turn; but the ambition to be a steamboatman always remained. I first wanted to be a cabin boy, so that I could come out with a white apron on and shake a tablecloth over the side, where all my old comrades could see

me; later I thought I would rather be the deck hand who stood on the end of the stage plank with the coil of rope in his hand, because he was particularly conspicuous.

Boy after boy managed to get on the river. The minister's son became an engineer. The doctor's and the postmaster's sons became "mud clerks"; [1] the wholesale liquor dealer's son became a barkeeper on a boat; four sons of the chief merchant, and two sons of the county judge, became pilots. Pilot was the grandest position of all. The pilot, even in those days of trivial wages, had a princely salary — from a hundred and fifty to two hundred and fifty dollars a month, and no board to pay. Two months of his wages would pay a preacher's salary for a year. Now some of us were left disconsolate. We could not get on the river — at least our parents would not let us.

So, by and by, I ran away. I said I would never come home again till I was a pilot and could come in glory.

During the two or two and a half years of my apprenticeship I served un-

[1] **"mud clerks"**: riverboat slang for the lowest of several clerks assisting the purser, the officer in charge of the ship's accounts. A "mud clerk" worked for nothing.

MARK TWAIN

der many pilots, and had experience of many kinds of steamboatmen and many varieties of steamboats. . . . I am to this day profiting somewhat by that experience; for in that brief, sharp schooling, I got personally and familiarly acquainted with about all the different types of human nature that are to be found in fiction, biography, or history.

The figure that comes before me oftenest, out of the shadows of that vanished time, is that of Brown, of the steamer *Pennsylvania*. He was a middle-aged, long, slim, bony, smooth-shaven, horse-faced, ignorant, stingy, malicious, snarling, fault-hunting, mote [1]-magnifying tyrant. I early got the habit of coming on watch with dread at my heart. No matter how good a time I might have been having with the off-watch below, and no matter how high my spirits might be when I started aloft, my soul became lead in my body the moment I approached the pilothouse.

I still remember the first time I ever entered the presence of that man. The boat had backed out from St. Louis and was "straightening down." I ascended to the pilothouse in high feather, and very proud to be semi-officially a member of the executive family of so fast and famous a boat. Brown was at the wheel. I paused in the middle of the room, all fixed to make my bow, but Brown did not look around. I thought he took a furtive glance at me out of the corner of his eye, but as not even this notice was repeated, I judged I had been mis-

[1] **mote:** a small particle, such as a speck of dust.

taken. By this time he was picking his way among some dangerous "breaks" abreast the woodyards; therefore it would not be proper to interrupt him; so I stepped softly to the high bench and took a seat.

There was silence for ten minutes; then my new boss turned and inspected me deliberately and painstakingly from head to heel for about — as it seemed to me — a quarter of an hour. After which he removed his countenance, and I saw it no more for some seconds; then it came around once more, and this question greeted me:

"Are you Horace Bixby's cub?"

"Yes, sir."

After this there was a pause and another inspection. Then:

"What's your name?"

I told him. He repeated it after me. It was probably the only thing he ever forgot; for although I was with him many months he never addressed himself to me in any other way than "Here!" and then his command followed.

"Where was you born?"

"In Florida, Missouri."

A pause. Then:

"Dern sight better stayed there!"

By means of a dozen or so of pretty direct questions, he pumped my family history out of me.

The leads [2] were going now in the first crossing. This interrupted the inquest.

It must have been all of fifteen minutes — fifteen minutes of dull, home-sick silence — before that long

[2] **leads** (ledz): weights lowered to test the depth of the river.

horse-face swung round upon me again — and then what a change! It was as red as fire, and every muscle in it was working. Now came this shriek:

"Here! You going to set there all day?"

I lit in the middle of the floor, shot there by the electric suddenness of the surprise. As soon as I could get my voice I said apologetically: "I have had no orders, sir."

"You've had no *orders!* My, what a fine bird we are! We must have *orders!* Our father was a *gentleman,* and *we've* been to *school.* Yes, *we* are a gentleman, *too,* and got to have *orders!* ORDERS, is it? ORDERS is what you want! Dod dern my skin, *I'll* learn you to swell yourself up and blow around *here* about your dod-derned *orders!* G'way from the wheel!" (I had approached it without knowing it.)

I moved back a step or two and stood as in a dream, all my senses stupefied by this frantic assault.

"What you standing there for? Take that ice pitcher down to the texas-tender![1] Come, move along, and don't you be all day about it!"

The moment I got back to the pilot-house Brown said:

"Here! What was you doing down there all this time?"

"I couldn't find the texas-tender; I had to go all the way to the pantry."

"Derned likely story! Fill up the stove."

I proceeded to do so. He watched

[1] **the texas-tender:** the waiter in the officer's quarters. The staterooms on Mississippi steamboats were named after the states. Since the officers' area was the largest, it was called the texas.

Looking at the Mississippi from the pilothouse. Notice the "backseat pilots."

me like a cat. Presently he shouted:

"Put down that shovel! Derndest numbskull I ever saw — ain't even got sense enough to load up a stove."

All through the watch this sort of thing went on. Yes, and the subsequent watches were much like it during a stretch of months. As I have said, I soon got the habit of coming on duty with dread. The moment I was in the presence, even in the darkest night, I could feel those yellow eyes upon me and knew their owner was watching for a pretext to spit out some venom on me. Preliminarily he would say:

"Here! Take the wheel."

Two minutes later:

"*Where* in the nation you going to? Pull her down! Pull her down!"

After another moment:

"Say! You going to hold her all day? Let her go — meet her! Meet her!"

Then he would jump from the bench, snatch the wheel from me, and meet her himself, pouring out wrath upon me all the time.

George Ritchie was the other pilot's cub. He was having good times now, for his boss, George Ealer, was as kind-hearted as Brown wasn't. Ritchie had steered for Brown the season before; consequently, he knew exactly how to entertain himself and plague me, all by the one operation. Whenever I took the wheel for a moment on Ealer's watch, Ritchie would sit back on the bench and play Brown, with continual ejaculations of "Snatch her! Snatch her! Derndest mud-cat I ever saw!" "Here! Where are you going *now?* Going to run over that snag?" "Pull her *down!* Don't you hear me? Pull her *down!*"

"There she goes! *Just* as I expected! I told you not to cramp that reef. G'way from the wheel!"

So I always had a rough time of it, no matter whose watch it was; and sometimes it seemed to me that Ritchie's good-natured badgering was pretty nearly as aggravating as Brown's dead-earnest nagging.

I often wanted to kill Brown, but this would not answer. A cub had to take everything his boss gave in the way of vigorous comment and criticism, and we all believed that there was a United States law making it a penitentiary offense to strike or threaten a pilot who was on duty.

Two trips later I got into serious trouble. Brown was steering; I was "pulling down." My younger brother [Henry] appeared on the hurricane deck, and shouted to Brown to stop at some landing or other, a mile or so below. Brown gave no intimation that he had heard anything. But that was his way: he never condescended to take notice of an underclerk. The wind was blowing; Brown was deaf (although he always pretended he wasn't), and I very much doubted if he had heard the order. If I had had two heads, I would have spoken; but as I had only one, it seemed judicious to take care of it; so I kept still.

Presently, sure enough, we went sailing by that plantation. Captain Klinefelter appeared on the deck, and said:

"Let her come around, sir, let her come around. Didn't Henry tell you to land here?"

"*No*, sir!"

"I sent him up to do it."

A steamboat "woods up" on the Mississippi. The pilothouse is on the top deck. (Currier and Ives print. Courtesy of Museum of the City of New York.)

"He *did* come up; and that's all the good it done, the dod-derned fool. He never said anything."

"Didn't *you* hear him?" asked the captain of me.

Of course I didn't want to be mixed up in this business, but there was no way to avoid it; so I said:

"Yes, sir."

I knew what Brown's next remark would be, before he uttered it. It was:

"Shut your mouth! You never heard anything of the kind."

I closed my mouth, according to instructions. An hour later Henry entered the pilothouse, unaware of what had been going on. He was a thoroughly inoffensive boy, and I was sorry to see him come for I knew Brown would have no pity on him. Brown began, straightway:

"Here! Why didn't you tell me we'd got to land at that plantation?"

"I did tell you, Mr. Brown."

"It's a lie!"

I said:

"You lie, yourself. He did tell you."

Brown glared at me in unaffected surprise; and for as much as a moment he was entirely speechless; then he shouted to me:

"I'll attend to your case in a half a minute!" then to Henry, "And you leave the pilothouse; out with you!"

It was pilot law and must be obeyed. The boy started out, and even had his foot on the upper step outside the door, when Brown, with a sudden access of fury, picked up a ten-pound lump of coal and sprang after him; but I was between, with a heavy stool, and I hit Brown a good honest blow which stretched him out.

I had committed the crime of crimes

— I had lifted my hand against a pilot on duty! I supposed I was booked for the penitentiary sure and couldn't be booked any surer if I went on and squared my long account with this person while I had the chance; consequently I stuck to him and pounded him with my fists a considerable time. I do not know how long; the pleasure of it probably made it seem longer than it really was; but in the end he struggled free and jumped up and sprang to the wheel: a very natural solicitude, for, all this time, here was this steamboat tearing down the river at the rate of fifteen miles an hour and nobody at the helm! However, Eagle Bend was two miles wide at this bankfull stage, and correspondingly long and deep; and the boat was steering herself straight down the middle and taking no chances. Still, that was only luck — a body *might* have found her charging into the woods.

Perceiving at a glance that the *Pennsylvania* was in no danger, Brown gathered up the big spyglass, war-club fashion, and ordered me out of the pilothouse with more than Comanche bluster. But I was not afraid of him now; so, instead of going, I tarried and criticized his grammar. I reformed his ferocious speeches for him and put them into good English, calling his attention to the advantages of pure English over the dialect of the Pennsylvania collieries[1] whence he was extracted. He could have done his part to admiration in a crossfire of mere vituperation,[2] of course; but he was not equipped for this species of controversy; so he presently laid aside his glass and took the wheel, muttering and shaking his head; and I retired to the bench. The racket had brought everybody to the hurricane deck, and I trembled when I saw the old captain looking up from amid the crowd. I said to myself, "Now I *am* done for!" for although, as a rule, he was so fatherly and indulgent toward the boat's family, and so patient of minor shortcomings, he could be stern enough when the fault was worth it.

I tried to imagine what he *would* do to a cub pilot who had been guilty of such a crime as mine, committed on a boat that was guard-deep[3] with costly freight and alive with passengers. Our watch was nearly ended. I thought I would go and hide somewhere till I got a chance to slide ashore. So I slipped out of the pilothouse and down the steps and around to the texas-door, and I was in the act of gliding within when the captain confronted me! I dropped my head, and he stood over me in silence a moment or two, then said impressively:

"Follow me."

I dropped into his wake; he led the way to his parlor in the forward end of the texas. We were alone now. He closed the afterdoor; then he moved slowly to the forward one and closed that. He sat down; I stood before him. He looked at me some little time, then said:

"So you have been fighting Mr. Brown?"

I answered meekly:

---

[1] **collieries** (kŏl'yər·ēz): coal mines.
[2] **vituperation** (vī·tōō'pə·rā'shən): bitter abusive language.

[3] The guard of a ship is an extension of its deck.

"Yes, sir."

"Do you know that that is a very serious matter?"

"Yes, sir."

"Are you aware that this boat was plowing down the river fully five minutes with no one at the wheel?"

"Yes, sir."

"Did you strike him first?"

"Yes, sir."

"What with?"

"A stool, sir."

"Hard?"

"Middling, sir."

"Did it knock him down?"

"He — he fell, sir."

"Did you follow it up? Did you do anything further?"

"Yes, sir."

"What did you do?"

"Pounded him, sir."

"Pounded him?"

"Yes, sir."

"Did you pound him much — that is, severely?"

"One might call it that, sir, maybe."

"I'm deuced glad of it! Hark ye, never mention that I said that. You have been guilty of a great crime; and don't you ever be guilty of it again, on this boat. *But* — lay for him ashore! Give him a good sound thrashing; do you hear? I'll pay the expenses. Now go — and mind you, not a word of this to anybody. Clear out with you! You've been guilty of a great crime, you whelp!"

I slid out, happy with the sense of a close shave and a mighty deliverance, and I heard him laughing to himself and slapping his fat thighs after I had closed his door.

When Brown came off watch he went straight to the captain, who was talking with some passengers on the boiler deck, and demanded that I be put ashore in New Orleans — and added:

"I'll never turn a wheel on this boat again while that cub stays."

The captain said:

"But he needn't come round when you are on watch, Mr. Brown."

"I won't even stay on the same boat with him. *One* of us has got to go ashore."

"Very well," said the captain, "let it be yourself," and resumed his talk with the passengers.

During the brief remainder of the trip I knew how an emancipated slave feels, for I was an emancipated slave myself.

RIVER SCHOOLING

1. How did Twain's experiences on the river profit him later?

2. How did Mark Twain describe Brown? What did his fight with Brown tell you about Twain?

3. Did Mark Twain's sense of humor show through in this story? What is humorous about a cub badgering a pilot about his grammar? Did you see any humor in Twain's relations with Ritchie?

4. Mark Twain talks about his brother Henry in this selection and in "Boyhood Reminiscences" (page 472). Does he feel the same way about Henry in each story?

5. What experiences do young people today look forward to, as Mark Twain looked forward to being a steamboat pilot? What jobs hold out the promise of adventure in the future?

6. Mention some conditions that have changed in America since Mark Twain's boyhood.

Twain called Brown a "middle-aged, long, slim, bony, smooth-shaven, horse-faced, ignorant, stingy, malicious, snarling, fault-hunting, mote-magnifying tyrant." This list of adjectives may have described Brown to some extent, but many of these words really tell how young Sam felt about Brown and how he wanted us to think of him. Name-calling is a device often used against people. In all our reading, we should recognize this device and realize that we might be receiving not an accurate description of a person, but rather what someone else wants us to think.

DESCRIPTION IN *HUCKLEBERRY FINN*

Mark Twain's greatest book, *The Adventures of Huckleberry Finn*, takes place on the Mississippi River. No doubt Mark Twain drew deeply from his own experiences on the river as he had Huck tell about how he and his friend Jim floated on a raft down the Mississippi. As a cub pilot, Sam Clemens must have seen many sunrises over the river, such as this one which Huck describes in Chapter 19:

"We set down on the sandy bottom where the water was about knee-deep and watched the daylight come. Not a sound anywheres — perfectly still — just like the whole world was asleep, only sometimes the bull frogs a-cluttering, maybe. The first thing to see, looking away over the water, was a kind of dull line — that was the woods on t'other side; you couldn't make nothing else out; then a pale place in the sky; then more paleness spreading around; then the river softened up away off, and warn't black any more, but gray; you could see little dark spots drifting along ever so far away — trading scows and such things — and long black streaks — rafts. Sometimes you could hear a sweep screaking or jumbled-up voices — it was so still and sounds come so far; and by and by you could see a streak on the water which you know by the look of the streak that there's a snag there in a swift current which breaks on it and makes that streak look that way; and you see the mist curl up off of the water, and the east reddens up, and the river, and you make out a log cabin on the edge of the woods, away on the bank on t'other side of the river, being a wood-yard, likely, and piled by them cheats so you can throw a dog through it anywheres; then the nice breeze springs up and comes fanning you from over there, so cool and fresh and sweet to smell on account of the woods and the flowers; but sometimes not that way, because they've left dead fish laying around, gars and such, and they do get pretty rank; and next you've got the full day, and everything smiling in the sun, and the songbirds just going it!"

What sounds do you hear and what sights meet your eyes as you watch this sunrise? Can you smell anything?

Think of a scene that you like as much as Huck liked the sunrise on the Mississippi. In a paragraph, describe the scene. Make your readers experience the scene with their senses.

From *The Adventures of Huckleberry Finn* by Mark Twain. Reprinted by permission of Harper & Row, Publishers.

["Mark Twain" is continued on page 497.]

MASTERPIECES OF ART

Winslow Homer (1836–1910)

Winslow Homer once was asked whether he ever changed the colors he saw before him when he was painting landscapes. "Never! Never!" Homer replied. "When I have selected the thing carefully, I paint it exactly as it appears." Even so, Homer included only those parts of a landscape that seemed significant to him, and it is because of this that his paintings are never cluttered with meaningless detail. We feel that Homer was actually present at every scene he painted, and indeed he was, at least when he made his preliminary sketches. Every painting he did shows his devotion to nature as he "saw" it.

Homer began his career as an illustrator in Boston. When he moved to New York City in 1859 to join the staff of *Harper's Weekly* magazine, he received an important assignment: he was to make illustrations of the War Between the States. Rather than drawing theatrical battle scenes, however, he depicted soldiers struggling with the everyday hardships of barren camp life.

After the war, Homer devoted most of his spare time to oil painting, choosing mainly mountain or farmyard scenes or views of people at the seashore, such as the small canvas titled *Long Branch, New Jersey* (PLATE 1). Notice that in this picture Homer painted the shadows — especially on the young ladies' billowing dresses — a slightly bluish color to show the light reflections from the sky. Crisp outdoor light can be found also in his early sea pictures of the 1870's, such as the famous *Breezing Up* (PLATE 2). To suggest the motion of the sailboat, Homer placed it off-center to the left. The clouds descending toward the horizon and the distant schooner help to balance the composition.

In 1873, Homer spent June and July at Gloucester, Massachusetts. There he began to paint a great deal in water color, a medium that was especially well suited to sketching out-of-doors. With a few broad areas of color he could make a finished painting right on the beach, without returning to his studio. Working this way, Homer created land-scapes and seascapes with extraordinary freshness and realism. Look, for example, at one of his later water colors, reproduced in PLATE 5.

By 1876 Homer's water colors were selling so well that he could abandon his illustrating job to devote himself entirely to painting. Un-fortunately, collectors soon grew tired of his work, and critics began calling him everything from an "*almost* distinguished painter" to a "failure." Bewildered by such attacks, Homer left for England in 1881, where for a year and a half he stayed at a small fishing village on the edge of the North Sea. There he made profound changes in his style and expressed a new theme — man's struggle with the mighty power of the sea. Against gray, stormy skies and the raging sea, he painted fishermen as heroic figures who risked their lives to make a living. When he returned to the United States, he found that his critics were thrilled by the drama of these new paintings. In *Eight Bells* (PLATE 3), a brewing storm is suggested by irregular patches of light on the sky and the water and on the coats and hats of the fishermen. Yet man seems in control of the situation, whereas in *The Gulf Stream* (PLATE 4), the power of the sea appears overwhelming.

From 1884 on, Homer turned away from the outside world and lived mainly at Prout's Neck, Maine. From his studio overlooking the ocean, he observed day-to-day changes in the weather and the moods of the sea, waiting until the moment when sky and sea created the exact mood he was looking for. Then he would paint the scene rapidly in powerful, broad strokes, completing his canvas in a few hours.

During this period, Homer also spent many happy summers in the Adirondack Mountains, where he painted scenes expressing the quiet majesty of the forests. *Huntsman and Dogs* (PLATE 6) is one of these. Despite its many realistic details, what we notice most of all is the grand sweep of the picture as it builds upward to the stalwart figure of the hunter.

Homer's most widely acclaimed canvases, however, are the ones he painted at Prout's Neck. In these dramatic compositions, man plays only a minor role, for Homer's main theme was the endless battle be-tween land and sea. In the last years of his life, his seascapes won him countless honors, and he was finally considered the greatest living painter in America. Homer cared little for such rewards. He still pre-ferred to be alone, grateful only for his small circle of friends. To the end he kept his eyes sharply focused on nature. He said, "The sun will not rise, or set, without my notice and thanks."

PLATE 1. WINSLOW HOMER (American, 1836–1910): *Long Branch, New Jersey.* 1869. Oil on canvas, 16 x 21¾ inches. (Courtesy, Museum of Fine Arts, Boston, Charles Henry Hayden Fund)

PLATE 2. WINSLOW HOMER (American, 1836–1910): *Breezing Up*. 1876. Oil on canvas, 24⅛ x 38⅛ inches. (National Gallery of Art, Washington, D.C., Gift of the W. L. and May T. Mellon Foundation)

PLATE 3. WINSLOW HOMER (American, 1836–1910): *Eight Bells*. 1886. Oil on canvas, 25 x 30 inches. (Addison Gallery of American Art, Phillips Academy, Andover, Massachusetts)

PLATE 4. WINSLOW HOMER (American, 1836–1910): *The Gulf Stream.* 1899. Oil on canvas, 28⅛ x 49⅛ inches. (The Metropolitan Museum of Art, New York, Wolfe Fund, 1906)

494

PLATE 5. WINSLOW HOMER (American, 1836–1910): *Fishing Boats, Key West.* 1903. Water color, 13⅝ x 21½ inches. (The Metropolitan Museum of Art, New York, Lazarus Fund, 1910)

PLATE 6. WINSLOW HOMER (*American, 1836–1910*): *Huntsman and Dogs.* 1891. Oil on canvas, 24¼ x 48 inches. (Philadelphia Museum of Art, William L. Elkins Collection)

The Celebrated Jumping Frog of Calaveras County

When Mark Twain went West to seek his fortune, a tall tale about a jumping frog was circulating among the mining camps. Twain wrote the story down, telling it as though it had been told to him in a Western dialect by a character named Simon Wheeler. Twain's story was an instant success, and the world discovered a new kind of humor — the broad humor of the American West.

I<small>N COMPLIANCE</small> with the request of a friend of mine, who wrote me from the East, I called on good-natured, garrulous[1] old Simon Wheeler and inquired after my friend's friend, Leonidas W. Smiley, as requested to do, and I hereunto append the result. I have a lurking suspicion that *Leonidas W.* Smiley is a myth; that my friend never knew such a personage;

[1] **garrulous** (gar′ə·ləs): long winded.

From *Sketches New and Old* by Mark Twain. Reprinted by permission of Harper & Row, Publishers.

and that he only conjectured that if I asked old Wheeler about him, it would remind him of his infamous *Jim* Smiley, and he would go to work and bore me to death with some exasperating reminiscence of him as long and as tedious as it should be useless to me. If that was the design, it succeeded.

I found Simon Wheeler dozing comfortably by the barroom stove of the dilapidated tavern in the decayed mining camp of Angel's, and I noticed that he was fat and baldheaded, and had an expression of winning gentleness and simplicity upon his tranquil countenance. He roused up, and gave me good day. I told him that a friend of mine had commissioned me to make some inquiries about a cherished companion of his boyhood named *Leonidas W.* Smiley — *Reverend Leonidas W.* Smiley, a young minister of the gospel, who he had heard was at one time a resident of Angel's Camp. I added that if Mr. Wheeler could tell me anything about this Reverend Leonidas W. Smiley, I would feel under many obligations to him.

Simon Wheeler backed me into a corner and blockaded me there with his chair, and then he sat down and reeled off the monotonous narrative which follows this paragraph. He never smiled, he never frowned, he never changed his voice from the gentle-flowing key to which he tuned his initial sentence, and he never betrayed the slightest suspicion of enthusiasm; but all through the interminable narrative there ran a vein of impressive earnestness and sincerity, which showed me plainly that, so far from his imagining that there was anything ridiculous or funny about his story, he regarded it as a really important matter and admired its two heroes as men of transcendent genius in *finesse*.[1] I let him go on in his own way and never interrupted him once.

"Reverend Leonidas W. H'm, Reverend Le — well, there was a feller here once by the name of *Jim* Smiley, in the winter of '49 — or maybe it was the spring of '50 — I don't recollect exactly, somehow though what makes me think it was one or the other is because I remember the big flume[2] warn't finished when he first come to the camp; but anyway, he was the curiousest man about always betting on anything that turned up you ever see, if he could get anybody to bet on the other side; and if he couldn't he'd change sides. Any way that suited the other man would

suit *him* — any way just so's he got a bet, *he* was satisfied. But still he was lucky, uncommon lucky; he most always come out winner. He was always ready and laying for a chance; there couldn't be no solit'ry thing mentioned but that feller'd offer to bet on it and take ary side you please, as I was just telling you. If there was a horse race, you'd find him flush or you'd find him busted at the end of it; if there was a dog fight, he'd bet on it; if there was a cat fight, he'd bet on it; if there was a chicken fight, he'd bet on it; why, if there was two birds setting on a fence, he would bet you which one would fly first; or if there was a camp meeting, he would be there reg'lar to bet on Parson Walker, which he judged to be the best exhorter about here, and so he was too, and a good man. If he even see a straddlebug start to go anywheres, he would bet you how long it would take him to get to — to wherever he was going to, and if you took him up, he would foller that straddlebug to Mexico but what he would find out where he was bound for and how long he was on the road. Lots of the boys here has seen that Smiley and can tell you about him. Why, it never made no difference to *him* — he'd bet on *any*thing — the dangdest feller. Parson Walker's wife laid very sick once, for a good while, and it seemed as if they warn't going to save her; but one morning he come in, and Smiley up and asked him how she was, and he said she was considerable better — thank the Lord for his inf'nite mercy — and coming on so smart that with the blessing of Prov'dence she'd get well yet; and Smiley, before he thought, says, 'Well, I'll resk two

---

[1] *finesse* (fi·nes'): craftiness, artful strategy.
[2] *flume* (floom): an inclined chute for carrying water.

and a half she don't anyway.'

"Thish-yer Smiley had a mare — the boys called her the fifteen-minute nag, but that was only in fun, you know, because of course she was faster than that — and he used to win money on that horse, for all she was so slow and always had the asthma or the distemper or the consumption or something of that kind. They used to give her two or three hundred yards' start and then pass her under way, but always at the end of the race she'd get excited and desperate like and come cavorting and straddling up and scattering her legs around limber, sometimes in the air and sometimes out to one side among the fences, and kicking up m-o-r-e dust and raising m-o-r-e racket with her coughing and sneezing and blowing her nose — and *always* fetch up at the stand just about a neck ahead, as near as you could cipher it down.

"And he had a little small bull pup, that to look at him you'd think he warn't worth a cent but to set around and look ornery and lay for a chance to steal something. But as soon as money was up on him he was a different dog; his underjaw'd begin to stick out like the fo'castle of a steamboat, and his teeth would uncover and shine like the furnaces. And a dog might tackle him and bullyrag him, and bite him, and throw him over his shoulder two or three times, and Andrew Jackson — which was the name of the pup — Andrew Jackson would never let on but what *he* was satisfied and hadn't expected nothing else — and the bets being doubled and doubled on the other side all the time, till the money was all up; and then all of a sudden he would grab that other dog jest by the j'int of his hind leg and freeze to it — not chaw, you understand, but only just grip and hang on till they throwed up the sponge, if it was a year. Smiley always come out winner on that pup, til he harnessed a dog once that didn't have no hind legs, because they'd been sawed off in a circular saw, and when the thing had gone along far enough, and the money was all up, and he come to make a snatch for his pet holt, he see in a minute how he'd been imposed on and how the other dog had him in the door, so to speak, and he 'peared surprised, and then he looked sorter discouragedlike, and didn't try no more to win the fight, and so he got shucked out bad. He give Smiley a look, as much as to say his heart was broke, and it was *his* fault for putting up a dog that hadn't no hind legs for him to take holt of, which was his main dependence in a fight, and then he limped off a piece and laid down and died. It was a good pup, was that Andrew Jackson, and would have made a name for hisself if he'd lived, for the stuff was in him and he had genius — I know it, because he hadn't no opportunities to speak of, and it don't stand to reason that a dog could make such a fight as he could under them circumstances if he hadn't no talent. It always makes me feel sorry when I think of that last fight of his'n, and the way it turned out.

"Well, thish-yer Smiley had rat tarriers, and chicken cocks, and tomcats and all them kind of things, till you couldn't rest, and you couldn't fetch nothing for him to bet on but he'd match you. He ketched a frog one day

and took him home and said he cal'lat-
ed to educate him; and so he never
done nothing for three months but set
in his back yard and learn that frog to
jump. And you bet you he *did* learn
him, too. He'd give him a little punch
behind, and the next minute you'd see
that frog whirling in the air like a
doughnut — see him turn one summer-
set, or maybe a couple, if he got a good
start, and come down flat-footed and
all right, like a cat. He got him up so
in the matter of ketching flies and kep'
him in practice so constant, that he'd
nail a fly every time as fur as he could
see him. Smiley said all a frog wanted
was education, and he could do 'most
anything — and I believe him. Why,
I've seen him set Dan'l Webster down
here on this floor — Dan'l Webster was
the name of the frog — and sing out,
'Flies, Dan'l, flies!' and quicker'n you
could wink he'd spring straight up and
snake a fly off'n the counter there and
flop down on the floor ag'in as solid as
a gob of mud and fall to scratching the
side of his head with his hind foot as
indifferent as if he hadn't no idea he'd
been doin' any more'n any frog might
do. You never see a frog so modest and
straightfor'ard as he was, for all he was
so gifted. And when it come to fair and
square jumping on a dead level, he

could get over more ground at one
straddle than any animal of his breed
you ever see. Jumping on a dead level
was his strong suit, you understand;
and when it come to that, Smiley would
ante up money on him as long as he
had a red. Smiley was monstrous proud
of his frog, and well he might be, for
fellers that had traveled and been ev-
erywheres all said he laid over any frog
that ever *they* see.

"Well, Smiley kep' the beast in a little lattice box, and he used to fetch him
downtown sometimes and lay for a bet.
One day a feller — a stranger in the
camp, he was — come acrost him with
his box, and says:

"'What might it be that you've got in
the box?'

"And Smiley says, sorter indifferent-
like, 'It might be a parrot or it might
be a canary, maybe, but it ain't — it's
only just a frog.'

"And the feller took it, and looked at
it careful, and turned it round this way
and that, and says, 'H'm — so 'tis. Well,
what's *he* good for?'

"'Well,' Smiley says, easy and careless, 'he's good enough for *one* thing, I
should judge — he can outjump any
frog in Calaveras County.'

"The feller took the box again and
took another long, particular look and
give it back to Smiley and says, very
deliberate, 'Well,' he says, 'I don't see
no p'ints about that frog that's any better'n any other frog.'

"'Maybe you don't,' Smiley says.
'Maybe you understand frogs and maybe you don't understand 'em; maybe
you've had experience, and maybe you
ain't only a amature, as it were. Any-
ways, I've got *my* opinion, and I'll resk

forty dollars that he can outjump any frog in Calaveras County.'

"And the feller studied a minute, and then says, kinder sadlike, 'Well, I'm only a stranger here, and I ain't got no frog; but if I had a frog, I'd bet you.'

"And then Smiley says, 'That's all right — that's all right — if you'll hold my box a minute, I'll go and get you a frog.' And so the feller took the box and put up his forty dollars along with Smiley's and set down to wait.

"So he set there a good while thinking and thinking to himself, and then he got the frog out and prized his mouth open and took a teaspoon and filled him full of quail shot — filled him pretty near up to his chin — and set him on the floor. Smiley he went to the swamp and slopped around in the mud for a long time, and finally he ketched a frog, and fetched him in, and give him to this feller, and says:

" 'Now, if you're ready, set him alongside of Dan'l, with his fore paws just even with Dan'l's, and I'll give the word.' Then he says, 'One — two — three — *git!*' and him and the feller touched up the frogs from behind, and the new frog hopped off lively, but Dan'l give a heave, and hysted up his shoulders — so — like a Frenchman, but it warn't no use — he couldn't budge; he was planted as solid as a church, and he couldn't no more stir than if he was anchored out. Smiley was a good deal surprised, and he was disgusted too, but he didn't have no idea what the matter was, of course.

"The feller took the money and started away; and when he was going out at the door, he sorter jerked his thumb over his shoulder — so — at Dan'l, and says again, very deliberate, 'Well,' he says, 'I don't see no p'ints about that frog that's any better'n any other frog.'

"Smiley he stood scratching his head and looking down at Dan'l a long time, and at last he says, 'I do wonder what in the nation that frog throw'd off for — I wonder if there ain't something the matter with him — he 'pears to look mighty baggy, somehow.' And he ketched Dan'l by the nap of the neck and hefted him and says, 'Why blame my cats if he don't weigh five pound!' and turned him upside down, and he belched out a double handful of shot. And then he see how it was, and he was the maddest man — he set the frog down and took out after that feller, but he never ketched him. And — "

(Here Simon Wheeler heard his name called from the front yard and got up to see what was wanted.) And turning to me as he moved away, he said: "Just set where you are, stranger, and rest easy — I ain't going to be gone a second."

But, by your leave, I did not think that a continuation of the history of the enterprising vagabond *Jim* Smiley would be likely to afford me much information concerning the Reverend *Leonidas W.* Smiley, and so I started away.

At the door I met the sociable Wheeler returning, and he buttonholed me and recommenced:

"Well, thish-yer Smiley had a yaller one-eyed cow that didn't have no tail, only just a short stump like a bannanner, and — "

However, lacking both time and inclination, I did not wait to hear about the afflicted cow, but took my leave.

A WESTERN YARN

This story is a good example of an American brand of humor known as the yarn. (Perhaps such stories are so-called because they roll on and on like a ball of yarn.) In a magazine article called "How to Tell a Story," Mark Twain himself described how such a humorous story should be told. It may be spun out at great length, wander about as much as it pleases, and arrive nowhere in particular. It is told gravely, as if the teller does not even dimly suspect that there is anything funny about it. Often the point of the yarn is dropped in a casual and indifferent way, as if the yarn spinner is unaware that it *is* the point of the story. It was part of Mark Twain's genius to be able to capture these qualities of oral storytelling in his own writing.

1. There is a story within a story in this Western yarn. Mark Twain made himself out to be the teller of the whole story. What kind of person did he pretend to be?

2. What kind of person was Wheeler, the teller of the story within this story?

3. What two persons were, perhaps, playing a joke on Mark Twain?

4. What examples were given to show that Jim Smiley was a real better? Describe the training of Dan'l Webster. How did the stranger outsmart Smiley?

5. Tell in detail how Simon Wheeler used the techniques of the yarn spinner, as described above.

LANGUAGE TO FIT THE CHARACTER

Simon Wheeler's yarn is told just as this long-winded miner would tell it himself. Here is a sentence from his tale, from the first paragraph on page 499.

"Thish-yer Smiley had a mare — the boys called her the fifteen-minute nag, but that was only in fun, you know, because of course she was faster than that — and he used to win money on that horse, for all she was so slow and always had the asthma or the distemper or the consumption or something of that kind."

To see how Wheeler's colorful and easy-going speech adds to the fun of this story, look at how his sentence would appear if it were retold in standard English, with all Wheeler's rambling interruptions omitted and his grammar and pronunciations revised.

Smiley had a mare that used to win money for him, in spite of the fact that it was so slow and always had asthma, distemper, consumption, or some similar disease.

Take the rest of this paragraph and rewrite it in standard English. Be sure to change Wheeler's colorful pronunciations. Then read aloud your paragraph and the one that Twain wrote for Wheeler. Which paragraph captures the real flavor of Wheeler's speech?

COMPOSITION:
FRAMING AN ANECDOTE

Mark Twain put the jumping frog story into a "frame"; that is, he didn't tell the yarn directly himself. Rather, he began by telling how he had been told to locate Simon Wheeler to find out about a man named Smiley. The yarn about the frog was then told to Twain by Simon Wheeler. Notice how Twain's words and sentences differ from those used by Simon Wheeler. Wheeler uses incorrect pronunciations and rambling sentences, and his frog yarn has all the qualities of a story told orally.

Think of a humorous anecdote that you can use as a "story within a story." Create a "frame" in which a suitable character tells this anecdote to you — just as Twain had Wheeler tell him the frog story. You might want to write the anecdote as this character would tell it aloud.

Lost in
a Snowstorm

In his book *Roughing It,* Mark Twain has a tenderfoot tell about the hardships of prospecting in Nevada. In the excerpt that follows, the narrator tells how he tried to find his way to Carson City in the Nevada Territory, with two companions — a Prussian named Ollendorff and an old man named Ballou. Mark Twain once made such a trip himself — with a German named Pfersdorff and an elderly blacksmith named Tillou.

THE NEXT MORNING it was still snowing furiously when we got away with our new stock of saddles and accouterments.[1] We mounted and started. The snow lay so deep on the ground that there was no sign of a road perceptible, and the snowfall was so thick that we could not see more than a hundred yards ahead, else we could have guided our course by the mountain ranges. The case looked dubious, but Ollendorff said his instinct was as sensitive as any compass and that he could "strike a beeline" for Carson City and never diverge from it. He said that if he were

---

[1] **accouterments** (ə·kōō′tər·mənts): equipment.

From *Roughing It,* pp. 220–232, by Mark Twain. Reprinted by permission of Harper & Row, Publishers.

to straggle a single point out of the true line his instinct would assail him like an outraged conscience. Consequently we dropped into his wake happy and content. For half an hour we poked along warily enough, but at the end of that time we came upon a fresh trail, and Ollendorff shouted proudly:

"I knew I was as dead certain as a compass, boys! Here we are, right in somebody's tracks that will hunt the way for us without any trouble. Let's hurry up and join company with the party."

So we put the horses into as much of a trot as the deep snow would allow, and before long it was evident that we were gaining on our predecessors, for the tracks grew more distinct. We hurried along, and at the end of an hour the tracks looked still newer and fresher — but what surprised us was that the *number* of travelers in advance of us seemed to steadily increase. We wondered how so large a party came to be traveling at such a time and in such a solitude. Somebody suggested that it must be a company of soldiers from the fort, and so we accepted that solution and jogged along a little faster still, for they could not be far off now. But the tracks still multiplied, and we began to think the platoon of soldiers was miraculously expanding into a regiment — Ballou said they had already increased to five hundred! Presently he stopped his horse and said:

"Boys, these are our own tracks, and we've actually been circussing round and round in a circle for more than two hours, out here in this blind desert! By George, this is perfectly hydraulic!"

Then the old man waxed wroth and abusive. He called Ollendorff all manner of hard names — said he never saw such a lurid fool as he was, and ended with the peculiarly venomous opinion that he "did not know as much as a logarithm!" [1]

We certainly had been following our own tracks. Ollendorff and his "mental compass" were in disgrace from that moment. After all our hard travel, here we were on the bank of the stream

---

[1] **logarithm:** a mathematical term. Ballou often misuses words.

again, with the inn beyond dimly outlined through the driving snowfall.

Presently the Overland stage forded the now fast-receding stream and started toward Carson on its first trip since the flood came. We hesitated no longer, now, but took up our march in its wake, and trotted merrily along, for we had good confidence in the driver's bump of locality. But our horses were no match for the fresh stage team. We were soon left out of sight; but it was no matter, for we had the deep ruts the wheels made for a guide. By this time it was three in the afternoon, and consequently it was not very long before night came — and not with a lingering twilight, but with a sudden shutting down like a cellar door, as is its habit in that country. The snowfall was still as thick as ever, and of course we could not see fifteen steps before us; but all about us the white glare of the snow bed enabled us to discern the smooth

sugar-loaf mounds made by the covered sage bushes, and just in front of us the two faint grooves which we knew were the steadily filling and slowly disappearing wheel tracks.

Now those sage bushes were all about the same height — three or four feet; they stood just about seven feet apart, all over the vast desert; each of them was a mere snow mound, now; in *any* direction that you proceeded (the same as in a well laid-out orchard) you would find yourself moving down a distinctly defined avenue, with a row of these snow mounds on either side of it — an avenue the customary width of a road, nice and level in its breadth, and rising at the sides in the most natural way, by reason of the mounds. But we had not thought of this. Then imagine the chilly thrill that shot through us when it finally occurred to us, far in the night, that since the last faint trace of the wheel tracks had long ago been buried from sight, we might now be wandering down a mere sage-brush avenue, miles away from the road and diverging further and further away from it all the time. Having a cake of ice slipped down one's back is placid comfort compared to it. There was a sudden leap and a stir of blood that had been asleep for an hour, and as sudden a rousing of all the drowsing activities in our minds and bodies. We were alive and awake at once — and shaking and quaking with consternation, too. There was an instant halting and dismounting, a bending low and an anxious scanning of the roadbed. Useless, of course, for if a faint depression could not be discerned from an altitude of four or five feet above it, it certainly could not

with one's nose nearly against it.

We seemed to be in a road, but that was no proof. We tested this by walking off in various directions — the regular snow mounds and the regular avenues between them convinced each man that *he* had found the true road, and that the others had found only false ones. Plainly, the situation was desperate. We were cold and stiff, and the horses were tired. We decided to build a sage-brush fire and camp out till morning. This was wise, because if we were wandering from the right road and the snowstorm continued another day, our case would be the next thing to hopeless if we kept on.

All agreed that a campfire was what would come nearest to saving us, now, and so we set about building it. We could find no matches, and so we tried to make shift with the pistols. Not a man in the party had ever tried to do such a thing before, but not a man in the party doubted that it *could* be done, and without any trouble — because every man in the party had read about it in books many a time and had naturally come to believe it, with trusting simplicity, just as he had long ago accepted and believed *that other* common book fraud about Indians and lost hunters making a fire by rubbing two dry sticks together.

We huddled together on our knees in the deep snow, and the horses put their noses together and bowed their patient heads over us; and while the feathery flakes eddied down and turned us into a group of white statuary, we proceeded with the momentous experiment. We broke twigs from a sage bush and piled them on a little cleared

We were miserable enough, before; we felt still more forlorn, now. Patiently, but with blighted hope, we broke more sticks and piled them, and once more the Prussian shot them into annihilation. Plainly, to light a fire with a pistol was an art requiring practice and experience, and the middle of a desert at midnight in a snowstorm was not a good place or time for the acquiring of the accomplishment. We gave it up and tried the other. Each man took a couple of sticks and fell to chafing them together. At the end of half an hour we were thoroughly chilled, and so were the sticks. We bitterly execrated [1] the Indians, the hunters, and the books that had betrayed us with the silly device, and wondered dismally what was next to be done. At this critical moment Mr. Ballou fished out four matches from the rubbish of an overlooked pocket. To have found four gold bars would have seemed poor and cheap good luck compared to this. One cannot think how good a match looks under such circumstances — or how lovable and precious and sacredly beautiful to the eye. This time we gathered sticks with high hopes; and when Mr. Ballou prepared to light the first match, there was an amount of interest centered upon him that pages of writing could not describe. The match burned hopefully a moment, and then went out. It could not have carried more regret with it if it had been a human life. The next match simply flashed and died. The wind puffed the third one out just as it was on the imminent verge of success. We gathered

place in the shelter of our bodies. In the course of ten or fifteen minutes all was ready, and then, while conversation ceased and our pulses beat low with anxious suspense, Ollendorff applied his revolver, pulled the trigger, and blew the pile clear out of the county! It was the flattest failure that ever was.

This was distressing, but it paled before a greater horror — the horses were gone! I had been appointed to hold the bridles, but in my absorbing anxiety over the pistol experiment I had unconsciously dropped them and the released animals had walked off in the storm. It was useless to try to follow them, for their footfalls could make no sound, and one could pass within two yards of the creatures and never see them. We gave them up without an effort at recovering them and cursed the lying books that said horses would stay by their masters for protection and companionship in a distressful time like ours.

---

[1] **execrated** (ek′sə·krāt·əd): cursed.

together closer than ever, and developed a solicitude that was rapt and painful, as Mr. Ballou scratched our last hope on his leg. It lit, burned blue and sickly, and then budded into a robust flame. Shading it with his hands, the old gentleman bent gradually down and every heart went with him — everybody, too, for that matter — and blood and breath stood still. The flame touched the sticks at last, took gradual hold upon them — hesitated — took a stronger hold — hesitated again — held its breath five heartbreaking seconds, then gave a sort of human gasp and went out.

Nobody said a word for several minutes. It was a solemn sort of silence; even the wind put on a stealthy, sinister quiet and made no more noise than the falling flakes of snow. Finally a sad-voiced conversation began, and it was soon apparent that in each of our hearts lay the conviction that this was our last night with the living. I had so hoped that I was the only one who felt so. When the others calmly acknowledged their conviction, it sounded like the summons itself. Ollendorff said:

"Brothers, let us die together. And let us go without one hard feeling towards each other. Let us forget and forgive bygones. I know that you have felt hard toward me for turning over the canoe and for knowing too much and leading you round and round in the snow — but I meant well; forgive me. I acknowledge freely that I have had hard feelings against Mr. Ballou for abusing me and calling me a logarithm, which is a thing I do not know what, but no doubt a thing considered disgraceful and unbecoming in America,

and it has scarcely been out of my mind and has hurt me a great deal — but let it go; I forgive Mr. Ballou with all my heart, and . . ."

Poor Ollendorff broke down and the tears came. He was not alone, for I was crying too, and so was Mr. Ballou. Ollendorff got his voice again and forgave me for things I had done and said. Then he got out his bottle of whisky and said that whether he lived or died he would never touch another drop. He said that he had given up all hope of life and, although ill-prepared, was ready to submit humbly to his fate; that he wished he could be spared a little longer, not for any selfish reason, but to make a thorough reform in his character and, by devoting himself to helping the poor, nursing the sick, and pleading with the people to guard themselves against the evils of intemperance, to make his life a beneficent example to the young and lay it down at last with the precious reflection that it had not been lived in vain. He ended by saying that his reform should begin at this moment, even here in the presence of death, since no longer time was to be vouchsafed [1] wherein to prosecute it to men's help and benefit — and with that he threw away the bottle of whisky.

Mr. Ballou made remarks of similar purport, and began the reform he could not live to continue, by throwing away the ancient pack of cards that had solaced our captivity during the flood and made it bearable. He said he never gambled but still was satisfied that the meddling with cards in any way was

[1] **vouchsafed:** granted.

immoral and injurious and no man could be wholly pure and blemishless without eschewing [1] them. "And therefore," continued he, "in doing this act I already feel more in sympathy with that spiritual saturnalia [2] necessary to entire and obsolete [3] reform." These rolling syllables touched him as no intelligible eloquence could have done, and the old man sobbed with a mournfulness not unmingled with satisfaction.

My own remarks were of the same tenor as those of my comrades, and I know that the feelings that prompted them were heartfelt and sincere. We were all sincere and all deeply moved and earnest, for we were in the presence of death and without hope. I threw away my pipe, and in doing it felt that at last I was free of a hated vice and one that had ridden me like a tyrant all my days. While I yet talked, the thought of the good I might have done in the world and the still greater good I might *now* do, with these new incentives and higher and better aims to guide me if I could only be spared a few years longer, overcame me, and the tears came again. We put our arms about each other's necks and awaited the warning drowsiness that precedes death by freezing.

It came stealing over us presently, and then we bade each other a last farewell. A delicious dreaminess wrought its web about my yielding senses, while the snowflakes wove a winding

sheet about my conquered body. Oblivion came. The battle of life was done.

I do not know how long I was in a state of forgetfulness, but it seemed an age. A vague consciousness grew upon me by degrees, and then came a gathering anguish of pain in my limbs and through all my body. I shuddered. The thought flitted through my brain, "This is death — this is the hereafter."

Then came a white upheaval at my side, and a voice said, with bitterness: "Will some gentleman be so good as to kick me behind?"

It was Ballou — at least it was a tousled snow image in a sitting posture, with Ballou's voice.

I rose up, and there in the gray dawn, not fifteen steps from us, were the frame buildings of a stage station, and under a shed stood our still saddled and bridled horses!

An arched snowdrift broke up, now, and Ollendorff emerged from it, and the three of us sat and stared at the houses without speaking a word. We really had nothing to say. The whole situation was so painfully ridiculous and humiliating that words were tame, and we did not know where to commence anyhow.

The joy in our hearts at our deliverance was poisoned, well-nigh dissipated, indeed. We presently began to grow pettish by degrees, and sullen; and then, angry at each other, angry at ourselves, angry at everything in general, we moodily dusted the snow from our clothing and in unsociable single file plowed our way to the horses, unsaddled them, and sought shelter in the station.

I have scarcely exaggerated a detail

---

[1] **eschewing** (es·chōo′ing): avoiding.

[2] **saturnalia:** a period of general lawlessness, or immorality. Ballou has used the wrong word.

[3] **obsolete:** no longer in use. Ballou has used the wrong word again; he means *absolute*.

of this curious and absurd adventure. It occurred almost exactly as I have stated it. We actually went into camp in a snowdrift in a desert, at midnight in a storm, forlorn and hopeless, within fifteen steps of a comfortable inn.

For two hours we sat apart in the station and ruminated in disgust. The mystery was gone, now, and it was plain enough why the horses had deserted us. Without a doubt they were under that shed a quarter of a minute after they had left us, and they must have overheard and enjoyed all our confessions and lamentations.

After breakfast we felt better, and the zest of life soon came back. The world looked bright again, and existence was as dear to us as ever. Presently an uneasiness came over me — grew upon me — assailed me without ceasing. Alas, my regeneration [1] was not complete — I wanted to smoke! I resisted with all my strength, but the

¹ **regeneration:** renewal of life.

flesh was weak. I wandered away alone and wrestled with myself an hour. I recalled my promises of reform and preached to myself persuasively, upbraidingly, exhaustively. But it was all vain; I shortly found myself sneaking among the snowdrifts hunting for my pipe. I discovered it after a considerable search and crept away to hide myself and enjoy it. I remained behind the barn a good while, asking myself how I would feel if my braver, stronger, truer comrades should catch me in my degradation. At last I lit the pipe, and no human being can feel meaner and baser than I did then. I was ashamed of being in my own pitiful company. Still dreading discovery, I felt that perhaps the further side of the barn would be somewhat safer, and so I turned the corner. As I turned the one corner, smoking, Ollendorff turned the other with his bottle to his lips, and between us sat unconscious Ballou deep in a game of "solitaire" with the old greasy cards!

Absurdity could go no farther. We shook hands and agreed to say no more about "reform" and "examples to the rising generation."

A REFORMATION

1. Ollendorff said his instinct was as sensitive as a compass. Was he right? Where did his instinct lead the men?

2. Ballou wounded Ollendorff's pride by saying that he " 'did not know as much as a logarithm.' " What did Ollendorff say about this remark later? Where did Ballou make mistakes in word choice?

3. Describe the efforts of the men to build a fire. What happened to the horses?

4. What bad habit did each man renounce? What happened the next day?

5. Mark Twain knew that people will laugh at characters who are in a predicament as a result of their own foolishness — so long as the results are not tragic. What kinds of characters were the three men in this story? How were they foolish? Which of their actions or reactions do you think was the funniest?

6. How did Mark Twain make fun of the tenderfoot and of book learning in this story?

7. One reason why people like Mark Twain's writing is that he was not afraid to laugh at himself. How did Mark Twain laugh at himself in this selection?

WORDS: WHICH MEANING?

In the first paragraph Twain says that the men dropped into Ollendorff's "wake." Perhaps you usually think of the word *wake* as a verb, meaning "emerge from sleep." But in this sentence *wake* is used as a noun. In a dictionary, you will see that one meaning for *wake* when used as a noun is this: "the track a ship leaves in passing through the water," hence, "any

track left by a moving thing." The context tells you that *wake* here refers to a track left by Ollendorff in the snow.

Use your dictionary and context clues to help you figure out the meaning of each of these italicized words, as it is used in this story.

" '. . . I was as *dead* certain as a compass . . .' " (See page 503.)

"Then the old man *waxed* wroth . . ." (See page 504.)

"My own remarks were of the same *tenor* . . ." (See page 508.)

COMPOSITION: TIME ORDER

To help his readers know when things happen in a story, an author uses words and phrases referring to time. Study the following passage from "Lost in a Snowstorm." This passage opens with a word indicating time: *presently*. Notice how other words in the sentence (in italics) help keep you on the right time track.

> "*Presently* the Overland stage forded the now fast-receding stream and started toward Carson on its first trip since the flood came. We hesitated no longer, *now*, but took up our march in its wake, and trotted merrily along, for we had good confidence in the driver's bump of locality. But our horses were no match for the fresh stage team. We were *soon* left out of sight; but it was no matter, for we had the deep ruts the wheels made for a guide. *By this time it was three in the afternoon*, and consequently it was not very long before night came — and not with a lingering twilight, but with a sudden shutting down like a cellar door . . ."

Write a short paragraph, perhaps telling about a time you were lost or had lost something. Use words and phrases to help your readers keep track of when the events happened.

Punch, Brothers, Punch

One of Mark Twain's trademarks is humorous exaggeration. In this famous story, he writes about a jingle someone made up about the colored tickets given out on buses and streetcars.

Wᴵˡˡ ᴛʜᴇ ʀᴇᴀᴅᴇʀ please to cast his eye over the following lines and see if he can discover anything harmful in them?

> Conductor, when you receive a
> fare,
> Punch in the presence of the pas-
> senjare!
> A blue trip slip for an eight-cent
> fare,
> A buff trip slip for a six-cent fare,
> A pink trip slip for a three-cent
> fare,
> Punch in the presence of the pas-
> senjare!
>
> CHORUS
>
> Punch, brothers! punch with care!
> Punch in the presence of the pas-
> senjare!

"Punch, Brothers, Punch" from *Tom Sawyer Abroad and Other Stories* by Mark Twain. Reprinted by permission of Harper & Row, Publishers.

I came across these jingling rhymes in a newspaper a little while ago and read them a couple of times. They took instant and entire possession of me. All through breakfast they went waltzing through my brain, and when, at last, I rolled up my napkin, I could not tell whether I had eaten anything or not. I had carefully laid out my day's work the day before — a thrilling tragedy in the novel which I am writing. I went to my den to begin my deed of blood. I took up my pen, but all I could get it to say was, "Punch in the presence of the passenjare." I fought hard for an hour, but it was useless. My head kept humming, "A blue trip slip for an eight-cent fare, a buff trip slip for a six-cent fare," and so on and so on, without peace or respite. The day's work was ruined — I could see that plainly enough. I gave up and drifted downtown and presently discovered that my feet were keeping time to that relentless jingle. When I could stand it no longer, I altered my step. But it did no good; those rhymes accommodated themselves to the new step and went on harassing me just as before. I returned home and suffered all the afternoon; suffered all through an unconscious and unrefreshing dinner; suffered and cried and jingled all through the evening; went to bed and rolled, tossed, and jingled right along, the same as ever; got up at midnight, frantic, and tried to read; but there was nothing visible upon the whirling page except "Punch! punch in the presence of the passenjare." By sunrise I was out of my mind, and everybody marveled and was distressed at the idiotic burden of my ravings — "Punch! oh, punch! punch in the presence of the passenjare!"

Two days later, on Saturday morning, I arose, a tottering wreck, and went forth to fulfill an engagement with a valued friend, the Reverend Mr. ——, to walk to the Talcott Tower, ten miles distant. He stared at me but asked no questions. We started. Mr. —— talked, talked, talked — as is his wont. I said nothing; I heard nothing. At the end of a mile, Mr. —— said:

"Mark, are you sick? I never saw a man look so haggard and worn and absent-minded. Say something, do!"

Drearily, without enthusiasm, I said, "Punch, brothers, punch with care! Punch in the presence of the passenjare!"

My friend eyed me blankly, looked perplexed, then said:

"I do not think I get your drift, Mark. There does not seem to be any relevancy [1] in what you have said, certainly nothing sad; and yet — maybe it was the way you *said* the words — I never heard anything that sounded so pathetic. What is —— "

[1] **relevancy**: relationship to what is going on.

But I heard no more. I was already far away with my pitiless, heartbreaking "blue trip slip for an eight-cent fare, buff trip slip for a six-cent fare, pink trip slip for a three-cent fare; punch in the presence of the passenjare." I do not know what occurred during the other nine miles. However, all of a sudden Mr. —— laid his hand on my shoulder and shouted:

"Oh, wake up! wake up! wake up! Don't sleep all day! Here we are at the Tower, man! I have talked myself deaf and dumb and blind, and I never got a response. Just look at this magnificent autumn landscape! Look at it! Look at it! Feast your eyes on it! You have traveled; you have seen boasted landscapes elsewhere. Come, now, deliver an honest opinion. What do you say to this?"

I sighed wearily, and murmured:

"A buff trip slip for a six-cent fare, a pink trip slip for a three-cent fare, punch in the presence of the passenjare."

Reverend Mr. —— stood there, very grave, full of concern, apparently, and looked long at me; then he said:

"Mark, there is something about this that I cannot understand. Those are about the same words you said before; there does not seem to be anything in them, and yet they nearly break my heart when you say them. Punch in the — how is it they go?"

I began at the beginning and repeated all the lines.

My friend's face lighted with interest. He said:

"Why, what a captivating jingle it is! It is almost music. It flows along so nicely. I have nearly caught the rhymes myself. Say them over just once more, and then I'll have them, sure."

I said them over. Then Mr. —— said them. He made one little mistake, which I corrected. The next time and the next he got them right. Now a great burden seemed to tumble from my shoulders. That torturing jingle departed out of my brain, and a grateful sense of rest and peace descended upon me. I was lighthearted enough to sing; and I did sing for half an hour, straight along, as we went jogging homeward. Then my freed tongue found blessed speech again, and the pent[1] talk of many a weary hour began to gush and flow. It flowed on and on, joyously, jubilantly, until the fountain was empty and dry. As I wrung my friend's hand at parting, I said:

"Haven't we had a royal good time! But now I remember, you haven't said a word for two hours. Come, come, out with something!"

The Reverend Mr. —— turned a lackluster eye upon me, drew a deep sigh, and said, without animation, without apparent consciousness:

"Punch, brothers, punch with care! Punch in the presence of the passenjare!"

A pang shot through me as I said to myself, "Poor fellow, poor fellow! *He* has got it now."

I did not see Mr. —— for two or three days after that. Then, on Tuesday evening, he staggered into my presence and sank rejectedly into a seat. He was pale, worn; he was a wreck. He lifted his faded eyes to my face and said:

"Ah, Mark, it was a ruinous invest-ment that I made in those heartless rhymes. They have ridden me like a nightmare, day and night, hour after hour, to this very moment. Since I saw you I have suffered the torments of the lost. Saturday evening I had a sudden call, by telegraph, and took the night train for Boston. The occasion was the death of a valued old friend who had requested that I should preach his funeral sermon. I took my seat in the cars and set myself to framing the discourse. But I never got beyond the opening paragraph; for then the train started and the car wheels began their 'clack-clack — clack-clack-clack! clack-clack — clack-clack-clack!' and right away those odious rhymes fitted themselves to that accompaniment. For an hour I sat there and set a syllable of those rhymes to every separate and distinct clack the car wheels made. Why, I was as fagged out, then, as if I had been chopping wood all day. My skull was splitting with a headache. It seemed to me that I must go mad if I sat there any longer; so I undressed and went to bed. I stretched myself out in my berth, and — well, you know what the result was. The thing went right along, just the same. 'Clack-clack-clack, a blue trip slip, clack-clack-clack, for an eight-cent fare; clack-clack-clack, a buff trip slip, clack-clack-clack, for a six-cent fare,' and so on, and so on, and so on — '*punch* in the presence of the passenjare!' Sleep? Not a single wink! I was almost a lunatic when I got to Boston. Don't ask me about the funeral. I did the best I could, but every solemn individual sentence was meshed and tangled and woven in and out with 'Punch, brothers, punch with care, punch in

---

[1] **pent**: repressed.

the presence of the passenjare.' And the most distressing thing was that my *delivery* dropped into the undulating[1] rhythm of those pulsing rhymes, and I could actually catch absent-minded people nodding *time* to the swing of it with their stupid heads. And, Mark, you may believe it or not, but before I got through, the entire assemblage were placidly bobbing their heads in solemn unison — mourners, undertaker, and all. The moment I had finished, I fled to the anteroom in a state bordering on frenzy. Of course it would be my luck to find a sorrowing and aged maiden aunt of the deceased there, who had arrived from Springfield too late to get into the church. She began to sob, and said:

" 'Oh, oh, he is gone, he is gone, and I didn't see him before he died!'

" 'Yes!' I said, 'he *is* gone, he *is* gone, he *is* gone — oh, *will* this suffering never cease!'

" 'You loved him, then! Oh, you too loved him!'

" 'Loved him! Loved *who?*'

" 'Why, my poor George! My poor nephew!'

" 'Oh — *him!* Yes — oh, yes, yes. Certainly — certainly. Punch — punch — oh, this misery will kill me!'

" 'Bless you! Bless you, sir, for these sweet words! *I*, too, suffer in this dear loss. Were you present during his last moments?'

" 'Yes. I — *whose* last moments?'

" '*His*. The dear departed's.'

" 'Yes! Oh, yes — yes — *yes!* I suppose so, I think so, *I* don't know! Oh, certainly — I was there — *I* was there!'

" 'Oh, what a privilege! What a precious privilege! And his last words — oh, tell me, tell me his last words! What did he say?'

" 'He said — he said — oh, my head, my head, my head! He said — he said — he never said *any*thing but "Punch, punch, *punch* in the presence of the passenjare!" Oh, leave me, madam! In the name of all that is generous, leave me to my madness, my misery, my despair! — a buff trip slip for a six-cent fare, a pink trip slip for a three-cent fare — endu-rance *can* no fur-ther go! — PUNCH in the presence of the passen-jare!' "

My friend's hopeless eyes rested upon mine a pregnant minute, and then he said impressively:

"Mark, you do not say anything. You do not offer me any hope. But, ah me, it is just as well — it is just as well. You could not do me any good. The time has long gone by when words could comfort me. Something tells me that my tongue is doomed to wag forever to the jigger of that remorseless jingle. There — there it is coming on me again: a blue trip slip for an eight-cent fare, a buff trip slip for a . . ."

Thus murmuring faint and fainter, my friend sank into a peaceful trance and forgot his sufferings in a blessed respite.[2]

How did I finally save him from an asylum? I took him to a neighboring university and made him discharge the burden of his persecuting rhymes into the eager ears of the poor, unthinking students. How is it with *them*, now? The result is too sad to tell. Why did I

---

[1] **undulating:** rising and falling.

[2] **respite** (res'pit): interval of rest.

write this article? It was for a worthy, even a noble, purpose. It was to warn you, reader, if you should come across those merciless rhymes, to avoid them — avoid them as you would a pestilence!

THE JINGLE

1. How did the lines of the jingle affect Mark Twain? How did he get rid of the jingle?

2. Tell the story of the jingle's effect upon the minister. What is humorous about the way the minister preached the sermon?

3. How did Mark Twain help his friend? Why did he write this article? What is funny in his purpose?

4. Almost all of Mark Twain's writings are characterized by exaggeration. How did he exaggerate in this article?

5. Catchy songs seem to take hold of people in the way this jingle captured the minds of Mark Twain and his friend. Over the years, radio and television have been full of such songs. Have any songs or commercials ever stuck in your mind? Give some examples.

BALANCED SENTENCE PARTS

Read aloud this sentence from "Punch, Brothers, Punch":

"That torturing jingle departed out of my brain, and a grateful sense of rest and peace descended upon me."

Notice that one part seems to balance the other neatly. Many compound sentences, joined by *and* or *but,* have this quality of balance. You can find other sentences like this in "Punch, Brothers, Punch." For example:

"Then my freed tongue found blessed speech again, and the pent talk of many a weary hour began to gush and flow."

Find two more sentences like this from the story, and then write two similar compound sentences of your own. Read all these sentences aloud to emphasize their balanced parts.

COMPOSITION: EXAGGERATION

In "Punch, Brothers, Punch," Mark Twain exaggerates, perhaps even more than he does in "The Celebrated Jumping Frog of Calaveras County" or "Lost in a Snowstorm." In this story about his obsession with a jingle, Twain took an experience that most of us have had, and he had fun blowing it into a wild tale.

Try your hand at writing this kind of exaggeration. The following titles may start your imagination whirling.

> That Rule!
> Ten-Dollar Words
> Our Neighbor's Dog
> Jabber! Jabber!

FURTHER READING OF MARK TWAIN

Probably you have already read *The Adventures of Tom Sawyer,* one of Twain's great novels. If you have not, you should delay no longer in becoming acquainted with Tom and Huck and with the funny and exciting adventures they have along the Mississippi River.

Below are listed a few more selections by Twain which you might enjoy reading. In almost all these selections, you will find evidence of Twain's genius for making people laugh.

> Chapters 1–4 of *The Autobiography of Mark Twain* (Charles Neider, editor).
> "Jim Baker's Bluejay Yarn" from *A Tramp Abroad.*
> "The Story of the Old Ram" from *Roughing It.*
> "I Find Fool Gold" from *Roughing It.*

ROBERT FROST
1874–1963

The "New England poet," Robert Frost, was born in California and named after the Southern general Robert E. Lee. When Frost was about ten years old, his father died, and his mother moved the family to New England, where Frost's father had once lived. From that time on, Robert Frost was to take a deep and abiding delight in the New England countryside.

After Frost had spent two unhappy years at college, his grandfather gave him a farm. Frost tried raising chickens; he also taught school, directed plays, and coached baseball. But all this time he was writing poetry.

Discouraged at his lack of recognition, Frost sold his farm at the end of ten years and took his family to England. There, when he was thirty-nine years old, his first book of poems, *A Boy's Will*, was published, and a second collection, *North of Boston*, followed a year later.

After the outbreak of World War I, Robert Frost returned to America. Now publishers were eager for his poems, and universities and colleges eager to hear his lectures and readings.

Over the next forty years, Frost lived close to the land and became America's unofficial poet laureate. Four times he received the Pulitzer prize. On his seventy-sixth and eighty-fifth birthdays, the United States Senate passed resolutions of good wishes to him. Frost was the first American poet to take part in the inauguration of a President. In January 1961, at the inauguration of John F. Kennedy, the aging poet recited from memory his poem "The Gift Outright."

Frost once said that a poem should begin in delight and end in wisdom. Beneath the simple language and familiar country themes of his poems, the reader shares in Robert Frost's delight and wisdom.

The Pasture

I'm going out to clean the pasture spring;
I'll only stop to rake the leaves away
(And wait to watch the water clear, I may):
I shan't be gone long. — You come too.

I'm going out to fetch the little calf   5
That's standing by the mother. It's so young
It totters when she licks it with her tongue.
I shan't be gone long. — You come too.

A Time to Talk

When a friend calls to me from the road
And slows his horse to a meaning walk,
I don't stand still and look around
On all the hills I haven't hoed,
And shout from where I am, "What is it?"   5
No, not as there is a time to talk.
I thrust my hoe in the mellow ground,
Blade-end up and five feet tall,
And plod: I go up to the stone wall
For a friendly visit.   10

THE POET'S THEMES

1. "The Pasture" reads like an invitation, and rightly so, for Frost often used these lines to introduce his collections of poems. How does the poet try to persuade you to come along? Can you feel the urgency of Frost's desire for company? If you go with the poet, what do you think you might learn?

2. In "A Time to Talk," what do you think the poet means by a "meaning walk" (line 2)? What would the poet not do when his friend slowed down? How would he assure his friend that he wanted to visit?

3. The loneliness of the human soul is a theme we find over and over again in Robert Frost's poems. Have you ever wanted someone to share things with you? What experiences do you like to share?

The Birthplace

Here further up the mountain slope
Than there was ever any hope,
My father built, enclosed a spring,
Strung chains of wall round everything,
Subdued the growth of earth to grass,   5
And brought our various lives to pass.
A dozen girls and boys we were.
The mountain seemed to like the stir,
And made of us a little while —
With always something in her smile.   10
Today she wouldn't know our name.
(No girl's, of course, has stayed the same.)
The mountain pushed us off her knees.
And now her lap is full of trees.

NATURE

1. What words and phrases suggest that the speaker's father had difficulties building this home on the mountain? Explain the meaning of line 5.

2. Why do you suppose the poet refers to the mountain as "her," not "him"? What does Frost mean in line 9 when he says that the mountain "made of us a little while"? What does line 12 mean? Why is it in parentheses?

3. In what ways is this the story of most birthplaces? How does line 13 describe what happens to almost everyone?

4. Reread Frost's biography (page 516.) Do you think this poem applies to his family?

The Road Not Taken

Two roads diverged in a yellow wood,
And sorry I could not travel both
And be one traveler, long I stood
And looked down one as far as I could
To where it bent in the undergrowth;   5

Then took the other, as just as fair,
And having perhaps the better claim,
Because it was grassy and wanted wear;
Though as for that the passing there
Had worn them really about the same,   10

And both that morning equally lay
In leaves no step had trodden black.
Oh, I kept the first for another day!
Yet knowing how way leads on to way,
I doubted if I should ever come back.   15

I shall be telling this with a sigh
Somewhere ages and ages hence:
Two roads diverged in a wood, and I —
I took the one less traveled by,
And that has made all the difference.   20

DEEPER MEANING

A poem can be interpreted in different ways by different readers. So it is with this well-known poem. However, all readers agree that in this poem Frost is talking about more than just roads.

1. When the speaker came to the fork in the road, what were his feelings? Why did he choose one road over the other? At the time, though, was there really any difference in the appearance of the roads? What do you think the poet meant when he said "knowing how way leads on to way" in line 14?

2. How does the last stanza indicate that this poem has a deeper meaning — that the poet's choice was not really between two roads? What do you think the two roads in the wood might stand for or symbolize?

3. Some people think that Frost was describing a particular type of person in this poem. Can the speaker make up his mind easily? After he has made his choice, what does he do?

4. As he did in most of his poems, Frost drew his inspiration from simple country things. What symbols might a city poet have used instead of roads in a wood?

Stopping by Woods on a Snowy Evening

Whose woods these are I think I know.
His house is in the village though;
He will not see me stopping here
To watch his woods fill up with snow.

The little horse must think it queer   5
To stop without a farmhouse near,
Between the woods and frozen lake
The darkest evening of the year.

He gives his harness bells a shake
To ask if there is some mistake.   10
The only other sound's the sweep
Of easy wind and downy flake.

The woods are lovely, dark and deep.
But I have promises to keep,
And miles to go before I sleep,   15
And miles to go before I sleep.

In "Stopping by Woods on a Snowy Evening," Frost describes a particular, everyday experience. He then wants his reader to unfold from this experience a general meaning — or, as he calls it, a "clarification of life." Most readers of this poem think that it tells more than the simple story of a man who stops to watch the falling snow. They feel that Frost has led them to realize that duties and obligations in life prevent them from enjoying the beauty of the world. Others think that Frost here is looking at the woods as a tempting escape from the world and its pressures.

1. Where is the speaker of this poem? What month of the year is it? Is the speaker alone or is someone with him? What has made the speaker stop his horse?

2. What picture does Frost make you see in stanza 2? What sounds do you hear in stanza 3?

3. With what three adjectives does Frost describe the woods? Why can't the speaker linger to look at the woods?

4. What do *you* think Frost is talking about in this poem?

5. Did Frost's description of his experience lead you to a clarification of any aspect of life? Explain your answer. What do you think the poet's "promises" might have been?

The Last Word of a Bluebird

As Told to a Child

As I went out a Crow
In a low voice said, "Oh,
I was looking for you.
How do you do?
I just came to tell you   5
To tell Lesley (will you?)
That her little Bluebird
Wanted me to bring word
That the north wind last night
That made the stars bright   10
And made ice on the trough

Almost made him cough
His tail feathers off.
He just had to fly!
But he sent her Good-bye   15
And said to be good,
And wear her red hood,
And look for skunk tracks
In the snow with an ax —
And do everything!   20
And perhaps in the spring
He would come back and sing."

1. Sometimes, as in this lyric, Frost showed a sly humor. Here he was addressing his young daughter, Lesley. What message was the crow relaying to Lesley?

2. How did Frost indicate in this poem that he was talking to a child? Compare the rhyme in this poem with that of other poems in this group. Read this poem aloud to feel its light, gay rhythm.

Mending Wall

Something there is that doesn't love a wall,
That sends the frozen ground-swell under it,
And spills the upper boulders in the sun;
And makes gaps even two can pass abreast.
The work of hunters is another thing: 5
I have come after them and made repair
Where they have left not one stone on a stone,
But they would have the rabbit out of hiding,
To please the yelping dogs. The gaps I mean,
No one has seen them made or heard them made,   10
But at spring mending-time we find them there.
I let my neighbor know beyond the hill;
And on a day we meet to walk the line
And set the wall between us once again.
We keep the wall between us as we go.   15
To each the boulders that have fallen to each.
And some are loaves and some so nearly balls
We have to use a spell to make them balance:
"Stay where you are until our backs are turned!"
We wear our fingers rough with handling them.   20
Oh, just another kind of outdoor game,
One on a side. It comes to little more:
There where it is we do not need the wall:

He is all pine and I am apple orchard.
My apple trees will never get across   25
And eat the cones under his pines, I tell him.
He only says, "Good fences make good neighbors."
Spring is the mischief in me, and I wonder
If I could put a notion in his head:
"*Why* do they make good neighbors? Isn't it   30
Where there are cows? But here there are no cows.
Before I built a wall I'd ask to know
What I was walling in or walling out,
And to whom I was like to give offense.
Something there is that doesn't love a wall,   35
That wants it down." I could say "Elves" to him,
But it's not elves exactly, and I'd rather
He said it for himself. I see him there
Bringing a stone grasped firmly by the top
In each hand, like an old-stone savage armed.   40
He moves in darkness as it seems to me,
Not of woods only and the shade of trees.
He will not go behind his father's saying,
And he likes having thought of it so well
He says again, "Good fences make good neighbors."   45

A CLARIFICATION

In this poem, as in "Stopping by Woods on a Snowy Evening," Frost starts with an ordinary, everyday experience — two New England farmers are working together in spring to repair the fence between their farms. As we read the poem, however, we begin to discover that Frost is making a general observation about human character: he is again leading us to a "clarification of life."

1. Frost says that "Something" doesn't like a wall. Tell what happens to stone fences in winter that leads Frost to say this.

2. Beginning with line 25, Frost carries on a dialogue with his neighbor. What does Frost say in lines 25–26? What is the neighbor's reply? Does the poet really express to his neighbor the ideas in lines 30–35? What does Frost mean when he says "Elves" in line 36?

3. Frost says that the neighbor appears to move in "darkness" (line 41). What does he mean? What does Frost mean by saying that the neighbor will not "go behind his father's saying"?

4. How does Frost make mending the wall a symbol of meaningless traditions and rituals? What point of view about people who perform such rituals is stated in lines 41–42?

5. Show that the statements made in the first and last lines of the poem reveal different attitudes. What does each statement reveal about the character of the person saying it? Do you see values in each point of view? With which do you agree?

6. Does this poem clarify anything for you? Explain.

Dust of Snow

The way a crow
Shook down on me
The dust of snow
From a hemlock tree

Has given my heart
A change of mood
And saved some part
Of a day I had rued.

The Armful

For every parcel I stoop down to seize,
I lose some other off my arms and knees,
And the whole pile is slipping, bottles, buns,
Extremes too hard to comprehend at once,
Yet nothing I should care to leave behind.   5
With all I have to hold with, hand and mind
And heart, if need be, I will do my best
To keep their building balanced at my breast.
I crouch down to prevent them as they fall;
Then sit down in the middle of them all.   10
I had to drop the armful in the road
And try to stack them in a better load.

Fire and Ice

Some say the world will end in fire,
Some say in ice.
From what I've tasted of desire
I hold with those who favor fire.
But if it had to perish twice,
I think I know enough of hate
To say that for destruction ice
Is also great
And would suffice.

What Fifty Said

When I was young my teachers were the old.
I gave up fire for form till I was cold.
I suffered like a metal being cast.
I went to school to age to learn the past.

Now I am old my teachers are the young.
What can't be molded must be cracked and sprung.
I strain at lessons fit to start a suture.
I go to school to youth to learn the future.

ROBERT FROST   525

Meaning. In introducing a collection of his poems, Robert Frost said that "a poem ends in a clarification of life — not necessarily a great clarification such as sects and cults are founded on, but in a momentary stay against confusion."

1. How had the speaker in "Dust of Snow" been feeling? How did he react to the dust of snow? Why do you think the snow changed his mood? Has anything like this ever changed your mood?

2. Put into your own words the experience described in "The Armful." Remembering that Frost often leads us into deeper meaning, can you think of other kinds of "armfuls" he might have had in mind? Have you ever felt as though you had an "armful"? When is it best to drop things and try to make "a better load"?

3. The little poem "Fire and Ice" is about a big idea. It deals with desires and hatreds, with the end of the world or of one person's world. Which did Frost think is the greater destructive force: desire or hate? How can either of these destroy a life? Can you give examples? How can they destroy the world?

4. What does "Fifty" say? What did the poet mean by saying that he "gave up fire for form"? Does the word *fire* have the same meaning here that it had in the poem "Fire and Ice"? What is meant by *cold* in line 2? Explain the comparison in line 3. What did the poet learn in school when he was young? From whom did he learn when he was young? How have things reversed completely now that the poet is old? What does line 6 mean?

Style. Frost's poems seem so simple and so much like ordinary conversation, that we often forget that rhyme and rhythm have been skillfully worked into them.

5. Look at "The Road Not Taken" and "Stopping By Woods on a Snowy Eve-

ning." Are their rhyme schemes regular?

6. Look back at "Dust of Snow." How many sentences make up this poem? The strangest word in the poem is probably *rued*. What does it mean?

7. Read "The Birthplace" aloud. Can you detect a definite rhythm? Does this poem really sound like ordinary conversation?

FURTHER READING OF ROBERT FROST

Below are a number of other poems by Robert Frost that you should enjoy reading and thinking about.

"The Figure in the Doorway"
"To a Young Wretch"
"A Minor Bird"
"Canis Major"
"The Tuft of Flowers"
"The Death of the Hired Man"
"Birches"
"Mowing"
"Two Tramps in Mud Time"
"A Leaf Treader"
"The Gift Outright"
"A Considerable Speck"
"A Prayer in Spring"
"Come In"
"Choose Something Like a Star"
"In Hardwood Groves"

The following suggestions will help you in your study of Frost's poems.

Read the poems for surface meaning.
   Who is the speaker?
   Can you understand all the words?
   Upon what experience or observation is the poem based?
Notice the poet's technique.
   Do you understand the comparisons?
   Are any symbols used?
Look for deeper meaning.
   Is the poet illustrating a general truth or clarifying some part of life?
Analyze your reaction to the poem.

JAMES THURBER

1894–1961

When James Thurber died, he had been blind for ten years. He was only seven when he lost his left eye in a boyhood game, and his right eye became diseased as a result. Yet even with impaired vision, Thurber could look at life playfully.

Thurber was born in Columbus, Ohio. After working as a newspaper reporter for a few years, he joined *The New Yorker* magazine in 1927, and he contributed humorous stories, essays, and drawings to this magazine for the rest of his life.

His friends have told how, in the early 1930's, Thurber would entertain people by acting out his stories, mostly about his family and their antics in Columbus, Ohio. Thurber would play all the characters himself, including the part of his dog Rex.

Thurber's famous story "The Secret Life of Walter Mitty" was made into a successful movie. He also wrote a series of modern fables, which were later collected into two books, and he produced hundreds of cartoons about cowering men, bossy women, and wise dogs. Thurber was coauthor of the well-known play, *The Male Animal*.

When Thurber died, his friend E. B. White wrote this about him in *The New Yorker:* "He was both a practitioner of humor and a defender of it. The day he died, I came on a letter from him. 'Every time is a time for humor,' he wrote. 'I write humor the way a surgeon operates, because it is a livelihood, because I have a great urge to do it, because many interesting challenges are set up, and because I have the hope it may do some good.'. . . During his happiest years, Thurber did not write the way a surgeon operates, he wrote the way a child skips rope, the way a mouse waltzes."

The Night
the Bed Fell

Thurber began to write down the funny stories about his family in Columbus, Ohio, and to publish them in *The New Yorker* under the general title "My Life and Hard Times." Eventually, these humorous sketches were collected into a book. One of his famous stories from this collection is "The Night the Bed Fell."

I SUPPOSE that the high-water mark of my youth in Columbus, Ohio, was the night the bed fell on my father. It makes a better recitation (unless, as some friends of mine have said, one has heard it five or six times) than it does a piece of writing, for it is almost necessary to throw furniture around, shake doors, and bark like a dog, to lend the proper atmosphere and verisimilitude [1] to what is admittedly a somewhat incredible tale. Still, it did take place.

It happened, then, that my father had decided to sleep in the attic one night, to be away where he could think. My mother opposed the notion strongly because, she said, the old wooden bed

---

[1] **verisimilitude** (ver'ə·si·mil'ə·tōōd): appearance of truth.

"The Night the Bed Fell" from *My Life and Hard Times* by James Thurber, Harper & Row, Publishers, copyright © 1933, 1961, by James Thurber. Originally appeared in *The New Yorker*. Reprinted by permission of Helen Thurber.

up there was unsafe; it was wobbly, and the heavy headboard would crash down on Father's head in case the bed fell, and kill him. There was no dissuading him, however, and at a quarter past ten he closed the attic door behind him and went up the narrow twisting stairs. We later heard ominous creakings as he crawled into bed. Grandfather, who usually slept in the attic bed when he was with us, had disappeared some days before. (On these occasions he was usually gone six or eight days and returned growling and out of temper, with the news that the Federal Union was run by a passel of blockheads and that the Army of the Potomac didn't have a chance.)

We had visiting us at this time a nervous first cousin of mine named Briggs Beall, who believed that he was likely to cease breathing when he was asleep. It was his feeling that if he were not awakened every hour during the night, he might die of suffocation. He had been accustomed to setting an alarm clock to ring at intervals until morning, but I persuaded him to abandon this. He slept in my room and I told him that I was such a light sleeper that if anybody quit breathing in the same room with me, I would wake instantly. He tested me the first night — which I had suspected he would — by holding his breath after my regular breathing had convinced him I was asleep. I was not asleep, however, and called to him. This seemed to allay his fears a little, but he took the precaution of putting a glass of spirits of camphor on a little table at the head of his bed. In case I didn't arouse him until he was almost gone, he said, he would sniff the camphor, a powerful reviver.

Briggs was not the only member of his family who had his crotchets.[1] Old Aunt Melissa Beall (who could whistle like a man, with two fingers in her mouth) suffered under the premonition that she was destined to die on South High Street because she had been born on South High Street and married on South High Street. Then there was Aunt Sarah Shoaf, who never went to bed at night without the fear that a burglar was going to get in and blow chloroform under her door through a tube. To avert this calamity — for she was in greater dread of anesthetics than of losing her household goods — she always piled her money, silverware, and other valuables in a neat stack just outside her bedroom, with a note reading "This is all I have. Please take it and do not use your chloroform, as this is all I have." Aunt Gracie Shoaf also had a burglar phobia, but she met it with more fortitude. She was confident that burglars had been getting into her house every night for forty years. The fact that she never missed anything was to her no proof to the contrary. She always

claimed that she scared them off before they could take anything, by throwing shoes down the hallway. When she went to bed, she piled, where she could get at them handily, all the shoes there were about her house. Five minutes after she had turned off the light, she would sit up in bed and say "Hark!" Her husband, who had learned to ignore the whole situation as long ago as 1903, would either be sound asleep or pretend to be sound asleep. In either case he would not respond to her tugging and pulling, so that presently she would arise, tiptoe to the door, open it slightly, and heave a shoe down the hall in one direction and its mate down the hall in the other direction. Some nights she threw them all, some nights only a couple of pairs.

But I am straying from the remarkable incidents that took place during the night that the bed fell on Father. By midnight we were all in bed. The layout of the rooms and the disposition of their occupants is important to an understanding of what later occurred. In the front room upstairs (just under Father's attic bedroom) were my mother and my brother Herman, who sometimes sang in his sleep, usually "Marching Through Georgia" or "Onward, Christian Soldiers." Briggs Beall and myself were in a room adjoining this one. My brother Roy was in a room across the hall from ours. Our bull terrier, Rex, slept in the hall.

My bed was an army cot, one of those affairs which are made wide enough to sleep on comfortably only by putting up, flat with the middle section, the two sides which ordinarily hang down like the sideboards of a

---

[1] **crotchets:** peculiarities.

drop-leaf table. When these sides are up, it is perilous to roll too far toward the edge, for then the cot is likely to tip completely over, bringing the whole bed down on top of one, with a tremendous banging crash. This, in fact, is precisely what happened about two o'clock in the morning. (It was my mother who, in recalling the scene later, first referred to it as "the night the bed fell on your father.")

Always a deep sleeper, slow to arouse (I had lied to Briggs), I was at first unconscious of what had happened when the iron cot rolled me onto the floor and toppled over on me. It left me still warmly bundled up and unhurt, for the bed rested above me like a canopy. Hence I did not wake up, only reached the edge of consciousness and went back. The racket, however, instantly awakened my mother, in the next room, who came to the immediate conclusion that her worst dread was realized: the big wooden bed upstairs had fallen on Father. She therefore screamed, "Let's go to your poor father!" It was this shout, rather than the noise of my cot falling, that awakened Herman, in the same room with her. He thought that Mother had become, for no apparent reason, hysterical. "You're all right, Mamma!" he shouted, trying to calm her. They exchanged shout for shout for perhaps ten seconds: "Let's go to your poor father!" and "You're all right!" That woke up Briggs. By this time I was conscious of what was going on, in a vague way, but did not yet realize that I was under my bed instead of on it. Briggs, awakening in the midst of loud shouts of fear and apprehension, came to the quick con-

clusion that he was suffocating and that we were all trying to "bring him out." With a low moan, he grasped the glass of camphor at the head of his bed and instead of sniffing it poured it over himself. The room reeked of camphor. "Ugf, ahfg," choked Briggs, like a drowning man, for he had almost succeeded in stopping his breath under the deluge of pungent spirits. He leaped out of bed and groped toward the open window, but he came up against one that was closed. With his hand, he beat out the glass, and I could hear it crash and tinkle on the alleyway below. It was at this juncture that I, in trying to get up, had the uncanny sensation of feeling my bed above me! Foggy with sleep, I now suspected, in my turn, that the whole uproar was being made in a frantic endeavor to extricate me from what must be an unheard-of and perilous situation. "Get me out of this!" I bawled. "Get me out!" I think I had the nightmarish belief that I was entombed in a mine. "Gugh," gasped Briggs, floundering in his camphor.

By this time my mother, still shouting, pursued by Herman, still shouting, was trying to open the door to the attic, in order to go up and get my father's body out of the wreckage. The door was stuck, however, and wouldn't yield. Her frantic pulls on it only added to the general banging and confusion. Roy and the dog were now up, the one shouting questions, the other barking.

Father, farthest away and soundest sleeper of all, had by this time been awakened by the battering on the attic door. He decided that the house was on fire. "I'm coming, I'm coming!" he wailed in a slow, sleepy voice — it took him many minutes to regain full consciousness. My mother, still believing he was caught under the bed, detected in his "I'm coming!" the mournful, resigned note of one who is preparing to meet his Maker. "He's dying!" she shouted.

"I'm all right!" Briggs yelled to reassure her. "I'm all right!" He still believed that it was his own closeness to death that was worrying Mother. I found at last the light switch in my room, unlocked the door, and Briggs and I joined the others at the attic door. The dog, who never did like Briggs, jumped for him — assuming that he was the culprit in whatever was going on — and Roy had to throw Rex and hold him. We could hear Father crawling out of bed upstairs. Roy pulled the attic door open with a mighty jerk, and Father came down the stairs, sleepy and irritable but safe and sound. My mother began to weep when she saw him. Rex began to howl. "What in the name of heaven is going on here?" asked Father.

The situation was finally put together like a gigantic jigsaw puzzle. Father caught a cold from prowling around in his bare feet, but there were no other bad results. "I'm glad," said Mother, who always looked on the bright side of things, "that your grandfather wasn't here."

THURBER'S HARD TIMES

Humor of Situation. Thurber enjoyed telling stories about his family's predicaments. The situations which ordinary people get themselves into become hilarious when James Thurber tells about them.

1. This particular situation began at the moment Thurber fell off his cot. Tell, in order, what happened to cause an uproarious chain reaction of events.

2. What effect did the *time* have upon the situation? Do things ever seem quite the same in daylight as they do in the middle of the night?

Humor of Character. What happened on the night the bed fell is funny because of the characters involved. Thurber spends a great deal of time describing the crotchets of his family.

3. What strange crotchet makes Briggs such a humorous character? How does Mother's character add to the humor of the situation?

4. Describe the crotchets of Grandfather, Aunt Melissa Beall, and Aunt Gracie Shoaf.

5. Why do you think Thurber digresses from his story to tell about the peculiarities of these other relatives?

SENTENCES: INTERRUPTERS

The second sentence of this story contains some words in parentheses. These words are meant to be a kind of humorous "aside," perhaps spoken out of the corner of the mouth. As we speak, we often interrupt our sentences in this way. Such an interruption is indicated by a change in the tone or pitch of the voice. In writing, such interruptions are usually put in parentheses or placed between dashes.

Find other interrupters in sentences in the second, third, and fourth paragraphs of the story. What would you do with the tone or pitch of your voice when you read these sentences aloud? Can you write a sentence that contains an interrupter?

The Dog That Bit People

Dogs fascinated James Thurber, and many of his stories tell about the incredible things that happened to his family and their famous dogs. Thurber loved most of his dogs, but there was an exception. This story tells about that dog.

Probably no one man should have as many dogs in his life as I have had, but there was more pleasure than distress in them for me except in the case of an Airedale named Muggs. He gave me more trouble than all the other fifty-four or -five put together, although my moment of keenest embarrassment was the time a Scotch terrier named Jeannie, who had just had four puppies in the shoe closet of a fourth-floor apartment in New York, had the fifth and last at the corner of — but we shall get around to that later on. Then, too, there was the prize-winning French poodle, a great big black poodle — none of your little, untroublesome white miniatures — who got sick riding in the rumble seat of a car with me on her way to the Greenwich Dog Show. She had a red rubber bib

tucked around her throat and, since a rainstorm came up when we were halfway through the Bronx, I had to hold over her a small green umbrella, really more of a parasol. The rain beat down fearfully, and suddenly the driver of the car drove into a big garage, filled with mechanics. It happened so quickly that I forgot to put the umbrella down, and I shall always remember the look of incredulity that came over the face of the garageman who came over to see what we wanted. "Get a load of this, Mac," he called to someone behind him.

But the Airedale, as I have said, was the worst of all my dogs. He really wasn't my dog, as a matter of fact; I came home from a vacation one summer to find that my brother Robert had bought him while I was away. A big, burly, choleric [1] dog, he always acted as if he thought I wasn't one of the family. There was a slight advantage in being one of the family, for he didn't bite the family as often as he bit strangers. Still, in the years that we had him he bit everybody but Mother, and he made a pass at her once but missed. That was during the month when we

[1] **choleric** (kol′ər·ik): bad tempered.

suddenly had mice, and Muggs refused to do anything about them. Nobody ever had mice exactly like the mice we had that month. They acted like pet mice, almost like mice somebody had trained. They were so friendly that one night when Mother entertained at dinner the Friraliras, a club she and my father had belonged to for twenty years, she put down a lot of little dishes with food in them on the pantry floor so that the mice would be satisfied with that and wouldn't come into the dining room. Muggs stayed out in the pantry with the mice, lying on the floor, growling to himself — not at the mice, but about all the people in the next room that he would have liked to get at. Mother slipped out into the pantry once to see how everything was going. Everything was going fine. It made her so mad to see Muggs lying there, oblivious of the mice — they came running up to her — that she slapped him and he slashed at her, but didn't make it. He was sorry immediately, Mother said. He was always sorry, she said, after he bit someone, but we could not understand how she figured this out. He didn't act sorry.

Mother used to send a box of candy every Christmas to the people the Airedale bit. The list finally contained forty or more names. Nobody could understand why we didn't get rid of the dog. I didn't understand it very well myself, but we didn't get rid of him. I think that one or two people tried to poison Muggs — he acted poisoned once in a while — and old Major Moberly fired at him once with his service revolver near the Seneca Hotel on East Broad Street — but Muggs lived to be almost eleven years old, and even when he could hardly get around, he bit a congressman who had called to see my father on business. My mother had never liked the congressman — she said the signs of his horoscope showed he couldn't be trusted (he was Saturn with the moon in Virgo) — but she sent him a box of candy that Christmas. He sent it right back, probably because he suspected it was trick candy. Mother persuaded herself it was all for the best that the dog had bitten him, even though Father lost an important business association because of it. "I wouldn't be associated with such a man," Mother said. "Muggs could read him like a book."

We used to take turns feeding Muggs to be on his good side, but that didn't always work. He was never in a very good humor, even after a meal. Nobody knew exactly what was the matter with him, but whatever it was it made him irascible,[1] especially in the mornings. Robert never felt very well in the morning either, especially before breakfast, and once when he came downstairs and found that Muggs had moodily chewed up the morning paper, he hit him in the face with a grapefruit and then jumped up on the dining-room table, scattering dishes and silverware and spilling the coffee. Muggs' first free leap carried him all the way across the table and into a brass fire screen in front of the gas grate, but he was back on his feet in a moment, and in the end he got Robert and gave him a pretty vicious bite

[1] **irascible** (i·ras′ə·bəl): irritable.

in the leg. Then he was all over it; he never bit anyone more than once at a time. Mother always mentioned that as an argument in his favor; she said he had a quick temper but that he didn't hold a grudge. She was forever defending him. I think she liked him because he wasn't well. "He's not strong," she would say, pityingly, but that was inaccurate; he may not have been well, but he was terribly strong.

One time my mother went to the Chittenden Hotel to call on a woman mental healer who was lecturing in Columbus on the subject of "Harmonious Vibrations." She wanted to find out if it was possible to get harmonious vibrations into a dog. "He's a large, tan-colored Airedale," Mother explained. The woman said she had never treated a dog, but she advised my mother to hold the thought that he did not bite and would not bite. Mother was holding the thought the very next morning when Muggs got the iceman, but she blamed that slip-up on the iceman. "If you didn't think he would bite you, he wouldn't," Mother told him. He stomped out of the house in a terrible jangle of vibrations.

One morning when Muggs bit me slightly, more or less in passing, I reached down and grabbed his short stumpy tail and hoisted him into the air. It was a foolhardy thing to do, and the last time I saw my mother, about six months ago, she said she didn't know what possessed me. I don't either, except that I was pretty mad. As long as I held the dog off the floor by his tail he couldn't get at me, but he twisted and jerked so, snarling all the time, that I realized I couldn't hold him that way very long. I carried him to the kitchen and flung him onto the floor and shut the door on him just as he crashed against it. But I forgot about the back stairs. Muggs went up the back stairs and down the front stairs and had me cornered in the living room. I managed to get up onto the mantelpiece above the fireplace, but it gave way and came down with a tremendous crash, throwing a large marble clock, several vases, and myself heavily to the floor. Muggs was so alarmed by the racket that when I picked myself up he had disappeared. We couldn't find him anywhere, although we whistled and shouted, until old Mrs. Detweiler called after dinner that night. Muggs had bitten her once, in the leg, and she came into the living room only after we assured her that Muggs had run away. She had just seated herself when, with a great growling and scratching of claws, Muggs emerged from under a davenport where he had been quietly hiding all the time and bit her again. Mother examined the bite and put arnica on it and told Mrs. Detweiler that it was only a bruise. "He just bumped you," she said. But Mrs. Detweiler left the house in a nasty state of mind.

Lots of people reported our Airedale to the police, but my father held a municipal office at the time and was on friendly terms with the police. Even so, the cops had been out a couple of times — once when Muggs bit Mrs. Rufus Sturtevant and again when he bit Lieutenant-Governor Malloy — but Mother told them that it hadn't been Muggs' fault but the fault of the people who were bitten. "When he starts for them, they scream," she explained, "and that excites him." The cops suggested that it might be a good idea to tie the dog up, but Mother said that it mortified him to be tied up and that he wouldn't eat when he was tied up.

Muggs at his meals was an unusual sight. Because of the fact that if you reached toward the floor he would bite you, we usually put his food plate on top of an old kitchen table with a bench alongside the table. Muggs would stand on the bench and eat. I remember that my mother's Uncle Horatio, who boasted that he was the third man up Missionary Ridge,[1] was splutteringly indignant when he found out that we fed the dog on a table because we were afraid to put his plate on the floor. He said he wasn't afraid of any dog that ever lived and that he would put the dog's plate on the floor if we would give it to him. Robert said that if Uncle Horatio had fed Muggs on the ground just before the battle, he would have been the first man up Missionary Ridge. Uncle Horatio was furious. "Bring him in! Bring him in now!" he shouted. "I'll feed the ——— on the floor!" Robert was all for giving him a chance, but my father wouldn't hear of it. He said that Muggs had already been fed. "I'll feed him again!" bawled Uncle Horatio. We had quite a time quieting him.

In his last year Muggs used to spend practically all of his time outdoors. He didn't like to stay in the house for some reason or other — perhaps it held too

---

[1] **Missionary Ridge:** the site of a decisive battle of the War Between the States.

many unpleasant memories for him. Anyway, it was hard to get him to come in, and as a result, the garbage man, the iceman, and the laundryman wouldn't come near the house. We had to haul the garbage down to the corner, take the laundry out and bring it back, and meet the iceman a block from home. After this had gone on for some time, we hit on an ingenious arrangement for getting the dog in the house so that we could lock him up while the gas meter was read, and so on. Muggs was afraid of only one thing, an electrical storm. Thunder and lightning frightened him out of his senses (I think he thought a storm had broken the day the mantelpiece fell). He would rush into the house and hide under a bed or in a clothes closet. So we fixed up a thunder machine out of a long narrow piece of sheet iron with a wooden handle on one end. Mother would shake this vigorously when she wanted to get Muggs into the house. It made an excellent imitation of thunder, but I suppose it was the most roundabout system for running a household that was ever devised. It took a lot out of Mother.

A few months before Muggs died, he got to "seeing things." He would rise slowly from the floor, growling low, and stalk stiff-legged and menacing toward nothing at all. Sometimes the Thing would be just a little to the right or left of a visitor. Once a Fuller Brush salesman got hysterics. Muggs came wandering into the room like Hamlet following his father's ghost. His eyes were fixed on a spot just to the left of the Fuller Brush man, who stood it until Muggs was about three slow, creeping paces from him. Then he shouted. Muggs wavered on past him into the hallway, grumbling to himself, but the Fuller Brush man went on shouting. I think Mother had to throw a pan of cold water on him before he stopped. That was the way she used to stop us boys when we got into fights.

Muggs died quite suddenly one night. Mother wanted to bury him in the family plot under a marble stone with some such inscription as "Flights of angels sing thee to thy rest," but we persuaded her it was against the law. In the end we just put up a smooth board above his grave along a lonely road. On the board I wrote with an indelible pencil *"Cave Canem."* [1] Mother was quite pleased with the simple, classic dignity of the old Latin epitaph.

[1] *"Cave Canem"*: "beware of the dog." In the days of ancient Rome, this warning was often put on the doorways of homes.

THURBER AND HIS DOGS

1. What other dogs caused Thurber some trouble and embarrassment? Why was Muggs the worst of all his dogs?

2. When did Muggs make "a pass" at Mother? How did Mother usually come to Muggs' defense? What advice did the mental healer give Mother?

3. What happened when Thurber foolishly hoisted Muggs into the air by his stumpy tail?

4. Tell about Muggs' other encounters with people. What kind of a character has Thurber created in Muggs?

Upside-down Situations. For some reason, people laugh at things that do not seem to fit together, that seem to be upside-down.

For example, we laugh when we see in the movies or on television a big man cowering before a little lady, or a burly wrestler dancing a dainty waltz. Such situations are called incongruous.

5. One incongruous situation in this story is that of the friendly mice. We do not expect to find mice behaving like these, nor do we expect to find a fierce dog lying among a group of mice and ignoring them. What other surprising and unusual situations involving Muggs and people add to the humor of this story? What is humorous about a family being ruled by an irritable dog?

COMPOUND WORDS

You know that we often create compound words in English, words like *halfway, mantelpiece,* and *silverware.* Sometimes we keep the identity of the original words by using a hyphen between them, as in words like *prize-winning, stiff-legged,* and *slip-up.* Often, compound words are written separately, but they still have the effect of one word, as in the words *fire screen, double exposure,* and *jet stream.*

Below are two lists of words; by combining a word in column A with a word in column B you can make seven compound words. Which words would be written as one word? Which would be hyphenated? Which would be written as separate words? Does each word keep its original meaning after it is compounded? Use a dictionary.

A	B
feather	seller
card	brain
hush	wise
first	file
length	class
moon	puppy
best	eyed

Memorial

We should never make the mistake of thinking that a humorist takes life lightly. James Thurber was one of America's funniest writers, but he felt very deeply about almost everything. The following essay about a poodle is one of Thurber's famous ones. It reveals the serious and tender side of the humorist.

S HE CAME all the way from Illinois by train in a big wooden crate many years ago, a frightened black poodle, not yet a year old. She felt terrible in body and worse in mind. These contraptions that men put on wheels, in contravention of that law of nature which holds that the feet must come in contact with the ground in traveling, dismayed her. She was never able to ride a thousand yards in an automobile without getting sick at her stomach, but she was always apologetic about this frailty, never, as she might well have been, reproachful.

She tried patiently at all times to understand Man's way of life: the rolling of his wheels, the raising of his voice, the ringing of his bells; his way of searching out with lights the dark protecting corners of the night; his habit of building his beds inside walls, high above the nurturing earth. She refused, with all courtesy, to accept his silly notion that it is better to bear puppies in a place made of machined wood and clean blue cloth than in the dark and warm dirt beneath the oak flooring of the barn.

The poodle was hand in glove with natural phenomena. She raised two litters of puppies, taking them in her stride, the way she took the lightning and the snow. One of these litters, which arrived ahead of schedule, was discovered under the barn floor by a little girl of two. The child gaily displayed on her right forearm the almost invisible and entirely painless marks of teeth which had gently induced her to put down the live black toys she had found and wanted to play with.

The poodle had no vices that I can think of, unless you could count her incurable appetite for the tender tips of the young asparagus in the garden and for the black raspberries when they ripened on the bushes in the orchard. Sometimes, as punishment for her depredations,[1] she walked into bees' nests or got her long shaggy ears tangled in fence wire. She never snarled about the penalties of existence or whimpered about the trials and

[1] **depredations** (dep′rə·dā′shənz): robberies.

"Memorial" and the accompanying drawing from *My World — And Welcome to It* by James Thurber, published by Harcourt, Brace & World, Inc., copyright © 1942 by James Thurber. Reprinted by permission of Helen Thurber.

JAMES THURBER   **537**

grotesqueries of life with Man.

She accepted gracefully the indignities of the clipping machine which, in her maiden days, periodically made a clown of her for the dog shows, in accordance with the stupid and unimaginative notion that this most sensitive and dignified of animals is at heart a buffoon. The poodle, which can look as husky as a briard when left shaggy, is an outdoor dog and can hold its own in the field with the best of the retrievers, including the Labrador.

The poodle won a great many ribbons in her bench days, but she would have traded all her medals for a dish of asparagus. She knew it was show time when the red rubber bib was tied around her neck. That meant a ride in a car to bedlam.

Like the great Gammeyer [1] of Tarkington's *Gentle Julia*, the poodle I knew seemed sometimes about to bridge the mysterious and conceivably narrow gap that separates instinct from reason. She could take part in your gaiety and your sorrow; she trembled to your uncertainties and lifted her head at your assurances. There were times when she seemed to come close to a pitying comprehension of the whole troubled scene and what lies behind it. If poodles, who walk so easily upon their hind legs, ever do learn the little tricks of speech and reason, I should not be surprised if they made a better job of it than Man, who would seem to be surely but not slowly slipping back to all fours.

The poodle kept her sight, her hearing, and her figure up to her quiet and dignified end. She knew that the Hand was upon her, and she accepted it with a grave and unapprehensive resignation. This, her dark intelligent eyes seemed to be trying to tell me, is simply the closing of full circle, this is the flower that grows out of Beginning; this — not to make it too hard for you, friend — is as natural as eating the raspberries and raising the puppies and riding into the rain.

THURBER IN A SERIOUS MOOD

1. Why is this essay called "Memorial"?

2. Thurber suggested that his poodle was at the mercy of Man's strange ways of life. How did the poodle's habits and attitudes differ from Man's? Whom does Thurber favor in this essay — his poodle or Man? Point to passages of the story to justify your answer.

3. What was the poodle's only "vice"? Does this "vice" make her seem wicked or more lovable? Explain.

4. What do you think Thurber meant when he said that the poodle "seemed sometimes about to bridge the mysterious and conceivably narrow gap that separates instinct from reason"?

5. Thurber thought that poodles might do a better job of using speech and reason than Man has done. What did he mean? Which of Man's uses of his speech and reason might Thurber have been concerned about?

6. How did the poodle seem to feel about death? Can you explain in your own words the last sentence of the essay?

7. Describe Thurber's attitude toward his patient black poodle. How does this attitude compare with the way he seemed to feel about Muggs? Can you find a reference to the poodle in the opening paragraphs of the story about Muggs?

[1] **Gammeyer:** the name of a remarkable poodle in Booth Tarkington's novel.

The Spreading "You Know"

Because humorists point out man's follies and weaknesses, we often find feelings of bitterness and pessimism in some types of humorous writing. But James Thurber never revealed such feelings. His mood as he looked at man was almost always sympathetic. In this essay, he takes delight in looking at the way man uses and misuses his language.

THE LATEST BLIGHT to afflict the spoken word in the United States is the rapidly spreading reiteration[1] of the phrase "*you* know." I don't know just when it began moving like a rainstorm through the language, but I tremble at its increasing garbling of meaning, ruining of rhythm, and drumming upon my hapless ears. One man, in a phone conversation with me last summer, used the phrase thirty-four times in about five minutes, by my own count; a young matron in Chicago got seven "*you* knows" into one wavy sentence; and I have also heard it as far west as Denver, where an otherwise charming woman at a garden

[1] **reiteration** (rē·it'ə·rā'shən): repetition.

"The Spreading 'You Know'" from *Lanterns and Lances* by James Thurber, Harper & Row, Publishers, copyright © 1961 by James Thurber. Reprinted by permission of Helen Thurber.

party in August said it almost as often as a whippoorwill says, "Whippoorwill." Once, speaking of whippoorwills, I was waked after midnight by one of those feathered hellions and lay there counting his chants. He got up to one hundred and fifty-eight and then suddenly said, "Whip —" and stopped dead. I like to believe that his mate, at the end of her patience, finally let him have it.

My unfortunate tendency to count "*you* knows" is practically making a female whippoorwill out of me. Listening to a radio commentator, not long ago, discussing the recent meeting of the United Nations, I thought I was going mad when I heard him using "you know" as a noun, until I realized that he had shortened United Nations Organization to UNO and was pronouncing it, you know, as if it were "*you* know."

A typical example of speech *you*-knowed to death goes like this: "The other day I saw, you know, Harry Johnson, the, you know, former publicity man for, you know, the Charteriss Publishing Company, and, you know, what he wanted to talk about, strangely enough, was, you know, something you'd never guess. . . ."

This curse may have originated simultaneously on Broadway and in Hollywood, where such curses often originate. About twenty-five years ago, or perhaps longer, theater and movie people jammed their sentences with "you know what I mean?" which was soon shortened to "you *know?*" That had followed the overuse, in the 1920's, of "you see?" or just plain "see?" These blights often disappear finally, but a few have stayed and will continue to stay, such as "Well" and "I mean to say" and "I mean" and "The fact is." Others seem to have mercifully passed out of lingo into limbo, such as, to go back a long way, "twenty-three, skid-doo" and "so's your old man" and "I don't know nothin' from nothin'" and "believe you me." About five years ago both men and women were saying things like "He has a new Cadillac job with a built-in bar deal in the back seat," and in 1958 almost everything anybody mentioned, or even wrote about, was "triggered." Arguments were triggered, and allergies, and divorces, and even love affairs. This gun-and-bomb verb seemed to make the jumpiest of the jumpy even jumpier, but it has almost died out now, and I trust that I have not triggered its revival.

It was in Paris, from late 1918 until early 1920, that there was a glut — an American glut, to be sure — of "You said it" and "You can say that again," and an American marine I knew, from Montana, could not speak any sentence of agreement or concurrence without saying, "It *is*, you *know.*" Fortunately, that perhaps original use of "*you*

know" did not seem to be imported into America.

I am reluctantly making notes for a possible future volume to be called *A Farewell to Speech* or *The Decline and Fall of the King's English.* I hope and pray that I shall not have to write the book. Maybe everything, or at least the language, will clear up before it is too late. Let's face it, it better had, that's for sure, and I don't mean maybe.

LOOKING AT LANGUAGE

1. Is the expression "*you* know" still overused by many persons? What other overworked words and phrases does Thurber mention? Are any of these still in common use?

2. What does Thurber mean when he says (page 539) that his tendency to count "*you* knows" is making a "female whippoorwill" out of him?

3. What is humorous about the last sentence of this essay? At what other points in the essay did Thurber use the very words he was making fun of?

4. What current expressions might be classed with "*you* know" and might have been included in this essay had Thurber written it today?

WORDS: CLICHÉS

In this essay Thurber points out one kind of language habit that garbles meaning. Another bad language habit is the use of overworked expressions, sometimes called clichés. Two commonly used clichés are "white as a sheet," and "a good round of applause." These phrases were effective when they were first used, but constant overuse has worn them out. Can you think of five other clichés?

Tales with a Twist

You have probably read some of Aesop's fables. In these shrewd stories from ancient Greece, animals think and talk like human beings, for the purpose of showing us our weaknesses and funny ways. James Thurber loved to imitate the style of these old fables, and also of fairy tales. In the following selections, he has given new twists to four old tales.

The Little Girl and the Wolf

One afternoon a big wolf waited in a dark forest for a little girl to come along carrying a basket of food to her grandmother. Finally a little girl did come along and she was carrying a basket of food. "Are you carrying that basket to your grandmother?" asked the wolf. The little girl said yes, she was. So the wolf asked her where her grandmother lived and the little girl told him and he disappeared into the wood.

When the little girl opened the door of her grandmother's house she saw that there was somebody in bed with a nightcap and nightgown on. She had approached no nearer than twenty-five feet from the bed when she saw that it was not her grandmother but the wolf, for even in a nightcap a wolf does not look any more like your grandmother than the Metro-Goldwyn lion looks like Calvin Coolidge. So the little girl took an automatic out of her basket and shot the wolf dead.

MORAL: IT IS NOT SO EASY TO FOOL LITTLE GIRLS NOWADAYS AS IT USED TO BE.

The Princess and the Tin Box

Once upon a time, in a far country, there lived a King whose daughter was the prettiest princess in the world. Her eyes were like the cornflower, her hair was sweeter than the hyacinth, and her throat made the swan look dusty.

From the time she was a year old, the Princess had been showered with presents. Her nursery looked like Cartier's [1] window. Her toys were all made of gold or platinum or diamonds or emeralds. She was not permitted to have wooden blocks or china dolls or rubber dogs or linen books, because such materials were considered cheap for the daughter of a King.

When she was seven, she was allowed to attend the wedding of her brother, and throw real pearls at the bride instead of rice. Only the nightingale, with his lyre of gold, was permitted to sing for the Princess. The common blackbird, with his boxwood flute, was kept out of the palace grounds. She walked in silver-and-samite slippers to a sapphire-and-topaz bathroom and slept in an ivory bed inlaid with rubies.

On the day the Princess was eighteen, the King sent a royal ambassador to the courts of five neighboring kingdoms to announce that he would give his daughter's hand in marriage to the prince who brought her the gift she liked the most.

The first prince to arrive at the palace rode a swift white stallion and laid at the feet of the Princess an enormous apple made of solid gold which he had taken from a dragon who had guarded it for a thousand years. It was placed on a long ebony table set up to hold the gifts of the Princess's suitors. The second prince, who came on a gray charger, brought her a nightingale made of a thousand diamonds, and it was placed beside the golden apple. The third prince, riding on a black horse, carried a great jewel box made of platinum and sapphires, and it was placed next to the diamond nightingale. The fourth prince, astride a fiery yellow horse, gave the Princess a gigantic heart made of rubies and pierced by an emerald arrow. It was placed next to the platinum-and-sapphire jewel box.

Now the fifth prince was the strongest and handsomest of all the five suitors, but he was the son of a poor king whose realm had been overrun by mice and locusts and wizards and mining engineers so that there was nothing much of value left in it. He came plodding up to the palace of the Princess on a plow horse and he brought her a small tin box filled with mica and feldspar and hornblende [2] which he had picked up on the way.

The other princes roared with disdainful laughter when they saw the tawdry [3] gift the fifth prince had brought to the Princess. But she examined it with great interest and

---

[1] **Cartier's** (kär'tē-āz): a very expensive jewelry store in New York City.

"The Princess and the Tin Box" from *The Beast in Me and Other Animals* by James Thurber, published by Harcourt, Brace & World, Inc., copyright © 1948 by James Thurber. Reprinted by permission of Helen Thurber.

[2] **mica and feldspar and hornblende:** three kinds of ordinary rock.

[3] **tawdry** (tô'drē): cheap.

squealed with delight, for all her life she had been glutted with precious stones and priceless metals, but she had never seen tin before or mica or feldspar or hornblende. The tin box was placed next to the ruby heart pierced with an emerald arrow.

"Now," the King said to his daughter, "you must select the gift you like best and marry the prince that brought it."

The Princess smiled and walked up to the table and picked up the present she liked the most. It was the platinum-and-sapphire jewel box, the gift of the third prince.

"The way I figure it," she said, "is this. It is a very large and expensive box, and when I am married, I will meet many admirers who will give me precious gems with which to fill it to the top. Therefore, it is the most valuable of all the gifts my suitors have brought me, and I like it the best."

The Princess married the third prince that very day in the midst of great merriment and high revelry. More than a hundred thousand pearls were thrown at her and she loved it.

MORAL: ALL THOSE WHO THOUGHT THAT THE PRINCESS WAS GOING TO SELECT THE TIN BOX FILLED WITH WORTHLESS STONES INSTEAD OF ONE OF THE OTHER GIFTS WILL KINDLY STAY AFTER CLASS AND WRITE ONE HUNDRED TIMES ON THE BLACKBOARD, "I WOULD RATHER HAVE A HUNK OF ALUMINUM SILICATE THAN A DIAMOND NECKLACE."

From *The Beast in Me and Other Animals* by James Thurber, published by Harcourt, Brace & World, Inc., copyright © 1948 by James Thurber. Reprinted by permission of Helen Thurber.

The Tiger Who Would Be King

One morning the tiger woke up in the jungle and told his mate that he was king of beasts.

"Leo, the lion, is king of beasts," she said.

"We need a change," said the tiger. "The creatures are crying for a change."

The tigress listened but she could hear no crying, except that of her cubs.

"I'll be king of beasts by the time the moon rises," said the tiger. "It will be a yellow moon with black stripes, in my honor."

"Oh, sure," said the tigress as she went to look after her young, one of whom, a male, very like his father, had got an imaginary thorn in his paw.

The tiger prowled through the jungle till he came to the lion's den. "Come out," he roared, "and greet the king of beasts! The king is dead, long live the king!"

Inside the den, the lioness woke her mate. "The king is here to see you," she said.

"What king?" he inquired, sleepily.

"The king of beasts," she said.

"I am the king of beasts," roared Leo, and he charged out of the den to defend his crown against the pretender.

It was a terrible fight, and it lasted until the setting of the sun. All the animals of the jungle joined in, some taking the side of the tiger and others the side of the lion. Every creature from the aardvark to the zebra took part in the struggle to overthrow the lion or to repulse the tiger, and some did not know which they were fighting for, and some fought for both, and some fought whoever was nearest, and some fought for the sake of fighting.

"What are we fighting for?" someone asked the aardvark.

"The old order," said the aardvark.

"What are we dying for?" someone asked the zebra.

"The new order," said the zebra.

When the moon rose, fevered and gibbous,[1] it shone upon a jungle in which nothing stirred except a macaw and a cockatoo, screaming in horror. All the beasts were dead except the tiger, and his days were numbered and his time was ticking away. He was monarch of all he surveyed, but it didn't seem to mean anything.

MORAL: YOU CAN'T VERY WELL BE KING OF BEASTS IF THERE AREN'T ANY.

[1] **gibbous** (gib′əs): irregularly rounded because it's not quite full.

"The Tiger Who Would Be King" and the accompanying drawing from *Further Fables for Our Time* by James Thurber, published by Simon and Schuster, Inc., copyright © 1956 by James Thurber. Reprinted by permission of Helen Thurber.

The Kingfisher and the Phoebe

A proud mother phoebe who had raised two broods of fledglings in the fair weather was at first dismayed and then delighted when one of the males of the second brood refused to leave the nest and fly away like the others. "I have raised a remarkable phoebe unlike any other phoebe," the mother bird decided. "He will become a great singer, greater than the nightingale."

She brought in a nightingale to teach her son to sing, and then a catbird, and then a mockingbird, but all the young phoebe could learn to sing was "Phoebe, Phoebe." And so the mother bird sent for Dr. Kingfisher, a bird psychologist, who examined the young phoebe carefully. "This phoebe is a phoebe like any other phoebe," he told the mother. "And all he will ever sing is 'Phoebe, Phoebe.'"

But the ambitious mother did not believe Dr. Kingfisher's prognosis. "Maybe he won't be a great singer, but he will be a great something," she insisted. "He will take the place of the eagle on the dollar or the canary in the gilded cage or the cuckoo in the cuckoo clock. You just wait."

"I'll wait," said Dr. Kingfisher, and he waited. But nothing happened. The phoebe went on being a phoebe and singing "Phoebe, Phoebe" like any other phoebe, and that was all.

MORAL: YOU CAN'T MAKE ANYTHING OUT OF COOKIE DOUGH EXCEPT COOKIES.

PARODY

A parody is a funny imitation of some serious work. When an author writes a parody, he wants to make us laugh, but he also may want to make us think.

1. What famous children's fairy tale did Thurber parody in "The Little Girl and the Wolf"? How does Thurber's story differ from the other one? Do you think Thurber was making fun of modern girls or of old-time stories? Do you agree with the moral of this story?

2. What standard kind of romantic tale was Thurber making fun of in "The Princess and the Tin Box"? In what ways does Thurber's story differ from the others? How did you expect the story to come out? (Would you have had to write on the blackboard?)

3. How did the behavior of the animals in "The Tiger Who Would Be King" remind you of human behavior? What started the jungle war in this fable? What terrible result of modern warfare might Thurber be warning us against?

4. What ambitions did the mother phoebe have for her son? Do people ever behave like this mother phoebe? Do you agree with this moral? Why?

COMPOSITION: WRITING PARODY

Make up a brief modern fable of your own, in which you have animals behave in the way human beings behave. (Perhaps you can have animals as astronauts or as passengers in "flying saucers.") Be sure to conclude your fable with a moral.

Or, are there any styles of writing or any standard plots that you would like to parody? Instead of writing a fable, you might want to write a story in which you imitate the style or the plot of a fairy tale, mystery story, television play, or movie.

Thurber's Cartoons

James Thurber is famous both as a cartoonist and as a writer. When his cartoons were first published in *The New Yorker*, hundreds of mothers sent in samples of their children's work, claiming that a four-year-old's scrawl was as good as Thurber's scribbling. James Thurber had great fun drawing pictures, and he didn't take his art seriously. Some people did, however. Thurber claimed that editors used to ask him if it was true that he drew his pictures under water.

The Hound and the Hat

"The Hound and the Hat" from *Thurber's Dogs* by James Thurber, published by Simon and Schuster, Inc., copyright © 1955 by James Thurber. Reprinted by permission of Helen Thurber.

"I wear it for luck."

"Well, if I called the wrong number, why did you answer the phone?"

WILLIAM
SHAKESPEARE
1564–1616

Almost everyone who visits England wants to see a small town northwest of London called Stratford-on-Avon, for Stratford-on-Avon is the birthplace of William Shakespeare. Here the visitor will see the house where Shakespeare was born; he will visit the old church where Shakespeare is buried; and he will, no doubt, stand in line at the Shakespeare Memorial Theater, built on the banks of the Avon River, hoping to get a ticket for a performance of one of Shakespeare's famous plays.

But Shakespeare did not stay long in his quiet home town. In his twenties he went to London, and after a time he joined a famous company of actors there. He was not a star actor; his lasting fame rests upon the plays that he wrote for this acting company — a great series of comedies, tragedies, and historic dramas. These plays are so great that they are still being acted all over the world.

Shakespeare began to write in the later years of the reign of Queen Elizabeth I, who died in 1603, but most of his greatest work was done during the reign of her successor, James I. In those days, London theaters attracted all kinds of people. Londoners would go to plays as eagerly as modern Americans flock to baseball or football games.

Shakespeare's plays were especially popular for various reasons. For one thing, Shakespeare wrote in magnificent language. The speeches of his characters gave audiences the same kind of thrill as audiences today feel on hearing popular singing groups. Moreover, of all the writers in the English language, Shakespeare had the greatest power to create living characters, men and women of all kinds and classes. His plays also have a unique kind of vitality; at each rereading they reveal new depths and meanings. Their colors never fade.

A Father's Advice to His Son

In Shakespeare's play *Hamlet,* a young man, Laertes, is about to leave home to go to France. Before the young man leaves, his father, Polonius, gives him this advice. These lines are from Act I, Scene iii, of *Hamlet.*

> . . . Give thy thoughts no tongue,
> Nor any unproportioned° thought his act.
> Be thou familiar, but by no means vulgar.
> Those friends thou hast, and their adoption tried,
> Grapple them to thy soul with hoops of steel,   5
> But do not dull thy palm with entertainment
> Of each new-hatched unfledged comrade. Beware
> Of entrance to a quarrel, but being in,
> Bear't that the opposed may beware of thee.
> Give every man thy ear, but few thy voice.   10
> Take each man's censure,° but reserve thy judgment.
> Costly thy habit as thy purse can buy,
> But not expressed in fancy — rich, not gaudy.
> For the apparel oft proclaims the man . . .
> Neither a borrower nor a lender be,   15
> For loan oft loses both itself and friend
> And borrowing dulls the edge of husbandry.°
> This above all: To thine own self be true,
> And it must follow, as the night the day,
> Thou canst not then be false to any man.   20

2. **unproportioned:** unsuitable. 11. **censure** (sen'shər): criticism or opinion. 17. **husbandry:** careful management of one's household; thrift.

ADVICE

1. This son was going away to a strange foreign city. What does his father tell him about making friends?

2. In lines 7–9, the son hears some advice about quarreling. What is he told?

3. What is the son told about clothes?

4. In line 16, the father says, a "loan oft loses both itself and friend." What do you think he means?

5. What basic philosophy does the father share with his son in the last three lines? How could someone be false to himself? (Have you read the story on page 144?)

A PARAPHRASE

"Don't tell what you're thinking!" This is how the father's first suggestion might be said in modern American English. Paraphrase, or express in your own words, the rest of his advice. What words would you use in place of *thou, hast, oft, thine,* and *canst?* How would you spell *bear't* (line 9)?

Above, a view of the Globe, the theater owned by Shakespeare and his friends. Note the spectators crowding to get in. Below, from left to right, stand some of Shakespeare's characters: King Henry V; the sharp-tongued Mistress Quickly; the brooding Prince Hamlet; Polonius; Juliet; and the Roman Coriolanus. Elizabethan audiences loved lavish costumes like these.

Good Name

In Shakespeare's tragedy called *Othello*, we see the terrible danger of jealousy and the harm that can come from gossip. Here, one of Shakespeare's characters, Iago, speaks some now-famous words about a good name. These lines come from Act III, Scene iii, of *Othello*.

Good name in man and woman . . .
Is the immediate jewel of their souls.
Who steals my purse steals trash — 'tis something, nothing,
'Twas mine, 'tis his, and has been slave to thousands —
But he that filches from me my good name
Robs me of that which not enriches him
And makes me poor indeed.

AN OBSERVATION

1. These lines are about a "good name." Can you define *name* as it is used here?

2. What is a good name compared to?

3. According to this speaker, why is it worse to lose a good name than to lose money? Do you agree with him? Why?

4. How can a good name be "filched," or stolen? Tell, for example, how gossip can ruin a good name.

5. Can you express line 6 in your own words?

6. Do you think a good name is precious? Why?

WORD DERIVATIONS

In the sixteenth century, a *filch* was a staff with a hook on the end, and in that day people used *filch* as a slang word meaning "to steal with a filch." In "Good Name," therefore, Shakespeare was using a slang word of his day. *Filch* is now an acceptable word, still meaning "to steal." Some other synonyms for the word *steal* are *pilfer, purloin, lift, swipe,* and *pinch.* The last three words are considered to be slang words at the present time. Can you guess at the origins of the three slang words?

READING SHAKESPEARE'S POETRY

Most of the lines in Shakespeare's plays, like the lines you have just read from *Othello* and *Hamlet*, are written in poetry. However, the last words in Shakespeare's lines usually do not rhyme. But in Shakespeare's poetry you *will* find a regular rhythm, and each line has been written with a certain number of heavily accented syllables. Notice, for example, that each line of the speech from *Hamlet* has five heavily accented syllables.

"Those friends thou hast, and their
     adoption tried,
   Grapple them to thy soul with hoops
     of steel"

Read aloud the speech from *Othello* and the one from *Hamlet* (page 550). After two or three readings, you should be able to feel the regular rhythm of the lines. When you read these lines aloud, do not read them as if you were reading prose, which is written without a regular rhythm. On the other hand, do not over-stress the rhythm, so that the effect is singsong.

Sonnet 71

No longer mourn for me when I am dead
Than you shall hear the surly sullen bell
Give warning to the world that I am fled
From this vile world, with vilest worms to dwell.

Nay, if you read this line, remember not   5
The hand that writ it, for I love you so
That I in your sweet thoughts would be forgot
If thinking on me then should make you woe.

Oh, if, I say, you look upon this verse
When I perhaps compounded am with clay,   10
Do not so much as my poor name rehearse,
But let your love even with my life decay,

Lest the wise world should look into your moan,
And mock you with me after I am gone.

A LOVE SONNET

Shakespeare wrote one hundred fifty-four sonnets, and among them are some of the best of the world's love poems. Sonnets are a special form of poetry, consisting always of fourteen lines.

1. In lines 1–4 of this sonnet, how long does the poet say his love should mourn for him? In lines 5–6, what request does he make about the lover's reading of the poem itself? How do lines 6–8 explain the requests in lines 1–6? Shakespeare hopes his lover will let her love die when he is dead. What lines tell you this?

2. Shakespeare always ended his sonnets with two rhyming lines, called a couplet. Restate in your own words the couplet that ends this sonnet.

WORD CHOICE

A great poet is able to use just the right combination of words to make his readers feel certain emotions.

In line 2 Shakespeare talks about a bell that will toll his death. Why does he call the bell "surly" and "sullen"? What do you think his purpose may have been in using the terms "vile world" and "vilest worms" in line 4? What emotion might the poet have aroused in his love by referring, in line 10, to his being "compounded . . . with clay"? What feeling for himself does he reveal in saying "my poor name" in line 11? Do you think he is sincere when he calls the world "wise," in line 13?

SENTENCES: A TIDY PLAN

This sonnet is made up of three sentences. The first four lines contain a single sentence. Can you find the second and third sentences of the sonnet? Which sentence, would you say, is the topic sentence of the sonnet, giving the main thought? What supporting ideas are provided by the other two sentences in the sonnet?

Advice to Actors

Not only was Shakespeare the most successful playwright of his time, but he was also a professional actor. In this speech from *Hamlet,* Act III, Scene ii, Shakespeare has his main character, a young intellectual named Hamlet, make the following remarks to a group of actors.

Speak the speech, I pray you, as I pronounced it to you, trippingly on the tongue. But if you mouth [1] it, as many of your players do, I had as lief [2] the town crier spoke my lines. Nor do not saw the air too much with your hand, thus, but use all gently. For in the very torrent, tempest, and, as I may say, whirlwind of passion, you must acquire and beget a temperance [3] that may give it smoothness. . . .

Be not too tame neither, but let your own discretion be your tutor. Suit the action to the word, the word to the action, with this special observance: that you o'erstep not the modesty of nature. For anything so overdone is from [4] the purpose of playing, whose end, both at the first and now, was and is to hold as 'twere the mirror up to Nature . . .

. . . And let those that play your clowns speak no more than is set down for them. For there be of them that will themselves laugh, to set on some quantity of barren spectators to laugh too, though in the meantime some necessary question of the play be then to be considered. That's villainous, and shows a most pitiful ambition in the fool that uses it. . . .

[1] **mouth:** ham.
[2] **lief:** soon.
[3] **temperance:** restraint.
[4] **from:** contrary to.

A LESSON IN ACTING

1. What does Hamlet mean when he tells the players to speak their lines "trippingly"? How do you think an actor would "mouth," or ham, a speech?

2. The verb *saw* in the third sentence means to cut or slice the air, with a motion like that of a saw. What do you think Hamlet is doing as he says this sentence?

3. In his second group of instructions, what does Hamlet say is the purpose of "playing," or acting? What do you think he means by the "modesty" of nature?

4. In Shakespeare's day, most plays included comic parts for clowns or fools. What warning does Hamlet give to the clowns, or to other actors with humorous lines? What are "barren spectators"?

5. Have you ever seen a movie or a television show in which actors violated Hamlet's advice on acting?

6. Some people do not believe that Shakespeare himself agreed with all that Hamlet says about acting. Do you agree with all of Hamlet's advice?

Pyramus and Thisby

FROM *A Midsummer Night's Dream*

Shakespeare's play *A Midsummer Night's Dream* is a remarkable mixture of dreamlike romance and hilarious comedy. The comedy in the play comes in the scenes in which a group of workingmen appear. These men have volunteered to present a play to help celebrate the wedding of their ruler, Theseus, the Duke of Athens. The men can hardly read or write. They have much difficulty figuring out the meaning of their lines and even more trouble in memorizing them. To make their scenes even funnier, Shakespeare has these men take themselves very seriously, and they have decided to dramatize a serious tragic story that was well known to theatergoers of Shakespeare's day — a tale of two young lovers named Pyramus and Thisby. The workingmen's bumbling efforts result in a play that has brought laughs to theatergoers for hundreds of years.

Characters

PETER QUINCE, *a carpenter, the director of the play, who also delivers the* PROLOGUE

NICK BOTTOM, *a weaver, who takes the part of the lover* PYRAMUS

FRANCIS FLUTE, *a bellows mender, who takes the part of* THISBY, *the beautiful and tragic heroine*

ROBIN STARVELING, *a tailor, who presents* MOONSHINE

TOM SNOUT, *a tinker, who plays the* WALL

SNUG, *a joiner, or cabinetmaker, who plays the* LION

THESEUS, *the Duke of Athens, in whose honor the play is presented*

HIPPOLYTA, *the bride of Theseus*

PHILOSTRATE, *an entertainment director at the palace*

COURTIERS (2) *and their* LADIES

ATTENDANTS *on Theseus and Hippolyta*

This is the first meeting of the workingmen who have decided to give a play in honor of the Duke's marriage. These amateur actors, as you will see, are all prepared to work hard — especially Bottom. Watch Bottom carefully! He loves long words but usually uses them in the wrong ways. As would be expected, he bosses everyone around, including Quince, the director of the play.

But let us look in on these would-be actors as Quince calls them together to assign parts.

[*The setting is the house of* QUINCE. *Enter* QUINCE, SNUG, BOTTOM, FLUTE, SNOUT, *and* STARVELING.]

QUINCE. Is all our company here?

BOTTOM. You were best to call them generally,[1] man by man, according to the script.

QUINCE. Here is the scroll of every man's name which is thought fit, through all Athens, to play in our interlude[2] before the Duke and the Duchess on his wedding day at night.

BOTTOM. First, good Peter Quince, say what the play treats on, then read the names of the actors, and so grow to a point.

QUINCE. Marry, our play is *The Most Lamentable Comedy and Most Cruel Death of Pyramus and Thisby.*

BOTTOM. A very good piece of work, I assure you, and a merry. Now, good Peter Quince, call forth your actors by the scroll. Masters, spread yourselves.

QUINCE. Answer as I call you. Nick Bottom, the weaver.

BOTTOM. Ready. Name what part I am for, and proceed.

QUINCE. You, Nick Bottom, are set down for Pyramus.

BOTTOM. What is Pyramus? A lover, or a tyrant?

QUINCE. A lover, that kills himself most gallant for love.

BOTTOM. That will ask some tears in the true performing of it. If I do it, let the audience look to their eyes! I will move storms, I will condole[3] in some measure. To the rest . . .

QUINCE. Francis Flute, the bellows mender.

FLUTE. Here, Peter Quince.

QUINCE. Flute, you must take Thisby on you.

FLUTE. What is Thisby? A wandering knight?

QUINCE. It is the lady that Pyramus must love.

---

[1] **generally:** Bottom gets his words wrong. He means *separately.*
[2] **interlude:** play.
[3] **condole:** This word means "to sympathize with." Bottom means *lament* or *weep.*

FLUTE. Nay, faith, let not me play a woman! I have a beard coming.

QUINCE. That's all one. You shall play it in a mask, and you may speak as small as you will.

BOTTOM. If I may hide my face, let me play Thisby too. I'll speak in a monstrous little voice, "Thisne, Thisne." "Ah Pyramus, my lover dear! Thy Thisby dear, and lady dear!"

QUINCE. No, no! You must play Pyramus, and Flute, you Thisby.

BOTTOM. Well, proceed.

QUINCE. Robin Starveling, the tailor.

STARVELING. Here, Peter Quince.

QUINCE. Robin Starveling, you must play Thisby's mother. Tom Snout, the tinker.

SNOUT. Here, Peter Quince.

QUINCE. You, Pyramus' father. Myself, Thisby's father. Snug, the joiner, you the lion's part. And, I hope, here is a play fitted.

SNUG. Have you the lion's part written? Pray you, if it be, give it me, for I am slow of study.

QUINCE. You may do it extempore,[1] for it is nothing but roaring.

BOTTOM. Let me play the lion too. I will roar so that I will do any man's heart good to hear me; I will roar so that I will make the Duke say, "Let him roar again! Let him roar again!"

QUINCE. If you should do it too terribly, you would fright the Duchess and the ladies, that they would shriek; and that were enough to hang us all.

ALL. That would hang us, every mother's son.

BOTTOM. I grant you, friends, if you should fright the ladies out of their wits, they would have no more discretion but to hang us; but I will aggravate[2] my voice so that I will roar you as gently as any sucking dove, I will roar you as if it were any nightingale.

QUINCE. You can play no part but Pyramus; for Pyramus is a sweet-faced man, a proper man as one shall see in a summer's day, a most lovely gentlemanlike man. Therefore you must needs play Pyramus.

BOTTOM. Well, I will undertake it. What beard were I best to play it in?

QUINCE. Why, what you will.

BOTTOM. I will discharge it in either your straw-color beard, your orange-tawny beard, your purple-in-grain[3] beard, or your French-crown-color beard, your perfect yellow.

QUINCE. Masters, here are your parts. And I am to entreat you, request you, and desire you, to know them by tomorrow night; and meet

---

[1] **extempore** (ik·stem'pə·rē); without preparation.
[2] **aggravate**: instead of *moderate* or *soften*.
[3] **purple-in-grain**: dyed purple.

me in the palace wood, a mile without the town, by moonlight. There will we rehearse, for if we meet in the city, we shall be dogged with company, and our devices known. In the meantime I will draw a bill of properties, such as our play wants. I pray you, fail me not.

BOTTOM. We will meet, and there we may rehearse most obscenely [1] and courageously. Take pains, be perfect. Adieu.

QUINCE. At the Duke's oak we meet.

[*Exit.*]

SCENE 2

[*The setting is a wood, near Athens. Enter* QUINCE, SNUG, BOTTOM, FLUTE, SNOUT, *and* STARVELING.]

BOTTOM. Are we all met?

QUINCE. Pat,[2] pat, and here's a marvelous convenient place for our rehearsal. This green plot shall be our stage, this hawthorn brake [3] our dressing room; and we will do it in action as we will do it before the Duke.

BOTTOM. Peter Quince ——

QUINCE. What sayest thou, bully Bottom?

BOTTOM. There are things in this comedy of Pyramus and Thisby that will never please. First, Pyramus must draw a sword to kill himself, which the ladies cannot abide. How answer you that?

SNOUT. By'r lakin, a parlous [4] fear!

---

[1] **obscenely:** instead of *obscurely.*
[2] **pat:** exactly, right on time.
[3] **hawthorn brake:** thicket (brake) of hawthorn bushes.
[4] **parlous:** an old-fashioned way of saying *perilous.*

STARVELING. I believe we must leave the killing out, when all is done.

BOTTOM. Not a whit. I have a device to make all well. Write me a prologue, and let the prologue seem to say we will do no harm with our swords, and that Pyramus is not killed indeed. And, for the more better assurance, tell them that I, Pyramus, am not Pyramus, but Bottom, the weaver. This will put them out of fear.

QUINCE. Well, we will have such a prologue, and it shall be written in eight and six.[1]

BOTTOM. No, make it two more. Let it be written in eight and eight.

SNOUT. Will not the ladies be afeard of the lion?

STARVELING. I fear it, I promise you.

BOTTOM. Masters, you ought to consider with yourselves. To bring in — God shield us — a lion among ladies is a most dreadful thing; for there is not a more fearful wild fowl than your lion living, and we ought to look to't.

SNOUT. Therefore another prologue must tell he is not a lion.

BOTTOM. Nay, you must name his name, and half his face must be seen through the lion's neck. And he himself must speak through, saying thus, or to the same defect — "Ladies" — or "Fair ladies — I would wish you" — or "I would request you" — or "I would entreat you — not to fear, not to tremble. My life for yours. If you think I come hither as a lion, it were pity of my life. No, I am no such thing, I am a man as other men are." And there indeed let him name his name and tell them plainly he is Snug, the joiner.

QUINCE. Well, it shall be so. But there is two hard things: that is, to bring the moonlight into a chamber, for, you know, Pyramus and Thisby meet by moonlight.

SNOUT. Doth the moon shine that night we play our play?

BOTTOM. A calendar, a calendar! Look in the almanac. Find out moonshine, find out moonshine!

QUINCE. Yes, it doth shine that night.

BOTTOM. Why, then may you leave a casement [2] of the great-chamber window, where we play, open, and the moon may shine in at the casement.

QUINCE. Aye, or else one must come in with a bush of thorns and a lantern [3] and say he comes to disfigure, or to present, the person of moonshine. Then, there is another thing. We must have a wall in the great chamber, for Pyramus and Thisby, says the story, did talk through the chink of a wall.

---

[1] **eight and six:** a common way in which ballads were written, using alternate lines of eight and six syllables.

[2] **casement:** hinged window.

[3] **bush . . . lantern:** supposedly carried by the man in the moon.

WILLIAM SHAKESPEARE   559

SNOUT. You can never bring in a wall. What say you, Bottom?

BOTTOM. Some man or other must present wall. And let him have some
plaster, or some loam, or some roughcast about him, to signify
wall. And let him hold his fingers thus, and through that cranny
shall Pyramus and Thisby whisper.

QUINCE. If that may be, then all is well. Come, sit down, every mother's
son, and rehearse your parts. Pyramus, you begin. When you
have spoken your speech, enter into that brake. And so everyone
according to his cue. Speak, Pyramus. Thisby, stand forth.

PYRAMUS [BOTTOM].
"Thisby, the flowers of odious savors sweet ——"

QUINCE. Odorous, odorous.

PYRAMUS [BOTTOM].
"—— odors savors sweet.
So hath thy breath, my dearest Thisby dear.
But hark, a voice! Stay thou but here awhile,
And by and by I will to thee appear."

[*Exit* PYRAMUS.]

FLUTE. Must I speak now?

QUINCE. Aye, marry must you, for you must understand he goes but to
see a noise that he heard, and is to come again.

THISBY [FLUTE].
"Most radiant Pyramus, most lily-white of hue,
Of color like the red rose on triumphant brier,
Most briskly juvenal,[1] and eke[2] most lovely too,
As true as truest horse, that yet would never tire,
I'll meet thee, Pyramus, at Ninny's tomb."

QUINCE. "Ninus's tomb," man. Why, you must not speak that yet. That
you answer to Pyramus. You speak all your part at once, cues
and all. Pyramus enter. Your cue is past. It is "never tire."

THISBY [FLUTE]. Oh —
"As true as truest horse, that yet would never tire."

*At this point in the proceedings, the rehearsal is broken up, and the
players scatter. We next meet our actor friends on their big night, when
the play — without benefit of even one more rehearsal — goes on the
boards before the Duke and his court. Bottom has warned the players
to eat no onion or garlic, for he wants to present a "sweet comedy" for
the Duke.*

---

[1] **juvenal**: youthful.
[2] **eke**: also.

SCENE 3

[The setting is a section of one of the rooms in the palace of THESEUS.
*The stage is bare except for several chairs placed to one side. As the
curtain opens,* THESEUS *enters with* HIPPOLYTA, *his bride,* PHILO-
STRATE, *two* COURTIERS *and their* LADIES, *and* ATTENDANTS. *They are
talking as they enter.]*

THESEUS.

     Where is our usual manager of mirth?
     What revels are in hand? Is there no play?
     Call Philostrate!

PHILOSTRATE *(stepping forward).*

               Here, mighty Theseus.

THESEUS.

     Say, what abridgement [1] have you for this evening?
     What masque? What music? How shall we beguile
     The lazy time, if not with some delight?

PHILOSTRATE *(having read the workingmen's play).*

     A play there is, my lord, some ten words long,
     Which is brief as I have known a play.
     But by ten words, my lord, it is too long,
     Which makes it tedious; for in all the play
     There is not one word apt, one player fitted.
     And tragical, my noble lord, it is,
     For Pyramus therein doth kill himself.
     Which, when I saw rehearsed, I must confess,

---

[1] **abridgment:** entertainment (to abridge, or shorten, the evening).

Made mine eyes water, but more merry tears
The passion of loud laughter never shed.

THESEUS (*becoming interested in the idea*). What are they that do
   play it?

PHILOSTRATE (*trying to discourage* THESEUS).
   Hard-handed men that work in Athens here,
   Which never labored in their minds till now,
   And now have toiled their unbreathed [1] memories
   With this same play, against [2] your nuptial.

THESEUS. And we will hear it.

PHILOSTRATE.
                   No, my noble lord,
   It is not for you; I have heard it over,
   And it is nothing, nothing in the world —
   Unless you can find sport in their intents,
   Extremely stretched [3] and learned with cruel pain,
   To do you service.

THESEUS.
              I will hear that play,
   For never anything can be amiss,
   When simpleness and duty tender it.
   Go, bring them in, and take your places, ladies.

[*Exit* PHILOSTRATE. *As* PHILOSTRATE *leaves to get the players,* THESEUS
*and the others go to the side of the stage and arrange themselves on
the side as an "audience."*]

HIPPOLYTA (*objecting mildly to* THESEUS's *decision*).
   He says they can do nothing in this kind.

THESEUS.
   The kinder we, to give them thanks for nothing.
   Our sport shall be to take what they mistake.

[*Re-enter* PHILOSTRATE.]

PHILOSTRATE. So please your Grace, the Prologue is addressed.

THESEUS. Let him approach.

[*Flourish of trumpets. Enter* QUINCE *for the* PROLOGUE.]

PROLOGUE [QUINCE] (*nervous and mixed up. He pays no attention to
     punctuation marks, and the meaning of the Prologue comes out
     garbled.*)

---

[1] **unbreathed**: unexercised.
[2] **against**: in anticipation of.
[3] The workingmen overreached (stretched) themselves.

"If we offend, it is with our good will.
That you should think, we come not to offend,
But with good will. To show our simple skill,
That is the true beginning of our end.
Consider, then, we come but in despite.[1]
We do not come, as minding to content you,
Our true intent is. All for your delight,
We are not here. That you should here repent you,
The actors are at hand, and, by their show,
You shall know all, that you are like to know."

THESEUS. This fellow does not stand upon points.[2]

FIRST COURTIER. He hath rid his prologue like a rough colt, he knows not
the stop. A good moral, my lord. It is not enough to speak, but
to speak true.

HIPPOLYTA. Indeed he hath played on his prologue like a child on a recorder — a sound, but not in control.

THESEUS. His speech was like a tangled chain — nothing impaired, but
all disordered. Who is next?

[*Enter* PYRAMUS *and* THISBY, *followed by* WALL, MOONSHINE, *and* LION.
*As each player is introduced, he steps forward and makes some kind
of self-conscious or exaggerated bit of action, ending with a bow to
the noble audience.*]

PROLOGUE [QUINCE].
"Gentles, perchance you wonder at this show,
But wonder on, till truth makes all things plain.
This man is Pyramus, if you would know.
This beauteous lady, Thisby is certain.
This man, with lime and roughcast, doth present
Wall, that vile Wall which did these lovers sunder,[3]
And through Wall's chink, poor souls, they are content
To whisper. At the which let no man wonder.
This man, with lantern, dog, and bush of thorn,
Presenteth Moonshine; for, if you will know,
By moonshine did these lovers think no scorn
To meet at Ninus's tomb, there, there to woo.
This grisly beast, which Lion hight [4] by name,
The trusty Thisby, coming first by night,
Did scare away, or rather did affright.

---

1 **despite:** ill will.
2 **stand upon points:** pay attention to punctuation marks.
3 **sunder:** separate.
4 **hight:** is called.

And, as she fled, her mantle she did fall,
Which Lion vile with bloody mouth did stain.
Anon comes Pyramus, sweet youth and tall,
And finds his trusty Thisby's mantle slain.
Whereat, with blade, with bloody blameful blade,
He bravely broached his boiling bloody breast.
And Thisby, tarrying in mulberry shade,
His dagger drew, and died. For all the rest,
Let Lion, Moonshine, Wall, and lovers twain
At large discourse, while here they do remain."

[*Exit* PROLOGUE, PYRAMUS, THISBY, LION, *and* MOONSHINE.]

THESEUS. I wonder if the lion be to speak.
SECOND COURTIER. No wonder, my Lord. One lion may, when many
    asses do.
WALL [SNOUT].
    "In this same interlude it doth befall
    That I, one Snout by name, present a wall,
    And such a wall, as I would have you think,
    That had in it a crannied hole or chink,
    Through which the lovers, Pyramus and Thisby,
    Did often whisper very secretly.
    This loam, this roughcast, and this stone doth show
    That I am that same wall. The truth is so.
         [*Whispers through chink*]
    And this the cranny is, right and sinister,[1]
    Through which the fearful lovers are to whisper."
THESEUS. Would you desire lime and hair to speak better?
SECOND COURTIER. It is the wittiest partition that I ever heard discourse,
    my lord.
THESEUS. Pyramus draws near the wall! Silence!

[PYRAMUS *re-enters.* BOTTOM *is strutting, conscious that he is the hero.*]

PYRAMUS [BOTTOM].
    "O grim-looked night! O night with hue so black!
    O night, which ever art when day is not!
    O night, O night! Alack, alack, alack,
    I fear my Thisby's promise is forgot!
    And thou, O Wall, O sweet, O lovely Wall,
    That stand'st between her father's ground and mine!

[1] **sinister:** left (rarely used this way today).

Thou Wall, O Wall, O sweet and lovely Wall,
Show me thy chink, to blink through with mine eyne!"
        [WALL *holds up his fingers.*]
Thanks, courteous Wall. Jove shield thee well for this!
"But what see I? No Thisby do I see.
O wicked Wall, through whom I see no bliss!
Cursed be thy stones for thus deceiving me!"
THESEUS. The wall, methinks, being sensible, should curse again.

[BOTTOM *is afraid* THESEUS *does not understand, so he drops out of
character and addresses* THESEUS *very seriously.*]

BOTTOM. No, in truth, sir, he should not. "Deceiving me" is Thisby's cue.
     She is to enter now, and I am to spy her through the wall. You
     shall see, it will fall pat as I told you. Yonder she comes.

        [THISBY *re-enters, on the other side of* WALL.]

THISBY [FLUTE].
     "O Wall, full often hast thou heard my moans,
     For parting my fair Pyramus and me!
     My cherry lips have often kissed thy stones,
     Thy stones with lime and hair knit up in thee."
PYRAMUS [BOTTOM].
     "I see a voice. Now will I to the chink,
     To spy if I can hear my Thisby's face.
     Thisby!"
THISBY [FLUTE].
     "My love thou art, my love I think."
PYRAMUS [BOTTOM].
     "Think what thou wilt, I am thy lover's grace;

And, like Limander,[1] am I trusty still."

THISBY [FLUTE].

"And I, like Helen,[2] till the Fates[3] me kill."

PYRAMUS [BOTTOM].

"Oh, kiss me through the hole of this vile wall!"

THISBY [FLUTE].

"I kiss the wall's hole, not your lips at all."

PYRAMUS [BOTTOM].

"Wilt thou at Ninny's tomb meet me straightway?"

THISBY [FLUTE].

" 'Tide life, 'tide death, I come without delay."

[*Exit* PYRAMUS *and* THISBY.]

WALL [SNOUT].

"Thus have I, Wall, my part dischargèd so;
And, being done, thus Wall away doth go."

[*Exit* WALL.]

THESEUS. Now is the mural down between the two neighbors.

SECOND COURTIER. No remedy, my lord, when walls are so willful to hear without warning.

HIPPOLYTA. This is the silliest stuff that I ever heard.

THESEUS. The best in this kind are but shadows, and the worst are no worse if imagination amend them.

HIPPOLYTA. It must be your imagination then, and not theirs.

THESEUS. If we imagine no worse of them than they of themselves, they may pass for excellent men. Here come two noble beasts in, a man and a lion.

[*Re-enter* LION *and* MOONSHINE.]

LION [SNUG].

"You, ladies, you, whose gentle hearts do fear
The smallest monstrous mouse that creeps on floor,
May now perchance both quake and tremble here,
When Lion rough in wildest rage doth roar.
Then know that I, one Snug, the joiner, am
A lion fell,[4] nor else no lion's dam;
For, if I should as Lion come in strife
Into this place, 'twere pity on my life."

---

[1] **Limander:** instead of *Leander*, a legendary Greek lover.
[2] **Helen:** instead of *Hero*, Leander's love. Helen was in another legend.
[3] **Fates:** in Greek mythology, three goddesses said to control the future.
[4] **fell:** fierce.

THESEUS. A very gentle beast, and of a good conscience.

SECOND COURTIER. The very best at a beast, my lord, that e'er I saw.

FIRST COURTIER. This lion is a very fox for his valor.

MOONSHINE [STARVELING].
"This lantern doth the hornèd moon present,
Myself the man in the moon do seem to be."

THESEUS. This is the greatest error of all the rest.
The man should be put into the lantern. How is it else the man
in the moon?

FIRST COURTIER. Proceed, Moon.

STARVELING (*dropping out of character*). All that I have to say is to tell
you that the lantern is the moon; I, the man in the moon; this
thornbush, my thornbush; and this dog, my dog.

SECOND COURTIER. Why, all these should be in the lantern, for all these
are in the moon. But silence! Here comes Thisby.

[*Re-enter* THISBY.]

THISBY [FLUTE].
"This is old Ninny's tomb. Where is my love?"

LION [SNUG] (*roaring*). "Oh! —— "

[THISBY *runs off.*]

SECOND COURTIER. Well roared, Lion!

THESEUS. Well run, Thisby!

HIPPOLYTA. Well shone, Moon! Truly, the moon shines with a good
grace.

[LION *shakes* THISBY's *mantle and exits.*]

THESEUS. Well moused, Lion!

FIRST COURTIER. And so the lion vanished.

SECOND COURTIER. And then came Pyramus.

[*Re-enter* PYRAMUS.]

PYRAMUS [BOTTOM].
"Sweet Moon, I thank thee for thy sunny beams,
I thank thee, Moon, for shining now so bright.
For, by thy gracious, golden, glittering gleams,
I trust to take of truest Thisby sight.
    But stay! Oh spite!
    But mark, poor knight!

What dreadful dole [1] is here!
Eyes, do you see?
How can it be?
Oh dainty duck! Oh dear!
Thy mantle good,
What, stained with blood!
Approach, ye Furies fell! [2]
O Fates, come, come,
Cut thread and thrum [3]
Quail, crush, conclude, and quell!"

THESEUS. This passion, and the death of a dear friend, would go near to make a man look sad.

HIPPOLYTA. Beshrew my heart, but I pity the man.

PYRAMUS [BOTTOM].

"O wherefore, Nature, didst thou lions frame?
Since Lion vile hath here deflowered my dear,
Which is — no, no — which was the fairest dame
That lived, that loved, that liked, that looked with cheer.
      Come, tears, confound!
      Out, sword, and wound
      The pap [4] of Pyramus.
      Aye, that left pap,
      Where heart doth hop.
            [*Stabs himself.*]
Thus die I, thus, thus, thus.
      Now am I dead,
      Now am I fled,
      My soul is in the sky.
      Tongue, lose thy light,
      Moon, take thy flight,
            [*Exit* MOONSHINE.]
Now die, die, die, die, die."
            [PYRAMUS *dies.*]

THESEUS. With the help of a surgeon he might yet recover, and prove an ass.

HIPPOLYTA. How chance Moonshine is gone before Thisby comes back and finds her lover?

---

1 **dole:** grief.
2 **Furies fell:** In Greek mythology, the Furies avenged unpunished crimes.
3 **thrum:** the very end of the thread. In other words, "destroy everything."
4 **pap:** breast.

THESEUS. She will find him by starlight. Here she comes, and her passion ends the play.

[*Re-enter* THISBY.]

HIPPOLYTA. Methinks she should not use a long one for such a Pyramus. I hope she will be brief.

THISBY [FLUTE].
        "Asleep, my love?
        What, dead, my dove?
        O Pyramus, arise!
        Speak, speak. Quite dumb?
        Dead, dead? A tomb
        Must cover thy sweet eyes.
        These lily lips,
        This cherry nose,
        These yellow cowslip cheeks,
        Are gone, are gone.
        Lovers, make moan.
        His eyes were green as leeks.[1]
        O Sisters Three,[2]
        Come, come to me,
        With hands as pale as milk;
        Lay them in gore,
        Since you have shore
        With shears his thread of silk.

[1] **leeks:** a type of herb, like an onion.
[2] **Sisters Three:** the three Fates, who spin the threads of each man's destiny.

Tongue, not a word.
Come, trusty sword,
Come, blade, my breast imbrue! [1]
[THISBY *stabs herself.*]
And, farewell, friends.
Thus Thisby ends.
Adieu, adieu, adieu!"
[THISBY *dies.*]

THESEUS. Moonshine and Lion are left to bury the dead.

SECOND COURTIER. Aye, and Wall too.

BOTTOM (*starting up*). No, I assure you; the wall is down that parted their fathers. Will it please you to see the epilogue?

THESEUS. No epilogue, I pray you, for your play needs not excuse. Never excuse, for when the players are all dead, there need none to be blamed. Marry, if he that writ it had played Pyramus and hanged himself in Thisby's garter, it would have been a fine tragedy. And so it is, truly, and very notably discharged.

[The End]

---

[1] **imbrue:** drench with blood.

SHAKESPEARE'S COMEDY

Comedy of Character. Bottom is one of Shakespeare's great comic characters. While the other workingmen are also humorous, Bottom dominates all the scenes with his blunders in language and with his great self-satisfaction.

1. Bottom has ideas on almost any subject or problem that comes up. Which speeches show this?

2. What fears does Bottom express about the audience's reaction to certain parts of the play? What is humorous about Bottom's solutions to these problems?

3. How do the other workingmen react to Bottom?

4. These workingmen are simple and uneducated. The story of Pyramus and Thisby comes from a legend told by a famous Roman writer. What is amusing about the workingmen dramatizing this particular legend?

5. How do the various members of the audience react to the production when it is finally staged?

6. Shakespeare has made up some amusing names for his workingmen. How do the names Bottom, Flute, Starveling, Snout, and Snug suit these characters?

Parody. Humorists often poke fun at certain styles of writing to make us laugh. In this play, Shakespeare makes fun of certain aspects of the theater. Shakespeare's audience knew the legend of Pyramus and Thisby very well. Many writers of his time would dramatize serious tragic legends just like this one, using poetic, flowery language, and paying careful attention to the number of syllables in each poetic line.

7. Read aloud Bottom's speech on pages 567–68. How does Bottom overuse such poetic devices as alliteration — the repetition of initial word sounds? How does he overuse rhyme?

8. Some writers in Shakespeare's day loved to use high-flown poetic comparisons. Can you find some ridiculous comparisons in Thisby's last speech?

9. How do you think Shakespeare uses Bottom to make fun of actors? Did Bottom and his friends fail to follow any of Hamlet's advice to actors (page 554)? If so, which ones?

10. At what point in the play might Shakespeare be poking fun at some kinds of theatergoers who cannot use their imaginations and need all kinds of elaborate props?

COMIC MISUSE OF WORDS

The pretensions of Bottom and his fellow actors extend into their use of words, for they were truly out of their element in presenting a tragic love story. They describe their production as a "most lamentable comedy." What is funny about this title? Was the play a comedy?

Sometimes the misuse of words produces hilarious effects. For example, look back at page 560, and see how Bottom confuses the words *odious, odorous,* and *odors,* with humorous results. (What are the differences in meaning among these words?)

Look back at the play and read the speeches in which Bottom speaks the following lines. He has bungled the words in italics. What words did he intend to use? Explain why each of these blunders is so funny.

". . . read the names of the actors, and so *grow* to a point." (See page 556.)

". . . saying thus, or to the same *defect* . . ." (See page 559.)

". . . he comes to *disfigure,* or to present, the person of moonshine." (See page 559.)

"*Quail,* crush, conclude, and quell!" (See page 568.)

SENTENCES:
"STANDING UPON POINTS"

Some people have a hard time reading poetry. They are uncertain about where they are to pause, where they are to come to full stops, and where they are to continue reading without pausing. Quince reads the prologue as some people read poetry. He pays little attention to punctuation and, consequently, pauses in the wrong places — with the result that the prologue's meaning is jumbled. Theseus, hearing the nonsensical results, says, "This fellow does not stand upon points."

Read this passage of the prologue aloud. Then try to punctuate it so that it makes sense.

"Consider, then, we come but in despite [ill will].
We do not come, as minding to content you,
Our true intent is. All for your delight,
We are not here. That you should here repent you,
The actors are at hand, and, by their show,
You shall know all, that you are like to know."

Whenever we write or read, we must "stand upon points" in order to have our audience get the right meaning. To illustrate this further, select a poem or a passage from some essay or story in this book, and have someone read it aloud as Quince read the prologue. (Do you feel like making remarks similar to those of Theseus, Hippolyta, and the Courtiers?)

How to Write About Literature

During your school career, you will often be asked to write about the stories, poems, and plays that you read. For example, you might be asked to write about the plot of a story, or about the meaning of a poem, or about the characters in a play. Sometimes, you will be asked to tell in a composition why you liked or disliked a piece of literature. At other times, you will be asked to make some general critical statement about something you have read.

When you write about literature, you use the techniques of exposition, that is, the techniques of explanatory writing. On pages 254–55, you learned how to write good paragraphs of exposition. By applying what you learned there, your writing about literature can be clear and forceful.

To summarize, here are the points you should keep in mind.

1. *Begin with a clearly phrased statement of your topic,* perhaps something like "I disliked this poem because I do not agree with the author," or "Mark Twain based many writings on his own experiences."

2. *Explain your topic statement in the sentences that follow.* Be sure to support the topic statement with forceful, specific details from the literature itself.

3. *Present your supporting details in some kind of logical order.* For example, you might discuss your supporting details in the order of their importance.

4. *Keep to the main point.* Do not wander off your subject and confuse your reader.

Suppose you were to write about the second topic statement above: "Mark Twain based many writings on his own experiences." The following outline lists some details you should use as evidence and shows how they might be organized.

The Topic Statement:
    Mark Twain based many writings on his own experiences.

Supporting Details:
    (1) In his autobiography, Twain says that certain people and incidents from his boyhood were used in *Tom Sawyer.* For example:
        (a) His brother Henry was Sid.
        (b) The sugar-bowl incident was true.
        (c) The incident with the cat and the Pain Killer was true.
    (2) In "Cub Pilot on the Mississippi," Twain tells about his own real-life experiences on the river.
    (3) "Lost in a Snowstorm" is set in Nevada, during gold-rush days. Mark Twain was in Nevada during these times. He once made the same trip described in this story, with two men having names similar to those in the story.

Now try arranging these details into a coherent composition.

Here are the skeletons of two paragraphs about James Thurber's writings. You have read several of his essays in this unit. Notice that some blank spaces have been left in these paragraphs. Where these blanks occur, provide specific details about James Thurber's writings to support each topic statement. Rewrite these paragraphs on a separate sheet of paper.

Things always seemed to be happening to James Thurber. He often wrote about the ridiculous predicaments people get into, or about the funny things they say. For example, in this unit, on pages ———, ———, and ———, are the funny essays ———, ———, and ———. They tell about ———, ———, and ———.

But sometimes Thurber says something very seriously. Deep thoughts lie behind the fable on page ———, called ———. These thoughts might be expressed like this: ———.

Now try it yourself. Here is a topic statement about Robert Frost to start you off. Complete the paragraph with specific details taken from the poems you have read in this unit.

The poems of Robert Frost tell of simple things, but beneath the simple exteriors lie deep thoughts and feelings.

Another kind of composition you will frequently be asked to write is a comparison or a contrast of two stories, poems, or plays. When you do this — when you state that two or more pieces of literature are similar or dissimilar — be sure to support your statement by citing specific lines or passages from the stories, poems, or plays.

A poem by Robert Frost is in the next column. After you read this poem several times, go back to page 517 and reread another poem by Frost, "A Time to Talk." Then, in a paragraph, write a comparison or a contrast of these two poems. Open your paragraph with a sentence stating whether the poems are alike or different in theme. Then use details to support this topic statement. In a second paragraph, tell which poem you prefer, and give at least one good reason for your choice. (Note: The phrase "sotto chants," in line 3, refers to the soft snatches of song the poet was singing.)

A Mood Apart
ROBERT FROST

Once down on my knees to growing plants
I prodded the earth with a lazy tool
In time with a medley of sotto chants;
But becoming aware of some boys from school
Who had stopped outside the fence to spy,
I stopped my song and almost heart,
For any eye is an evil eye
That looks in on to a mood apart.

ART AND LITERATURE

Many times our appreciation of a painting is deepened when we read what someone has written about it. For example, the full pages of paintings in this textbook are accompanied by commentary. Notice how the writer of the commentary often refers directly to a painting whenever he makes a general statement about an artist's technique. For example, in the third paragraph of the commentary on page 489, this general statement is made: "Crisp outdoor light can be found . . . in his early sea pictures . . ." To illustrate this general statement, the writer directs us to look at PLATE 2.

Here are two more general statements about Winslow Homer's paintings. Choose one and develop it into a full paragraph. Refer to specific details in the paintings as you tell whether you agree or disagree with the statement.

Many of Winslow Homer's paintings tell a story of men pitched in a struggle against the sea. (See pages 491–96.)

Winslow Homer's paintings are unlike Georges Braque's. (See page 405.)

PART FOUR

Our Heritage from Rome

Unit 9

UNIT 9 Our Heritage from Rome

Today, as astronauts soar into space exploring areas that may lead some modern Columbus to a distant planet, their rockets bear ancient names. Mercury, Gemini, Atlas, Saturn, Titan are all names that were once borne by Greek and Roman gods and goddesses.

In addition to the words, the ideas of the ancients have echoed through the centuries. While many great ideas and institutions originated with the Greeks, it was the Romans who spread them throughout the world. America feels everywhere the influence of ancient Rome. Our ideas of law and the very structure of our government, our alphabet, and our calendar are part of this heritage. And, with the remainder of the world, we share the great masterpieces of Latin literature.

Men have always looked to the past for help in understanding the present. It was a Roman, Cicero, who said "Not to know what happened before you were born is to remain forever a child." This unit will give you a glimpse into the history of a people to whom we owe much.

The Wooden Horse by Bella Koral:
    An adventure set in prerecorded time, where a great city is destroyed by a famous act of treachery.

The Adventures of Aeneas by Virgil:
    Incidents from the great Latin epic, about the man said to be the forebearer of the Roman race.

How Horatius Held the Bridge by Henry W. Lanier:
    The legend of how Rome's great republican government was snatched from destruction by a single soldier.

The Battle of Zama by Robert Silverberg:
    The true story of how Rome met the elephants of Carthage.

Julius Caesar by Plutarch:
    A biography of the most famous Roman of them all — the political and military genius who became Rome's first dictator.

The Eruption of Vesuvius by Pliny:
    An eyewitness report by the man who refused to give in to panic during one of the worst natural disasters in history.

The Heart of the City by Gilbert Highet:
    A contemporary writer's thoughts on ancient Rome.

The Wooden Horse

BELLA KORAL

Legend tells us that the founders of the ancient Roman race came from a great city that had once flourished in Asia Minor. This city was named Troy. According to an old tradition, a band of Trojans were forced to flee their homeland and settle down in Italy after Troy had been savagely destroyed by the Greek army. The destruction of Troy is historically true. But since ancient people liked a good story, you will find that in the tale of Troy's downfall, fact mixes easily with legend.

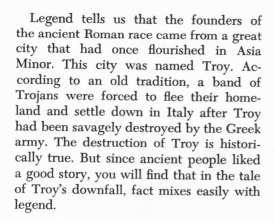

About four thousand years ago, a great city stood on the shores of the Aegean Sea, near the mouth of the Hellespont. That great city is entirely gone, and people in our time have found relics of it by digging deep into the ground. And the name Hellespont, like the name of the city — Troy — is part of ancient legends and writings. The actual waterway still exists and is called the Dardanelles, which you can find on the map; but Troy is no more.

"The Wooden Horse" by Bella Koral. Reprinted by permission of the author.

The walls of this great city were so high that no enemy could climb over them. And they were so thick and strong that no enemy could break through them or batter them down. And the gates of the city were well defended by its ablest and bravest soldiers.

Yet, proud and glorious though its history had been and confident as the Trojans were that their city would live forever, Troy at last fell upon evil days. This was because Paris, a prince of Troy, stole Helen, the most beautiful woman in the world, away from her husband Menelaus,[1] a king of the Greeks.

To avenge this great wrong, Menelaus called together all the heroes and great warriors of his country, among them the wise and courageous Ulysses. In two years of preparation, the Greeks assembled a tremendous army. They set sail for Troy in a fleet of a thousand ships. They landed on the beaches of the coastal plain before the city, and there the heroes made camp.

[1] Menelaus (men′ə·lā′əs).

The Trojans, too, were well prepared for battle, and their old King, Priam, gathered many brave fighters and chieftains about him. The Greeks defied the Trojans to engage in battle.

For nine long years the Greeks laid siege to Troy. Many fierce battles were fought outside the gates, and many were the noble heroes who were slain on both sides, for the chief warriors would engage in single combat as their armies stood by, and the old people and children of Troy would come out to watch the contests from the city's walls. On both sides, the warriors were equally valiant, so that the Trojans could not rid their beaches of the invaders, nor could the Greeks force their way into the city. Both sides suffered and struggled, and the weary siege dragged on and on. Finally the Greeks began to despair of ever conquering Troy in outright battle.

"For nine years we have been laying siege to Troy. Our bravest comrades are dead. Still the city is not ours, and Menelaus has not been avenged for the theft of Helen," the Greek soldiers grumbled.

"To fight any longer is useless. Let us give up this hopeless struggle! Our wives and children will learn to forget their husbands and fathers. We long to see our homes once more," they whispered at night among themselves.

Agamemnon,[1] chief of the Greek army, came to Ulysses. "Surely you, with your great cleverness and wisdom, can find a way to subdue the Trojans and save us," he urged.

After long consideration, Ulysses

[1] **Agamemnon** (ag'ə·mem'non): brother of Menelaus.

thought of a plan which the Greek chieftains decided to carry out.

Ulysses ordered his men, with the aid of a Greek sculptor, to build a colossal horse of wood. It was so huge and spacious that it could hold a hundred armed men within its hollow body. It was fitted with a door so skillfully concealed that no one could possibly notice it. One night, under the cloak of darkness, Ulysses, Menelaus, Agamemnon, and others of the Greek heroes, fully armed, crept into the wooden figure. The door was shut upon them, and the rest of the Greek army broke up camp and set sail, leaving the enormous wooden horse on the beach.

The Greeks pretended they were abandoning the siege and were sailing for home. But once out of sight of Troy, they anchored behind a somewhat distant neighboring island where they were well hidden from their enemies.

When the sun rose the next morning, there was not a Greek ship to be seen on the shore and not a single tent on the plain. Only the huge wooden horse remained. Like wildfire, the exciting news spread throughout the city. "The Greeks have fled! The Greeks have fled! They have left at last!" cried the people. Hundreds of eager men, women, and children ran toward the city's walls and gazed with happy, straining eyes toward the last straggling ship as it disappeared around the bend of the distant island.

Then the Trojans went wild with delight. The long years of siege were over, they thought. Everywhere there were embraces, kisses, and joyous shouts of laughter.

The newly found peace and liberty were wonderful to a people long besieged. They surged forward to the city gates, which were soon flung wide open, and quickly the crowds streamed over the site of the deserted enemy camp.

Now they saw the great wooden figure of the horse, resting on a wide platform of wood. Slowly they drew near it. Gazing and wondering, they walked round and round the colossal image. Touching it curiously, as little children will a strange object, they marveled at its tremendous height and girth.

"Perhaps it is a peace offering from the Greeks to the goddess Athene," said one Trojan to another. A few cautious ones continued to be afraid of the strange wooden creature, but others, becoming bolder, thought it should be carried back into the city as a war trophy.

At this, Laocoon,[1] priest of Neptune, god of the sea, came forward. "Trojans," warned the old man, "put no trust in this horse. Have you so soon forgotten the sad years of siege and suffering? Whatever this is, I fear the Greeks, even when they bear gifts," he cried.

Suddenly a great uproar was heard; the priest's warning was drowned in the hubbub that followed. "It's a Greek! A Greek!" A poor wretched fellow wearing Greek garments was dragged forward, his hands tightly bound. The ragged, badly beaten captive had been found by some shepherds, hiding among the reeds along the shore.

The captured Greek in reality was Sinon, a trusted friend of the crafty Ulysses, and he had been left behind by his companions to deceive the Tro-

[1] **Laocoon** (lā·ok′ə·won).

jans into taking the wooden horse within their gates.

"Do not kill me," he begged his Trojan captors. "It is true that I am a Greek, but I escaped from my cruel countrymen when they were about to sacrifice me to the gods."

Sinon was brought before the Trojan chiefs, who promised to spare his life if he would tell them the truth about the wooden horse. "The wooden horse," he told them, "was built by my countrymen as an offering to appease the goddess Athene. It was made so large so that you would be unable to take it within your walls. For," he went on lying craftily, "those who own this wooden horse will gain the favor and protection of Athene. If once the horse stands within the walls of Troy, the city can never be captured!"

At first the Trojans doubted the spy's story, but after a while Sinon convinced them that if they took the sacred object the Greeks had left behind them into their city, they would have happiness and prosperity forever.

Soon they devised a scheme for taking the huge figure into the city. Putting rollers under the wooden platform on which the horse stood, they fastened long ropes about its legs and began dragging the immense image across the plain toward the walls of Troy.

Again, out of the crowd, came the voice of the aged priest, Laocoon. "Men of Troy," he cried, "beware, beware of the treacherous Greeks. Cast the horse into the sea or burn it, for it will bring you only misery and ruin!" As he spoke, he hurled his spear against the side of the horse, and it resounded with a hollow clang of armor.

While some people were again persuaded to doubt and were standing about discussing the priest's warning, an event occurred before their very eyes which seemed an omen direct from the gods. Out of the sea rose two immense serpents. With rearing heads, their eyes and tongues flashing flames before them, they swiftly glided through the terrified, panic-stricken crowd and made straight for Laocoon and his two sons.

Before they could escape, the two serpents entwined their coiling, slimy bodies about the three unfortunate men and crushed them to death. The monsters then slipped away again into the sea, as quickly and silently as they had come.

The Trojans, frozen with horror at this dreadful scene, were sure that this punishment had come to Laocoon for his words against the wooden horse. "He has been doomed for his sacrilege against this gift," they cried. "We will offer thanks to our protector Athene and bring the sacred image into our city."

Amid great acclaim, many willing hands dragged and pushed the great horse on its rolling platform over the plain, and little by little it approached the gate. When it was reached, they found that the opening was too narrow to admit the horse. So they pulled down part of the wall and made a breach to allow the wooden horse to be brought into the city. "Now," said the Trojans, "our city is safe from every enemy," and they draped wreaths and garlands of flowers around the horse.

That night they had a great feast of wild merrymaking to celebrate the end of nine years of anxious watching and suffering. For the first time in nine years, no one was on guard on the walls of Troy. On that night all went to sleep, secure in the belief that the gods were on their side.

When the noises of the city had died down and the streets were quiet and empty, Sinon, as had been planned, opened the cunningly concealed trap door in the side of the wooden horse. Out of it came the hero Ulysses, Menelaus, and the many other hidden Greeks. They set up a beacon light as a signal to the Greek army, for during the night the ships that had anchored behind the island had sailed back again toward the Trojan shore.

Soon, thousands of Greek soldiers swarmed through the streets of a proud city sunken in darkness and sleep. It was to the sounds of battle that the Trojans awoke from their dreams of peace. So the prophecy of Laocoon was fulfilled.

Priam, the King, and his noblest warriors were killed. Greek soldiers robbed the palaces and plundered the city of all its wealth and treasure. Helpless, the Trojans watched as their glorious city, set to the torch, burned to its very foundations.

Then the Greeks set sail for their own country, taking with them many Trojan captives. With them they took also the fair Helen, for whose sake the dreadful war had been waged. At last she had awakened from the spell that the goddess Venus had cast upon her, and she was eager to behold again her native land.

But the glory of Troy was gone forever. Nothing but smouldering ruins and the everlasting renown of its valiant heroes remained of the wondrous, rich city on the shores of the Aegean.

THE FALL OF TROY

1. Why were the Greeks and Trojans fighting? Why had the Greek soldiers begun to grumble? Describe Ulysses' plan.

2. How did the Trojans react to the Greeks' withdrawal? How did Laocoon warn them about the wooden horse? What part did Sinon play in the plot? Describe the outcome of Ulysses' plan.

3. What is your reaction to the cause of the Trojan war? Compare causes of modern wars with the cause of this one.

4. Why did Laocoon say, ". . . I fear the Greeks, even when they bear gifts?" This quotation is used today as a warning against gifts which seem suspicious. Can you think of any situations to which this warning might apply?

5. How did you feel about the way the Trojans reacted to the wooden horse and to Laocoon's prophecy? What characteristics of the Trojans led to their defeat?

COMPOSITION: PARAGRAPHING

Most compositions consist of a number of paragraphs. As a writer goes from one topic to another, he usually starts a new paragraph. Notice the first three paragraphs of "The Wooden Horse." Each paragraph is about a different topic. The topic of the first paragraph, for example, is that Troy exists no longer. What is the topic of the second paragraph? the third?

Write about a place that is familiar to you — a shopping center, your neighborhood, your city. In each of three different paragraphs, describe or explain a different thing about this place. Develop each paragraph with several sentences of detail.

The Adventures of Aeneas

VIRGIL

Retold by H. A. Guerber

Between the years 30 and 19 B.C., a Roman writer named Virgil took the legends about the founding of Rome and wove them into a long adventure story. According to these legends, a Trojan named Aeneas had fled the burning city of Troy and, after many adventures, had landed in Italy.

Virgil wanted to glorify Rome and her founders. In his long story, we find that Aeneas is not an ordinary mortal but the son of a goddess. Nor, according to Virgil, was the kidnap of Helen really the cause of Troy's collapse. Troy fell because it was the will of the gods that Aeneas should leave Troy and go to Italy, and that his descendants should found the city of Rome.

Virgil's great story became the national epic of Rome. Roman children studied it as a textbook. The following selection tells you part of Virgil's book-length story of Aeneas.

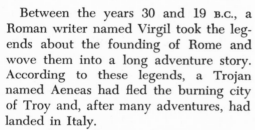

You HAVE already heard how the Greeks entered the city of Troy in the dead of night, massacred the inhabitants, and set fire to the beautiful build-

ings which had been the pride and delight of King Priam. Now you shall hear how Virgil relates the escape of some of the Trojans from general destruction.

Unconscious of coming danger, Aeneas, son of Venus and Anchises,[1] lay fast asleep in his palace. But the gods had not doomed him to perish, and they sent the ghost of Hector[2] to warn him in a dream to arise, leave the city, and fly to some distant land.

Awakened at last by the ever-increasing tumult outside, Aeneas seized his arms and hastened forth, attended by many of his fellow citizens, to ascertain the cause of the great uproar. A few minutes later he discovered that the Greek army had entered the town and was even now killing, plundering, and burning without mercy. The men were all slain, but the fairest women were dragged away to be sold as slaves

---

[1] **Venus and Anchises** (an·kī′sēz): According to Roman legend, Venus was the goddess of love. She fell in love with a mortal, Anchises, of the royal house of Troy, and bore him a son, Aeneas.

[2] **Hector:** the greatest Trojan warrior, killed by the Greeks.

in Greece. Among them, Aeneas beheld in the hands of Agamemnon's soldiers [1] the unfortunate daughter of Priam, Cassandra, whom the gods had endowed with prophetic powers, but whom no one would heed.

Aeneas, seeing that there was no hope of saving the doomed city, quickly disguised himself in a Greek armor that he tore from the corpse of one of his foes and rushed on to the palace, hoping to save the aged King, who, at the first alarm, had seized his weapons, determined to fight to the very last.

Hecuba, Priam's wife, was clinging to him, imploring him to remain, when suddenly one of their sons rushed into their presence, closely followed by the son of Achilles, [2] who thrust his sword into the youth and then murdered Priam also.

Aeneas, who arrived just too late to stop this frightful catastrophe, now suddenly remembered that a similar fate awaited his aged father, Anchises, his wife, Creusa, and his little son, Iulus, [3] who were at home without any protector near them. The hero, therefore, madly cut his way through the foe and rushed through the once magnificent palace that was now stripped of its rarest treasures and desecrated by an enemy's tread.

There, in one of the abandoned halls, he saw Helen, the fair cause of all this war and bloodshed, and for a moment he determined to take her life. But before he could do so, Venus, his mother, stayed his hand and bade him remember that the immortal gods had long ago decreed that the city should fall and that Helen was merely the pretext used to induce the rival nations to fly to arms.

To convince him further of the truth of her assertions, she enabled him to see what was hidden from mortal eyes: the deities Neptune, Minerva, Juno, and even Jupiter fighting and leveling the walls with mighty blows. She then vehemently implored her son to leave this scene of carnage [4] and to fly with his family and followers to some safe place outside the city, where he could embark and sail away to a more fortunate land. Her entreaties finally prevailed.

Aeneas rushed home and bade his father prepare to leave Troy, but Anchises obstinately refused to leave his post, until he saw a bright flame hover for a moment above his grandson's head, a sign which he interpreted as an omen that his race should endure. He no longer resisted; and, as he was too weak to walk, Aeneas bade him hold the Lares and Penates, [5] and, taking him on his back, carried him off, while with one hand he led his little son and bade Creusa closely follow him.

A trysting place near a ruined temple had already been appointed for his servants, and there Aeneas turned his steps. When he arrived, he found many awaiting him, and he counted them carefully to make sure none were missing. All were there except Creusa, his beloved young wife, and he retraced

---

[1] **Agamemnon's** (ag'ə·mem'nonz) **soldiers:** Agamemnon was chief of the Greek army.

[2] **Achilles** (ə·kil'ēz): the Greek warrior who killed Priam's son Hector.

[3] **Iulus** (ī·yōō'ləs).

[4] **carnage** (kär'nij): bloody slaughter.

[5] **Lares** (lâr'ēz) **and Penates** (pə·nā'tēz): household gods.

his steps with anxious haste, hoping to find her still alive. But on the threshold of his once happy home, he met her disembodied spirit and heard her bid him seek the banks of the Tiber,[1] where a beautiful young bride would comfort him for her loss. This speech ended, Creusa's ghost vanished, and Aeneas sadly returned to the ruined temple, where he found many fugitives ready to follow him wherever he might go and eager to obey his every command. Their preparations for departure were speedily completed, the sails unfurled, and the little exiled band soon lost sight of the shores of Troy.

[Weeping, the band of Trojans left their country, but their trials had only just begun. For seven hard years Aeneas and his companions roamed over the Mediterranean in search of a new home. Finally,

---

[1] **Tiber:** river in central Italy.

with the help of the gods — except for Juno, who nursed a deep hatred for the Trojan race — the group of weary travelers landed on Italy's shores.]

Aeneas led his companions to the mouth of the Tiber, whose course they followed until they reached Latium,[2] where their wanderings were to cease. Latinus, King of the country, received them hospitably and promised the hand of his daughter, Lavinia, in marriage to Aeneas.

Lavinia was very beautiful, and had already had many suitors, among whom was Turnus, a neighboring prince, who boasted of the most exalted rank. The Queen, Amata, especially favored this youth, and the King would gladly have received him for a son-in-law had he not twice been warned by the gods to reserve his daughter for a foreign prince, who had now appeared.

In spite of all the years which had elapsed, Juno had not yet forgotten her hatred of the Trojan race, and, afraid that her enemy's course should now prove too smooth, she sent Alecto, the Fury,[3] down upon earth to stir up war and goad Amata to madness. The Fury executed both commands, and Amata fled to the woods, where she concealed her daughter, Lavinia, to keep her safe for Turnus, whom she preferred to Aeneas.

Because Aeneas's son and some companions had unfortunately wounded a pet stag, a brawl ensued, which, incited by Alecto, soon developed into a bloody war. Hostilities having begun,

---

[2] **Latium** (lā′shē·əm): an ancient country in central Italy.

[3] **Fury:** in mythology, one of three goddesses who avenge unpunished crimes.

Turnus, with the various Latin chiefs, immediately besought Latinus to open the gates of Janus's temple.[1] He refused; but Juno, afraid that even now her plans might come to nothing, came down from Olympus and with her own hand flung wide the brazen doors. This unexpected apparition kindled a general ardor, and new troops came to the aid of Turnus.

Surprised to see Latinus's friendly offers of hospitality so suddenly withdrawn, Aeneas made rapid preparations for war, and sailed farther up the Tiber to secure the aid of Evander, King of the Tuscans, the hereditary foe of the Latins. This monarch, too old to lead his troops in person, nevertheless promised his aid and sent his beloved son, Pallas, in his place to command the troops he supplied.

Juno, still implacable,[2] had in the meantime informed Turnus of Aeneas's departure, and urged him to set fire to the Trojan fleet — a suggestion which Turnus joyfully obeyed. The Trojans, headed by young Iulus, Aeneas's son, defended themselves with their usual courage; but, seeing the enemy would soon overpower them, they dispatched Nisus and Euryalus,[3] two of their number, to warn Aeneas of their danger and to entreat him to hasten up with his reinforcements. These unfortunate youths passed through the camp unseen but farther on fell into the hands of a troop of enemy horsemen, who cruelly put them to death and then hurried to lend assistance to Turnus. Next, some of the Trojan vessels were fired by the enemy, but, instead of being consumed by the flames, they were changed into water nymphs by the intervention of the gods and, sailing down the Tiber, met Aeneas and warned him to hasten to his son's rescue.

In the meanwhile, Venus, who befriended the Trojans, had sought Vulcan's[4] detested abode and had prevailed upon him to forge a beautiful

---

[1] **Janus's temple:** Janus was a Latin god who presided over the beginning of things. When war was declared, the bronze, or "brazen," gates to Janus's temple were traditionally left open so he could help the Latin soldiers. A coin showing Janus is on page iii.

[2] **implacable** (im·plā′kə·bəl): unrelenting; merciless.

[3] **Nisus** (nī′səs) **and Euryalus** (yōō′rə·ləs).

[4] **Vulcan's:** Vulcan was the Roman god of fire and metalworking.

armor for Aeneas. On the shield were depicted many of the stirring scenes in the lives of the future descendants of Aeneas, the heroes of Roman history. As soon as this armor was completed, Venus brought it to her son, who donned it with visible pleasure and, encouraged by his mother's words, prepared to meet the Latins and hold his own.

Venus and Juno were not the only deities interested in the coming struggle, for all the gods, having watched Aeneas's career, were anxious about his fate. Seeing this, and fearful that their interference should still further endanger the hero whom he favored, Jupiter assembled the gods on high Olympus and sternly forbade their taking any active part in the coming strife, under penalty of his severe displeasure.

Aeneas and his Tuscan allies arrived on the battle scene just in time to give the necessary support to the almost exhausted Trojans; now the fight raged more fiercely than ever, and prodigies of valor were accomplished on both sides, until finally young Pallas fell, slain by Turnus. When aware of the death of this promising young prince,

Aeneas' heart was filled with grief, for he could imagine the sorrow of the aged Evander when he saw his son's corpse brought home for burial; and he then and there registered a solemn vow to avenge Pallas' death by slaying Turnus.

In the meantime, Juno, suspecting what Aeneas's purpose would be and afraid to allow Turnus to encounter such a formidable antagonist as Aeneas, had determined to lure her favorite away from the field. To do this, she assumed the form of Aeneas, challenged Turnus, and, as soon as he began the fight, fled toward the river and took refuge on one of the vessels, closely pursued by him. No sooner did she see him safe on board, than she loosed the vessel from its moorings and allowed it to drift downstream, bearing Turnus away from the scene of battle. Aware now of the delusion, Turnus raved and accused the gods, and then eagerly watched for an opportunity to land and make his way, alone and on foot, back to the scene of conflict.

During Turnus's involuntary absence, Aeneas had ranged all over the battlefield in search of him and had encountered and slain many warriors. The dead and dying covered the field when Latinus, weary of bloodshed, summoned a council and again vainly tried to make peace. But his efforts were of no avail. The war was renewed more fiercely than ever. In the very midst of the fray, Aeneas suddenly felt himself wounded by an arrow sent by some mysterious hand. He hastened to seek aid, but the barb could not be removed nor the wound dressed until Venus brought a magic herb that instantly healed the hero and enabled him to return to the fight with unabated strength and energy.

The tide was now decidedly turning in favor of the Trojans; for Amata, the Latin Queen, sorry for her ill-advised opposition to her daughter's marriage to Aeneas, brought Lavinia home, and hanged herself in a fit of remorse.

Aeneas, appearing once more on the battlefield, finally encountered the long sought Turnus, who had made his way back. The two heroes instantly closed in deadly fight; but, in spite of his bravery, Turnus was finally obliged to succumb, and he sank to the ground, frankly acknowledging himself beaten as he exhaled his last sigh.

With the death of Turnus the war came to an end. A lasting peace was made with Latinus, and the brave Trojan hero, whose woes were now over, was united in marriage to Lavinia. With Latinus, he ruled the Latins and founded a city, which he called Lavinia in honor of his bride and which became, for a time, the capital of Latium.

Aeneas, as the gods had predicted, became the father of a son named Aeneas Silvia, who founded Alba Longa, where his descendants reigned for many a year and where one of his race gave birth to Remus and Romulus, the founders of Rome.

FROM TROY TO LATIUM

1. Describe Aeneas's last hours in Troy. What advice did he get from the gods and from Hector's ghost? What happened to Aeneas's wife, to King Priam, and to the King's son? Why didn't Aeneas kill Helen, as he wished to do?

2. What started the war between the Latins and the Trojans? What part did the gods and goddesses play in the war? Trace the conflict between Aeneas and Turnus from its beginning to its end.

3. How were Latinus and Aeneas related to the founders of Rome?

4. According to the great Roman writer Virgil, the founders of Rome were descendants of Aeneas, the son of the goddess Venus. Why do you think Romans liked to relate their founders to the gods? Where did Virgil show favoritism toward the Trojans? Point out passages of this story which indicate that Virgil was trying to show that the founding of Rome was divinely inspired.

5. Aeneas, the hero of this story, was regarded by the Romans as the father of their country. Do Americans also have favorite stories about the father of their country? Do these stories idealize Washington in the ways that Aeneas was idealized? Explain.

LATIN AND GREEK NAMES

Virgil's *Aeneid* describes how the survivors of the Trojan War left their burning city and founded a new race of people in Italy. Through reading this story, you might have noted a few explanations for the derivations of some words. For example, we call the language of the ancient Romans *Latin*. From what you read in this story, tell where the word *Latin* comes from. What does the last sentence of this story tell about how Rome got its name?

Many other words used today are derived from the names the Romans and Greeks gave to their gods, goddesses, and heroes. Here is a list of some of these names. A dictionary will give you some information about the people they named in ancient Greece and Rome. In what different ways are the names of these divinities and heroes used today?

Ajax	Fury	Mars
Atlas	Sphinx	Venus

SENTENCES:
WORD GROUPS AS NOUNS

In the third paragraph of this selection is a sentence in which a lengthy group of words (in italics) serves as a noun:

> "A few minutes later he discovered *that the Greek army had entered the town and was even now killing, plundering, and burning without mercy.*"

The entire group of words beginning with the word *that* acts as a unit and serves as a noun. This word group is in the object position in the sentence. (It does the same job as the words *a fact* would do in this position in the sentence.)

Here is another lengthy word group acting as a single unit in a sentence. It, too, is used as a noun and is in the object position. (It does the same job as the words *the story* would do in this position in the sentence.)

> "You have already heard *how the Greeks entered the city of Troy in the dead of night, massacred the inhabitants, and set fire to the beautiful buildings which had been the pride and delight of King Priam.*"

Complete the following sentences with word groups. Note that any group you add will serve as a noun. Which word group will be in an object position? Which will be used as a complement? Which groups will be used as subjects?

Aeneas remembered how _____.

Juno's plan was to _____.

That _____ seemed impossible to Turnus.

To _____ was important in Aeneas's plans.

OUTLINING

H. A. Guerber's summary of part of Virgil's story of Aeneas has been divided into two parts. The first ten paragraphs tell what happened to Aeneas as Troy burned. The last fifteen paragraphs tell about Aeneas's conquest of Latium.

By outlining this story, you will see more clearly how all the details relate to the two main parts of the story.

Below are listed the topics of all the paragraphs in this story — except for the first and last paragraphs. Arrange these topics in the order in which they occur, and put them under one of these main topics: I. *Nine events occurred while Aeneas was in Troy.* II. *Fourteen events happened while Aeneas was in Latium.*

Aeneas is visited by Hector's ghost.

Aeneas is received in Latium.

Aeneas remembers his family.

Amata favors Turnus's suit.

Priam is killed.

Jupiter forbids the gods to interfere in the battle.

Juno sends a Fury to make Amata mad.

Pallas is killed.

Aeneas sees the Greeks plunder Troy and capture the women.

Turnus sets fire to the Trojan fleet.

Aeneas sees Helen.

The war between Turnus and Aeneas begins.

Venus tells Aeneas to leave Troy.

Juno lures Turnus away from battle.

Aeneas persuades his father to leave.

Aeneas is wounded as the battle continues.

Aeneas kills Turnus.

Amata brings Lavinia home.

Aeneas makes peace with Latinus.

Aeneas goes to save Priam.

The ghost of Creusa talks to Aeneas.

Aeneas goes to secure the help of the Tuscans.

Venus gives Aeneas armor.

Roman Art

One of the most modern civilizations the world has ever known developed over two thousand years ago. A small hill town in ancient Italy gradually became a world power, conquering much of what we now call Europe and the Near East. This was the period of the Roman Empire.

The larger the Roman Empire grew, the more difficult it was to manage. The chief problem was one of defense, for all the empire's outlying provinces had to be protected constantly against barbarian invasion. Fortunately, the Romans were skillful planners and builders. Along the borders of their provinces they erected massive stone walls, some over twelve feet high and eight feet thick. And to make it possible for the Imperial Army to move swiftly from one trouble spot to another, Roman engineers built hundreds of miles of long, straight roads. Most of these led finally toward the city of Rome itself, the heart of the empire.

The city's population grew so fast that soon entirely new types of buildings were required to accommodate large public gatherings. For example, a huge sports arena seating over forty thousand spectators was needed. Roman architects solved this problem in two ways. First, they discovered that by supporting such a structure on wide-spanned arches, they could distribute its weight over a much greater area than was possible with columns, which had to be placed close together. By setting rows of arches one above another, they could support the weight of a building several stories high. Second, they found that they could build more efficiently with concrete — a mixture of sand, pebbles, lime, and water which hardens to the strength of solid stone in molds of any shape or size. Using these techniques, the Romans built the largest sports arena in ancient history: the Colosseum (PLATE 1). This great oval structure, though now in ruins, is still one of the world's most impressive buildings. The Colosseum has a special meaning for us today, for it is the grandfather of our modern football stadium.

Another problem the Romans had to face was the need for a fresh water supply in the large cities of the empire. The public baths in Rome, for instance, required millions of gallons a day to fill their huge indoor pools. Roman engineers met this need by building miles and miles of long troughs, known as "aqueducts," that carried water to the cities from far-off mountain streams. Some of these ancient aqueducts are still in excellent condition. One of these is the great Pont du Gard (PLATE 2), near the town of Nîmes in southern France. This aqueduct soars 180 feet high in some parts of the countryside.

The Romans were also great builders of monuments. They often celebrated the return to Rome of a victorious general by erecting a triumphal arch in his honor. A few of these arches, such as the Arch of Constantine (PLATE 3), stand today on their original sites.

One of the most famous of all Roman buildings is a massive, domed structure known as the Pantheon. This building was originally intended to be a temple to the seven Roman gods of the planets. Perhaps the best-known picture of its breathtaking interior is an eighteenth-century painting by Panini (PLATE 4), which represents it much as it looks today. If you can imagine standing beneath an enormous upside-down teacup — 110 feet high and 110 feet across, with a circular opening at the top which is 30 feet in diameter — you might get some idea of the strange feeling of space under this huge dome.

Now let's look at some pictures of Roman people. In PLATE 5 we see the hard, rugged face of a Roman citizen. Portrait sculpture of this type was done to preserve the likeness of the head of a family after his death. A truly Roman style developed in these portrait busts. This style was more realistic than that of most Greek sculpture, which Roman artists greatly admired and often copied. For example, the marble portrait of an elegant Roman lady shown in PLATE 6 comes close to the Greek ideal of beauty.

In PLATE 7 we see a statue of the Emperor Trajan. Statues of this sort could be found in the forum, or civic center, of every town in the empire, for many Roman emperors thought of themselves almost as gods and wanted to instill this image in the minds of the citizens.

Our last picture (PLATE 8) is a detail from a wall painting that once was part of a room in a country villa about a hundred miles south of Rome. This picture of a maiden gathering flowers is often titled *Flora*, after the name of the Roman goddess of flowers and spring.

PLATE 1. THE COLOSSEUM (Roman, A.D. 70–82). Height is 157 feet, 6 inches; length is 620 feet; width is 513 feet. Arena is 287 by 180 feet. (Rome)

PLATE 2. PONT DU GARD (Roman, A.D. early 1st century). Aqueduct, 900 feet long, rises 180 feet above the River Gard. (Nîmes, France)

PLATE 3. ARCH OF CONSTANTINE (Roman, A.D. 312). Built in honor of Constantine's victory over Maxentius. Height is 67 feet, 7 inches; width is 82 feet. (Rome)

PLATE 4. THE INTERIOR OF THE PANTHEON. Painting by Giovanni Paolo Panini (Italian, about 1692–1765/68). Oil on canvas, 50½ x 39 inches. (National Gallery of Art, Washington, D.C., Samuel H. Kress Collection). PANTHEON: Roman, completed in A.D. 27 and rebuilt, after fire, about A.D. 120–24; height from floor to ceiling is 142 feet, 6 inches.

PLATE 5. PORTRAIT OF UNKNOWN ROMAN
(Roman, A.D. early 1st century). Marble, life size.
(The Metropolitan Museum of Art, New York,
Rogers Fund, 1912)

PLATE 6. PORTRAIT OF A LADY
(Roman, A.D. 1st century). Marble,
life size. (Capitoline Museums,
Rome)

PLATE 7. EMPEROR TRAJAN (Roman, A.D. 2nd century). Marble, 6 feet 5 inches high. (Courtesy of the Fogg Art Museum, Harvard University, Cambridge, Massachusetts, Alpheus Hyatt Fund)

PLATE 8. FLORA (Roman, A.D. 1st century). Detail of wall painting from Stabiae. Entire painting is 15½ inches by 12½ inches. (National Museum, Naples)

How Horatius Held the Bridge

HENRY W. LANIER

Tradition records that Rome had seven kings. Romulus was the first, and a tyrant named Tarquin was the seventh and the last. By the time Tarquin came to rule, Rome had become the largest and richest city in all Italy, and the city's aristocracy began to resent the King. In 510 B.C. Tarquin was overthrown, and from then on, the Romans despised the title "king." At this time, the Romans began their great republic, a form of government which was to last for five hundred years. But at first the republic had to struggle to endure. One of the legends told in Rome was about a man named Horatius, whose bravery saved the infant republic from the threats of the deposed King.

THE LAST of the Roman kings was Tarquin the Proud. He came to the throne by murder and held it by tyranny. After twenty-five years of misrule, the people revolted under the leadership of his nephew, who had only escaped his father's and brother's fate by pretending to be half-witted and meekly accept-

"How Horatius Held the Bridge" by Henry W. Lanier. Reprinted by permission of The Estate of Henry W. Lanier.

ing the name of Brutus (stupid). The tyrant, Tarquin the Proud, was driven out.

Tarquin raised an army among the Tuscans and led it against Rome, but it was defeated, though his son and Brutus killed each other in battle. Again and again the deposed King tried to regain his throne.

At last he formed an alliance with Lars Porsena of Clusium, a powerful prince to the north of Rome, who took up the fugitive's cause as his own. When the Romans refused Porsena's demands to reinstate their former ruler, he warned them when and where he meant to attack, and he gathered all his forces for the effort.

Word came of his approach. The people were filled with terror, for this was one of the foremost powers of Italy which was descending upon them. Moreover, the Tuscan ranks were swelled with their bitterest enemies: deserters and exiles and all who envied their growing power; and they knew only too well what bloody Tarquin's course would be if he succeeded in his attempts.

But the consuls,[1] Publicola and Lucretius, as if to show their disregard of the enemy, proceeded to build the new walled city of Sigliura and place within it a colony of seven hundred men.

This bravado had little effect upon Porsena, at least.

He assaulted the town, drove out the garrison, and sent them flying in disorder toward Rome. Nor did he give them any chance to recover, but followed so hard upon them that a panic seized the citizens. The gates must be kept open to admit their own people, but the foe was so close upon their heels that it looked as if this meant letting him in also. The walls of Rome, they felt, were impregnable[2] against anybody; a victorious enemy actually within the gates was another matter.

Great was the confusion as the press of battle swayed to and fro by the Tiber's side. The Romans fought valiantly but they were outnumbered, and, in spite of their utmost efforts, they were being forced back upon the wooden bridge spanning the Tiber River.

The river was the main natural defense of the city on the west; once in possession of the Sublician Bridge, an enemy had a direct entrance, so that the struggle for possession became more and more desperate.

At the critical instant, the consul Publicola sallied out of the gate with a chosen band. For a time his onslaught drove the Tuscans back. But before long he fell, desperately wounded; his followers carried him back out of the fight, and the pressure at the bridge head was renewed.

The other consul, Lucretius, attacked bravely also. He too fell wounded. With both leaders gone, the Romans lost heart and retreated before the fierce onslaughts. A dash of the invaders captured the Janiculum,[3] and from thence the Tuscan host pressed triumphantly forward.

---

[1] **consuls:** In the Roman republic, the consuls were the two chief executives, elected annually.

[2] **impregnable** (im·preg′nə·bəl): firmly resistant.

[3] **Janiculum** (jə·nik′yə·ləm): a hill on which a defense post was built, located on the side of the Tiber opposite from Rome.

There was clearly but one chance left. The bridge must be destroyed. If they could break it down before Porsena's army could pass, "Father Tiber" would guard his chosen town. For the river was in flood, and it would be a bold man who would even venture to try to cross it in the face of a hostile force.

All this was clear as day to those in command. What was not clear at all was how the Tuscans were to be held back even for the short time required to saw and hack through the bridge timbers on the city side. To be sure, it was a narrow passage where a few men side by side could guard the way. But where were there any who would attempt such a foolhardy feat?

It looked like certain death. Even if one were a warrior stout enough to defend himself from those fierce war-wolves thronging forward so eagerly, what would happen when the bridge fell behind him?

There was a moment's silence in the hurried council of war, as the menacing facts impressed themselves on every mind.

Then up stood one, Horatius. He was nephew to Horatius the consul, and came of that line which had made the name memorable in the tremendous combat between the Horatii and Curiatii [1] in the reign of Tullius Hostilius. He bore his own record upon his face, for he had received in the wars such a wound between the eyes that at first glance he seemed to have but one great eye in his forehead. Hence he was called Cyclops,[2] the one-eyed, which had somehow been converted by the ignorant populace into Cocles.[3]

He bade his disheartened comrades face the grim truth: the one chance for safety lay in facing the enemy.

"Let him who thinks to escape death by deserting his post reflect that if he flies, there soon will be more of the enemy in the Palatium and Capital [4] than now are in the Janiculum.

"Besides, death comes to all: how can a man die better than in defending his home and gods?

"Do ye break down the bridge, by sword, by fire, or by any means whatever. What one man can do to hold back the foe, that will I do."

Like a lion among a frightened flock, he strode across to the first entrance to the bridge. Breasting the current of those whose backs were toward the enemy, he reached the narrow passage, and the exulting Tuscans paused in sheer surprise at the sight.

Two Romans there were who were inspired by his example. Spurius Lartius and Herminius, patricians [5] both and proved warriors, rushed forward and took their places, one on his right hand, the other on his left.

The road to Rome was guarded. It was three men against an army. But they were three who were concerned only to purchase with their lives the minutes necessary to destroy the

---

[1] **Horatii** (hə·rā′shē·ī) **and Curiatii** (kyōōr′ē·ā′shē·ī): According to Roman legend, three brothers named Horatius, representing Rome, killed three other brothers, the Curatii, representing Rome's enemy Alba.

[2] **Cyclops** (sī′klops): This word means, literally, "round-eyed."

[3] **Cocles** (kō′klēz).

[4] **Palatium** (pə·lā′shē·əm) **and Capital:** two hills in Rome, on which were located the imperial buildings and the temples.

[5] **patricians** (pə·trish′ənz): aristocrats.

bridge behind them. And already their comrades, shamed into action by their devotion, were hacking desperately at the timbers.

The Tuscan warriors were not slow to accept the challenge. Their champions sprang forward from the ranks into the confined space. Warily the three met the onset. Swords and spears flashed upon their ready shields. Their own weapons flashed in the sunlight, then bit deeply into their assailants, cleaving through armor and flesh.

One after another of the assailants went down, and were dragged away to make room for a fresh attack. Battered, and covered with blood and sweat, Horatius and his supporters glared at each fresh adversary like some wild boars surrounded by baying hounds, awaiting the instant to strike a fatal blow.

Never a word spoke they, but strained their ears backward for the sounds of ax and lever which came from the rear.

Maddened by the check and by the sudden obstacle to the easy victory that had lain before them, the Tuscans attacked more furiously than ever. Bitter was the chagrin [1] of Porsena to see his doughtiest [2] warriors laid low, his whole vast force held back by that thin wall of human courage.

A shout from behind made even the combatants turn. "It falls! It falls!" ran the cry from those who wrought so eagerly at destruction. "Back, Horatius! Back, Lartius! Back, Herminius!"

The leader of the three looked round. Coolly he bade his comrades to retreat. They darted back, and as they sped to safety the timbers cracked beneath their feet.

In a frenzy of rage the assailants hurled a perfect cloud of spears upon the solitary defender. Skillfully protecting himself with his shield, he defied them with taunts that bit deeper than their weapons.

"Slaves are ye all," he called, "slaves

[1] **chagrin** (shə·grin′): distress, disappointment.
[2] **doughtiest** (dou′tē·ist): bravest.

of haughty tyrants. Ye have lost your own freedom, yet ye think to take away the liberty of Romans."

There was a mighty crash, above which rose the triumphant shouts of the Romans. The great bridge collapsed into a mass of wreckage, and the swift waters of the Tiber seized hold of truss and girder. Horatius was cut off between the gap and the threatening mass of the enemy.

There was a moment's pause as the realization sank into their minds. Then there rose a hoarse cry from a thousand throats, demanding vengeance on the one who had wrecked their hopes.

Horatius sprang to the edge of the shattered bridge. He raised his hand aloft.

"Holy Father Tiber," cried he, "receive these arms and this thy soldier in thy propitious [1] stream."

With this invocation, he leaped into the flood. A silence fell upon friend and foe alike as the gallant warrior reappeared on the surface and, encumbered as he was by his heavy armor, struck out for the city's shore.

Recovering themselves, many of the Tuscans hurled javelins at him as he strove against the buffeting waves and current. One of these wounded him in the thigh, but with powerful strokes he rose dripping from the shallows among the cheering multitude of his countrymen. He had saved Rome, and Rome gave him full meed [2] of gratitude.

Publicola, the consul, decreed that, in spite of the public scarcity, every citizen should present to him one day's provisions for his maintenance; and

[1] **propitious** (prō·pish'əs): kindly, gracious.
[2] **meed**: reward.

even the women were proud to be among the hundreds of thousands who thus honored the one-eyed and now lamed hero. He was granted as much land as he could encircle with a plow in a day. And a brazen statue of him was set up in the temple of Vulcan, that future generations might ever remember the son of Rome who was ready to give her all, including life itself.

A GREAT ROMAN HERO

1. How did Tarquin the Proud's attempts to regain his throne lead to the fight at the Sublician bridge? Why was the bridge of such strategic importance? What events led up to the decision to destroy the bridge?

2. Who was Horatius? Describe him. What did he say to the council of war? Tell about the main events of Horatius's fight with the Tuscans, including the dramatic outcome. How did Rome show her gratitude to Horatius?

3. The Romans were practical men, skilled in war, and completely devoted to their country. Horatius was one of their great heroes. Can you guess why? Why would Horatius's defense of the bridge be a story that Roman parents would tell their sons?

4. The actions of Horatius had a tremendous effect upon the history of Rome. Can you think of other men who have had such a great influence upon the history of their countries? Tell about some of them.

5. Do you remember what Horatius said about death? Skim page 599 to find his remark. Have men usually agreed with Horatius? Explain your answer.

6. What American heroes do we remember as the Romans remembered Horatius? Compare their characters and their deeds with those of Horatius.

The Battle of Zama

ROBERT SILVERBERG

In "The Adventures of Aeneas" (page 582) you read of how Aeneas and his followers settled in Italy, and of how, many years later, Aeneas's descendants founded Rome. At about the same time that Rome was being settled, another group of people were developing a city on the opposite shore of the Mediterranean, in North Africa, a city called Carthage. During the years that Rome was expanding her power, Carthage, too, was steadily growing in strength and wealth. The shippers and roving merchants of Carthage made her a wealthy city, and while Rome became the military master of Europe, Carthage held naval sway over the Mediterranean world.

The two giants came into conflict in a series of bitter wars. The final battle in the long history of hostilities between Rome and Carthage was fought in 202 B.C., at a town southwest of Carthage called Zama.

Because the stakes were so tremendous, the Battle of Zama was one of the most important battles in man's history — for the victor in this battle could win domination of the world.

E**IGHTY** dull-gray elephants formed the front line of the enemy army confronting the legions of Rome. Massive, ponderous, the huge beasts lashed their trunks through the air as they awaited the order to charge the foe. It was an array calculated to strike terror into any army — even the mighty warriors of Rome!

The year was 202 B.C. The rising power of Rome stood massed against the forces of her great rival, the city of Carthage in North Africa. For more than sixty years, Rome and Carthage had been fighting a desperate struggle. The prize to the winner was world power; the share of the loser, destruction and oblivion.

The war had gone with Rome. Carthage had been driven back, yielding its empire bit by agonizing bit to the onrushing Romans. The Roman military skill had proven unsurpassable. And Rome had the confident conviction that destiny was on her side.

But one man had arisen to block the Roman dream of world conquest. He was the great Carthaginian general,

Hannibal, who had taken command of the armies of Carthage in 218 B.C. Hannibal was a military genius who kept tottering Carthage from disaster and brought the cold chill of fear to Roman hearts. For sixteen years Hannibal had outgeneraled the Romans — until the Battle of Zama.

He was a crafty man. He had spies lurking everywhere, bringing him news from Rome often before the Roman armies had received it. He wore disguises himself to go on spying missions from time to time. He was worshiped by his soldiers. His word was law.

The Roman historian Dio Cassius wrote of him, "He could lower the superb, elevate the humble, inspire here terror, there confidence; all this in a moment whenever he chose." The great historian Livy said, "His fearlessness in encountering dangers, and his prudence when in the midst of them, were extreme."

The great weapons of the one-eyed [1] Hannibal were three in number: his wild, spirited, fighting men; his wonderful strategic skill; and his force of enormous, terrifying, trained war elephants. In 218 B.C., Hannibal had launched an army from Spain, just across the Mediterranean from Carthage, and had driven eastward through what is now France and was then called Gaul. He had crossed the Alps with his elephants and had struck deep into Italy. Though his armies had suffered heavily, they annihilated the Romans at every battle.

The Roman generals were stunned by Hannibal's successes. "His soldiers are only barbarians," they exclaimed in bewilderment. "They are scarcely trained. They fight like wild men. And yet they defeat us!"

Rome's soldiers were indeed better trained in the arts of war. But no Roman general had the insight, the daring, the sparkling brilliance of Hannibal. He knew how to outguess, how to outfeint, how to outmaneuver. He had smashed every Roman army that had come against him, and had taken firm possession of much of southern Italy. All that had remained was for him to march on Rome and take the city. The upstart Roman nation would be vanquished at last.

Hannibal never took his opportunity. He might have marched in 216 B.C., after shattering the Roman forces at Cannae.[2] His cavalry general, Maharbal, had urged him vigorously: "Now is the time to march on Rome, Hannibal! The city will be yours."

Hannibal had refused to march. The infuriated Maharbal had cried, "Of a truth the gods have not bestowed all things upon the same person. You know how to conquer, Hannibal; but you do not know how to make use of your victory."

History would have been vastly different if Hannibal had captured Rome in 216 B.C. But he had felt that Rome was too strong. He had not had the ships to blockade Rome by sea, nor the troops to lay siege effectively by land. He had decided instead to encircle Rome by capturing her colonies in Spain, Sardinia, and Sicily, and by win-

---

[1] **one-eyed:** Hannibal lost the sight of one eye in 217 B.C., during a battle against the Romans.

[2] **Cannae** (kan′ē): an ancient town in southern Italy.

ning the walled cities of Italy that paid tribute to Rome. Hannibal had switched from the offensive to the defensive after he had captured the territory surrounding Rome. He had concentrated on keeping his gains in Italy, hoping that Rome would weaken in time.

Rome had not weakened. But neither had Rome attempted to drive Hannibal out of Italy. The stalemated war had dragged on and on, Hannibal holding to his captured land and Rome making only a token attempt to dislodge him. Rome's leading general, Fabius, was called "Cunctator," [1] the "Delayer," because he had held back and refused to make a direct assault against Hannibal.

But new Roman generals had arisen who resolved to crush Carthage. One of them, Scipio,[2] had driven the Carthaginians out of Spain. At the battle of the Metaurus, in 207 B.C., Hannibal's brother Hasdrubal had been routed and his severed head sent contemptuously to Hannibal by the Romans. Hannibal himself had remained in the "boot" of Italy, too strong to be driven out but not strong enough to extend his conquests to Rome herself.

While Hannibal had held tight in southern Italy, Scipio had taken the offensive across the Mediterranean into Africa, virtually to Carthage's own doorstep. With Scipio's armies almost at the city walls, the Carthaginians had panicked and sent for Hannibal, telling him to come back from Italy to defend the homeland.

Hannibal had not been willing to give up his hard-won position in Italy.

But Carthage herself was in danger. Indeed, before Hannibal could set sail for Rome, Carthage had been forced to beg for peace. Scipio's armies had surrounded the city and a peace treaty was being negotiated with the Romans when electrifying news had reached Carthage.

"Hannibal has landed! Hannibal is on his way to save us!"

With an army of 20,000 men, Hannibal had landed on African shores. Immediately the jubilant Carthaginians had broken off the peace talks and treacherously imprisoned the Roman envoys. Scipio and the Roman soldiers had been taken by surprise and found themselves in a ticklish spot. They were on hostile soil, far from home, with the enemy's most dreaded general approaching. To make things worse for the Romans, Scipio did not even have his full army with him for, during the peace talks, he had sent some of his troops to go to the aid of an ally of Rome nearby, Masinissa, King of Numidia.[3]

In this tight spot Scipio had chosen the path of boldness. He had known that sooner or later he would have to face the invincible Hannibal, and he did not want to do it near Carthage, where Hannibal would easily be able to obtain reinforcements and supplies. Calling his generals together, Scipio had declared, "We will move inland and force Hannibal to follow us."

The Roman legions had set out for the valley of the Bagradas, a rich, fertile area that produced much of Car-

---

[1] "Cunctator" (kungk·tā′tər).
[2] Scipio (sip′ē·ō).

[3] Numidia (noo·mid′ē·ə): an ancient kingdom in northern Africa, roughly corresponding to modern Algeria.

thage's food and grain. As they had passed through the farmlands, the Romans burned, plundered, and looted, destroying Hannibal's supply lines. In order to put a stop to this destruction, Hannibal had found himself compelled to leave the security of his base at Carthage and follow Scipio into the interior to defeat him there.

Hannibal had struck camp and set out after Scipio. He had marched toward the town of Zama, five days' march southwest of Carthage. But before his armies could encounter those of Scipio, bad news for Carthage had arrived:

"Masinissa has joined Scipio!" a breathless messenger had cried. "He has come with 6,000 infantrymen and 4,000 cavalry!"

Hannibal was dismayed. His own army numbered about 50,000, as against only 36,000 for the combined forces of Scipio and Masinissa. But the Roman soldiers were far more capable, man for man, and their cavalry would far outnumber Hannibal's now.

For the first time in his sixteen-year career as Carthage's general, Hannibal saw possible defeat. Under the blazing African sun he had gone out to parley with Scipio as the opposing forces arrayed themselves at the town of Zama.

The two commanders, accompanied only by interpreters, had met in the open space between the two armies. Hannibal offered a treaty in which Carthage would relinquish all claim to Sicily, Sardinia, and Spain.

But Scipio had already had one taste of Carthaginian treachery in treaty signing, and he was wary. Besides, he felt that his forces were stronger than Hannibal's. So he had haughtily brushed aside Hannibal's proposal. "I cannot again trust the word of a Carthaginian," he had declared.

"Then we must do battle," Hannibal had said.

"If we must, we shall," Scipio had answered. "The attack will commence at dawn."

Hannibal knew all too well how weak his army was, despite its size. He had three infantry groups: his own tried and true men, veterans of his many Italian campaigns; the troops of his other brother, Mago, who had just died; and a hastily assembled force of new recruits.

Hannibal put Mago's men in the front line. They were not Carthaginians, but tough, well-trained men from Gaul and Liguria (western Italy). Right behind them, he assembled the large force of inexperienced recruits. And in the third line, two hundred yards to the rear of the second, he arrayed his own battle-hardened Carthaginians.

In his past battles with the Romans, Hannibal had had strong cavalry divisions that he had used to outflank the enemy. At his great victory of Cannae he had sent his cavalry around to attack the Romans from the rear, causing great devastation. But at Zama he had only 2,000 cavalry; Scipio had at least three times as many. There could be no outflanking today. Hannibal could hope for success only by a direct head-on attack. He put a thousand Carthaginian cavalry on the right wing, a thousand Numidians on the left to serve as shields for his infantry.

His most spectacular force consisted

of eighty elephants — more than he had ever used in one battle before. Hannibal placed the great beasts along the front line, in front of Mago's Ligurian and Gallic soldiers. His strategy was simple. The charging elephants, Hannibal hoped, would throw the Romans into confusion and disorder. Mago's experienced troops would break through the Roman lines, scattering them. Then the second wave, the game but inexperienced new recruits, would charge in, making up in number what they lacked in skill. And finally, with the Romans in disarray, Hannibal's own picked troops of the third line would swoop in for the *coup de grâce*.[1]

On the other side of the field, Scipio was using the traditional Roman battle formation with some special adaptations to suit the situation. His troops were of four types: *hastati* (javelin throwers); *principes* (spearmen); *triarii* (veteran spearmen); and *velites* (light infantry). The usual arrangement was to place the *hastati* in the first line, the *principes* in the second, and the *triarii* in the third, using the *velites* as flankers. This Scipio did. But instead of arranging his men in alternating checkerboard fashion from row to row to present a solid front, Scipio left wide aisles through which he planned to let the Carthaginian elephants pass. Also, he drew the *triarii* farther back than usual, to give them room to cope with the rampaging elephants. On his left flank, Scipio placed his own cavalry, under Laelius; on the right wing, he put Masinissa's Numidian force, both infantry and cavalry.

---

[1] *coup de grâce* (kōō'də-gräs'): finishing blow.

Hannibal gave the order for the elephants to charge. Eighty gigantic "living tanks" thundered toward the waiting Romans as the battle began. Dust rose high. But Scipio had a surprise planned. The men in his front line suddenly whipped out trumpets! A terrifying clamor split the air!

The shrill trumpet calls terrified the elephants. In fright, the unwieldy beasts turned back. Only a few continued on, smashing through and doing great damage among Scipio's troops. But most of the elephants charged Hannibal's own lines in their bewilderment. Spurred on by the shrieking trumpets, the panicky animals hurtled into Hannibal's left wing of cavalry just as the horsemen were about to attack. The cavalry was thrown into confusion, and Masinissa and his Numidians took advantage of the crisis to charge in, driving Hannibal's entire left cavalry wing from the field.

The same thing was happening on the right. There, the Roman cavalry under Laelius was routing Hannibal's other cavalry wing and driving it, too, into retreat.

Those elephants that had not turned back against Hannibal plowed forward. But Scipio's cunningly devised aisles now opened wide, and the elephants continued on, passing harmlessly through the Roman legions and on into the open fields beyond. Hannibal now found himself at the outset of the battle stripped of his cavalry and his elephants both — thanks to Scipio's idea of using trumpets to frighten the mighty beasts.

The first phase of the battle was over. Now, as the sun rose blisteringly in the cloudless blue sky, a brutal frontal attack started. The front lines of both armies collided with a ringing clang of shields. The veteran Ligurians and Gauls that Mago had trained performed valiantly, and for a while held the upper hand.

But as each front-line Roman fell, another stepped forward to take his place. On the Carthaginian side it was otherwise. The untrained recruits of Hannibal's second line held back in fear. Slowly, the ranks of Mago's men were thinned. The Carthaginian front line was forced steadily back.

"Where's the second line?" Mago's men asked each other in the heat of the battle. "Why aren't they supporting us?"

"They're afraid!" someone shouted. "They aren't going to fight!"

Sudden panic swept the Carthaginian front line. Feeling that they had been betrayed by the men behind them, they turned to flee. But now, the hesitant second line closed ranks against their own allies. Under orders to hold their formation no matter what, they refused to let the fleeing Gauls and Ligurians break through. A battle broke out between Hannibal's own first and second lines, while the gleeful Romans completed their massacre of Hannibal's front-line men.

Belatedly the second line showed heroism. Now that the soldiers of Mago's army were gone, the raw recruits of the second line had to bear the brunt of Scipio's assault. They rose to the challenge, holding off the *hastati,* or javelin wielders. The ground was covered with corpses and was slippery with blood.

The Romans, who had scented victory half an hour before, were troubled by this unexpected display of valor on the part of Hannibal's unskilled second line. The *hastati* wavered, and their tight formation began to break up as fallen corpses interfered with their positions. "When they had surmounted the obstacles," wrote the historian Polybius, "the two lines charged each other with the greatest fire and fury. Being nearly equal in spirit, number, courage, and arms, the battle was for a long time undecided, the men in their obstinate valor falling dead without giving way a step."

During all this, Hannibal kept his third line back, out of the fray. They were his most experienced soldiers, and he was saving them. He did not believe in sending a line into battle while the line in front was still unbroken.

The *hastati* and the *principes* surged forward, and even the *triarii,* Scipio's third line, entered the fray. The Carthaginian second line gave way steadily, and finally broke into flight.

Now the battle entered its final stage. In the words of Livy, the Romans "had penetrated to their real antagonists, men equal to them in the nature of their arms, in their experience of war, in the fame of their achievements."

The advantage now appeared to lie with Hannibal. He still had the nucleus of his army intact — 24,000 superb fighting men, skilled in battle, and completely fresh and rested. Against them, Scipio could only throw some 20,000 men, many of them already weary from the struggle against Hannibal's second line.

Once again Scipio showed his bold inventive nature. He called his troops together and, with the enemy only a few hunded yards away, completely rearranged his forces. Instead of a wide frontage that overlapped the Carthaginian line, he now drew his *hastati* together in a concentrated unit that was as solid as possible. He sent the *principes* and *triarii* out on the flanks to reinforce the front line, stringing them out on a wide arc.

Scipio's idea was to smash powerfully into the Carthaginian lines with his massed *hastati*, and then to encircle the enemy with the *principes* and *triarii*. This, he hoped, would put Hannibal's army in a position where it could be easily attacked when the cavalry under Masinissa and Laelius returned from its pursuit of Hannibal's horsemen.

Masinissa and Laelius, though, had apparently been too energetic in their chase, and had gone far from the battlefield. Scipio was compelled to fight a delaying action until they returned. His tired men struggled doggedly against Hannibal's rested veterans, and the issue hung in doubt as the long day waned and the sun began to slip toward the horizon.

Then, in the literal nick of time, the Roman cavalry appeared. The horsemen charged the rear of Hannibal's army. Hannibal's infantry, pinned by foot soldiers in front, cavalry behind, was cut to pieces. The battle ended in a rout. The Roman cries of victory were loud. The Carthaginians fought virtually to the last man. When all was clearly lost, Hannibal and a few of his aides made their escape.

Scipio now turned toward Carthage. Capture of Carthage itself was out of the question; the city was magnificently fortified, and Scipio's decimated [1] army was in no condition to mount a prolonged siege. Scipio offered peace terms to Carthage, and the war-weary city, at Hannibal's advice, accepted. Under the terms of peace, Carthage agreed to pay Rome a tribute of ten thousand talents of silver (some $15,-000,000) over the next fifty years, to hand all its warships and elephants over to Rome, and to carry on no future war without Rome's consent.

Hannibal was chosen by his defeated people to head the government of Carthage, and he ruled wisely until 196 B.C., when he was compelled by Roman schemes to flee into exile. For the next thirteen years he lived abroad, planning campaigns against Rome that were never carried out and fighting the battles of other kings. In 183 B.C., a cowardly king who had hired Hannibal as a general agreed to turn him over to the Romans. But the noble Carthagin-

[1] **decimated** (des'ə·māt·ed): almost entirely wiped out.

ian cheated his lifelong enemies by taking poison before they could seize him.

The Battle of Zama is one of the great turning points in world history because it marked the end of Carthage's hopes of destroying the rising power of Rome. So long as Carthage had the brilliant Hannibal, there was the possibility of ultimate victory over Rome. At Zama, Hannibal tasted defeat for the first time, and Carthage never recovered.

And so Rome, which only a century before had been master merely of a small section of Italy, extended its sway to Spain, Sicily, North Africa, and the entire western Mediterranean area, without a challenger. The city of Carthage, the sole rival to Rome's sway, had been destroyed. For the next six hundred years — a time longer than that from Columbus's to our own — Rome would rule the world.

A TURNING POINT IN HISTORY

1. Until the Battle of Zama, Hannibal was a success. What qualities contributed to his success? What three great weapons did he have? What decision, made in 216 B.C., may have led to his downfall?

2. Trace the events that led up to the Battle of Zama.

3. How were Hannibal's elephants used against him? What other strategies of Scipio led to victory for the Romans? What weaknesses of Hannibal's army led to his defeat?

4. What happened to Hannibal and to Carthage after the battle? Why is the Battle of Zama considered one of the turning points in world history?

5. What does this account of the Battle of Zama tell you about the Romans?

6. Name some battles of modern times that might be called turning points in history.

WORDS FROM LATIN

The results of the Battle of Zama affected the course of world history. As Rome sent its armies around the world, their Latin language greatly influenced the languages of many peoples. Our English language, for example, shows strong Latin influence. Over sixty percent of the words in English are derived from Latin.

Even today we make use of Latin when we make up a word to name a new machine or a new concept. For example, the word *airplane* was taken from two Latin words: *aer* meaning "air" and *planus* meaning "level" (referring to the level surface of the airplane). Here are some other aviation words. Look each word up in a dictionary to see which Latin word or words it comes from.

motor	propeller
aviator	supersonic
jet	turboprop

LOOKING AT PARAGRAPHS

A good author separates his material into paragraphs as a help to the reader. Each paragraph should help move a composition forward.

Beginning on page 602 four paragraphs tell about Hannibal. The topic sentence of the first of these paragraphs is "But one man had arisen to block the Roman dream of world conquest." Instead of taking one paragraph to tell about Hannibal, the author uses four. Some of these paragraphs have topic sentences, but some do not. Which paragraphs do have topic sentences? What main idea about Hannibal does each paragraph contain?

Julius Caesar

PLUTARCH

To many people, the word *Rome* immediately calls to mind the name *Julius Caesar*. Perhaps no other man so well represents the genius of Rome, and perhaps no other Roman had such a great effect on the course of world events, for Caesar's military victories helped Rome to expand her rule over Europe.

Though Rome's power was great when Caesar was a young man, her formerly great republican form of government was tottering. The city was experiencing a series of bloody purges and civil wars, and general after general was trying to seize control of the government.

As this selection from Plutarch's biography opens, Caesar had already been elected to a one-year term as consul, and had, thus, been one of the chief magistrates of the Roman republic. To strengthen his position further, Caesar had made friends with two of Rome's most powerful politicians, Crassus and Pompey. His hold on Pompey was tightened when Caesar betrothed his daughter, Julia, to him. Yet Caesar was using Pompey for his own ambitions, and the alliance between the two men was shaky and dangerous.

Knowing that military experience would help his political career, Caesar soon took command of four legions of soldiers and

"Julius Caesar" from *Plutarch: Ten Famous Lives* by Charles A. Robinson, Jr., copyright © 1962 by Charles A. Robinson, Jr. Reprinted by permission of E. P. Dutton & Co., Inc.

a five-year assignment to the provinces of Gaul, an area roughly corresponding to modern France. Caesar was to bring Gaul to her knees.

THE PERIOD of those many expeditions in which he subdued Gaul showed Caesar to be a soldier and general not in the least inferior to any of the greatest commanders who have ever appeared at the heads of armies. The difficulty and extent of the country he subdued; the number and strength of the enemy he defeated; the wildness and perfidiousness [1] of the tribes and his goodwill toward them; his clemency to the conquered; his gifts and kindnesses to his soldiers — what other general in history can match this? During the ten years he ultimately spent in Gaul, he captured eight hundred towns, subdued three hundred states, and, of the three million men who opposed him, he killed one million and captured another million.

Caesar inspired his men with his own love of honor and passion for distinction. By generously distributing money and honors he showed that he

---

[1] **perfidiousness** (pər·fid′ē·əs·nes): treachery.

was not heaping up wealth from the wars for his own luxury, but that it was a reward for valor. Moreover, there was no danger to which he did not willingly expose himself, no labor from which he shrank. Although the soldiers were not mystified by his contempt of danger, because they knew how much he coveted honor, they were astonished by his enduring so much hardship beyond his natural strength. For Caesar was of a slight build, had a soft and white skin, and was subject to epilepsy.[1] However, he did not make his bodily weakness a pretext for ease, but rather used war as the best possible medicine; by fatiguing journeys, simple diet, frequent sleeping outdoors, and continual exercise, he fortified his body against all attacks. He slept generally in his chariots or while he was carried in a litter.[2] In the daytime he was thus carried to forts, garrisons, and camps, one servant sitting with him, who used to write down what he dictated as he went.

After settling the affairs in Gaul, Caesar spent the winter by the Po,[3] in order to carry out his plans at Rome. He gave money to his candidates for office, so that they could corrupt the people and buy their votes and then, when elected, advance his own power. More significant was the fact that the most powerful men in Rome came to see him at Luca,[4] among them Pompey and Crassus, and in all about two hundred senators. It was decided at Luca that Pompey and Crassus should be consuls the next year and that Caesar's command in Gaul should be extended for another five years.

After this, Caesar returned to Gaul, where he found that German tribes had crossed the Rhine and stirred up revolts. So Caesar made this a pretext for invading the land of the Germans, being ambitious to be the first man to cross the Rhine with an army. He built a bridge across the river, though it was wide at this point. The current was swift and dashed trunks of trees against the foundations of the bridge. Caesar, however, drove great piles of wood into the bottom of the river just before the bridge, and these caught the trees and other things floating down and thus protected the bridge.

The bridge was completed in ten days. The Suevi, who were the most warlike people in all Germany, fled before his approach. After he had burned the countryside, Caesar returned to Gaul eighteen days later.

Caesar's expedition to Britain was the most famous example of his courage. He was the first who brought a navy into the western ocean or who sailed into the Atlantic with an army to make war. Historians had actually doubted the existence of the island, considering it a mere name or piece of fiction, and so Caesar may be said to have carried the Roman Empire beyond the limits of the known world. He crossed twice from Gaul and fought several battles. But he did not win much for himself, since the islanders were very poor. Accordingly, he took hostages from the king and, after im-

[1] **epilepsy:** a disease marked by attacks of unconsciousness, sometimes accompanied by convulsions.
[2] **litter:** a couch between poles carried by men or by horses.
[3] **Po:** a river in northern Italy.
[4] **Luca:** a city in north-central Italy.

posing a tribute, left Britain.

Caesar's troops were now so numerous that he had to distribute them in various camps for winter quarters. Then, according to custom, he went to Italy. Scattered revolts brought him back soon to Gaul; and, in the course of the winter, he visited every part of the country. But after a while, the seeds of war, which had long since been secretly sown by the most powerful men in those warlike nations, broke forth into the greatest and most dangerous war that was ever fought there. More men had gathered for it, youthful and vigorous and well armed; they had much money; their towns were strongly fortified. Besides, it was winter, and the rivers were frozen, the woods were covered with snow, paths were obliterated, and there were overflowing marshes. It seemed unlikely, therefore, that Caesar would march against the rebels. The general who was in supreme command of the rebels was Vercingetorix,[1] chief of the Arverni.

But Caesar was gifted above all other men with the faculty of making the right use of everything in war, and especially in seizing the right moment. Therefore, as soon as he heard of the revolt, he advanced quickly in the terrible weather with his army. In fact, in the time that it would have taken an ordinary messenger to cover the distance, Caesar appeared with all his army, ravaged the country, reduced outposts, and captured towns.

Even the Haedui,[2] who had hitherto been friends of the Roman people and had been honored by them, joined the rebels. Accordingly Caesar struck out for the land of the Sequani, who were his friends. At this point tens of thousands of the enemy set upon him, but after much slaughter he won a victory.

The rest of the enemy fled with Vercingetorix into a town called Alesia. Caesar besieged it, though the height of the walls and the number of defenders made it appear impregnable.[3] Then suddenly, from outside the walls, Caesar was assailed by a greater danger than can be described. For the best men of Gaul, picked out of each nation and well-armed, came to the relief of Alesia. There were 300,000 of these men, and inside the town were 170,000 more. And so Caesar was shut up between the two forces. He now built two walls, one toward the town, and the other against the relieving army, for he knew that he would be ruined if the enemy joined forces.

The danger that Caesar underwent at Alesia justly gained him great honor and gave him the opportunity of showing his valor as no other contest had done. But it seems extraordinary that he was able to defeat thousands of men outside the town without those inside being able to see it. Even the Romans guarding the wall next to the town did not know of it, until finally they heard the cries of the men and women inside who spied the Roman soldiers carrying into their camp great quantities of shields adorned with gold and silver, and breastplates stained with blood, besides cups and tents made in the Gallic fashion. Just as fast as that did a vast army vanish like a ghost or dream, most

[1] **Vercingetorix** (vûr′sin·jet′ər·iks).
[2] **Haedui** (hed′yōō·ī).

[3] **impregnable** (im·preg′nə·bəl): resistant to force.

of them being killed on the spot.

At last those who were in Alesia surrendered. Vercingetorix put on his best armor, adorned his horse, and rode out of the gates to Caesar; then he dismounted and threw off his armor and remained quietly sitting at Caesar's feet until he was led away for the triumph in Rome.

Back in Gaul, Caesar had received letters announcing that his daughter, Julia, Pompey's wife, had died in childbirth; soon afterward the child also died. Both Caesar and Pompey were much affected by Julia's death; as were also their friends, for they felt that the alliance was broken which had kept the troubled state in peace.

Caesar had long ago resolved upon Pompey's overthrow, as had Pompey, for that matter, on his. The fear of Crassus had kept them in peace, but Crassus had recently been killed. And so, if one of them wished to make himself the greatest man in Rome, he had only to overthrow the other.

Rome itself was now the scene of election riots and murders. Some thought that the only hope lay in monarchy. Others tried to reconcile Pompey and Caesar, but they would not yield, and finally two of Caesar's friends — Antony and Curio — were driven out of the senate house with insults. This gave Caesar the chance to inflame his soldiers, for he showed them two reputable Romans of authority who had been forced to escape in a hired wagon, dressed as slaves.

Caesar was now in Gaul on the southern side of the Alps, with 300 cavalry and 5,000 infantry; the rest of his army was beyond the Alps, with orders to follow. But Caesar felt that here, at the beginning of his design, he did not need large forces; he planned, rather, to astound his enemies with the speed and boldness of his plan. This particular day he spent in public as a spectator at gladiatorial games.[1] Then, a little before night, he dressed and went into the hall and chatted for some time with those he had invited to supper. When it began to grow dark, he rose from the table and made his excuses to the company. Then he and a few friends drove off in hired wagons, some going one way and some another — so that no one could suspect what they were up to — until at last he came to the River Rubicon, which divides Cisalpine[2] Gaul from Italy proper.

Caesar now began to reflect upon the danger, and he wavered when he considered the greatness of the enterprise. He checked himself and halted while he turned things over in his mind. He discussed the matter at some length with friends who were with him, estimating how many calamities his passing of that small river would bring on mankind and what a tale about it would be transmitted to posterity. At last, in a sort of passion, throwing aside calculation and abandoning himself to what might come, he used the proverb of people entering upon dangerous attempts, "The die is cast," and crossed the river. He then pushed south as fast as possible.

Wide gates, so to speak, were now thrown open to let in war upon every

[1] **gladiatorial games:** public entertainments in which slaves, captives, or paid freemen fought other men or animals.
[2] **Cisalpine** (sĭs·ăl′pĭn) **Gaul:** the part of Gaul south of the Alps.

land and sea. Men and women fled, in
their consternation, from one town of
Italy to another. The city of Rome was
overrun with a deluge of people flying
in from all the neighboring places.
Magistrates could no longer govern, nor
could the eloquence of an orator quiet
the mob.

Pompey at this time had more forces
than Caesar. But he did not think
clearly and believed false reports that
Caesar was close at hand. He was carried away by the general panic. And so
he issued an edict that the city was in
a state of anarchy [1] and left it, ordering
the senators to follow him unless they
preferred tyranny to their country and
liberty.

Pompey fled south all the way to
Brundisium [2] and shipped the consuls
and soldiers across the Adriatic Sea.
He himself soon followed, on Caesar's

approach. But Caesar could not pursue
him, since he had no boats, and therefore turned back to Rome. He had
made himself master of all Italy, without bloodshed, in sixty days.

Caesar arranged things in Rome and
then went off to Spain, so that no enemy would be left behind him when he
marched against Pompey. Back in
Rome, he stopped only briefly and then
hastened with all speed to Brundisium.
It was the beginning of January and
the winter storms made it difficult for
him to transport his troops across the
Adriatic. Finally this was done, and
Caesar was joined by Antony and other
friends. After several skirmishes, both
Pompey and Caesar moved their armies into Greece.

The two armies now encamped at
Pharsalus, in Thessaly.[3] Pompey was
still against fighting, because of certain
omens. His friends, on the other hand,
acted as if they had already won the

---

[1] **anarchy** (an′ər·kē): lawless confusion and
political disorder.
[2] **Brundisium** (brun·diz′ē·əm): a seaport in
southeastern Italy, now called Brindisi.

[3] **Thessaly** (thes′ə·lē): in ancient times, a
division of northern Greece.

battle, and some even sent messages to Rome to rent houses for them fit for consuls and praetors,[1] so sure were they of themselves. The cavalry was especially anxious to fight, being splendidly armed and mounted on fine horses; also, they numbered 7,000 to Caesar's 1,000. Similarly, Pompey had 45,000 infantry to Caesar's 22,000.

Caesar collected together his soldiers and told them that reinforcements were on the way, but they called out to him not to wait. As soon as the sacrifices had been made to the gods, the seer[2] told him that within three days he would come to a decisive action.

The night before the battle, as Caesar was making the rounds about midnight, there was a light seen in the heavens, very bright and flaming, which seemed to pass over Caesar's camp and fall into Pompey's. In the morning, Caesar's soldiers saw panic among the enemy.

The signal for battle was now given on both sides. Pompey ordered the infantry not to break their order, but to stand their ground and receive the enemy's first attack till they came within a javelin's throw. Caesar, in his own writings, blames Pompey's generalship in this regard: Pompey should have realized, says Caesar, how the first encounter, when made on the run, gives weight to the blows and actually fires the men's spirits into a flame.

While the infantry was engaged on the flank, Pompey's cavalry rode up confidently and opened their ranks wide, so that they could surround

Caesar's right wing. At this very moment, Caesar's six cohorts of infantry, which he had moved up from the rear and had stationed behind his right wing, rushed out and attacked the cavalry. They now followed the special instructions which Caesar had given them. This was that they were not to throw their javelins from a distance nor were they to strike at the legs and thighs of the enemy. They must aim at their faces. Caesar had noted that most of Pompey's men were young, not accustomed to battles and wounds; they were naturally vain, being in the flower of their youth, and would not wish to risk either death now or a scar for the future. And that is the way it worked out. For Pompey's cavalry could not stand the sight of the javelins, but turned and covered their faces. Now in disorder, they fled and ruined everything. With Pompey's cavalry beaten back, Caesar's men outflanked the infantry and cut it to pieces.

When Pompey, who was commanding the other wing of his army, saw the cavalry broken and fleeing, he was no longer himself. He forgot that he was Pompey the Great and, like someone whom the gods have deprived of his senses, retired to his tent. He did not say a word, but just sat there, until his whole army was routed and the enemy appeared upon the defenses which had been thrown up before his camp. Then he seemed to recover his senses, and with the words, "What, are they in the camp too?" he took off his general's uniform and put on ordinary clothes. He then stole off and made his way to Egypt.

After the victory Caesar pardoned

---

[1] **praetors** (prē′tərz): government officials, in charge of administering justice.
[2] **seer** (sē′ər): prophet.

his opponents, including Brutus — who afterward was to kill him. He then set off in pursuit of Pompey, but when he reached Alexandria, in Egypt, he learned that Pompey had been murdered. This caused Caesar to weep, for, as he wrote friends in Rome, his greatest desire was always to save the lives of fellow citizens who had fought against him.

Caesar passed on to Syria and Asia Minor. At Zela, in Pontus,[1] he destroyed Pharnaces,[2] an enemy of Rome, and sent the senate a message that expressed the promptness and rapidity of his action: "I came, I saw, I conquered."

His victories brought war at long last to an end. Triumphs, banquets, and other celebrations were held in Rome on a magnificent scale. But a census of the people showed that Rome's population had declined from 320,000 to 150,000. So great a waste had the civil wars made in Rome alone, to say nothing of the other parts of Italy and the provinces.

The Romans, hoping that the government of a single person would give them time to breathe after so many civil wars and calamities, made Caesar dictator for life. This was an out-and-out tyranny, for his power was both absolute and perpetual. But Caesar was moderate and even gave offices to those who had fought against him, such as Brutus and Cassius. He entertained the common people with more feasting and free gifts of grain and founded colonies at Carthage and Corinth, which

Rome had destroyed a century earlier. The colonies provided a good place for his soldiers to settle.

Caesar was born to do great things, and had a passion for honor. His noble exploits merely inflamed him with a passion to accomplish even more. But Caesar's desire to be king brought on him open and mortal hatred.

One day, when a festival was being celebrated in the Forum, Caesar was dressed in his triumphal robe and seated on a golden chair at the speaker's platform, or rostra. Antony, who was then consul, came up to Caesar and offered him a diadem[3] wreathed with laurel. There was a slight shout of approval from the crowd, and when Caesar refused it, there was universal applause. It was offered a second time and again refused, and again all applauded. Caesar, finding that this idea could not succeed, ordered the diadem to be carried into the Capitol.

Such matters made the multitude think of Marcus Brutus, whose paternal ancestor centuries earlier had slain the

[1] **Pontus:** an ancient country in Asia Minor, on the Black Sea.
[2] **Pharnaces** (fär′nə·sēz): King of Pontus.

[3] **diadem** (dī′ə·dem): here, an ornamental headband, a badge of royalty.

last of Rome's kings. But the honors and favors he had received from Caesar took the edge off Brutus's desire to overthrow the new monarchy. Those who looked on Brutus to effect the change would put papers near his official chair, with sentences such as, "You are asleep, Brutus," "You are no longer Brutus." Cassius, too, because of a private grudge against Caesar, was eager to be done with him. Caesar had his suspicions of Cassius and once remarked to a friend, "What do you think Cassius is aiming at? I don't like him; he looks so pale." He added that he feared pale, lean fellows, meaning Cassius and Brutus.

Fate, however, is to all appearances more unavoidable than expected. Many strange prodigies [1] and apparitions were now observed. As to the lights in the heavens, the noises heard in the night, and the wild birds which perched in the Forum, these are perhaps not worth noticing in a case as great as this. But, it is also said that a seer warned Caesar to watch for a great danger on the Ides of March.[2] When this day arrived, Caesar met the seer as he was going into the senate house and said jokingly to him, "Well, the Ides of March have come." The seer answered calmly, "Yes, they have come, but they are not yet past."

The day before his assassination, Caesar dined with Lepidus. As he was signing some letters at the table, the question came up as to what kind of death was best. Caesar answered im-

mediately, "A sudden one." Later, when he was in bed, all the doors and windows of the house flew open together; he was startled at the noise and the light which broke into the room, and he sat up in bed. By the light of the moon he could see his wife, Calpurnia, fast asleep, but he also heard her utter in her dream some indistinct words and inarticulate groans. Later on, she said that she had been dreaming that she was weeping over Caesar, holding him butchered in her arms.

In the morning, Calpurnia urged Caesar to postpone the meeting of the senate to another day, but he would not hear of it. After he left his house, a teacher of Greek philosophy, who knew of the conspiracy, slipped Caesar a piece of paper and said, "Read this, Caesar, alone and quickly." Caesar tried to read it, but could not, on account of the crowd pressing in on him. But he kept the note in his hand till he entered the senate.

All these things might happen by chance. But the place that was destined for the scene of the murder — where the senate was then meeting — was the same in which Pompey's statue stood. A supernatural force seemed to guide affairs to this spot. In fact, just before the murder, Cassius looked at Pompey's statue and silently implored his aid.

When Caesar entered, the senate rose in respect, and then some of the confederates pressed up to him, pretending that they had petitions. As he seated himself, Cimber seized his toga and pulled it down from his neck, which was the signal for the assault. Casca gave him the first cut in the neck, nei-

---

[1] **prodigies:** here, ominous signs of something to come.
[2] **Ides of March:** the fifteenth of March on the Roman calendar.

ther a mortal nor a dangerous blow, for he was probably too nervous, here at the beginning. Caesar immediately turned around and seized the dagger and kept hold of it. And both cried out, Caesar in Latin, "Vile Casca, what does this mean?" And Casca, in Greek, to his brother, "Brother, help!"

The conspirators now closed in on Caesar from every side, with their drawn daggers in their hands. No matter which way Caesar turned, he was met with blows; he could see weapons leveled at his face and eyes; on all sides he was surrounded by wild beasts. The conspirators had agreed that each of them should make a stab at Caesar and taste of his blood. And so Brutus also stabbed him. When Caesar saw Brutus's dagger, he covered his face with his toga and let himself fall at the foot of the pedestal on which Pompey's statue stood, thus spattering it with his blood. It seemed as if Pompey himself had presided, as it were, over the revenge on his enemy, who lay here at his feet and breathed out his last with twenty-three wounds in his body.

The senators, who had not been part of the conspiracy, now fled out of doors and filled the people with so much alarm that some shut up their houses, and others left their shops. Everyone seemed to run this way and that. Antony and Lepidus, Caesar's most faithful friends, who had been kept out of the senate house during the murder, sneaked off and hid in friends' houses. Brutus and his followers, still hot from their deed, marched in a body from the senate house to the Capitol and called on people, as they passed them, to resume their liberty.

Next day, Brutus and the others came down from the Capitol and addressed the people, who showed by their silence that they pitied Caesar and respected Brutus. Then the senate passed an amnesty [1] for what was past and took steps to reconcile all parties. The senate ordered that Caesar should receive divine honors, and that no act of his was to be revoked. At the same time, it gave Brutus and his followers the command of provinces and other important posts. And so, people thought that everything had been brought to a happy conclusion.

But when Caesar's will was opened and it was found that he had left a considerable legacy to each Roman citizen, and then when his body was carried through the Forum all mangled with wounds, the people could contain themselves no longer. They heaped together a pile of benches, railings, and tables, and then set Caesar's corpse on top and set fire to it all. [2]

Caesar died in his fifty-sixth year, not having survived Pompey by much more than four years. The empire and power which he sought through his life with so much risk, he finally achieved with much difficulty, but he got little from it except glory. But the great genius, which attended him through his lifetime, even after his death remained as the avenger of his murder, pursuing through every sea and land all those connected with it and allowing none to escape.

The most remarkable of mere hu-

---

[1] amnesty: general pardon.
[2] Those Romans who could afford to do so had their relatives' bodies burned and their ashes preserved. The very poor or the scorned were buried in common pits in a public cemetery.

man coincidences was that which befell Cassius, who, when he was defeated by Antony and Octavian at Philippi,[1] killed himself with the same dagger which he had used against Caesar; Brutus also committed suicide after that battle. But the most extraordinary supernatural happenings were the great comet, which shone very bright for seven nights after Caesar's death and then disappeared, and the dimness of the sun. The sun remained pale and dull all that year, never really shining at sunrise and not giving much heat. Consequently, the air was damp and the fruits never properly ripened.

[1] **Philippi** (fi·lip′ī): an ancient town in northern Macedonia, Greece.

CAESAR

1. This selection from Plutarch's account of the life of Caesar tells a great deal about Caesar the army commander. In what ways was Caesar a courageous and imaginative general, especially at Alesia? Why was the expedition to Britain a famous example of his courage?

2. Caesar had great political ambitions, and some people claim he used his military victories for political advancement. His great chance was taken when he decided to march through Italy, overthrow Pompey, and take control of Rome. Tell how Caesar did this. When he crossed the Rubicon, why did Caesar say, "The die is cast" (page 613)?

3. Describe the battle in Greece between Pompey and Caesar.

4. What did the Roman people do for Caesar after he returned to Rome following his victory over Pompey and other enemies?

5. Why did Caesar become so mortally hated? What was the significance of Antony's offering Caesar a crown? Why did the crowd applaud when Caesar rejected it? Describe Caesar's assassination.

6. Plutarch mentions several signs that should have warned Caesar that his life was in danger. What were these signs? Does Plutarch make it seem as if Caesar's murder were destined by fate and, therefore, unavoidable? Explain.

7. What attitude do you think Plutarch had toward Caesar? What attitude might someone else take toward Caesar?

8. What is your opinion of Caesar from reading this account by Plutarch? Can you think of other men in history who were assassinated? What were the reasons for these acts? How did these men compare with Caesar?

9. Can you think of other men who have sought power, as Caesar did? Compare these men to Caesar. Did they show both good and bad qualities, as Caesar did? Explain.

10. Plutarch wrote several biographies of famous men, and he had strong motives for writing these biographies. He wanted his readers to learn something from the lives of great men. What lesson do you think he wished readers to draw from this life of Julius Caesar?

11. What references did you find in this narrative to other selections included in this unit on Rome? What do you remember about Brutus's paternal ancestor, mentioned on page 616? The city of Carthage is also referred to on page 616. What do you recall about its destruction?

WORDS FROM LATIN

We read here that Caesar was seated at the speaker's plattorm, or rostra. *Rostra* is a Latin word meaning "beaks." In the days of ancient Rome, the speaker's platform was decorated with parts captured from enemy ships, and often these parts consisted of a beaked head that was used on the prow of a ship for ramming. Today we use the word *rostrum* to mean a speaker's pulpit or platform — not realizing that we are really using the Latin word for "beak."

Many words that we have taken over from Latin have interesting stories behind them. Tracing the history of words and seeing how they have changed in meaning is fascinating. Find the answers to the questions below. You might discover interesting and surprising facts about the history of each word. You will have to use a dictionary.

candidate: What does this word have to do with being "clothed in white"?

senate: How does "old" figure in the meaning of this word?

infantry: Why do you think this word came from one meaning "youth"?

suitor: What does a suitor have to do with "one who follows"?

lunatic: Why would the "moon" be part of this word?

caper: How does "goat" figure in the meaning of this word?

SENTENCES: GROUP MODIFIERS

Groups of words that are used as modifiers are often longer than the basic sentence itself. Notice how this is true of the group modifier in the following sentence:

"He was the first *who brought a navy into the western ocean or who sailed into the Atlantic with an army to make war.*"

How might the ideas in this sentence have been expressed in two shorter sentences?

Notice the long group modifier in the following sentence. How could the ideas in this sentence have been expressed in two separate sentences?

"After this, Caesar returned to Gaul, *where he found that German tribes had crossed the Rhine and stirred up revolts.*"

Expand the following sentences by adding group modifiers.

The general who _____ was Vercingetorix.

Alesia was a town in Gaul where _____.

Caesar's wife had dreamed that _____.

Caesar was murdered because _____.

OUTLINING

In this section of Plutarch's biographical narrative about Julius Caesar, several broad topics about Caesar's career are developed. Below are listed fifteen general topics that this selection discusses in some detail. Referring closely to the story itself, list at least one or two subtopics under each general topic in this list.

   I. The characteristics of Caesar
  II. The winter by the Po
 III. The invasion of Germany
 IV. The invasion of Britain
  V. The battle with Vercingetorix
 VI. The break with Pompey
VII. The march to Rome
VIII. Pompey's flight
 IX. The battle with Pompey in Greece
  X. Caesar made dictator for life
 XI. The offering of the diadem
XII. Plots against Caesar
XIII. Portents of danger
XIV. The assassination
 XV. Results of the murder

For example, under topic I, you might begin with the following three subtopics:

  I. The characteristics of Caesar
    A. Skillful as a soldier and as a general
    B. Generous with the wealth he got from his wars
    C. Brave in the face of danger

Lines from Julius Caesar

WILLIAM SHAKESPEARE

William Shakespeare, the great English dramatist, wrote a play about Julius Caesar. Many people believe that Shakespeare based his play on Plutarch's life of Caesar, part of which formed the preceding selection. Here are some famous lines from Shakespeare's play.

Cassius Speaks of Caesar to Brutus

At the opening of the play, Cassius, one of the conspirators, tries to turn Brutus against Caesar. It is important to the conspirators that they win over Brutus, a member of an old and respected family of Rome. These lines are from Act I, Scene ii, of *Julius Caesar*. Cassius is speaking of Caesar.

> Why, man, he doth bestride the narrow world
> Like a Colossus, and we petty men
> Walk under his huge legs and peep about
> To find ourselves dishonorable graves.
> Men at some time are masters of their fates.
> The fault, dear Brutus, is not in our stars,
> But in ourselves, that we are underlings.

Caesar to Antony

Caesar notices Cassius talking to Brutus. Caesar's remarks to his friend Antony foreshadow the conspiracy against him. These lines are from Act I, Scene ii. Caesar is speaking.

> Let me have men about me that are fat,
> Sleek-headed men, and such as sleep o' nights.
> Yon Cassius has a lean and hungry look.
> He thinks too much, such men are dangerous.

Caesar to Calpurnia

On the morning of his murder, Caesar's wife says that she has had strange dreams, and she urges Caesar to stay at home that day. But Caesar does not heed her, and he speaks these memorable lines in Act II, Scene ii.

Cowards die many times before their deaths,
The valiant never taste of death but once.
Of all the wonders that I yet have heard,
It seems to me most strange that men should fear,
Seeing that death, a necessary end,
Will come when it will come.

Antony's Oration at Caesar's Funeral

Caesar has been assassinated. Brutus delivers the funeral address and tries to win over the people with his arguments against Caesar. Although advised against it, Brutus allows Antony, Caesar's close friend, to speak also. Here is Antony's famous speech to the Romans from Act III, Scene ii.

Friends, Romans, countrymen, lend me your ears.
I come to bury Caesar, not to praise him.
The evil that men do lives after them,
The good is oft interred ° with their bones.
So let it be with Caesar. The noble Brutus   5
Hath told you Caesar was ambitious.
If it were so, it was a grievous fault,
And grievously hath Caesar answered it.
Here, under leave of Brutus and the rest —
For Brutus is an honorable man,   10
So are they all, all honorable men —
Come I to speak in Caesar's funeral.
He was my friend, faithful and just to me.
But Brutus says he was ambitious,
And Brutus is an honorable man.   15
He hath brought many captives home to Rome,
Whose ransoms did the general coffers ° fill.

4. **interred** (in·tûrd′): buried.   17. **coffers:** safes, boxes in which treasures are kept.

Did this in Caesar seem ambitious?
When that the poor have cried, Caesar hath wept —
Ambition should be made of sterner stuff.   20
Yet Brutus says he was ambitious,
And Brutus is an honorable man.
You all did see that on the Lupercal °
I thrice presented him a kingly crown,
Which he did thrice refuse. Was this ambition?   25
Yet Brutus says he was ambitious,
And, sure, he is an honorable man.
I speak not to disprove what Brutus spoke,
But here I am to speak what I do know.
You all did love him once, not without cause: 30
What cause withholds you then to mourn for him?
O judgment, thou art fled to brutish beasts,
And men have lost their reason! Bear with me,
My heart is in the coffin there with Caesar,
And I must pause till it come back to me.   35

23. **Lupercal** (lōō′pər·kal): an ancient Roman festival celebrated on February 15.

Antony Speaks of Brutus

Antony's speech arouses the mob and starts a civil war. After much bloodshed, the conspirators are defeated, and Cassius and Brutus kill themselves to avoid capture. At the close of the play, in Act V, Scene v, Antony looks sadly on the body of Brutus and says these words.

This was the noblest Roman of them all.
All the conspirators, save only he,
Did what they did in envy of great Caesar.
He only, in general honest thought
And common good to all, made one of them.
His life was gentle, and the elements
So mixed in him that Nature might stand up
And say to all the world, "This was a man."

THOUGHTS FROM SHAKESPEARE

1. Cassius compared Caesar to a Colossus. The Colossus was a gigantic bronze statue of the god Apollo which bestrode the entrance to the harbor of the ancient city of Rhodes. What did Cassius picture other men doing around this "Colossus"? Centuries ago people used to think that the movement of the stars influenced man's fate. What did Cassius think of this idea?

2. What kind of men did Caesar say he mistrusted? Look back at page 617, in Plutarch's life of Caesar. Can you find these same words used there?

3. What did Caesar mean when he said "Cowards die many times before their deaths"? What did Caesar think of the fear of death? Look back to page 617 of Plutarch's life of Caesar. How does Caesar's remark about death there compare with what Shakespeare had him say?

4. What did Antony mean when he said "the good is oft interred" with men's bones? What did Antony keep saying about Brutus? Do you think he meant what he said? How did Antony try to convince the mob that Brutus had been wrong about Caesar's being ambitious? According to Plutarch (page 616), was Caesar sincere in the action described by Antony in lines 23–25? What did Antony mean when he said, "My heart is in the coffin there with Caesar"? How did Antony feel about Caesar?

5. Why did Antony call Brutus "the noblest Roman of them all"? What did he say were the motives of the other conspirators? What did Antony mean by saying that, in Brutus, "the elements [were] so mixed in him that Nature might . . . say . . . 'This was a man' "? Look back at Plutarch's life of Caesar, on page 618. How did Caesar, according to Plutarch, react when he saw Brutus stabbing him? How do you think Caesar felt about Brutus?

The Eruption of Vesuvius

PLINY

Without warning, on August 24, A.D. 79, a terrible catastrophe occurred in southern Italy. The volcanic mountain called Vesuvius, silent and inactive for almost a thousand years, suddenly erupted, spewing tons of molten lava and heavy ashes over the countryside and burying thousands of people in the thriving towns nearby.

About twenty-seven years after this event, the Roman historian Tacitus contacted a lawyer named Pliny, asking for an eyewitness account of this disaster. Pliny had been only seventeen at the time the mountain exploded. He had been living with his uncle, who was commander of the fleet, at a city called Misenum, located about twenty miles from Vesuvius.

Here is Pliny's report of the tragedy.

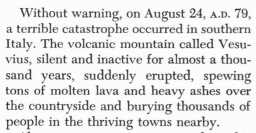OU ASK that I write you how my uncle died, in order that you may hand down a more reliable account to posterity. I am grateful to you, for I realize that his death will be crowned with immortal glory, if it is commemorated by you. . . .

"The Eruption of Vesuvius — Pliny's Letters to Tacitus," translated by Alfred P. Dorjahn, from *Latin Literature in Translation*, edited by K. Guinagh and A. P. Dorjahn. Reprinted by permission of David McKay Company, Inc.

He was at Misenum and commanding the fleet in person. On August 24 [in A.D. 79], at about one o'clock in the afternoon, my mother pointed out to him a cloud of unusual size and appearance. He was through with his sun bath and his cold bath and had partaken of his lunch while reclining, and was now engaged in study. He demanded his sandals and went to a higher place, where the phenomenon could best be observed. Since we were watching from a distance, it was not clear from what mountain it arose, but later we learned that it was Vesuvius. Its appearance and form were more like an umbrella-shaped pine than any other tree, for the cloud seemed to rise to a great height on a tall trunk and to spread out into several branches. I imagine a strong breeze forced it upward and then died down, whereupon the cloud, being unsupported or yielding to its own weight, drifted off laterally. Sometimes it was white, while at others it was dark and spotted, depending upon whether it had carried aloft earth or ashes.

To a learned man like my uncle, the

phenomenon seemed remarkable and worth observing at closer range. He ordered a swift vessel to be made ready and granted me permission to accompany him. I replied that I preferred to study, and by chance he himself had given me something to write. As he was leaving the house, he received a note from Rectina, the wife of Tascus, who was terrified by the imminence of the danger, for their villa was situated at the base of Vesuvius, and the only escape was by boat. The note begged my uncle to rescue them from such great peril. He changed his plan and turned from scholarly pursuits to heroic deeds. He ordered the battleships launched and went on board in person, determined to bring aid not only to Rectina, but also to others — for there are many villas on that charming shore. He was hastening in the direction from which others were fleeing, and steering a straight and direct course toward danger, so devoid of fear that he could dictate to his secretary and make notes on all the quakes and shapes of that terrible disaster, as he observed them with his own eyes. Now ashes were falling on the ships, hotter and thicker as they drew nearer, and now, pumice stones, blackened, charred, and cracked by fire; now the waters suddenly grew shallow, and the shore was obstructed by landslides from the mountain. After hesitating a moment and wondering whether he should turn back, he soon said to the helmsman, who was urging him to do so, "Fortune aids the brave; straight ahead to Pomponianus." Pomponianus was then at Stabiae, separated from us by half the extent of the bay, for here there is an indentation of the sea, and the shore winds and curves gradually. Although the danger had not yet reached Stabiae, it was in plain sight and would be hard upon the population as soon as it spread more widely. Pomponianus, accordingly, had already put his belongings on boats and was determined to flee, as soon as the unfavorable wind should drop. My uncle, carried along by this same breeze, which was most favorable to him, embraced his terrified friend, comforted and encouraged him, and, to relieve his friend's fear by his own composure, he asked to be shown to the bath. Having bathed, he came to the table, dined, and was in high spirits, or pretended to be so, which was an equally courageous thing to do.

From Vesuvius, meanwhile, widespread fires and tall flames were gleaming in many places, and their glare and brightness were intensified by the darkness of night. To relieve their fear, my uncle kept saying that fires had been left burning by the frightened rustics [1] and that their empty houses were now burning in the deserted districts. Thereupon he retired and slept most soundly; his snoring, which was rather loud and resounding as a result of his corpulence,[2] was heard by those who were standing watch at his door. But the courtyard from which his quarters were reached was now raised to a higher level by the mixture of ashes and pumice stones that filled it. As a result, he would have had no place of exit, if he had remained longer

---

[1] **rustics:** country people.
[2] **corpulence** (kôr′pyə·ləns): heaviness.

Fronto, a wealthy citizen of Pompeii, had this seaside scene painted on the wall of his home. Before Vesuvius erupted, many homes in Pompeii were gracious villas like these.

in his chamber. When he had been awakened, he came out and returned to Pomponianus and the rest, who had stayed up all night. Together they considered the question of remaining in the house or wandering in the open. The house was swaying as a result of the frequent and violent earthquake shocks and, just as if torn from its foundation, seemed to totter now in this direction and now in that. Under the open sky, however, the falling pumice stones, though light and porous, were feared. A comparison of the dangers induced them to choose the latter plan. In reaching this decision my uncle was guided by reason, the rest by fear. They used towels to tie on the pillows which they had placed over their heads. This was their only protection against the falling stones and ashes.

Elsewhere it was already day, but here the night was blacker and denser than ever, being relieved, however, by many torches and various lights. It was decided to go to the shore and observe from close range whether it was possible to put out to sea. But the sea was still wild and running in a contrary direction. There my uncle lay down on a discarded sail, called repeatedly for cold water, and drank it. Then flames and the smell of sulfur, which warned them that more flames were about to burst forth, frightened the rest into flight but barely roused my uncle from his coma. Supported by two slaves he rose up, but straightway fell helplessly, because, I suppose, his breathing was obstructed by the heavy atmosphere, and his windpipe was blocked; it was naturally weak and contracted and often inflamed. When day returned, the third from that on which he last beheld the light, his body was found, untouched and unharmed, and clothed in the garments he had put on. The position of his body gave the appearance of sleep rather than of death.

Meanwhile my mother and I were

at Misenum. . . . After my uncle had departed, I devoted the remaining time to my studies, for I had remained at home on that very account. Soon I had my bath, then dinner, and then a brief and restless sleep. For several days previous, there had been tremors of the earth, but they were less terrifying because they are common in Campania.[1] On that night, however, they were so severe that you would think that all things were not moved, but overturned. My mother rushed into my chamber; I, in turn, was rising, intending to awaken her if she should be sleeping. We sat down in the courtyard of the house, which separated our house from the sea by a short distance. I do not know whether I should attribute my conduct to firmness of character or lack of foresight; I was not yet eighteen. At any rate, I asked for a book of Livy[2] and read as if I were unconcerned; I even made excerpts, as I had begun to do. A friend of my uncle, who had recently come to him from Spain, upon seeing my mother and me sitting there and me even reading, upbraided her patience and my unconcern. But I remained no less intent on my book.

Already it was after six o'clock in the morning, but still the light was uncertain and rather hazy. Since the houses around us were swaying, great and certain destruction threatened us, although we were in an open yet narrow place. Then, finally, we decided to leave the town. The terrified crowd followed us, motivated by a thought-less fear that resembled prudence, and preferring the judgment of others to their own. We were pushed and forced forward by a long line. When we had got beyond the line of houses, we halted. There we had many strange and terrifying experiences. The vehicles that we had ordered to be brought forward moved back and forth, although they stood on absolutely level ground, and did not even remain stationary when stones were propped under them.

Moreover, we saw the sea drawn back upon itself and then forced out, as it were, by the earthquake. At any rate, the shore had advanced and many animals of the sea were left on the dry sand. In the other direction a dark and dreadful cloud, broken by twisting and vibrating streaks of fiery vapor, opened into long fingers of flame that resembled lightning, but were larger.

Then that same friend from Spain spoke with greater vehemence and earnestness and said: "If your uncle — your brother — is still alive, it is his wish that you should be saved. If he is dead, it is his wish that you should survive." We replied that we could not permit ourselves to think of our safety while we were uncertain of his. Without further delay he hurried away and took himself from the danger at full speed.

A little later that cloud descended upon the earth and concealed the sea; it had already encompassed and hidden Capri and obscured our view of the promontory[3] of Misenum. Then my mother begged, urged, and ordered me

---

[1] **Campania** (kam·pā′nē·ə): a region of southern Italy.

[2] **Livy** (59 B.C.–A.D. 17): a Roman historian.

[3] **promontory** (prom′ən·tôr′ē): a high point of land extending into the sea.

A quiet Vesuvius looks down on what remains of the Temple of Apollo in Pompeii.

to escape in any way I could, saying that a young man would be able to do so and that she, hindered by her age and her weight, would die peacefully if she had not become the cause of my death. I declared that I would not save myself unless I saved her too, and, taking her hand, I made her walk more quickly. Reluctantly she obeyed, and she accused herself of delaying me. Already ashes were falling, but only in a light shower. I looked back: a dense darkness overhung behind us and followed us like a torrent pouring over the land. "Let us turn aside," I said, "while we are able to see, lest we stumble on the road and be trampled upon by the crowd following us." We had hardly sat down, when a peculiar darkness surrounded us, resembling not a moonless or cloudy night, but a closed room with the light extinguished. You could hear the shrieks of women, the cries of children, and the shouts of men. With their shouts some were seeking their parents, others their children, and still others their wives; by their voices they recognized them. Some were lamenting their own misfortune, others that of their loved ones; there were some, who, through fear of death, were praying for death. Many raised their hands to the gods, but more believed that no gods remained anywhere and that the end of the world had come that night.

Nor were those lacking who augmented [1] the real dangers by imaginary and fictitious terrors. There were those who said that certain buildings at Misenum had fallen and that others were aflame; the reports were false, but they fell upon believing ears. Gradually it grew light again, but this appeared to us to be not the light of day but an indication of approaching fire. And fire it was, but it did not come very near. Then it grew dark again, and a second time ashes fell in a thick and heavy shower. We got up repeatedly and shook them off, or we would have been buried and crushed by their weight.

Gradually the darkness became less obscure and vanished into a sort of smoke or mist. Soon genuine daylight appeared, and the sun even shone, but with a lurid light, as if there were an eclipse. To our yet frightened eyes all things appeared changed and covered with deep ashes, as if with snow. Having returned to Misenum and refreshed ourselves, we spent an anxious and harried night, in hope and fear, but mostly in fear, for the earthquake continued. Many people who had gone mad were making grim jests about their own misfortunes and those of

[1] **augmented:** intensified.

others, with terrible prophecies. Not even then, however, although we had experienced danger and were expecting more, did we think of leaving Misenum until we should hear about my uncle.

A PERSONAL EXPERIENCE

1. Who was at the house at Misenum on August 24? Describe the cloud that these people saw. Why did Pliny's uncle leave on the ship?

2. Why was the uncle unable to rescue his friend and others from their villas near Vesuvius? Tell how the uncle died.

3. Describe what Pliny saw as the mountain was erupting. What did the visitor from Spain say? How did people react to the terrifying things happening to them? Why did Pliny remain at Misenum?

4. How did Pliny feel about his uncle? What kind of a person was his uncle?

5. From what he said in this letter, and from what he didn't say, what is your opinion of Pliny himself?

6. Have you ever experienced any kind of natural disaster — a flood, a hurricane, a tornado? Did these Romans behave in the way most people would act in an emergency? Give examples to support your opinion.

WORDS FROM LATIN

The first sentence of Pliny's letter ends with the word *posterity*. *Posterity* is derived from the Latin word *posterus*, meaning "coming after." We use the word *posterity* to mean "descendants" or "future generations" (those who "come after").

A related Latin word is *post*, which we use as a prefix to mean "after," "later," or "behind." *Post* is combined with many English words (as in *postmortem, post-orbital, postwar*).

You can increase your vocabulary by becoming interested in the derivations of words. Look in a large dictionary to find the Latin derivation of each of the following words (all from Pliny's letter).

immortal	dictate
commemorate	secretary
imminent	corpulence

SENTENCES:
FUNCTIONS OF WORD GROUPS

The first sentence in Pliny's letter is quoted below. Notice that each group of words in italics functions as a single unit in the sentence:

> "You ask [*that I write you how my uncle died,*] [*in order that you may hand down a more reliable account to posterity*]."

The first group of words in italics, beginning with the word *that*, works as a single unit in acting as the object of the verb. It does the same job as the single word *favors* in the sentence "You ask favors." The second word group in this sentence, beginning with the words *in order that*, works as a modifier of the whole sentence, telling why Pliny has been asked to tell how his uncle died.

Here is another sentence from Pliny's letter. Notice the long, modifying word groups in italics.

> "As he was leaving the house, he received a note from Rectina, the wife of Tascus, [*who was terrified by the imminence of the danger,*] [*for their villa was situated at the base of Vesuvius, and the only escape was by boat.*]"

What word is modified by the group modifier introduced by *who*? What words are modified by the group modifier introduced by the word *for*?

The Heart of the City

GILBERT HIGHET

After ruling the world for centuries, the great Roman Empire eventually began to decline in power. By A.D. 410, barbarians from northern Europe had made their way into Italy, and the city of Rome began to suffer wave after wave of invasions by these hordes of peoples. The tottering empire fell completely when a barbarian leader deposed the last Roman emperor.

But in a sense, the best of the Roman spirit has lived on. Rome left the world a legacy of law, of language, and of literature. In the following essay, a noted writer and professor of Latin describes his feelings as he stands in modern Rome and looks upon the remains of the Forum of the ancient city — once the heart of Rome's vital public life.

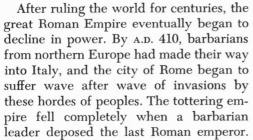

THE HEART of the city of Rome, the vital center of a republic that lived for nearly five centuries and the ceremonial nucleus of the empire that succeeded it, was an oblong area of land called the Forum. The word means only "the place outside." Originally it

was the cemetery outside the walls of the small hilltop citadel which was the earliest Rome; the marketplace for the citizens and neighbors; and the meeting place where the inhabitants could debate their own affairs at ease, celebrate religious and official ceremonies, and hold athletic contests. As Rome rose into a large city, then into a strong nation, and at last into a world power, the Forum grew more grand, more formal, more crowded with people, and more surrounded and cluttered with shops and monuments and important buildings. Something of this profuse confusion is still to be seen in it.

Centuries later, as Rome fell into decay — after the city was abandoned for the new imperial capitals at Milan and Constantinople, after it was sacked by barbarians and suffered depopulation, floods, earthquakes, landslides, and other natural disasters — the Forum was gradually deserted, emptied of its fine statues and stones, and filled with earth and ruins until its level rose above its original pavement. By the twelfth century of the Christian era, it had become a majestic desolation. The solemn processions led through Rome by the Popes avoided it entirely.

During the Renaissance,[1] when other parts of Rome were being excavated and re-explored, the Roman Forum was still further forgotten. Many buildings were torn down and the level of the Forum was raised even more. It became merely a halting place for cattle, and it remained so until the beginning of the nineteenth century, when excavation of the magnificent old square really began.

During the last century or so, the Forum has been largely cleared. It is not all clear yet. The task is hard — not because any great mass of material still remains to be moved, but because here, more than anywhere else, many ancient Romes lie close together. It is difficult, often impossible, to reveal one Rome without destroying others. Christian churches are constructed inside pagan temples. Official buildings of the early empire were restored and enlarged by later emperors. Near one entrance to the Forum lie the faint and mysterious relics of the grave of the founder of Rome, Romulus. A short walk away there is a Christian church that was originally a pagan temple dedicated to another Romulus, an imperial prince who died in boyhood a thousand years and more after the city was founded.

The result is that when we first walk through the Forum, or stand above it on the Palatine Hill,[2] looking down, we are confused and a little disappointed. It looks too small, too crowded, and too disorderly to have been a worthy center for so much reverence and a focus for so much ambition. And, when it was filled with all the buildings, whose foundations and broken columns we now see, it may have looked like an outdoor art exhibition.

---

[1] **Renaissance** (ren'ə·säns'): a period that began in the 1300's, when people became interested again in Greek and Roman culture.

[2] **Palatine** (pal'ə·tīn) **Hill:** the central hill of the seven on which Rome was built. At one time it held the homes (palaces) of wealthy Romans. Later the emperor's palace was located there.

A model of ancient Rome showing the Colosseum, a temple, and an aqueduct. Thousands of Romans once poured through the narrow streets to the Colosseum to watch men and beasts fight to the death.

The stately ruins of the Forum — the "heart of the city" as it looks today. Here Romans once gathered to do business, to meet friends, and to gossip.

This is true. The Romans themselves felt it, because they were constantly renewing and improving the Forum, clearing spaces and building colonnades in which citizens could walk without discomfort; diverting business and traffic into other new forums; and finally, under the empire, building larger and less cluttered squares elsewhere, for those great official ceremonies in which the emperors and their subjects delighted.

But it tells us two things about Rome. First, it shows us how human the ancient Romans were. Reading their hard, monumental prose and their lofty, controlled poetry, studying the records of their vast political schemes, their military and engineering feats, their wise legislation and their humane provincial administration, we are apt to think of them as distant figures, hardly human, statues rather than people. One of the chief difficulties which teachers of classical literature meet is the difficulty of convincing young readers that, behind the smooth artistic surface of Virgil's poetry or Cicero's [1] prose, there are conflicts as violent and painful as those which agitated the soul of Shakespeare; and the historian can be misled into forgetting the humanity of the Romans. However, it is not possible to pass an hour in the Roman Forum without reliving the events of Roman history and seeing them as vivid, comprehensible, and close to our own lives. On this spot, the body of Julius Caesar was burned after his assassination. Here is the base of the platform called the rostra: Cicero spoke to the people

[1] Cicero (106–43 B.C.) was a great Roman statesman, orator, and writer.

from it, and his head and hands were nailed to it after his murder, by the order of Caesar's heir, Mark Antony. Here are the pedestals on which the statues of great dignitaries once stood. On the slabs of marble left from the floors of great public buildings here and there, we can see the gaming boards scratched by idlers; and sometimes, as we look at the fine sculptured relics of sacrificial processions, we can almost hear the grave voices of the officiating priest calling for silence.

The Forum also shows us one of the essential strengths of the Roman people: their reverence for tradition. That is why it was so crowded. That is why it is now so wonderfully confused — because they preserved everything that had ever been valuable for them. Emperors ruling a vast and complex empire would still, with complete solemnity and with no trace of hypocrisy, take part in rites that were largely incomprehensible, repeat religious formulas that went back before the beginnings of the written Latin language. Ancient customs were maintained long after their origin and meaning had been forgotten. Venerable relics were carefully preserved, repaired, restored; buildings of remote antiquity were rebuilt, but never quite abolished. So the crowded and untidy Forum is a living monument to the crowded and intricate history of Rome.

The most sacred thing in Rome was simply a burning fire. It lived in the sanctuary of Vesta, whose name means "hearth." It was tended by sacred maidens. It burned for a thousand years and more, until a Christian emperor had it extinguished. We can still see the precinct of Vesta, with the mutilated statues of the priestesses, in the Forum. This was not the worship of fire as an element, nothing so complex. It was the cult of hearth and home. Closely connected with it was another simple cult: the worship of the spirits protecting the food store, the Penates.[1] The worship of Vesta and the Penates was symbolic of the idea that Rome was itself a single home, sacred as all homes should be, which grew outwards into a city containing several groups of citizens (who all were, or ought to be, members of the same family), then into an ever broadening empire always centered on Rome and its hearth fire, and finally into an entire world of fellow citizens.

Here too, along the eastern side of the Forum, is the oldest street in Rome, the Sacred Road. It slopes down from a ridge of the Palatine Hill into the valley of the Forum, runs past the ruins of great porticos[2] and temples, and finally turns into the ascent toward the Capitol. Although it was occasionally realigned and although the buildings around it kept changing, the street itself followed essentially the same line as it does today. This old road was most important when it was the scene of that peculiarly Roman ceremony, the triumphal procession of a victorious general — a fantastic blend of ancient ritual, modern power-politics, sacral formality, and truly Italian informality. The general, reaching the pinnacle of earthly felicity,[3] wore

[1] **Penates** (pə·nā′tēz).
[2] **porticos:** covered arcades, with roofs supported by columns.
[3] **felicity:** happiness.

a magnificent robe of crimson and gold, a sumptuous tunic embroidered with figures of victory, and a golden crown. The crown was held above his head, partly because it was too heavy for him to wear and partly so that he should remember it was not his to own forever. It symbolized the fact that he had almost crossed the line between humanity and divinity: he was nearly a god. His face was painted red. The Romans themselves did not know why, or did not say; but we believe it was a symbol of blood, his own strength, and the strength of the defeated enemy. The custom surely went back to a remote epoch when the victorious general was felt to have taken the blood from the enemies of his state and given new blood to his own countrymen.

Behind the general marched, or lurched, his soldiers, usually singing disrespectful songs about their leader. Yet they were not arrested or even discouraged. They were felt to be doing the right thing. Caesar himself scarcely dared to object. Such behavior took the curse off the triumphant general's good luck. It diverted the energy of any enemy who might put the evil eye on him. A Roman triumph was a combination of grave political and military thanksgiving with jolly, carefree human irreverence. The general was almost divine. The soldiers were human, all too human. Such was the ancient tradition.

Then came the symbols of the general's victories: his booty — gold dishes, rich clothes and tapestries, jewels, works of art; and models of his battles and sieges, in the form of floats showing

The ghostly ruins of an aqueduct. Centuries ago it carried pure spring water into Rome.

the cities he had captured, the rivers he had crossed, the tribes he had subdued. There were the prisoners he had taken, headed by their princes and their captains, such as had not been wise enough to commit suicide before their capture. And there were priests and musicians and dancers and jesters, and the relatives of the general and his friends and dependents, and the friends of the returned soldiers, and Roman prisoners set free by their victories, and hundreds of grateful people. They all marched along the Sacred Road, singing and rejoicing. At this corner, on the northwest of the Forum, where we can stand today, the procession broke up. The soldiers went off to mingle with the crowd, to spend their back pay and their share of the plunder on jollification. The chief prisoners went down to the cells hidden below the spurs[1] of the Capitol Hill, there to be executed. This was a rare and cruel ceremony. It took place after a triumph because a triumph was an ancient ritual, going back to the era when every war was a holy war and had to be concluded by a sacrifice to the gods who had granted victory. Meanwhile, the general with his suite and with attendant priests climbed the Capitol Hill to offer, with white bulls, gratitude to supreme Jupiter. That was Rome: power, efficiency, cruelty, frank humanity, frequent gaiety, and grave reverence for the gods.

Above the Forum on one side towers the Palatine. Diagonally opposite it, there rises the Capitoline Hill. On both these hills there were ancient relics and sanctuaries. But the Capitoline held the temple of the supreme deity, Jupiter. As the disease of absolutism[2] ate deeper and deeper into the spirit of the Romans, the two hills became competitors. The mad emperor, Caligula,[3] after deciding that he himself was a god, built a passageway high in the air across the Forum, between the two hills, so that he could "visit Jupiter." A later emperor called himself "the Thunderer" and his palace "Sacred," as though he had outstripped the sky god. And yet the sanctity of the shrine of Jupiter and the ancient citadel of Rome remained. It was always the greatest and most august[4] temple in the city, until the early Christian emperors closed all the pagan sanctuaries.

For centuries afterwards, the Capitol was a lonely place of ruins. A few convents and churches were built on its slopes, but its meaning was forgotten. In the Renaissance, the grandeur, if not the sanctity of the place, was recaptured by Michelangelo.[5] He designed splendid palaces in the classical style to occupy three sides of the new square, and a noble staircase to approach it on the fourth. The city councilors of Rome now meet in one of the palaces. The other palaces are filled with strange relics of the past — portraits of emperors and philosophers, an exquisite Venus, fantastic figures created by the Oriental cults that insinu-

---

[1] **spurs:** projecting parts.

[2] **absolutism** (ab′sə·lōō·tiz′əm): a form of government in which one person has all the power, the opposite of democracy.

[3] **Caligula** (kə·lig′yə·lə) (A.D. 12–41).

[4] **august** (ô·gust′): awe-inspiring, majestic.

[5] **Michelangelo** (mī′kəl·an′jə·lō) (1475–1564): great Italian sculptor, painter, architect, and poet.

ated themselves into imperial Rome, a model of the city, a copy of the law validating the power of the emperor, vases, mosaics, reliefs, magnificent junk, beautiful debris. In the courtyard and along the corridors there stand colossal fragments from the monuments of the later empire — an enormous head of the Emperor Constantine; a giant foot with large marble veins; titanic square-nailed hands, their forefingers pointing to heaven.

On one side of the hill, difficult of access from above and impossible from below, is a steep cliff. A hundred feet or so beneath its rim there are boulders and then the roadway leading down to the corner of the Forum. This is the famous Tarpeian Rock. Convicted traitors to the republic were not stoned, or burned, or hanged: they were thrown off this cliff, as though the protecting divinities of the state rejected them.

Capitol, Forum, Palatine — the three names were once merely local names in an insignificant village settlement: the Head place (because of its abrupt contours, or because a huge skull was found in it when the foundations of the temple were laid?); the Outside place, for marketing and meeting the neighbors; and the Grazing place. But now they have entered the languages of many peoples and have brought with them the meanings given them by the history of our Roman ancestors. A *palace* is the home of a powerful ruler whose acts may not lightly be questioned and whose person is sacrosanct.[1] A *forum* is the meeting place of free

[1] **sacrosanct** (sak′rō·sangkt): sacred in some way.

men who want to exchange goods and services, ideas, and diversions. A *capitol* is the center of civil government and stands for the administration of law above all individuals or parties. It was the Greeks, in their city-states, who first conceived and practiced democracy. It was the Romans who worked out most of its harder implications and who most spectacularly failed to cure its most dangerous weaknesses.

This is the center of Rome. It was once the center of the world. It is still one of the roots of our life. Within this small mile dwelt many of the men whose names have become permanent ideals, and were born many of the institutions which we now accept without question as natural to our lives. The Roman poets and thinkers proved, in the end, to be builders and civilizers as great as the Roman generals, engineers, and statesmen. For them, too, this was the center of the world.

Here are three thousand years of history. The stones are dead. The history is alive, running through our hearts and through our minds. Walking among the stupendous ruins, we still feel the power of the Romans and the tragedy of their failure; and we remember that it was one of their greatest poets who gave them the counsel which, to their sorrow, they abandoned:

> Bow down to God, you Romans,
> and rule the world.

ROME'S HEART

1. What happened to the Forum over the years?

2. Why was it difficult to excavate and clear the Forum?

3. How does the Forum show us that the ancient Romans were very human? What does it show us about one of the strengths of the Romans — their reverence for tradition? What was the most sacred thing in Rome?

4. Describe the triumphal procession of a victorious Roman general.

5. On page 637, the author says that three names — Capitol, Forum, and Palatine — have entered the languages of many peoples. What did these names mean to the ancient Romans? How do we use these names or their derivatives today?

6. In what ways was the Forum "the heart of the city"? Can you think of any particular place that might be called the "heart" of a modern city? Explain.

7. On page 636, the author says "That was Rome: power, efficiency, cruelty, frank humanity, frequent gaiety, and grave reverence for the gods." Using what you know of the Romans, can you explain what this statement means?

8. The lines that conclude this essay were written by Horace (65–8 B.C.). Can you explain what they mean? How can they be applied to other great ruling powers?

WORDS FROM LATIN

In Rome, says Gilbert Highet, many of the institutions natural to our lives were born. Our calendar, for instance, something we use daily, owes much to the work of Julius Caesar, the great Roman general and politician whom you read about on pages 610–19. Look in a dictionary at the derivations of the names of the months. You will find that the month July was named for Julius Caesar, and that a later emperor, Augustus, renamed another summer month after himself. What months are derived from other Roman names or words? What stories lie behind the names of these months?

COMPOSITION: WRITING A SUMMARY

To write an intelligent summary of a piece of literature, you must be sure that you understand how the writer has related and arranged his facts and ideas. In fact, before you write a summary of an essay like this one by Gilbert Highet, it is a good idea to make a brief outline.

Begin your outline by listing the eight major ideas of the essay.

    I. The heart of ancient Rome was the Forum.

   II. The Forum later became a desolation.

 III. It was difficult to clear the Forum.

 IV. The Forum tells us two things about the Romans.

   V. The Sacred Road was the scene of a peculiarly Roman ceremony.

 VI. The Capitoline and Palatine hills rise near the Forum.

VII. The names Capitol, Forum, and Palatine have entered the languages of many peoples.

VIII. Rome is still one of the roots of our life.

Next, list the important details used to support each of these major topics. For example, under the first topic you might list these details:

    I. The heart of ancient Rome was the Forum.
       A. The word *forum* means "the place outside."
       B. Originally the forum was a cemetery, a marketplace, and a meeting place.
       C. It was the vital center of the republic.
       D. It was the ceremonial nucleus of the empire.

Refer closely to the essay when listing the important details that support the other major topics. Then write your summary, using a paragraph for each major topic.

Exposition

More and more of your schoolwork in all subjects will involve reading exposition — the kind of writing that explains something. How can you improve your ability to read and understand a long selection that is packed with information?

Let us examine a long passage from "The Heart of the City" by Gilbert Highet.

Here . . . along the eastern side of the Forum is the oldest street in Rome, the Sacred Road. It slopes down from a ridge of the Palatine Hill into the valley of the Forum, runs past the ruins of great porticos and temples, and finally turns into the ascent toward the Capitol. Although it was occasionally realigned and although the buildings around it kept changing, the street itself followed essentially the same line as it does today. This old road was most important when it was the scene of that peculiarly Roman ceremony, the triumphal procession of a victorious general — a fantastic blend of ancient ritual, modern power-politics, sacral formality, and truly Italian informality. The general, reaching the pinnacle of earthly felicity, wore a magnificent robe of crimson and gold, a sumptuous tunic embroidered with figures of victory, and a golden crown. The crown was held above his head, partly because it was too heavy for him to wear and partly so that he should remember it was not his to own forever. It symbolized the fact that he had almost crossed the line between humanity and divinity: he was nearly a god. His face was painted red. The Romans themselves did not know why, or did not say; but we believe it was a symbol of blood — his own strength and the strength of the defeated enemy. The custom surely went back to a remote epoch when the victorious general was felt to have taken the blood from the enemies of his state and given new blood to his own countrymen.

Behind the general marched, or lurched, his soldiers, usually singing disrespectful songs about their leader. Yet they were not arrested or even discouraged. They were felt to be doing the right thing. Caesar himself scarcely dared to object. Such behavior took the curse off the triumphant general's good luck. It diverted the energy of any enemy who might put the evil eye on him. A Roman triumph was a combination of grave political and military thanksgiving with jolly, carefree human irreverence. The general was almost divine. The soldiers were human, all too human. Such was the ancient tradition.

(pages 634–35)

1. *A long passage like this one contains many details, and it is your job, first, to realize that these details really support or add up to a certain main idea.* Often an author will summarize his main idea in a single sentence. You might find this sentence at the head of the paragraph (as the "topic" sentence), or at the end of the paragraph (as the "clincher" sentence). At other times, you will find this summarizing sentence buried in the middle of the paragraph, as it is in the first paragraph of this passage. Go back now and notice how the fourth sentence serves as a key to the whole first paragraph.

Read this key sentence closely again. Rituals are ceremonies performed over and over again. Which details in this paragraph told you about the rituals found in the procession? What did the author mean when he said that power-politics were a part of the procession? The word *sacral* refers to religious rites. What was the sacral formality in the procession?

Note that the last detail in this topic sentence is not explained until we read the second paragraph. How does this paragraph show the procession's informality?

Can you find in the second paragraph a sentence that presents the main idea of that paragraph? What details in both paragraphs help explain the generalization made in this key sentence?

2. *After you have found the main ideas, it is your job to find and remember those details that are most important.* For example, it is not especially important to remember that the Roman general's robe was red, but it is important to remember that his face was smeared with red paint and the possible reason why this was done. This detail is important because it tells us that blood symbolized strength to the Romans. Here are four other details in the first paragraph. Which details are most important? Why?

a. The general's crown was heavy.
b. The crown was held above the general's head to remind him that it was not his to own forever.
c. The crown symbolized the fact that the general had almost crossed the line between humanity and divinity.
d. The crown was gold.

Turn back now to pages 635–36 of "The Heart of the City," and reread the paragraph that follows the two model paragraphs. Which sentence states the main idea in this paragraph? How does the writer explain this main idea in the rest of the paragraph? Which are the important details in this paragraph?

WRITING A REPORT

When you write a report, you use the techniques of exposition in presenting your information. How can you learn to write a report with greater ease?

1. *As you read books and articles in doing your research, take notes of the summary sentences and important details.*

2. *Organize the information you have gathered.* Making an outline of how you plan to organize your topic is the best way to begin your report.

3. *Devote a paragraph for each major point on your outline.* Remember that each paragraph should tell about a main idea supported by specific details.

Choose one of the following topics or one of your own for a report.

The First Airplane Flight
The History of Baseball
Indians in the United States Today

ART AND LITERATURE

Perhaps you would like to look more closely into some scenes from Roman history and write about what you discover there. The Roman art on pages 591–96 might help you choose a subject. For example:

PLATE 1: What terrible and bloody spectacles were witnessed by the walls of the Colosseum?

PLATES 5 and 6: What was everyday life like in the city of ancient Rome?

PLATE 8: This painting was found on the wall of a home which had been buried under tons of debris, spewed out by the volcano Vesuvius. What can you discover about the towns of Pompeii and Herculaneum, whose inhabitants were struck down by sudden death so many centuries ago? (Use the letter on page 625 as part of your reference material.)

Authors' Biographies

If you are curious about some of the authors included in this book, you can learn more about them in this miniature biographical dictionary. Much more information about all the writers, of course, can be found in more complete biographical books — the kind of reference sources you should become acquainted with.

ROBERT BENCHLEY (1889–1945) Phillips Exeter Academy still remembers the paper Benchley wrote as a student when he was assigned to write about "something practical." The paper was called "How to Embalm a Corpse." Benchley's humor centers around the problems of the average middle-class man in America. Benchley looked exactly like his own characters, whose spectacles slip down their noses and who stumble over chairs and bump into doors. He was not only a humorist but also a drama critic, a contributor to magazines, and a radio and motion picture performer. His humorous essay "Your Change" is on page 383.

RAY BRADBURY (1920–   ) When science-fiction writer Ray Bradbury first published a timetable for man's conquest of the moon and beyond, people laughed. Now nobody laughs. Strangely enough, despite his intense interest in man's technical achievements, Bradbury avoids flying, has never learned to drive a car, and often bicycles on business errands. He has published well over a thousand stories and has written novels, plays, and film scripts. Bradbury believes in letting his characters make their own story: "Only the character knows where he's going. It is up to the writer to let him have his head." One of his stories (*not* science fiction), "The Drummer Boy of Shiloh," can be found on page 202.

ROBERT BURNS (1759–1796) Scotland's foremost poet was born in a two-room clay cottage, on a poor and stony farm. He had only three years' schooling, which his father struggled to supplement as best he could. Burns worked hard at farm tasks, but he spent his spare time greedily reading Scottish literature and the Bible. Young Bobby was handsome and lively, but romantic complications made life so difficult for him that he set about writing a volume of poems to raise money to go to Jamaica. The poems made such a sensation in Scotland that Burns decided to go to Edinburgh instead of Jamaica. For a time he was adored by society there, but people turned away from him when they realized he was still an earthy farm boy, not given to polite city ways. Back he went to the farm, where he married one of his sweethearts, Jean. In the Highlands he eked out a meager living and wrote some of his finest poetry. Some of the poems are of such lyrical beauty that they have been set to music—"Auld Lang Syne" and "Flow Gently, Sweet Afton," for example. His famous poem "Jean" is on page 456. Burns's last years were made wretched by ill health and poverty. He was only thirty-seven when he died.

LEWIS CARROLL (1832–1898) "Lewis Carroll," famous for the fantasies, *Alice in Wonderland* (1865) and *Through the*

Looking Glass (1872), is the penname of Charles Lutwidge Dodgson. Dodgson was an English mathematician who wrote technical articles under his real name. His famed nonsense poem, "Jabberwocky," on page 435, is from *Through the Looking Glass*. Most English children of the nineteenth century knew this poem by heart. In fact, some of its nonsense words are found in the conversation of the schoolboys in Rudyard Kipling's famous novel *Stalky & Co*. The Girls' Latin School in Boston even asked Carroll's permission to name their school magazine *The Jabberwock*. The church in the small English village where Lewis Carroll grew up now has a stained glass window showing the characters from *Alice in Wonderland*.

JOHN CIARDI (1916–) As poetry editor of the *Saturday Review*, Ciardi has expressed a dislike for most children's poems because they seem written with a sponge dipped in warm milk and sprinkled with sugar. Believing that children are capable of violent emotions, Ciardi has captured a large audience among the young with his own poetry. One of his poems, "The River Is a Piece of Sky," can be found on page 451.

ARTHUR C. CLARKE (1917–) "If this book seems completely reasonable and . . . convincing, I will not have succeeded in looking very far ahead; for the one fact about the future of which we can be certain is that it will be utterly fantastic." So Arthur C. Clarke writes about his book, *Profiles of the Future* (1962). A science-fiction writer, Clarke has sold over two million books in fifteen languages and has written more than three hundred articles and short stories. During service in the Royal Air Force, as early as 1945, Clarke proposed the use of satellites for

communication. His article "Where's Everybody?" (page 423) suggests some surprising answers to a much-discussed question.

STEPHEN CRANE (1871–1900) Stephen Crane began as a free-lance writer in New York City, where he was hungry and ill most of the time. His first novel, a shocking story about the derelicts of the city, was looked on as too outspoken and was not successful. But in 1895, with *The Red Badge of Courage*, a story about the War Between the States, Crane found himself famous. People thought Crane must be a veteran, for he wrote of war with great vividness and understanding. He replied that what he knew about courage he had discovered on the football field. After publication of this novel, newspaper editors thought of Crane whenever a war broke out. He was sent out as a war correspondent on a private military expedition to Cuba in 1896, but the ship was wrecked. After twenty-seven terrible hours, Crane and four others reached the Florida coast in a dinghy. One of his companions was dead. You can read about this experience in his famous story "The Open Boat." As a star reporter, Crane traveled widely, but the hardships he went through affected his health. His early death was a tragic loss to American literature. His brief poem "Think As I Think," on page 132, shows his concern for personal honesty.

E. E. CUMMINGS (1894–1962) By nature, Edward Estlin Cummings was shy and extremely sensitive, with the "breathtakingly clean vision" of a child put out into an un-innocent world. Before America entered World War I, he went to France as an ambulance driver and there gathered material for his prose work, *The Enormous Room* (1922). It has been called one of the best "direct observation" war books to be written by an American. He is best known, however, for his lyric poetry, which he punctuates and arranges in strange ways. One of his poems, "what if a much of a which of wind," can be found on page 462.

EMILY DICKINSON (1830–1886) Emily Dickinson lived and died in the house in Amherst, Massachusetts, where she had been born. For most of her adult life, she traveled no farther than her own garden. She had no great knowledge of literature, and she wrote her poems in the meters she found in her hymnbook. Yet in her poems she reveals herself as a daring and honest thinker, with a deep sense of the mystery of things. Everything she wrote was highly personal, yet it was not petty. Friends knew that Emily Dickinson, during her hidden life, had written a few poems. Sometimes she sent a poem out to a neighbor with a basket of cookies. But after her death, even her sister was astounded to discover that in her room were bundles containing almost 1,800 poems. "We Never Know How High" (page 98), "A Word" (page 132), and "I Like to See It Lap the Miles" (page 465) show the interesting workings of this poet's mind.

T. S. ELIOT (1888–1965) Born in St. Louis, Missouri, Thomas Stearns Eliot received intensive intellectual training. From 1941 on, he made his home in England. Even during his undergraduate days, Eliot wrote poetry. His fame may be dated from 1922, with the publication of a long and difficult poem called *The Waste Land*, the title of the poem referring to the modern world. In this and other early works, Eliot saw modern man lost in a world that appears to have no meaning. "Prelude I: The Winter Evening" (page 452) is from this period. His later poems are different. They show his acceptance of a religious faith. Eliot was an intellectual who could also be very funny. As gifts for his friends, he often wrote poems about cats. His cat poems are collected in a volume called *Old Possum's Book of Practical Cats*. One of these poems, "The Naming of Cats," can be found on page 439. Old Possum is Eliot himself; the nickname was given to him by his friend, poet Ezra Pound.

RALPH WALDO EMERSON (1803–1882) After Emerson read the newspapers, he would often walk through the woods around Concord, Massachusetts, to recover his sense of peace with the universe. Although he lived in a time made chaotic by the War Between the States, Emerson remained an idealist and believed in man's innate goodness. He was an immensely popular lecturer, as well as an essayist and poet. Emerson's idealistic teachings had a great influence on the leaders of his time. He called for reforms in theology, education, and social welfare. Emerson was often called upon to speak on important public occasions. His poem, "The Concord Hymn" (page 176), was written for ceremonies commemorating the first battle in the American Revolution.

PAUL GALLICO (1897–   ) While a cub sports writer, Paul Gallico was sent to interview Jack Dempsey, then the heavyweight boxing champion. Gallico, who had never boxed before, asked for a round with Dempsey. Afterwards he said, "I knew all that there was to know about being hit in the prize ring." Such interest in all of his assignments helped Gallico become one of the highest paid sports writers in New York City. One of his articles, "Lou Gehrig's Epic of Courage," can be found on page 87. In 1936, Gallico left sports writing to become a free-lance fiction writer. Perhaps the most popular of his books is *The Snow Goose*, the legend of a lonely hunchback, a girl, and a white goose said to have flown over the ships that rescued soldiers from Dunkirk during World War II. Gallico has created a memorable character in Mrs. 'Arris, the remarkable Cockney scrub woman who makes trips abroad (*Mrs. 'Arris Goes to Paris*, *Mrs. 'Arris Goes to New York*). His story about Thomasina, the marvelous cat, has been made into a movie.

EDITH HAMILTON (1867–1963) When Edith Hamilton was a child, most people thought it was unladylike to study. Her father, however, began to teach her Latin when she was only seven. Soon after, she learned Greek. Miss Hamilton was the first woman to enter the University of Munich in Germany, but she was not allowed to sit with the men. She would take her notes at a little desk on the platform, beside the teacher. Miss Hamilton was headmistress of the Bryn Mawr School in Baltimore, Maryland, where she passed on her love of the classical world to her students. When she retired, she began to write about the Greeks and Romans, whose literature had given her so much pleasure. Two of her most important books are *The Greek Way* and *The Roman Way*. Her retelling of the myth about Baucis and Philemon is on page 103. In her ninetieth year, Miss Hamilton was made an honorary citizen of Athens, a fitting reward for one who so loved Greece.

THOMAS HARDY (1840–1928) Thomas Hardy was a frail child whose formal schooling lasted only eight years. At sixteen, he was apprenticed to an architect, but he wrote in his spare time. When his first novel was rejected, he destroyed the manuscript. Despite this failure, he was determined to make his career as a writer, and he eventually did so. He is famous for his novels, which present tragic heroes defeated in their struggle against environment and chance. Hardy is an important figure in the revolt against the self-satisfied, narrow world of late nineteenth-century England. For the last thirty years of his life, he devoted himself to poetry. One of his poems, "Last Week in October," is on page 461.

O. HENRY (1862–1910) "O. Henry" was the penname of William Sydney Porter, who, as a freckled boy in Greensboro, North Carolina, used to spin yarns for his friends. Poor health sent O. Henry to the Southwest, and there he found trouble. Shortly after he had left a job as clerk in a bank, funds were found missing. When O. Henry was summoned to trial for embezzlement, he fled the country in panic, even though it now seems that inefficient methods at the bank were probably responsible. He first caught a train to New Orleans, where he unloaded bananas for a while. Next stop was Honduras, where he met the outlaw Al Jennings. With Jennings, O. Henry traveled to South America and Mexico, but he returned home when he was notified that his wife was ill. Once he was back in the country, he was jailed, but his prison term was not all unpleasant. He was allowed to work in the pharmacy, sleep in the prison hospital, and even roam the streets at night. In prison he resumed writing stories, something he had attempted several times before. In fact, his famous penname was probably adopted from the name of a prison guard, Orrin Henry. Shortly after his release from jail, O. Henry went to New York, where he haunted parks, streets, and restaurants, talking with all sorts of people and looking for story material. Soon he built up an enviable reputation as a writer. His output was tremendous. In one year he wrote sixty-five stories. His stories are noted for their unusual surprise endings, and they have been widely imitated. A classic example, "The Ransom of Red Chief," is on page 283.

GILBERT HIGHET (1906–) "Teaching is an art, not a science" is the basic theme of Gilbert Highet's book, *The Art of Teaching* (1951), and, as a professor of Latin at Columbia University, he has put his beliefs into practice. A student once described him in action: "He sings, points at students, acts, strides about the room . . . waves his handkerchief . . . and explodes his sentences." Highet was born in Scotland, but he now makes his home in America, a country he was drawn to by its vitality. He has written many books, criticisms, and translations. His essay on Rome, "The Heart of the City," appears on page 631.

OLIVER WENDELL HOLMES (1809–1894) Witty, energetic, and popular, Oliver Wendell Holmes seemed to be able to do many things at one time. He was a great teacher at Harvard Medical School, a distinguished physician, and a steadily productive writer. His best known poems, apart from "Old Ironsides," which can be found on page 177, are "The Chambered Nautilus" and "The Deacon's Masterpiece or 'The Wonderful One-Hoss Shay.'" The name "Sherlock Holmes," one of the famous characters in English fiction (page 301), was coined from Holmes's name.

HOMER   According to tradition, Homer was a blind poet of Greece who lived around 700 or 800 B.C. He is said to have wandered from place to place telling over and over again, in poetic language, exciting stories about great events that had taken place about four or five hundred years before. At some point, Homer is supposed to have written down these stories in verse. We may as well continue to believe this about Homer, since nothing else about him has ever been discovered. The two long narrative poems, or epics, which he is supposed to have set down in writing are the *Iliad* and the *Odyssey*. The *Iliad* tells how the Greeks besieged the town of Troy (also known as Ilium) in Asia Minor. The *Odyssey* relates the adventures of one of the Greek heroes of Troy, Odysseus, who met so many misfortunes after the end of the war that ten whole years went by before he reached home again. Most people think that Homer did not actually compose the *Iliad* or the *Odyssey* himself. They think that Homer merely collected and retold many shorter tales that had been told by various bards all over the Greek-speaking world. According to this view, the stories had no one author, unless it was the Greek people themselves. Fortunately, we do not have to make up our minds about the question of authorship in order to enjoy the adventures of Odysseus. The oxen of the sun, the one-eyed giant (page 15), the sirens, the dread whirlpools, and the enchantress who turned the sailors into pigs — these and many other adventures in the *Odyssey* (as well as those in the *Iliad*) will continue to be told for as long as there are men, women, and children to listen.

LANGSTON HUGHES (1902–1967) After working at jobs which had taken him as far afield as France, Holland, and Africa, American-born Langston Hughes took a job as bus boy in a hotel in Washington where poet Vachel Lindsay was staying. One day, Hughes left three of his poems beside Mr. Lindsay's plate in the dining room, and Lindsay subsequently attracted the attention of the literary world to the young poet. Hughes's poems, which are full of the rhythms of Negro folk music and jazz, have been translated into many languages. One of his poems, "Kid in the Park," is on page 463.

WASHINGTON IRVING (1783–1859) It is fitting that the first highly successful professional American writer should have been named after the first president of the country. Washington Irving's first dabbling in literature came when he wrote sketches for a gossipy New York paper called *Salmagundi,* published by Irving, his brother, and a friend. This was followed by a sprightly and irreverent history of New York, a book which annoyed some solemn members of New York's old Dutch families. Irving spent many years in Europe. There he became friendly with Sir Walter Scott and was inspired to give Americans the same sense of a romantic past that Europe possessed. His fame was established with the publication of *The Sketch Book,* in which two enduring legends appeared, "The Legend of Sleepy Hollow" (page 259) and "Rip Van Winkle." With this book, Irving helped defeat the British notion that no writer of any worth could come from "the colonies." Irving served as American minister to Spain for a time, and he found Spain fascinating. He wrote several books about the country, including *The Alhambra,* a collection of stories about captured princesses, Moorish castles, magicians, and knights.

HENRY WADSWORTH LONGFEL–LOW (1807–1882) People were drawn to Longfellow for his goodness, his charm, and his intelligence. A descendant of John and Priscilla Alden, whose love story he was to tell in his long poem *The Courtship of Miles Standish,* Longfellow was born in Portland, Maine, and received a good education. The book that first captured his imagination was Washington Irving's *The Sketch Book.* Like Irving, Longfellow was to draw much of his inspiration from the American continent. Among his most popular poems are *Evangeline,* about two tragically separated lovers, and *Hiawatha,* about an Indian boy. His famed poem about the great American patriot, Paul Revere, is on page 171. The tragic death, by burning, of his second wife made it impossible for Longfellow to go on with his creative work for a time. But he met this sorrow with patience and courage, and it is, in fact, these virtues which Longfellow frequently praised in his poetry. He was immensely popular in America throughout his life. His poems were bought in the same way that best-selling novels are bought today.

PHYLLIS MC GINLEY (1905–   ) "At the age of six, I went introspective and turned out this little stunner —

> Sometimes in the evening
>   When the sky is red and pink
> I love to lie in a hammock
>   And think and think and think.

— which must be the beginning of my life-long preference for composing my stuff in a horizontal position." In this way, Phyllis McGinley writes about herself. Her light verse is highly praised, and she is regarded as an expert writer of satire. In 1961 she received the Pulitzer prize for her collection of poetry called *Times Three.* Besides poetry, she has published stories for children, such as *The Horse Who Lived Upstairs* (1944) and *Boys Are Awful* (1962), essays, lyrics for a Broadway revue, and film scripts. Her poems "A Choice of Weapons" and "A Garland of Precepts" can be found on pages 132 and 133.

EDNA ST. VINCENT MILLAY (1892–1950) Encouraged by her mother, Edna St. Vincent Millay began to write poetry in her childhood. By the time she graduated from Vassar College, she had published her first book of poems. She is best known for her sonnets, which have an appealing lyrical quality. Besides her poetry about nature, Miss Millay also wrote poems on the rights of women. She lived in Greenwich Village in New York, during its "golden age," when, to quote her, everyone was "very, very poor and very, very merry." One of her poems, "Exiled," can be found on page 458.

A. A. MILNE (1882–1956) Alan Alexander Milne's other writings have been overshadowed by his famous creations, Christopher Robin (who was his young son) and Winnie the Pooh. Nevertheless, Milne wrote several excellent comic plays, such as *Mr. Pim Passes By* and *The Ugly Duckling*, which appears on page 363. Milne served in World War I, and he wrote his first play at the Western Front.

OGDEN NASH (1902–   ) A "worsifier," as he once called himself, Ogden Nash used the best as well as the worst rhymes he could dream up. He was born in Rye, New York, of a distinguished family. (One relative gave his name to Nashville, Tennessee.) He tried several jobs, including that of bond salesman (he sold one bond — to his godmother), before he settled down to write humorous verse. He once said that he could say things in verse which he would be tarred and feathered for saying in prose. Nash has made recordings of many of his verses. Four of his poems are on page 438.

PLINY (THE YOUNGER) (A.D. 62–113) Pliny was a citizen of ancient Rome. After the death of his father, he was adopted by his wealthy uncle, Pliny the Elder, a famous naturalist, who perished in the eruption of Vesuvius in A.D. 79. Young Pliny's own description of this disaster is on page 625. Pliny was a bright lawyer who rose quickly in rank and became governor of a Roman province in Asia Minor. Volumes of Pliny's letters — to friends as well as to emperors — have come down to us. They give us a valuable account of how cultured people lived in the days of the Roman empire.

PLUTARCH (A.D. 46?–120?) Plutarch was a Greek who was famous for his vast learning. He was inclined toward mysticism in religion and he served as a priest in the temple of Apollo. Of all Plutarch's works, the book most admired is his *Parallel Lives*. In order to inspire his readers to noble works, Plutarch would write about a great Greek statesman or general and then do the same for a Roman statesman or general. He then would draw comparisons between the two men and point out a moral. Plutarch's "lives" have been popular for centuries. When Shakespeare was writing his play *Julius Caesar*, he drew heavily on Plutarch's life of Caesar. (See the life of Caesar on page 610, and lines from Shakespeare's play on page 621.) Plutarch used many anecdotes and gossipy stories in his *Lives*, and parts of them are probably not true. But his purpose was not to write history, but to give a picture of a real living human being, in all his pettiness as well as in his nobility. In this, most people agree that Plutarch succeeded.

EDGAR ALLAN POE (1809–1849) Orphaned at the age of two, Edgar Allan Poe lived with foster parents until disagreements over his handling of money drove him from home. He attended the University of Virginia and West Point for brief periods, and later worked on the staffs of newspapers in Richmond, Baltimore, Philadelphia, and New York. An erratic temperament and alcoholism, however, kept him from a steady job. Apart from his deep love for his young wife, who died from a long illness in 1847, his life was shrouded in poverty and unhappiness. Best known for his short stories, which are full of mystery and horror, Poe also wrote poetry and criticism. One of his most famous poems is "The Raven" (page 444). His writings first received full recognition in Europe, especially in France. He is now recognized as one of the most important American authors of the nineteenth century.

HOWARD PYLE (1853–1911) This famous writer and illustrator thought that his bright and happy childhood in Wilmington, Delaware, must have been responsible for making him what he was. Pyle recalls that he spent many hours reading and rereading romantic tales from the Arabian nights and Grimm's fairy tales. When he grew up, Pyle became an author and illustrator of children's stories. At one time Pyle ran an art school at Chadds Ford, Pennsylvania, and one of his pupils was the noted illustrator N. C. Wyeth, father of the contemporary artist, Andrew Wyeth. Pyle's tales of the sea, of pirates, of colonial days, and of medieval times are still immensely popular. He has been called "the father of American illustrators." There were so many copies made of *The Merry Adventures of Robin Hood* that the plates almost wore out. A story from this book is on page 32.

CONRAD RICHTER (1890–   ) As a child, Conrad Richter had lived in many small villages in Pennsylvania, and he had listened eagerly to stories told by descendants of pioneers. When he grew up and went West, he resumed his childhood practice of talking to local inhabitants. In this way he collected material for his stories about frontier life in the Southwest. His story "Smoke over the Prairie" can be found on page 212. Richter received the Pulitzer prize in 1951 for *The Town*, a novel of American pioneer life. One of his other novels, *The Light in the Forest* (1953), is told from the point of view of a white boy who for eleven years was the captive of an Indian tribe. A companion novel is *A Country of Strangers* (1966), which tells the tragic story of Stone Girl, another white child who had been kidnaped by the Indians and later returned against her will to her white family.

EDWIN ARLINGTON ROBINSON (1869–1935) All his life, Robinson looked on poetry as his true vocation. After two years at Harvard, he supported himself, far from grandly, by doing odd jobs in New York City. There he saw little of other people and devoted himself to writing. One poem attracted the attention of President Theodore Roosevelt. The President made Robinson's life more comfortable by giving him a modest salary as a clerk in a customhouse. Fame descended on Robinson when he was almost fifty. He was honored with the Pulitzer prize three times, and in the last years of his life he was considered America's greatest living poet. His lyric "The Dark Hills" is on page 461. Many of Robinson's poems are studies of sad people with names like Cliff Klingenhagen and Miniver Cheevy, who live in a place called Tilbury Town. Later in his life he wrote poems about King Arthur and his knights.

THEODORE ROETHKE (1908–1963) "This book unfolds a man. Its two hundred poems reveal, in root, bud, and flower, a way of knowing how to be alive." This description of Roethke's collected poems expresses the unique quality in his poetry. He makes us feel that what we know, however familiar it may be, is wonderful and that reality is better than dreams or fancies. "Night Journey" is on page 464. His collection of poems called *The Waking* won the Pulitzer prize in 1954.

CARL SANDBURG (1878–1967) "I'll probably die propped up in bed trying to write a poem about America" is the way that Carl Sandburg tried to express the particular nature of his poetry, which deals with all aspects of American life. After working at many odd jobs as a youth, traveling as a hobo to the West, and serving in the Spanish-American War, Sandburg finally settled down to write a biography of Abraham Lincoln, who had captured his imagination as a child. The writing took fifteen years. For a few months each year, Sandburg would take a rest (and earn money) by touring the country with his guitar, singing songs. His monumental six-volume biography of Lincoln won the Pulitzer prize for history in 1940. Among his books are the *Rootabaga Stories* (1922), written especially for children, and his widely admired story of his boyhood in Galesburg, Illinois, *Always the Young Strangers* (1952). One of his poems, "Fog," is on page 451.

SIR WALTER SCOTT (1771–1832) Known as "the Wizard of the North" to readers of his day, Sir Walter Scott wrote novels and poems about Scotland's romantic past. With their detailed stories of adventure and their "supernatural" overtones, his books influenced the development of the historical novel in England, France, and America. One of his famous novels is *Ivanhoe*. His poem "Lochinvar," on page 441, is from a long narrative poem called *Marmion* (1808). The story of

Lochinvar is supposedly told by a lady who has come to the Scottish court to try to rescue her imprisoned husband.

PERCY BYSSHE SHELLEY (1792–1822) Gentle and imaginative even as a boy, Shelley was often teased by his classmates and branded "Mad Shelley." As he grew older, he was looked on as a dangerous radical. He rejected the beliefs held by most people, and he struggled continuously against injustice and authority of all kinds. Shelley became one of England's noted poets of the Romantic period. One poem, "A Widow Bird," can be found on page 453. Along with Byron and some other English friends, Shelley eventually moved to Italy, where he wrote some of his best poems. Shelley was intensely sensitive, and he had a superstitious fear of water. Ironically, he was drowned during a squall at sea.

ROBERT LOUIS STEVENSON (1850–1894) Named "Tusitala," or teller of tales, by the natives of Samoa, Robert Louis Stevenson wrote short stories and novels which are famous for their excitement and adventure. Stevenson was afflicted with tuberculosis and was forced to leave the damp climate of Scotland where he was born. His life was a courageous fight against death, but his sufferings did not stifle the gaiety and imagination of his writings. He was not concerned with the deep problems of life, but he loved a good story. The most famous of his novels are *Treasure Island* (1883) and *Kidnaped* (1886). A dramatization of his short story, "The Sire de Maletroit's Door," is on page 333. Stevenson lies buried on a windy peak on a South Sea Island. One of his verses is his epitaph.

"Here he lies where he longed to be.
Home is the sailor, home from the sea,
And the hunter home from the hill."

EDWIN WAY TEALE (1899–   ) Edwin Way Teale decided to be a naturalist and author at a very early age. By the time he was nine, he had written a book (unpublished) called *Tales of Lone Oak*. (He spelled it "tails.") In order to buy a box camera for his nature work, he once picked 20,000 strawberries on his grandfather's farm. It was not, however, until he was 42 that he could resign as a regular feature writer with *Popular Science Monthly* and fulfill his childhood ambition. Since then, Teale has combined scientific knowledge with a poetic feeling for nature and has produced books rated as American nature classics. On page 417 are excerpts from his great series of books called *Circle of the Seasons*. Teale lives with his wife in Connecticut, where he has cut trails through his woods for his nature observation.

ALFRED, LORD TENNYSON (1809–1892) Tennyson grew up in the peaceful isolation of the English countryside. He attended school for only four or five years, and received most of his education from his father, who was a brilliant but melancholy man. Tennyson began publishing while he was in his teens, but a savage review of his work and the death of a close friend caused him to publish nothing for ten years. His attempt to overcome his loss and his long search for the meaning of human life are revealed in his greatest work, a long poem titled *In Memoriam*, which was not published until 1850. In that same year, Tennyson was named England's poet laureate, and he married a girl to whom he had been engaged for twelve years. As poet laureate, Tennyson wrote poems commemorating national events. One of these, "The Charge of the Light Brigade" (page 58), immortalizes a heroic but senseless incident in the Crimean War. Perhaps the best-known poems of Tennyson's later life are the *Idylls of the King*, which relate the glories and the decline of King Arthur's court.

VIRGIL (70–19 B.C.) The greatest Roman writer was really not born in Rome at all. Publius Vergilius Maro was born on his father's farm near Mantua, in what was then Cisalpine Gaul. The family was reasonably well off, and Virgil was given a good education in Rome. His talent as a writer was recognized early. During those times most writers had to find a wealthy and influential patron to help support them while they wrote. Virgil was fortunate in finding a good patron who was also a close associate of the emperor. For ten years Virgil worked on his literary masterpiece, the *Aeneid*. His intention was to give Rome an epic story to match the great epic of Greece, the *Iliad*. The long poem he produced had a vast panorama. Its hero was a Trojan named Aeneas, who fled the burning town of Troy and made his way to Italy, where he fathered the Roman race. Virgil was a careful and superb craftsman. Before his story was finished, he was suddenly taken ill. He ordered his friends to have the manuscript destroyed, saying that it needed three years' more work to make it perfect. This was not done, for the Roman emperor forbade his friends to carry out Virgil's request. As a consequence one of the world's literary masterpieces was saved. A summary of some of Aeneas's adventures appears on page 582.

WALT WHITMAN (1819–1892) Whitman was born on Long Island, in New York, and he frequently visited Coney Island, in those years a bare unfrequented shore, where he loved to race up the beach reciting Shakespeare to the surf. For several years, Whitman worked as a newspaperman, but he also became interested in writing poetry. A trip to Chicago and New Orleans gave him a greater appreciation of his country and changed the well-dressed newspaper man to a roughly dressed, bearded poet. The first edition of *Leaves of Grass* came out in 1855. Nothing quite like it had ever appeared before. Many people were thrilled by Whitman's vigorous acceptance of life in all its strange variety and by his belief in democracy, in a great world where men and women would live in comradeship, free from restrictions of the past. Other people disliked Whitman for his frankness. Then the War Between the States transformed the poet's existence. He spent several years as a voluntary nurse, helping the wounded who filled military hospitals. One of Whitman's famous poems, "O Captain! My Captain!" was written when he heard the news of Lincoln's assassination in 1865. The poem is on page 210.

JOHN GREENLEAF WHITTIER (1807–1892) Whittier was born to Quaker parents in Haverhill, Massachusetts. He made up for his limited schooling by reading widely. One of Whittier's poems attracted the attention of William Lloyd Garrison, a vigorous opponent of slavery, and Whittier was decisively influenced by him. Beginning in 1833, Whittier devoted thirty years to a writing and speaking crusade against slavery. He spoke out fearlessly, and sometimes he had to face angry mobs. Whittier had a burning zeal for reform, but he also found poetic inspiration in other themes. Some of his best-known poems, such as "Barbara Frietchie" and "Skipper Ireson's Ride," are based on old American legends. Whittier's most beloved poem, however, is a long poem called *Snowbound* (1866), which describes the poet's own tranquil boyhood on a New England farm. One of Whittier's recollections from *Snowbound* is on page 455.

THORNTON WILDER (1897–) In 1927, Thornton Wilder first achieved fame (and the Pulitzer prize) with his novel *The Bridge of San Luis Rey* — the story of five people who were killed when a bridge in Peru collapsed in the early eighteenth century. But Wilder is noted as an important American dramatist, especially for the plays *Our Town* and *The Happy Journey to Trenton and Camden* (page 351). His best plays are known for their touches of fantasy and their experiments in theatrical technique. At one point, for example, in his play *The Skin of Our Teeth*, the audience is asked to send up its chairs to keep the fire going against the approaching Ice Age. Interested in acting, Wilder has taken parts in summer productions. He likes to write what he wishes when he wishes, and he says that his best ideas come in the shower.

WILLIAM CARLOS WILLIAMS (1883–1963) A practicing physician in New Jersey, William Carlos Williams was a poet in his spare time. Both his poetry and his medicine were necessary to him: "I've been writing, trying to get a few things said, ever since I started to study medicine. One feeds the other, in a manner of speaking." One of his poems, "The Lonely Street," is on page 452.

WILLIAM WORDSWORTH (1770–1850) A familiar sight to the inhabitants of the Lake District in England was the tall, imposing figure of William Wordsworth, tramping over the moors, reciting his poetry aloud. Wordsworth was one of the founders of the Romantic movement. His poetry reflects this movement's concern with simple, everyday subjects, and its deep love of nature. Wordsworth was appointed poet laureate of England in 1843. "Daffodils," one of his best-known poems, can be found on page 454.

THE READING PROGRAM

These charts have been designed to show the sequence of skills that are presented in The Reading Program and in The Composition Program. Hence, skills are not listed in alphabetical order, but in the order in which they are first presented in the textbook.

Words: Sound, Structure, Meaning

Sound and spelling 14
Pronunciation related to function and meaning 24
Context clues to meaning 31, 480, 510
Archaic words 41, 443
Inflections 57
Suffixes that form adjectives and verbs 78, 400
Word classes and meaning 96, 112
Roots of words 106, 131, 154, 201, 248, 630
Prefixes and meaning 117, 131, 143, 154, 422
Synonyms and meaning 170
Words coined to imitate sounds 207
Word histories 233, 253, 430, 552, 587, 609, 619, 630, 638
Words used for effect (often humorous) 292, 319, 571
Colloquial or informal usage 380, 502
Compound words 536
Clichés 540

Sentence Structure and Style in Prose

Punctuation and meaning 14
Pitch, stress, and pause 14, 350
Word order and meaning 25
Three basic sentence patterns 31
Compound parts 41, 156, 248, 330, 515
Noun modifiers 78, 100
Verb modifiers 97
Adverb clause placement 106
Adjective phrase and clause placement 117
Oral style 138, 143
Reducing long sentences 154, 234, 416
Verbs that describe action 156
Variety in sentence lengths 255, 480
Modifiers and basic sentence structure 281, 328, 620, 630
The connective *but* 384
Parenthetical expressions (interrupters) 531
Word groups functioning as nouns 588, 630

Reading Prose for Comprehension

Reading words in groups 97
Recognizing important details in description 99
Recognizing the general impression created in description 99
Understanding specific words and comparisons in description 99
Remembering important supporting details in narration 155
Recognizing the main event in narration 156
Understanding transitional expressions and relationships among details 209, 254
Finding topic statements in exposition 254, 431, 639
Noting supporting details in exposition 254, 431, 640
Seeing logical relationships between paragraphs in exposition 254
Finding the narrator of a story 329
Finding the details that set time, place, and mood in a story 329
Noting the organization of an essay or article 415, 430
Outlining a selection 588, 620, 638
Finding the main ideas in a series of paragraphs 609
Distinguishing between important details and less important details 640

Reading Prose to Recognize Literary Techniques

Point of view and its effect in stories   131, 138, 292, 329
Propaganda   170
Figurative language   207, 389
Evaluating a writer's accuracy, clarity, and conclusions   255, 432
Characterization in a short story   280, 319
Suspense in a short story   281
Effect in a short story   281
Plot in a short story   291, 318
Foreshadowing in a short story   292
Irony in a short story   292
Elements in a detective story   318
Theme in a short story   327
Plot in a play   349, 378
Characterization in a play   349, 361, 378
Setting of a play   349, 361
Conflict in a play   349, 350, 361
Climax in a play   350
Understanding and interpreting stage directions   350, 362, 378, 379
Theme in a play   362, 378
Using imagination in reading a play   380
Humorous essay   384
Finding the author's purpose in nonfiction   384, 388, 399, 415, 421, 429, 431
Style in an essay   384
Reacting to nonfiction   384, 389, 400, 416, 422, 430
Editorial   388
Tone in nonfiction   389, 400, 422
Biography   399

Familiar essay   415
Personal journal   421
Article   429
Differentiating between fact and opinion   430
Sensing a writer's personality   432
Name-calling   488
Western yarn   502
Techniques of humorous writing   531, 536, 570
Incongruity in humor   536
Parody   545, 570

"Practice in Reading and Writing" Sections

(unit closings that form the core of The Reading Program and The Composition Program)

Description   99–100
Narration   155–56
Exposition   254–55
Stories   329–30
Dialogue   379–80
Nonfiction   431–32
Poetry   466–67
How to Write About Literature   572–73
Exposition   639–40

Reading Poetry

Sound, including rhyme   59, 63, 440, 448, 460
Sentences in poetry   133, 178, 443, 466, 553, 571
Connotations and word choice   175, 448, 453, 553
Poetic exaggeration   176
A poet's style   440, 517, 521, 526
Rhythm   440, 460, 526, 552
Total effect   440
Deeper meanings   448, 463, 519, 521, 523, 526
Alliteration   448, 571
Images   450
Personification   453, 460
A poet's purpose   465
Figurative language   466

THE COMPOSITION PROGRAM

Many of the exercises on sentences, charted under The Reading Program, on page 652, can also be used to improve writing skills.

Assignments Based on Models

DESCRIPTION

Specific details in description *25, 282*
"Odysseus and the Cyclops," Homer *25*
"The Legend of Sleepy Hollow," Washington Irving *282*
Unity in description *31*
"Sir Gawain," Dorothy Heiderstadt
Sensory details in description *41, 57, 488*
"Will Stutely's Rescue," Howard Pyle *41*
"Top Man," James Ramsey Ullman *57*
FROM *Huckleberry Finn*, Mark Twain *488*
Total impression in description *78*
"My Friend Flicka," Mary O'Hara
Sensory details and general impression in description *100*
Practice in Reading and Writing: Description
Specific details and general impression in a description of an imaginary person *100*
Practice in Reading and Writing: Description
Character description revealing thoughts and feelings *328*
"The Apprentice," Dorothy Canfield

NARRATION

Related events in narration *106*
"Baucis and Philemon," Edith Hamilton *112, 510*
Chronological order in narration
"Midas," Olivia E. Coolidge *112*
"Lost in a Snowstorm," Mark Twain *510*
Dialogue within a narrative *131*
"Weep No More, My Lady," James Street
A narrative combining all the techniques of effective narration *156*
Practice in Reading and Writing: Narration
A story about a personal experience or a fictional event *329*
Practice in Reading and Writing: Stories
A dramatic dialogue *380*
Practice in Reading and Writing: Dialogue

EXPOSITION

Supporting a topic sentence with an anecdote *248*
"Incandescent Genius," C. B. Wall
Supporting a topic sentence with specific details *253, 255, 400, 416*
"Sing an Old Song," Eleanor R. Van Zandt *253*
Practice in Reading and Writing: Exposition *255*
"George Washington Carver," Florence Crannell Means *400*
"An Old-fashioned Iowa Christmas," Paul Engle *416*
Unity in an expository paragraph *389*
"Mary White," William Allen White
A summarizing sentence in an expository paragraph *422*
"From Spring to Summer," Edwin Way Teale

Assignments Based on Selections

DESCRIPTION

Character sketch emphasizing one personal quality 97
"Lou Gehrig's Epic of Courage," Paul Gallico
Description that creates a mood 448
"The Raven," Edgar Allan Poe

NARRATION

Personal narrative 154
"As the Night the Day," Abioseh Nicol
A humorous personal anecdote 480
"Boyhood Reminiscences," Mark Twain
A fictional anecdote framed within a story 502
"The Celebrated Jumping Frog of Calaveras County," Mark Twain
An exaggerated story 515
"Punch, Brothers, Punch," Mark Twain
A parody 545
Fables, James Thurber

EXPOSITION

Paraphrasing a poem 98, 467, 550
"We Never Know How High," Emily Dickinson 98
Practice in Reading and Writing: Poetry 467
"A Father's Advice to His Son," William Shakespeare 550
Developing a topic sentence 170, 234, 572
"Salt-Water Tea," Esther Forbes 170
"Smoke over the Prairie," Conrad Richter 234
Practice in Writing: How to Write About Literature 572

Explaining what, why, and how 175
"Paul Revere's Ride," Henry Wadsworth Longfellow
Expressing and supporting a personal opinion 201, 350, 432
"The Man Without a Country," Edward Everett Hale 201
The Sire de Malétroit's Door, Robert Louis Stevenson 350
Practice in Reading and Writing: Nonfiction 432
Presenting a contrast or comparison 362, 573
The Happy Journey to Trenton and Camden, Thornton Wilder 362
Practice in Writing: How to Write About Literature 573
Presenting an argument 378
The Ugly Duckling, A. A. Milne
Summary of a poem explaining a personal reaction 443
"Lochinvar," Sir Walter Scott
Paragraphing 581
"The Wooden Horse," Bella Koral
Summary of an essay showing how details are related 638
"The Heart of the City," Gilbert Highet
A report 640
Practice in Reading and Writing: Exposition

WRITING POETRY

Haiku-style poems 450
Five Japanese Poems
Short poem, in free verse style 467
Practice in Reading and Writing: Poetry

Assignments Based on Art
(under the heading *Art and Literature*)

A description of a scene in a painting, supplying sensory details and conveying a general impression 100
A narrative about events leading up to the scene depicted in a painting 156
A comparison or contrast of two paintings 255
A story based on a painting, describing the action depicted 330
A dialogue between the people in a painting 380
An informal essay explaining a viewpoint toward a painting 432
Poems expressing reactions to paintings 467
Supporting a general statement about some paintings by citing specific details 573
A report about some aspect of ancient Rome 640

Index of Contents by Types

MYTHS, LEGENDS, FABLES, FOLK TALES

Adventures of Aeneas, The, Virgil, retold by
  H. A. Guerber, 582
Baucis and Philemon, retold by Edith Hamilton,
  103
Gift and the Giver, The, retold by Russell G.
  Davis and Brent K. Ashabranner, 114
How Horatius Held the Bridge, retold by Henry
  W. Lanier, 597
Kingfisher and the Phoebe, The, James Thurber,
  545
Little Girl and the Wolf, The, James Thurber,
  541
Midas, retold by Olivia E. Coolidge, 107
Odysseus and the Cyclops, Homer, translated by
  Samuel Butler, 15
Princess and the Tin Box, The, James Thurber,
  542
Sir Gawain, retold by Dorothy Heiderstadt, 26
Tiger Who Would Be King, The, James Thurber,
  544
Will Stutely's Rescue, Howard Pyle, 32
Wooden Horse, The, retold by Bella Koral, 577

STORIES

Apprentice, The, Dorothy Canfield, 320
As the Night the Day, Abioseh Nicol, 144
*Celebrated Jumping Frog of Calaveras County,
  The,* Mark Twain, 497
Drummer Boy of Shiloh, The, Ray Bradbury, 202
Legend of Sleepy Hollow, The, Washington Ir-
  ving, 259
Man Without a Country, The, Edward Everett
  Hale, 187
My Friend Flicka, Mary O'Hara, 64
Ransom of Red Chief, The, O. Henry, 283
Red-headed League, The, Sir Arthur Conan
  Doyle, 301
Salt-Water Tea, Esther Forbes, 159
Smoke over the Prairie, Conrad Richter, 212
Top Man, James Ramsey Ullman, 42
Weep No More, My Lady, James Street, 118

NONFICTION (INCLUDING ESSAYS, ARTICLES, AND BIOGRAPHIES)

Battle of Zama, The, Robert Silverberg, 602
Boyhood Reminiscences, Mark Twain, 472
Countess and the Impossible, The, Richard Y.
  Thurman, 139
Cub Pilot on the Mississippi, Mark Twain, 481
Dog That Bit People, The, James Thurber, 532
Eruption of Vesuvius, The, Pliny, 625
First Pitch, Robert Creamer, 409
From Spring to Summer, Edwin Way Teale, 417
Gettysburg Address, The, Abraham Lincoln, 208
George Washington Carver, Florence Crannell
  Means, 390
Heart of the City, The, Gilbert Highet, 631
Incandescent Genius, C. B. Wall, 235
Julius Caesar, Plutarch, 610
Lost in a Snowstorm, Mark Twain, 503
Lou Gehrig's Epic of Courage, Paul Gallico, 87
Mama and the Graduation Present, Kathryn
  Forbes, 134
Mary White, William Allen White, 385
Memorial, James Thurber, 537
Night the Bed Fell, The, James Thurber, 528
Old-fashioned Iowa Christmas, An, Paul Engle,
  410
Punch, Brothers, Punch, Mark Twain, 511
Sing an Old Song, Eleanor R. Van Zandt, 249
Spreading "You Know," The, James Thurber, 539
Where's Everybody? Arthur C. Clarke, 423
Your Change, Robert Benchley, 383

PLAYS

Happy Journey to Trenton and Camden, The,
  Thornton Wilder, 351
Pyramus and Thisby, William Shakespeare, 555
Sire de Maletroit's Door, The, Robert Louis Ste-
  venson, adapted for television by Reginald
  Denham and Mary Orr, 333
Stone, The, Jerome Ross and Larry Marcus, 3
Ugly Duckling, The, A. A. Milne, 363

POETRY

Advice to Actors, from *Hamlet,* William Shake-
  speare, 554
Antony's Oration at Caesar's Funeral, from *Julius
  Caesar,* William Shakespeare, 622
Antony Speaks of Brutus, from *Julius Caesar,*
  William Shakespeare, 624
Armful, The, Robert Frost, 524
Birthplace, The, Robert Frost, 518
Blind Men and the Elephant, The, John Godfrey
  Saxe, 113
Caesar to Antony, from *Julius Caesar,* William
  Shakespeare, 621
Caesar to Calpurnia, from *Julius Caesar,* William
  Shakespeare, 622

Casey at the Bat, Ernest Lawrence Thayer, 436
Cassius Speaks of Caesar to Brutus, from Julius
Caesar, William Shakespeare, 621
Charge of the Light Brigade, The, Alfred, Lord
Tennyson, 58
Choice of Weapons, A, Phyllis McGinley, 132
Concord Hymn, The, Ralph Waldo Emerson, 176
Crossing a Creek, Herbert Clark Johnson, 456
Daffodils, The, William Wordsworth, 454
Dark Hills, The, Edwin Arlington Robinson, 461
Dunkirk, Robert Nathan, 60
Dust of Snow, Robert Frost, 524
Eel, The, Ogden Nash, 438
Exiled, Edna St. Vincent Millay, 458
Father's Advice to His Son, A, from Hamlet,
William Shakespeare, 550
Fire and Ice, Robert Frost, 525
Fog, Carl Sandburg, 451
Garland of Precepts, A, Phyllis McGinley, 133
Good Name, from Othello, William Shakespeare,
552
Hearth Fire, The, John Greenleaf Whittier, 455
High Flight, Pilot-Officer John Gillespie Magee,
Jr., RCAF, 458
I Like to See It Lap the Miles, Emily Dickinson,
465
Jabberwocky, Lewis Carroll, 435
Japanese Poems, 449
Jean, Robert Burns, 456
Kid in the Park, Langston Hughes, 463
Last Week in October, Thomas Hardy, 461
Last Word of a Bluebird, The, Robert Frost, 521
Lochinvar, Sir Walter Scott, 441

Lonely Street, The, William Carlos Williams,
452
Mending Wall, Robert Frost, 522
Mood Apart, A, Robert Frost, 573
Naming of Cats, The, T. S. Eliot, 439
Night Journey, Theodore Roethke, 464
O Captain! My Captain! Walt Whitman, 210
Old Ironsides, Oliver Wendell Holmes, 177
Panther, The, Ogden Nash, 438
Pasture, The, Robert Frost, 517
Paul Revere's Ride, Henry Wadsworth Longfel-
low, 171
Poetry, Eleanor Farjeon, 449
Porcupine, The, Ogden Nash, 438
Prelude I: The Winter Evening, T. S. Eliot, 452
Raven, The, Edgar Allan Poe, 444
River Is a Piece of Sky, The, John Ciardi, 451
Road Not Taken, The, Robert Frost, 519
Sonnet 71, William Shakespeare, 553
Stopping by Woods on a Snowy Evening, Robert
Frost, 520
Termite, The, Ogden Nash, 438
Think As I Think, Stephen Crane, 132
Time to Talk, A, Robert Frost, 517
We Never Know How High, Emily Dickinson,
98
What Fifty Said, Robert Frost, 525
what if a much of a which of a wind, E. E. Cum-
mings, 462
Widow Bird, A, Percy Bysshe Shelley, 453
Wise Old Apple Tree in Spring, The, Robert
Hillyer, 457
Word, A, Emily Dickinson, 132

PICTURE ACKNOWLEDGMENTS

Page xvi, (left) Collection of American Literature, Yale University Library, (right) Dick Han-
ley from Photo Researchers; 2, Russ Kinne from
Photo Researchers; 82, 83, Scala from Shostal;
85, John R. Freeman (Photographers) Ltd., London; 86, Meyer Erwin; 87, New York Yankees; 90,
93, Wide World Photos; 102, Thomas Hollyman
from Photo Researchers; 134, Essex Institute,
Salem, Mass.; 158, Susan McCartney; 205, Library of Congress; 209, Culver Pictures; 211,
(top) Meserve Collection, (bottom) Lloyd Osten-
dorf; 235, Bettmann Archive; 236, 245, Erik S.
Monberg; 256, (left) Harbrace Photo, (right)
Slim Aarons from Photo Researchers; 258, Fritz
Henle from Photo Researchers; 297, J. E. Bulloz;
298, Musées Nationaux; 332, Susan McCartney;
381, (top left) Bettmann Archive, (bottom left)
Photo courtesy of the American Museum – Hayden Planetarium, (right) Jack Zehrt from
Shostal; 382, F. B. Grunzweig from Photo Researchers; 385, 388, The Emporia Gazette; 390,
395, Bettmann Archive; 409, Jack Zehrt from
Shostal; 410, Harbrace Photo; 417, Jim The-
ologos; 419, Harbrace Photo; 423, 425, Photo
courtesy of the American Museum – Hayden
Planetarium; 434, Peter Sahula from Photo Researchers; 459, Manley Photo from Shostal; 468,
(left) Bettmann Archive, (right) Thomas Hollyman from Photo Researchers; 470, Susan Mc-
Cartney; 471, Chicago Historical Society; 481,
483, Bettmann Archive; 485, Harbrace Photo;
493, George Cushing; 516, Clyde Hare; 527,
Henri Cartier-Bresson from Magnum Photos; 549,
Bettmann Archive; 574, (left) A. L. Goldman
from Rapho Guillumette, (right) Richard Cac-
cese from Shostal; 576, Susan McCartney from
Photo Researchers; 591, Ray Manley from Shostal; 592, (top) William G. Froelich, (bottom)
Ray Manley from Shostal; 594, (top) Harbrace
Photo, (bottom) Oscar Savio; 596, Scala from
Shostal; 625, Fritz Henle from Photo Researchers; 627, R. V. Schoder, S.J.; 629, Fritz Henle
from Photo Researchers; 631, American Numismatic Society, Harbrace Photo; 632, 633,
Scala from Shostal; 635, Erich Lessing from Magnum Photos.

INDEX OF FINE ART

Balla, Giacomo, *Dog on a Leash*, 295

Bingham, George Caleb, *Shooting for the Beef*, 185

Braque, Georges, *Musical Forms with the Words* Fête *and* Journ, 405

Bruegel, Pieter, the Elder, *The Peasant Wedding*, 86

Cézanne, Paul, *Still Life with Ginger Jar and Eggplants*, 404

Copley, John Singleton, *Paul Revere*, 181

Cotán, Juan Sánchez, *Still Life: Quince, Cabbage, Melon and Cucumber*, 403

Currier and Ives, *"Wooding Up" on the Mississippi*, 485

Géricault, Théodore, *The Derby at Epsom*, 298

Hals, Frans, *The Laughing Cavalier*, 85

Hicks, Edward, *The Peaceable Kingdom*, 186

Homer, Winslow:
Breezing Up, 492
Eight Bells, 493
Fishing Boats, Key West, 495
Gulf Stream, The, 494
Huntsman and Dogs, 496
Long Branch, New Jersey, 491

Hooch, Pieter de, *Courtyard of a House in Delft*, 84

Manet, Édouard, *The Races at Longchamp*, 299

Marin, John, *Fifth Avenue at Forty-second Street*, 300

Moses, Grandma, *Out for the Christmas Trees*, 412 (details from, 410, 413, 414)

Mount, William Sidney, *Raffling for the Goose*, 184

Panini, Giovanni Paolo, *The Interior of the Pantheon*, 593

Rembrandt van Rijn, *The Polish Rider*, 81

Roman art:
Arch of Constantine, 592
Colosseum, The, 591
Emperor Trajan (sculpture), 595
Flora (wall painting from Stabiae), 596
Fronto's House in Pompeii (wall painting from), 627
Pantheon, The (depicted in a painting by Giovanni Paolo Panini), 593
Pont du Gard (aqueduct), 592
Portrait of a Lady (sculpture), 594
Portrait of Unknown Roman (sculpture), 594

Rubens, Peter Paul, *Henry IV at the Battle of Ivry*, 297

Ruisdael, Jacob van, *The Mill at Wijk-bij-Duurstede*, 406

Seurat, Georges, *The Bridge at Courbevoie*, 408

Stage Master (stained glass), 470

Trumbull, John, *The Battle of Bunker's Hill*, 182 (detail from, 183)

Uccello, Paolo, *Battle of San Romano*, 296

Van Gogh, Vincent, *Cypresses*, 407

Velásquez, Diego, *The Surrender of Breda*, 82 (detail from, 83)

ARTISTS' CREDITS

Glossary

Anyone who reads and writes English today knows that a dictionary is an essential reference tool. All our modern dictionaries are the descendants of a great dictionary, a massive two-volume dictionary completed in 1755 by the famous British literary man, Doctor Samuel Johnson. Modern dictionaries are compiled more scientifically, but they are less enjoyable to read than the dictionary written by Doctor Johnson. Occasionally, one of Doctor Johnson's definitions reveals a personal prejudice or a sense of humor. For example, he calls a writer of dictionaries a "harmless drudge." Oats are defined as "a grain which in England is generally given to horses, but in Scotland supports the people." The English language was greatly affected by Doctor Johnson's dictionary. Up to the eighteenth century, there were no rules for using English. Words were spelled any way people chose to spell them, and if someone wanted a new word, he just made one up. Doctor Johnson regulated the spellings and the uses of English words. Today the English language still shows the effects of his mammoth work. It was Doctor Johnson who made official the *k* in *know*, the *gh* in *light,* and the *b* in *debt*. He also made the *p* in *receipt* official, but declined to do the same for *conceit* and *deceit*.

The words listed in the glossary in the following pages are found in the selections in this textbook. The pronunciation system is that of Funk & Wagnalls *Standard College Dictionary*, and the definitions are based on those in the Funk & Wagnalls dictionary. You can use this glossary as you would a dictionary — to look up words that are unfamiliar to you. Strictly speaking, the word *glossary* means a collection of technical, obscure, or foreign words found in a certain field of work. Of course, the words in this glossary are not "technical, obscure, or foreign," but are those that might present difficulty as you read the selections in this textbook.

The pronunciations listed in this glossary are the pronunciations generally used by educated people. But, of course, all educated people do not pronounce all words in the same way. For example, the word *forest* is pronounced differently in Boston, in Chicago, in Atlanta, and in Spokane. For some words, the glossary lists different pronunciations, but, of course, there is not space to record the many variations. When two or more pronunciations are indicated for a word, the one listed first is the one that the editors of the *Standard College Dictionary* believe most frequent in northern and western sections of the United States, but other pronunciations are equally acceptable.

Many words in the English language have several meanings. In this glossary, the meanings given are the ones that apply to the words as they are used in the selections in the textbook. In most cases, when the meaning of a word as it is used in the textbook is an unusual one, its more common meaning is also given. Definitions are always listed according to frequency of use.

For more information about the words in this glossary, consult a dictionary.

A

abandon (ə·ban′dən) *v.* **1.** To give up wholly; to desert. **2.** To yield without restraint, as to one's feelings.

abash (ə·bash′) *v.* To embarrass or make ashamed. — **abashed** *adj.*

abate (ə·bāt′) *v.* To reduce in quantity, force, or intensity.

abhor (ab·hôr′) *v.* To detest; loathe.

abide (ə·bīd′) *v.* To dwell; live; reside.

abode (ə·bōd′) *n.* A dwelling or home.

abominable (ə·bom′in·ə·bəl) *adj.* Hateful; detestable. — **abominably** *adv.*

abound (ə·bound′) *v.* To be plentiful; have plenty; be full.

abstract (ab·strakt′) *adj.* **1.** Not concrete: *abstract* truth. **2.** Theoretical, not practical. — *v.* To take away; remove.

abut (ə·but′) *v.* To border on; end at.

abyss (ə·bis′) *n.* **1.** A bottomless gulf. **2.** Any great depth or void: an *abyss* of shame.

accede (ak·sēd′) *v.* To agree; assent.

access (ak′ses) *n.* Admittance; entrance.

acclimate (ə·klī′mit, ak′lə·māt) *v.* To become accustomed to a foreign climate or to a new environment.

accommodate (ə·kom′ə·dāt) *v.* To adjust or conform, as to new conditions.

acute (ə·kyōot′) *adj.* Keen; sensitive; sharp.

adamant (ad′ə·mant) *adj.* Immovable; unyielding.

adjacent (ə·jā′sənt) *adj.* Near; close at hand; adjoining.

adversary (ad′vər·ser′ē) *n.* An opponent; enemy.

advocate (ad′və·kāt) *v.* To recommend; speak or write in favor of.

affinity (ə·fin′ə·tē) *n.* A natural attraction or inclination.

affirm (ə·fûrm′) *v.* To declare or state positively.

afflict (ə·flikt′) *v.* To trouble; cause distress to. — **afflicted** *adj.*

aghast (ə·gast′) *adj.* Terrified; amazed; horrified.

agitate (aj′ə·tāt) *v.* **1.** To disturb or shake up: The wind *agitates* the sea. **2.** To excite or perturb: Sorrow *agitates* the heart. **3.** To keep before the public, as a controversial issue. — **agitated** *adj.*

alien (āl′yən) *adj.* Foreign; strange.

allay (ə·lā′) *v.* **1.** To lessen; reduce the intensity of. **2.** To lay to rest, as fears.

allege (ə·lej′) *v.* To state to be true without proof; affirm.

allude (ə·lōōd′) *v.* To refer to indirectly.

allure (ə·lōor′) *v.* To attract or entice; tempt.

animated (an′ə·mā′tid) *adj.* Lively.

annihilate (ə·nī′ə·lāt) *v.* To destroy completely. — **annihilation** *n.*

antagonist (an·tag′ə·nist) *n.* Enemy; opponent; adversary.

appall (ə·pôl′) *v.* To fill with horror; shock. — **appalling** *adj.*

apparition (ap′ə·rish′ən) *n.* A ghost; phantom; specter.

appease (ə·pēz′) *v.* **1.** To soothe or calm; pacify. **2.** To satisfy: *Appease* your hunger with this bread.

append (ə·pend′) *v.* **1.** To add. **2.** To hang or attach: to *append* a seal.

apprehension (ap′rə·hen′shən) *n.* Fear, distrust, or dread of the future.

arbitrary (är′bə·trer′ē) *adj.* Based on personal opinion, judgment, or prejudice.

archaic (är·kā′ik) *adj.* Belonging to an earlier time; no longer in use.

ardent (är′dənt) *adj.* Passionate; intense; eager.

ardor (är′dər) *n.* Eagerness; zeal; enthusiasm.

arduous (är′jōō·əs) *adj.* Difficult; laborious.

ascertain (as′ər·tān′) *v.* To make sure or certain; determine.

askew (ə·skyōo′) *adv.* In a slanting position or manner; to one side; awry.

assail (ə·sāl′) *v.* To attack violently; assault.

assent (ə·sent′) *v.* To agree; consent.

assuage (ə·swāj′) *v.* **1.** To make less harsh or severe. **2.** To satisfy, as thirst.

astound (ə·stound′) *v.* To overcome with wonder; amaze; astonish.

astute (ə·stōot′) *adj.* Keen; sharp; clever. — **astuteness** *n.*

asunder (ə·sun′dər) *adv.* Apart; into pieces.

audacious (ô·dā′shəs) *adj.* Showing no fear; bold; daring.

audible (ô′də·bəl) *adj.* Loud enough to be heard.

auspices (ôs′pə·sēz) *n.* **1.** Influence or guidance; patronage. **2.** Omens or signs.

auspicious (ôs·pish′əs) *adj.* Fortunate; hopeful; promising.

avail (ə·vāl′) *v.* Serve; be of use or advantage.

avenge (ə·venj′) *v.* To punish for or in behalf of: They *avenged* his murder.

awe (ô) *n.* Reverential fear.

B

balm (bäm) *n.* Anything that soothes or heals.

---

barbarous (bär′bər·əs) *adj.* Primitive; uncivilized. — **barbarian** *n.*

barren (bar′ən) *adj.* Not fruitful; not productive: *barren* land; a *barren* mind.

batter (bat′ər) *v.* To beat; strike repeated blows upon.

beatific (bē′ə·tif′ik) *adj.* Giving or showing bliss or blessedness.

beguile (bi·gīl′) *v.* 1. To deceive by trickery. 2. To while away pleasantly, as time. 3. To charm; amuse.

benefactor (ben′ə·fak′tər) *n.* One who does good or gives help; a patron.

beneficent (bə·nef′ə·sənt) *adj.* Bringing about or doing good.

benign (bi·nīn′) *adj.* Kindly; mild; gentle.

bevy (bev′ē) *n.* A group, especially of girls or women.

bizarre (bi·zär′) *adj.* Odd; fantastic; eccentric; grotesque.

bland (bland) *adj.* 1. Gentle and soothing. 2. Not stimulating; mild.

blight (blīt) *v.* To destroy; ruin.

boding (bō′ding) *adj.* Predicting evil.

booty (bōō′tē) *n.* Plunder; loot; goods taken in war.

brazen (brā′zən) *adj.* 1. Made of brass. 2. Resembling brass in hardness, color, sound, etc. 3. Shameless; impudent.

breach (brēch) *n.* A breaking, especially of a contract, law, or rule.

buffet (buf′it) *v.* To strike repeatedly; knock about.

buffoon (bu·fōōn′) *n.* A clown; jester.

bulbous (bul′bəs) *adj.* Shaped like a bulb; swollen: a *bulbous* nose.

bunting (bun′ting) *n.* 1. A material used for flags. 2. Flags, banners, etc., collectively.

buoyancy (boi′ən·sē) *n.* 1. The ability to keep afloat. 2. Cheerfulness. — **buoyant** *adj.*

burnish (bûr′nish) *v.* To polish or make shiny.

C

cache (kash) *n.* A hiding place or storage place; also, the things stored.

capacious (kə·pā′shəs) *adj.* Able to contain much; roomy; large.

caper (kā′pər) *n.* A wild prank; escapade; lark or spree. — Also *v.*

capitulate (kə·pich′ōō·lāt) *v.* 1. To surrender under certain terms. 2. To give up.

caprice (kə·prēs′) *n.* A sudden change of mind or action without adequate motivation; a whim.

captivate (kap′tə·vāt) *v.* To fascinate; charm.

chafe (chāf) *v.* To rub, especially to make either sore or warm by rubbing.

chaos (kā′os) *n.* Complete disorder or confusion.

chastise (chas·tīz′) *v.* To punish, especially by beating. — **chastisement** *n.*

chortle (chôr′təl) *n.* A chuckle; joyful vocal sound.

chronic (kron′ik) *adj.* Habitual; prolonged; lingering.

clamor (klam′ər) *v.* To cry out; shout.

cleave (klēv) *v.* 1. To split or cut. 2. To stick to; adhere.

clemency (klem′ən·sē) *n.* Mildness; mercy.

collaborate (kə·lab′ə·rāt) *v.* To work or cooperate with another person.

colossal (kə·los′əl) *adj.* Enormous; huge.

combustible (kəm·bus′tə·bəl) *adj.* Capable of burning; easily ignited; flammable.

commend (kə·mend′) *v.* To recommend.

compassion (kəm·pash′ən) *n.* A feeling of pity for another.

compel (kəm·pel′) *v.* To force to do something.

compensate (kom′pən·sāt′) *v.* 1. To make suitable amends; pay. 2. To make up for something. — **compensation** *n.*

competent (kom′pə·tənt) *adj.* Able; capable.

compile (kəm·pīl′) *v.* To put together or collect; gather.

compliance (kəm·plī′əns) *n.* Obedience; yielding; consent.

composure (kəm·pō′zhər) *n.* Calmness; serenity.

comprehensible (kom′pri·hen′sə·bəl) *adj.* Easily understood; intelligible.

compress (kəm·pres′) *v.* To press together; squeeze together.

compunction (kəm·pungk′shən) *n.* Pity or regret.

con (kon) *v.* To study carefully.

concede (kən·sēd′) *v.* To acknowledge; admit.

concur (kən·kûr′) *v.* To agree or approve.

concurrent (kən·kûr′ənt) *adj.* Occurring together at the same time or place; existing together.

condescend (kon′di·send′) *v.* To lower oneself; stoop to do something.

confront (kən·frunt′) *v.* To stand or to put face to face with.

conjecture (kən·jek′chər) *v.* To guess; suppose; infer.

consecrate (kon′sə·krāt) *v.* To set apart as sacred; dedicate.

consequential (kon′sə·kwen′shəl) *adj.* 1. Following as an effect. 2. Important.

consign (kən·sīn′) *v.* To give up or turn over; transfer.

consternation (kon′stər·nā′shən) *n.* Sudden fear or amazement; panic.

contemplative (kən·tem′plə·tiv) *adj.* Meditative; thoughtful.

contemptuous (kən·temp′chōō·əs) *adj.* Scornful; disdainful. — **contemptuously** *adv.*

contend (kən·tend′) *v.* To oppose; compete.

contort (kən·tôrt′) v. To twist out of shape.

contravene (kon′trə·vēn′) v. To conflict; oppose or contradict.

convey (kən·vā′) v. To carry from one place to another; transport.

convoy (kon′voi) v. To escort; accompany.

cordial (kôr′jəl) adj. Warm; hearty; sincere. — **cordially** adv.

cosmic (koz′mik) adj. Of or relating to the universe or cosmos.

countenance (koun′tə·nəns) n. The face or features. — v. To approve; encourage.

courier (koor′ē·ər) n. A messenger, especially one on official business.

covert (kuv′ərt) adj. Concealed; secret. — n. 1. A covering. 2. A shelter or hiding place.

covet (kuv′it) v. To want very much; especially, to desire something which belongs to someone else.

credible (kred′ə·bəl) adj. Believable.

crescendo (krə·shen′dō) n. A gradual increase in the volume of sound.

cult (kult) n. A religion; system of religious observances: the *cult* of Aphrodite.

cunning (kun′ing) adj. Shrewd; clever.

curt (kûrt) adj. Brief and abrupt; blunt.

D

dank (dangk) adj. Unpleasantly damp; cold and wet.

dauntless (dônt′lis) adj. Fearless; not to be frightened.

declaim (di·klām′) v. To recite; quote.

decry (di·krī′) n. To condemn or denounce.

deem (dēm) v. To believe; judge; think.

deference (def′ər·əns) n. Respect; regard.

degrade (di·grād′) v. To lower in character or morals. — **degradation** n.

demeanor (di·mē′nər) n. Deportment; behavior; bearing.

demented (di·men′tid) adj. Insane; deprived of mental powers.

denizen (den′ə·zən) n. An inhabitant; one who lives in a place.

denote (di·nōt′) v. To indicate: signify.

depose (di·pōz′) v. To remove from office or position; oust.

deprecate (dep′rə·kāt) v. To disapprove of or express regret for.

depreciate (di·prē′shē·āt) v. 1. To lessen in value or price. 2. To belittle.

descry (di·skrī′) v. 1. To discover with the eye, as something distant; detect. 2. To discover by observation or investigation.

desecrate (des′ə·krāt) v. To change from using something for holy purposes to using it for evil purposes.

despotic (di·spot′ik) adj. Tyrannical.

detain (di·tān′) v. To delay; stop.

detract (di·trakt′) v. To take away from; lessen.

devious (dē′vē·əs) adj. 1. Rambling; swerving. 2. Straying from the proper way; erring.

devise (di·vīz′) v. To form in the mind; invent; plan.

devoid (di·void′) adj. Not possessing; lacking; free from.

diligent (dil′ə·jent) adj. Busy; industrious; painstaking.

din (din) n. A loud, continuous noise.

direful (dīr′fool) adj. Dreadful; terrible.

disapprobation (dis′ap·rə·bā′shən) n. Disapproval.

disconcert (dis′kən·sûrt′) v. To confuse; upset.

disconsolate (dis·kon′sə·lit) adj. Gloomy; sad; downcast.

discordant (dis·kôr′dənt) adj. Harsh; disagreeable; clashing. — **discordantly** adv.

discourse (dis′kôrs) n. A formal treatment of a subject, as a sermon.

discreet (dis·krēt′) adj. Careful not to do or say the wrong thing, especially in dealing with others.

disdainful (dis·dān′fəl) adj. Scornful; arrogant. — **disdainfully** adv.

disintegrate (dis·in′tə·grāt) v. To break down into fragments; crumble. — **disintegration** n.

dismember (dis·mem′bər) v. To tear apart; mangle.

disperse (dis·pûrs′) v. To scatter in various directions.

disreputable (dis·rep′yə·tə·bəl) adj. Having a bad name; not respected; not esteemed.

dissipate (dis′ə·pāt) v. 1. To drive away; dispel. 2. To waste; spend foolishly.

dissuade (di·swād′) v. To alter or change the intentions or plans of someone by advice or persuasion.

diverge (di·vûrj′) v. To move in different directions from one point; deviate.

diverse (di·vûrs′) adj. Varied; different.

divert (di·vûrt′) v. 1. To distract the attention of. 2. To entertain; amuse. — **diversion** n.

divine (di·vīn′) adj. God-like. — v. To guess.

divulge (di·vulj′) v. To disclose; reveal.

dogged (dôg′id) adj. Stubborn; obstinate. — **doggedly** adv.

doleful (dōl′fəl) adj. Sad; mournful.

don (don) v. To put on, as a garment.

---

dormant (dôr′mənt) *adj.* Motionless, as if asleep; inactive.

drone (drōn) *n.* 1. The male bee. 2. A loafer; an idler.

dubious (dōō′bē-əs) *adj.* Doubtful; uncertain.

duly (dōō′lē) *adv.* Properly; fitly.

duplicity (dōō-plis′ə-tē) *n.* Trickery; double-dealing; deceitfulness.

E

eccentric (ek-sen′trik) *adj.* Odd; different in behavior, appearance, or opinions.

ecstasy (ek′stə-sē) *n.* Intense delight; rapture.

eddy (ed′ē) *v.* To move in backward circles (used of air or water).

edict (ē′dikt) *n.* An official decree.

egotism (ē′gə-tiz′əm) *n.* Selfishness; conceit.

ejaculate (i-jak′yə-lāt) *v.* To speak out suddenly; exclaim.

elocution (el′ə-kyōō′shən) *n.* Public speaking, including vocal delivery and gesture.

eloquence (el′ə-kwəns) *n.* Forceful, moving, or persuasive speaking or writing.

elusive (i-lōō′siv) *adj.* Hard to understand or perceive: an *elusive* fragrance.

emancipate (i-man′sə-pāt) *v.* To set free. — **emancipation** *n.*

embellish (im-bel′ish) *v.* 1. To decorate or adorn; beautify. 2. To make more interesting by adding fictional details.

eminent (em′ə-nənt) *adj.* Prominent; notable; important.

emit (i-mit′) *v.* To send forth or give off (light, heat, sound, etc.).

encompass (in-kum′pəs) *v.* Encircle; surround.

endearment (in-dir′mənt) *n.* A loving word or act.

endeavor (in-dev′ər) *v.* To try; make an effort to do.

enrapture (in-rap′chər) *v.* To delight intensely.

enterprising (en′tər-prī′zing) *adj.* Energetic; bold; venturesome; full of initiative.

enthrall (in-thrôl′) *v.* To charm; fascinate.

entrails (en′trālz) *n.* The inner parts of a man or animal; intestines.

entreat (in-trēt′) *v.* To beg earnestly; implore. — **entreaty** *n.*

enumerate (i-nōō′mə-rāt) *v.* To name one by one; list.

epilogue (ep′ə-lôg) *n.* A short portion added on to a work of literature to complete or conclude the story.

epitaph (ep′ə-taf) *n.* Something spoken or written in memory of the dead.

epoch (ep′ək) *n.* A point in time marked by a new development: the atomic *epoch* in history.

errant (er′ənt) *adj.* 1. Roving; wandering. 2. Straying from the proper course or standard.

exasperate (ig-zas′pə-rāt) *v.* To make very annoyed or angry; infuriate.

excavate (eks′kə-vāt) *v.* To dig out; uncover; unearth.

exhilarate (ig-zil′ə-rāt) *v.* To set aglow with happiness or elation; make cheerful. — **exhilaration** *n.*

exhort (ig-zôrt′) *v.* To urge strongly; advise or recommend earnestly.

exotic (ig-zot′ik) *adj.* 1. Foreign; not native: an *exotic* plant. 2. Strangely different and fascinating: *exotic* customs.

expiate (ek′spē-āt) *v.* To pay the penalty for or to make up for. — **expiation** *n.*

expire (ik-spīr′) *v.* 1. To come to an end, as a contract. 2. To breathe air out of the lungs; exhale. 3. To die.

exploit (eks′ploit) *n.* A deed or act; brilliant feat.

extemporary (ik-stem′pə-rer′ē) *adj.* Without preparation; impromptu. Also *extemporaneous* and *extempore*.

extricate (eks′trə-kāt) *v.* To disentangle; get free from.

exult (ig-zult′) *v.* To rejoice greatly; triumph. — **exultant** *adj.*

F

falter (fôl′tər) *v.* 1. To waver; be uncertain; hesitate. 2. To speak haltingly; stammer.

farce (färs) *n.* A comedy; an absurd or ridiculous situation.

feign (fān) *v.* 1. To pretend: to *feign* madness. 2. To counterfeit: to *feign* another's signature. — **feigned** *adj.*

ferment (fər-ment′) *v.* To be agitated; seethe.

fervent (fûr′vənt) *adj.* Enthusiastic; intense; ardent.

fervor (fûr′vər) *n.* Intensity; passion; great warmth.

festoon (fes-tōōn′) *v.* To decorate with flowers, ribbon, etc., in chains or links.

filly (fil′ē) *n.* 1. A young female horse. 2. A high-spirited young girl.

firmament (fûr′mə-mənt) *n.* The heavens; sky.

flaunt (flônt) *v.* To make a bold display of.

flinch (flinch) *v.* To shrink back; wince.

florid (flôr′id) *adj.* 1. Red-faced; ruddy; flushed. 2. Too ornate; flowery: *florid* architecture; a *florid* writing style.

flounder (floun′dər) *v.* To struggle clumsily; move awkwardly.

flourish (flûr′ish) *v.* 1. To thrive 2. To display or wave about.

fluctuate (fluk′chōō-āt) *v.* To change or vary often and irregularly; waver.

forfeit (fôr′fit) *v.* To lose as a penalty or punishment.

forlorn (fôr·lôrn′) *adj.* 1. Abandoned. 2. Cheerless; desolate: *a forlorn countryside.*

formidable (fôr′mi·də·bəl) *adj.* 1. Dreaded or feared because of size or strength: *a formidable enemy.* 2. Very difficult: *a formidable task.*

fortify (fôr′tə·fī) *v.* 1. To make strong; reinforce against attack. 2. To encourage.

fortitude (fôr′tə·tōōd) *n.* Courage; bravery.

fossil (fos′əl) *n.* 1. Remains of animals (or plants) preserved in rock. 2. *Informal* Someone who is out of date or old.

fraud (frôd) *n.* Trickery; deception.

fraudulent (frô′jə·lənt) *adj.* Dishonest; deceitful.

fray (frā) *n.* Fight; battle; conflict.

furbish (fûr′bish) *v.* 1. To make bright by rubbing. 2. To restore to brightness or beauty.

furrow (fûr′ō) *v.* 1. To make deep grooves in. 2. To make wrinkles in. — **furrowed** *adj.*

furtive (fûr′tiv) *adj.* Secret; sly; shifty.

G

gait (gāt) *n.* Manner of walking or moving on foot.

galactic (gə·lak′tik) *adj.* Pertaining to systems of stars.

gambol (gam′bəl) *n.* A frolic; playful skipping about.

gamut (gam′ət) *n.* The whole range of anything: *the gamut of emotions.*

gape (gāp) *v.* 1. To stare, with the mouth open wide, as in surprise. 2. To be open wide, as a mouth is in yawning.

garble (gär′bəl) *v.* To mix up or confuse.

gargoyle (gär′goil) *n.* A distorted figure of a human or animal, used as an ornament on the corner of a building.

garner (gär′nər) *v.* To gather up; accumulate.

germinate (jûr′mə·nāt) *v.* To grow or develop; sprout.

gesticulate (jes·tik′yə·lāt) *v.* To make gestures; use motions with or instead of speech.

giddy (gid′ē) *adj.* 1. Silly; not responsible. 2. Dizzy.

gild (gild) *v.* 1. To cover with gold paint or gold leaf. 2. To brighten or adorn.

gingerly (jin′jer·lē) *adv.* In a careful, cautious manner.

glint (glint) *v.* To shine; gleam.

goad (gōd) *v.* To drive or urge into action.

gorge (gôrj) *n.* A narrow, deep ravine, especially with a stream running through it. — *v.* To stuff with food; gulp down.

gratify (grat′ə·fī) *v.* To give pleasure or satisfaction to; satisfy.

grizzled (griz′əld) *adj.* Gray-haired.

gross (grōs) *adj.* 1. Total: *gross income.* 2. Obviously bad or wrong: *gross errors.* 3. Excessively fat or large. 4. Coarse; vulgar.

grotesque (grō·tesk′) *adj.* Distorted; fantastic; outlandish.

grovel (gruv′əl) *v.* 1. To lie or crawl face downward, as in fear. 2. To act with despicable humility; lower oneself, as from fear.

grueling (grōō′əl·ing) *adj.* Exhausting; causing extreme fatigue.

gullible (gul′ə·bəl) *adj.* Easily fooled or cheated.

gusto (gus′tō) *n.* Enjoyment; enthusiasm; zest.

guttural (gut′ər·əl) *adj.* Having a harsh, throaty sound.

H

haggard (hag′ərd) *adj.* Worn-out looking; gaunt.

hale (hāl) *adj.* Healthy; hearty; robust.

hallow (hal′ō) *v.* To make holy; consecrate.

hapless (hap′lis) *adj.* Unfortunate; unlucky.

harass (har′əs, hə·ras′) *v.* To trouble; annoy.

harbinger (här′bin·jər) *n.* A herald; forerunner.

hardy (här′dē) *adj.* Robust; tough; brave.

harry (har′ē) *v.* To trouble; torment; harass.

hellion (hel′yən) *n.* A person or animal that enjoys making mischief.

herald (her′əld) *n.* Any bearer of important news; a messenger.

heretical (hə·ret′i·kəl) *adj.* Different from established beliefs, especially of religion; dissenting.

homage (hom′ij) *n.* Respect or honor.

hostile (hos′təl) *adj.* Unfriendly; antagonistic.

hovel (huv′əl) *n.* A small hut or shed.

hover (huv′ər) *v.* To remain suspended in or near one place in the air.

husbandry (huz′bən·drē) *n.* The occupation or business of farming.

I

ignoble (ig·nō′bəl) *adj.* Dishonorable; low.

imbibe (im·bīb′) *v.* 1. To drink. 2. To absorb; take in.

PRONUNCIATION KEY: **a**dd, **ā**ce, c**â**re, p**ä**lm; **e**nd, **ē**ven; **i**t, **ī**ce; **o**dd, **ō**pen, **ô**rder; t**ŏŏ**k, p**ōō**l; **u**p, b**û**rn; **ə** = **a** in *above*, **e** in *sicken*, **i** in *flexible*, **o** in *melon*, **u** in *focus*; **yōō** = **u** in *fuse*; **oi**l; p**ou**t; **ch**eck; **g**o; **r**in**g**; **th**in; **th**is; **zh**, vision.

immanent (im'ə·nənt) *adj.* **1.** Existing or remaining within. **2.** Of God, pervading all creation.

imminent (im'ə·nənt) *adj.* About to happen; threatening, said especially of danger.

impair (im·pâr') *v.* To make worse; weaken; damage.

impartiality (im'pär·shē·al'ə·tē) *n.* Freedom from prejudice; fairness.

impassive (im·pas'iv) *adj.* Calm; serene.

impediment (im·ped'ə·mənt) *n.* An obstacle; hindrance.

imperceptible (im'pər·sep'tə·bəl) *adj.* Barely able to be discerned or perceived: an *imperceptible* improvement.

imperious (im·pir'ē·əs) *adj.* Commanding; domineering; arrogant.

impertinent (im·pûr'tə·nənt) *adj.* Disrespectful; bold; unmannerly; impudent.

impervious (im·pûr'vē·əs) *adj.* Not interested in or open to; not receiving: a mind *impervious* to reason.

impetuous (im·pech'ōō·əs) *adj.* Impulsive; hasty; reckless.

impious (im'pē·əs) *adj.* Lacking in respect or reverence.

implacable (im·plā'kə·bəl) *adj.* Unable to be pacified; unrelenting; unforgiving.

implicit (im·plis'it) *adj.* **1.** Absolute; unreserved: *implicit* confidence. **2.** Understood, but not specifically expressed: *implicit* agreement.

implore (im·plôr') *v.* To beg; entreat; beseech.

imply (im·plī') *v.* To indicate or suggest without stating; hint. **— implication** *n.*

impregnable (im·preg'nə·bəl) *adj.* Incapable of being taken by force.

impromptu (im·promp'tōō) *adj.* Made, done, or spoken on the spur of the moment, without preparation.

impropriety (im'prō·prī'ə·tē) *n.* An improper action.

inarticulate (in'är·tik'yə·lit) *adj.* **1.** Uttered without the distinct sounds of spoken language: *inarticulate* cries. **2.** Incapable of speech.

incentive (in·sen'tiv) *n.* A stimulus to action.

incite (in·sīt') *v.* To spur on to action; urge on; stir up.

inconsequential (in'kon·sə·kwen'shəl) *adj.* Unimportant; trivial.

inconsolable (in'kən·sō'lə·bəl) *adj.* Not to be comforted or cheered up; dejected.

incredible (in·kred'ə·bəl) *adj.* Impossible to believe; unbelievable. **— incredibly** *adv.*

incredulous (in·krej'ə·ləs) *adj.* Unwilling or unable to believe; doubting.

indomitable (im·dom'i·tə·bəl) *adj.* Not easily defeated or discouraged; unyielding.

indulge (in·dulj') *v.* **1.** To yield to or gratify: to *indulge* a love of good food. **2.** To yield to the whims of; humor: to *indulge* a child.

inept (in·ept') *adj.* Clumsy; awkward; incompetent.

inert (in·ûrt') *adj.* Without power to move; inactive.

inevitable (in·ev'ə·tə·bəl) *adj.* Certain; unavoidable.

inexorable (in·ek'sər·ə·bəl) *adj.* Unyielding; unalterable; relentless.

infernal (in·fûr'nəl) *adj.* Hellish; hateful.

infinite (in'fə·nit) *adj.* **1.** Having no boundaries or limits; extending without end: *infinite* space. **2.** Very numerous: an *infinite* supply.

inflame (in·flām') *v.* To excite to violent emotion or activity.

inflexible (in·flek'sə·bəl) *adj.* Stubborn; unyielding; unbending.

infuse (in·fyōōz') *v.* **1.** To instill, as principles. **2.** To pour in.

ingenious (in·jēn'yəs) *adj.* Clever; skillful. **— ingenuity** *n.*

ingratiate (in·grā'shē·āt) *v.* To deliberately bring oneself into favor or confidence with.

inimitable (in·im'ə·tə·bəl) *adj.* Not to be imitated; matchless.

innate (i·nāt') *adj.* Inborn: an *innate* love of music.

innovation (in'ə·vā'shən) *n.* Something new.

insinuate (in·sin'yōō·āt) *v.* **1.** To hint or suggest slyly. **2.** To introduce gradually: to *insinuate* mistrust.

insolent (in'sə·lənt) *adj.* Impertinent; disrespectful; arrogant. **— insolently** *adv.*

instigate (in'stə·gāt) *v.* **1.** To spur on to do some deed. **2.** To bring about by inciting; provoke: to *instigate* treason.

insubstantial (in'səb·stan'shəl) *adj.* Not real; imaginary; dreamlike.

insuperable (in·sōō'pər·ə·bəl) *adj.* Not to be surmounted or overcome.

integrity (in·teg'rə·tē) *n.* Honesty; uprightness of character.

intelligible (in·tel'ə·jə·bəl) *adj.* Clear; capable of being understood.

intemperance (in·tem'pər·əns) *n.* Lack of moderation; especially, drinking too much alcohol.

interloper (in'tər·lōp'ər) *n.* An intruder; a meddler in others' affairs.

interminable (in·tûr'mə·nə·bəl) *adj.* Having no end; endless. **— interminably** *adv.*

intervene (in'tər·vēn') *v.* **1.** To interfere. **2.** To be located between.

intimate (in'tə·mit) *adj.* **1.** Close in friendship. **2.** Deeply personal: *intimate* thoughts. **3.** Resulting from close study or familiarity with: *intimate* knowledge of a crime.

intimate (in'tə·māt) *v.* To hint; imply. **— intimation** *n.*

intolerable (in·tol′ər·ə·bəl) *adj.* Unable to be borne or endured; insufferable.

intricate (in′tri·kit) *adj.* 1. Complicated; entangled: an *intricate* knot. 2. Complex; puzzling; difficult to follow or understand.

intrigue (in·trēg′) *v.* To arouse the interest and curiosity of; fascinate.

introspection (in·trə·spek′shən) *n.* The observation of one's own thoughts and emotions. — **introspective** *adj.*

invariable (·in·vâr′ē·ə·bəl) *adj.* Unchangeable; constant. — **invariably** *adv.*

invincible (in·vin′sə·bəl) *adj.* Not to be overcome; unconquerable. — **invincibly** *adv.*

irascible (i·ras′ə·bəl) *adj.* Irritable; quick-tempered.

irk (ûrk) *v.* To annoy or tire; vex.

irreparable (i·rep′ər·ə·bəl) *adj.* Unable to be repaired or remedied.

itinerant (ī·tin′ər·ənt) *adj.* Going from place to place; wandering.

J

jubilant (jōo′bə·lənt) *adj.* Extremely joyful; in high spirits; triumphant.

judicious (jōo·dish′əs) *adj.* Having or exercising good judgment. — **judiciousness** *n.*

juncture (jungk′chər) *n.* 1. A joining. 2. A point in time.

L

labyrinth (lab′ə·rinth) *n.* An arrangement of winding paths planned to confuse; maze.

lackadaisical (lak′ə·dā′zi·kəl) *adj.* Without energy; listless; languid.

lackluster (lak′lus′tər) *adj.* Dull; lacking brightness.

lament (lə·ment′) *v.* To feel grief, regret, or sorrow for. — **lamentation** *n.*

languid (lang′gwid) *adj.* Lacking liveliness or animation; listless; weak.

languor (lang′gər) *n.* A lack of energy or enthusiasm.

latent (lā′tənt) *adj.* Undeveloped; not apparent.

lath (lath) *n.* A thin strip of wood or metal. — **lathlike** *adj.*

legible (lej′ə·bəl) *adj.* Capable of being read; easy to read: *legible* handwriting.

lethargy (leth′ər·jē) *n.* A state of dullness or inaction; stupor; apathy.

limber (lim′bər) *adj.* Bending easily; flexible.

listless (list′lis) *adj.* Languid; indifferent; showing lack of energy or interest.

lithe (līth) *adj.* Graceful; limber.

loath (lōth) *adj.* Unwilling; reluctant.

loathe (lōth) *v.* To hate; detest; abhor.

loiter (loi′tər) *v.* To linger idly or aimlessly; loaf; dawdle. — **loiterer** *n.*

loom (lōom) *v.* 1. To appear dimly or indistinctly, as through a mist. 2. To appear to the mind as large or threatening.

lope (lōp) *v.* To run with a steady, swinging stride.

lubberly (lub′ər·ly) *adj.* Awkward; clumsy.

ludicrous (lōo′də·krəs) *adj.* Ridiculous; absurd.

luminosity (lōo′mə·nos′ə·tē) *n.* Light; glow; the state of shining.

lurid (lōor′id) *adj.* 1. Shocking; vivid; sensational. 2. Giving out or having a yellowish-red glare.

lurk (lûrk) *v.* 1. To lie hidden. 2. To exist unobserved. 3. To move secretly.

M

macabre (mə·kä′brə) *adj.* Suggesting death and decay; gruesome; ghastly.

machination (mak′ə·nā′shən) *n.* A scheming or contriving.

magnitude (mag′nə·tōod) *n.* Size; extent.

malevolent (mə·lev′ə·lent) *adj.* Wishing evil toward others.

malice (mal′is) *n.* Spite; ill will; wish to do harm. — **malicious** *adj.*

malignant (mə·lig′nənt) *adj.* Harmful; malicious.

manifest (man′ə·fest) *adj.* Plain; apparent; evident; obvious.

manifold (man′ə·fōld) *adj.* Many; varied; complex.

maraud (mə·rôd′) *v.* To raid; plunder or pillage.

maxim (mak′sim) *n.* A proverb; brief statement of a general truth.

meager (mē′gər) *adj.* Scanty; insufficient.

medium (mē′dē·əm) *n.* A means or agency: Money is a *medium* of exchange.

melancholy (mel′ən·kol′ē) *adj.* Gloomy; sad; depressed.

menace (men′is) *v.* To threaten.

mercenary (mûr′sə·ner′ē) *n.* A hired soldier in foreign service. — *adj.* Greedy.

meticulous (mə·tik′yə·les) *adj.* Extremely precise about minor details.

mettle (met′l) *n.* Courage; pluck; spirit.

minute (mi·nōot′) *adj.* Exceedingly small.

mishap (mis′hap) *n.* An unfortunate accident.

molder (mōl′dər) *v.* To decay little by little; crumble.

PRONUNCIATION KEY: **a**dd, **ā**ce, **c**âre, **p**älm; **e**nd, **ē**ven; **i**t, **ī**ce; **o**dd, **ō**pen, **ô**rder; t**ŏŏ**k, p**ōō**l; **u**p, b**û**rn; ə = a in *above*, e in *sicken*, i in *flexible*, o in *melon*, u in *focus*; y**ōō** = u in *fuse*; **oil**; **pout**; **ch**eck; **go**; **ring**; **th**in; **th**is; **zh**, vision.

monumental (mon'yə·men'təl) *adj.* Enduring; impressive.

mortal (môr'təl) *adj.* 1. Subject to death. 2. Causing or liable to cause death; fatal.

myriad (mir'ē·əd) *adj.* Composed of a very large number.

N

naive (nä·ēv') *adj.* Simple; unaffected; lacking worldly experience.

nocturnal (nok·tûr'nəl) *adj.* Of, pertaining to, or occurring at night.

nominal (nom'ə·nəl) *adj.* Slight; trifling: for *nominal* services.

novel (nov'əl) *adj.* New, strange, or unusual.

nurture (nûr'chər) *n.* To feed or support; nourish.

O

obese (ō·bēs') *adj.* Very fat.

oblique (ə·blēk') *adj.* 1. Slanting; sloping. 2. Not direct or straightforward: *oblique* praise.

obliterate (ə·blit'ə·rāt) *v.* To blot or wipe out; leave no trace of.

oblivion (ə·bliv'ē·ən) *n.* Forgetfulness.

obstinate (ob'stə·nit) *adj.* Stubborn; unyielding in opinion or action.

odious (ō'dē·əs) *adj.* Offensive; hateful; repulsive.

ominous (om'ə·nəs) *adj.* Threatening; prophetic of evil. — **omen** *n.*

opulence (op'yə·ləns) *n.* 1. Wealth; richness. 2. Abundance; luxuriance.

P

pacific (pə·sif'ik) *adj.* Peaceful; calm.

palatable (pal'it·ə·bəl) *adj.* 1. Tasty. 2. Agreeable.

paltry (pôl'trē) *adj.* Worthless; trifling; petty.

pandemonium (pan'də·mō'nē·əm) *n.* Riotous uproar; disorder.

paroxysm (par'ək·siz'əm) *n.* A sudden outburst, as of emotion or action.

patronize (pā'trən·īz) *v.* 1. To show favor to in an affected manner. 2. To trade with as a regular customer.

peaked (pē'kid) *adj.* Thin or sickly-looking.

pedagogue (ped'ə·gog) *n.* A schoolmaster; educator.

peerless (pir'lis) *adj.* Unequaled; matchless.

pending (pen'ding) *adj.* 1. Unfinished; undecided. 2. Imminent; impending.

pensive (pen'siv) *adj.* Thoughtful; meditative; reflective.

perception (pər·sep'shən) *n.* Sensation; realization; knowledge.

perennial (pə·ren'ē·əl) *adj.* Everlasting; unceasing; continuing through the years.

perspective (pər·spek'tiv) *n.* 1. The art of painting objects in a way that conveys the impression of depth and distance. 2. Judgment of facts with regard to their relative importance.

pervade (pər·vād') *v.* To spread through; permeate.

phenomenon (fi·nom'ə·non) *n.* Something unusual or marvelous.

phobia (fō'bē·ə) *n.* 1. A persistent fear. 2. A strong dislike.

pinnacle (pin'ə·kəl) *n.* The highest point; peak; summit.

pique (pēk) *v.* 1. To arouse resentment in. 2. To arouse or stimulate; provoke.

placid (plas'id) *adj.* Calm; not easily disturbed.

plague (plāg) *v.* To annoy; torment. — **plagued** *adj.*

plunder (plun'dər) *v.* To rob violently; loot. — *n.* Booty; the spoils of war.

poignant (poin'yənt) *adj.* Painful to the feelings: *poignant* grief.

poise (poiz) *v.* To balance or be balanced. — *n.* Dignity or self-possession.

pompous (pom'pəs) *adj.* Conceited; puffed up; self-important.

ponderous (pon'dər·əs) *adj.* Huge; heavy; bulky.

pore (pôr) *v.* To study or read with care: with *over*.

portal (pôr'təl) *n.* An entrance, door, or gate.

portentous (pôr·ten'təs) *adj.* Bearing signs of something to come or happen, especially of something momentous or terrible; ominous.

portly (pôrt'lē) *adj.* Stout.

posterity (pos·ter'ə·tē) *n.* Future generations.

potent (pōt'nt) *adj.* Powerful.

precipice (pres'i·pis) *n.* A high vertical or overhanging face of rock; the brink of a cliff.

precipitous (pri·sip'ə·təs) *adj.* 1. Very steep. 2. Hasty.

predecessor (pred'ə·ses'ər) *n.* One who has gone before.

preeminent (prē·em'ə·nənt) *adj.* Outstanding; conspicuous. — **preeminently** *adv.*

premonition (prē'mə·nish'ən) *n.* An instinctive feeling about something coming in the future.

pretension (pri·ten'shən) *n.* 1. A claim put forward. 2. Affectation; display. 3. A bold assertion.

pretext (prē'tekst) *n.* An excuse or reason made up to hide the real one.

prevail (pri·vāl') *v.* To be victorious; triumph or conquer.

prey (prā) *v.* 1. To seize for food: Cats *prey* on birds. 2. To influence in a harmful or wearing way: The threats *preyed* on his mind.

primeval (prī·mē'vəl) *adj.* Belonging to very earliest times, such as before man appeared on earth; primitive.

prodigality (prod'ə·gal'ə·tē) *n.* Abundance; generosity; lavishness.

prodigious (prə·dij'əs) *adj.* Extraordinary; amazing.

profound (prə·found') *adj.* Deep; lasting.

profuse (prə·fyōōs') *adj.* Overflowing; abundant; excessive.

propound (prə·pound') *v.* To put forward for consideration; submit or suggest.

protract (prō·trakt') *v.* To prolong; lengthen the time of.

providence (prov'ə·dəns) *n.* 1. The care taken by God over the universe. 2. Care for the future. — **providential** *adj.*

pungent (pun'jənt) *adj.* Keen; penetrating to the senses: a *pungent* odor.

purport (pûr'pôrt) *n.* Meaning or intention; purpose.

R

radius (rā'dē·əs) *n.* 1. A straight line from the center of a circle to its circumference or boundary line. 2. Scope or limit, as of activity.

rampant (ram'pənt) *adj.* 1. Wild; unrestrained. 2. Standing on the hind legs; rearing.

rant (rant) *v.* To speak loudly or violently; rave.

rapt (rapt) *adj.* Deeply interested; absorbed; intent.

rash (rash) *adj.* Reckless; heedless of danger.

rational (rash'ən·əl) *adj.* Reasonable; able to think clearly.

ravage (rav'ij) *v.* To destroy or lay waste to.

recommence (rē'kə·mens') *v.* To begin again.

regal (rē'gəl) *adj.* Royal; fit for a king.

reiterate (rē·it'ə·rāt) *v.* To repeat.

relent (ri·lent') *v.* To soften in temper; become more gentle or relaxed.

relentless (ri·lent'lis) *adj.* 1. Continuous: 2. Pitiless; unmerciful; unfeeling.

relic (rel'ik) *n.* A fragment or portion of something which has been destroyed.

rend (rend) *v.* To tear apart by force; split or break.

rendezvous (rän'dā·vōō) *n.* 1. An appointed place of meeting. 2. A meeting or an appointment to meet.

renown (ri·noun') *n.* Fame; celebrity.

replenish (ri·plen'ish) *v.* To fill up again; restore.

repose (ri·pōz') *n.* Rest, especially lying down.

repress (ri·pres') *v.* To keep under control.

reproach (ri·prōch') *v.* To blame.

repulse (ri·puls') *v.* To drive back; repel.

reputable (rep'yə·tə·bəl) *adj.* Of good reputation; honorable.

resound (ri·zound') *v.* To echo.

respite (res'pit) *n.* Postponement or delay; interval of rest.

resplendent (ri·splen'dənt) *adj.* Shining bright; splendid; gorgeous.

restorative (ri·stôr'ə·tiv) *adj.* Tending or able to restore.

retort (ri·tôrt') *v.* 1. To reply back to in the same way you have been addressed, as hurling back one accusation for another. 2. To answer sharply.

revels (rev'əlz) *n.* Celebrations; festivities.

revenue (rev'ə·nyōō) *n.* Income.

reverberate (ri·vûr'bə·rāt) *v.* To re-echo.

revere (ri·vir') *v.* To regard with respect.

reverie (rev'ər·ē) *n.* Dreaming; especially, daydreaming.

revoke (ri·vōk') *v.* To cancel; repeal.

revulsion (ri·vul'shən) *n.* A drawing back from something; strong reaction or withdrawal.

rout (rout) *n.* A disorderly retreat or flight from defeat.

rueful (rōō'fəl) *adj.* Sorrowful; regretful.

ruminate (rōō'mə·nāt) *v.* To meditate or reflect about; ponder.

ruse (rōōz) *n.* An action intended to mislead or deceive; a trick.

S

sack (sak) *v.* 1. To loot; pillage or plunder a captured city.

sacrilege (sak'rə·lij) *n.* The act of treating something holy with disrespect.

sagacity (sə·gas'ə·tē) *n.* Wisdom; shrewdness; good judgment.

sage (sāj) *adj.* Wise; prudent. — Also *n.* — **sagely** *adv.*

salutary (sal'yə·ter'ē) *adj.* Doing good; wholesome; beneficial.

saunter (sôn'tər) *v.* To walk in a leisurely or lounging way; stroll.

scan (skan) *v.* 1. To examine closely or in detail. 2. To read hastily; glance over.

scathing (skā'thing) *adj.* Severe; merciless.

scepter (sep'tər) *n.* A staff or wand carried as the badge of royal power.

scrutiny (skrōō'tə·nē) *n.* A close examination or investigation.

seep (sēp) *v.* To soak through; ooze.

sever (sev'ər) *v.* To cut off.

sham (sham) *n.* A pretense; deception.

PRONUNCIATION KEY: add, āce, câre, pälm; end, ēven; it, īce; odd, ōpen, ôrder; tŏŏk, pōōl; up, bûrn; ə = a in *above*, e in *sicken*, i in *flexible*, o in *melon*, u in *focus*; yōō = u in *fuse*; oil; pout; check; go; ring; thin; this; zh, vision.

shamble (sham'bəl) v. To walk with shuffling or unsteady steps.

sheath (shēth) n. A case or covering, as for a sword.

sheer (shir) adj. 1. Downright; with no modifying conditions: *sheer* folly. 2. Steep: a *sheer* precipice.

shirk (shûrk) v. To avoid doing something that should be done. — **shirker** n.

sibilant (sib'ə·lənt) adj. Hissing.

simultaneous (sī'məl·tā'nē·us) adj. Happening, done, or existing at the same time. — **simultaneously** adv.

sojourn (sō'jûrn) v. To stay temporarily.

solace (sol'is) n. Comfort in time of trouble.

solicitude (sə·lis'ə·tōod) n. Care; concern.

sophistication (sə·fis'tə·kā'shən) n. Wisdom in worldly matters.

sough (suf) v. To make a sighing sound; moan, as the wind.

sovereignty (sov'rən·tē) n. Supreme authority; highest power.

Spartan (spär'tən) adj. Hardy; austere, that is, able to do without things that make for comfort and ease.

spasm (spaz'əm) n. A sudden, short-lived burst of activity or energy.

spawn (spôn) v. 1. To deposit eggs, as some fish do. 2. To give rise to; bring forth, especially in great quantities.

spectral (spek'trəl) adj. Ghostly.

speculation (spek'yə·lā'shən) n. 1. The act of guessing. 2. A risky business transaction that offers possibility of profit.

sphinx (sfingks) n. 1. In Greek mythology, a monster who destroyed people who couldn't guess her riddle. 2. Any mysterious person.

splayed (splād) adj. Spread out; turned outward.

stalk (stôk) v. 1. To pursue or hunt stealthily, as game. 2. To walk in a stiff manner. 3. To move through or follow, as an evil: Famine *stalked* the land.

stalwart (stôl'wərt) adj. Tall and strong; big.

stealthy (stel'thē) adj. Secret; sly; furtive.

steep (stēp) v. To soak; saturate.

stifle (stī'fəl) v. To hold or keep back; repress, as sobs.

stilted (stil'tid) adj. Unnaturally formal in manner.

stint (stint) v. To limit, as in amount or share; be sparing.

stoic (stō'ik) adj. Indifferent to pain and pleasure.

stout (stout) adj. 1. Strong; firm; tough. 2. Fat; thickset.

stratagem (strat'ə·jəm) n. A trick.

stripling (strip'ling) n. A very young man.

stupor (stōo'pər) n. A condition in which the senses are dulled.

subjugate (sub'jōo·gāt) v. 1. To subdue.

2. To cause to undergo something; to subject.

submerge (səb·mûrj') v. 1. To put into or under water or other liquid. 2. To cover up; hide.

subsequent (sub'sə·kwənt) adj. Following in time, place, order, or as a result.

successor (sək·ses'ər) n. One who comes after another person.

succumb (sə·kum') v. 1. To give way; yield. 2. To die.

suffice (sə·fīs') v. To be enough; satisfy.

sullen (sul'ən) adj. Stubbornly ill-humored; glum; melancholy. — **sullenly** adv.

sumptuous (sump'chōo·əs) adj. Lavish; expensive; luxurious.

sunder (sun'dər) v. To break apart; disunite.

supple (sup'əl) adj. Easily bent; flexible.

supplement (sup'lə·ment) v. To make additions to; add to.

suppliant (sup'lē·ənt) n. One who asks earnestly or begs for something.

surge (sûrj) v. To roll onward, as waves; swell or heave.

surmise (sər·mīz') v. To guess; suppose.

surmount (sər·mount') v. 1. To overcome. 2. To put above or on top of.

swain (swān) n. A country boy or young man.

symmetrical (si·met'ri·kəl) adj. Regular; well-proportioned; with corresponding parts.

synthetic (sin·thet'ik) adj. Produced artificially rather than occurring naturally.

T

tactful (takt'fəl) adj. Considerate of the feelings of others.

taunt (tônt) v. To provoke with hurtful or sarcastic remarks.

taut (tôt) adj. Stretched tight; tense.

tawdry (tô'drē) adj. Showy and cheap; gaudy.

tedious (tē'dē·əs) adj. Boring; tiresome.

tenacious (ti·nā'shəs) adj. Stubborn; obstinate. — **tenacity** n.

terminate (tûr'mə·nāt) v. To end; finish; put a stop to.

tether (teth'er) v. To tie up an animal; fasten with a rope.

thwart (thwôrt) v. To prevent the accomplishment of; frustrate; foil.

titanic (tī·tan'ik) adj. Of great size; huge.

titter (tit'ər) v. To laugh in a suppressed way; snicker or giggle.

tonic (ton'ik) n. Something stimulating or invigorating, such as a medicine.

totter (tot'ər) v. 1. To walk unsteadily. 2. To shake or sway, as if about to fall.

tranquil (trang'kwil) adj. Calm; quiet. — **tranquillity** n.

transcribe (tran·skrīb') *v.* To write over; copy or recopy.

transfigure (trans·fig'yər) *v.* To change the outward form or appearance of.

transfix (trans·fiks') *v.* 1. To pierce through. 2. To make motionless, as with emotion.

translucent (trans·lōō'sənt) *adj.* Allowing the passage of light, but not permitting a clear view of anything beyond; semitransparent.

transmit (trans·mit') *v.* To send from one person or place to another; forward.

tremor (trem'ər) *n.* A shaking or shiver.

tryst (trist) *n.* An appointment; a prearranged meeting.

tumult (tōō'mult) *n.* An uproar or hubbub. — **tumultuous** *adj.*

turbulent (tûr'byə·lənt) *adj.* Agitated; disturbed; wild. — **turbulence** *n.*

turmoil (tûr'moil) *n.* Confused movement; tumult.

U

ultimate (ul'tə·mit) *adj.* 1. Final. 2. Most distant; deepest; furthest.

uncanny (un·kan'ē) *adj.* Strange; weird; unnatural.

uncongenial (un·kən·jēn'yəl) *adj.* Not agreeable; unsympathetic.

uncouth (un·kōōth') *adj.* Rough; crude; unrefined.

unique (yōō·nēk') *adj.* Without equal or like; being the only one of its kind.

unruly (un·rōō'lē) *adj.* Not cared for; rough.

upbraid (up·brād') *v.* To scold or reproach.

V

validate (val'ə·dāt) *v.* To confirm or ratify.

valor (val'ər) *n.* Courage; bravery.

vanquish (vang'kwish) *v.* To conquer; defeat; overcome.

veer (vir) *v.* To change course or direction; swerve or shift position.

vehement (vē'ə·mənt) *adj.* Marked by passionate or strong feelings; violent. — **vehemence** *n.*

venerable (ven'ər·ə·bəl) *adj.* Entitled to respect because of age, position, etc.

venom (ven'əm) *n.* Spite; malice. — **venomous** *adj.*

venture (ven'chər) *v.* To run the risk of; take the chance of.

vex (veks) *v.* To irritate; disturb; annoy.

vindicate (vin'də·kāt) *v.* 1. To clear of accusation or suspicion. 2. To support or maintain as a right or claim. 3. To justify.

virility (və·ril'ə·tē) *n.* Masculinity; strength.

voracious (vô·rā'shəs) *adj.* Greedy; ravenous.

vulnerable (vul'nər·ə·bəl) *adj.* Capable of being hurt.

W

wan (won) *adj.* 1. Pale. 2. Indicating sickness or unhappiness: a *wan* smile.

wane (wān) *v.* To grow smaller; decline gradually.

wanton (won'tən) *adj.* Unjust; malicious; unprovoked: *wanton* savagery.

wary (wâr'ē) *adj.* Carefully watching and guarding. — **warily** *adv.*

waver (wā'vər) *v.* To falter; be hesitant or uncertain.

weld (weld) *v.* To connect or unite.

wend (wend) *v.* To go on one's way; proceed.

whimsical (hwim'zi·kəl) *adj.* 1. Having fanciful ideas. 2. Fantastic; quaint.

winsome (win'səm) *adj.* Pleasing; attractive; winning.

wrath (rath) *n.* Violent rage; fury; extreme anger.

writhe (rīth). *v.* To twist or distort the body, as in pain.

PRONUNCIATION KEY: add, āce, câre, pälm; end, ēven; it, īce; odd, ōpen, ôrder; tŏŏk, pōōl; up, bûrn; ə = a in *above*, e in *sicken*, i in *flexible*, o in *melon*, u in *focus*; yōō = u in *fuse*; oil; pout; check; go; ring; thin; this; zh, vision.

Index of Authors and Titles

The page numbers in italics show where a brief biography of the author is located.

Adventures of Aeneas, The, 582
Advice to Actors, 554
Antony's Oration at Caesar's Funeral, 622
Antony Speaks of Brutus, 624
Apprentice, The, 320
Armful, The, 524
Ashabranner, Brent K., 114
As the Night the Day, 144

Battle of Zama, The, 602
Baucis and Philemon, 103
Benchley, Robert, 383, *641*
Birthplace, The, 518
Blind Men and the Elephant, The, 113
Boyhood Reminiscences, 472
Bradbury, Ray, 202, *641*
Burns, Robert, 456, *641*
Butler, Samuel, 15

Caesar to Antony, 621
Caesar to Calpurnia, 622
Canfield, Dorothy, 320
Carroll, Lewis, 435, *641*
Casey at the Bat, 436
Cassius Speaks of Caesar to Brutus, 621
Celebrated Jumping Frog of Calaveras County, The, 497
Charge of the Light Brigade, The, 58
Choice of Weapons, A, 132
Ciardi, John, 451, *642*
Clarke, Arthur C., 423, *642*
Concord Hymn, The, 176
Coolidge, Olivia E., 107
Countess and the Impossible, The, 139
Crane, Stephen, 132, *642*
Creamer, Robert, 409
Crossing a Creek, 456
Cub Pilot on the Mississippi, 481
Cummings, E. E., 462, *642*

Daffodils, The, 454
Dark Hills, The, 461
Davis, Russell G., 114
Denham, Reginald, 333
Dickinson, Emily, 98, 132, 465, *643*
Dog That Bit People, The, 532
Doyle, Sir Arthur Conan, 301
Drummer Boy of Shiloh, The, 202
Dunkirk, 60
Dust of Snow, 524

Eel, The, 438
Eliot, T. S. 439, 452, *643*
Emerson, Ralph Waldo, 176, *643*
Engle, Paul, 410
Eruption of Vesuvius, The, 625
Exiled, 458

Farjeon, Eleanor, 449
Father's Advice to His Son, A, 550
Fire and Ice, 525
First Pitch, 409
Fog, 451
Forbes, Esther, 159
Forbes, Kathryn, 134
From Spring to Summer, 417
Frost, Robert, *516,* 517–26, 573

Gallico, Paul, 87, *643*
Garland of Precepts, A, 133
George Washington Carver, 390
Gettysburg Address, The, 208
Gift and the Giver, The, 114
Good Name, 552
Guerber, H. A., 582

Hale, Edward Everett, 187
Hamilton, Edith, 103, *644*
Happy Journey to Trenton and Camden, The, 351
Hardy, Thomas, 461, *644*
Hearth Fire, The, 455
Heart of the City, The, 631
Heiderstadt, Dorothy, 26
Henry, O., 283, *644*
High Flight, 458
Highet, Gilbert, 631, *645*
Hillyer, Robert, 457
Holmes, Oliver Wendell, 177, *645*
Homer, 15, *645*
How Horatius Held the Bridge, 597
Hughes, Langston, 463, *645*

I Like to See It Lap the Miles, 465
Incandescent Genius, 235
Irving, Washington, 259, *646*

Jabberwocky, 435
Japanese Poems, 449
Jean, 456
Johnson, Herbert Clark, 456
Julius Caesar, 610

Kid in the Park, 463
Kingfisher and the Phoebe, The, 545
Koral, Bella, 577

Lanier, Henry W., 597
Last Week in October, 461
Last Word of a Bluebird, The, 521
Legend of Sleepy Hollow, The, 259
Lincoln, Abraham, 208
Little Girl and the Wolf, The, 541
Lochinvar, 441
Lonely Street, The, 452
Longfellow, Henry Wadsworth, 171, 646
Lost in a Snowstorm, 503
Lou Gehrig's Epic of Courage, 87

Magee, John Gillespie, Jr., 458
Mama and the Graduation Present, 134
Man Without a Country, The, 187
Marcus, Larry, 3
Mary White, 385
McGinley, Phyllis, 132, 133, 646
Means, Florence Crannell, 390
Memorial, 537
Mending Wall, 522
Midas, 107
Millay, Edna St. Vincent, 458, 647
Milne, A. A., 363, 647
Mood Apart, A, 573
My Friend Flicka, 64

Naming of Cats, The, 439
Nash, Ogden, 438, 647
Nathan, Robert, 60
Nicol, Abioseh, 144
Night Journey, 464
Night the Bed Fell, The, 528

O Captain! My Captain! 210
Odysseus and the Cyclops, 15
O'Hara, Mary, 64
Old-fashioned Iowa Christmas, An, 410
Old Ironsides, 177
Orr, Mary, 333

Panther, The, 438
Pasture, The, 517
Paul Revere's Ride, 171
Pliny, 625, 647
Plutarch, 610, 647
Poe, Edgar Allan, 444, 647
Poetry, 449
Porcupine, The, 438
Prelude I: The Winter Evening, 452
Princess and the Tin Box, The, 542
Punch, Brothers, Punch, 511
Pyle, Howard, 32, 648
Pyramus and Thisby, 555

Ransom of Red Chief, The, 283
Raven, The, 444
Red-headed League, The, 301

Richter, Conrad, 212, 648
River Is a Piece of Sky, The, 451
Road Not Taken, The, 519
Robinson, Edwin Arlington, 461, 648
Roethke, Theodore, 464, 648
Ross, Jerome, 3

Salt-Water Tea, 159
Sandburg, Carl, 451, 649
Saxe, John Godfrey, 113
Scott, Sir Walter, 441, 649
Shakespeare, William, 549, 550–71, 621–24
Shelley, Percy Bysshe, 453, 649
Silverberg, Robert, 602
Sing an Old Song, 249
Sire de Maletroit's Door, The, 333
Sir Gawain, 26
Smoke over the Prairie, 212
Sonnet 71, 553
Spreading "You Know," The, 539
Stevenson, Robert Louis, 333, 649
Stone, The, 3
Stopping by Woods on a Snowy Evening, 520
Street, James, 118

Teale, Edwin Way, 417, 650
Tennyson, Alfred, Lord, 58, 650
Termite, The, 438
Thayer, Ernest Lawrence, 436
Think As I Think, 132
Thurber, James, 527, 528–48
Thurber's Cartoons, 546
Thurman, Richard Y., 139
Tiger Who Would Be King, The, 544
Time to Talk, A, 517
Top Man, 42
Twain, Mark, 471, 472–515

Ugly Duckling, The, 363
Ullman, James Ramsey, 42

Van Zandt, Eleanor R., 249
Virgil, 582, 650

Wall, C. B., 235
Weep No More, My Lady, 118
We Never Know How High, 98
What Fifty Said, 525
what if a much of a which of a wind, 462
Where's Everybody? 423
White, William Allen, 385
Whitman, Walt, 210, 650
Whittier, John Greenleaf, 455, 651
Widow Bird, A, 453
Wilder, Thornton, 351, 651
Williams, William Carlos, 452, 651
Will Stutely's Rescue, 32
Wise Old Apple Tree in Spring, The, 457
Wooden Horse, The, 577
Word, A, 132
Wordsworth, William, 454, 651

Your Change, 383

C
D
E
F
G
H
I
J